MW00825263

Suzuki GSX-R600 & 750
Service and Repair Manual

by Matthew Coombs

Models covered

(4790 - 4AP1 - 304)

GSX-R600K6, K7, K8 and K9. 599cc. 2006 to 2009
GSX-R750K6, K7, K8 and K9. 750cc. 2006 to 2009

© **Haynes Publishing 2016**

ABCDE
FGHIJ
KLMNO

A book in the **Haynes Service and Repair Manual Series**

Printed in the USA

All rights reserved. No part of this book may be reproduced or transmitted in any form or by any means, electronic or mechanical, including photocopying, recording or by any information storage or retrieval system, without permission in writing from the copyright holder.

ISBN 978 1 78521 043 3

British Library Cataloguing in Publication Data
A catalogue record for this book is available from the British Library

Library of Congress Control Number 2008938307

Haynes Publishing
Sparkford, Yeovil, Somerset BA22 7JJ, England

Haynes North America, Inc
861 Lawrence Drive, Newbury Park, California 91320, USA

Haynes Publishing Nordiska AB
Box 1504, 751 45 Uppsala, Sweden

Printed using 33-lb Resolute Book 65 4.0 from Resolute Forest Products Calhoun, TN mill. Resolute is a member of World Wildlife Fund's Climate Savers programme committed to significantly reducing GHG emissions. This paper uses 50% less wood fibre than traditional offset. The Calhoun Mill is certified to the following sustainable forest management and chain of custody standards: SFI, PEFC and FSC Controlled Wood.

Contents

LIVING WITH YOUR SUZUKI GSX-R

Introduction

Pre-ride checks

MAINTENANCE

Routine maintenance and servicing

Contents

Suzuki
Every Which Way

by Julian Ryder

From Textile Machinery to Motorcycles

Suzuki were the second of Japan's Big Four motorcycle manufacturers to enter the business, and like Honda they started by bolting small two-stroke motors to bicycles. Unlike Honda, they had manufactured other products before turning to transportation in the aftermath of World War II.

In fact Suzuki has been in business since the first decade of the 20th-Century when Michio Suzuki manufactured textile machinery.

The desperate need for transport in post-war Japan saw Suzuki make their first motorised bicycle in 1952, and the fact that by 1954 the company had changed its name to Suzuki Motor Company shows how quickly the sideline took over the whole company's activities. In their first full manufacturing year,

Suzuki made nearly 4500 bikes and rapidly expanded into the world markets with a range of two-strokes.

Suzuki didn't make a four-stroke until 1977 when the GS750 double-overhead-cam across-the-frame four arrived. This was several years after Honda and Kawasaki had established the air-cooled four as the industry standard, but no motorcycle epitomises the era of what came to be known as the Universal

The T500 two-stroke twin

One of the later GT750 'kettle' models with front disc brakes

50 cc racer won six of the eight world titles chalked up by Suzuki during the 1960s as well as providing Mitsuo Itoh with the distinction of being the only Japanese rider to win an Isle of Man TT. Mr Itoh still works for Suzuki, he's in charge of their racing program.

Europe got the benefit of Suzuki's two-stroke expertise in a succession of air-cooled twins, the six-speed 250 cc Super Six being the most memorable, but the arrival in 1968 of the first of a series of 500 cc twins which were good looking, robust and versatile marked the start of mainstream success.

So confident were Suzuki of their two-stroke expertise that they even applied it to the burgeoning Superbike sector. The GT750 water-cooled triple arrived in 1972. It was big, fast and comfortable although the handling and stopping power did draw some comment. Whatever the drawbacks of the road bike, the engine was immensely successful in Superbike and Formula 750 racing. The roadster has its devotees, though, and is now a sought-after bike on the classic Japanese scene. Do not refer to it as the Water Buffalo in such company. Joking aside, the later disc-braked versions were quite civilised, but the audacious idea of using a big two-stroke motor in what was essentially a touring bike was a surprising success until the fuel crisis of the mid-'70s effectively killed off big strokers.

The same could be said of Suzuki's only real lemon, the RE5. This is still the only mass-produced bike to use the rotary (or Wankel) engine but never sold well. Fuel consumption in the mid-teens allied to frightening complexity and excess weight meant the RE5 was a non-starter in the sales race.

Japanese motorcycle better than the GS. So well engineered were the original fours that you can clearly see their genes in the GS500 twins that are still going strong in the mid-1990s. Suzuki's ability to prolong the life of their products this way means that they are often thought of as a conservative company. This is hardly fair if you look at some of their landmark designs, most of which have been commercial as well as critical successes.

Two-stroke Success

Early racing efforts were bolstered by the arrival of Ernst Degner who defected from the East German MZ team at the Swedish GP of 1961, bringing with him the rotary-valve secrets of design genius Walter Kaaden. The new Suzuki 50 cc racer won its first GP on the Isle of Man the following year and winning the title easily. Only Honda and Ralph Bryans interrupted Suzuki's run of 50 cc titles from 1962 to 1968.

The arrival of the twin-cylinder 125 racer in 1963 enabled Hugh Anderson to win both 50 and 125 world titles. You may not think 50 cc racing would be exciting - until you learn that the final incarnation of the thing had 14 gears and could do well over 100 mph on fast circuits. Before pulling out of GPs in 1967 the

Suzuki's GT250X7 was an instant hit in the popular 250 cc 'learner' sector

The GS400 was the first in a line of four-stroke twins

Development of the Four-stroke range

When Suzuki got round to building a four-stroke they did a very good job of it. The GS fours were built in 550, 650, 750, 850, 1000 and 1100 cc sizes in sports, custom, roadster and even shaft-driven touring forms over many years. The GS1000 was in on the start of Superbike racing in the early 1970s and the GS850 shaft-driven tourer was around nearly 15 years later. The fours spawned a line of 400, 425, 450 and 500 cc GS twins that were essentially the middle half of the four with all their reliability. If there was ever a criticism of the GS models it was that with the exception of the GS1000S of 1980, colloquially known as the ice-cream van, the range was visually uninspiring.

They nearly made the same mistake when they launched the four-valve-head GSX750 in 1979. Fortunately, the original twin-shock version was soon replaced by the 'E'-model with Full-Floater rear suspension and a full set of all the gadgets the Japanese industry was then keen on and has since forgotten about, like 16-inch front wheels and anti-dive forks. The air-cooled GSX was like the GS built in 550, 750 and 1100 cc versions with a variety of half, full and touring fairings, but the GSX that is best remembered is the Katana that first appeared in 1981. The power was provided by an 1000 or 1100 cc GSX motor, but wrapped around it was the most outrageous styling package to come out of Japan. Designed by Hans Muth of Target

Design, the Katana looked like nothing seen before or since. At the time there was as much anti feeling as praise, but now it is rightly regarded as a classic, a true milestone in motorcycle design. The factory have even started making 250 and 400 cc fours for the home market with the same styling as the 1981 bike.

Just to remind us that they'd still been building two-strokes for the likes of Barry Sheene, in 1986 Suzuki marketed a road-going version of their RG500 square-four racer which had put an end to the era of the four-stroke in 500 GPs when it appeared in 1974. In 1976 Suzuki not only won their first 500 title with Sheene, they sold RG500s over the counter and won every GP with them - with the exception of the Isle of Man TT which the works riders boycotted. Ten years on, the RG500 Gamma gave road riders the nearest experience they'd ever get to riding a GP bike. The fearsome beast could top 140 mph and only weighed 340 lb - the other alleged GP replicas were pussy cats compared to the Gamma's man-eating tiger.

The RG only lasted a few years and is already firmly in the category of collector's item; its four-stroke equivalent, the GSX-R, is still with us and looks like being so for many years. You have to look back to 1985 and its launch to realise just what a revolutionary step the GSX-R750 was: quite simply it was the first race replica. Not a bike dressed up to look like a race bike, but a genuine racer with lights on, a bike that could be taken straight to the track and win.

The first GSX-R, the 750, had a completely new motor cooled by oil rather than water and an aluminium cradle frame. It was sparse, a little twitchy and very, very fast. This time Suzuki got the looks right, blue and white bodywork based on the factory's racing colours and endurance-racer lookalike twin headlights. And then came the 1100 - the big GSX-R got progressively more brutal as it chased the Yamaha EXUP for the heavyweight championship.

And alongside all these mould-breaking

The GS750 led the way for a series of four cylinder models

Later four-stroke models, like this GSX1100, were fitted with 16v engines

designs, Suzuki were also making the best looking custom bikes to come out of Japan, the Intruders; the first race replica trail bike, the DR350; the sharpest 250 Supersports, the RGV250; and a bargain-basement 600, the Bandit. The Bandit proved so popular they went on to build 1200 and 750 cc versions of it. I suppose that's predictable, a range of four-stroke fours just like the GS and GSXs. It's just like the company really, sometimes predictable, admittedly - but never boring.

Hot Stuff

You now where you are with a GSX-R, the initials say it all. The first one to hit the streets of the UK, Europe and the USA, an oil-cooled 750, appeared in 1985 and founded the race-replica craze. Actually, it wasn't so much a replica as a real racer with lights on. There had been a 400 cc GSX-R on the Japanese home market the year before the 750 but that only escaped the home country to run in the F3 TT on the Isle of Man or as a grey import. The big banger, the 1100 cc GSX-R, hit us in '86.

The first major revision of the GSX-R came in 1992, when the 750 and 1100 got water cooling – the W suffix was attached as a clue. A 600 cc version was also produced, but only sold in a few countries. It was merely a sleeved-down version of the 750 – literally the only dimension that differed from the bigger bike was the cylinder bore. Even

knowledgeable GSX-R fans will give you an argument if you tell them there was a 600 cc version before 1997, but it really did exist.

We had to wait until 1997 for a 600 cc GSX-R that was really a different bike in its own right. It came on the back of the second complete revamp of the GSX-R750 that produced the WT with SRAD ram-air induction, the first GSX-R to feature a beam frame rather than the now rather quaintly old-fashioned double cradle every model, no matter what capacity,

had used. Again the 750 was launched a year before the 600. The SRAD models used an identical main frame but the smaller bike had a shorter swinging arm. It was the lightest bike in the now very competitive supersport class at 195 kg (430 lb) and made a claimed 100 hp at 12,000 rpm. It was also a peaky, skittish, cramped machine much happier on the track than on the road. In other words, a real GSX-R. Not surprisingly, it won back-to-back British Supersport titles in 1998 and '99 and in '98 Fabrizio Pirovano won the inaugural World title with team-mate Stephane Chambon retaining the crown for Suzuki in '99.

However, things move quicker in the supersport class than any other sector, mainly because the racing formula allows many fewer modifications from stock than the superbike formula, especially in the chassis department. Again the 750 got the upgrade first, in 2000, with the 600 having to wait until the following year. Once more the motor got lighter, the chassis got shorter and the power output went up. This was the first time fuel-injection was used on GSX-R models. It weighed 161 kg (355 lb) and made 115 hp at 13,000 rpm. Karl Harris won the British Supersport title first time out in 2001.

Such is the pace of development that the GSX-R now gets a radical update every two years to keep it competitive on the track – something it needs to be if it's to be desirable in the showroom. The 750 and 600 now get their updates simultaneously, the 2004 models were effectively new motorcycles, recognisable by their black frames and radial brakes – straight from MotoGP. This was the first time the 600 got upside-down forks. The 2006 models were also very different from their predecessors – shorter, lower, lighter and more powerful and identifiable by their underslung exhausts.

For 2008 the major improvements were in software rather than hardware with selectable engine mapping and dual throttle butterflies. One set is connected to the

The 2006 GSX-R600K6

The 2008 GSX-R750K8

twistgrip in conventional fashion, the second set is controlled by the engine management electronics and moves under control of the central processor to keep the intake stream velocity as near to optimum as possible.

Although the engine may look as the same as its predecessor there are again major internal changes. The 600 now weighs 163 kg (360 lb), that's 36 kg (80 lb) lighter than the first true 600 cc GSX-R of 1997. Power has gone up from a claimed 97 hp to what is reckoned to between 120 and 125 hp.

The development history of the GSX-R is the history of modern sportsbike design. If you write out the spec sheet of the GSX-R600 without any numbers on it (power output, weight, wheelbase etc) it doesn't change. Any GSX-R600 has a twin-spar aluminium frame and an across-the-frame four-cylinder engine. However the latest bike is 18% lighter than the first one and makes 25% more power. Suzuki aren't alone in making that sort of progress, but where other manufacturers have switched the focus of their supersports 600s between road and track, the GSX-R has always been a hard-edged sportster. Suzuki have even kept faith with the 750 cc class the original GSX-R invented. That was the capacity limit for four-cylinder machines under the original World Superbike Championship regulations, and there's something rather pleasing about a 750 GSX-R being at the cutting edge of biking more than twenty years after the first one necessitated the coining of the phrase 'race replica.'

Acknowledgements

Our thanks are due to V & J Motorcycles of Yeovil and Fowlers Motorcycles of Bristol and who supplied the machines featured in the illustrations throughout this manual. We would also like to thank NGK Spark Plugs (UK) Ltd for supplying the colour spark plug condition photographs, the Avon Rubber Company for supplying information on tyre fitting and Draper Tools Ltd for some of the workshop tools shown.

Thanks are also due to Julian Ryder who wrote the introduction 'Every Which Way' and to Suzuki (GB) Ltd who supplied model photographs.

About this Manual

The aim of this manual is to help you get the best value from your motorcycle. It can do so in several ways. It can help you decide what work must be done, even if you choose to have it done by a dealer; it provides information and procedures for routine maintenance and servicing; and it offers diagnostic and repair procedures to follow when trouble occurs.

We hope you use the manual to tackle the work yourself. For many simpler jobs, doing it yourself may be quicker than arranging an appointment to get the motorcycle into a dealer and making the trips to leave it and pick it up. More importantly, a lot of money can be saved by avoiding the expense the shop must pass on to you to cover its labour and overhead costs. An added benefit is the sense of satisfaction and accomplishment that you feel after doing the job yourself.

References to the left or right side of the motorcycle assume you are sitting on the seat, facing forward.

We take great pride in the accuracy of information given in this manual, but motorcycle manufacturers make alterations and design changes during the production run of a particular motorcycle of which they do not inform us. No liability can be accepted by the authors or publishers for loss, damage or injury caused by any errors in, or omissions from, the information given.

Other books of interest from Haynes

See the Haynes website www.haynes.co.uk for details

Illegal Copying

It is the policy of Haynes Publishing to actively protect its Copyrights and Trade Marks. Legal action will be taken against anyone who unlawfully copies the cover or contents of this Manual. This includes all forms of unauthorised copying including digital, mechanical, and electronic in any form. Authorisation from Haynes Publishing will only be provided expressly and in writing. Illegal copying will also be reported to the appropriate statutory authorities.

Frame and engine numbers

The frame serial number is stamped into the right-hand side of the steering head and is also repeated on the VIN plate. The engine number is stamped into the right-hand side of the crankcase. Both of these numbers should be recorded and kept in a safe place so they can be furnished to law enforcement officials in the event of a theft. The throttle bodies also have an identification number stamped into them.

The frame serial number and engine serial number should also be kept in a handy place (such as with your driving licence) so they are always available when purchasing or ordering parts for your machine.

The frame number (arrowed) is on the right-hand side of the steering head

Model code identification

The procedures in this manual identify the bikes by engine size (e.g. GSX-R600), then if further clarification is required also by the model suffix code (e.g. GSX-R600**K5**). The model code corresponds to the production year (which may not necessarily be the same as the year of first registration).

K6	2006
K7	2007
K8	2008
K9	2009

The model code can be established from the frame number (see below).

Model	Market	Initial frame number
GSX-R600K6 and K7	UK and EU	JS1CE111100100001-
GSX-R600U2K6 and K7	EU (restricted)	JS1CE211100100001-
GSX-R600U3K6 and K7	EU (restricted)	JS1CE311100100001-
GSX-R600K6	US and Canada	JS1GN7DA 62100001-
GSX-R600K7	US and Canada	JS1GN7DA 72100001-
GSX-R600K8 and K9	UK and EU	JS1CV111100100001-
GSX-R600U2K8 and K9	EU (restricted)	JS1CV211100100001-
GSX-R600U3K8 and K9	EU (restricted)	JS1CV311100100001-
GSX-R600K8	US and Canada	JS1GN7EA 82100001-
GSX-R600K9	US and Canada	JS1GN7EA 92100001-
GSX-R750K6 and K7	UK and EU	JS1CF111100100001-
GSX-R750U2K6 and K7	EU (restricted)	JS1CF211100100001-
GSX-R750K6	US and Canada	JS1GR7KA 62100001-
GSX-R750K7	US and Canada	JS1GR7KA 72100001-
GSX-R750K8 and K9	UK and EU	JS1CW111100100001-
GSX-R750U2K8 and K9	EU (restricted)	JS1CW211100100001-
GSX-R750K8	US and Canada	JS1GR7LA 82100001-
GSX-R600K9	US and Canada	JS1GR7LA 92100001-

On K6 and K7 models the VIN plate (arrowed) is behind the left-hand fairing side panel

On K8 and K9 models the VIN plate (arrowed) is on the main frame spar

The engine number (arrowed) is stamped into the right-hand side of the crankcase

Buying spare parts

Once you have found all the identification numbers, record them for reference when buying parts. Since the manufacturers change specifications, parts and vendors (companies that manufacture various components on the machine), providing the ID numbers is the only way to be reasonably sure that you are buying the correct parts.

Whenever possible, take the worn part to the dealer so direct comparison with the new component can be made. Along the trail from the manufacturer to the parts shelf, there are

numerous places that the part can end up with the wrong number or be listed incorrectly.

The two places to purchase new parts for your motorcycle the franchised or main dealer and the parts/accessories store differ in the type of parts they carry. While dealers can obtain every single genuine part for your motorcycle, the accessory store is usually limited to normal high wear items such as chains and sprockets, brake pads, spark plugs and cables, and to tune-up parts and various engine gaskets, etc. Rarely will an accessory outlet have major suspension

components, camshafts, transmission gears, or engine cases.

Used parts can be obtained from breakers yards for roughly half the price of new ones, but you can't always be sure of what you're getting. Once again, take your worn part to the breaker for direct comparison, or when ordering by mail order make sure that you can return it if you are not happy.

Whether buying new, used or rebuilt parts, the best course is to deal directly with someone who specialises in your particular make.

GSX-R600/750-K6 and K7 (2006 and 2007)

The engine is a liquid cooled four-cylinder with double overhead camshafts driven by chain off the right-hand end of the crankshaft. The crankcase is a two-piece arrangement that divides horizontally. The only structural difference between the 600 and the 750 is in the incorporation of a balancer shaft in the crankcase of the 750. Drive is transmitted to the six-speed gearbox via a conventional wet multi-plate clutch with slipper mechanism to control back-torque, and to the rear wheel by chain and sprockets.

The chassis comprises a compact, twin-spar aluminium alloy frame with a bolt-on rear sub-frame and triangulated swingarm. Front suspension is via upside-down forks with three-way adjustment. A mechanical steering damper is fitted as standard. Rear suspension has a rising rate, three-way adjustable aluminium-bodied mono-shock.

The front brake system has twin discs with radially mounted four piston calipers and a radially mounted master cylinder, while the rear system has a single disc and a single piston sliding caliper.

Fuel injection is managed by Suzuki's Dual Throttle Valve (SDTV) system, which incorporates an automatic fast idle system for cold starting.

GSX-R600/750-K8 and K9 (2008 and 2009)

The K8 models feature a number of changes, the most significant being the introduction of a drive mode selection switch (S-DMS, or Suzuki Drive Mode Selector). allowing the rider to chose between three different engine maps (controlling fuel and ignition parameters).

Other changes include new shape combustion chambers and 8-nozzle injectors, a redesigned exhaust system, an electronically controlled steering damper, new wheels, new triple headlights, a slightly larger capacity fuel tank and a redesigned fairing.

Bike spec

Engine

Type	Liquid cooled, in-line 4-cylinder
Capacity	
600 models	599 cc
750 models	750 cc
Bore x stroke	
600 models	67.0 x 42.5 mm
750 models	70.0 x 48.7 mm
Compression ratio	
600 models	
K6 and K7	12.5:1
K8 and K9	12.8:1
750 models	12.5:1
Camshafts	DOHC, chain driven
Valves	4 valves per cylinder
Fuel system	SDTV (Suzuki Dual Throttle Valve) fuel injection
Clutch	Wet multi-plate with slipper mechanism, cable operated
Transmission	6-speed constant mesh
Final drive chain	
600-K6 and K7 models	RK 525SMOZ7Y (114 links)
600-K8 and K9 models	RK 525SMOZ8 (114 links)
750 models	RK 525ROZ5Y (116 links)
Final drive sprockets	
600 models	16 tooth front, 43 tooth rear
750 models	17 tooth front, 45 tooth rear

Chassis

Type	Twin spar, aluminium alloy
Rake	23.45°
Trail	97 mm
Front suspension	
Type	Showa upside down 41 mm telescopic forks
Travel	120 mm
Adjustments	Spring pre-load, compression and rebound damping
Rear suspension	
Type	Rising rate linkage with single Showa shock
Wheel travel	130 mm
Adjustments	Spring pre-load, compression and rebound damping
Tyre sizes	
Front	120/70 ZR 17 58W
Rear	180/55 ZR 17 73W
Brakes	
Front	Twin 310 mm discs with opposed four-piston Tokico calipers
Rear	Single 220 mm disc with single-piston sliding Tokico caliper

Weights and dimensions

Overall length	2040 mm
Overall width.	715 mm
Overall height	1125 mm
Wheelbase	
All 600 models, 750-K6 and K7	1400 mm
750-K8 and K9	1405 mm
Seat height	810 mm
Ground clearance.	130 mm
Dry weight*	
600-K6 and K7 models.	161 kg
600-K8 and K9 models.	165 kg
750-K6 and K7 models.	163 kg
750-K8 and K9 models.	167 kg

*For all California models add 1kg

Capacities

Fuel tank	
K6 and K7 models	16.5 litres
K8 and K9 models	17.0 litres

*For all California models reduce by 1 litre

Engine oil capacity	
Oil change.	2.2 litres
Oil and filter change	2.5 litres
Following engine overhaul – dry engine, new filter.	2.9 litres
Coolant capacity (inc. reservoir).	2.65 litres

Professional mechanics are trained in safe working procedures. However enthusiastic you may be about getting on with the job at hand, take the time to ensure that your safety is not put at risk. A moment's lack of attention can result in an accident, as can failure to observe simple precautions.

There will always be new ways of having accidents, and the following is not a comprehensive list of all dangers; it is intended rather to make you aware of the risks and to encourage a safe approach to all work you carry out on your bike.

Asbestos

● Certain friction, insulating, sealing and other products - such as brake pads, clutch linings, gaskets, etc. - contain asbestos. Extreme care must be taken to avoid inhalation of dust from such products since it is hazardous to health. If in doubt, assume that they do contain asbestos.

Fire

● Remember at all times that petrol is highly flammable. Never smoke or have any kind of naked flame around, when working on the vehicle. But the risk does not end there - a spark caused by an electrical short-circuit, by two metal surfaces contacting each other, by careless use of tools, or even by static electricity built up in your body under certain conditions, can ignite petrol vapour, which in a confined space is highly explosive. Never use petrol as a cleaning solvent. Use an approved safety solvent.

● Always disconnect the battery earth terminal before working on any part of the fuel or electrical system, and never risk spilling fuel on to a hot engine or exhaust.

● It is recommended that a fire extinguisher of a type suitable for fuel and electrical fires is kept handy in the garage or workplace at all times. Never try to extinguish a fuel or electrical fire with water.

Fumes

● Certain fumes are highly toxic and can quickly cause unconsciousness and even death if inhaled to any extent. Petrol vapour comes into this category, as do the vapours from certain solvents such as trichloroethylene. Any draining or pouring of such volatile fluids should be done in a well ventilated area.

● When using cleaning fluids and solvents, read the instructions carefully. Never use materials from unmarked containers - they may give off poisonous vapours.

● Never run the engine of a motor vehicle in an enclosed space such as a garage. Exhaust fumes contain carbon monoxide which is extremely poisonous; if you need to run the engine, always do so in the open air or at least have the rear of the vehicle outside the workplace.

The battery

● Never cause a spark, or allow a naked light near the vehicle's battery. It will normally be giving off a certain amount of hydrogen gas, which is highly explosive.

● Always disconnect the battery ground (earth) terminal before working on the fuel or electrical systems (except where noted).

● If possible, loosen the filler plugs or cover when charging the battery from an external source. Do not charge at an excessive rate or the battery may burst.

● Take care when topping up, cleaning or carrying the battery. The acid electrolyte, evenwhen diluted, is very corrosive and should not be allowed to contact the eyes or skin. Always wear rubber gloves and goggles or a face shield. If you ever need to prepare electrolyte yourself, always add the acid slowly to the water; never add the water to the acid.

Electricity

● When using an electric power tool, inspection light etc., always ensure that the appliance is correctly connected to its plug and that, where necessary, it is properly grounded (earthed). Do not use such appliances in damp conditions and, again, beware of creating a spark or applying excessive heat in the vicinity of fuel or fuel vapour. Also ensure that the appliances meet national safety standards.

● A severe electric shock can result from touching certain parts of the electrical system, such as the spark plug wires (HT leads), when the engine is running or being cranked, particularly if components are damp or the insulation is defective. Where an electronic ignition system is used, the secondary (HT) voltage is much higher and could prove fatal.

Remember...

✗ **Don't** start the engine without first ascertaining that the transmission is in neutral.

✗ **Don't** suddenly remove the pressure cap from a hot cooling system - cover it with a cloth and release the pressure gradually first, or you may get scalded by escaping coolant.

✗ **Don't** attempt to drain oil until you are sure it has cooled sufficiently to avoid scalding you.

✗ **Don't** grasp any part of the engine or exhaust system without first ascertaining that it is cool enough not to burn you.

✗ **Don't** allow brake fluid or antifreeze to contact the machine's paintwork or plastic components.

✗ **Don't** siphon toxic liquids such as fuel, hydraulic fluid or antifreeze by mouth, or allow them to remain on your skin.

✗ **Don't** inhale dust - it may be injurious to health (see Asbestos heading).

✗ **Don't** allow any spilled oil or grease to remain on the floor - wipe it up right away, before someone slips on it.

✗ **Don't** use ill-fitting spanners or other tools which may slip and cause injury.

✗ **Don't** lift a heavy component which may be beyond your capability - get assistance.

✗ **Don't** rush to finish a job or take unverified short cuts.

✗ **Don't** allow children or animals in or around an unattended vehicle.

✗ **Don't** inflate a tyre above the recommended pressure. Apart from overstressing the carcass, in extreme cases the tyre may blow off forcibly.

✔ **Do** ensure that the machine is supported securely at all times. This is especially important when the machine is blocked up to aid wheel or fork removal.

✔ **Do** take care when attempting to loosen a stubborn nut or bolt. It is generally better to pull on a spanner, rather than push, so that if you slip, you fall away from the machine rather than onto it.

✔ **Do** wear eye protection when using power tools such as drill, sander, bench grinder etc.

✔ **Do** use a barrier cream on your hands prior to undertaking dirty jobs - it will protect your skin from infection as well as making the dirt easier to remove afterwards; but make sure your hands aren't left slippery. Note that long-term contact with used engine oil can be a health hazard.

✔ **Do** keep loose clothing (cuffs, ties etc. and long hair) well out of the way of moving mechanical parts.

✔ **Do** remove rings, wristwatch etc., before working on the vehicle - especially the electrical system.

✔ **Do** keep your work area tidy - it is only too easy to fall over articles left lying around.

✔ **Do** exercise caution when compressing springs for removal or installation. Ensure that the tension is applied and released in a controlled manner, using suitable tools which preclude the possibility of the spring escaping violently.

✔ **Do** ensure that any lifting tackle used has a safe working load rating adequate for the job.

✔ **Do** get someone to check periodically that all is well, when working alone on the vehicle.

✔ **Do** carry out work in a logical sequence and check that everything is correctly assembled and tightened afterwards.

✔ **Do** remember that your vehicle's safety affects that of yourself and others. If in doubt on any point, get professional advice.

● If in spite of following these precautions, you are unfortunate enough to injure yourself, seek medical attention as soon as possible.

Engine oil level

Before you start:
✔ Start the engine and allow it to reach normal operating temperature.
Caution: Do not run the engine in an enclosed space such as a garage or workshop.
✔ Stop the engine and allow the motorcycle to stand undisturbed for a few minutes to allow the oil level to stabilise. Make sure the motorcycle is on level ground and held upright whilst the oil level is checked.

Bike care:
● If you have to add oil frequently, you should check whether you have any oil leaks. If there is no sign of oil leakage from the joints and gaskets the engine could be burning oil (see *Fault Finding*).

The correct oil
● Modern, high-revving engines place great demands on their oil. It is very important that the correct oil for your bike is used.
● Always top up with a good quality motorcycle oil of the specified type and viscosity and do not overfill the engine. A different viscosity oil can be used if required (see oil viscosity chart). Do not use oils marked 'Energy Conserving' or car motor oils.

Oil type	API grade SF/SG or SH/SJ, or JASO grade MA motorcycle oil
Oil viscosity	SAE 10W40

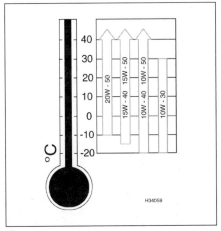

Select the oil best suited to your conditions

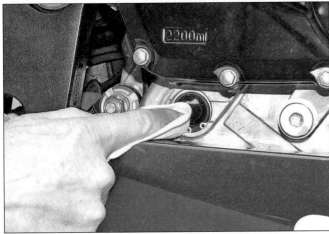

1 Wipe the oil level window in the right-hand side of the engine so that it is clean.

2 With the motorcycle held upright, the oil level must lie between the upper and lower level lines (arrowed).

3 If the level is on or below the lower line, remove the filler cap from the top of the clutch cover.

4 Top the engine up with the recommended grade and type of oil, to bring the level almost up to the upper line on the window. Do not overfill. Refit the filler cap.

Coolant level

> ⚠ **Warning: DO NOT remove the radiator pressure cap to add coolant. Topping up is done via the coolant reservoir tank filler. DO NOT leave open containers of coolant about, as it is poisonous.**

Before you start:

✔ Make sure you have a supply of coolant available – either one of the 'off the shelf' pre-mixed coolant products or a prepared mixture of 50% distilled water and 50% corrosion inhibited ethylene glycol anti-freeze.
✔ The motorcycle must be positioned on level ground with the engine cold.
✔ The coolant reservoir is located on the inside of the right-hand fairing side panel and is visible by looking over the front wheel from the left-hand side.

Bike care:

● Use only the specified coolant mixture. It is important that anti-freeze is used in the system all year round, and not just in the winter. Do not top the system up using only water, as the system will become too diluted.
● Do not overfill the reservoir tank. If the coolant is significantly above the 'F' level line at any time, the surplus should be siphoned or drained off to prevent the possibility of it being expelled out of the overflow hose.
● If the coolant level falls steadily, check the system for leaks (see Chapter 1). If no leaks are found and the level continues to fall, it is recommended that the machine is taken to a Suzuki dealer for a pressure test.

1 The coolant level should be between the 'F' and 'L' level lines (arrowed) on the reservoir (shown with fairing side panel removed for clarity). If topping up is required, remove the right-hand fairing side panel (see Chapter 7).

2 Remove the reservoir filler cap.

3 Top the coolant level up with the recommended coolant mixture, using a funnel to avoid spillage. Fit the cap securely, then install the side panel.

Suspension, steering and drive chain

Suspension and steering:

● Check that the front and rear suspension operates smoothly without binding.
● Check that the suspension is adjusted as required.
● Check that the steering moves smoothly from lock-to-lock (taking into account the resistance of the steering damper).

Drive chain:

● Check that the drive chain slack isn't excessive, and adjust if necessary (see Chapter 1).
● If the chain looks dry, lubricate it (see Chapter 1).

Brake fluid levels

> ⚠ **Warning: Brake hydraulic fluid can harm your eyes and damage painted surfaces, so use extreme caution when handling and pouring it and cover surrounding surfaces with rag. Do not use fluid that has been standing open for some time, as it absorbs moisture from the air which can cause a dangerous loss of braking effectiveness.**

Before you start:

✔ Support the motorcycle in an upright position when checking the fluid level.
✔ When checking the level in the front master cylinder position the handlebars so the reservoir is as level as possible.

✔ The rear master cylinder reservoir is located on the inside of the rear sub-frame on the right-hand side of the machine.
✔ If topping up is necessary, make sure you have a supply of DOT 4 hydraulic fluid.
✔ Wrap a rag around the reservoir being worked on to ensure that any spillage does not come into contact with painted surfaces.

Bike care:

● The fluid level in the front and rear brake master cylinder reservoirs will drop slightly as the brake pads wear down. If the fluid level is low check the brake pads for wear (see Chapter 1), and replace them with new ones if necessary (see Chapter 6). Do not top the reservoir(s) up until the new pads have been fitted, and then check to see if topping up is still necessary – when the caliper pistons are pushed back to accommodate the extra thickness of the new pads some fluid will be displaced back into the reservoir. The difference between the UPPER and LOWER levels in the reservoir should equate to the amount of fluid that will be displaced during the lifetime of a brake pad.
● If any fluid reservoir requires repeated topping-up this is an indication of an hydraulic leak somewhere in the system, which should be investigated immediately.
● Check for signs of fluid leakage from the hydraulic hoses and components – if found, rectify immediately.
● Check the operation of both brakes before taking the machine on the road; if there is evidence of air in the system (spongy feel to lever or pedal), it must be bled as described in Chapter 6.

FRONT BRAKE

Steps 1–5

REAR BRAKE

Steps 6–11

1 The front brake fluid level is visible through the reservoir body – it must be between the UPPER and LOWER level lines (arrowed).

2 If the level is on or below the LOWER level line, remove the reservoir cap clamp screw, then unscrew the cap and remove the diaphragm plate and the diaphragm.

3 Top up with new DOT 4 brake fluid, until the level is just below the UPPER level line. Do not overfill the reservoir, and take care to avoid spills (see **Warning** above).

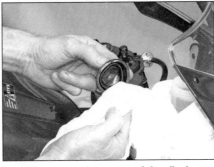

4 Wipe any moisture out of the diaphragm using an absorbent lint-free cloth.

5 Ensure that the diaphragm is correctly seated before installing the plate and cap. Tighten the cap and the clamp screw securely.

6 The rear brake fluid level is visible through the reservoir body – the fluid level must be between the UPPER and LOWER level lines (arrowed).

7 If the level is on or below the LOWER level line, undo the reservoir mounting bolt and manoeuvre the reservoir out so the cover is accessible.

8 Undo the reservoir cover screws and remove the cover, plate and diaphragm.

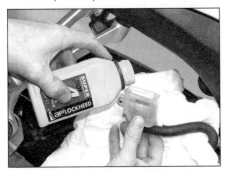

9 Top up with new DOT 4 brake fluid, until the level is just below the UPPER level line. Do not overfill the reservoir, and take care to avoid spills (see **Warning** above).

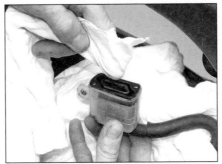

10 Wipe any moisture out of the diaphragm using an absorbent lint-free cloth.

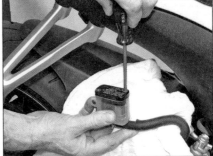

11 Ensure that the diaphragm is correctly seated before fitting the plate and the cover and tightening the screws. Fit the reservoir onto its bracket.

Tyres

The correct pressures:

● The tyres must be checked when **cold**, not immediately after riding. Note that low tyre pressures may cause the tyre to slip on the rim or come off. High tyre pressures will cause abnormal tread wear and unsafe handling.

● Use an accurate pressure gauge. Many garage forecourt gauges are wildly inaccurate. If you buy your own, spend as much as you can justify on a quality gauge.

● Proper air pressure will increase tyre life and provide maximum stability and ride comfort.

600 models

Tyre pressures (cold)	Front	Rear
Solo	36 psi (2.5 Bar)	36 psi (2.5 Bar)
With passenger	36 psi (2.5 Bar)	42 psi (2.9 Bar)

750 models

Tyre pressures (cold)	Front	Rear
Solo	36 psi (2.5 Bar)	42 psi (2.9 Bar)
With passenger	36 psi (2.5 Bar)	42 psi (2.9 Bar)

Tyre care:

● Check the tyres carefully for cuts, tears, embedded nails or other sharp objects and excessive wear. Riding the motorcycle with damaged or worn tyres is extremely dangerous, as traction and handling are directly affected.

● Check the condition of the tyre valve and ensure the dust cap is in place.

● Pick out any objects which have become embedded in the tyre tread. If left, they will eventually penetrate through the casing and cause a puncture.

● If tyre damage is apparent, or unexplained loss of pressure is experienced, seek the advice of a tyre fitting specialist without delay.

Tyre tread depth:

● At the time of writing UK law requires that tread depth must be at least 1 mm over 3/4 of the tread breadth all the way around the tyre, with no bald patches. Many riders, however, consider 2 mm tread depth minimum to be a safer limit. The manufacturer's recommended minimum tread depth is given below.

● Many tyres now incorporate wear indicators in the tread. Identify the triangular pointer or 'TWI' mark on the tyre sidewall to locate the indicator bar and renew the tyre if the tread has worn down to the bar.

Minimum tyre tread depths	
Front	1.6 mm
Rear	2.0 mm

1 Remove the cap from the valve – if there isn't one there, fit a new one.

2 Check the tyre pressures when the tyres are cold and keep them properly inflated. Fit the cap on completion.

3 Measure tread depth at the centre of the tyre using a tread depth gauge.

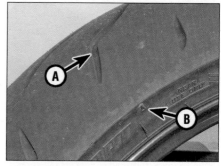

4 Tyre tread wear indicator bar (A) and its location marking (usually either an arrow, a triangle or the letters TWI) on the sidewall (B).

Legal and safety checks

Lighting and signalling:

● Take a minute to check that the headlights, tail light, brake light, instrument lights and turn signals all work correctly.

● Check that the horn sounds when the switch is operated.

● A working speedometer graduated in mph is a statutory requirement in the UK.

Safety:

● Check that the throttle grip rotates smoothly and snaps shut when released, in all steering positions. Also check for the correct amount of freeplay (see Chapter 1).

● Check that the steering moves freely from lock-to-lock.

● Check that the brake lever and pedal, clutch lever and gearchange lever operate smoothly. Lubricate them at the specified intervals or when necessary (see Chapter 1).

● Check that the engine shuts off when the kill switch is operated.

● Check that sidestand return spring holds the stand securely up when retracted.

Fuel:

● This may seem obvious, but check that you have enough fuel to complete your journey. If you notice signs of fuel leakage – rectify the cause immediately.

● Ensure you use the correct grade unleaded fuel – see Chapter 4 Specifications.

Chapter 1
Routine maintenance and Servicing

Contents Section number

Degrees of difficulty

Easy, suitable for novice with little experience | **Fairly easy,** suitable for beginner with some experience | **Fairly difficult,** suitable for competent DIY mechanic | **Difficult,** suitable for experienced DIY mechanic | **Very difficult,** suitable for expert DIY or professional

Engine

Valve clearances (COLD engine)
- Intake valves . . . . 0.08 to 0.18 mm
- Exhaust valves . . . . 0.18 to 0.28 mm

Spark plugs

   K6 and K7 models
- Standard . . . . NGK CR9E or Nippondenso U27ESR-N
- For cold climate (below 5°C) . . . . NGK CR8E or Nippondenso U24ESR-N
- For extended high speed riding . . . . NGK CR10E or Nippondenso U31ESR-N
- Electrode gap . . . . 0.7 to 0.8 mm

   K8 and K9 models (iridium plugs)
- Standard . . . . NGK CR9EIA-9 or Nippondenso IU27D
- For cold climate (below 5°C) . . . . NGK CR8EIA-9 or Nippondenso IU24D
- For extended high speed riding . . . . NGK CR10EIA-9or Nippondenso IU31D
- Electrode gap . . . . 0.8 to 0.9 mm

Engine idle speed
- 600 models . . . . 1300 ± 100 rpm
- 750 models . . . . 1200 ± 100 rpm

Clutch release mechanism screw (see Section 8) . . . . 1/2 turn out

Frame and cycle parts

Drive chain
- Freeplay . . . . 20 to 30 mm
- Stretch limit (21 pin length – see text) . . . . 319.4 mm

Cable freeplay
- Clutch cable . . . . 10 to 15 mm
- Throttle cable . . . . 2 to 4 mm

Rear brake pedal height . . . . 65 to 75 mm

Tyre pressures (cold) and tread depth . . . . see *Pre-ride checks*

Lubricants and fluids

Drive chain lubricant . . . . Aerosol chain lubricant suitable for O-ring chains or heavy motor oil (such as gear oil)

Engine oil type . . . . API grade SF/SG or SH/SJ, or JASO grade MA, 4-stroke motorcycle oil

Engine oil viscosity . . . . SAE 10W40 (but see *Pre-ride checks*)

Engine oil capacity
- Oil change . . . . 2.2 litres
- Oil and filter change . . . . 2.5 litres
- Following engine overhaul – dry engine, new filter . . . . 2.9 litres

Coolant type . . . . 50% distilled water, 50% corrosion inhibited ethylene glycol anti-freeze, or pre-mix coolant

Coolant capacity
- Engine and radiator . . . . 2.40 litres
- Reservoir . . . . 0.25 litre

Brake fluid . . . . DOT 4

Front fork oil . . . . see Chapter 5

Steering head bearings . . . . Lithium-based multi-purpose grease

Wheel bearings (unsealed) . . . . Lithium-based multi-purpose grease

Swingarm pivot bearings . . . . Lithium-based multi-purpose grease

Suspension linkage bearings . . . . Lithium-based multi-purpose grease

Bearing seal lips . . . . Lithium-based multi-purpose grease

Gearchange lever/rear brake pedal/footrest pivots . . . . Lithium-based multi-purpose grease

Front brake lever and clutch lever pivots . . . . Lithium-based multi-purpose grease

Cables . . . . Aerosol cable lubricant

Sidestand pivot and spring hook . . . . Lithium-based multi-purpose grease

Throttle grip . . . . Multi-purpose grease or dry film lubricant

Torque settings

Clutch release mechanism cap . . . . 11 Nm

Engine oil drain plug . . . . 23 Nm

Fork clamp bolts . . . . 23 Nm

Handlebar clamp bolts . . . . 23 Nm

Oil filter . . . . 20 Nm

Rear axle nut . . . . 100 Nm

Spark plugs . . . . 11 Nm

Steering stem nut . . . . 90 Nm

Timing inspection cap . . . . 11 Nm

Pre-ride

☐ See 'Pre-ride checks' at the beginning of this manual.

After the initial 600 miles (1000 km)

Note: *This check is usually performed by a Suzuki dealer after the first 600 miles (1000 km) from new. Thereafter, maintenance is carried out according to the following intervals of the schedule.*

Every 600 miles (1000 km)

☐ Check, adjust, clean and lubricate the drive chain (Section 1)

Every 4000 miles (6000 km) or 12 months

Carry out all the items under the pre-ride checks and the 600 mile (1000 km) check, plus the following:

☐ Check for drive chain and sprocket wear and chain stretch (Section 1)
☐ Clean the air filter element (Section 2)
☐ Check the spark plugs (Section 3)
☐ Check the fuel system hoses and components (Section 4)
☐ Change the engine oil (Section 5)
☐ Check and adjust the engine idle speed (Section 6)
☐ Check throttle cable operation and freeplay (Section 7)
☐ Check/adjust the clutch cable freeplay and if necessary adjust the clutch release mechanism (Section 8)
☐ Check the cooling system (Section 9)
☐ Check the brake system (Section 10)
☐ Check the brake pads for wear (Section 10)
☐ Check the tyre and wheel condition, and the tyre tread depth (Section 11 and *Pre-ride checks*)
☐ Check the tightness of all nuts and bolts (Section 12)
☐ Check and lubricate the sidestand pivot, lever pivots and cables (Section 13)

Every 7500 miles (12,000 km) or two years

Carry out all the items under the 4000 mile (6000 km) check, plus the following:

☐ Replace the spark plugs with new ones (Section 3)
☐ Check throttle valve synchronisation (Section 14)
☐ Check the operation of the PAIR system and on California models check the EVAP system (Section 15)
☐ Check the steering head bearing freeplay (Section 16)
☐ Check the front and rear suspension (Section 17)
☐ Check the operation of the exhaust control valve (Section 18)

Note: *Always perform the pre-ride inspection at every maintenance interval (in addition to the procedures listed). The intervals listed below are the intervals recommended by the manufacturer for each particular operation during the model years covered in this manual. Your owner's manual may have different intervals for your model.*

Every 11,000 miles (18,000 km) or three years

Carry out all the items under the 4000 mile (6000 km) check, plus the following:

☐ Replace the air filter element with a new one (Section 2)
☐ Change the engine oil and fit a new oil filter (Section 5)

Every 14,500 miles (24,000 km) or four years

Carry out all the items under the 7500 mile (12,000 km) check, plus the following:

☐ Check the valve clearances (Section 19)

Every two years

☐ Change the coolant (Section 9)
☐ Change the brake fluid (Section 10)

Every four years

☐ Replace the brake hoses with new ones (Section 10)

Non-scheduled maintenance

Note: *These items are not part of the manufacturer's mileage or time maintenance schedule, but are, in the author's opinion, necessary to ensure trouble-free running of the motorcycle.*

☐ Replace the fuel filter with a new one (Section 4)
☐ Renew the fuel system, PAIR system, and on California models the EVAP system, hoses (Section 4)
☐ Replace the cooling system hoses with new ones (Section 9)
☐ Replace the brake master cylinder and caliper seals with new ones (Section 10)
☐ Check the wheel bearings (Section 11)
☐ Re-grease the steering head bearings (Section 16)
☐ Change the front fork oil (Section 17)
☐ Re-grease the swingarm and suspension linkage bearings (Section 17)
☐ Check the sidestand and starter interlock (safety) circuit (Section 20)
☐ Check the battery (Section 21)

Component locations on right-hand side

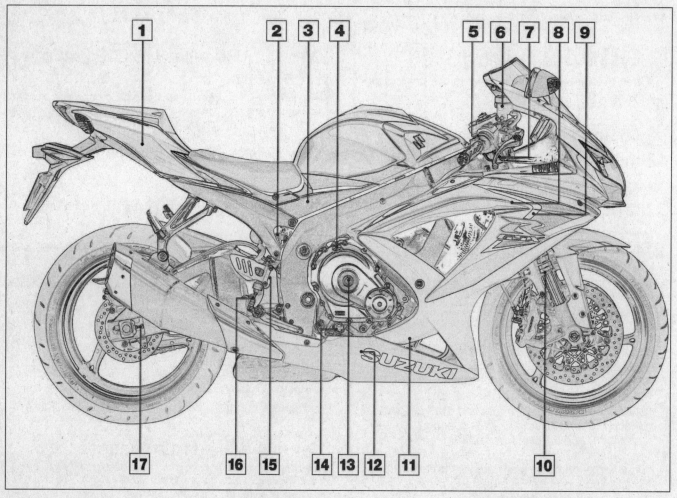

1 Exhaust control valve servo – K6/K7
2 Rear brake fluid reservoir
3 Exhaust control valve servo – K8/K9
4 Engine oil filler cap
5 Steering head bearing adjuster
6 Front brake fluid reservoir

7 Throttle cable adjuster
8 Radiator pressure cap
9 Coolant reservoir
10 Fork oil seals
11 Engine oil filter
12 Exhaust control valve

13 Clutch release mechanism
14 Engine oil level window
15 Rear brake light switch
16 Rear brake pedal height adjuster
17 Drive chain adjuster

Component locations on left-hand side

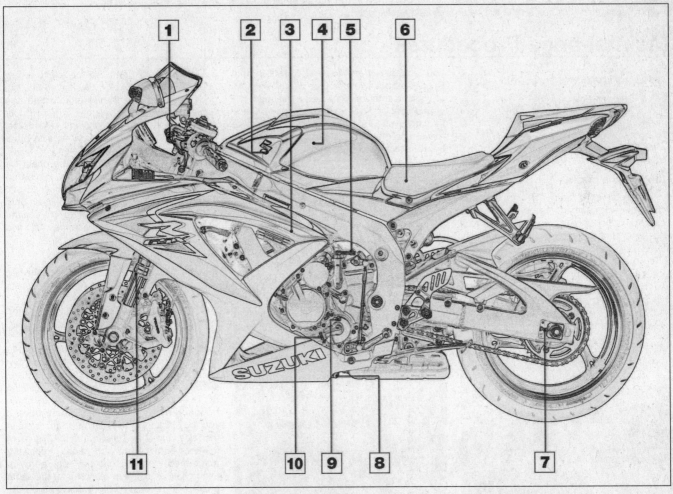

1 Clutch cable upper adjuster
2 Air filter
3 Idle speed adjuster – K6/K7
4 Fuel filter

5 Clutch cable lower adjuster
6 Battery
7 Drive chain adjuster
8 Engine oil drain plug

9 Cooling system bleed bolt
10 Radiator hose disconnection point for
   coolant drain
11 Fork oil seals

1 This Chapter is designed to help the home mechanic maintain his/her motorcycle for safety, economy, long life and peak performance.

2 Deciding where to start or plug into the routine maintenance schedule depends on several factors. If the warranty period on your motorcycle has just expired, and if it has been maintained according to the warranty standards, you may want to pick up routine maintenance as it coincides with the next mileage or calendar interval. If you have owned the machine for some time but have never performed any maintenance on it, then you may want to start at the nearest interval and include some additional procedures to ensure that nothing important is overlooked. If you have just had a major engine overhaul, then you may want to start the maintenance routine from the beginning. If you have a used machine and have no knowledge of its history or maintenance record, you may desire to combine all the checks into one large service initially and then settle into the maintenance schedule prescribed.

3 Before beginning any maintenance or repair, the machine should be cleaned thoroughly. Cleaning will help ensure that dirt does not contaminate the engine and will allow you to detect wear and damage that could otherwise easily go unnoticed.

4 Certain maintenance information is sometimes printed on decals attached to the motorcycle. If the information on the decals differs from that included here, use the information on the decal.

Maintenance Procedures

1 Drive chain and sprockets

Check, adjust, clean and lubricate the drive chain

Check chain slack

1 A neglected drive chain won't last long and will quickly damage the sprockets. Routine chain adjustment and lubrication isn't difficult and will ensure maximum chain and sprocket life.

2 To check the chain, place the bike on its sidestand and shift the transmission into neutral. Make sure the ignition switch is OFF.

3 Push up on the bottom run of the chain midway between the two sprockets and measure the amount of slack, then compare your measurement to that listed in this Chapter's Specifications (see illustration). As the chain stretches with wear, adjustment will periodically be necessary (see below). Since the chain will rarely wear evenly, roll the bike forward so that another section of chain can be checked (having an assistant to do this makes the task a lot easier); do this several times to check the entire length of chain, and mark the tightest spot.

Caution: Riding the bike with excess slack in the chain could lead to damage.

4 In some cases where lubrication has been neglected, corrosion and galling may cause the links to bind and kink, which effectively shortens the chain's length and makes it tight (see illustration). Thoroughly clean and work free any such links, then highlight them with a marker pen or paint. After the bike has been ridden repeat the measurement for slack in the highlighted area. If the chain has kinked again and is still tight, replace it with a new one (see Chapter 6). A rusty, kinked or worn chain will damage the sprockets and can damage transmission bearings. If in any doubt as to the condition of a chain, it is far better to fit a new one than risk damage to other components and possibly yourself.

5 Check the entire length of the chain for damaged rollers, loose links and pins, and missing O-rings, and replace it with a new one if necessary. **Note:** *Never fit a new chain onto old sprockets, and never use the old chain if you fit new sprockets – replace the chain and sprockets as a set.*

Adjust chain slack

6 Move the bike so that the chain is positioned with the tightest point at the centre of its bottom run, then put it on the sidestand.

7 On US and Canada models, where fitted remove the split pin from the rear axle nut. Discard it as a new one must be used.

8 Slacken the rear axle nut (see illustration).

9 Slacken the adjuster bolt locknut, then turn the adjuster bolt on each side evenly until the amount of freeplay specified at the beginning of the Chapter is obtained at the centre of the bottom run of the chain (see illustration). If you are slackening the chain turn the bolts in then push the wheel forwards so the alignment markers contact the bolt heads. Following adjustment, check that the rear edge of each chain adjustment marker is in the same position in relation to the index lines on the swingarm (see illustration). It is important the same index lines on each side align with the

1.3 Push up on the chain and measure the slack

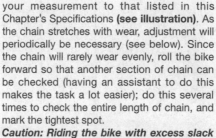

1.4 Neglect has caused the links in this chain to kink

1.8 Slacken the axle nut (arrowed)

1.9a Loosen the adjuster locknut (A) then turn the adjuster bolt (B) as required

1.9b Adjuster blocks must align with same marks on both sides of the swingarm

1.10 Tighten the axle nut to the correct torque

1.13 Apply lubricant to the overlap between the chain sideplates

rear edge of the marker; if not, the rear wheel will be out of alignment with the front. If there is a discrepancy in the marker positions, adjust one of them so that its position is exactly the same as the other. Check the chain freeplay again as described above and readjust if necessary. If the rear edge of the adjustment marker reaches the last index lines either the chain has stretched excessively (see below to measure the amount of stretch), or it has too many links it (see Specifications) – in either case it must be replaced with a new one (see Chapter 6).

10 Tighten the axle nut to the torque setting specified at the beginning of the Chapter **(see illustration)**. Recheck the adjustment as above, then check that the wheel runs freely. Make sure that the adjuster bolt heads are set against the alignment markers, turning them out slightly if necessary, then tighten the locknuts.

11 On US and Canada models, where fitted install a new split pin and secure it correctly.

Clean and lubricate the chain

12 If required, wash the chain in paraffin (kerosene) or a suitable non-flammable or high flash-point solvent that will not damage the O-rings, using a soft brush to work any dirt out if necessary. Wipe the cleaner off the chain and allow it to dry, using compressed air if available. If the chain is excessively dirty remove it from the machine and allow it to soak in the paraffin or solvent (see Chapter 6). *Caution: Don't use petrol (gasoline), an unsuitable solvent or other cleaning*

fluids which might damage the internal sealing properties of the chain. Don't use high-pressure water to clean the chain. The entire process shouldn't take longer than ten minutes, otherwise the O-rings could be damaged.

13 The best time to lubricate the chain is after the motorcycle has been ridden. When the chain is warm, the lubricant will penetrate the joints between the sideplates better than when cold. **Note:** *Suzuki specifies a heavy motor oil (such as gear oil) or an aerosol chain lube that it is suitable for O-ring or X-ring (sealed) chains; do not use any other chain lubricants – the solvents could damage the chain's sealing rings.* Apply the oil to the area where the sideplates overlap – not the middle of the rollers **(see illustration)**.

> **HAYNES HiNT** *Apply the lubricant to the top of the lower chain run, so centrifugal force will work the oil into the chain when the bike is moving. After applying the lubricant, let it soak in a few minutes before wiping off any excess.*

> ⚠ *Warning: Take care not to get any lubricant on the tyres or brake system components – hold a piece of card between them and the chain as a shield. If any of the lubricant inadvertently contacts them, clean it off thoroughly using a suitable solvent or dedicated brake cleaner before riding the machine.*

Check the drive chain stretch and sprocket wear

14 Check the entire length of the chain for damaged rollers, loose links and pins, and missing O-rings. Fit a new chain if damage is found. **Note:** *Never fit a new chain onto old sprockets, and never use the old chain if you fit new sprockets – replace the chain and sprockets as a set.*

15 Remove the front sprocket cover (see Chapter 6). Check the teeth on the front sprocket and the rear sprocket for wear **(see illustration)**. If the sprocket teeth are worn excessively, replace the chain and both sprockets with a new set.

16 Inspect the drive chain slider on the front of the swingarm for excessive wear and damage. Remove the swingarm and replace the slider with a new one if necessary (see Chapter 6).

17 Measure the amount of chain stretch as follows:

18 On US and Canada models, where fitted remove the split pin from the rear axle nut. Discard it as a new one must be used.

19 Slacken the rear axle nut **(see illustration 1.8)**.

20 Slacken the adjuster bolt locknuts, then turn the adjuster bolts out evenly until the chain is tight, but not taut **(see illustration 1.9a)**. Measure along the bottom run the length of 21 pins (from the centre of the 1st pin to the centre of the 21st pin) and compare the result to the stretch limit specified at the beginning of the Chapter **(see illustration)**. Rotate the rear wheel so that several sections of the chain can be measured, then calculate the average. If the chain stretch measurement exceeds the service limit it must be replaced with a new one (see Chapter 6). **Note:** *Never fit a new chain onto old sprockets, and never use the old chain if you fit new sprockets – replace the chain and sprockets as a set..*

21 If the chain is good, reset the adjusters so that there is the correct amount of freeplay (see Steps 9 to 11).

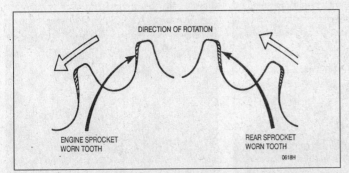

DIRECTION OF ROTATION

ENGINE SPROCKET WORN TOOTH

REAR SPROCKET WORN TOOTH

0618H

1.15 Check the sprockets in the areas indicated to see if they are worn excessively

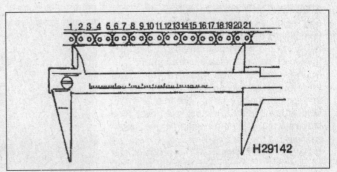

1 2 3 4 5 6 7 8 9 10 11 12 13 14 15 16 17 18 19 20 21

H29142

1.20 Measure the distance between the 1st and 21st pins to determine chain stretch

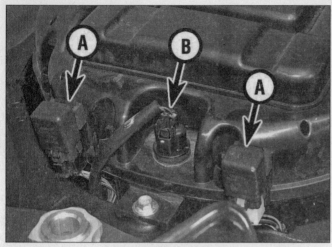

2.2 Displace the relays (A) and disconnect the wiring connector (B)

2.3 Release the clamp and detach the hose (arrowed)

2.4a Undo the screws (arrowed) . . .

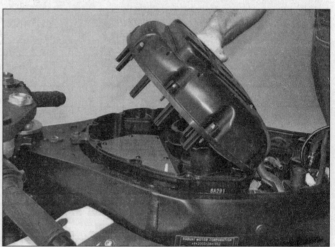

2.4b . . . remove the cover . . .

2   Air filter

Caution: If the machine is continually ridden in dusty conditions, the filter should be cleaned more frequently.

1 Raise the fuel tank (see Chapter 4).
2 On K6 and K7 models displace the relays and the IAT sensor from the front of the cover **(see illustration)**.
3 Detach the crankcase breather hose from the top of the cover **(see illustration)**.
4 Undo the air filter cover screws, not forgetting the recessed one in the middle, and remove the rear ones – the front and side screws are captive. Remove the cover **(see illustrations)**. Note the position of the rubber seal around the edge of the cover.
5 Withdraw the filter from the housing **(see illustration)**. Note the position of the filter seal.
6 Tap the filter on a hard surface to dislodge any dirt. DO NOT use compressed air to clean

the filter element. If the element is damaged or extremely dirty, fit a new one.
7 Ensure the inside of the filter housing is clean.
8 Release the clip and remove the cap from the drain on the back of the filter housing on the left-hand side and allow any fluid to drain, then install the cap and secure it with the clip **(see illustration)**.
9 Ensure the filter seal is correctly located in the housing, then install the filter with the meshed

side facing up **(see illustration 2.5)**. Make sure the seal is properly seated around the edge of the cover and fit the cover **(see illustration 2.4b)**. Install the cover screws and tighten them **(see illustration 2.4a)**.
10 Connect the crankcase breather hose and fit the clamp **(see illustration 2.3)**. On K6 and K7 models fit the relays and the IAT sensor **(see illustration 2.2)**. Lower the fuel tank (see Chapter 4).

2.5 . . . then lift out the filter

2.8 Filter housing drain cap (arrowed)

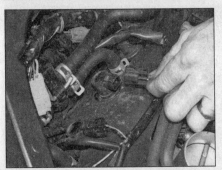

3.3 Disconnect the wiring connector . . .

3.4 . . . then pull the coil off the spark plug

3.5 Removing a spark plug using the socket and spanner supplied in the toolkit

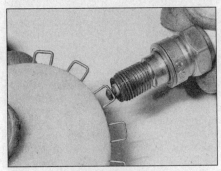

3.6a Using a wire gauge to measure the spark plug electrode gap

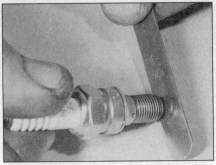

3.6b Using a feeler gauge to measure the spark plug electrode gap

3.6c Adjust the electrode gap by bending the side electrode only

3 Spark plugs

Special tool: *On K6 and K7 models, which are fitted with conventional plugs, a set of feeler gauges or a wire gauge is necessary for this job. On K8 and K9 models, which are fitted with Iridium plugs, a wire gauge is necessary for this job – feeler blades should not be used.*
Note: *The spark plug caps are integral with the ignition coils. To avoid damaging the wiring, always disconnect the wiring connectors before removing the coils. Do not attempt to lever the coils off the plugs or pull them off with pliers. Do not drop the coils.*

1 Make sure your spark plug socket is the correct size before attempting to remove the plugs – a suitable one is supplied in the motorcycle's tool kit which is stored under the passenger seat. Make sure the ignition is switched OFF.
2 To access the spark plugs, remove the air filter housing (see Chapter 4).
3 Disconnect each coil's wiring connector **(see illustration)**.
4 Clean the area around the coil seal to prevent any dirt falling into the spark plug channel, then pull the coil off each spark plug **(see illustration)**.
5 Using either the plug socket supplied in the bike's toolkit or a deep socket type wrench, unscrew each plug from the cylinder head **(see illustration)**. Lay each plug out in relation to its cylinder; if any plug shows up a problem

it will then be easy to identify the troublesome cylinder.
6 On K6 and K7 models, look for excessive deposits and evidence of a cracked or chipped insulator around the centre electrode. Compare your spark plugs to the colour spark plug reading chart at the end of this manual. If in doubt concerning the condition of the plugs, install new ones – the expense is minimal. Inspect the electrodes for wear. Both the centre and side electrodes should have square edges and the side electrode should be of uniform thickness. If the electrodes are not excessively worn, and if the deposits can be easily removed with a wire brush, the plugs can be re-used. Before installing the plugs, make sure they are the correct type and heat range (see Specifications), and measure the gap between the electrodes **(see illustrations)**. Compare the gap to that

specified and adjust as necessary. If the gap must be adjusted, bend the side electrode only and be very careful not to chip or crack the insulator nose **(see illustration)**. Make sure the washer is in place before installing each plug.
7 On K8 and K9 models, check the condition of the electrodes, referring to the spark plug reading chart at the end of this manual if signs of contamination are evident. Note that contaminated iridium plugs should not be cleaned – discard them and install new ones. Examine the pointed iridium-tipped centre electrode; if the tip has rounded off, the plug is worn **(see illustration)**. Measure the gap between the two electrodes with a wire type gauge only **(see illustrations)** – do not use blade type feeler gauges because the iridium tip might be damaged. The gap should be as given in the Specifications at the beginning of

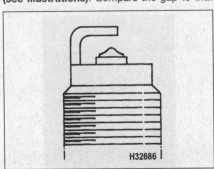

H32686

3.7a If the centre electrode has rounded off fit new plugs

3.7b Measure the gap using a wire gauge rather than a feeler blade gauge

3.9 Fit the plug into the tool and thread it into the head

this chapter; if the electrodes have worn and the gap is wider than it should be, or for some reason the gap is narrower than it should be (if the plug has been dropped for instance) a new plug must be installed. Do not bend the outer electrode to adjust the gap.

8 Check the threads, the washer and the ceramic insulator body for cracks and other damage.

9 Fit the plug into the end of the tool, then use the tool to insert the plug **(see illustration)**. Since the cylinder head is made of aluminium, which is soft and easily damaged, thread the plug as far as possible into the head turning the tool by hand. Once the plug is finger-tight, the job can be finished with a spanner on the tool supplied or a socket drive **(see illustration 3.5)**. If a torque wrench can be applied, tighten the spark plugs to the torque setting specified at the beginning of the Chapter. Otherwise, tighten them according the instructions on the box – generally if new plugs are being used, tighten them by 1/2 a turn after the washer has seated, and if the old plugs are being reused, tighten them by 1/8 to 1/4 turn after they have seated. Do not over-tighten them.

> **HAYNES HiNT** You can slip a short length of hose over the end of the plug to use as a tool to thread it into place. The hose will grip the plug well enough to turn it, but will start to slip if the plug begins to cross-thread in the hole – this will prevent damaged threads.

4.1 Check the fuel tank hoses . . .

10 Fit the coils onto the plugs and push them down lightly so they are felt to connect **(see illustration 3.4)**. Connect the coil wiring connectors **(see illustration 3.3)**.
11 Install the air filter housing (see Chapter 4).

> **HAYNES HiNT** Stripped plug threads in the cylinder head can be repaired with a thread insert – see 'Tools and Workshop Tips' in the Reference section.

4 Fuel system

> ⚠ **Warning: Petrol (gasoline) is extremely flammable, so take extra precautions when you work on any part of the fuel system. Don't smoke or allow open flames or bare light bulbs near the work area, and don't work in a garage where a natural gas-type appliance is present. If you spill any fuel on your skin, rinse it off immediately with soap and water. When you perform any kind of work on the fuel system, wear safety glasses and have a fire extinguisher suitable for a Class B type fire (flammable liquids) on hand.**

Check fuel hoses, EVAP hoses and system components

1 Raise the fuel tank (see Chapter 4) and check the tank, its breather and overflow hoses, and the fuel supply hose for signs of leaks, deterioration or damage, and make sure they are all securely connected **(see illustration)**. In particular check that there are no leaks from the fuel hose or hose unions. Replace any hose that is cracked or deteriorated with a new one.
2 If the joint between the fuel pump mounting plate and the underside of the tank is leaking, make sure the mounting bolts are tightened to the specified torque setting **(see illustration)** (see Chapter 4); if the leak persists, remove the pump and fit a new gasket (see Chapter 4).
3 Inspect the joints between the fuel rails, the injectors and the throttle bodies. If there are

4.2 . . . and around the pump base

any leaks, remove the fuel rail assembly and fit new seals and O-rings to the injectors (see Chapter 4). Make sure all the throttle body hoses are secure and in good condition.

Filter renewal and strainer cleaning

4 Cleaning and/or renewal of the fuel strainer and filter is advised after a particularly high mileage has been covered, although no interval is specified by Suzuki. It is also necessary if fuel starvation is suspected.
5 The filter and strainer are integral with the fuel pump. Remove the pump from the fuel tank and disassemble it as required filter (see Chapter 4).

Hose renewal

6 The fuel and air system hoses (see Step 1) should be replaced with new ones at the first signs of deterioration, or if preferred every four years or so regardless of their apparent condition. On California models, also replace the EVAP emission control system hoses (see Chapter 4).
7 Remove the fuel tank and the air filter housing. Refer to Chapter 4 and disconnect the various hoses from the fuel tank, air filter housing, throttle bodies, sensors and the PAIR control valve, noting the routing of each one and how it is secured. **Note:** It is advisable to make a sketch of the hoses before removing them to ensure they are correctly installed.
8 Where appropriate, secure each new hose to its unions using new clips. Run the engine and check that the fuel system is working correctly before taking the machine out on the road.

5 Engine oil and filter

Oil change

> ⚠ **Warning: Be careful when draining the oil, as the exhaust pipes, the engine, and the oil itself can cause severe burns.**

1 Regular oil and filter changes are the single most important maintenance procedure you can perform on a motorcycle. The oil not only lubricates the internal parts of the engine, transmission and clutch, but it also acts as a coolant, a cleaner, a sealant, and a protector. Because of these demands, the oil takes a terrific amount of abuse and should be drained and the engine refilled with new oil of the correct type and grade at the specified service interval. The oil filter should be changed with every third oil change.
2 Before changing the oil, warm up the engine so the oil will drain easily.
3 Support the bike on its sidestand, and position a drain tray below the engine. Unscrew the oil filler cap from the clutch cover to vent the crankcase and to act as a

5.3 Unscrew the oil filler cap . . .

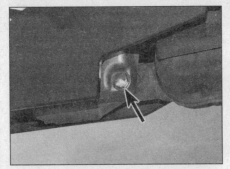

5.4a . . . then unscrew the drain plug (arrowed) . . .

5.4b . . . and allow the oil to drain

reminder that there is no oil in the engine **(see illustration)**.

4 Unscrew the oil drain plug and allow the oil to flow into the drain tray **(see illustrations)**. Note the magnet inside the plug and clean off any metal swarf. Check the condition of the sealing washer on the drain plug and fit a new one if it is damaged or worn – you will probably need to cut the old one off **(see illustration)**. It is good practice to fit a new washer whenever the drain plug is removed.

 To help determine whether any abnormal or excessive engine wear is occurring, place a strainer between the engine and the drain tray so that any debris in the oil is filtered out and can be examined. If there are flakes or chips of metal in the oil or on the drain plug magnet, then something is drastically wrong internally and the engine will have to be disassembled for inspection and repair. If there are pieces of fibre-like material in the oil, the clutch is wearing excessively and should be checked.

5 When the oil has completely drained, fit the plug into the sump, using a new sealing washer if necessary, and tighten it to the torque setting specified at the beginning of this Chapter **(see illustration)**. Avoid overtightening, as damage to the sump will result.

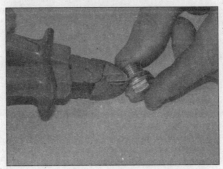

5.4c Clean the magnetic tip and cut the old washer off

5.5 Fit a new sealing washer and tighten the plug to the specified torque

6 Refill the engine with the correct amount and type of oil (see Specifications) **(see illustration)**. With the motorcycle held upright on level ground, the oil level should lie between the upper and lower level lines on the inspection window (see *Pre-ride checks)* **(see illustration)**. Install the filler cap. Start the engine and let it run for two or three minutes (make sure that the oil pressure warning symbol and the warning light extinguish after a few seconds). Shut it off, wait a few minutes, then recheck the oil level. If necessary, add more oil to bring the level up to the upper line on the window. Check that there are no leaks from around the drain plug.

7 The oil drained from the engine should be disposed of properly. Check with your local refuse disposal company, disposal facility or environmental agency to see whether they will accept the used oil for recycling. Don't pour used oil into drains or onto the ground.

OIL CARE
FOLLOW THE CODE

OIL BANK LINE
0800 66 33 66
www.oilbankline.org.uk

Note: It is antisocial and illegal to dump oil down the drain. In the UK, call this number free to find the location of your local recycling bank. in the USA, note that any oil supplier must accept used oil for recycling.

5.6a Pour in the oil . . .

5.6b . . . to the correct level, between the lines (arrowed) – do not overfill

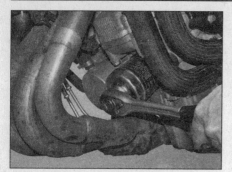

5.10a Unscrew the filter . . .

5.10b . . . and drain it into the tray

5.11 Smear the seal with clean oil then thread the filter onto the engine

Oil and oil filter change

Special tool: *A filter removing tool is necessary for this job.*

 Warning: Be careful when draining the oil, as the exhaust pipes, the engine, and the oil itself can cause severe burns.

8 Remove the left-hand fairing side panel (see Chapter 7).

9 Drain the engine oil as described above.

10 Now place the drain tray below the oil filter, which is on the front, left-hand side of the engine. Clean the crankcase around the filter, then unscrew the filter using a filter adapter (Suzuki service tool (Pt. No. 09915-40610) or an aftermarket alternative), or a strap or chain type filter removing tool, and tip any residual oil into the drain tray **(see illustrations)**.

11 Smear clean engine oil onto the seal of the new filter, then screw it onto the engine by hand until the seal just seats **(see illustration)**. Using a filter adapter (DO NOT use a strap or chain type removing tool), tighten the filter to the torque setting specified at the beginning of the Chapter if you have the correct tools, or by a further two whole turns.

12 Wipe any oil off the exhaust pipes to prevent smoking when the engine is started and refill the engine with oil as described in Step 6.

6 Idle speed

K6 and K7 models

1 Start the engine and run it up to normal operating temperature.

2 Place the motorcycle on its sidestand, with the engine idling and the transmission in neutral. Check that the engine speed shown by the tachometer is within the range given in the Specifications at the beginning of this Chapter.

3 If adjustment is required, for easiest access to the adjuster remove the left-hand fairing side panel (see Chapter 7), but note that it can be reached without doing so **(see illustration)**. Turn the adjuster until the correct idle speed is shown on the tachometer. Turn

the screw clockwise to increase idle speed, and anti-clockwise to decrease it. **Note:** *The fast idle mechanism for cold starting is actuated automatically by the STV servo and should cancel when engine coolant temperature, ambient temperature and lapsed time parameters are reached. If the idle speed cannot be adjusted correctly, check for a possible fault in the coolant temperature sensor or sensor wiring (see Chapter 4, Section 11). Details on adjusting the fast idle speed are given in Chapter 4, Section 16.*

4 Snap the throttle open and shut a few times, then recheck the idle speed. If necessary, repeat the adjustment procedure.

5 If a smooth, steady idle can't be achieved, the throttle valves may need synchronising (see Section 14).

K8 and K9 models

6 Idle speed is controlled automatically by the ECU via the idle speed control valve (ISCV) in the throttle bodies. It is not adjustable manually, and can only be reset electronically using the Suzuki diagnosis system (SDS) equipment. If engine idle speed is not within the range given in the Specifications at the beginning of this Chapter refer to Chapter 4 for checks that can be made on the ISCV.

7 Throttle cables

1 Make sure the throttle twistgrip rotates easily from fully closed to fully open with the

front wheel turned at various angles. The twistgrip should return automatically from fully open to fully closed when released.

2 If the throttle sticks, this is probably due to a cable fault. Remove the cables (see Chapter 4) and lubricate them (see Section 13). If the inner cables still do not run smoothly in the outer cables, replace them with new ones.

3 With the cables removed, check that the twistgrip turns smoothly around the handlebar – dirt combined with a lack of lubrication can cause the action to be stiff. Remove, clean and lightly grease the twistgrip pulley and the inside of the twistgrip housing if necessary (see Chapter 5, Section 5). Install the lubricated or new cables, making sure they are correctly routed (see Chapter 4). If this fails to improve the operation of the throttle, the fault could lie in the throttle bodies. Remove the air filter housing and check the action of the throttle pulley (see Chapter 4).

4 With the throttle operating smoothly, check that the amount of freeplay in the cables, measured in terms of twistgrip rotation before the throttle opens, is within the range given in the specifications at the beginning of this Chapter **(see illustration)**. If it is incorrect, adjust the cables as follows.

5 Where fitted, pull the rubber boot off the cable adjuster **(see illustration 7.6)**.

6 Loosen the locknut on the accelerator (throttle opening) cable and turn the adjuster until the specified amount of freeplay is

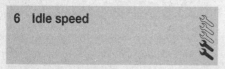

6.3 Idle speed adjuster (arrowed) on K6 and K7 models

7.4 Throttle cable freeplay is measured in terms of twistgrip rotation

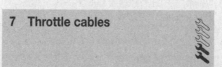

7.6 Loosen the locknut and turn the adjuster as required

8.4 Measuring clutch lever freeplay

8.5 Adjusting clutch lever freeplay

obtained, then retighten the locknut **(see illustration)**.

7 If the cables cannot be adjusted as specified, install new ones (see Chapter 4).

 Warning: Turn the handlebars all the way through their travel with the engine idling. Idle speed should not change. If it does, the cables may be routed incorrectly. Correct this condition before riding the bike.

8 Check that the throttle twistgrip operates smoothly and snaps shut quickly when released.

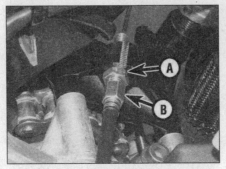

8.9 Slacken the locknut (A) and turn the adjuster (B) as required

8.10 Unscrew the cover . . .

8 Clutch

Cable adjustment

1 Check that the clutch lever operates smoothly and easily.

2 If the lever action is heavy or stiff, remove the cable (see Chapter 2) and lubricate it (see Section 13). If the inner cable still does not run smoothly in the outer cable, fit a new cable. Install the lubricated or new cable (see Chapter 2).

3 If the lever itself is stiff, remove the lever from its bracket (see Chapter 5) and check for damage or distortion, or any other cause, and remedy as necessary. Clean and lubricate the pivot bolt and contact areas (see Section 13).

4 Adjustment of the clutch cable is necessary to compensate for stretch in the cable. Check

that the clutch lever freeplay, measured at the end of the lever, is within the range given in the specifications at the beginning of this Chapter **(see illustration)**.

5 If adjustment is required, turn the handlebar lever adjuster in or out until the correct amount of freeplay is obtained **(see illustration)**. The adjuster spring will hold the adjuster in place once adjustment has been made. If the adjuster is nearly all the way out of the lever bracket, follow the release mechanism adjustment procedure given in the following Steps.

Release mechanism adjustment

6 Periodic adjustment of the clutch release mechanism is necessary to compensate for wear of the clutch plates and ensure smooth operation of the clutch and transmission.

7 Turn the cable adjuster at the handlebar lever fully in **(see illustration 8.5)**.

8 Raise the fuel tank (see Chapter 4).

9 Loosen the locknut on the adjuster at the lower end of the cable and turn the adjuster until the specified amount of freeplay is obtained at the clutch lever **(see illustration)**. Tighten the locknut.

10 Unscrew the clutch release mechanism cap from the clutch cover on the right-hand side of the engine **(see illustration)**.

11 Counter-hold the release mechanism adjuster screw and loosen the locknut **(see illustrations)**. Counter-hold the hex on the pushrod piece and turn the adjuster out two or three turns, then turn the adjuster in until resistance can just be felt, and finally turn the adjuster out 1/2 turn. Now hold the adjuster to prevent it turning and tighten the locknut. Again loosen the locknut on the adjuster at the lower end of the cable and turn the adjuster until the specified amount of freeplay is obtained at the clutch lever **(see illustration 8.9)**. Tighten the locknut.

12 Subsequent adjustments can be made using the lever adjuster only (see Step 5). If the specified amount of freeplay cannot be obtained at the clutch lever, fit a new cable.

13 Check the condition of the O-ring on the release mechanism cap and fit a new one if necessary, then thread the cap into the clutch cover and tighten it to the torque setting specified at the beginning of the Chapter **(see illustration 8.10)**.

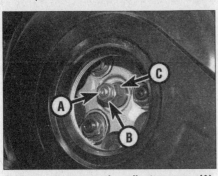

8.11a . . . to access the adjuster screw (A), locknut (B) and pushrod piece hex (C) . . .

8.11b . . . and adjust as described

9.2 Check the hoses as described

9.3 Check the drain hole (arrowed) and around the pump for leakage

9 Cooling system

Check

 Warning: The engine must be cool before beginning this procedure.

1 Check the coolant level (see *Pre-ride checks*).

2 Remove the fairing side panels (see Chapter 7) and check the cooling system for evidence of leaks. Examine each coolant hose along its entire length. Look for cracks, abrasions and other damage. Squeeze each hose at various points **(see illustration)**. They should feel firm, yet pliable, and return to their original shape when released. If they are cracked or hard, fit new ones (see Chapter 3).

3 Check for evidence of leaks at each cooling system joint and ensure the hose clips are tightened securely. Check around the bottom of the water pump, which is on the left-hand side of the engine. If the pump cover is leaking, fit a new cover O-ring (see Chapter 3). If coolant is leaking from the drain hole on the underside of the pump (between the pump and the crankcase), the internal

mechanical seal or the sealing washer has failed and should be replaced with a new one (see Chapter 3) **(see illustration)**. If oil is leaking from the drain hole, the internal oil seal has failed (see Chapter 3). If oil is leaking from between the pump and the crankcase, the pump body O-ring has failed (see Chapter 3).

4 Check the radiator for leaks and other damage. Leaks in the radiator leave tell-tale scale deposits or coolant stains on the outside of the core below the leak. If leaks are noted, remove the radiator (see Chapter 3) and have it repaired by a specialist.

Caution: Do not use a liquid leak stopping compound to try to repair leaks.

5 Check the radiator fins for mud, dirt and insects, which may impede the flow of air through the radiator. If the fins are dirty, remove the radiator (see Chapter 3) and clean it using water or low pressure compressed air directed through the fins from the back. If the fins are bent or distorted, straighten them carefully with a screwdriver. If there is substantial damage to the radiator's surface area replace it with a new one.

 Warning: Do not remove the pressure cap when the engine is hot. It is good practice to cover the cap with a heavy cloth and turn the cap slowly anti-clockwise. If you hear a hissing sound (indicating that there is still pressure in the system), wait until it stops, then continue turning the cap until it can be removed.

6 Remove the pressure cap from the radiator filler neck by turning it anti-clockwise until it reaches the stop. Now press down on the cap and continue turning it until it can be removed **(see illustration)**.

7 Check the condition of the coolant in the system. If it is rust-coloured or if accumulations of scale are visible, drain, flush and refill the system with new coolant (see below). Check the cap seal for cracks and other damage. If in doubt about the pressure cap's condition, have it tested by a Suzuki dealer or fit a new one.

8 Check the antifreeze content of the coolant with an antifreeze hydrometer. If the system has not been topped-up with the correct coolant mixture (see *Pre-ride checks*) the coolant will be too weak to offer adequate protection. If the hydrometer indicates a weak mixture, drain, flush and refill the system (see below).

9 Install the pressure cap – align the tabs on the cap with the cut-outs in the filler neck, then press the cap down and turn it clockwise until it is tight **(see illustration 9.6)**.

10 Start the engine and let it reach normal operating temperature, then check that here are no leaks. As the coolant temperature increases, the fan should come on automatically, controlled by the engine coolant temperature (ECT) sensor via the electronic control module (ECM), and the temperature should begin to drop. If it does not, refer to Chapter 3 to check the fan, fan relay and fan circuit, and to Chapter 4 to check the ECT sensor.

11 If the coolant level is consistently low, and no evidence of leaks can be found, have the entire system pressure checked by a Suzuki dealer.

Change the coolant

 Warning: Allow the engine to cool completely before performing this maintenance operation. Also, don't allow antifreeze to come into contact with your skin or the painted surfaces of the motorcycle. Rinse off spills immediately with plenty of water. Antifreeze is highly toxic if ingested. Never leave antifreeze lying around in an open container or in puddles on the floor; children and pets are attracted by its sweet smell and may drink it. Check with local authorities (councils) about disposing of antifreeze. Many communities have collection centres which will see that antifreeze is disposed of safely. Antifreeze is also combustible, so don't store it near open flames.

9.6 Turn the cap slowly anticlockwise to release any pressure in the system

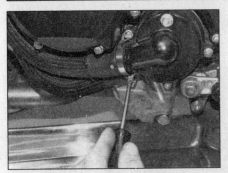

9.13a Slacken the clamp . . .

9.13b . . . then detach the hose and drain the cooling system

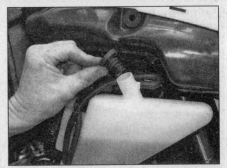

9.14a Remove the cap . . .

Draining

12 Support the motorcycle upright on a level surface using an auxiliary stand. Remove the fairing side panels (see Chapter 7). Cover the radiator pressure cap with a heavy cloth then remove it by turning it anti-clockwise until it reaches a stop. If you hear a hissing sound (indicating there is still pressure in the system), wait until it stops. Now press down on the cap and continue turning the cap until it can be removed **(see illustration 9.6)**.

13 Position a suitable container beneath the water pump on the left-hand side of the engine. Loosen the clip securing the radiator hose to the pump cover, then pull the hose off its union and allow the coolant to drain completely from the system **(see illustrations)**.

14 Remove the reservoir cap, then detach the overflow hose from the bottom of the reservoir and drain the coolant **(see illustrations)**. Rinse the inside of the reservoir with clean water. Reconnect the overflow hose.

Flushing

15 Flush the radiator with clean water by inserting a garden hose in the filler neck. Allow the water to run through until it is clear. If there is a lot of rust in the water, remove the radiator and have it cleaned professionally (see Chapter 3).

16 Reconnect the radiator hose to the water pump and tighten the clip.

17 Fill the cooling system via the radiator with clean water mixed with a flushing compound. Make sure the flushing compound is compatible with aluminium components, and follow the manufacturer's instructions carefully. Rock the machine from side to side to bleed any trapped air from the system and top up as necessary. When the system is full (all the way up to the top of the radiator filler neck), fit the pressure cap.

18 Fill the coolant reservoir to the F level line with clean water and fit the cap.

19 Start the engine and allow it to reach normal operating temperature. Let it run for about ten minutes.

20 Stop the engine and let it cool for a while. Cover the pressure cap with a heavy rag and turn it anti-clockwise to the stop. If you hear a hissing sound (indicating there is pressure in the system), wait until it stops. Now press

9.14b . . . then detach the hose (arrowed) and drain the reservoir

down on the cap and continue turning it until it can be removed.

21 Drain the system once again.

22 Refill the system with clean water, fit the radiator cap and repeat the procedure in Steps 19 to 21.

23 Drain the coolant reservoir, then ensure the overflow hose is properly fitted and secured with its clip (see Step 14).

Refilling

24 Fit the radiator hose onto the water pump and tighten the clip.

25 Fill the system via the radiator with the proper coolant mixture (see this Chapter's Specifications) **(see illustration)**. **Note:** *Pour the coolant into the radiator slowly to minimise the amount of air entering the system.* Rock the machine from side to side to bleed any trapped air from the system and top up as necessary. Repeat until no more air comes out.

9.26 . . . then fill the reservoir to the F line

9.25 Fill the system as described . . .

26 Fill the coolant reservoir to the F level line with coolant mixture and fit the cap **(see illustration)**.

27 Start the engine and allow it to idle for 2 to 3 minutes. Flick the throttle twistgrip part open 3 or 4 times, so that the engine speed rises to approximately 4000 – 5000 rpm, then stop the engine. Any air trapped in the system should bleed back to the radiator filler neck.

28 Hold some rag against the water pump cover, then loosen the air bleed screw in the top of the cover and allow any trapped air to escape until only coolant comes out, then tighten the screw **(see illustration)**.

29 Top the coolant level up to the radiator filler neck as necessary, then fit the pressure cap.

30 Run the engine and check the system for leaks.

31 Install the remaining components in the reverse order of removal. After the engine has

9.28 Slacken the air bleed bolt (arrowed) and let any air escape

been run a few times check the level in the reservoir.

32 Do not dispose of the old coolant by pouring it down the drain. Instead pour it into a heavy plastic container, cap it tightly and take it into an authorised disposal site or service station – see **Warning** on page 1•14.

Hose renewal

33 The hoses will deteriorate with age and should be replaced with new ones regardless of their apparent condition (see Chapter 3).
34 After fitting new hoses refill the system with new coolant and bleed the system as described above.

10 Brake system

Brake system check

1 A routine general check of the brake system will ensure that any problems are discovered and remedied before the rider's safety is jeopardised.
2 Check the brake lever and pedal for loose fixings, improper or rough action, excessive play, bends, and other damage. Replace any damaged parts with new ones (see Chapter 5). Clean and lubricate the lever and pedal pivots if their action is stiff or rough (see Section 13).
3 Make sure all brake system components and bolts are tight. Check the brake pads for wear (see below) and make sure the fluid level in the reservoirs is correct (see *Pre-ride checks*). Look for leaks at the hose connections and check for cracks in the hoses **(see illustration)**. If the lever or pedal is spongy, bleed the brakes (see Chapter 6).
4 Make sure the brake light operates when the front brake lever is pulled in. The front brake light switch is not adjustable. If it fails to operate properly, check it (see Chapter 8).
5 Make sure the brake light is activated just

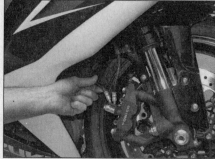

10.3 Flex the brake hoses and check for cracks, bulges and leaking fluid

10.5b ... hold the switch (A) and turn the adjuster (B) as required

10.5a The brake light switch (arrowed) is on the inside of the footrest bracket . . .

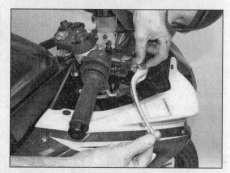

10.6 Adjusting front brake lever span

before the rear brake takes effect. The switch is mounted behind the rider's right-hand footrest bracket **(see illustration)**. If adjustment is necessary, hold the switch and turn the adjuster nut on the switch body **(see illustration)**. If the brake light comes on too late, turn the ring clockwise. If the brake light comes on too soon or is permanently on, turn the ring anti-clockwise. If the switch doesn't operate the brake light, check the bulb, the switch and the circuit (see Chapter 8).
6 The front brake lever has a span adjuster which alters the distance of the lever from the handlebar. Each of the six settings is identified by a number on the adjuster which aligns with

the arrow on the lever bracket. Pull the lever away from the handlebar and turn the adjuster dial until the setting which best suits the rider is obtained **(see illustration)**. When making adjustment ensure that the pin set in the lever bracket is engaged in its detent in the adjuster.
7 Check the position of the rear brake pedal. The distance between the top edge of the brake pedal and the top of the rider's footrest should be within the range specified at the beginning of this Chapter **(see illustration)**. To adjust the pedal height, loosen the locknut on the top of the master cylinder pushrod clevis, then turn the pushrod using the hex at the top until the pedal is at the correct height **(see illustration)**. Tighten

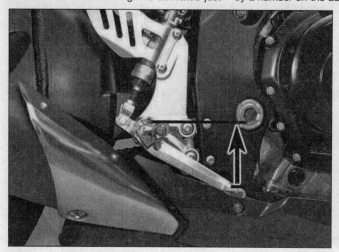

10.7a Check the setting of the brake pedal

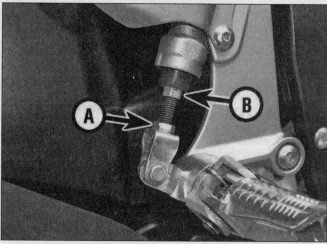

10.7b To adjust it slacken the locknut (A) and turn the pushrod (B)

10.8a Front brake pad wear indicators (arrowed)

10.8b Rear brake pad wear indicator (arrowed)

the locknut securely and check the setting of the rear brake light switch (see Step 5).

Brake pad wear check

8 Each brake pad has wear indicator lines, grooves or cut-outs in the friction material that should be plainly visible from the most obvious vantage point, but note that an accumulation of road dirt and brake dust could make them difficult to see **(see illustrations)**.

9 If the indicators aren't visible, then the amount of friction material remaining should be, and it will be obvious when the pads need replacing – if necessary remove the pad spring, displace the caliper itself, or use a mirror to improve your view (see Chapter 6). **Note:** *Some after-market pads may use different indicators to those on the original equipment.*

10 If the pads are dirty or if you are in doubt as to the amount of friction material remaining, remove them for inspection of the friction material (see Chapter 6). Suzuki do not specify a minimum thickness, but anything less than 1 mm is worn.

11 If the pads are worn to or beyond the wear indicator or there is little friction material remaining, they must be replaced with new ones, though it is advisable to replace the pads before they become this worn. If the pads are excessively worn, check the brake discs (see

Chapter 6). If the pads appear to be wearing unevenly, remove the caliper and check the operation of the pistons (see Chapter 6).

12 Refer to Chapter 6 for details of pad removal and installation.

Brake fluid change

13 The brake fluid should be changed at the prescribed interval or whenever a master cylinder or caliper overhaul is carried out. Refer to Chapter 6, Section 11 for details. Ensure that all the old fluid is be pumped from the hydraulic system and that the level in the fluid reservoir is checked and the brakes tested before riding the motorcycle.

Brake hoses

14 The hoses will deteriorate with age and should be replaced with new ones regardless of their apparent condition (see Chapter 6).

15 Always use new sealing washers when fitting the hoses. Refill the system with new brake fluid and bleed the system as described in Chapter 6.

Brake caliper and master cylinder seals

16 Brake system seals will deteriorate over a period of time and lose their effectiveness, leading to sticky operation of the brake master cylinders or the pistons in the brake calipers,

or fluid loss. Although seal replacement is not subject to a specific time or mileage interval, it is advised after a high mileage has been covered and particularly if fluid leakage or a sticking caliper action is apparent.

17 Replace all the seals in each caliper as a set – a rebuild kit for each caliper is available; master cylinder seals are supplied as a kit along with a new piston and spring (see Chapter 6).

11 Wheels and tyres

Wheels

1 Cast wheels are virtually maintenance free, but they should be kept clean and checked periodically for cracks and other damage. Also check the wheel runout and alignment (see Chapter 6). Never attempt to repair damaged cast wheels; they must be renewed if damaged. Check that any wheel balance weights are fixed firmly to the wheel rim **(see illustration)**. If you suspect that a weight has fallen off, have the wheel rebalanced by a motorcycle tyre specialist.

Tyres

2 Check the tyre condition and tread depth thoroughly – see *Pre-ride checks*. Check the valve rubber for signs of damage or deterioration and have it renewed if necessary by a tyre fitting specialist. Also, make sure the valve stem cap is in place and tight.

Wheel bearings

3 Wheel bearings will wear over a considerable mileage and should be checked periodically to avoid handling problems.

4 Support the motorcycle upright using an auxiliary stand so that the wheel being examined is off the ground. Check for any play in the bearings by pushing and pulling the wheel against the hub **(see illustration)**.

11.1 Check that any wheel balance weights are firmly attached (arrowed)

11.4 Check for play in the wheel bearings

Also rotate the wheel and check that it turns smoothly and without any grating noises.

5 If any play is detected in the hub, or if the wheel does not rotate smoothly (and this is not due to brake or transmission drag), the wheel should be removed and the bearings inspected for wear or damage (see Chapter 6).

12 Nuts and bolts

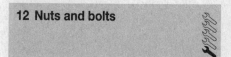

1 Since vibration of the machine tends to loosen fasteners, all nuts, bolts, screws, etc. should be periodically checked for proper tightness.

2 Pay particular attention to the following, referring to the relevant Chapter:

   Spark plugs
   Engine oil drain plug
   Lever and pedal bolts
   Footrest assembly bolts
   Sidestand assembly bolts
   Engine mounting bolts
   Shock absorber and suspension linkage bolts; swingarm pivot bolt, nut and locknut
   Handlebar clamp bolts
   Front fork clamp bolts (top and bottom yoke) and fork top bolts
   Steering stem nut
   Steering damper bolts
   Front axle bolt and axle clamp bolts
   Rear axle nut
   Front and rear sprocket nuts
   Brake caliper and master cylinder mounting bolts, brake caliper body bolts
   Brake hose banjo bolts and caliper bleed valves
   Brake disc bolts
   Exhaust system bolts/nuts

3 If a torque wrench is available, use it along with the torque settings given at the beginning of the relevant Chapter.

13 Stand, lever pivot and cable lubrication

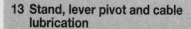

Pivot points

1 Since the controls, cables and various other components of a motorcycle are exposed to the elements, they should be checked and lubricated periodically to ensure safe and trouble-free operation.

2 The footrest pivots, clutch and brake lever pivots, brake pedal and gearchange lever pivots and linkage and sidestand pivot should be lubricated frequently. In order for the lubricant to be applied where it will do the most good, the component should be disassembled (see Chapter 5). The lubricant recommended by Suzuki for each application is listed at the beginning of the Chapter. If chain or cable lubricant is being used, it can be

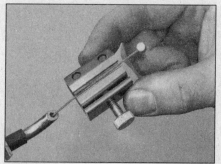

13.3a Fit the cable into the adapter . . .

applied to the pivot joint gaps and will usually work its way into the areas where friction occurs, so less disassembly of the component is needed (however it is always better to do so and clean off all corrosion, dirt and old lubricant first). If motor oil or light grease is being used, apply it sparingly as it may attract dirt (which could cause the controls to bind or wear at an accelerated rate). **Note:** *One of the best lubricants for the control lever pivots is a dry-film lubricant (available from many sources by different names).*

Cables

3 To lubricate the cables, disconnect the relevant cable at its upper end, then lubricate it with a pressure adapter and aerosol lubricant **(see illustrations)**. See Chapter 4 for throttle cable removal procedures, and Chapter 2 for the clutch cable.

14 Throttle valve synchronisation

K6 and K7 models

Special tool: *A set of vacuum gauges is necessary for this job.*

 Warning: Petrol (gasoline) is extremely flammable, so take extra precautions when you work on any part of the fuel system. Don't smoke or allow open flames or bare light bulbs near the work area, and don't work in a garage where a natural gas-type appliance is present. If you spill any fuel on your skin, rinse it off immediately with soap and water. When you perform any kind of work on the fuel system, wear safety glasses and have a fire extinguisher suitable for a Class B type fire (flammable liquids) on hand.

Warning: Take great care not to burn your hand on the hot engine unit when accessing the gauge take-off points on the throttle bodies. Do not allow exhaust gases to build up in the work area; either perform the check outside or use an exhaust gas extraction system.

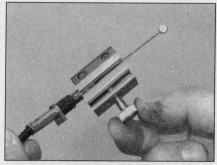

13.3b . . . and tighten the screw to seal it in . . .

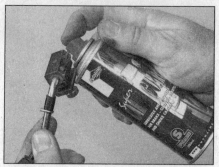

13.3c . . . then apply the lubricant using the nozzle provided inserted in the hole in the adapter

1 Throttle valves that are out of synchronisation will result in increased fuel consumption, increased engine temperature, less than ideal throttle response and higher vibration levels. Synchronisation is the process of adjusting the throttle valves so they each pass the same amount of fuel/air mixture to their respective cylinders. This is done by measuring the vacuum produced in each intake tract as the piston descends on its induction stroke and adjusting the throttle valves accordingly.

2 To synchronise the throttle valves you will need a set of vacuum gauges or calibrated tubes to measure engine vacuum. The equipment used should be suitable for a four cylinder engine and come complete with the necessary adapters and hoses to fit the take-off points on the throttle bodies. **Note:** *Because of the nature of the synchronisation procedure and the need for special instruments, most owners leave the task to a Suzuki dealer.*

3 Start the engine and let it run until it reaches normal operating temperature, then shut it off.

4 Remove the air filter housing (see Chapter 4). Remove the intake air temperature (IAT) sensor from the housing and reconnect it to its wiring connector on the bike. Disconnect the intake air pressure (IAP) sensor wiring connector **(see illustration)**.

5 Visually identify the synchronisation screw situated in the throttle valve linkage between each throttle body pair, and the idle air screw for each throttle body **(see illustrations)**. Note that the synchronisation screw synchronises

14.4 Disconnect the IAP sensor wiring connector (arrowed)

14.5a Throttle valve synchronising screw (arrowed)

14.5b Idle air screws (arrowed)

the throttle body pair for cylinders 1 and 2 to the pair for cylinders 3 and 4 – if throttle bodies 1 and 2 or 3 and 4 are out of synchronisation with each other they can be adjusted individually using the idle air screws, as described later.

Caution: To avoid the possibility of drawing dirt into the engine secure a fine mesh material (stockings for example) over the throttle body inlets to act as a temporary filter.

6 Disconnect the vacuum hose from the take-off stub on each throttle body **(see illustration)**. Connect the vacuum gauge hoses to the take-off stubs. Make sure they are a good fit because any air leaks will result in false readings.

7 Start the engine and if necessary adjust the idle speed to the level specified at the beginning of this Chapter using the idle speed adjuster screw **(see illustration 6.3)**. If using vacuum gauges fitted with damping adjustment, set this so that the needle flutter is just eliminated but so that they can still respond to small changes in pressure.

8 The vacuum readings for both pairs of throttle bodies should be the same. If the vacuum readings differ, turn the synchronisation screw until the readings are the same **(see illustration 14.5a)**. **Note:** *Do not press on the screw whilst adjusting it, otherwise a false reading will be obtained.*

Ensure the idle speed remains at the specified level throughout the procedure and adjust it if necessary.

9 When both pairs are synchronised, open and close the throttle twistgrip quickly to settle the linkage, and recheck the gauge readings, readjusting if necessary.

10 If the individual throttle bodies are out of balance with each other, further adjustment can be made using the idle air screws **(see illustration 14.5b)**. Start by turning the screw for the throttle body displaying the higher vacuum reading of Nos. 1 and 2 valves until they both read the same, then repeat for Nos. 3 and 4 until they are equal. Finally set both pairs equal by adjusting the synchronisation screw as in Step 8. If synchronisation is still not possible, remove the throttle bodies, then remove the air screws and clean through all passages using a fuel injection system aerosol spray, blowing them through afterwards with compressed air (see Chapter 4) – before removing the screws, turn them in until they seat lightly, counting and recording the exact number of turns so they can be reset in the same position.

11 When the adjustment is complete, turn the engine OFF. Disconnect the vacuum gauge hoses and refit the vacuum hoses (see Step 6).

12 If fitted, remove any temporary filter from the throttle body inlets. Connect the

IAP sensor wiring connector **(see illustration 14.4)**. Install the air filter housing (see Chapter 4).

13 Start the engine and re-check the idle speed; use the adjuster screw to correct it if necessary.

14 Lower the fuel tank.

K8 and K9 models

15 Throttle valve synchronisation on these models can only be carried with the Suzuki diagnosis system (SDS) tools and software connected to the ECM. Take the bike to a Suzuki dealer that has this equipment.

---

15 Emission control systems

PAIR (pulse secondary air injection) system

1 To reduce the amount of unburned hydrocarbons released in the exhaust gases, a pulse secondary air injection (PAIR) system is fitted. The system consists of the control valve (mounted above the valve cover), the reed valves (incorporated in the valve cover), and the hoses **(see illustration)**. The control valve is actuated electronically by the ECM.

14.6 Disconnect the vacuum hose from the take-off stub on each throttle body (centre two arrowed)

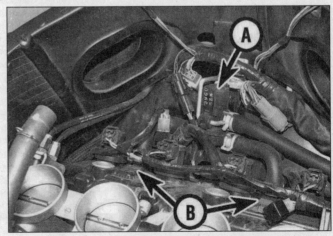

15.1 PAIR control valve (A), reed valve housings (B) and hoses

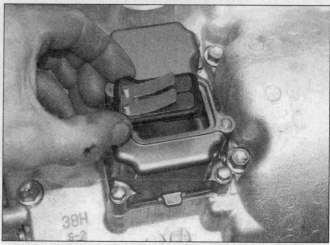

15.6a Crankcase breather hose (A) and reed valve housing (B)

15.6b Clean up the reed valve and its housing if necessary

2 Under certain operating conditions, the PAIR control valve allows filtered air to be drawn through it, the reed valves and cylinder head passages and into the exhaust ports. The air mixes with the exhaust gases, causing any unburned particles of the fuel in the mixture to be burnt in the exhaust port/pipes. This process changes a considerable amount of hydrocarbons and carbon monoxide into relatively harmless carbon dioxide and water. The reed valves are fitted to prevent the flow of exhaust gases back into the control valve and air filter housing.

3 The system is not adjustable and requires little maintenance, only to ensure that the hoses are in good condition and are securely connected at each end, and that there is no build-up of carbon fouling the reed valves – remove the air filter housing to access and inspect the components (see Chapter 4). Replace any hoses that are cracked, split or generally deteriorated with new ones. The reed valves can be checked for any build-up of carbon by unscrewing the cover bolts – if any is found, clean up the valves and their housings.

4 Refer to Chapter 4 for further details, and for checks on the system if it is believed to be faulty.

Crankcase breather system

5 This system prevents the escape of blow-by

16.4 Checking for play in the steering head bearings

gases from the combustion chambers, and of oil vapour from the crankcase, into the atmosphere by routing it back from the crankcase to the combustion chamber via a reed valve, the air filter housing and throttle bodies to be reburnt. A breather chamber in the top of the crankcase separates most of the oil and routes it back to the sump.

6 The only maintenance requirement is to check that the hose between the top of the crankcase and the top of the air filter housing is in good condition and is securely connected at each end **(see illustration)** – raise the fuel tank for access (see Chapter 4). Replace the hose with a new one if it is cracked, split or generally deteriorated. The reed valve can be checked for any build-up of carbon by unscrewing the breather chamber cover bolts, but it is necessary to remove the throttle bodies to do so (see Chapter 4) – if any carbon is found, clean up the valve and the housing **(see illustration)**.

EVAP system (California models)

7 This system prevents the escape of fuel vapour into the atmosphere by storing it in a charcoal-filled canister.

8 When the engine is not running, excess fuel vapour from the tank is fed into the canister. When the engine is started, intake manifold depression draws the vapour from the canister into the throttle bodies to be burned during the normal combustion process. On K6 and K7 models the vapour passes through a tank pressure control valve on its way to the canister. On K7 and K8 models a purge control solenoid valve between the canister and the throttle bodies opens on receipt of a signal from the ECM.

9 The canister has a one way valve which allows air to be drawn into the system as the volume of fuel decreases in the tank. The system also has a shut-off valve between the tank and the canister which prevents any fuel escaping through it in the event of the bike falling over.

10 The system is not adjustable. The only maintenance requirement is to check that

all the hoses are in good condition and are securely connected at each end – raise the fuel tank (see Chapter 4) and remove the seat cowling (see Chapter 7) for access. Replace any hoses that are cracked, split or generally deteriorated with new ones.

11 Refer to Chapter 4 for checks on the various valves in the system if it is believed to be faulty.

Caution: Fuel vapour is toxic. A small amount of vapour will be present in the valve when it is removed from the bike. Take care not to inhale the vapour when checking the valve.

16 Steering head bearings

Freeplay check and adjustment

1 Steering head bearings can become dented, rough or loose during normal use of the machine. Steering head bearings that are loose, too tight or worn will cause handling problems that are potentially dangerous.

Check

2 Remove the steering damper to allow free movement of the steering (see Chapter 5). Support the motorcycle in an upright position using an auxiliary stand, then raise the front wheel off the ground by placing a support under the engine.

3 Point the front wheel straight ahead and slowly turn the handlebars from lock to lock. Any indents or roughness in the bearing races will be felt and if the bearings are too tight the bars will not move smoothly and freely. If the bearings are damaged they should be replaced with new ones (see Chapter 5). If the bearings are too tight, adjust them as described below.

4 Next, grasp the forks and try to move them forwards and backwards **(see illustration)**. Any looseness in the steering head bearings will be felt as front to back movement of the forks.

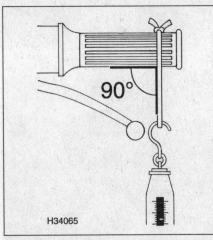

16.5 Checking the bearing loading with a spring balance

16.6 Unscrew the bolt (arrowed) and displace the reservoir

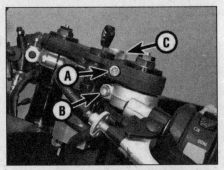

16.7 Loosen the fork clamp bolt (A) and the handlebar clamp bolt (B) on each side and the steering stem nut (C)

Note: *Freeplay in the fork due to worn fork bushes can be misinterpreted as steering head bearing play.* If play is felt in the steering head bearings, adjust them as described below.

5 If a spring balance is available, the bearing loading can be checked by applying a measured pull on the handlebar ends. Attach one end of the balance to the outer end of a handlebar grip (not the end-weight) and set the front wheel in the straight-ahead position. Now pull on the balance, making sure the balance is at right angles to the handlebar **(see illustration)**. If the bearing is adjusted correctly, the steering should start to turn when between 200 and 500 grams register on the balance scale. Connect the balance to the other handlebar and check the loading again – the result should be the same. If the loading is not within the specified range adjust the bearings.

Adjustment

6 Although not essential, it is wise to raise the fuel tank to avoid the possibility of damage should a tool slip while adjustment is being made (see Chapter 4). Alternatively cover it in plenty of rag. Unscrew the brake fluid reservoir bolt and displace the reservoir to access the clamp bolt in the top yoke **(see illustration)**.
7 Loosen the fork clamp bolts in the top yoke, the handlebar clamp bolts and the steering

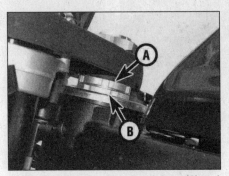

16.8a Slacken the adjuster locknut (A) and turn the adjuster nut (B) . . .

stem nut **(see illustration)**. Do not loosen the lower yoke bolts.
8 Using a slim C-spanner or a suitable drift located in one of the notches, loosen the adjuster locknut **(see illustrations)**; now loosen or tighten the adjuster nut as required using the same tool until the bearings are set correctly as described in Steps 3, 4 and 5.
Caution: Take great care not to overtighten the adjuster nut – excessive pressure will cause premature failure of the bearings.
9 With the bearings correctly adjusted, tighten the locknut against the adjuster nut, making sure the adjuster nut does not turn as you do so. Now tighten the steering stem nut and then the fork clamp bolts in the top yoke to the torque settings specified at the beginning of this Chapter **(see illustration 16.7)**. Make sure each handlebar is seated against the

16.8b . . . using a C-spanner or drift as shown

underside of the top yoke with the lug located in its hole, then tighten the clamp bolts to the specified torque **(see illustration)**.
10 Check the bearing adjustment as described above and re-adjust if necessary. Install the remaining components in the reverse order of removal.

Lubrication

11 Over a considerable time the grease in the bearings will be dispersed or will harden allowing the ingress of dirt and water.
12 The steering head should be disassembled periodically and the bearings cleaned and re-greased (see Chapter 5, Section 10).

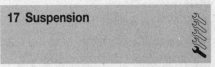

17 Suspension

1 The suspension components must be in top operating condition to ensure rider safety. Loose, worn or damaged suspension parts decrease the motorcycle's stability and control.

Front suspension check

2 While standing alongside the motorcycle, apply the front brake and push on the handlebars to compress the forks several times **(see illustration)**. They should move up-and-down smoothly without binding. If binding is felt, the forks should be disassembled and inspected (see Chapter 5).

16.9 Make sure the lug on each handlebar clamp locates in its hole (arrowed) in the underside of the yoke

17.2 Check the action of the forks by compressing and releasing them

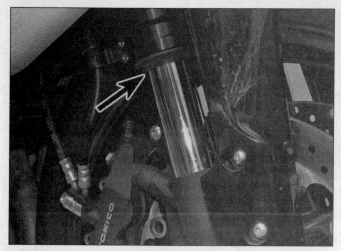

17.4 Check for oil leaks around the seals (arrow) and for pitting on the inner tubes

17.8 Check the action of the rear suspension by compressing and releasing it

3 Inspect the fork tubes for scratches, corrosion and pitting which will cause premature seal failure – if the damage is excessive, new tubes should be installed (see Chapter 5).

4 Inspect the area below the dust seal for signs of oil leaks, then carefully lever off the dust seal using a flat-bladed screwdriver and inspect the area around the fork seal **(see illustration)**. If leaks are evident, the seals must be replaced with new ones (see Chapter 5).

5 The forks are adjustable for spring pre-load, rebound damping and compression damping and it is essential that both fork legs are adjusted equally (see Chapter 5).

6 Check the tightness of all suspension nuts and bolts to be sure none have worked loose, referring to the torque settings specified at the beginning of Chapter 5.

Rear suspension check

7 Inspect the rear shock for fluid leaks and tightness of its mountings. If leaks are found, a new shock must be installed or advice sought from a suspension specialist on overhauling the shock (see Chapter 5).

8 With the aid of an assistant to support the bike, compress the rear suspension several times **(see illustration)**. It should move up and down freely without binding. If binding is felt, the worn or faulty component must be identified and renewed. The problem could be caused by the shock absorber, the suspension linkage components or the swingarm components.

9 Support the motorcycle using an auxiliary stand so that the rear wheel is off the ground. Grasp the swingarm and rock it from side to side – there should be no discernible movement at the rear **(see illustration)**. If there's a little movement or a clicking can be heard, check the tightness of all the rear suspension mounting bolts and nuts, referring to the torque settings specified at the beginning of Chapter 5, and re-check for movement.

10 Grasp the top of the rear wheel and pull it upwards – there should be no discernible freeplay before the shock absorber begins to compress **(see illustration)**. Any freeplay indicates worn bearings in the suspension linkage or swingarm, or worn shock absorber mountings. The worn components must be replaced with new ones (see Chapter 5).

11 To make a more accurate assessment of the swingarm bearings, remove the rear wheel (see Chapter 6) and the bolt securing the suspension linkage to the swingarm (see Chapter 5). Grasp the rear of the swingarm with one hand and place your other hand at the junction of the swingarm and the frame. Try to move the rear of the swingarm from side-to-side. Any wear in the bearings will be felt as movement between the swingarm and the frame at the front. If there is any wear, the swingarm will be felt to move forwards and backwards at the front (not from side-to-side). Next, move the swingarm up and down through its full travel. It should move freely, without any binding or rough spots. If the swingarm bearings are worn or if the swingarm does not move freely, new bearings must be fitted (see Chapter 5).

Front fork oil change

12 Although there is no set interval for changing the fork oil, note that the oil will degrade over a period of time and lose its damping qualities. Refer to Chapter 5, Sections 6 and 7 for details of front fork removal, oil draining and refilling. The forks do not need to be completely disassembled to change the oil.

Rear suspension bearing lubrication

13 Although there is no set interval for regreasing the suspension linkage and swingarm bearings, over a considerable mileage the grease in the bearings will be washed out or will harden allowing the ingress of dirt and water.

14 The suspension linkage and the swingarm should be disassembled periodically and the bearings cleaned and re-greased as necessary (see Chapter 5, Sections 13 and 16).

18 Exhaust control valve

1 The exhaust control valve is located inside the single pipe section of the exhaust system just ahead of the collector box under

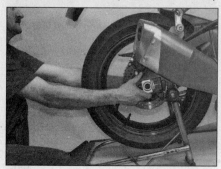

17.9 Checking for play in the swingarm bearings

17.10 Checking for play in the shock mountings and suspension linkage

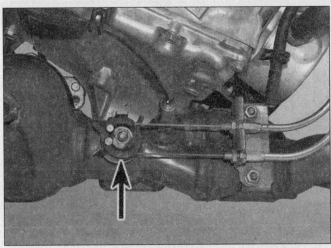

18.1a Exhaust control valve (arrowed) and its cables

18.1b Exhaust control valve servo (arrowed) – K6 and K7 models

the engine **(see illustration)**. The valve is connected by two cables to a servo located behind the seat cowling on the right-hand side on K6 and K7 models, and under the fuel tank on the right-hand side on K8 and K9 models **(see illustrations)**. The servo is actuated by the engine control module (ECM).

2 To check the operation of the system remove the right-hand side panel on all models (see Chapter 7), the seat cowling on K6 and K7 models (see Chapter 7), and on K8 and K9 models raise the fuel tank and support it on its prop (see Chapter 4). Make sure the servo is securely mounted and the cables are held securely in the bracket on the exhaust. Turn the ignition ON and observe the movement of the servo pulley, cables and valve (this is a function which occurs each time the ignition is turned on).

3 If the servo pulley does not move, check the operation of the servo (see Chapter 4). If the pulley tries to move but can't because the cables or the valve have seized, or if the cable action is stiff or juddery, check the condition and adjustment of the cables and the operation

of the valve (see Chapter 4). **Note:** *Before the cables are adjusted or disconnected the servo pulley should be set in the adjustment position with the use of a Suzuki mode select switch, service tool Pt. No. 09930-82710.*

19 Valve clearances

Special tool: *A set of feeler gauges is necessary for this job.*

Check

1 The engine must be completely cool for this maintenance procedure, so let the machine sit overnight before beginning.

2 Remove the right-hand fairing side panel (see Chapter 7), the spark plugs (see Section 3) and the valve cover (see Chapter 2). The cylinders are numbered 1 to 4 from left to right, viewed as normally seated on the bike.

3 Make a chart or sketch of all valve positions so that a note of each clearance can be made against the relevant valve.

18.1c Exhaust control valve servo (arrowed) – K8 and K9 models

4 Unscrew the timing inspection cap from the right-hand side of the engine **(see illustration)**. Discard the cap O-ring as new one should be fitted on reassembly. The engine needs to be turned, which is done using a socket on the timing rotor bolt, and turned it in its normal direction of rotation (clockwise) only **(see illustration)**.

5 Turn the engine clockwise until the line on

19.4a Unscrew the timing inspection cap and discard the O-ring

19.4b Turn the crankshaft in a clockwise direction

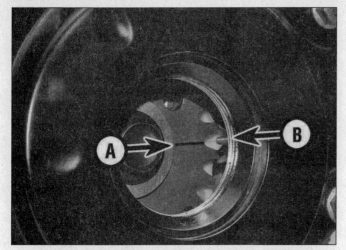

19.5a Align the line (A, highlighted) with the rib (B)

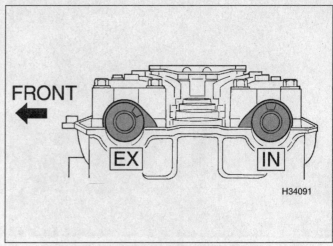

FRONT

EX   IN

H34091

19.5b Exhaust and intake camshaft cut-outs for checking Nos. 2 and 4 intake valves and Nos. 3 and 4 exhaust valves

19.6 Checking the valve clearance with a feeler gauge

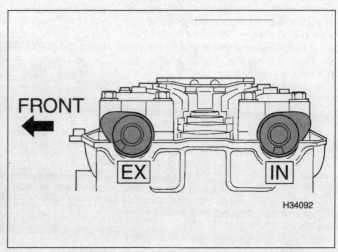

FRONT

EX   IN

H34092

19.7 Exhaust and intake camshaft cut-outs for checking Nos. 1 and 3 intake valves and Nos. 1 and 2 exhaust valves

the timing rotor aligns with the rib inside the timing inspection hole, and the cut-out in the left-hand end of the exhaust camshaft is at about 2 o'clock and the cut-out in the end of the intake camshaft is at 12 o'clock (see illustrations).

6 Check the clearances on the No. 2 and No. 4 intake valves and the No. 3 and No. 4 exhaust valves as follows. Insert a feeler gauge of the same thickness as the correct valve clearance (see Specifications at the beginning of this Chapter) between the base of the camshaft lobe and the cam follower of each valve in turn. The gauge should be a firm sliding fit – you should feel a slight drag when you pull the gauge out (see illustration). If not, use the feeler gauges to obtain the exact clearance. Record the measured clearances on your chart. Note: *The intake and exhaust valve clearances are different.*

7 Now turn the engine clockwise through 360° so that the line on the timing rotor again aligns with the rib inside the timing inspection hole.

The cut-out in the exhaust camshaft should now be at about 8 o'clock and the cut-out in the intake camshaft should be at 6 o'clock (see illustration).

8 Check the clearances on the No. 1 and No. 3 intake valves and the No. 1 and No. 2

exhaust valves as described in Step 6. Record the measured clearances on your chart.

Adjustment

9 When all clearances have been measured and recorded, identify whether the clearance

19.11a Lift out the cam follower using a magnet . . .

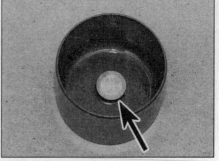

19.11b . . . and retrieve the shim from inside the follower . . .

19.11c . . . or from the top of the valve

19.12 Measuring the shim thickness with a micrometer

on any valve falls outside that specified. If it does, the shim between the follower and the valve must be replaced with one of a thickness which will restore the correct clearance.

10 To change the shims the camshafts must be removed (see Chapter 2). Place rags over the spark plug holes and the cam chain tunnel to prevent a shim dropping into the engine on removal.

11 Lift out the cam follower of the valve in

question using a magnet **(see illustration)**. Retrieve the shim from either the inside of the follower or pick it out of the top of the valve using a magnet, a small screwdriver with a dab of grease on it (the shim will stick to the grease), or a pair of pliers **(see illustrations)**. Do not allow the shim to fall into the engine.

12 The shim size should be marked on its upper face – a shim marked 170 is 1.70 mm

thick – but the shim should be measured with a micrometer to check that it has not worn **(see illustration)**. If the shim has worn undersize, this must be taken into account and the valve clearance adjusted accordingly.

13 Using the appropriate shim selection chart, find where the measured valve clearance and existing shim thickness values intersect and read off the shim size required **(see illustrations)**.

MEASURED TAPPET CLEARANCE (mm)	PRESENT SHIM SIZE (mm)																				
	1.20	1.25	1.30	1.35	1.40	1.45	1.50	1.55	1.60	1.65	1.70	1.75	1.80	1.85	1.90	1.95	2.00	2.05	2.10	2.15	2.20
0.00 - 0.02			1.20	1.25	1.30	1.35	1.40	1.45	1.50	1.55	1.60	1.65	1.70	1.75	1.80	1.85	1.90	1.95	2.00	2.05	2.10
0.03 - 0.07		1.20	1.25	1.30	1.35	1.40	1.45	1.50	1.55	1.60	1.65	1.70	1.75	1.80	1.85	1.90	1.95	2.00	2.05	2.10	2.15
0.08 - 0.18	SPECIFIED CLEARANCE/NO ADJUSTMENT REQUIRED																				
0.19 - 0.28	1.30	1.35	1.40	1.45	1.50	1.55	1.60	1.65	1.70	1.75	1.80	1.85	1.90	1.95	2.00	2.05	2.10	2.15	2.20	2.20	
0.29 - 0.33	1.35	1.40	1.45	1.50	1.55	1.60	1.65	1.70	1.75	1.80	1.85	1.90	1.95	2.00	2.05	2.10	2.15	2.20			
0.34 - 0.38	1.40	1.45	1.50	1.55	1.60	1.65	1.70	1.75	1.80	1.85	1.90	1.95	2.00	2.05	2.10	2.15	2.20				
0.39 - 0.43	1.45	1.50	1.55	1.60	1.65	1.70	1.75	1.80	1.85	1.90	1.95	2.00	2.05	2.10	2.15	2.20					
0.44 - 0.48	1.50	1.55	1.60	1.65	1.70	1.75	1.80	1.85	1.90	1.95	2.00	2.05	2.10	2.15	2.20						
0.49 - 0.53	1.55	1.60	1.65	1.70	1.75	1.80	1.85	1.90	1.95	2.00	2.05	2.10	2.15	2.20							
0.54 - 0.58	1.60	1.65	1.70	1.75	1.80	1.85	1.90	1.95	2.00	2.05	2.10	2.15	2.20								
0.59 - 0.63	1.65	1.70	1.75	1.80	1.85	1.90	1.95	2.00	2.05	2.10	2.15	2.20									
0.64 - 0.68	1.70	1.75	1.80	1.85	1.90	1.95	2.00	2.05	2.10	2.15	2.20										
0.69 - 0.73	1.75	1.80	1.85	1.90	1.95	2.00	2.05	2.10	2.15	2.20											
0.74 - 0.78	1.80	1.85	1.90	1.95	2.00	2.05	2.10	2.15	2.20												
0.79 - 0.83	1.85	1.90	1.95	2.00	2.05	2.10	2.15	2.20													
0.84 - 0.88	1.90	1.95	2.00	2.05	2.10	2.15	2.20														
0.89 - 0.93	1.95	2.00	2.05	2.10	2.15	2.20															
0.94 - 0.98	2.00	2.05	2.10	2.15	2.20																
0.99 - 1.03	2.05	2.10	2.15	2.20																	
1.04 - 1.08	2.10	2.15	2.20																		
1.09 - 1.13	2.15	2.20																			
1.14 - 1.18	2.20																				

H31236

19.13a Shim selection chart – intake valves

MEASURED TAPPET CLEARANCE (mm)	PRESENT SHIM SIZE (mm)																				
	1.20	1.25	1.30	1.35	1.40	1.45	1.50	1.55	1.60	1.65	1.70	1.75	1.80	1.85	1.90	1.95	2.00	2.05	2.10	2.15	2.20
0.03 - 0.07				1.20	1.25	1.30	1.35	1.40	1.45	1.50	1.55	1.60	1.65	1.70	1.75	1.80	1.85	1.90	1.95	2.00	2.05
0.08 - 0.12			1.20	1.25	1.30	1.35	1.40	1.45	1.50	1.55	1.60	1.65	1.70	1.75	1.80	1.85	1.90	1.95	2.00	2.05	2.10
0.13 - 0.17		1.20	1.25	1.30	1.35	1.40	1.45	1.50	1.55	1.60	1.65	1.70	1.75	1.80	1.85	1.90	1.95	2.00	2.05	2.10	2.15
0.18 - 0.28	SPECIFIED CLEARANCE/NO ADJUSTMENT REQUIRED																				
0.29 - 0.38	1.30	1.35	1.40	1.45	1.50	1.55	1.60	1.65	1.70	1.75	1.80	1.85	1.90	1.95	2.00	2.05	2.10	2.15	2.20	2.20	
0.39 - 0.43	1.35	1.40	1.45	1.50	1.55	1.60	1.65	1.70	1.75	1.80	1.85	1.90	1.95	2.00	2.05	2.10	2.15	2.20			
0.44 - 0.48	1.40	1.45	1.50	1.55	1.60	1.65	1.70	1.75	1.80	1.85	1.90	1.95	2.00	2.05	2.10	2.15	2.20				
0.49 - 0.53	1.45	1.50	1.55	1.60	1.65	1.70	1.75	1.80	1.85	1.90	1.95	2.00	2.05	2.10	2.15	2.20					
0.54 - 0.58	1.50	1.55	1.60	1.65	1.70	1.75	1.80	1.85	1.90	1.95	2.00	2.05	2.10	2.15	2.20						
0.59 - 0.63	1.55	1.60	1.65	1.70	1.75	1.80	1.85	1.90	1.95	2.00	2.05	2.10	2.15	2.20							
0.64 - 0.68	1.60	1.65	1.70	1.75	1.80	1.85	1.90	1.95	2.00	2.05	2.10	2.15	2.20								
0.69 - 0.73	1.65	1.70	1.75	1.80	1.85	1.90	1.95	2.00	2.05	2.10	2.15	2.20									
0.74 - 0.78	1.70	1.75	1.80	1.85	1.90	1.95	2.00	2.05	2.10	2.15	2.20										
0.79 - 0.83	1.75	1.80	1.85	1.90	1.95	2.00	2.05	2.10	2.15	2.20											
0.84 - 0.88	1.80	1.85	1.90	1.95	2.00	2.05	2.10	2.15	2.20												
0.89 - 0.93	1.85	1.90	1.95	2.00	2.05	2.10	2.15	2.20													
0.94 - 0.98	1.90	1.95	2.00	2.05	2.10	2.15	2.20														
0.99 - 1.03	1.95	2.00	2.05	2.10	2.15	2.20															
1.04 - 1.08	2.00	2.05	2.10	2.15	2.20																
1.09 - 1.13	2.05	2.10	2.15	2.20																	
1.14 - 1.18	2.10	2.15	2.20																		
1.19 - 1.23	2.15	2.20																			
1.24 - 1.28	2.20																				

H31237

19.13b Shim selection chart – exhaust valves

14 New shims are available in 0.05 mm increments from 1.200 to 2.200 mm and can be obtained from a Suzuki dealer. **Note:** *If the required replacement shim is greater than 2.20 mm (the largest available), the valve is probably not seating correctly due to a build-up of carbon deposits or valve damage. Remove the valve for checking (see Chapter 2).*

15 When replacing a shim, lubricate it both sides with engine oil and fit it into its recess in the top of the valve with the size marking facing up **(see illustration 19.11c)**. Check that the shim is correctly seated, then lubricate the follower with engine oil or molybdenum disulphide oil (a 50/50 mixture of molybdenum paste and engine oil) and fit it onto the valve **(see illustration)**. Repeat the process for any other valves as required, then install the camshafts (see Chapter 2).

16 Rotate the crankshaft several turns to seat the new shim(s), then check the clearances again.

17 Fit a new O-ring on the timing inspection cap **(see illustration)** and smear it with engine oil, then tighten the cap to the specified torque setting.

18 Install the remaining components in the reverse order of removal.

19.15 Lubricate the follower and fit it onto the valve

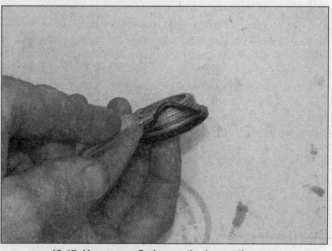

19.17 Use a new O-ring on the inspection cap

20 Sidestand and starter interlock circuit

1 Check the stand springs for damage and distortion. The springs must be capable of retracting the stand fully and holding it retracted when the motorcycle is in use. If a spring is sagged or broken it must be replaced with a new one.

2 Lubricate the stand pivot regularly (see Section 13).

3 Check the stand and its mount for bends and cracks, and that the bolts and nut are tightened to the correct torque settings (see Chapter 5). If necessary a stand can often be repaired by welding.

4 Check the operation of the starter interlock circuit by shifting the transmission into neutral, retracting the stand, pulling in the clutch lever and starting the engine. Pull in the clutch lever and select a gear. Extend the sidestand. The engine should stop as the sidestand is extended. Also check that the engine cannot be started when the sidestand is down and the engine is in gear, and that the engine stops if a gear is selected with the engine running and the sidestand down. If the circuit does not operate as described, check the various switches (sidestand, gear position and clutch) and the diodes in the circuit (see Chapter 4 for the gear position switch and Chapter 8 for the rest).

21 Battery

1 All models are fitted with a sealed MF (maintenance free) battery. **Note:** *Do not attempt to remove the battery caps to check the electrolyte level or battery specific gravity. Removal will damage the caps, resulting in electrolyte leakage and battery damage.* All that should be done is to check that the terminals are clean and tight and that the casing is not damaged or leaking. See Chapter 8 for further details and charging information.

2 If the machine is not in regular use, remove the battery and give it a refresher charge every month to six weeks.

Chapter 2
Engine, clutch and transmission

Contents

Degrees of difficulty

Easy, suitable for novice with little experience

Fairly easy, suitable for beginner with some experience

Fairly difficult, suitable for competent DIY mechanic

Difficult, suitable for experienced DIY mechanic

Very difficult, suitable for expert DIY or professional

Specifications – 600 models

General

Type	Four-stroke in-line four
Capacity	599 cc
Bore	67.0 mm
Stroke	42.5 mm
Compression ratio	
K6 and K7 models	12.5 to 1
K8 and K9 models	12.8 to 1
Clutch	Wet multi-plate
Transmission	6-speed constant mesh
Final drive	Chain

Cylinder compression

Standard	171 to 228 psi (12 to 16 Bars)*
Minimum	128 psi (9 Bars)*
Maximum difference between cylinders	28 psi (2 Bars)*

Note: If all cylinders record less than the standard (even if they are above the minimum), or if the difference between any two cylinders is greater than the maximum, or if any one cylinder is less than the minimum, the engine should be overhauled.

Lubrication system

Oil pressure	14 to 57 psi (1 to 4 Bars) at 3000 rpm, oil at 60°C

Camshafts

Intake lobe height	
K6 and K7 models	
Standard	36.58 to 36.63 mm
Service limit (min)	36.28 mm
K8 and K9 models	
Standard	36.18 to 36.23 mm
Service limit (min)	35.88 mm
Exhaust lobe height	
Standard	35.98 to 36.03 mm
Service limit (min)	35.68 mm
Journal diameter	23.959 to 23.980 mm
Camshaft holder journal diameter	24.012 to 24.025 mm
Journal oil clearance	
Standard	0.032 to 0.066 mm
Service limit (max)	0.15 mm
Runout (max)	0.10 mm

Cylinder head

Warpage (max)	0.20 mm

Valves, guides and springs

Valve clearances	see Chapter 1
Intake valves	
Head diameter	27.2 mm
Stem diameter	4.475 to 4.490 mm
Guide bore diameter	4.500 to 4.512 mm
Stem-to-guide clearance	0.010 to 0.037 mm
Side clearance, wobble (max) – see text	0.25 mm
Seat width	0.9 to 1.1 mm
Head runout (max)	0.03 mm
Stem runout (max)	0.05 mm
Exhaust valves	
Head diameter	22.0 mm
Stem diameter	4.455 to 4.470 mm
Guide bore diameter	4.500 to 4.512 mm
Stem-to-guide clearance	0.030 to 0.057 mm
Side clearance, wobble (max) – see text	0.25 mm
Seat width	0.9 to 1.1 mm
Head runout (max)	0.03 mm
Stem runout (max)	0.05 mm
Valve spring free length (min)	
K6 and K7 models	38.1 mm
K8 and K9 models	39.4 mm

Clutch

Friction plate
  Quantity
    K6 and K7 models   8
    K8 and K9 models   9
  Thickness
    Standard. . . . .   2.72 to 2.88 mm
    Service limit (min) . . . .   2.42 mm
  Tab width
    Standard
      K6 and K7 models . . . .   13.85 to 14.04 mm
      K8 and K9 models . . . .   13.85 to 13.96 mm
    Service limit (min) . . . .   13.05 mm
Plain plate
  Quantity
    K6 and K7 models   7
    K8 and K9 models   8
  Warpage (max) . . . .   0.1 mm
Spring free length
  Standard. . . . .   56.0 mm
  Service limit . . . .   53.2 mm
Slipper mechanism adjuster screw protrusion. . . . .   0.2 to 0.4 mm
Spring washer min free height . . . .   4.30 mm

Cylinders

Bore standard dimension. . . . .   67.000 to 67.015 mm
Warpage of gasket face (max) . . . .   0.20 mm

Pistons

Piston diameter (measured 15 mm up from skirt, at 90° to piston pin axis)
  Standard. . . . .   66.965 to 66.980 mm
  Service limit (min) . . . .   66.880 mm
Piston-to-bore clearance
  Standard. . . . .   0.030 to 0.040 mm
  Service limit (min) . . . .   0.120 mm
Piston pin diameter
  Standard. . . . .   13.995 to 14.000 mm
  Service limit (min) . . . .   13.980 mm
Piston pin bore diameter in piston
  Standard. . . . .   14.002 to 14.008 mm
  Service limit (max) . . . .   14.030 mm

Piston rings

Ring end gap (free)
  Top ring
    Standard. . . . .   5.5 mm (approx.)
    Service limit (min) . . . .   4.4 mm
  2nd ring
    K6 and K7 models
      Standard. . . . .   8.5 mm
      Service limit (min) . . . .   6.8 mm
    K8 and K9 models
      Standard. . . . .   7.5 mm
      Service limit (min) . . . .   6.0 mm
Ring end gap (installed) – top and second ring . . . .   0.06 to 0.21 mm
Service limit (max) . . . .   0.50 mm
Ring thickness
  Top ring. . . . .   0.97 to 0.99 mm
  2nd ring. . . . .   0.77 to 0.79 mm
Ring groove width in piston
  Top ring. . . . .   1.01 to 1.03 mm
  2nd ring. . . . .   0.81 to 0.83 mm
  Oil ring . . . .   1.51 to 1.53 mm
Ring-to-groove clearance
  Top ring (max). . . . .   0.18 mm
  2nd ring (max). . . . .   0.15 mm

Transmission

Gear ratios (no. of teeth)

Primary reduction	1.974 to 1 (77/39)
Final reduction	2.687 to 1 (43/16)
1st gear.	2.785 to 1 (39/14)
2nd gear	2.052 to 1 (39/19)
3rd gear	1.714 to 1 (36/21)
4th gear	1.500 to 1 (36/24)
5th gear	1.347 to 1 (31/23)
6th gear	1.208 to 1 (29/24)

Selector drum and forks

Selector fork-to-groove clearance

Standard.	0.1 to 0.3 mm
Service limit (max)	0.5 mm
Selector fork end thickness	4.8 to 4.9 mm
Selector fork groove width.	5.0 to 5.1 mm

Connecting rods

Small-end internal diameter

Standard.	14.010 to 14.018 mm
Service limit (max)	14.040 mm

Big-end side clearance

Standard.	0.10 to 0.20 mm
Service limit (max)	0.30 mm
Big-end width.	19.95 to 20.00 mm
Crankpin width.	20.10 to 20.15 mm

Big-end ID

Code 1	34.000 to 34.008 mm
Code 2	34.008 to 34.016 mm

Crankpin OD

Code 1	30.992 to 31.000 mm
Code 2	30.984 to 30.992 mm
Code 3	30.976 to 30.984 mm

Big-end oil clearance

Standard.	0.032 to 0.056 mm
Service limit (max)	0.08 mm

Crankshaft and bearings

Main bearing journal OD

Code A	29.994 to 30.000 mm
Code B	29.988 to 29.994 mm
Code C	29.982 to 29.988 mm

Crankcase seat ID

Code A	33.000 to 33.006 mm
Code B	33.006 to 33.012 mm
Code C	33.012 to 33.018 mm

Main bearing oil clearance

Standard.	0.010 to 0.028 mm
Service limit (max)	0.080 mm
Runout (max)	0.05 mm
Thrust bearing clearance	0.055 to 0.110 mm

Thrust bearing thickness

Right-hand side	2.425 to 2.450 mm
Left-hand side	Selective fit (see text)

Torque wrench settings – see end of Specifications

Specifications – 750 models

General

Type	Four-stroke in-line four
Capacity	750 cc
Bore	70.0 mm
Stroke	48.7 mm
Compression ratio	12.5 to 1
Clutch	Wet multi-plate
Transmission	6-speed constant mesh
Final drive	Chain

Cylinder compression

Standard	185 to 242 psi (13 to 17 Bars)*
Minimum	142 psi (10 Bars)*
Maximum difference between cylinders	28 psi (2 Bars)*

Note: If all cylinders record less than the standard (even if they are above the minimum), or if the difference between any two cylinders is greater than the maximum, or if any one cylinder is less than the minimum, the engine should be overhauled.

Lubrication system

Oil pressure	14 to 57 psi (1 to 4 Bars) at 3000 rpm, oil at 60°C

Camshafts

Intake lobe height	
K6 and K7 models	
Standard	36.78 to 36.83 mm
Service limit (min)	36.48 mm
K8 and K9 models	
Standard	36.58 to 36.63 mm
Service limit (min)	36.28 mm
Exhaust lobe height	
K6 and K7 models	
Standard	35.38 to 35.43 mm
Service limit (min)	35.08 mm
K8 and K9 models	
Standard	35.98 to 36.03 mm
Service limit (min)	35.68 mm
Journal diameter	23.959 to 23.980 mm
Journal holder diameter	24.012 to 24.025 mm
Journal oil clearance	
Standard	0.032 to 0.066 mm
Service limit (max)	0.15 mm
Runout (max)	0.10 mm

Cylinder head

Warpage (max)	0.20 mm

Valves, guides and springs

Valve clearances	see Chapter 1
Intake valve	
Head diameter	29.0 mm
Stem diameter	4.475 to 4.490 mm
Guide bore diameter	4.500 to 4.512 mm
Stem-to-guide clearance	0.010 to 0.037 mm
Side clearance, wobble (max) – see text	0.25 mm
Seat width	0.9 to 1.1 mm
Head runout (max)	0.03 mm
Stem runout (max)	0.05 mm
Exhaust valve	
Head diameter	23.0 mm
Stem diameter	4.455 to 4.470 mm
Guide bore diameter	4.500 to 4.512 mm
Stem-to-guide clearance	0.030 to 0.057 mm
Side clearance, wobble (max) – see text	0.25 mm
Seat width	0.9 to 1.1 mm
Head runout (max)	0.03 mm
Stem runout (max)	0.05 mm
Valve spring free length (min)	37.1 mm

Clutch

Friction plate
  Quantity 9
  Thickness
    Standard . . . . 2.72 to 2.88 mm
    Service limit (min) . . . . 2.42 mm
  Tab width
    Standard
      K6 and K7 models . . . . 13.85 to 14.04 mm
      K8 and K9 models . . . . 13.85 to 13.96 mm
    Service limit (min) . . . . 13.05 mm
Plain plate
  Quantity 8
  Warpage (max) . . . . 0.1 mm
Spring free length
  Standard . . . . 56.0 mm
  Service limit . . . . 53.2 mm
Slipper mechanism adjuster screw protrusion . . . . 0.2 to 0.4 mm
Spring washer min free height . . . . 4.30 mm

Cylinders

Bore standard dimension . . . . 70.000 to 70.015 mm
Warpage of gasket face (max) . . . . 0.20 mm

Pistons

Piston diameter (measured 15 mm up from skirt, at 90° to piston pin axis)
  Standard . . . . 69.965 to 69.980 mm
  Service limit (min) . . . . 69.880 mm
Piston-to-bore clearance
  Standard . . . . 0.030 to 0.040 mm
  Service limit (max) . . . . 0.120 mm
Piston pin diameter
  Standard . . . . 14.995 to 15.000 mm
  Service limit (min) . . . . 14.980 mm
Piston pin bore diameter in piston
  Standard . . . . 15.002 to 15.008 mm
  Service limit (max) . . . . 15.030 mm

Piston rings

Ring end gap (free)
  Top ring
    Standard . . . . 9.2 mm (approx.)
    Service limit (min) . . . . 7.3 mm
  2nd ring
    Standard . . . . 7.3 mm (approx.)
    Service limit (min) . . . . 5.8 mm
Ring end gap (installed) – top and second rings . . . . 0.06 to 0.21 mm
Service limit (max) . . . . 0.50 mm
Ring thickness
  Top ring . . . . 0.97 to 0.99 mm
  2nd ring . . . . 0.77 to 0.79 mm
Ring groove width in piston
  Top ring . . . . 1.01 to 1.03 mm
  2nd ring . . . . 0.81 to 0.83 mm
  Oil ring . . . . 1.51 to 1.53 mm
Ring-to-groove clearance
  Top ring (max) . . . . 0.18 mm
  2nd ring (max) . . . . 0.15 mm

Transmission

Gear ratios (no. of teeth)
  Primary reduction . . . . 1.761 to 1 (74/42)
  Final reduction . . . . 2.647 to 1 (45/17)
  1st gear . . . . 2.785 to 1 (39/14)
  2nd gear . . . . 2.052 to 1 (39/19)
  3rd gear . . . . 1.714 to 1 (36/21)
  4th gear . . . . 1.500 to 1 (36/24)
  5th gear . . . . 1.347 to 1 (31/23)
  6th gear . . . . 1.208 to 1 (29/24)

Selector drum and forks

Selector fork-to-gear groove clearance
  Standard.. 0.1 to 0.3 mm
  Service limit (max) .... 0.5 mm
Selector fork end thickness .... 4.8 to 4.9 mm
Selector fork groove width in gears .... 5.0 to 5.1 mm

Connecting rods

Small-end internal diameter
  Standard.. 15.010 to 15.018 mm
  Service limit (max) .... 15.040 mm
Big-end side clearance
  Standard.. 0.1 to 0.2 mm
  Service limit (max) .... 0.3 mm
Big-end width.. 19.95 to 20.00 mm
Crankpin width... 20.10 to 20.15 mm
Big-end ID
  Code 1 .... 36.000 to 36.008 mm
  Code 2 .... 36.008 to 36.016 mm
Crankpin OD
  Code 1 .... 32.992 to 33.000 mm
  Code 2 .... 32.984 to 32.992 mm
  Code 3 .... 32.976 to 32.984 mm
Big-end oil clearance
  Standard.. 0.032 to 0.056 mm
  Service limit (max) .... 0.08 mm

Crankshaft and bearings

Main bearing journal OD
  Code A .... 31.994 to 32.000 mm
  Code B .... 31.988 to 31.994 mm
  Code C .... 31.982 to 31.988 mm
Crankcase seat ID
  Code A .... 35.000 to 35.006 mm
  Code B .... 35.006 to 35.012 mm
  Code C .... 35.012 to 35.018 mm
Main bearing oil clearance
  Standard.. 0.010 to 0.028 mm
  Service limit (max) .... 0.080 mm
Runout (max) .... 0.05 mm
Thrust bearing clearance .... 0.055 to 0.110 mm
Thrust bearing thickness
  Right-hand side .... 2.425 to 2.450 mm
  Left-hand side .... Selective fit (see text)

Balancer shaft and bearings

Balancer shaft oil clearance
  Standard.. 0.028 to 0.052 mm
  Service limit (max) .... 0.080 mm
Shaft bearing journal OD
  Code A .... 22.984 to 22.992 mm
  Code B .... 22.976 to 22.984 mm
Crankcase seat ID
  Code A .... 26.000 to 26.008 mm
  Code B .... 26.008 to 26.016 mm

Torque wrench settings – 600 and 750

Alternator cover bolts	10 Nm
Alternator stator bolts	11 Nm
Alternator rotor bolt	120 Nm
Cam chain guide blade bolt	23 Nm
Cam chain tensioner blade bolt	23 Nm
Cam chain tensioner cap bolt – 600K6 and K7	23 Nm
Cam chain tensioner inspection cap – 600K8 and K9, all 750 models	23 Nm
Cam chain tensioner mounting bolts	10 Nm
Camshaft holder bolts	10 Nm
Clutch centre nut	95 Nm
Clutch cover bolts	10 Nm
Clutch slipper mechanism adjuster screw locknuts	23 Nm
Clutch spring bolts	10 Nm
Connecting rod cap bolts	
Initial setting	15 Nm
Final angle setting	+90°
Coolant inlet union bolts	10 Nm
Crankcase bolts	
6 mm bolts	
Initial setting	6 Nm
Final setting	11 Nm
8 mm bolt with threadlock	
Initial setting	15 Nm
Final setting	22 Nm
All other 8 mm bolts	
Initial setting	15 Nm
Final setting	26 Nm
9 mm bolts (crankshaft journal bolts)	
Initial setting	18 Nm
Final setting	+50°
Crankcase breather cover bolts	10 Nm
Cylinder block water jacket plug	9.5 Nm
Cylinder head 6 mm bolts	10 Nm
Cylinder head 10 mm bolts	
Initial setting	31 Nm (see Section 9)
Final angle setting	+60°
Engine mountings	
Rear mounting adjuster bolts	23 Nm
Rear mounting adjuster bolt locknuts	45 Nm
Rear mounting bolt nuts	75 Nm
Front mounting bolts	55 Nm
Front mounting lug pinch bolt	23 Nm
Gearchange selector drum bearing/fork shaft retainer screws	10 Nm
Gearchange selector drum cam centre bolt	13 Nm
Gearchange shaft return spring post bolt	19 Nm
Gearchange stopper arm bolt	10 Nm
Main oil gallery plugs	
Internal (M12)	15 Nm
External (M16)	35 Nm
Oil cooler mounting bolts	10 Nm
Oil jet (for alternator)	
K6 and K7 models	22 Nm
K8 and K9 models	27 Nm
Oil pump mounting bolts	10 Nm
Oil sump bolts	10 Nm
Piston oil jet bolts	10 Nm
Starter clutch housing bolts	
K6 and K7 models	10 Nm
K8 and K9 models	13 Nm
Starter reduction gear cover bolts	10 Nm
Timing inspection cap	11 Nm
Timing rotor bolt	54 Nm
Transmission output shaft bearing housing screws	12 Nm
Transmission output shaft oil seal retainer screws	12 Nm
Valve cover bolts	14 Nm

1 General information

The engine/transmission unit is a water-cooled, four cylinder in-line design fitted across the frame. The valves are operated by double overhead camshafts which are chain driven off the crankshaft. The engine/ transmission unit is constructed from aluminium alloy with the crankcase divided horizontally into two sections. On 750 models a balancer shaft is gear driven off the crankshaft.

The crankcase incorporates a wet sump, pressure-fed lubrication system which uses a gear-driven, dual-rotor oil pump. A crankcase mounted oil cooler works in conjunction with the engine cooling system.

Power from the crankshaft is transferred via a wet, multi-plate type clutch to a six-speed, constant-mesh transmission unit. Final drive to the rear wheel is by chain and sprockets.

2 Component access

Operations possible with the engine in the frame

The components listed below can be removed without having to remove the engine from the frame. If however, a number of areas require attention at the same time, removal of the engine is recommended.

Valve cover
Cam chain tensioner
Camshafts
Starter motor (see Chapter 8)
Alternator (see Chapter 8)
Starter clutch and idle gear
Ignition timing rotor and crankshaft position sensor
Cam chain and tensioner blade
Clutch
Gearchange mechanism
Oil cooler
Water pump (see Chapter 3)

Operations requiring engine removal

It is necessary to remove the engine from the frame to gain access to the following components.

Cylinder head
Cam chain front guide blade
Oil sump, oil strainer and pressure relief valve
Oil pump
Pistons/connecting rod assemblies
Crankshaft and bearings
Transmission shafts
Selector drum and forks
Balancer shaft (750 models)

3 Engine wear assessment

Cylinder compression check

Special tool: *A compression gauge with adaptor to fit the spark plug hole (use either the Suzuki gauge and adapter (pt. Nos. 09915-64512 and 09913-10750) or aftermarket versions) are needed. Depending on the outcome of the initial test, a squirt-type oil can may also be needed.*

1 Poor engine performance may be caused by leaking valves, incorrect valve clearances, a leaking head gasket, or worn pistons, piston rings or cylinder walls. A cylinder compression check will highlight these conditions and can also indicate the presence of excessive carbon deposits in the cylinder head, and a leakdown test (for which special equipment is needed – consult a Suzuki dealer) will pinpoint the actual cause(s) of the problem.

2 Start by making sure the valve clearances are correctly set (see Chapter 1) and that the cylinder head bolts are tightened to the correct torque setting (see Section 9). Also make sure the battery has sufficient charge.

3 Run the engine until it is at normal operating temperature. Remove the spark plugs (see Chapter 1).

4 Fit the gauge into the No. 1 cylinder spark plug hole – if the rubber cone type is used keep the gauge pressed onto the hole throughout the test to maintain a good seal.

5 With the ignition switch ON, the kill switch set to RUN, the clutch lever pulled in and the throttle held fully open, turn the engine over on the starter motor until the gauge reading has built up and stabilised **(see illustration)**.

6 Compare the reading on the gauge to the cylinder compression figure specified for your model at the beginning of the Chapter. Repeat for the remaining cylinders.

7 If the reading is low, it could be due to a worn cylinder bore, piston or rings, failure of the head gasket, or worn valve seats. To determine which is the cause, pour a small quantity of engine oil into the spark plug hole to seal the rings, then repeat the compression test. If the figures are noticeably higher the

cause is worn cylinder, piston or rings. If there is no change the cause is a leaking head gasket or worn valve seats.

8 If the reading is high there could be a build-up of carbon deposits in the combustion chamber, or the cylinder head gasket is too thin. Remove the cylinder head and scrape all deposits off the piston and the cylinder head, and on installation fit a new gasket.

Engine oil pressure check

9 The oil pressure 'oil can' symbol and the warning light should illuminate when the ignition switch is turned ON, and they should extinguish when the engine is started – this serves as a check that the LED is sound. If the oil pressure light comes on whilst the engine is running, low oil pressure is indicated – stop the engine immediately and carry out an oil level check (see *Pre-ride checks*).

10 An oil pressure check must be carried out if the warning light comes on when the engine is running yet the oil level is good. It can also provide useful information about the condition of the engine's lubrication system.

11 To check the oil pressure, a suitable gauge, hose and adapter (which screws into the crankcase) will be needed. Suzuki produce service tools Pt. Nos. 09915-77331, 09915-74521 and 09915-74540 for this purpose.

12 Remove the fairing right-hand side-panel (see Chapter 7).

13 Position a suitable container below the main oil gallery plug on the right-hand side of the engine to catch any spilled oil. Unscrew the plug and swiftly screw the gauge adapter into the crankcase threads **(see illustration)**. Connect the hose and gauge to the adapter. If much oil is lost, replenish it to the correct level before proceeding (see *Pre-ride checks*).

14 Warm the engine up to normal operating temperature (between 10 and 20 minutes running at 2000 rpm) then increase the engine speed to 3000 rpm whilst watching the gauge reading. The oil pressure should be within the range given in the Specifications at the beginning of this Chapter. Turn the engine OFF.

15 If the pressure is significantly lower than the standard, either the pressure regulator is stuck open, the oil pump is faulty, the oil strainer or filter is blocked, or there is other engine

3.5 Checking cylinder compression

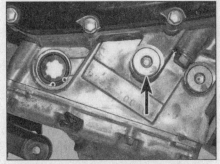

3.13 Main oil gallery plug (arrowed)

damage. Begin diagnosis by checking the oil filter, strainer and regulator, then the oil pump (see Section 18). If these items are good, it is likely the bearing oil clearances are excessive and the engine needs to be overhauled.

16 If the pressure is too high, either an oil passage is clogged, the regulator is stuck closed or the wrong grade of oil is being used.

17 Fit a new O-ring onto the main oil gallery plug. Disconnect the hose and gauge from the adapter and unscrew the adapter from the crankcase. Fit the plug and tighten it to the torque setting specified at the beginning of this Chapter.

⚠️ *Warning: Be careful when removing the pressure gauge adapter as the exhaust pipes, the engine and the oil itself can cause severe burns.*

18 Check the engine oil level (see *Pre-ride) checks*) then install the remaining components in the reverse order of removal.

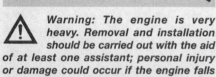

4 Engine removal and installation

⚠️ *Warning: The engine is very heavy. Removal and installation should be carried out with the aid of at least one assistant; personal injury or damage could occur if the engine falls or is dropped. If available, an hydraulic or mechanical floor jack should be used to support and lower or raise the engine.*

Special tool: *A peg spanner is required to loosen and tighten the engine mounting locknuts and adjusters. If the Suzuki service tool (Pt .No. 09940-14990 or 14980 – check with your dealer) is not available, a suitable peg spanner will have to be obtained or fabricated (see **Tool Tip**).*

Removal

1 If the engine is dirty, particularly around its mountings, wash it thoroughly before starting any major dismantling work. This will make work much easier and rule out the possibility of dirt falling into some vital component.

2 Support the bike in an upright position using an auxiliary stand. Work can be made easier by raising the machine to a suitable working height on an hydraulic ramp or a suitable platform. Make sure the motorcycle is

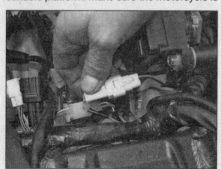

4.15a Disconnect the CKP sensor wiring connector . . .

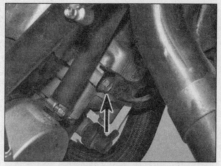

4.8 Unscrew the bolt (arrowed) and remove the bracket

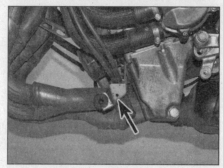

4.13 Remove the bracket (arrowed), noting how it fits

secure and will not topple over (see *Tools and Workshop Tips* in the Reference section).

3 Remove the seats, the fairing and the fairing side panels (see Chapter 7).

4 Disconnect the negative (-) lead from the battery (see Chapter 8).

5 Drain the engine oil and the coolant (see Chapter 1).

6 Remove the fuel tank and the air filter housing (see Chapter 4). Remove the fuel tank drain and breather hoses, noting their routing.

7 Remove the throttle bodies (see Chapter 4). Plug the engine intake manifolds with clean rag to prevent debris falling into the engine.

8 Remove the radiator and the coolant reservoir, detaching the hoses from the engine and oil cooler (see Chapter 3). Remove the radiator bracket, noting how it locates **(see illustration)**.

9 Remove the exhaust system (see Chapter 4).

10 On K6 and K7 models remove the horn and the regulator/rectifier (see Chapter 8).

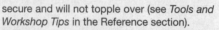

4.15b . . . the GP sensor wiring connector . . .

4.12 Remove the deflector panel

4.14 Pull the boot off the switch, undo the screw and detach the wire

11 On K8 and K9 models remove the horn (see Chapter 8).

12 Release and remove the heat deflector panel, noting how it locates **(see illustration)**.

13 On K6 and K7 models release and remove the fairing side panel bracket, noting how it locates **(see illustration)**.

14 Disconnect the wire from the oil pressure switch **(see illustration)**. Release the wire from its clip on the engine and secure it clear, noting its routing.

15 Trace the crankshaft position (CKP) sensor wiring from the timing rotor cover on the right-hand side of the engine and disconnect it at the connector **(see illustration)**. Trace the gear position (GP) sensor wiring from the lower left-hand side of the crankcase and disconnect it at the connector **(see illustration)**. Disconnect the coolant temperature (ECT) sensor wiring connector **(see illustration)**.

16 Pull back the boot on the starter motor

4.15c . . . and the ECT sensor wiring connector (arrowed)

4.16a Displace the boot then unscrew the nut and disconnect the lead

4.16b Disconnect the engine earth (ground) wiring connector

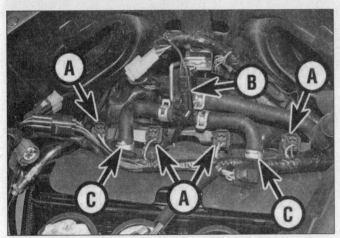

4.17 Disconnect the wiring connectors (A) and remove the coils, then disconnect the CMP sensor wiring connector (B), and detach the PAIR hoses (C)

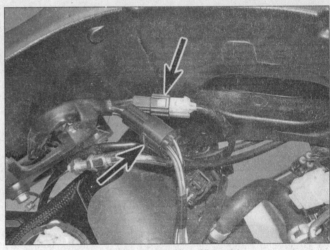

4.18a Disconnect the regulator/rectifier wiring connectors (arrowed) . . .

terminal, then undo the nut and disconnect the lead (see illustration). Disconnect the engine earth lead wiring connector (see illustration).

17 Disconnect the ignition coil wiring connectors and remove the coils (see illustration). Disconnect the camshaft position (CMP) sensor wiring connector. Secure the wiring clear of the engine. Detach the PAIR system hoses from their unions on the valve cover. Remove the PAIR control valve if required (see Chapter 4).

18 On K8 and K9 models disconnect the regulator/rectifier wiring connectors. Remove the rubber shield from the top of the valve cover (see illustrations).

19 Release all wiring from any clips or ties on the engine, noting its routing, and secure it clear of the engine.

20 If required, remove the oil filter (see Chapter 1).

21 Remove the front sprocket cover (see Chapter 6). Unscrew the gearchange lever brackets and remove the lever and linkage assembly (see illustration). Remove the clutch pushrod for safekeeping (see illustration). Remove the front sprocket (see Chapter 6).

22 At this point, position an hydraulic or

4.18b . . . and remove the rubber shield

4.21a Unscrew the bolts (arrowed) and remove the lever assembly

4.21b Withdraw the clutch pushrod

4.22 Support the weight of the engine on a jack

4.23 Unscrew and remove the front left-hand mounting bolt

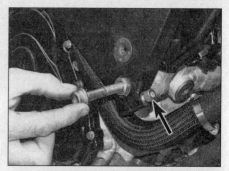

4.24 Loosen the pinch bolt (arrowed) then unscrew and remove the mounting bolt

4.25 Unscrew the nut from each end of the upper and lower rear mounting bolts

4.26a This is the Suzuki tool . . .

4.26b . . . for undoing the locknut

mechanical jack under the engine with a block of wood between the jack head and sump. Make sure the jack is centrally positioned so the engine will not topple in any direction when the last mounting bolt is removed. Take the weight of the engine on the jack, but make sure the jack is not lifting it as the engine bolts will then be difficult to remove **(see illustration)**.

23 Undo and remove the front left-hand engine mounting bolt **(see illustration)**.

24 Loosen the front right-hand engine mounting spacer pinch bolt **(see illustration)**. Undo and remove the front right-hand mounting bolt. **Note:** *The front left-hand and right-hand bolts are different lengths – do not mix them up.*

25 Undo the nuts on the upper and lower rear engine mounting bolts but do not remove the bolts **(see illustration)**. **Note:** *The rear mounting bolt nuts are self-locking, and Suzuki*

advise that they should only be used once. Obtain new nuts before installing the engine.

26 Using either the Suzuki service tool or a suitable peg spanner (see **Tool Tip**), undo the locknut on the lower adjuster bolt in the right-hand side of the frame **(see illustrations)**. Now use a 19 mm hex socket (a bi-hex one won't work) and turn the adjuster bolt anti-clockwise as far as it will go without becoming tight **(see illustration)**.

27 Follow Step 26 and undo the locknut on the upper adjuster bolt, then turn the adjuster bolt anti-clockwise to loosen it fully **(see illustrations 4.26a, b and c)**.

28 Check that all wiring, cables and hoses are disconnected and clear of the engine. Make sure the engine is properly supported on the jack and have an assistant support it as well.

29 Withdraw the upper and lower rear mounting bolts **(see illustrations)**. Carefully lower the

TOOL TIP

For the locknut, a peg "socket" can be made by cutting an old socket as shown – measure the width and depth of the slots in the locknut to determine the size of the castellations on the socket. If an old socket is not available, castellations can be welded onto a suitable nut.

4.26c Use a 19 mm hex socket to turn the adjuster (arrowed)

4.29a Withdraw the upper . . .

4.29b . . . and lower rear mounting bolts . . .

4.29c . . . slip the chain off the end of the shaft . . .

4.29d . . . and remove the engine

engine, remembering to lift the drive chain off the transmission output shaft, then manoeuvre the engine out of the frame **(see illustrations)**.

30 If required, remove the spacer for the front right-hand mounting bolt and thread the adjuster bolts for the rear mountings out of the frame from the inside **(see illustration)**.

Installation

31 Clean the threads of the engine mounting bolts and, if removed, the rear mounting adjuster bolts.

32 If removed, thread the adjuster bolts for the rear engine mountings all the way into the frame from the inside **(see illustration 4.30)**. If removed, fit the spacer into the front right-hand mounting, making sure the shouldered end faces the inside **(see illustration 4.30)**.

33 With the aid of an assistant place the engine unit under the frame then on top of the jack and block of wood and carefully raise it into position in the frame, remembering to lift the drive chain over the output shaft **(see illustrations 4.29d and c)**. Ensure no wires, cables or hoses become trapped between the engine and the frame.

34 Align the bolt holes and slide the rear mounting bolts through from the left-hand side **(see illustration 4.29b and a)**.

35 Install the front mounting bolts and tighten

them finger-tight **(see illustrations 4.24 and 23)**. **Note:** *The right-hand bolt is longer than the left-hand bolt.*

36 Turn the adjuster bolts clockwise so they contact the engine and tighten them to the torque setting specified at the beginning of this Chapter **(see illustration 4.26c)**.

37 Fit the adjuster locknuts and tighten them to the specified torque setting, using the same tool as for removal, making sure the adjuster bolts do not turn with them **(see illustrations 4.26b and a)**.

38 Fit the new self-locking nuts onto the rear mounting bolts and tighten them finger-tight **(see illustration 4.25)**.

39 Ensure that the front mounting bolts are still finger-tight, then tighten the nuts on the rear mounting bolts to the torque setting specified at the beginning of this Chapter. Now tighten the left-hand and right-hand front bolts to the torque setting specified at the beginning of this Chapter. Finally tighten the spacer pinch bolt on the right-hand mounting lug to the specified torque setting **(see illustration)**.

40 The remainder of the installation procedure is the reverse of removal, noting the following points.

● Make sure all wires, cables and hoses are correctly routed and connected, and secured by the relevant clips or ties.

● Tighten all bolts to the specified torque settings where given.
● Adjust the throttle and clutch cable freeplay (see Chapter 1).
● Adjust the drive chain (see Chapter 1).
● Refill the engine with oil and coolant (see Chapter 1 and *Pre-ride checks*).
● Prior to installing the fairing side panels start the engine and check that there is no coolant or oil leakage.

5 Engine overhaul – general information

1 Before beginning the engine overhaul, read through the related procedures to familiarise yourself with the scope and requirements of the job. Overhauling an engine is not all that difficult, but it is time consuming. Check on the availability of parts and make sure that any necessary special tools are obtained in advance.

2 Most work can be done with typical workshop hand tools, although a number of precision measuring tools are required for inspecting parts to determine if they are worn.

3 To ensure maximum life and minimum trouble from a rebuilt engine, everything must be assembled with care in a spotlessly clean environment.

Disassembly

4 Before disassembling the engine clean and degrease its external surfaces. This will prevent contamination of the engine internals, and will also make working a lot easier and cleaner. Use a proprietary engine cleaner such as Gunk or alternatively a high flash-point solvent, such as paraffin (kerosene). Use a brush to work the cleaner into the recesses of the engine casings. Take care not to get solvent or water into the electrical components and intake and exhaust ports.

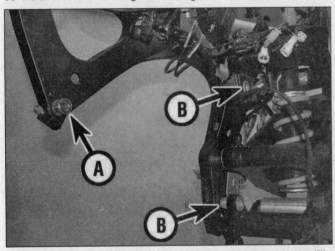

4.30 If required remove the spacer (A) and the adjuster bolts (B)

4.39 Do not forget to tighten the spacer pinch bolt (arrowed)

Warning: Do not use petrol (gasoline) as a cleaning agent because of the risk of fire.

5 When clean and dry, position the engine on the workbench, leaving suitable clear area for working. Make sure the engine is stable at all times – some strategically placed blocks of wood under the crankcase or engine covers will help support it and keep it stable. Note that the engine will have to be moved around as you work on it. Gather a selection of small containers, plastic bags and some labels so that parts can be grouped together in an easily identifiable manner. Also get some paper and a pen so that notes can be taken. You will also need a supply of clean rag, which should be as absorbent as possible.

6 Before commencing work, read through the appropriate section so that some idea of the necessary procedure can be gained. When removing components it should be noted that great force is seldom required. In many cases, a component's reluctance to be removed is indicative of an incorrect approach or removal method – if in any doubt, re-check with the text. In cases where fasteners have corroded, apply penetrating oil or WD40 before disassembly.

7 When disassembling the engine, keep 'mated' parts together (e.g. valve assemblies, pistons and connecting rods, clutch plates etc. that have been in contact with each other during engine operation). These 'mated' parts must be reused or renewed as assemblies.

8 Disassembly should be done in the following general order with reference to the appropriate Sections.

> *Remove the valve cover*
> *Remove the cam chain tensioner*
> *Remove the camshafts*
> *Remove the cylinder head*
> *Remove the tensioner blade, timing rotor, am chain, and front guide blade*
> *Remove the starter motor*
> *Remove the alternator and starter clutch*
> *Remove the clutch*
> *Remove the gearchange mechanism*
> *Remove the oil sump, strainer and pressure regulator*
> *Remove the oil pump*
> *Separate the crankcases*
> *Remove the transmission shafts/gears*
> *Remove the selector drum and forks*
> *Remove the crankshaft and connecting rod assemblies*
> *Remove the balancer shaft (750 models only)*

Reassembly

9 Reassembly is accomplished by reversing the general disassembly sequence.

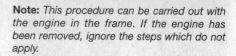

6 Valve cover

Note: *This procedure can be carried out with the engine in the frame. If the engine has been removed, ignore the steps which do not apply.*

Removal

1 Remove the fairing side panels (see Chapter 7).

2 Remove the fuel tank and air filter housing (see Chapter 4). Loosen the clamp screws securing the throttle bodies to the intake adapters – one screw on each side secures both bodies for that side **(see illustration)**. Lift the assembly out of the intake adapters and move it back slightly so it is out of the way.

3 Remove the PAIR system control valve along with its hoses (see Chapter 4).

4 Disconnect the ignition coil wiring connectors and remove the coils **(see illustration 4.17)**. Disconnect the camshaft position sensor wiring connector. On K8 and K9 models remove the rubber shield **(see illustration 4.18b)**.

5 Unscrew the radiator mounting bolts and displace the radiator forwards – there is no need to drain the coolant or detach the hoses.

6 On K6 and K7 models remove the regulator/rectifier and horn assembly (see Chapter 8).

7 On K8 and K9 models remove the horn (see Chapter 8).

8 Release and remove the heat deflector panel, noting how it locates **(see illustration 4.12)**.

9 Unscrew the valve cover bolts and remove them along with their sealing washers **(see illustration)**. Discard the washers as new ones must be fitted on reassembly.

10 Lift the valve cover off the cylinder head

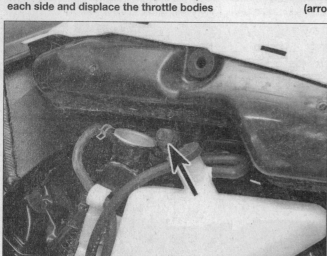

6.2 Slacken the clamp screw (arrowed) on each side and displace the throttle bodies

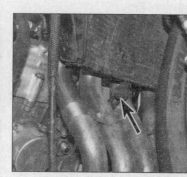

6.5a Unscrew the bottom bolt (arrowed) . . .

6.5b . . . and the top bolt (arrowed) on each side

6.9 Unscrew the valve cover bolts (arrowed) . . .

6.10 . . . and remove the cover

6.11a Lift the seals from the camshaft holders . . .

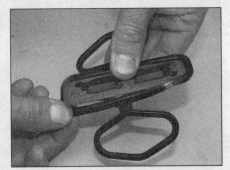

6.11b . . . and remove the reed valves

6.13 Locate the tab on the seal in the curbed section on the camshaft holder (arrowed)

6.14a Fit the lipped side of the new gasket into the groove in the cover

evenly and in a criss-cross sequence starting from the centre and working outwards to the torque setting specified at the beginning of this Chapter **(see illustration)**.

16 Install the remaining components in the reverse order of removal.

7 Cam chain tensioner

Note: *This procedure can be carried out with the engine in the frame. If the engine has been removed, ignore the steps which do not apply.*

Removal

1 Remove the valve cover (see Section 6). Remove the spark plugs (see Chapter 1).
2 Unscrew the timing inspection cap from the right-hand side of the engine **(see illustration 8.2)**. Discard the O-ring as a new one must be fitted on reassembly. Using a socket on the timing rotor bolt, turn the engine in a clockwise direction until the line on the rotor aligns with the rib inside the inspection hole, and the number 1 arrow on the exhaust camshaft sprocket points forwards and is level with the top surface on the cylinder head **(see illustrations 8.3a, b and c)**.

(see illustration). If it is stuck, do not try to lever it off with a screwdriver. Tap around the joint with a soft-faced mallet to dislodge it. Discard the cover gasket as a new one must be fitted on reassembly.

11 Remove the reed valve/spark plug passage seals, then ease the reed valves from the seals, noting how they fit **(see illustrations)**. Discard the seals as new ones must be used.

Installation

12 Clean the mating surfaces of the cylinder head and cover with a suitable solvent to remove all traces of old sealant and gasket.
13 Fit the reed valves into the new reed

valve/spark plug passage seals **(see illustration 6.11b)**. Make sure they are the correct way round and they locate correctly. Fit the seals onto the camshaft holders, making sure they locate correctly **(see illustration)**.
14 Lay the new gasket onto the valve cover, making sure it locates correctly in its groove and using dabs of grease to hold it in place **(see illustration)**. Apply a suitable, non-permanent sealant to the corners of the camshaft end caps **(see illustration)**.
15 Position the cover on the cylinder head, making sure the gasket stays in place **(see illustration 6.10)**. Install the cover bolts with new sealing washers and tighten the bolts

6.14b Apply sealant to the end caps for the cut-outs

6.15 Use new sealing washers

7.3 Secure the chain to the sprockets with cable-ties to prevent the chain jumping teeth

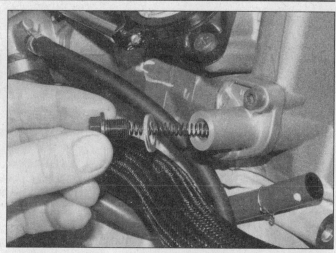

7.4a Unscrew the cap bolt, remove the spring and discard the sealing washer

7.4b Tensioner bolts (arrowed) – 600 K6/K7

7.5 Tensioner bolts (arrowed) – 600 K8/K9, all 750

3 To prevent the possibility of the cam chain jumping teeth on the camshaft sprockets with the tensioner removed, fit a cable-tie through one hole in each sprocket and around the cam chain and pull them tight **(see illustration)**.

4 On 600K6 and K7 models unscrew the tensioner cap bolt and withdraw the spring from the tensioner **(see illustration)**. Discard

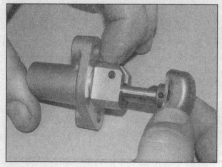

7.6 Lift the catch to retract the tensioner pushrod

the sealing washer as a new one must be used. Unscrew the tensioner mounting bolts and withdraw the tensioner **(see illustration)**. Discard the gasket as a new one must be fitted on reassembly.

5 On 600K8 and K9 and all 750 models unscrew the tensioner mounting bolts and withdraw the tensioner **(see illustration)**. Discard the gasket as a new one must be fitted on reassembly.

Caution: Do not rotate the engine with the cam chain tensioner removed.

Inspection

6 On 600K6 and K7 models examine the tensioner components for signs of wear or damage. Release the catch and push the plunger into the tensioner body **(see illustration)**. Insert the spring and check that the tensioner plunger extends under spring pressure. Check that the ratchet and teeth are not worn or damaged. If any components are worn or damaged replace them with new ones.

7 On 600K8 and K9 and all 750 models examine

the tensioner for signs of wear or damage. Hold the top of the tensioner body and the bottom of the plunger and compress them while turning the plunger clockwise until the groove in the plunger reaches the outer circlip in the body, then locate the circlip in the groove and release the plunger, which should now be locked retracted by the circlip **(see illustrations)**. If the plunger groove goes beyond the outer circlip and the inner circlip locates in it, push its tip away to expand it and allow the plunger to extend so the groove reaches the outer circlip, then locate that in the groove and release the plunger. Now turn the plunger more than 90° clockwise. Tap the end of the plunger and check that the circlip releases itself and the plunger springs out. If the plunger is difficult to compress because of trapped oil inside the tensioner push the tip of the inner circlip to expand it and withdraw the plunger assembly **(see illustrations)**. Drain the oil and clean all components, then smear all components with clean oil and reassemble the tensioner as shown in the sequence **(see illustrations)**.

7.7a Compress the tensioner while turning the plunger . . .

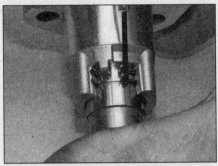

7.7b . . . then press and hold the circlip in the groove and release the plunger . . .

7.7c . . . so it is held in the retracted position

7.7d Push the end of the inner circlip away . . .

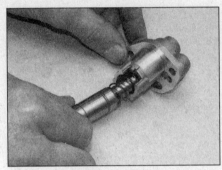

7.7e . . . to release the plunger assembly from the body

7.7f Contracting circlip (with closer spaced ends) fits in the inner groove in the body, and the expanding circlip with (wider spaced ends) fits in the outer groove

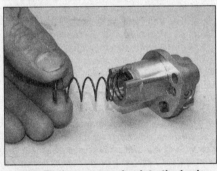

7.7g Fit the outer spring into the body

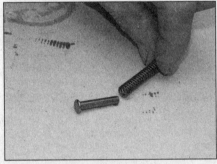

7.7h Fit the pin into the inner spring . . .

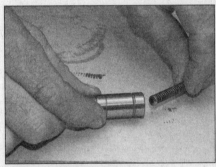

7.7i . . . then fit the pin end of the spring into the plunger

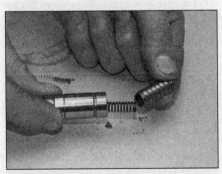

7.7j Fit the threaded piece over the inner spring . . .

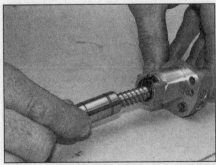

7.7k . . . then fit the assembly into the tensioner body . . .

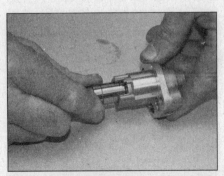

7.7l . . . locating the inner circlip in the first groove in the plunger so it is held in its expanded state

7.8 Remove and clean the oil jet

7.9 Use a new gasket and make sure it is the correct way round

7.10a This is the correct way for the gasket so both the oil jet and the oil passage are exposed by the oval cut-out in the gasket (arrowed)

7.10b This is the wrong way round – the oil passage is exposed, but the oil jet will be covered when the tensioner is installed (arrowed)

7.10c Install the tensioner and tighten the bolts

7.12a Unscrew the cap, noting the sealing washer

7.12b Press the plunger into the body to release the circlip . . .

7.12c . . . then allow the plunger to extend

8 Remove the cam chain tensioner oil jet from the cylinder head **(see illustration)**. Remove the O-ring, then clean the jet with solvent and blow it through, with compressed air if available. Fit an new O-ring and smear it with clean oil, then fit the jet back into the head.

Installation

9 On 600K6 and K7 models release the catch and push the plunger into the tensioner body **(see illustration 7.6)**. Fit the tensioner using a new gasket and tighten the mounting bolts to the torque setting specified at the beginning of the Chapter – make sure the gasket is fitted the correct way round so that both the oil jet in the head and the passage in the tensioner are left uncovered by the oval cut-out in the gasket **(see illustration)**. Install the spring and the cap bolt with a new sealing washer and tighten the bolt to the specified torque **(see illustration 7.4a)**. Note that a clicking noise that is the plunger extending should be heard as the cap bolt is installed.

10 On 600K8 and K9 and all 750 models, hold the top of the tensioner body and the bottom of the plunger and compress them while turning the plunger clockwise until the groove in the plunger reaches the outer circlip in the body, then locate the circlip in the groove and release the plunger, which should now be locked retracted by the circlip **(see illustrations 7.7a, b and c)**. If the plunger groove goes beyond the outer circlip and the inner circlip locates in it, push its tip away to expand it and allow the plunger to extend so the groove reaches the outer circlip, then locate that in the groove and release the plunger. Now turn the plunger more than 90° clockwise. If the plunger is difficult to compress because of trapped oil inside the tensioner push the tip of the inner circlip to expand it and withdraw the plunger assembly **(see illustrations 7.7d and e)**. Drain the oil and clean all components, then smear all components with clean oil and reassemble the tensioner as shown in the sequence **(see illustrations 7.7f to l)**. Fit a new gasket onto the body – note that it is very important that the gasket is fitted the correct way round as shown in illustration 7.10a with the cut-out in the gasket correctly aligned with that in the tensioner so that both the oil jet in the head and the passage in the tensioner are uncovered **(see illustrations)**. Fit the tensioner into the cylinder head **(see illustration)**. Tighten the mounting bolts to the torque setting specified at the beginning of this Chapter.

11 On 600K6 and K7 models turn the engine about 180° anti-clockwise – the pressure exerted by the tensioner blade on the plunger by turning the engine in the wrong direction will release the plunger. Now turn the engine 180° clockwise to reset the timing marks (Step 2).

12 On 600 K8 and K9 and all 750 models unscrew the tensioner inspection cap **(see illustration)**. Using a screwdriver press the plunger head into the tensioner body so that the circlip releases and the plunger extends **(see illustration)**. Fit the inspection cap, using a new sealing washer if necessary, and tighten it to the specified torque.

13 Check that the sprocket markings are still correctly aligned as in Step 2, and that the cam chain is tensioned. Remove the cable-ties from the sprockets. Rotate the engine clockwise a couple of times and recheck that the sprocket markings and timing rotor markings are in alignment.

14 Fit a new O-ring on the timing inspection cap and smear it with engine oil then tighten the cap to the specified torque setting. Install the remaining components in the reverse order of removal.

8 Camshafts and followers

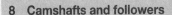

Note: *This procedure can be carried out with the engine in the frame. If the engine has been removed, ignore the steps which do not apply.*

Removal

1 Remove the valve cover (see Section 6). Remove the spark plugs (see Chapter 1).

2 Unscrew the timing inspection cap from the right-hand side of the engine **(see illustration)**. Discard the cap O-ring as a new one must be fitted on reassembly.

3 Using a socket on the timing rotor bolt, turn the engine in a clockwise direction until the scribe line on the timing rotor aligns with the rib inside the inspection hole, and the number 1 arrow on the exhaust camshaft sprocket points forwards and is level with the top surface on the cylinder head **(see illustrations)**.

4 Remove the cam chain tensioner (see Section 7, Step 4 or 5).

5 Before disturbing the camshaft holders, check for identification markings – the holder above the Nos. 1 and 2 cylinders is marked A, and the holder above Nos. 3 and 4 is marked B, and the arrow next to each letter points to the front of the engine **(see illustration)**. These markings ensure that the holders can be matched up to their original camshafts on installation. If no markings are visible, make your own using a felt pen.

8.2 Remove the timing inspection cap and discard the O-ring

6 Unscrew the holder bolts evenly and a little at a time in the **reverse** of the numerical tightening sequence shown and as marked on each holder **(see illustrations 8.31a and b)**. Where a bolt is marked twice, (i.e. with two different numbers), this means that it must be slackened twice during one round of the sequence. While loosening the bolts make sure that the holder is lifting squarely away

8.3a Turn the crankshaft in a clockwise direction

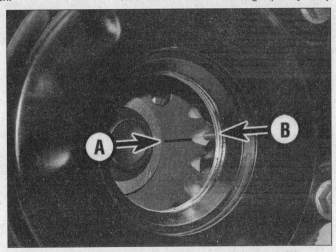

8.3b Align the scribe line (A, highlighted) with the rib (B) . . .

8.3c . . . and the No. 1 arrow with the top surface of the cylinder head

8.5 Camshaft holder identification and orientation marks (highlighted and arrowed)

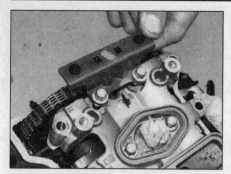

8.7a Lift off the top guide . . .

8.7b . . . then remove the holders, noting the dowels

8.7c Remove the intake camshaft first . . .

from the cylinder head and is not sticking on the locating dowels.

Caution: If the bolts are loosened carelessly and the holder does not come away from the head squarely, the holder is likely to break. If this happens the complete cylinder head assembly must be renewed; the holders are matched to the cylinder head and cannot be renewed separately. Also, a camshaft could be damaged if the holder bolts are not loosened evenly and the pressure from a depressed valve causes the shaft to bend.

7 Remove the bolts, noting those with copper washers, then remove the cam chain top guide, noting how it fits **(see illustration)**. Lift off the camshaft holders and remove the dowels for safekeeping if they are loose **(see illustration)**. Slip the cam chain off the intake camshaft sprocket and lift the camshaft out of the head, then remove the exhaust camshaft **(see illustration)**. **Note:** *Secure the cam chain to some convenient point with wire or a cable-tie to prevent it falling into the engine.* The camshafts are marked for identification. The intake camshaft is marked 'IN' and the exhaust camshaft is marked 'EX' **(see illustration)**. Remove the air passage O-rings from the underside of each holder and the spark plug bore O-rings from their grooves in the bores and discard them as new ones must be used **(see illustrations)**.

8 If the cam followers and shims are being removed, obtain a container which is divided into sixteen compartments, and label each compartment with the location of its corresponding valve in the cylinder head. If a

8.7d . . . then the exhaust

8.7f Remove the O-rings (arrowed) from the holders . . .

8.7e Camshaft identification marks

8.7g . . . and from the spark plug bores

container is not available, use labelled plastic bags. **Note:** *It is essential that the followers and shims are stored according to their position in the head and fitted back on their original valves otherwise all the clearances will be wrong.* Lift each cam follower out of the cylinder head using a magnet or suction tool

(such as a valve lapping tool) **(see illustration)**. Retrieve the shim from either the inside of the follower or pick it out of the top of the valve, using a magnet or a small screwdriver with a dab of grease on it (the shim will stick to the grease) **(see illustrations)**. Do not allow the shim to fall into the engine.

8.8a Lift out each follower . . .

8.8b . . . and remove the shim (arrowed) from inside it . . .

8.8c . . . or from the top of the valve

8.10 Inspect the camshaft journals for wear and damage

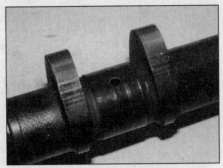

8.11a Inspect the camshaft lobes for wear . . .

8.11b . . . here's an example of spalling requiring repair or renewal

9 Cover the cylinder head to prevent anything falling into the engine.

Inspection

10 Inspect the bearing surfaces of the head and the holders and the corresponding journals on the camshaft. Look for score marks, deep scratches and evidence of spalling (a pitted appearance) **(see illustration).**

11 Check the camshaft lobes for heat discoloration (blue appearance), score marks, chipped areas, flat spots and spalling **(see illustrations).** Measure the height of each lobe with a micrometer and compare the results to the Specifications at the beginning of this Chapter **(see illustration).** If damage is noted or wear is excessive, the camshaft must be replaced with a new one.

12 Check camshaft runout by supporting each end of the camshaft on V-blocks, and measuring any runout at the journals using a dial gauge (see *Tools and Workshop Tips* in the *Reference* section). If the runout exceeds the specified limit the camshaft must be replaced with a new one.

13 If removed, inspect the outer surfaces of the cam followers for evidence of wear, scoring or other damage **(see illustration 8.25).** If the surface of a follower is in poor condition, it is probable that the bore in which it works is also damaged. Remove the valves (see Section 10) and measure the internal diameter of the follower bore in different places to determine wear. If the bore is seriously out-of-round the cylinder head will have to be replaced with a new one.

 HAYNES HiNT *Refer to Tools and Workshop Tips in the Reference section for details of how to read a micrometer and dial gauge.*

14 The camshaft journal oil clearance should now be checked. There are two possible ways of doing this, either by direct measurement (see Steps 15 to 17) or by the use of a product known as Plastigauge (see Steps 18 to 21). If Plastigauge is used and the oil clearance is excessive, use direct measurement to determine whether it is the camshaft or the holder that is worn.

15 If direct measurement is to be used, make sure the camshaft holder dowels are in position then fit the holders onto the cylinder head (without the camshafts), making sure they are in their correct location **(see illustrations 8.7b and 8.5).** Tighten the holder bolts evenly to the specified torque setting **(see illustrations 8.31a and b).**

16 Make a chart or sketch of the cylinder head so that a note of each measurement can be made against the appropriate bearing surface. Using telescoping gauges and a micrometer (see *Tools and Workshop Tips*), measure the internal diameter of each holder journal and record it on the chart. Now measure the diameter of the corresponding camshaft journals with a micrometer **(see illustration).**

17 To determine the journal oil clearance, subtract the camshaft journal diameter from the internal holder journal diameter. Compare the result to the clearance specified. If the clearance is greater than specified, compare the individual measurements of the camshaft journal and the holder to those specified and replace whichever component is beyond its service limit with a new one.

18 If the Plastigauge method is to be used, clean the camshafts and the bearing surfaces in the cylinder head and camshaft holder with a clean, lint-free cloth. Lay the camshafts in place in the cylinder head **(see illustrations 8.7d and c). Note:** *Check that the valve timing marks are correctly aligned when installing the camshaft to avoid valve damage.*

19 Cut strips of Plastigauge and lay one piece on each camshaft journal, along the camshaft centreline **(see illustration).** Make sure the camshaft holder dowels are in position then fit the holders, making sure each is in its correct location **(see illustration 8.7b and 8.5).** Tighten the holder bolts evenly and a little at a time in the correct numerical sequence shown and as marked on the holder to the specified torque setting **(see illustrations 8.31a and b). Note:** *The camshaft must not rotate during this procedure.*

20 Now unscrew the bolts evenly and a little at a time in the reverse of the numerical sequence and carefully lift off the camshaft holders.

21 To determine the oil clearance, compare the crushed Plastigauge (at its widest point) on each journal to the scale printed on the

8.11c Measuring a camshaft lobe with a micrometer

8.16 Measuring a camshaft journal with a micrometer

8.19 Lay a strip of Plastigauge across each journal, along the camshaft centreline (arrowed)

8.21 Compare the width of the crushed Plastigauge with the scale provided

8.25 Fit the follower onto the valve

Plastigauge container **(see illustration)**. Compare the results to this Chapter's Specifications. If the oil clearance is greater than specified, follow Steps 15 and 16 to determine which component is worn beyond its service limit.

22 Check the camshaft sprockets for wear, chipped teeth and other damage. The camshaft sprockets are integral with the camshafts, the crankshaft sprocket is integral with the ignition timing rotor.

23 If the sprockets on the camshafts are worn, the chain and the drive sprocket on the crankshaft are probably worn as well and should be checked (see Section 11).

Installation

24 Make sure the bearing surfaces in the cylinder head, on the camshafts and in the holders are clean, then liberally apply molybdenum oil (a 50/50 mixture of molybdenum paste and engine oil) to each of

them. Also apply oil to the camshaft lobes and the followers.

25 If removed, lubricate each shim and fit it into its recess in the top of the valve, with the size marking on each shim facing up **(see illustration 8.8c)**. Check that the shim is correctly seated, then install the follower **(see illustration)**. **Note:** *It is most important that the shims and followers are returned to their original valves otherwise the valve clearances will be inaccurate.*

26 Ensure that the scribe line on the timing rotor still aligns with the rib inside the inspection hole **(see illustration 8.3b)**. If it is necessary to turn the crankshaft to restore the alignment, hold the cam chain up to prevent it jamming between the crankcase and the crankshaft sprocket.

27 Keeping the front run of the cam chain taut, lay the exhaust camshaft (identified by EX) onto the cylinder head with the number 1 arrow on the sprocket pointing forwards and level with the top surface on the cylinder

head and engage the chain on the sprocket, pulling up on the front run so there is no slack between the drive sprocket on the crankshaft and the sprocket on the camshaft **(see illustration 8.7d and 8.3c)**.

28 Tie the chain onto the sprocket with a cable-tie so it cannot jump teeth **(see illustration)**.

29 Starting with the cam chain pin that is directly above the number 2 arrow as the first pin, count 12 pins along the chain towards the intake side. Lay the intake camshaft (identified by IN) into the cylinder head **(see illustration 8.7c)** and engage the intake camshaft sprocket with the chain so that the 12th pin is directly above the arrow marked 3 on the sprocket **(see illustration)**. Lock the chain and the intake camshaft sprocket in position with a cable-tie, then check that everything aligns as described in Steps 26, 27 and 29, and make adjustments as necessary.

30 Fit new O-rings into the grooves in the spark plug bores. Fit new air passage O-rings

8.28 With the chain tight in the front run and the timing mark correctly aligned tie the chain to the sprocket

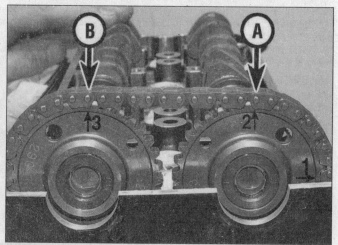

8.29 With the cam chain pin above the No. 2 arrow (A) as the 1st pin, engage the 12th pin with the No. 3 arrow (B)

8.30a Fit a new O-ring (arrowed) into the groove in each bore

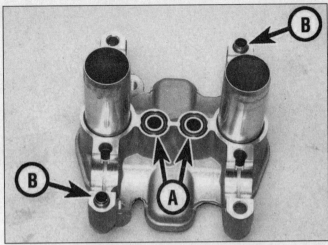

8.30b Fit new O-rings (A) and make sure the dowels (B) are in place

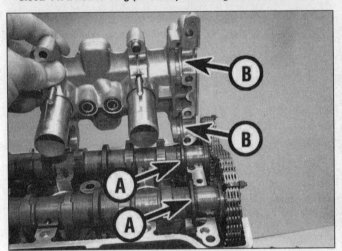

8.31a Make sure each rib (A) locates in its channel (B)

8.31b Fit new sealing washers to the bolts adjacent the plug bores

onto the underside of each camshaft holder and make sure the dowels are fitted (see illustrations).

31 Fit the holders, making sure they are in their correct locations (see Step 5), and make sure the ribbed section on the right-hand end of each camshaft locates in its channel in the holder (see illustration). Install the cam chain top guide (see illustration 8.7a). Fit the holder bolts, making sure the copper sealing washers are on the bolts to the front and back of each spark plug bore (see illustration). Now tighten the bolts evenly and a little at a time in the numerical tightening sequence marked on each holder and as shown to the specified torque setting (see illustrations) Where a bolt is marked twice, (i.e. with two

8.31c The number of each bolt is marked adjacent to it on the holder

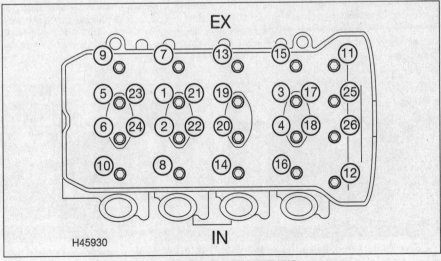

8.31d Camshaft holder bolt TIGHTENING sequence

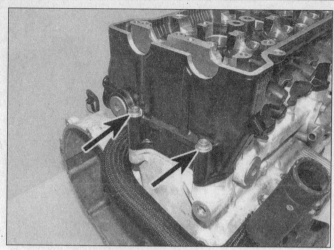

9.4 Undo and remove the 6 mm bolts (arrowed) . . .

9.5 . . . then loosen the 10 mm bolts (arrowed) in a criss-cross pattern from the outside to the centre

different numbers), this means that it must be tightened twice during one round of the sequence. **Note:** *The camshaft holder bolts are of the high tensile type. Don't use any other type of bolt.* As you tighten the bolts make sure the ribbed sections seat in the channels, if not the camshafts will be out of alignment and the bolts will go prematurely tight (if this happens do not force the bolts or something expensive will break!).

Caution: The camshaft is likely to break if it is tightened down onto the closed valves before the open valves. The holders are likely to break if they are not tightened down evenly and squarely.

32 Install the cam chain tensioner (see Section 7). Cut the cable-ties on the cam chain sprockets. Turn the engine clockwise two complete revolutions and ensure that everything still aligns (see Steps 26, 27 and 29) and that the camshafts are not pinched by the holders.

33 Check the valve clearances and adjust them if necessary (see Chapter 1). Install the remaining components in the reverse order of removal. Fit a new O-ring on the timing inspection cap and smear it with engine oil, then tighten the cap to the specified torque setting.

9 Cylinder head removal and installation

Note: *To remove the cylinder head the engine must be removed from the frame.*

Removal

1 Remove the engine from the frame (see Section 4).
2 Remove the camshafts, cam followers and shims (see Section 8).
3 If required remove the thermostat and its housing, and the ECT sensor (see Chapter 3).
4 The cylinder head is secured by two 6 mm bolts and ten 10 mm bolts. First unscrew and remove the 6 mm bolts **(see illustration)**.
5 Working from the outside to the centre in a criss-cross pattern, loosen the 10 mm bolts evenly and a little at a time until they are all slack, then remove the bolts and their washers **(see illustration)**.
6 Lift the head off the upper crankcase, passing the cam chain down through the tunnel as you do **(see illustration)**. If the head is stuck, tap around the joint with a soft-faced mallet to free it. Do not attempt to free the head by levering it off – you'll damage the sealing surfaces.

7 Secure the cam chain to prevent it falling into the engine and stuff a clean rag into the cam chain tunnel to prevent any debris falling in. Remove the old cylinder head gasket.
8 If they are loose, remove the two dowels from the rear edge of the upper crankcase for safekeeping **(see illustration 9.13)**. If either appears to be missing it is probably stuck in the underside of the cylinder head.
9 Inspect the cylinder head gasket and the mating surfaces on the cylinder head and upper crankcase for signs of leakage, which could indicate that the head is distorted. If necessary, check the cylinder head with a straight-edge (see Section 10). Discard the old head gasket as a new one must be fitted on reassembly.
10 If required, unscrew the bolts securing the intake adapters and remove the adapters, noting how they fit **(see illustration)**. Discard the O-rings as new ones must be fitted on reassembly.

Installation

11 Clean the mating surfaces of the cylinder head and upper crankcase with a suitable solvent to remove all traces of old gasket. If a scraper is used, take care not to scratch or gouge the soft aluminium. Ensure none of the old gasket material falls into the crankcase, the cylinder bores or the oil and coolant passages.

> **HAYNES HINT** *Refer to Tools and Workshop Tips for details of gasket removal methods.*

12 If removed, fit new O-rings smeared with grease into the grooves in the intake rubbers, then fit the adapters with the UP mark at the top **(see illustration 9.10)**. Apply a suitable non-permanent thread locking compound to the bolts and tighten them.
13 If removed, fit the two dowels into the upper crankcase, then fit the new head gasket

9.6 Carefully lift the head up off the crankcase

9.10 Each intake adapter is secured by two bolts (arrowed)

(see illustration). Make sure the gasket locates over the dowels and that all the holes are correctly aligned.

14 Remove any rag from the cam chain tunnel. Fit the head onto the upper crankcase, locating it on the dowels – keep the cam chain taut and pass it up through the tunnel as the head is fitted (see illustration 9.6). Secure the cam chain.

15 Apply clean engine oil to the washers on the cylinder head 10 mm bolts and to the bolt threads. Fit the bolts and tighten them finger-tight (see illustration).

16 Working from the centre to the outside in a criss-cross pattern, tighten the 10 mm bolts evenly and a little at a time to the initial torque setting specified at the beginning of this Chapter (see illustration 9.5). On K6 and K7 models now slacken the bolts off in a reverse of the tightening sequence, i.e. from the outside to the centre, then tighten them again from the centre to the outside to the same initial torque setting. On all models finally tighten the bolts from the centre to the outside through the specified final angle setting using a degree disc (see illustration).

17 Install the 6 mm bolts and tighten them to the specified torque setting (see illustration).

18 Install the remaining components in the reverse order of removal (Steps 3 to 1), referring to the relevant Sections and Chapters.

9.13 Fit the new gasket making sure it locates over the dowels (arrowed)

9.16 Tighten the bolts as described using a degree disc for the final stage

9.15 Lubricate the washers and threads of the 10 mm head bolts

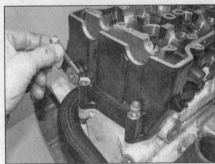

9.17 Install and tighten the 6 mm bolts

10 Cylinder head and valve overhaul

1 Because of the complex nature of this job and the special tools and equipment required, most owners leave servicing of the valves, valve seats and valve guides to a professional. However, you can make an initial assessment of whether the valves are seating correctly, and therefore sealing, by pouring a small amount of solvent into each of the intake and exhaust ports in turn. If the solvent leaks past any valve into the combustion chamber area the valve is not seating correctly and sealing.

2 With the correct tools (a valve spring

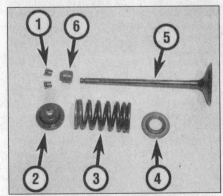

10.5 Valve components

1 *Collets*
2 *Spring retainer*
3 *Spring*
4 *Spring seat*
5 *Valve*
6 *Valve stem seal*

compressor is essential – make sure it is suitable for motorcycle work), you can also remove the valves and associated components from the cylinder head, clean them and check them for wear to assess the extent of the work needed, and, unless seat cutting or guide replacement is required, grind in the valves and reassemble them in the head.

3 A dealer service department or engine specialist can replace the guides and re-cut the valve seats.

4 After the valve service has been performed, be sure to clean it very thoroughly before installation on the engine to remove any metal particles or abrasive grit that may still be present from the valve service operations. Use compressed air, if available, to blow out all the holes and passages.

Disassembly

5 Before proceeding, arrange to label and

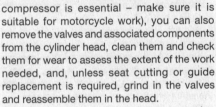

10.6a Make sure the spring compressor is a good fit on the top . . .

store the valves along with their related components in such a way that they can be returned to their original locations without getting mixed up (see illustration). Either use the same container as the cam followers and shims are stored in (see Section 8), or obtain a separate container and label each compartment accordingly. Alternatively, labelled plastic bags will do just as well.

6 Compress the valve spring on the first valve with a spring compressor, making sure it is correctly located onto each end of the valve assembly. On the top of the valve the adaptor needs to be about the same size as the spring retainer – if it is too big it will contact the follower bore and mark it, and if it is too small it will be difficult to remove and install the collets (see illustration). On the underside of the head make sure the plate on the compressor only contacts the valve and not the soft aluminium of the head (see illustration) – if

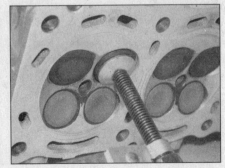

10.6b . . . and the bottom of the valve assembly

10.7a Remove the collets . . .

10.7b . . . then the spring retainer . . .

10.7c . . . valve spring . . .

10.7d . . . and the valve

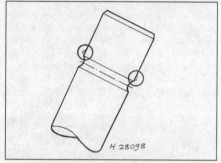

10.7e If necessary, deburr the area above the collet groove (circled)

the plate is too big for the valve, use a spacer between them. Do not compress the springs any more than is absolutely necessary.

Caution: Take great care not to mark the cam follower bore with the spring compressor.

7 Remove the collets, using either needle-nose pliers, tweezers, a magnet or a screwdriver with a dab of grease on it **(see illustration)**. Carefully release the valve spring compressor and remove the spring retainer, noting which way up it fits, the spring and the valve **(see illustrations)**. If the valve binds in the guide and won't pull through, push it back into the head and deburr the area around the

collet groove with a very fine file or whetstone **(see illustration)**.

8 Pull the valve stem seal off the top of the valve guide with pliers and discard it (the old seals should never be reused), then remove the spring seat noting which way up, it fits – using a magnet is the easiest way to remove the seat from the head **(see illustrations)**.

9 Repeat the procedure for the remaining valves. Remember to keep the parts for each valve together so they can be reinstalled in the same location.

10 Clean the cylinder head with solvent and dry it thoroughly. Compressed air will speed the drying process and ensure that all holes

and recessed areas are clean. **Note:** *Do not use a wire brush mounted in a drill motor to clean the combustion chambers as the head material is soft and may be scratched or eroded away by the wire brush.*

11 Clean all of the valve springs, collets, retainers and spring seats with solvent and dry them thoroughly. Do the parts from one valve at a time so that no mixing of parts between valves occurs.

12 Scrape off any deposits that may have formed on the valve. Again, make sure the valves do not get mixed up.

Inspection

13 Inspect the cylinder head very carefully for cracks and other damage. If cracks are found, a new head will be required. Check the cam bearing surfaces for wear and evidence of seizure. Check the camshafts for wear as well (see Section 8).

14 Using a precision straight-edge and a feeler gauge, check the head gasket mating surface for warpage. Refer to *Tools and Workshop Tips* in the Reference section for details of how to use the straight-edge. If the head is warped beyond the limit specified at the beginning of this Chapter, consult your Suzuki dealer or take it to a specialist repair shop for rectification.

15 Examine the valve seats in the combustion

10.8a Pull the stem seal off with pliers . . .

10.8b . . . then remove the spring seat

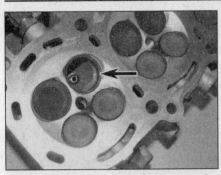

10.15 Examine the valve seat (arrowed) and measure its width

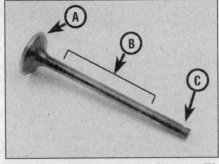

10.16 Examine the valve face (A), stem (B) and collet groove (C)

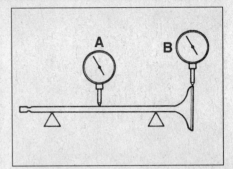

10.18 Measure the valve stem runout (A) and valve head runout (B)

chamber **(see illustration)**. If they are pitted, cracked or burned, the head will require work beyond the scope of the home mechanic. Measure the valve seat width and compare it to this Chapter's Specifications. If it exceeds the service limit, or if it varies around its circumference, consult your Suzuki dealer or take the head to a specialist repair shop for rectification.

Caution: Do not grind or lap the valves, otherwise their surface coating will be damaged.

16 Examine each valve face for cracks, pits and burned spots.

17 Check the valve stem and the collet groove area for wear and damage **(see illustration 10.16)**. Rotate the valve and check for any obvious indication that it is bent. Check the end of the stem for pitting and excessive wear.

18 Using V-blocks and a dial gauge,

measure the valve stem runout and the valve head runout and compare the results to the Specifications **(see illustration)**. If either measurement exceeds the service limit, a new valve must be fitted.

19 Clean the valve guides to remove any carbon build-up, then install each valve in its guide in turn so that its face is 10 mm above the seat. Mount a dial gauge against the side of the valve face and measure the amount of side clearance (wobble) between the valve stem and its guide in two directions **(see illustration)**.

20 If the side clearance exceeds the limit specified, remove the valve and measure the valve stem diameter at three points along the stem **(see illustration)**. Also measure the inside diameter of the guide with a small hole gauge and micrometer **(see illustration)**. Measure the guides at each end and at the centre to determine if they are worn unevenly. Subtract the stem diameter from the valve

guide inside diameter to obtain the valve stem-to-guide clearance. If the stem-to-guide clearance is greater than specified, renew whichever of the components is worn beyond its specifications. If the valve guide is within specifications, but is worn unevenly, it should be renewed.

21 Check the end of each valve spring for wear. Measure the spring free length and compare it to that listed in the specifications **(see illustration)**. If any spring is shorter than specified it has sagged and must be renewed.

22 Place each spring upright on a flat surface and check it for bend with a set square **(see illustration)**. If the bend in any spring is excessive, it must be replaced with a new one.

23 Check the spring retainers and collets for wear and damage. Any questionable parts should not be reused, as extensive damage will occur in the event of failure during engine operation.

24 If the inspection indicates that no overhaul

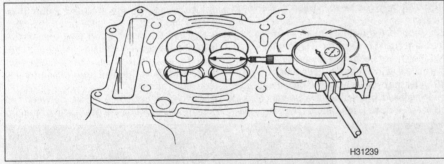

10.19 Measure the amount of 'wobble' as shown

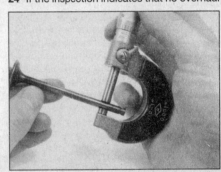

10.20a Measuring the valve stem diameter with a micrometer

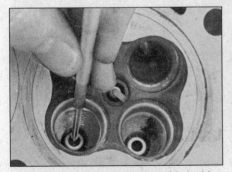

10.20b Measuring the valve guide inside diameter with a small hole gauge

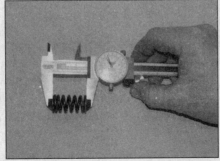

10.21 Measuring valve spring free length

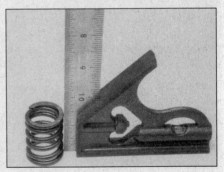

10.22 Check that the springs are not bent

10.25a Install the spring seat shouldered side up

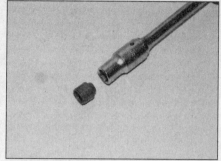

10.25b Press the stem seal into place with a suitably sized socket

  HAYNES HiNT *Check for proper sealing of the valves by pouring a small amount of solvent into each of the valve ports. If the solvent leaks past any valve into the combustion chamber the valve grinding operation on that valve should be repeated.*

10.29 Tap each valve stem lightly to seat the collets

work is required, the valve components can be reinstalled in the head.

Reassembly

25 Working on one valve at a time, lay the spring seat in place in the cylinder head with its shouldered side facing up so that it fits into the base of the spring (see illustration). Lubricate the new valve stem seal with molybdenum oil (a 50/50 mixture of molybdenum paste and engine oil) and fit it onto the valve guide. Use an appropriate size deep socket to push the seal squarely over the end of the guide until it is felt to clip into place (see illustration).
26 Coat the valve stem with molybdenum

oil, then slip it into its guide, rotating it slowly to avoid damaging the seal (see illustration 10.7d). Check that the valve moves up and down freely in the guide. Next, install the valve spring, with its closer-wound coils facing down into the cylinder head, followed by the spring retainer, with its shouldered side facing down into the top of the spring (see illustrations 10.7c and b).
27 Apply a small amount of grease to the collets to help hold them in place. Compress the spring with the valve spring compressor and install the collets (see illustration 10.7a). When compressing the spring, depress it only as far as is absolutely necessary to slip the collets into place. Make certain that the collets are securely located in the collet groove and release the spring compressor.
28 Repeat the procedure for the remaining valves. Remember to keep the parts for each valve together and separate from the other valves so they can be reinstalled in the same location.
29 Support the cylinder head on blocks so the valves can't contact the work surface, then tap the end of each valve stem lightly to seat the collets in their grooves (see illustration).
30 After the cylinder head and camshafts have been installed, check the valve clearances and adjust as required (see Chapter 1).

11 Cam chain, tensioner blade and guides

Note: *The cam chain and tensioner blade can be removed with the engine in the frame. To remove the front guide blade the engine must be removed from the frame and the cylinder head removed.*
1 Except in cases of oil starvation, the cam chain should wear very little (see illustration). If the chain has stretched excessively and can no longer be correctly tensioned by the cam chain tensioner, it is likely that the chain guides and tensioner blade will be worn and in need of renewal as well. Also check the condition of the camshaft sprockets (see Section 8) and crankshaft sprocket (see Step 9). **Note:** *Check the operation of the cam chain tensioner if the chain is slack but appears to be in good condition.*

Removal

2 Remove the camshafts (see Section 8). The cam chain top guide is secured by two of the camshaft holder bolts, and is removed as part of the camshaft removal procedure before removing the cylinder head (see illustration 8.7a).
3 Remove the clutch cover (see Section 13, following the relevant Steps).
4 Undo the pivot bolt securing the tensioner blade and draw the blade out of the engine (see illustration).
5 Wedge a stout piece of rag between the primary drive and driven gear teeth at the top

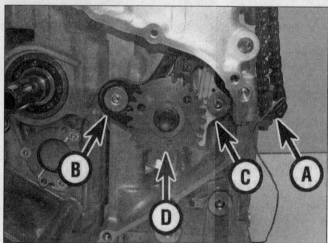

11.1 Cam chain (A), tensioner blade (B), front guide blade (C), timing rotor (D)

11.4 Unscrew the pivot bolt and remove the tensioner blade

11.5a Unscrew the bolt . . .

11.5b . . . then draw the rotor off and disengage it from the chain . . .

11.5c . . . then remove the chain

11.6 Unscrew the pivot bolt and remove the guide blade

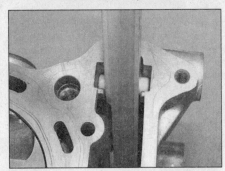

11.10a Make sure the lugs seat correctly

11.10b Apply threadlock to the pivot bolts

– this will prevent rotation while unscrewing the timing rotor bolt. Unscrew the rotor bolt **(see illustration)**. Slide the rotor towards the end of the crankshaft and disengage the cam chain from the sprocket behind the rotor **(see illustration)**. Remove the rotor, then remove the cam chain **(see illustration)**.

6 Remove the cylinder head (Section 9). Undo the pivot bolt securing the front guide blade and draw the blade out of the top of the engine **(see illustration)**.

Inspection

7 Examine the sliding surface of the guides and tensioner blade for signs of wear or damage. Check them carefully for cracks in the surface and along the edges. Install new components if necessary.

8 Lay the chain on the work surface and pull it taut. Check all round the chain; if there is any discernible slack between the links, or if there is any doubt about its condition, fit a new chain.

9 Inspect the teeth of the sprocket. If there are any signs of wear or damage, fit a new sprocket. It is good practice to renew the chain and sprocket at the same time.

Installation

10 Installation is the reverse of removal, noting the following:
● Fit the front guide blade first, then the cam chain and timing rotor, then the tensioner blade.
● Make sure the lugs on the front guide blade seat correctly **(see illustration)**.
● Apply a suitable, non-permanent locking compound to the threads of the blade pivot bolts **(see illustration)**. Tighten the pivot bolts to the specified torque setting.

● Fit the chain onto the sprocket teeth immediately behind the rotor, not those on the inner end **(see illustration 11.5b)**. Align the wide splines on the crankshaft and timing rotor and slide the rotor on with the sprocket on the inside.
● Secure the upper end of the chain with wire or a cable-tie.
● Wedge the rag between the primary drive and driven gear teeth at the bottom. Fit the washer with the timing rotor bolt and tighten the bolt to the specified torque setting **(see illustration 11.5a)**.

12 Alternator and starter clutch

Note: *This procedure can be carried out with the engine in the frame. If the engine has been removed, ignore the steps which do not apply.*

12.3a Alternator wiring connector (arrowed) – K6 and K7 models

Check

1 A preliminary check of the starter clutch and gears can be made by removing the starter motor (see Chapter 8), then turning the reduction gear by hand via the starter motor orifice – the gear should turn freely anti-clockwise as you look at it from the right-hand side of the engine, and should lock when turned clockwise. If not the starter clutch is faulty or the reduction and idle gears are jammed.

Removal

2 Remove the left-hand fairing side panel (see Chapter 7). If required drain the engine oil (see Chapter 1). Alternatively position a suitable receptacle underneath the alternator cover to catch any oil when the cover is removed.

3 Remove the air filter housing (see Chapter 4). Trace the wiring from the alternator cover and disconnect it at the wiring connector **(see illustrations)**. Free the wiring from any clips

12.3b Alternator wiring connector (arrowed) – K8 and K9 models

12.4 Unscrew the bolts (arrowed) and remove the cover

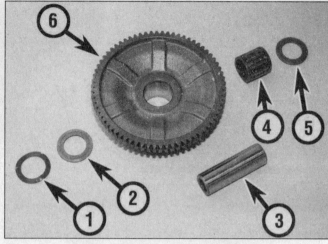

12.5 Reduction gear components

1 Wave washer
2 Outer thrust washer
3 Shaft
4 Bearing
5 Inner thrust washer
6 Reduction gear

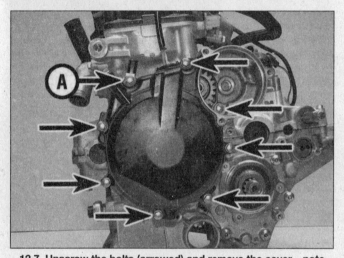

12.7 Unscrew the bolts (arrowed) and remove the cover – note the wiring clamp (A)

12.8 Remove the idle gear and its shaft

or ties and feed it through to the cover, noting its routing.

4 Undo the reduction gear cover bolts and remove the cover (see illustration). Remove and discard the O-ring as a new one must be used.

5 Remove the wave washer and outer thrust washer from the reduction gear shaft, then hold the shaft and slide the gear off, noting which way round it fits (see illustration and 12.27c and d).

6 Remove the bearing, the inner thrust washer and the shaft (see illustrations 12.27b and a).

7 Undo the alternator cover bolts, noting the wiring clamp, and remove the cover – you will have to pull it off against the force of the magnets (see illustration). Remove the gasket and discard it. Note the position of the dowel and remove it for safe-keeping if loose. If the starter motor has not been removed discard its O-ring – a new one must be used.

8 Withdraw the idle gear shaft and remove the gear, noting which way round it fits (see illustration).

9 Before proceeding further, the operation of

the starter clutch can be checked while it is in situ. Check that the driven gear on the back of the alternator rotor is able to rotate freely clockwise as you look at it, but locks when rotated anti-clockwise.

10 To remove the alternator rotor bolt it is necessary to stop the crankshaft from turning. Suzuki produces a Service Tool (Pt. No. 09930-44520) to do this. Alternatively, a large spanner can be applied to the two flats

12.10 Counter-hold the rotor as described and unscrew the bolt

machined into the boss in the rotor. With the rotor held, unscrew and remove the bolt (see illustration).

11 To remove the rotor from the crankshaft taper it is necessary to use a rotor puller. Suzuki produces a service tool (Pt. No. 09930-34980) to do this. Thread a suitable M12 bolt 28 to 38 mm long into the end of the crankshaft for the puller to bear on (see illustration). Thread the puller fully onto the

12.11a Thread the bolt into the end of the crankshaft . . .

12.11b . . . then thread the puller onto the rotor

12.11c Counter-hold the body of the puller and turn the bolt until the rotor is displaced

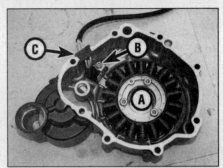

12.12 Stator bolts (A), wiring clamp bolt (B) and wiring grommet (C)

12.13 Driven gear should rotate freely anti-clockwise

12.15 Check the driven gear hub (A), the bush (B) and the sprags (C)

12.16a Counter-hold the rotor using a strap . . .

centre of the rotor **(see illustration)**. Hold the puller with a large spanner to stop it and the crankshaft turning, then turn the puller centre bolt until the rotor is free of the crankshaft taper **(see illustration)** – note that the bolts in some pullers are reverse threaded, so you may have to turn it anti-clockwise rather than clockwise to thread it into the puller. Remove the puller, then undo the M12 bolt and remove the rotor – the starter driven gear should come with it, but if not slide it off the crankshaft.

12 If required unscrew the bolts securing the stator in the cover, and the bolt securing the wiring clamp, then remove the assembly, noting how the wiring grommet fits **(see illustration)**.

Inspection

13 With the alternator rotor face down, check that the starter driven gear rotates freely in

an anti-clockwise direction and locks against the starter clutch in a clockwise direction **(see illustration)**. If it doesn't, replace the starter clutch with a new one (Step 16).

14 Withdraw the driven gear from the starter clutch **(see illustration 12.15)**. If it appears stuck, rotate the gear anti-clockwise as you withdraw it to free it from the clutch sprags.

15 Check the bearing surfaces on the outer surface of the starter driven gear hub, the bush on the inner surface, and the condition of the sprags inside the clutch housing **(see illustration)**. If there are signs of excessive wear, or the sprags are damaged, marked or pitted, the starter clutch assembly should be replaced with a new one.

16 To remove the starter clutch counter-hold the rotor using a strap or a spanner on the flats and unscrew the bolts on its inside, then remove the clutch housing from the back **(see**

illustrations). Release the sprag assembly from the housing **(see illustration)**. Fit the new sprag assembly into the housing with the wider rim of the sprag assembly locating in the recessed side of the housing. Fit the rotor onto the housing. Clean the housing bolt threads and apply a suitable thread lock. Tighten the bolts to the torque setting specified at the beginning of the Chapter while holding the rotor as before.

17 Check the condition of the needle roller bearing and the idle and reduction gear shafts and bearing surfaces and replace them with new ones if wear or damage is evident.

18 Examine the teeth of the starter gear train and the corresponding teeth of the starter motor drive shaft. Renew the gears and/or starter motor if worn or chipped teeth are discovered on related gears. Also check the gear shafts for damage, and check that the

12.16b . . . or a spanner, and unscrew the bolts . . .

12.16c . . . then detach the housing from the rotor . . .

12.16d . . . and the starter clutch from the housing

12.21 Clean the tapered section of the crankshaft (A) and lubricate the flat section (B) – do not get oil on the tapered section

12.22 Slide the rotor onto the shaft

12.23a Fit the bolt . . .

12.23b . . . and tighten it to the specified torque

12.25a Apply sealant to the crankcase joints and the wiring grommet

12.25b Locate the new gasket over the dowel (arrowed) . . .

gears are not a loose fit on the shafts. Replace the shafts with new ones if necessary.

Installation

19 Clean all old gasket and sealant from the covers and crankcase.

20 Apply a suitable sealant to the cut-out for the alternator stator wiring grommet. Fit the stator into the cover, aligning the grommet with the cut-out in the cover (see illustration 12.12). Fit the stator and wiring clamp bolts and tighten the stator bolts to the specified torque setting.

21 Clean the tapered end of the crankshaft and the corresponding mating surface on the inside of the alternator rotor with a suitable solvent (see illustration). Lubricate the innermost flat section of the crankshaft that the driven gear bush runs on with oil. Lubricate the starter clutch sprags with oil, then fit the starter driven gear into the starter clutch, turning it anti-clockwise as you do.

22 Make sure that no metal objects have attached themselves to the magnet on the inside of the rotor, then slide the rotor onto the shaft (see illustration).

23 Fit the rotor bolt and tighten it to the torque setting specified at the beginning of this Chapter, using the method employed on removal to prevent the rotor from turning (see illustrations).

24 Lubricate the idle gear shaft and its bore holes in both the crankcase and the alternator cover with molybdenum oil (a 50/50 mixture of molybdenum paste and engine oil). Position the idle gear, engaging its teeth with those of the starter driven gear, and slide the shaft through the gear and into its bore in the crankcase (see illustration 12.8).

25 Apply a suitable sealant across the crankcase joints and to the flat face of the stator wiring grommet (see illustration). If the starter motor has not been removed fit a new

O-ring smeared with grease onto it. If removed, fit the dowel into the crankcase and fit a new alternator cover gasket, making sure it locates correctly onto the dowel (see illustrations). Fit the cover, noting that it will be forcibly drawn on by the magnets, so make sure it is correctly aligned. Fit the bolts and tighten them evenly in a criss-cross pattern to the specified torque setting, not forgetting the wiring clamp with the upper front bolt (see illustration 12.7).

26 Feed the alternator wiring back to its connector, making sure it is correctly routed and secured by any clips or ties, and reconnect it (see illustration 12.3a or b).

27 Lubricate the reduction gear shaft, its bore holes in the covers, and the needle bearing with molybdenum oil (a 50/50 mixture of molybdenum paste and engine oil). Fit the shaft into its bore in the crankcase, then slide on the inner thrust washer and the needle bearing (see illustrations). Slide the gear

12.25c . . . then fit the cover

12.27a Fit the shaft and the inner thrust washer . . .

12.27b . . . then slide on the bearing

12.27c Fit the gear onto the bearing . . .

12.27d . . . then fit the outer thrust washer and the wave washer

onto the shaft and fit it over the bearing, making sure the smaller pinion faces inwards and meshes correctly with the teeth of the idle gear, and the larger pinion meshes with the starter motor drive shaft **(see illustration)**. Fit the outer thrust washer followed by the wave washer onto the end of the shaft **(see illustration)**.

28 Fit a new O-ring smeared with grease onto the idle gear cover **(see illustration)**. Fit the cover and tighten the bolts to the specified torque **(see illustration)**.

29 Refill or top up the engine oil as required (see Chapter 1 or *Pre-ride checks*).

30 Install the air filter housing (see Chapter 4) and the left-hand fairing side panel (see Chapter 7).

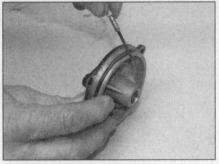

12.28a Fit a new O-ring into the groove . . .

12.28b . . . then fit the cover

13 Clutch

Note: *This procedure can be carried out with the engine in the frame. If the engine has been removed, ignore the steps which do not apply.*

Removal

1 Remove the fairing right-hand side panel (see Chapter 7). If required drain the engine oil (see Chapter 1). Alternatively position a suitable receptacle underneath the clutch cover to catch any oil when the cover is removed.

2 Raise the fuel tank (see Chapter 4). Trace the CKP sensor wiring from the top of the clutch cover and disconnect it at the connector **(see illustration 4.15a)**. Release the wiring from

any clips or ties and feed it down to the cover, noting its routing.

3 Undo the cover bolts, noting the sealing washer fitted on the upper front bolt, and remove the cover **(see illustration)**. Remove the gasket and discard it. Note the position of the locating dowels and remove them for safe-keeping if loose.

4 Undo the clutch spring bolts a little at a time in a criss-cross pattern, then remove the bolts and the springs **(see illustration)**.

5 Remove the clutch pressure plate, then

13.3 Clutch cover bolts (arrowed). Note the sealing washer (A)

13.4 Unscrew the bolts (arrowed) and remove the springs

13.5a Remove the pressure plate . . .

13.5b . . . then withdraw the clutch lifter with its thrust washer (A) and release bearing (B)

13.5c If required withdraw the right-hand pushrod

remove the clutch lifter with the thrust washer release bearing (see illustrations). If required withdraw the right-hand pushrod from the centre of the gearbox and input shaft – you will need to use a magnet or hook it out using a piece of wire (see illustration).

6 Note the location of the outer friction plate tabs offset in the shallow slots, then withdraw the clutch plates from the clutch housing, hooking out the inner ones (see illustration). Keep them in their original order, even if the plates are being replaced with new ones. Note that if you are just fitting new clutch plates and are not fully disassembling the clutch, you can go straight to the installation procedure at Step 31.

7 Withdraw the anti-judder spring and the spring seat, hooking them out with wire or using a magnet (see illustration).

8 The rim of the clutch nut is staked onto the input shaft (see illustration). Unstake it using a hammer and small chisel, taking care not to damage the shaft.

9 To loosen the clutch nut the input shaft must be locked using one of the following methods:

● If the engine is in the frame, engage 1st gear and have an assistant hold the rear brake on hard with the rear tyre in firm contact with the ground.

● Use the Suzuki service tool (Pt. No. 09920-53740) to engage the clutch centre splines.

● Use a commercially available clutch holding tool which will engage the clutch centre splines. That shown in illustration 13.9 is of the self-locking type.

Caution: The clutch nut is extremely tight. If a clutch holding tool is used, ensure it does not slip and damage the clutch.

Unscrew the nut and remove the dished washer and plain washer from the input shaft, noting which way round the dished washer fits (see illustration). Note: *If the nut has been reused several times or if it was damaged when it was unstaked, discard it and fit a new one on reassembly.*

10 Remove the clutch centre from the shaft (see illustration). Remove the clutch slipper mechanism drive and driven cams, diaphragm springs and the seating washer from the back of the clutch centre, noting how they fit (see illustrations 13.28d, c, b and a). Remove the outer thrust washer from the shaft (see illustration).

13.6 Remove the clutch plate pack from the clutch housing

13.7 Remove the anti-judder spring and spring seat using a magnet if required

13.8 The clutch nut is staked onto the input shaft – unstake it before unscrewing it

13.9 Counter-holding the clutch using a commercially available tool while unscrewing the clutch nut

13.10a Remove the clutch centre . . .

13.10b . . . then the outer thrust washer

13.11a Withdraw the sleeve and needle bearing using a magnet to draw them out . . .

11 Withdraw the sleeve and needle bearing from the centre of the clutch housing and manoeuvre the housing out of the crankcase **(see illustrations)**. **Note:** *In certain positions the primary driven gear on the back of the clutch housing may bind on the adjacent crankshaft web. If necessary rotate the crankshaft clockwise using a spanner or socket on the timing rotor bolt* **(see illustration 8.3a)** *until the web is clear of the gear, then remove the housing.*

12 If required withdraw the sleeve, and on K8 and K9 models the needle bearing, from the centre of the oil pump drive sprocket, then disengage the chain and remove the sprocket **(see illustrations)**.

13 Remove the inner thrust washer from the shaft, noting which way round it fits **(see illustration)**.

Inspection

14 After an extended period of service the clutch friction plates will wear and promote clutch slip. Measure the thickness of each friction plate and the width of their tabs using a Vernier caliper **(see illustrations)**. If any plate has worn to or beyond the service limits given in the Specifications at the beginning of this Chapter, the friction plates must be replaced with a new set. Also, if any of the plates smell burnt or are glazed, they must be replaced as a set. Friction plate identification is as follows:

● *600K6 and K7 models – one friction plate with an internal diameter of 118 mm, six*

13.11b . . . then manoeuvre out the clutch housing

13.12b . . . then disengage the chain and remove the sprocket . . .

with an internal diameter of 111 mm and with a purple ID mark, and one with an internal diameter of 111 mm and a black ID mark.

● *750K6 and K7 models – one friction plate with an internal diameter of 118 mm, seven with an internal diameter of 111 mm and with a purple ID mark, and one with an internal diameter of 111 mm and a black ID mark.*

● *All K8 and K9 models – one friction plate with an internal diameter of 118 mm and 36 friction pads, seven with an internal diameter of 111 mm and 48 friction pads, and one with an internal diameter of 111 mm and 36 friction pads.*

15 The plain plates should not show any signs of excess heating (bluing). Check for warpage using a surface plate and feeler

13.12a Draw out the sleeve and on K8 and K9 models the bearing . . .

13.13 . . . and remove the inner thrust washer

gauges **(see illustration)**. If any plate exceeds the maximum permissible warpage, or shows signs of bluing, all plain plates must be replaced as a new set. Plain plate identification is as follows:

● *600K6 and K7 models – none, one or two 2.3 mm thick plain plates, five to seven 2.6 mm thick plain plates, making a total of seven; any 2.3 mm plates should be located at the outer end of the clutch.*

● *All other models – none, one or two 1.6 mm thick plain plates, six to eight 2.0 mm thick plain plates, making a total of eight; any 1.6 mm plates should be located at the outer end of the clutch.*

16 Inspect the clutch assembly for burrs and indentations on the tabs of the friction plates and/or the slots in the housing with which they

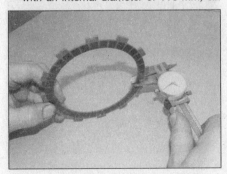

13.14a Measure the thickness of the friction plates . . .

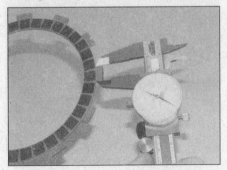

13.14b . . . and the width of the tabs

13.15 Check the plain plates for warpage

13.16a Inspect the slots in the housing and the edges of the tabs

13.16b Inspect the slots in the clutch centre and the tongues on the plate

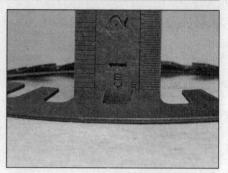

13.18a Measure the free height of each spring

engage **(see illustration)**. Similarly check for wear between the inner tongues of the plain plates and the slots in the clutch centre **(see illustration)**. Wear of this nature will cause clutch drag and slow disengagement during gear changes, since the plates will snag when the pressure plate is lifted. With care, a small amount of wear can be corrected by dressing with a fine file, but if this is excessive the worn components should be replaced with new ones.

17 Check that the threads for the spring bolts in the clutch centre are in good condition.

18 Inspect the anti-judder spring and the spring seat for signs of wear or distortion and replace if necessary. Check the diaphragm springs for distortion and measure the free height of each and replace them with new ones if they have sagged below the specified

amount **(see illustration)**. Check the slipper clutch drive and driven cams for wear and replace them with new ones if necessary **(see illustration)**. The slipper mechanism is adjustable and should be checked for correct setting – assemble the anti-judder spring seat and spring and the friction and plain plates in the clutch centre, then fit the pressure plate and the springs and tighten the bolts to the specified torque setting (see Steps 30 to 32) **(see illustration)**. Turn the assembly upside down and measure the amount of protrusion of the adjuster screws above the flat surface using feeler gauges and a plate or a Vernier caliper as shown, taking three measurements **(see illustration)**. The amount should be within the limits specified at the beginning of the Chapter, and all three screws should be the same. If not, loosen the locknuts and

adjust the screws as required until they are, then tighten the locknuts to the specified torque **(see illustration)**.

19 Check the pressure plate, thrust washer, release bearing, clutch lifter and right-hand pushrod for signs of roughness, wear or damage, and replace any parts necessary with new ones **(see illustrations 13.5a, b and c)**. Check that the pushrod is straight by rolling it on a flat surface. Remove the front sprocket cover (see Chapter 6). Withdraw the left-hand pushrod and check that in the same way **(see illustration 4.21b)**. Check the pushrod oil seal for signs of leakage – if necessary unscrew the retainer bolts, then hook the seal out **(see illustration)**. Press a new seal into place. Clean the retainer bolt threads and apply a thread locking compound then fit the retainer and tighten the bolts.

13.18b Check the mating dogs and slots on the drive and driven cams . . .

13.18c . . . and on the driven cam and clutch centre for wear

13.18d Assemble the plates as described

13.18e Check the protrusion of the adjuster screws as shown

13.18f If adjustment is necessary loosen the locknuts (arrowed) and turn the adjuster screws

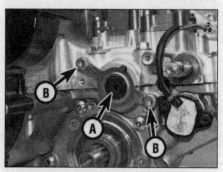

13.19 Check the pushrod oil seal (A) – if necessary unscrew the bolts (B), remove the retainer and fit a new seal

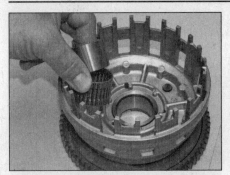

13.20a Inspect the bearing surface in the clutch housing, the needle bearing and the input shaft sleeve . . .

13.20b . . . and the oil pump driven sprocket, bearing and sleeve

13.21 Check the cush-drive springs (A) and primary driven gear teeth (B)

20 Inspect the related bearing surfaces of the clutch housing, the needle bearing, the sleeve and the input shaft for wear (see illustration). Similarly check the oil pump drive sprocket components (see illustration).
21 The clutch housing incorporates a cush-drive mechanism; check that the springs are not loose or broken and that there is no backlash between the housing and the primary driven gear, otherwise replace the housing with a new one (see illustration).
22 Check the teeth of the primary driven gear on the back of the clutch housing and the corresponding teeth of the primary drive gear on the crankshaft (see illustration). Replace the clutch housing with a new one if any teeth are worn or chipped. The primary drive gear

is an integral part of the crankshaft (see Section 28).
23 Measure the free length of each clutch spring (see illustration). If any spring is shorter than the specified service limit, the clutch springs must be renewed as a set.

Installation

24 Remove all traces of old gasket from the crankcase and clutch cover surfaces.
25 Slide the inner thrust washer, with its flat surface facing out, onto the transmission input shaft (see illustration 13.13).
26 Fit the oil pump drive sprocket onto the shaft, making sure the drive tabs on the sprocket face out, and fit the chain round it

(see illustration 13.12b). Lubricate the sleeve, and on K8 and K9 models the needle bearing, with oil and fit it/them into the centre of the sprocket (see illustration).
27 Lubricate the clutch housing needle roller bearing and sleeve with clean engine oil. Slide the clutch housing onto the input shaft, making sure the primary drive gears engage and the oil pump sprocket drive tabs locate in their cut-outs (see illustration). Hold the housing in position and slide the sleeve and needle roller bearing into the middle of the housing (see illustration). Hold the chain and turn the clutch housing to ensure the drive sprocket has engaged (see illustration).
28 Fit the outer thrust washer (see illustration 13.10b). Fit the slipper

13.22 Inspect the teeth on the crankshaft primary drive gear (arrowed)

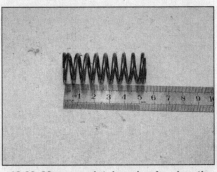

13.23 Measure clutch spring free length

13.26 Slide the sleeve and bearing where fitted into the centre of the drive sprocket

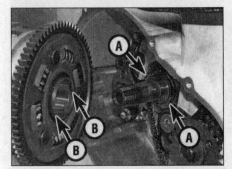

13.27a Slide the housing onto the shaft, aligning and engaging the drive tabs (A) with the cut-outs (B), and engage the gears, . . .

13.27b . . . then slide the bearing and sleeve onto the shaft and into the housing

13.27c Turn the housing to check that the oil pump drive sprocket has engaged

13.28a Fit the seating washer, locating the tabs in the cut-outs, . . .

13.28b . . . and the diaphragm springs onto the back of the clutch centre . . .

13.28c . . . then fit the driven cam over the dogs and onto the springs . . .

13.28d . . . and fit the drive cam into the driven cam

13.29a Fit the plain washer and the dished washer . . .

13.29b . . . and the clutch nut . . .

13.29c . . . then tighten the nut to the specified torque . . .

13.29d . . . and stake its rim into a spline on the shaft

mechanism seating washer onto the back of the clutch centre, followed by the diaphragm springs **(see illustrations)**. Apply a small amount of molybdenum oil (a 50/50 mixture of molybdenum paste and engine oil) to the contact surfaces on the clutch centre and the driven and drive cams, then fit the cams onto the clutch centre – the lipped side of the driven cam with the deeper straight sided dog slots fits down onto the springs and clutch centre dogs **(see illustrations)**. Fit the clutch centre onto the shaft **(see illustration 13.10a)**.

29 Fit the plain washer then the dished washer with its raised inner edge facing out **(see illustration)**. Fit the clutch nut with the shoulder facing out **(see illustration)**. Using the method employed on removal to lock the input shaft, tighten the nut to the torque setting specified at the beginning of the Chapter **(see illustration)**. Stake the nut to secure it on the shaft using a punch **(see illustration)**.

30 Fit the spring seat then the anti-judder spring with its outer edge raised off the spring seat **(see illustrations)**.

31 Build up the plates in the clutch housing in the order described below, according to model – coat each plate with clean engine oil before installing it:

600K6 and K7 models: There is one friction plate with an internal diameter of 118 mm – this is the innermost plate and fits over the anti-judder spring and seat; there are six friction plates with purple paint and an internal diameter of 111 mm, and there is one friction plate with black paint and an internal diameter of 111 mm – this is the outermost plate. There are none, one or two 2.3 mm thick plain plates, with the remaining plain plates being 2.6 mm thick. Fit the innermost friction plate over the anti-judder spring and its seat. Now alternate plain and purple-marked friction plates to build up the clutch, placing any thinner (2.3 mm) plain plates at the outer end of the pack. Finish with the outermost friction plate, and locate its tabs in the shallow slots in the housing.

13.30a Fit the spring seat and the spring, making sure they are the correct way round . . .

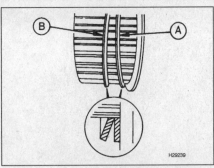

13.30b . . . correct fitting of spring seat (A) and anti-judder spring (B)

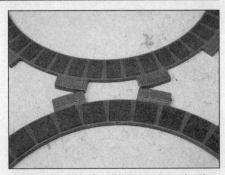

13.31a Identify the different plates by the different number of friction pads and the internal diameter

750K6 and K7 models: There is one friction plate with an internal diameter of 118 mm – this is the innermost plate and fits over the anti-judder spring and seat; there are seven friction plates with purple paint and an internal diameter of 111 mm, and there is one friction plate with black paint and an internal diameter of 111 mm – this is the outermost plate. There are none, one or two 1.6 mm thick plain plates with the remaining plain plates being 2.0 mm thick. Fit the innermost friction plate over the anti-judder spring and its seat. Now alternate plain and purple-marked friction plates to build up the clutch, placing any thinner (1.6 mm) plain plates at the outer end of the pack. Finish with the outermost friction plate, and locate its tabs in the shallow slots in the housing.

All K8 and K9 models: There is one friction plate with 36 friction pads and an internal diameter of 118 mm – this is the innermost plate and fits over the anti-judder spring and seat; there are seven friction plates with 48 friction pads and an internal diameter of 111 mm, and there is one friction plate with 36 friction pads and an internal diameter of 111 mm – this is the outermost plate **(see illustration)**. There are none, one or two 1.6 mm thick plain plates with the remaining plain plates being 2.0 mm thick. Fit the innermost friction plate over the anti-judder spring and its seat **(see illustration)**. Now alternate plain and 48 face friction plates to build up the clutch, placing any thinner (1.6 mm) plain plates at the outer end of the pack **(see illustration)**. Finish with the outermost friction

plate, and locate its tabs in the shallow slots in the housing **(see illustration)**.

32 Fit the right-hand pushrod if removed **(see illustration 13.5c)**. Fit the needle bearing and thrust washer onto the clutch lifter then slide the lifter into the shaft **(see illustration 13.5b)**. Fit the pressure plate, aligning the wide castellation on its inner face with the wide slot in the clutch centre, and locating the other castellations in the slots in the centre **(see illustration)**. Fit the springs and the bolts, then tighten the bolts evenly in a criss-cross pattern to the specified torque setting **(see illustration)**.

33 If removed, fit the clutch cover dowels. Apply a smear of suitable sealant across the crankcase joints and to the CKP sensor wiring

13.31b Fit the innermost friction plate over the anti-judder spring . . .

13.31c . . . then fit alternate plain plates . . .

13.31d . . . and friction plates as described . . .

13.31e . . . locating the tabs of the outermost friction plate in the shallow slots

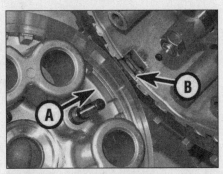

13.32a Align the wide castellation (A) with the wide slot (B)

13.32b Fit the springs and bolts and tighten the bolts as described to the specified torque

13.33a Apply some sealant to the crankcase joints

13.33b Locate the new gasket onto the dowels (arrowed) . . .

its connector, making sure it is correctly routed and secured by any clips or ties, and reconnect it **(see illustration 4.15a)**. Lower the fuel tank (see Chapter 4).
35 Refill or top up the engine oil as required (see Chapter 1 or *Pre-ride checks*).
36 Check the clutch release mechanism adjustment (see Chapter 1).
37 Install the right-hand fairing side panel (see Chapter 7).

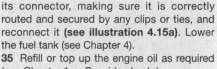
14 Clutch cable and release mechanism

13.33c . . . then fit the cover

13.33d Use a new sealing washer

Removal

1 Remove the right-hand fairing side panel (see Chapter 7). Raise the fuel tank (see Chapter 4).
2 On K8 and K9 models free the cable from the guide on the right-hand side of the frame **(see illustration)**.
3 Turn the handlebar lever adjuster fully in so there is no tension in the cable (see Chapter 1) **(see illustration)**.
4 Loosen the cable adjuster locknut **(see illustration)**. Unscrew the release arm pinch bolt and draw the arm up off the shaft, noting how the return spring ends locate **(see illustration)**. Turn the arm over and detach the cable end, noting how it fits **(see illustration)**. Thread the adjuster out of the sprocket cover **(see illustration)**. Remove the return

grommet in the cover **(see illustration)**. Fit the new cover gasket, making sure it locates correctly onto the dowels **(see illustration)**. Fit the cover bolts, using a new sealing

washer on the upper front bolt, and tighten them evenly in a criss-cross sequence to the specified torque **(see illustration)**.
34 Feed the CKP sensor wiring back to

14.2 Unscrew the bolt (arrowed) to release the cable

14.3 Thread the adjuster fully into the lever bracket

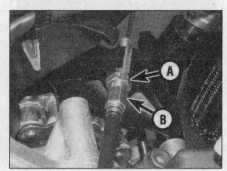

14.4a Slacken the locknut (A) on the adjuster (B)

14.4b Unscrew the bolt . . .

14.4c . . . then lift the arm off the shaft and detach the cable

14.4d Thread the adjuster out of the cover

14.4e Remove the return spring and the washer for safekeeping

14.5a Pull the outer cable out of the adjuster . . .

14.5b . . . then free the cable end from the lever

spring, noting how it fits, and the washer for safekeeping (see illustration).

5 Align the slot in the cable adjuster at the lever end with the slot in the lever bracket, then pull the outer cable end from the socket in the adjuster and release the inner cable from the lever (see illustrations). Remove the cable from the machine, noting its routing.

Before removing the cable from the bike, tape the lower end of the new cable to the upper end of the old cable. Slowly pull the lower end of the old cable out, guiding the new cable down into position. Using this method will ensure the cable is routed correctly.

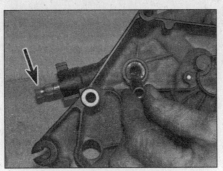

14.6 Remove the pushrod piece and withdraw the shaft (arrowed)

14.9 Make sure the arm is correctly aligned and the return spring ends (arrowed) are correctly located

6 If required, remove the front sprocket cover (see Chapter 6) and inspect the clutch release mechanism. Check the mechanism for smooth operation and any signs of wear or damage. If necessary remove the pushrod piece, and the return spring and the washer if not already done, and withdraw the shaft (see illustration). Check the condition of the oil seals and bearings and replace them with new ones if necessary. Otherwise clean and regrease the shaft, pushrod cap, bearings and seals.

7 If required, withdraw the left-hand clutch pushrod (see illustration 4.21b). Clean the pushrod and lubricate it with a smear of grease before installing it. Check the pushrod oil seal for signs of leakage – seal replacement is covered in Section 13, Step 19.

8 Grease the shaft before installing it. Fit the pushrod piece closed end first against the cut-out in the shaft so it sits flush with the seal (see illustration 14.6). Turn the shaft and make sure the pushrod piece moves out.

Installation

9 Installation is the reverse of removal, noting the following:
● Ensure the cable is correctly routed.
● Lubricate the cable ends with grease.
● Fit the washer onto the top of the shaft, then fit the return spring (see

illustration 14.4e). Align the punch mark on the release mechanism arm with the line on the shaft end, and make sure the return spring ends locate correctly (see illustration).
● Check the clutch release mechanism adjustment and cable adjustment (see Chapter 1).

15 Gearchange mechanism

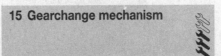

Note: *This procedure can be carried out with the engine in the frame. If the engine has been removed, ignore the steps which do not apply.*

15.2 Remove the circlip and slide off the washer

Removal

1 Remove the clutch (see Section 13). Make sure the transmission is in neutral. Remove the front sprocket cover (see Chapter 6).

2 Remove the circlip from the left-hand end of the gearchange shaft and slide off the washer (see illustration).

3 Working on the right-hand side of the engine, note how the gearchange shaft return spring ends fit on each side of the locating pin in the crankcase, and how the selector arm pawls engage with the pins on the gearchange cam (see illustration 15.18). Withdraw the gearchange shaft from the crankcase, noting the thrust washer (see illustration).

4 Note how the stopper arm roller locates in the neutral detent on the gearchange cam

15.3 Withdraw the gearchange shaft, noting the thrust washer

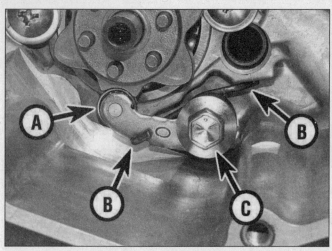

15.4 Note how the roller (A) locates in neutral detent and how the return spring ends (B) locate, then unscrew the bolt (C)

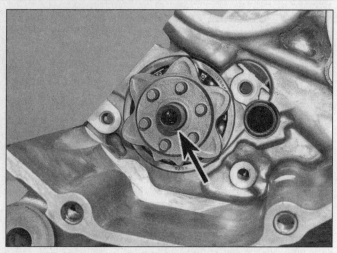

15.5 Unscrew the bolt (arrowed) and remove the cam

(see illustration). Undo the stopper arm pivot bolt and remove the arm, spacer and return spring.

5 If required, unscrew the selector drum centre bolt and remove the gearchange cam **(see illustration)**. *Note the position of the cam as the selector drum is likely to rotate when the centre bolt is undone.* Remove the locating pin from the end of the selector drum if it is loose and store it with the cam for safekeeping (see Section 23).

6 If required, undo the bolts securing the gear position sensor on the left-hand side of the crankcase and remove it **(see illustration)**.

Note how the pin on the sensor locates in the offset hole in the end of the selector drum. Disconnect the wiring connector and note the routing of the wiring. Discard the sensor O-ring as a new one must be fitted on reassembly.

Inspection

7 Inspect the stopper arm return spring and the gearchange shaft return spring. If they are fatigued, worn or damaged they must be replaced with new ones. The shaft return spring is retained by a circlip **(see illustration)** – slide it down the length of the shaft after

releasing it from the groove, do not stretch it over the shaft. Note which way round the spring is fitted and how it locates on the tab on the selector arm. Ensure the circlip is correctly located in its groove after fitting the new spring, then slide the thrust washer back onto the shaft.

8 The gearchange shaft return spring ends locate on each side of a post bolt **(see illustration)**. Check that the bolt is tight; if loose, remove it, then clean the threads and apply a suitable non-permanent thread-locking compound before tightening it to the torque setting specified at the beginning of the Chapter.

9 Check the gearchange shaft is straight and look for damage to the splines on the end **(see illustration)**. If the shaft is bent you can attempt to straighten it, but if the splines are damaged the shaft must be replaced with a new one.

10 Check the condition of the shaft oil seal in the left-hand side of the crankcase. If it is damaged or deteriorated it must be replaced with a new one. Lever out the old seal **(see illustration)**. Check the bearing behind it, replacing it with a new one if necessary before fitting a new seal (see Step 11). Press or drive the new seal in squarely, with its lip facing

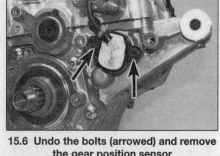

15.6 Undo the bolts (arrowed) and remove the gear position sensor

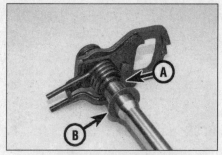

15.7 Gearchange shaft return spring is retained by a circlip (A). Note the thrust washer (B) and slide it off first

15.8 Make sure the bolt (arrowed) is tight

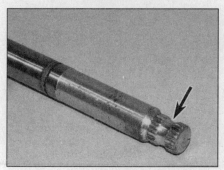

15.9 Check the splines (arrowed) on the end of the shaft

15.10a Lever out the old seal . . .

15.10b . . . and press the new one into place

inward, using a seal driver or suitable socket **(see illustration)**.

11 Check that the gearchange shaft needle bearings rotate freely and have no sign of freeplay between them and the crankcase **(see illustration)**. To remove the bearings, draw them out of the crankcase with a bearing puller, noting that once removed they cannot be re-used. Drive the new bearings into place, making sure they enter squarely. Refer to *Tools and Workshop Tips* in the Reference Section for more information on bearings and how to remove and install them.

12 Check the selector arm pawls for wear **(see illustration)**. The outer arm can be replaced with a new one separately by removing the screw, washer and spring and drawing the arm off the shaft **(see illustration)**. Note that the arm is fitted with the pawls facing inwards. The inner arm is integral with the gearchange shaft.

15.11 Check the bearing (arrowed) on each side of the crankcase

13 Inspect the lobes and the pins on the gearchange cam and check that the stopper arm roller turns freely **(see illustrations 15.5 and 4)**. Fit the stopper arm onto the pivot bolt – the arm should be a light fit on the shoulder with no appreciable freeplay between them. Renew any worn or damaged parts as necessary.

14 Check the gear position sensor pin for wear and damage and replace the sensor with a new one if necessary.

Installation

15 If removed, fit the pin in the end of the selector drum, then fit the gearchange cam, locating the pin in the recess in the back of the cam. Clean the threads of the centre bolt, then apply a suitable non-permanent thread-locking compound. Fit the bolt and tighten it to the torque setting specified at the beginning of this Chapter **(see illustration 15.5)**.

16 Ensure the selector drum is in the neutral position with the neutral detent in the gearchange cam at about 8 o'clock **(see illustration 15.4)**. Apply a suitable non-permanent thread locking compound to the stopper arm pivot bolt threads. Slide the stopper arm and the spacer onto the bolt, with the roller on the arm facing away from the bolt head and the flanged end of the spacer against the arm, then fit the return spring over the spacer and locate its curved end in the cut-out in the arm **(see illustration)**. Fit the stopper arm and tighten the bolt to the specified torque setting **(see illustration)** – make sure the shoulder under the head of the bolt locates inside the hole in the stopper arm as the pressure of the spring will push it off-centre – when the bolt is tight all components should be pressed together with no gap between the bolt head and the arm **(see illustration)**. Make sure the spring ends locate correctly against the arm and the crankcase, and the roller is in the neutral detent on the cam **(see illustration 15.4)**.

17 Check that the gearchange shaft return spring is properly positioned and that the circlip is in its groove, then slide the thrust washer onto the shaft **(see illustration 15.7)**. Lightly grease the inside of the gearchange shaft oil seal. Slide the shaft into place from the right-hand side **(see illustration 15.3)**.

18 Locate the selector arm pawls onto the pins on the selector cam and the ends of the return spring onto each side of the post bolt **(see illustration)**.

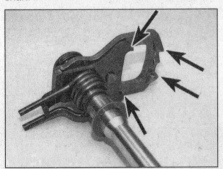

15.12a Check the selector arm pawls (arrowed) for wear

15.12b The outer arm is retained by a screw (arrowed)

15.16a Assemble the stopper arm components as shown . . .

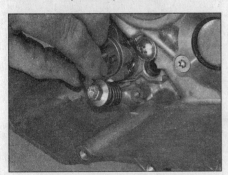

15.16b . . . then fit them onto the crankcase and tighten the bolt . . .

15.16c . . . making sure everything locates correctly as described

15.18 Make sure the return spring ends and arm locate correctly

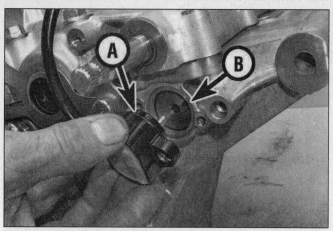

15.20 Fit a new O-ring (A) and locate the pin in the offset hole (B)

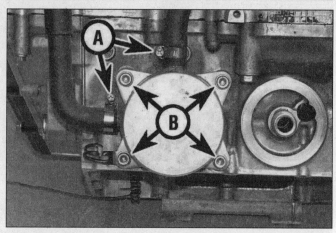

16.2 Slacken the clips (A) and detach the hoses. Cooler mounting bolts (B)

19 Fit the washer and circlip onto the left-hand end of the gearchange shaft (see illustration 15.2).

20 If removed install the gear position sensor using a new O-ring smeared with grease, locating the pin in the offset hole in the selector drum end (see illustration). Apply some threadlock to the bolts. Route the wiring and connect the wiring connector.

21 Install the remaining components in the reverse order of removal.

16.3a Remove the cooler . . .

16 Oil cooler

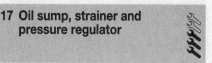

Note: *This procedure can be carried out with the engine in the frame. If the engine has been removed, ignore the steps which do not apply.*

Removal

1 Remove the fairing side panels (see Chapter 7). Drain the engine oil and the coolant (see Chapter 1).

2 Loosen the clips securing the coolant hoses to the unions on the oil cooler and detach the hoses (see illustration) – if the engine has been removed and is being disassembled you may not need to do this.

3 Unscrew the cooler mounting bolts, noting the hose clamp with the bottom right-hand bolt, and remove the cooler (see illustration). Discard the O-ring as a new one must be fitted on reassembly (see illustration).

Installation

4 Installation is the reverse of removal, noting the following:

● Smear the new O-ring with grease and make sure it seats in the groove in the cooler body (see illustration 16.3b).

● Apply a suitable thread locking compound to the mounting bolts and tighten them to the specified torque setting.

● Replenish the engine oil and refill the cooling system (see Chapter 1 and *Pre-ride checks*).

17 Oil sump, strainer and pressure regulator

Note: *To remove the sump the engine must be removed from the frame.*

Removal

1 Remove the engine from the frame (see Section 4).

2 Unscrew the sump and sump plate bolts, loosening them evenly in a criss-cross pattern to prevent distortion, noting the position of the longer bolts and those with the sealing washer and the wiring clamp (see illustration). Lift

16.3b . . . and discard the O-ring

17.2 Sump and sump plate bolts (arrowed) – note the bolt with sealing washer (A) and the wiring clamp (B)

17.3 Remove the oil strainer . . .

17.4 . . . and the pressure regulator

17.7 Clean the mesh (arrowed) inside the strainer

the sump off towards the front of the engine to prevent the gasket dislodging the strainer (this won't happen if the gasket sticks to the crankcase rather than the sump). Discard the sealing washer as a new one must be fitted on reassembly.

3 Remove the strainer, noting how it is aligned **(see illustration)**. Discard the O-ring as a new one must be fitted.

4 If required, pull the pressure regulator out of its socket **(see illustration)**.

5 Remove all traces of old gasket from the sump and crankcase mating surfaces – take care not to scratch or gouge the aluminium.

Inspection

6 Clean the sump thoroughly.

7 Wash the oil strainer with a suitable solvent and remove any debris caught in the mesh, using compressed air if available **(see illustration)**. Inspect the strainer for any signs of wear or damage and renew it if necessary.

8 Clean the pressure regulator. Push the plunger into the regulator body and check that it moves freely against the spring pressure **(see illustration)**.

Installation

9 Smear the new pressure regulator O-ring with grease and fit it into the groove **(see illustration)**. Press the regulator firmly into its socket **(see illustration 17.4)**.

10 Smear the new oil strainer O-ring with grease and fit it into the groove **(see illustration)**. Press the strainer into its socket , aligning it so the cut-out in the tab locates over the projection on the socket rim **(see illustration)**.

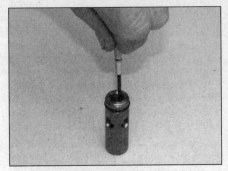

17.8 Checking the operation of the pressure regulator

17.10a Fit a new O-ring onto the strainer . . .

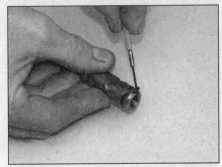

17.9 Fit a new O-ring onto the regulator

17.10b . . . and make sure it locates correctly over the tab (arrowed)

11 Clean the threads of the sump plate bolts and apply fresh thread lock to them.

12 Lay a new gasket onto the crankcase, making sure the holes align correctly **(see illustration)**.

13 Position the sump and sump plate on the crankcase **(see illustrations)**. Install the bolts,

using a new sealing washer on the one bolt and not forgetting the clamp with the other, and fitting the longer bolts through the sump plate **(see illustration 17.2)**. Tighten the bolts evenly in a criss-cross pattern to the specified torque setting.

17.12 Align the new gasket with the bolt holes . . .

17.13a . . . then fit the sump . . .

17.13b . . . and the sump plate (arrowed)

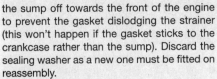

18.2a Lock the sprocket and unscrew the bolt

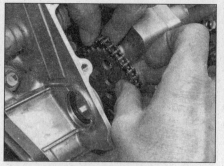

18.2b Remove the sprocket . . .

18.2c . . . and retrieve the washer

14 Install the engine (see Section 4).
15 Replenish the engine with oil and check the level (see Chapter 1 and *Pre-ride checks*). Start the engine and check that there are no leaks around the sump, then install the fairing side panels (see Chapter 7).

18 Oil pump

Note: *To remove the oil pump the engine must be removed from the frame.*

Removal

1 Remove the sump (see Section 17).
2 Use a screwdriver to lock the oil pump driven sprocket and unscrew the sprocket bolt **(see illustration)**. Slide the sprocket off the shaft and disengage it from the chain **(see illustration)**. Remove the washer **(see illustration)**. Note

that if the clutch, drive sprocket and chain have been removed it is not necessary to remove the driven sprocket, unless required.
3 Unscrew the bolts securing the pump to the crankcase and withdraw the pump **(see illustration)**.
4 Remove the O-ring from the oil passage and discard it as a new one must be fitted on reassembly **(see illustration)**. Remove the two locating dowels if loose **(see illustration 18.7)**.

Inspection

5 Inspect the pump body for any obvious damage such as cracks or distortion, and check that the shaft rotates freely and without any side-to-side play or excessive endfloat.
6 The internal components of the pump are not available separately and Suzuki provides no specifications for checking the pump components for wear. If an oil pressure check has been carried out there is low oil pressure, and other possible

causes listed in Section 3 have been ruled out, replace the pump with a new one.

Installation

7 Fit a new O-ring smeared with grease into the oil passage **(see illustration 18.4)**. Fit the dowels if removed **(see illustration)**.
8 Fit the pump onto the dowels, aligning and engaging the cut-out in the oil pump shaft end with the tabbed end of the water pump shaft **(see illustration)**. Fit the bolts and tighten them to the specified torque setting **(see illustration)**.
9 Fit the washer onto the shaft **(see illustration 18.2c)**. Engage the driven sprocket with the chain and fit it onto the shaft **(see illustration 18.2b)** – fit a small screwdriver into the gap between the oil pump and water pump shafts to keep the pump shaft fully protruded and so you can wiggle them to help align the flats for the driven sprocket **(see illustration)**. Apply some threadlock to the bolt, then lock the

18.3 Unscrew the bolts (arrowed) and remove the pump

18.4 Remove the O-ring

18.7 Make sure the dowels (arrowed) are in place

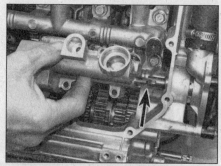

18.8a Engage the shafts (arrowed) and locate the pump on the dowels . . .

18.8b . . . then fit the bolts and tighten them

18.9a Use a screwdriver between the shafts as shown to make it easier to fit the sprocket

sprocket using a screwdriver and tighten the bolt **(see illustration and 18.2a)**.

10 Install the sump (see Section 17).

19 Crankcase separation and reassembly

Separation

1 To gain access to the crankshaft, balancer shaft (750 models), pistons and rings, connecting rods, transmission shafts and selector drum and forks, and all related bearings, the upper and lower crankcase must be separated.

2 To enable the crankcases to be separated, remove the engine from the frame (see Section 4).

3 Before separating the crankcases, remove the clutch (see Section 13), the gearchange mechanism (see Section 15), the water pump (Chapter 3), the oil cooler (Section 16), the oil sump, oil strainer and pressure regulator (see Section 17) and the oil pump (see Section 18). If

18.9b Apply threadlock to the sprocket bolt

you are removing the crankshaft also remove the cam chain (see Section 11) and the alternator and starter clutch (see Section 12). If you are removing the piston and connecting rod assemblies remove the cylinder head (see Section 9).

4 Unscrew the clutch pushrod oil seal retainer bolts and remove the retainer **(see illustration 13.19)**. Undo the bolts securing the reed valve cover to the breather housing and remove the

cover and the reed valve **(see illustration)**. Undo the bolts securing the crankcase breather housing to the upper crankcase and remove the housing; Remove and discard the gasket as a new one must be fitted.

5 Make a cardboard template punched with holes to match all the bolts in each crankcase half – as each crankcase bolt is removed, store it, along with any washer fitted with it, in its relative position in the template **(see illustration)**. This will ensure all bolts and washers are installed in the correct location on reassembly. Note that new copper sealing washers should be used on assembly where fitted, but keep the old ones with the bolts for the time being as a guide for reassembly.

6 With the engine right way up unscrew the bolts in the top of the crankcase, noting the positions of those with copper washers – undo the 6 mm bolts first, then undo the 8 mm bolts, starting with those around the edge of the crankcase and working to the centre **(see illustrations)**. Remove them and fit them in the template.

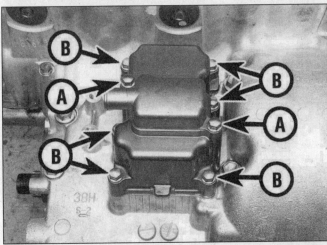

19.4 Undo the bolts (A) and remove the cover, then the bolts (B) and remove the housing

19.5 Example of a cardboard template for the crankcase bolts

19.6a Unscrew the bolts at the front (arrowed) . . .

19.6b . . . and those at the back (arrowed) – note the bolts with copper washers (A), and the earth lead (B)

19.8 Unscrew the bolts (arrowed)

19.9 Unscrew the 9 mm bolts in reverse of the tightening sequence shown – bolts 7 to 10 have copper sealing washers

7 Turn the engine upside down. Support it on wood blocks if required.

8 Unscrew the 6 mm and 8 mm bolts along the front of the crankcase, starting at the sides and working to the centre **(see illustration)**. Remove them and fit them in the template.

9 Now unscrew the 9 mm crankshaft journal bolts a little at a time in the **reverse** order of the tightening sequence shown until they are all finger-tight, then remove the bolts and fit them in the template **(see illustration)**.

10 Carefully lift the lower crankcase off the upper crankcase, using a soft-faced mallet to tap around the joint to initially separate the

halves if necessary **(see illustration)**. Note: *If the halves do not separate easily, make sure all fasteners have been removed.*

11 The lower crankcase, which contains the transmission output shaft and its selector forks and shaft and the selector drum, will come away leaving the transmission input shaft along with its selector fork and shaft, the crankshaft, and on 750 models the balancer shaft, in the upper crankcase. Take care not to dislodge the bearing shells from their seats in the lower crankcase.

12 Note the location of the three dowels and remove them for safekeeping if they are

loose **(see illustration)**. Also remove the oil passage O-ring, the balancer shaft seal and the clutch pushrod seal and discard them as new ones must be fitted on reassembly **(see illustrations)**.

13 Refer to Sections 20 onwards for the removal and installation of the components housed in the crankcases.

Reassembly

14 Remove all traces of old sealant from the crankcase mating surfaces with a suitable solvent and clean the threads of all the crankcase bolts – note that the 8 mm bolt on the right-hand corner of the lower crankcase comes pre-coated with a thread locking compound. Suzuki specify to use a new bolt when reassembling the crankcases, but if necessary you can clean of all of the old coating and apply fresh threadlock. Also clean any old gasket off the breather housing, clutch and alternator cover mating surfaces.

15 Ensure that all components and their bearings are in place in the crankcases. Check that the crankshaft thrust bearings are correctly located in the upper crankcase (see Section 28).

16 If removed, fit the locating dowels into the upper crankcase **(see illustration 19.12a)**. Fit a new oil passage O-ring, balancer shaft seal

19.10 Lift the lower crankcase off the upper crankcase

19.12a Remove the dowels (arrowed), if loose . . .

19.12b . . . the oil passage O-ring . . .

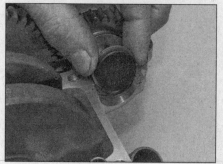

19.12c . . . the balancer shaft seal . . .

19.12d . . . and the clutch pushrod seal

19.18a Apply the sealant . . .

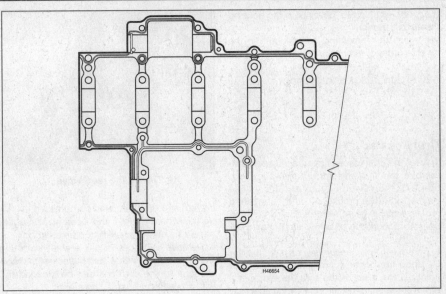

19.18b . . . to the shaded area

and clutch pushrod seal **(see illustrations 19.12b, c and d)**.

17 Check that the lower main bearing shells, and on 750 models the lower balancer shaft shells, are correctly located in the lower crankcase. If not already done lubricate all bearing shells and journals.

18 Apply a thin coating of suitable sealant to the mating surface of the lower crankcase **(see illustrations)**. Make sure the selector drum is positioned so that the neutral detent in the gearchange cam will align with the stopper arm when it is installed (see Section 15). Make sure the combined 3rd/4th gear pinion on the transmission input shaft is positioned centrally between its adjacent pinions so that it is not engaged with either, i.e. everything is in the neutral position to ensure the input shaft selector fork guide pin locates in its groove in the selector drum when the crankcases are joined.

Caution: Do not apply an excessive amount of sealant as it will ooze out when the case halves are assembled and may obstruct oil passages. Do not apply the sealant on or too close to any of the bearing shells or surfaces.

19 Carefully fit the lower crankcase onto the upper crankcase, making sure the dowels and oil seals locate correctly into the lower crankcase, and that the input shaft selector fork guide pin locates in its groove in the selector drum **(see illustration 19.10)**.

20 Check that the lower crankcase is correctly seated. **Note:** *The crankcases should fit together without being forced. If the casings are not correctly seated, remove the lower crankcase and investigate the problem. Do*

not attempt to pull the casings together using the crankcase bolts as they will crack and be ruined.

21 Install the ten 9 mm crankshaft journal bolts in their original locations, using new copper washers on the outer bolts **(see illustration 19.9)**. Secure all the bolts finger-tight, then tighten them a little at a time in the numerical sequence shown, to the initial torque setting specified at the beginning of this Chapter.

22 Now tighten each bolt in sequence and in one continuous movement through the specified angle to the final setting using a torque angle gauge. **Note:** *If a torque angle gauge is not available, paint one small reference mark on the top of each bolt and another on the bolt seat 50° clockwise after tightening them to the initial torque setting. Then, using a ring spanner so that you can see the marks, tighten the bolts until the marks align.*

23 Fit the 6 mm and 8 mm bolts into the front of the crankcase **(see illustration 19.8)**, either using a new pre-coated 8 mm bolt on the right-hand corner, or applying fresh threadlock to the original bolt **(see illustration)**. First tighten the bolts a little at a time in a

criss-cross pattern to the initial torque setting specified, then tighten them to the final torque setting.

24 Turn the engine the right way up. Fit the upper crankcase bolts, using new sealing washers where applicable, and not forgetting the earth lead **(see illustrations 19.6a and b)**. First tighten the bolts a little at a time in a criss-cross pattern to the initial torque setting specified, then tighten them to the final torque setting.

25 With all crankcase bolts tightened, check that the crankshaft and transmission shafts rotate smoothly and easily. Rotate the selector drum by hand and select each gear in turn whilst rotating the input shaft. Check that all gears can be selected and that the shafts rotate freely in every gear. If there are any signs of undue stiffness, tight or rough spots, or of any other problem, the fault must be rectified before proceeding further.

26 Clean the clutch pushrod oil seal retainer bolt threads and apply a thread locking compound then fit the retainer and tighten the bolts **(see illustration 13.19)**.

27 Fit a new crankcase breather housing gasket, then install the housing **(see illustrations)**. Fit

19.23 Use a new bolt or apply threadlock to the old one

19.27a Fit the new gasket . . .

19.27b . . . and the breather housing

the reed valve and its cover onto the housing **(see illustrations)**.

28 Install the remaining components in the reverse order of removal.

20 Crankcases and cylinder bores

Crankcases

1 After the crankcases have been separated, remove the transmission shafts (see Section 21), the selector drum and forks (see Section 23), the crankshaft and connecting rod assemblies (see Sections 25 and 28), and on 750 models the balancer shaft (see Section 29).

2 Remove the oil pressure switch (see Chapter 8). Undo the bolts securing the coolant inlet union to the front of the cylinder block and remove the union; discard the O-ring as a new one must be fitted on reassembly.

3 Undo the bolts securing the piston oil jets in the upper crankcase and remove the jets, noting how they fit **(see illustration)**. Remove the O-rings and discard them as new ones must be fitted. Unscrew the transmission oil jet from the lower crankcase **(see illustration)**.

4 Unscrew the water jacket plugs from the front and back of the cylinder block and the main oil galley plugs from the lower crankcase. Discard the O-rings and sealing washers as new ones must be fitted. Unscrew the alternator oil jet.

5 Clean the crankcases thoroughly with clean

19.27c Fit the reed valve . . .

solvent and dry them with compressed air. All oil passages, oil jets and coolant passages should be blown out with compressed air.

6 Remove all traces of old sealant from the mating surfaces with a suitable solvent. Minor damage to the surfaces can be cleaned up with a fine file or sharpening stone.

Caution: Be very careful not to nick or gouge the crankcase mating surfaces or oil leaks will result. Check the crankcases very carefully for cracks and other damage.

7 Small cracks or holes in aluminium castings may be repaired with an epoxy resin adhesive as a temporary measure. Permanent repairs can only be effected by argon-arc welding, and only a specialist in this process is in a position to advise on the economy or practical aspect of such a repair, although low-temperature DIY weld kits are available for small repairs. If any damage is found that can't be repaired, renew the crankcase halves as a set.

19.27d . . . and its cover

8 Damaged threads can be economically reclaimed by using a diamond section wire insert, of the Heli-Coil type, which is easily fitted after drilling and re-tapping the affected thread.

9 Sheared studs or screws can usually be removed with stud extractors, which consist of a tapered, left-thread screw of very hard steel. These are inserted into a pre-drilled hole in the stud, and usually succeed in dislodging the most stubborn stud or screw.

HAYNES HiNT *Refer to Tools and Workshop Tips for details of installing a thread insert and using screw extractors.*

10 Always clean the crankcases thoroughly after any repair work to ensure no dirt or metal swarf is trapped inside when the engine is rebuilt.

11 Fit a new O-ring onto the base of each piston oil jet and smear it with clean engine oil **(see illustration)**. Push each jet into its bore in the upper crankcase, making sure the oil nozzle points up into the cylinder **(see illustration)**. Apply a suitable non-permanent thread locking compound to the jet bolts and tighten them to the specified torque setting **(see illustration)**. Install the transmission oil jet **(see illustration 20.3b)**.

12 Fit new sealing washers to the oil gallery plugs then install the plugs and tighten them to the specified torque settings. Fit new O-rings to the water jacket plugs and smear them with coolant then tighten the plugs to the specified torque setting. Clean the threads of the oil jet for the alternator, then apply a suitable

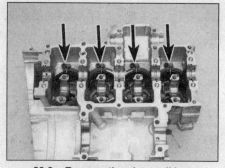

20.3a Remove the piston oil jets (arrowed) . . .

20.3b . . . and the transmission oil jet (arrowed)

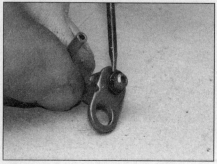

20.11a Fit a new O-ring onto each jet . . .

20.11b . . . then fit the jet . . .

20.11c . . . and secure it with a threadlocked bolt

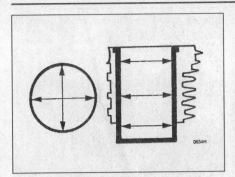

20.17 Measure the cylinder bore in the directions shown with a telescoping gauge

non-permanent thread locking compound and tighten it to the specified torque.
13 Fit a new O-ring into the groove in the cylinder block coolant union. Lubricate the O-ring with coolant, then fit the union and tighten the union bolts to the specified torque setting.
14 Install the remaining components in the reverse order of removal.

Cylinder bores

15 Using a precision straight-edge and a feeler gauge, check the head gasket mating surface for warpage. Refer to *Tools and Workshop Tips* in the Reference section for details of how to use the straight-edge. If the block is warped beyond the limit specified at the beginning of this Chapter, consult your Suzuki dealer or take it to a specialist repair shop for rectification.
16 Check the cylinder walls carefully for scratches and score marks. If the cylinders are badly scratched, scuffed or scored, the crankcase set must be replaced with a new one. The cylinder bores should not be honed.
17 The standard bore diameter range is given in the specifications. Suzuki do not specify a service limit for bore wear, but you can use telescoping gauges and a micrometer (see *Tools and Workshop Tips*) to check the dimensions of each cylinder to assess the amount of wear, taper and ovality. Measure near the top (but below the level of the top piston ring at TDC), centre and bottom (but above the level of the oil ring at BDC) of the bore, both parallel to and across the crankshaft axis **(see illustration)**. Compare the results to the standard bore

diameter range in the specifications at the beginning of this Chapter. If the cylinder bore is worn a new set of crankcases must be fitted.
18 If the precision measuring tools are not available, take the upper crankcase to a Suzuki dealer or specialist motorcycle repair shop for assessment.

21 Transmission shaft removal and installation

Note: *To remove the transmission shafts the engine must be removed from the frame.*

Removal

1 Separate the crankcases (see Section 19).
2 Remove the selector fork shaft retainer from the upper crankcase **(see illustration 23.4a)**. Remove the input shaft selector fork and shaft **(see illustration 23.4b)**.

21.6 Undo the screws (arrowed) and remove the seal housing

21.7b Thread two of the screws into the threaded holes as described . . .

21.3 Remove the input shaft . . .

21.4 . . . and its bearing half-ring retainer and dowel pin

3 Lift the input shaft out of the crankcase **(see illustration)**.
4 Remove the bearing half-ring retainer and the bearing locating pin noting how they fit **(see illustration)**. If they are not in their slots or holes in the crankcase, remove them from the bearings themselves on the shaft.
5 Remove the selector drum and the output shaft selector forks and shaft (see Section 23).
6 Undo the oil seal housing screws and remove the housing – the seal comes with it **(see illustration)**. Remove and discard the O-ring fitted around it **(see illustration 21.16c)**.
7 Undo the left-hand bearing housing screws **(see illustration)**. Thread two of the housing screws into the threaded holes in the housing and continue to screw them in evenly and a little at a time after they have contacted the crankcase – this will draw the bearing housing out, displacing the spacer as it does **(see illustrations)**. Remove the

21.7a Undo the screws (arrowed)

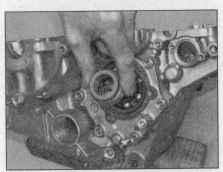

21.7c . . . to displace the spacer . . .

21.7d . . . and the housing

21.8a Undo the screws (arrowed)

21.8b Thread two of the screws into the threaded holes as described . . .

21.8c . . . to displace the housing

21.9 Draw the output shaft out of the crankcase

21.12 Lubricate the bearing (arrowed) with oil

Installation

11 Slide the output shaft into the left-hand side of the crankcase (see illustration 21.9).

12 Lubricate the right-hand bearing with oil (see illustration). Fit the right-hand bearing housing into the crankcase and onto the shaft end, pushing it on as far as it will go. Clean the threads of the housing screws and apply a suitable threadlock, then tighten them evenly and a little at a time in a criss-cross pattern to draw the housing squarely onto the shaft if it wouldn't push on all the way (see illustration 21.8a). When the housing seats, tighten the screws to the torque setting specified at the beginning of the Chapter.

13 Fit the dowel for the left-hand bearing housing into the crankcase if removed (see illustration). Fit a new O-ring smeared with grease into the groove in the bearing housing (see illustration).

14 Lubricate the left-hand bearing with oil. Fit the left-hand bearing housing over the shaft and into the crankcase, pushing it on as far as it will go (see illustration 21.7d). Clean the threads of the housing screws and apply a suitable threadlock, then tighten them evenly and a little at a time in a criss-cross pattern to draw the housing squarely onto the shaft if it wouldn't push on all the way (see illustration). When the housing seats, tighten the screws to the specified torque setting.

15 Fit a new O-ring smeared with grease into the groove in the spacer (see illustration). Slide the spacer onto the shaft and push it up against the bearing inner race (see illustration).

spacer and the housing as they become free (see illustrations). Remove and discard the O-rings fitted inside the spacer and around the bearing housing (see illustrations 21.15a and 13b). Remove the dowel if it is loose (see illustration 21.13a).

8 Repeat the procedure to remove the right-hand bearing housing, except there is no spacer (see illustrations).

9 Draw the output shaft out to the left of the crankcase (see illustration).

10 If required, the shafts can be disassembled and inspected for wear or damage (see Section 22).

21.13a Fit the dowel . . .

21.13b . . . and a new O-ring

21.14 Apply threadlock to the screws and tighten them as described

21.15a Fit a new O-ring into the groove on the inside . . .

21.15b . . . then push the spacer onto the shaft

21.16a Remove the oil seal . . .

21.16b . . . and drive a new one in until it seats

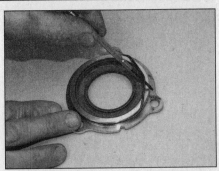

21.16c Fit a new O-ring into the groove . . .

16 Remove the oil seal from the housing – drive it out from the outside using a suitable socket **(see illustration)**. Fit a new seal and drive it in from the inside until it seats **(see illustration)**. Fit a new O-ring smeared with grease into the groove in the housing **(see illustration)**. Smear the seal lips with grease. Fit the housing over the shaft end and spacer and onto the crankcase **(see illustration)**. Clean the threads of the screws and apply a suitable threadlock, then tighten them to the specified torque setting.
17 Install the output shaft selector forks and shaft and the selector drum (see Section 23).
18 Fit the input shaft bearing half-ring retainer into its slot and the bearing locating pin into its hole in the upper crankcase **(see illustration 21.4)**.
19 Lower the input shaft into position in the upper crankcase **(see illustration 21.3)**. Ensure the hole in the needle bearing engages correctly on the pin, the ball bearing locating

21.16d . . . then fit the seal housing

pin faces forward and locates in its recess, and the groove in the bearing engages correctly with the half-ring retainer **(see illustration)**.
20 Fit the input shaft selector fork into the groove in its pinion and lay the shaft in the crankcase **(see illustration 23.4b)**. Fit the shaft retainer **(see illustration 23.4a)**.

21.19 Locating pin fits into recess (A) and groove fits onto half-ring retainer (B)

21 Make sure the transmission shafts are correctly seated and rotate freely.
Caution: If any of the bearing locating pins, half-ring retainers or dowel pins are not properly installed, the crankcase halves will not seat correctly.
22 Reassemble the crankcases (see Section 19).

22 Transmission shaft overhaul

Note: *References to the right- and left-hand ends of the transmission shafts are made as though they are installed in the engine and the engine is the correct way up.*
1 Remove the transmission shafts (see Section 21). Always disassemble them separately to avoid mixing up the components **(see illustration)**.

> **HAYNES HINT** *When disassembling the transmission shafts, place the parts on a long rod or thread a wire through them to keep them in order and facing the proper direction.*

Input shaft disassembly

2 Remove the needle bearing and dished oil seal from the left-hand end of the shaft **(see illustration 22.22)**.
3 Locate the circlip behind the 6th gear

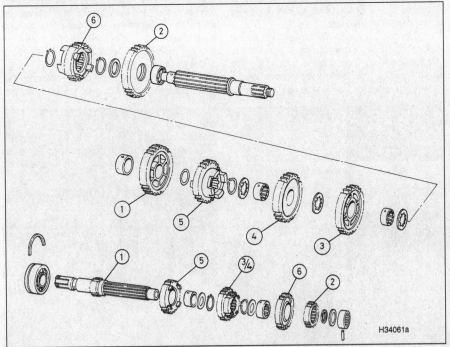

22.1 Transmission shaft components
Numbers indicate gears

H34061a

22.3a Slide the circlip towards the 3rd/4th gear pinion (arrowed)

22.3b Slide the gears back to expose the snap-ring (A) . . .

22.3c . . . and remove the snap-ring

pinion. Use circlip pliers to spread the circlip and slide it toward the 3rd/4th gear pinion **(see illustration)**. Slide the 6th and 2nd gear pinions towards the 3rd/4th gear pinion to expose the snap-ring on the end of the shaft and remove the snap ring **(see illustrations)**.

4 Slide the 2nd gear pinion and the 6th gear pinion and bush off the shaft **(see illustrations 22.21a, 22.20c and b)**.

5 Slide off the splined washer, then remove the circlip and slide the combined 3rd/4th gear pinion off the shaft **(see illustrations 22.20a, 22.19b and 19a)**.

6 Remove the circlip securing the 5th gear pinion, then slide the thrust washer, 5th gear pinion and its bush off the shaft **(see illustrations 22.18d, c, b and a)**.

7 The 1st gear pinion is integral with the shaft **(see illustration)**.

Input shaft inspection

8 Wash all the components in clean solvent and dry them off.

9 Check the gear teeth for cracking, chipping, pitting and other obvious wear or damage. Any pinion that is damaged must be replaced with a new one. Inspect the dogs and the dog holes in the pinions for cracks, chips, and excessive wear especially in the form

of rounded edges. Make sure mating gears engage properly. Replace the paired gears with a new set if necessary.

10 Measure the selector fork groove width and the fork to groove clearance (see Section 23).

11 Check for signs of scoring or bluing on the pinions, bushes and shaft. This could be caused by overheating due to inadequate lubrication. Check that all the oil holes and passages are clear. Replace any damaged pinions or bushes with new ones.

12 Check that each pinion moves freely on the shaft or bush but without undue freeplay. Check that each bush moves freely on the shaft but without undue freeplay.

13 The shaft is unlikely to sustain damage unless the engine has seized, placing an unusually high loading on the transmission, or the machine has covered a very high mileage. Check the surface of the shaft, especially where a pinion turns on it, and replace the shaft with a new one if it has scored or picked up, or if there is any wear.

14 Refer to *Tools and Workshop Tips* in the *Reference* Section and check the bearings. The ball bearing should be a tight fit on the shaft. Replace the bearing with a new one if it is worn, loose or damaged; use a bearing

puller to remove it and protect the end of the shaft with a piece of soft metal (brass or aluminium) **(see illustration)**. Install the new bearing using a press and a length of tubing which bears only on the bearing's inner race. Install the needle roller bearing on the shaft and check it for play or roughness. Replace the bearing with a new one if it is worn or damaged.

15 Check the needle bearing oil seal and replace it with a new one it if is damaged or deteriorated.

16 Check the washers and replace any that are bent or worn with new ones. Discard the circlips and the snap-ring as new ones must be fitted on reassembly.

Input shaft reassembly

17 During reassembly, apply clean engine oil to the mating surfaces of the shaft, pinions and bushes. When installing the circlips and snap-ring, do not expand their ends any further than is necessary. Install the stamped circlips so that the chamfered side faces the pinion it secures (see *Correct fitting of a stamped circlip* illustration in *Tools and Workshop Tips* of the *Reference* Section).

18 Slide the 5th gear bush all the way onto the shaft, then slide the 5th gear pinion onto the

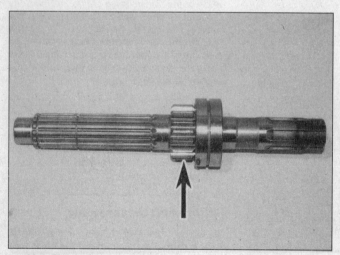

22.7 The 1st gear pinion is integral with the shaft (arrowed)

22.14 Protect the end of the shaft with a piece of soft metal (arrowed) when removing the bearing

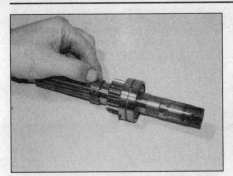

22.18a Slide on the 5th gear bush . . .

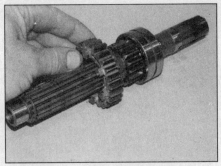

22.18b . . . the 5th gear pinion . . .

22.18c . . . and the washer . . .

22.18d . . . and secure them with the circlip

22.19a Slide on the 3rd /4th gear pinion

22.19b Slide the circlip past its groove (arrowed)

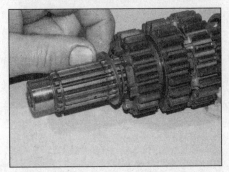

22.20a Slide on the splined washer . . .

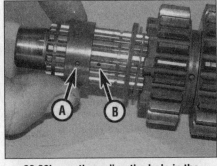

22.20b . . . then align the hole in the splined bush (A) with the hole in the shaft (B) and fit the bush

22.20c Fit the 6th gear pinion onto the bush

bush, with its dogs facing away from the integral 1st gear (see illustrations). Slide on the washer, then fit the circlip, making sure it is properly seated in its groove (see illustrations).

19 Slide the combined 3rd/4th gear pinion onto the shaft, so that the larger (4th gear) pinion faces the 5th gear pinion dogs (see illustration). Fit the circlip onto the shaft but do not locate it in its groove – slide it past the groove and as far towards the 3rd/4th gear pinion as possible (see illustration).

20 Slide on the splined washer, then the 6th gear pinion splined bush, aligning the oil hole in the bush with the hole in the shaft (see illustrations). Fit the 6th gear pinion onto the bush, with its dogs facing the dogs on the 3rd gear pinion (see illustration).

21 Slide the 2nd gear pinion onto the shaft with its recessed side facing outwards, away

from the 6th gear pinion (see illustration). Secure the pinion with the snap-ring, making sure it is properly seated in its groove (see illustration 22.3c). Now slide the 6th and 2nd

22.21a Slide on the 2nd gear pinion and secure it with the snap-ring

gear pinions up to the snap ring to expose the groove for the 3rd/4th gear pinion circlip, then move the circlip along the shaft and fit it into the groove (see illustration).

22.21b Slide the circlip into its groove

22.22 Install the bearing

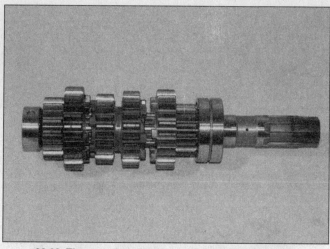

22.23 The completed input shaft should look like this

22 Fit the dished oil seal and needle bearing onto the end of the shaft **(see illustration)**.
23 Check that all components have been correctly installed **(see illustration)**.

Output shaft disassembly

24 Slide the 1st gear pinion and its bush off the shaft, followed by the thrust washer and the 5th gear pinion **(see illustrations 22.38b and a, 22.37b and a)**.
25 Remove the circlip securing the 4th gear pinion, then slide the splined washer, 4th gear pinion and its bush off the shaft **(see illustrations 22.36b and a, 22.35c and b)**.
26 Slide off the splined washer, followed by the 3rd gear pinion and its bush, and the splined washer **(see illustrations 22.35a, 22.34c and b and a)**.
27 Remove the circlip securing the 6th gear pinion, then slide the pinion off the shaft **(see illustrations 22.33b and a)**.
28 Remove the circlip securing the 2nd gear pinion, then slide the thrust washer, the 2nd gear pinion and its bush off the shaft **(see illustrations 22.32d, c, b and a)**.

Output shaft inspection

29 Refer to Steps 8 to 13, and 15 and 16, above.
30 Refer to *Tools and Workshop Tips* in the

Reference Section and check the bearings. To remove the left-hand bearing from its housing, support the housing on blocks and drive the bearing squarely out from the inside, using a bearing driver or socket that bears on the inner race. Drive the new bearing squarely in from the outside until it seats, using a driver or socket that bears on the outer race. The right-hand bearing is integral with the housing and must be replaced as such.

Output shaft reassembly

31 During reassembly, apply clean engine oil to the mating surfaces of the shaft, pinions and bushes. When installing the circlips, do not expand their ends any further than is necessary. Install the stamped circlips so that their chamfered side faces the pinion it secures (see *Correct fitting of a stamped circlip* illustration in *Tools and Workshop Tips* in the *Reference* Section).
32 Slide the 2nd gear pinion bush all the way onto the shaft, then slide the 2nd gear pinion (flat side faces towards the bearing) onto the bush, followed by the thrust washer **(see illustrations)**. Secure them in place with the circlip, making sure it is properly seated in its groove **(see illustration)**.
33 Slide the 6th gear pinion onto the shaft with its selector fork groove facing away from the 2nd gear pinion, and secure it in place with

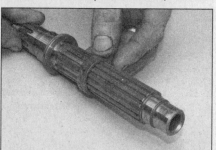

22.32a Slide on the 2nd gear bush . . .

22.32b . . . the 2nd gear pinion . . .

22.32c . . . and the washer . . .

22.32d . . . then fit the circlip into the groove . . .

22.32e . . . locating its ends as shown

22.33a Slide on the 6th gear pinion . . .

22.33b . . . then fit the circlip . . .

22.33c . . . locating its ends as shown

22.34a Slide on the splined washer . . .

22.34b . . . and the bush, aligning the oil holes

22.34c Fit the 3rd gear pinion onto the bush

the circlip, making sure it is properly seated in its groove (see illustrations).

34 Slide on the splined washer and the 3rd gear pinion bush, aligning the oil hole in the bush with the hole in the shaft (see illustration). Fit the 3rd gear pinion onto the

bush so that its open side faces the 6th gear pinion (see illustrations).

35 Slide on the splined washer and the 4th gear pinion bush, aligning the oil hole in the bush with the hole in the shaft (see illustration). Fit the 4th gear pinion onto the

bush so that its open side faces away from the 3rd gear pinion (see illustrations).

36 Slide on the splined washer, then fit the circlip, making sure it is properly seated in its groove (see illustrations).

37 Slide the 5th gear pinion onto the shaft

22.35a Slide on the splined washer . . .

22.35b . . . and the bush, aligning the oil holes

22.35c Fit the 4th gear pinion onto the bush

22.36a Slide on the splined washer . . .

22.36b . . . then fit the circlip . . .

22.36c . . . locating its ends as shown

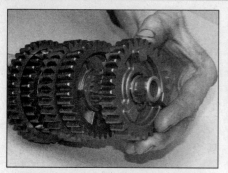

22.37a Slide on the 5th gear pinion . . .

22.37b . . . and the thrust washer

22.38a Slide on the bush . . .

with its selector fork groove facing the 4th gear pinion, followed by the thrust washer **(see illustrations)**.

38 Slide on the 1st gear pinion bush, then fit the pinion onto the bush with its open side facing the 5th gear pinion **(see illustrations)**.

39 Check that all components have been correctly installed **(see illustration)**.

23 Selector drum and forks

22.38b . . . then fit the 1st gear pinion

22.39 The completed output shaft should look like this

Note: *To remove the selector drum and forks the engine must be removed from the frame.*

Removal

1 Separate the crankcases (see Section 19).

2 If not already done, remove the gear position sensor (see Section 15).

3 Before removing the selector forks, mark each fork for identification using a felt pen and note which way round they fit, as an aid to installation. Note how the guide pin on each fork locates in the groove in the selector drum.

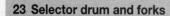

23.4a Remove the shaft retainer . . .

23.4b . . . then lift the shaft and fork out

4 Remove the selector fork shaft retainer from the upper crankcase, noting how its rim locates in the groove **(see illustration)**. Remove the selector fork and shaft **(see illustration)**.

5 Unscrew the output shaft selector fork shaft and selector drum bearing retainer screws **(see illustration)**.

6 Support the selector forks and withdraw the shaft **(see illustration)**.

7 Withdraw the selector drum from the crankcase **(see illustration)**. Remove the forks and slide them onto the shaft the correct way round **(see illustration)**.

8 To remove the gearchange cam from the end of the selector drum, pass a steel rod through the drum to hold it while unscrewing the centre bolt **(see illustration 23.16)**. The cam locates on a pin in the end of the selector

23.5 Undo the screws (arrowed)

23.6 Withdraw the shaft . . .

23.7a . . . then withdraw the selector drum . . .

23.7b . . . and remove the forks

23.8 Unscrew the centre bolt and remove the gearchange cam. Note the pin (arrowed)

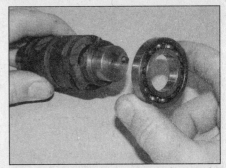

23.9 Pull the bearing off the selector drum

23.10a Check the fork ends and the grooves in the pinion

23.10b Measuring fork-to-groove clearance

drum **(see illustration)**. Remove the pin for safekeeping if it is loose.

9 If necessary, pull the caged ball bearing off the end of the selector drum **(see illustration)**.

Inspection

10 Inspect the selector forks for any signs of wear or damage, especially around the fork ends where they engage with the groove in the pinion **(see illustration)**. With the fork engaged with its gear pinion groove, measure the fork-to-groove clearance using a feeler gauge, and compare the result to the specifications at the beginning of this Chapter **(see illustration)**. If the clearance exceeds the service limit specified, measure the thickness of the fork ends and the width of the groove and compare the results with the specifications **(see illustrations)**. Replace whichever components are worn beyond their specifications with new ones.

11 Check the internal bearing surface of each fork for wear and pitting and check that the forks fit correctly on their shafts **(see illustration)** – they should move freely with a light fit but no appreciable freeplay. Check

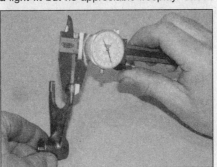

23.10c Measuring the thickness of the fork ends . . .

that the fork shaft holes in the crankcases are not worn or damaged.

12 Check each selector fork shaft is straight by rolling it on a flat surface. A bent shaft will cause difficulty in selecting gears and make the gearchange action heavy. Replace the shafts with new ones if bent. Check closely to see if the forks are bent. If the forks are in any way damaged they must be replaced with new ones.

13 Check the guide pins and the grooves in the selector drum for signs of wear or damage **(see illustration)**.

14 Check that the selector drum bearings rotate freely and have no sign of freeplay between them and the crankcase. A needle bearing is on the left-hand end in the crankcase **(see illustration)**. A caged ball bearing is on the right-hand end of the selector drum **(see illustration 23.9)**. Refer to *Tools and Workshop Tips* in the Reference

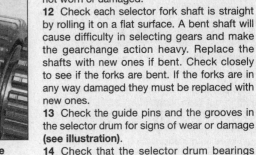

23.10d . . . and the width of the gear pinion groove

23.11 Check the bearing surface (arrowed) and the fit of each fork on its shaft

23.13 Check the guide pin (arrowed) and its groove in the selector drum

23.14 Selector drum needle bearing (arrowed)

23.16 Counter-hold the drum and tighten the bolt to the specified torque

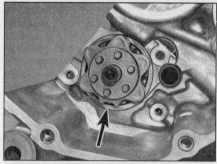

23.17 Align the neutral detent as shown for installation of the stopper arm (arrowed)

23.18 Slide the shaft through the forks and locate the guide pins in their grooves

Section for information on bearings and how to remove and install them.

15 If required and not already done, check the condition of the gearchange mechanism components (see Section 15).

Installation

16 If removed, fit the caged ball bearing onto the selector drum with the marked side facing out **(see illustration 23.9)**. Fit the pin in the end of the drum if removed. Fit the gearchange cam ensuring it locates onto the pin **(see illustration 23.8)**. Apply a suitable non-permanent thread locking compound to the centre bolt threads, then hold the drum as on disassembly and tighten the bolt to the specified torque setting **(see illustration)**.

17 Locate the output shaft selector forks in their pinions **(see illustration 23.7b)**. Slide the drum into the crankcase **(see illustration 23.7a)**. Rotate the drum so that the neutral detent in the gearchange cam is positioned to align with the stopper arm **(see illustration)**. Install the stopper arm now so it keeps the drum in neutral (see Section 15, Step 16).

18 Lubricate the output shaft selector fork shaft with clean engine oil and slide it into its bore in the crankcase and through the forks, locating the fork guide pins in their grooves in the selector drum **(see illustration)**.

19 Apply a suitable non-permanent thread locking compound to the threads of the selector drum bearing/fork shaft retaining screws and tighten them to the specified torque setting **(see illustration 23.5)**.

20 Fit the input shaft selector fork into the groove in its pinion and lay the shaft in the crankcase **(see illustration 23.4b)**. Fit the retainer, locating its rim in the groove **(see illustration 23.4a)**.

21 Reassemble the crankcases (see Section 19). Install the gear position sensor (see Section 15).

24 Connecting rod and main bearing information

1 Even though new main and connecting rod bearings are generally fitted during engine

overhaul, the old bearings should be retained for close examination as they may reveal valuable information about the condition of the engine.

2 Bearing failure occurs mainly because of lack of lubrication, the presence of dirt or other foreign particles, overloading the engine and/or corrosion. Regardless of the cause of bearing failure, it must be corrected before the engine is reassembled to prevent it from happening again.

3 When examining the bearings, lay them out on a clean surface in the same general position as their location on the crankshaft journals. This will enable you to match any noted bearing problems with the corresponding crankshaft journal.

4 Dirt and other foreign particles get into the engine in a variety of ways. They may be left in the engine during assembly or they may pass through filters or breathers, then get into the oil and from there into the bearings. Metal chips from machining operations and normal engine wear are often present. Abrasives are sometimes left in engine components after reconditioning operations, especially when parts are not thoroughly cleaned using the proper cleaning methods. Whatever the source, foreign objects often end up imbedded in the soft bearing material and are easily recognised. Large particles will not imbed in the bearing and will score or gouge the bearing and journal. The best prevention for this cause of bearing failure is to clean all parts thoroughly and keep everything spotlessly clean during engine reassembly. Regular oil and filter changes are also recommended.

5 Lack of lubrication or lubrication breakdown has a number of interrelated causes. Excessive heat (which thins the oil), overloading (which squeezes the oil from the bearing face) and oil leakage or throw off (from excessive bearing clearances, worn oil pump or high engine speeds) all contribute to lubrication breakdown. Blocked oil passages will starve a bearing of lubrication and destroy it. When lack of lubrication is the cause of bearing failure, the bearing material is wiped or extruded from the steel backing of the bearing. Temperatures may increase to the point where the steel backing and the journal turn blue from overheating.

HAYNES HiNT *Refer to Tools and Workshop Tips for bearing fault finding.*

6 Riding habits can have a definite effect on bearing life. Full throttle low, speed operation, or labouring the engine, puts very high loads on bearings, which tend to squeeze out the oil film. These loads cause the bearings to flex, which produces fine cracks in the bearing face (fatigue failure). Eventually the bearing material will loosen in pieces and tear away from the steel backing. Short trip riding leads to corrosion of bearings, as insufficient engine heat is produced to drive off the condensed water and corrosive gases produced. These products collect in the engine oil, forming acid and sludge. As the oil is carried to the engine bearings, the acid attacks and corrodes the bearing material.

7 Incorrect bearing installation during engine assembly will lead to bearing failure as well. Tight fitting bearings which leave insufficient bearing oil clearances result in oil starvation. Dirt or foreign particles trapped behind a bearing insert result in high spots on the bearing which lead to failure.

8 To avoid bearing problems, clean all parts thoroughly before reassembly, double check all bearing clearance measurements and lubricate the new bearings with clean engine oil during installation.

25 Connecting rods and bearings

Note: *To remove the connecting rods the engine must be removed from the frame.*

Removal

1 Separate the crankcases (see Section 19).

2 Before detaching the piston/connecting rod assemblies from the crankshaft, measure the big-end side clearance on each rod with a

25.2 Use a feeler gauge to measure the clearance (gap) between the big-end and the crank web

25.4a Unscrew the bolts (arrowed) and remove the cap and bearing shell from the crankpin . . .

25.4b . . . tapping the bolt heads help to dislodge the rod and cap

feeler gauge **(see illustration)**. If the clearance on any rod is greater than the service limit listed in the Specifications at the beginning of this Chapter, measure the big-end and crankpin widths as described in Step 11.

3 Using paint or a felt marker pen, mark the relevant cylinder identity on each connecting rod and cap. Mark across the cap-to-connecting rod join and note which side of the rod faces the front of the engine to ensure that the cap and rod are fitted the correct way around on reassembly. Cylinders are numbered 1 to 4, from the left to the right side of the engine. The indent on the top of the piston faces the front (exhaust side) of the engine. **Note:** *The number already across the rod and cap indicates rod bearing size, not cylinder number* **(see illustration 25.26)**. *This number faces the rear of the engine.*

4 Working on one connecting rod at a time, unscrew the connecting rod cap bolts and remove the cap, complete with the lower bearing shell, from the crankpin **(see illustration)** – to ease removal tap on the bolt heads when they are partially unscrewed and this will dislodge the rod **(see illustration)**. Detach the rod, complete with the upper bearing shell, from the crankpin **(see illustration)**. **Note:** *If you are only removing one connecting rod, the crankshaft can be left in place and the rod/piston manoeuvred out the top of the bore as described in Step 6. If, however, all rods require attention, it is advisable to remove the crankshaft.*

5 Remove the crankshaft, the upper bearing shells and the crankshaft thrust bearings

25.4c After removing the cap push the rod clear of the pin

(see Section 28). On 750 models, remove the balancer shaft from the front of the crankcase (see Section 29).

6 Turn the crankcase on its side. Push each piston/connecting rod assembly to the top end of the cylinder bore and remove it, making sure the rod does not mark the bore **(see illustration)**. Note the indent on the top of each piston which should face the front (exhaust side).

Caution: Do not try to remove the piston/ connecting rod from the bottom of the cylinder bore. The piston will not pass the crankcase main bearing webs.

7 Fit the related bearing shells (if removed), bearing cap and bolts on each connecting rod assembly so that they are all kept together as a matched set. Note how the locating pins in the cap fit into the rod. **Note:** *It is not*

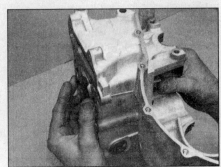

25.6 Push the rod up so the piston comes out the top of the bore

necessary to renew the big-end bolts when the connecting rods are removed, only if they show signs of damage.

8 Remove the pistons from the connecting rods (see Section 26).

Inspection

9 Check the connecting rods for cracks and other obvious damage.

10 Apply clean engine oil to the piston pin, insert it into its connecting rod small-end and check for any freeplay between the two **(see illustration)**. If there is freeplay, measure the pin external diameter in the middle and the small-end bore diameter and compare the measurements to the specifications at the beginning of this Chapter **(see illustrations)**. Replace components that are worn beyond the service limit with new ones.

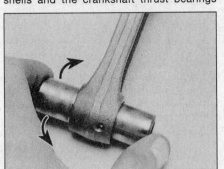

25.10a Check for freeplay between the piston pin and connecting rod

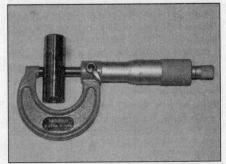

25.10b Measuring the external diameter of the piston pin . . .

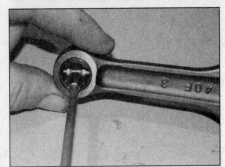

25.10c . . . and the small-end bore

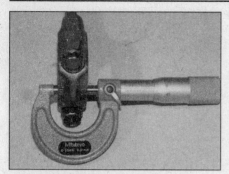

25.11a Measure the width of the connecting rod . . .

25.11b . . . and the corresponding crankpin

25.15 Remove the shells from the rods and caps

11 If the side clearance measured in Step 2 exceeds the service limit, measure the width of the connecting rod big-end and the width of the crankpin **(see illustrations)**. Compare the results to the specifications at the beginning of this Chapter, and replace whichever component exceeds those specifications with a new one.

12 Refer to Section 24 and examine the connecting rod bearing shells. If they are scored, badly scuffed or appear to have seized, new shells must be installed. Always renew the shells in the connecting rods as a set. If any are badly damaged, check the corresponding crankpin. Evidence of extreme heat, such as discoloration, indicates that lubrication failure has occurred. Be sure to check the oil pump, pressure regulator and all oil holes and passages thoroughly before reassembling the engine.

13 Have the rods checked by a Suzuki dealer if you are in doubt about their straightness.

Oil clearance check

14 Whether new bearing shells are being fitted or the original ones are being re-used, the connecting rod big-end bearing oil clearance should be checked prior to reassembly. Bearing oil clearance is measured with a product known as Plastigauge.

15 Remove the bearing shells from the rods and caps, keeping them in order **(see illustration)**. Clean the backs of the bearing shells, the bearing locations in both the connecting rod and cap, and the crankpin journal with a suitable solvent.

16 Press the bearing shells into their

locations, ensuring that the tab on each shell engages the notch in the connecting rod or cap. Make sure the bearings are fitted in the correct locations and take care not to touch any shell's bearing surface with your fingers.

17 Support the crankshaft so it cannot roll. Cut an appropriate size length of Plastigauge (it should be slightly shorter than the width of the crankpin) and place it on the crankpin journal to be checked **(see illustration 28.15)**. Do not place Plastigauge over the oil holes in the journal.

18 Fit the connecting rod and cap onto the crankpin, ensuring that the rod is fitted the correct way round and that the previously made markings and the cap locating pins align.

19 Tighten the bearing cap bolts in two stages, first to the initial torque setting specified, and then to the final angle setting specified **(see illustration 25.39)**. It is essential that, throughout this procedure, the connecting rod does not rotate on the crankshaft.

20 Undo the cap bolts and remove the cap and connecting rod from the crankshaft, again taking great care that the rod does not rotate on the crankshaft.

21 Compare the width of the crushed Plastigauge on the crankpin to the scale printed on the Plastigauge envelope to obtain the connecting rod bearing oil clearance **(see illustration 28.19)**. Compare the reading to the specifications at the beginning of this Chapter. If the clearance is within the range specified and the bearings are in perfect condition, they can be reused.

22 Carefully scrape away all traces of the Plastigauge from the crankpin journal and

bearing shells using a fingernail or other object which will not score the bearing surfaces.

23 If the oil clearance is beyond the service limit, first check the crankpin journal size code. The crankpin journal size code is stamped on the inner left-hand crankshaft web and will be either a 1, 2 or 3 **(see illustration)**. Measure the actual diameter of the crankpin journal with a micrometer and compare the result with the Specifications at the beginning of this Chapter **(see illustration)**. For example, on 600 models, if the journal being measured is code 1, the Specifications indicate that the service limit for that journal is 30.992 mm. If the journal diameter is larger than the service limit, new bearing shells can be fitted (see Steps 26 and 27). If the journal diameter is smaller than the service limit, the crankshaft must be replaced with a new one.

24 Repeat the oil clearance check for the remaining connecting rods. Always renew all of the shells (on all four rods) at the same time.

25 Install the new shells and check the oil clearance once again.

Bearing shell selection

26 New shells for the big-end bearings are supplied on a selected fit basis. Size codes for the crankpin journals are stamped on the inner left-hand crankshaft web and will be either a 1, 2 or 3 **(see illustration 25.23a)**. The first (top) number is for the left-hand (No. 1 cylinder) journal, and so on. Each connecting rod size code is marked on the flat face of the connecting rod and cap and will be either a 1 or 2 **(see illustration)**.

27 A corresponding range of bearing shells is available. To select the correct shells, use the

25.23a Crankpin journal size codes (arrowed)

25.23b Measuring a crankpin

25.26 Connecting rod size code

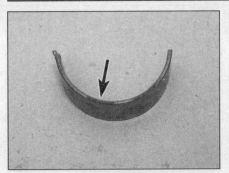

25.27 The colour code is marked on the side of the shell

table to cross-refer the crankpin journal size code with the connecting rod size code to determine the colour-code for the shells required. For example, if the connecting rod size code is 2, and the crankpin size code is 3, then the bearing required is Yellow. The colour is marked on the side of the shell **(see illustration)**.

Connecting rod code	Crankpin code 1	2	3
1	Green	Black	Brown
2	Black	Brown	Yellow

Installation

28 Fit the pistons onto the connecting rods if they were removed (see Section 26).

29 Ensure that the backs of the bearing shells, the bearing seats in the caps and rods and the crankpin journals are clean. If new shells are being fitted, ensure that all traces of protective grease are removed using paraffin (kerosene). Dry the shells, caps, rods and journals with a clean, lint-free cloth.

30 Fit the shells into the rods and caps, making sure the tab locates in the notch **(see illustration 25.15)**. If the old shells are being reused make sure each is returned to its original location.

31 Lubricate the pistons, rings and cylinder bore with clean engine oil. Stagger the piston ring end gaps (see Section 27). If available, use a piston ring compressor to aid installation.

32 If a ring compressor is available fit it around the piston and over the rings, then tighten it so the rings are compressed into their grooves **(see illustration)**.

33 Insert the piston/connecting rod assembly into the top of its cylinder, taking care not to

25.32 Fit the ring compressor and tighten it around the piston

25.34 Tap the piston into the cylinder then remove the compressor

allow the connecting rod to mark the bore **(see illustration)**. Make sure the indent on the top of the piston faces the front (exhaust side) of the engine.

34 If a ring compressor is being used tap the top of the piston with a soft tool so the piston enters the bore **(see illustration)** – when it is fully in, the ring compressor frees itself and can be removed.

35 If a ring compressor is not available, carefully compress and feed each piston ring into the bore as the piston is inserted **(see illustration)**.

36 Double-check that all rods and pistons have been correctly installed (see Step 3). Position the rods for Nos. 1 and 4 cylinders against the back of the crankcase, and the Nos. 2 and 3 cylinders against the front of the crankcase. Make sure all the bearing shells are in place then lubricate them with molybdenum oil (a 50/50 mixture of molybdenum paste and clean engine oil).

25.33 Insert the piston/connecting rod assembly into the top of the cylinder

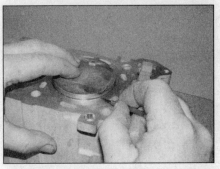

25.35 Carefully feed in each piston ring

37 Install the crankshaft thrust bearings, main bearing shells and crankshaft (see Section 28). On 750 models install the balancer shaft (see Section 29).

38 Lubricate the threads of the cap bolts with clean engine oil and fit them into the caps. Working on one connecting rod at a time, pull the rod onto the crankpin and fit the cap onto the rod, making sure it is the right way round and that the previously made markings and the cap locating pins align **(see illustrations)**. Tighten the bolts finger-tight at this stage. Check to make sure that all components have been returned to their original locations using the marks made on disassembly (Step 3).

39 Now tighten the bolts to the initial torque setting specified. Finally tighten each bolt in one continuous movement through the specified angle to the final setting using a torque angle gauge **(see illustration)**. If tightening is paused between the initial

25.38a Pull each rod up onto its crankpin . . .

25.38b . . . then fit the caps and tighten the bolts finger-tight

25.39 Tighten the cap bolts to the final setting with an angle gauge

and final settings, slacken the bolt to below the initial setting and repeat the procedure. **Note:** *If a torque angle gauge is not available, paint one small reference mark on the top of each bolt and another on the bolt seat 90° clockwise after tightening them to the initial torque setting. Then, using a ring spanner so that you can see the marks, tighten the bolts until the marks align.*

40 Rotate the crankshaft and check that the rods move smoothly and freely on the crankpins. If there are any signs of roughness or tightness, remove the rods and re-check the bearing clearance. Sometimes tapping the connecting rod cap bolts will relieve tightness.

41 Install the remaining components in the reverse order of disassembly.

26 Pistons

Note: *To remove the pistons the engine must be removed from the frame.*

Removal

1 Remove the piston/connecting rod assemblies (see Section 25).

2 Before removing the piston from the connecting rod, ensure it is marked with its cylinder identity. Cylinders are numbered 1 to 4, from the left to right side of the engine. If the piston is going to be cleaned, scratch the identity lightly on the inside of the piston skirt. Each piston must be installed in its original cylinder on reassembly. Note the indent on the top of each piston which faces the front (exhaust side) of the engine **(see illustration 25.33)**; if this is not visible, mark the piston accordingly so that it can be installed the correct way round.

3 Carefully prise out the circlip on one side of the piston using needle-nose pliers or a small flat-bladed screwdriver inserted into the notch **(see illustration)**. Push the piston pin out from the other side to free the piston from the connecting rod **(see illustration)**. Remove the other circlip and discard them as new ones must be used. When the piston has been removed, install its pin back into its bore so that related parts do not get mixed up.

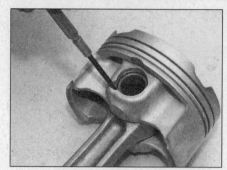
26.3a Prise out the circlip . . .

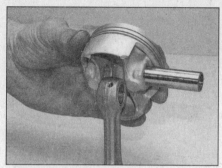
26.3b . . . then push out the piston pin

HAYNES HiNT *If a piston pin is a tight fit in the piston bosses, heat the piston gently with a hot air gun – this will expand the alloy piston sufficiently to release its grip on the pin. If the piston pin is particularly stubborn, extract it using a drawbolt tool, but be careful to protect the piston's working surfaces – see Tools and Workshop Tips in the Reference section.*

4 Remove the piston rings (see Section 27).

5 Clean all traces of carbon from the tops of the pistons. A hand-held wire brush or a piece of fine emery cloth can be used once most of the deposits have been scraped away. Do not, under any circumstances, use a wire brush mounted in a drill motor; the piston material is soft and will be eroded away by the wire brush.

6 Use a piston ring groove cleaning tool to remove any carbon deposits from the ring grooves. If a tool is not available, a piece broken off an old ring will do the job. Be very careful to remove only the carbon deposits. Do not remove any metal and do not nick or gouge the sides of the ring grooves.

7 Once the carbon has been removed, clean the pistons with a suitable solvent and dry them thoroughly. If the identification previously marked on the piston is cleaned off, be sure to re-mark it with the correct identity. Make sure the oil return holes at the back of the oil ring groove are clear.

Inspection

8 Carefully inspect each piston for cracks around the skirt, at the pin bosses and at the ring lands. Normal piston wear appears as even, vertical wear on the thrust surfaces of the piston and slight looseness of the top ring in its groove. If the skirt is scored or scuffed, the engine may have been suffering from overheating and/or abnormal combustion, which caused excessively high operating temperatures. The oil pump should be checked thoroughly. If wear is apparent on just one piston, check whether the piston oil jet set in the crankcase for that piston/cylinder is clear (see Section 20).

9 A hole in the top of the piston, in one extreme, or burned areas around the edge of the piston crown, indicate that pre-ignition or knocking under load have occurred. If you find evidence of any problems the cause must be corrected or the damage will occur again (see *Fault Finding* in the *Reference* section).

10 Check the piston-to-bore clearance by measuring the bore (see Section 20) and the piston diameter. Make sure each piston is matched to its correct cylinder. Measure the piston 15 mm up from the bottom of the skirt and at 90° to the piston pin axis **(see illustration)**. Subtract the piston diameter from the bore diameter to obtain the clearance. If it is greater than the figure specified at the beginning of this Chapter, check whether it is the bore or piston that is worn. If the piston diameter is less that the service limit, new pistons and rings should be fitted. If the cylinder bore is worn a new set of crankcases must be fitted.

11 Measure the piston ring-to-groove clearance by fitting each ring in its groove and slipping a feeler gauge in beside it **(see illustration)**. Make sure you have the correct ring for the groove. Check the clearance at three or four locations around the groove. If the clearance is greater than specified, renew both the piston and rings as a set. If new rings are being used, measure the clearance using the new rings. If the clearance is greater than that specified, the piston is worn and must be renewed.

12 Apply clean engine oil to the piston pin,

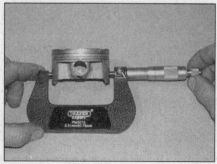
26.10 Measuring the piston diameter

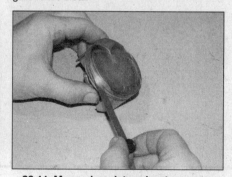
26.11 Measuring piston ring-to-groove clearance

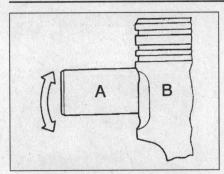

26.12a Slip the pin (A) into the piston (B) and try to rock it back and forth. If its loose, renew the piston and pin

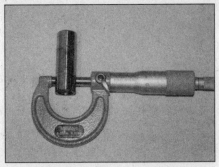

26.12b Measuring the external diameter of the pin . . .

26.12c . . . and the internal diameter of the pin bore

insert it into the piston and check for any freeplay between the two **(see illustration)**. Measure the pin external diameter at each end and the pin bores in the piston and compare the results to the Specifications at the beginning of this Chapter **(see illustrations)**. Repeat the measurements between the pin and the connecting rod small-end (see Section 25, Step 10). Renew components that are worn beyond the specified limits.

Installation

13 Inspect and install the piston rings (see Section 27).

14 Fit a **new** circlip into one side of the piston (never re-use old circlips) **(see illustration 26.15b)**. Lubricate the piston pin, the piston pin bore and the connecting rod small-end bore with clean engine oil.

15 Fit the piston on its correct connecting rod **(see illustration 26.3b)** – make sure the indent on the top of the piston is on the opposite side to the mark on the connecting rod big-end **(see illustration)**. Insert the piston pin from the side without the circlip. Secure the pin with the other **new** circlip **(see illustration)**. When installing the circlips, compress them only just enough to fit them in the piston, and make sure they are properly seated in their grooves with the open end away from the removal notch.

16 Install the piston/connecting rod assembly (see Section 25).

26.15a Make sure the mark on the rod (A) faces the opposite way to the mark on the piston (B)

27 Piston rings

Removal

Note: *It is good practice to replace the piston rings with new ones when an engine is being overhauled.*

1 Remove the piston/connecting rod assemblies (see Section 25).

2 Using your thumbs or a piston ring removal and installation tool, carefully remove the rings from the pistons, working on one piston at a time **(see illustrations 27.12, 11, and 9c, b and a)**. Do not nick or gouge the pistons in the process. Carefully note which way up each ring fits and in which groove as they

26.15b Fit the circlip into its groove

must be installed in their original positions if being re-used. The upper surface of the top two rings should have a manufacturer's letter or letters at one end – IT or IR on the top ring, and T or R on the second **(see illustration)**. The rings can also be identified by their different cross-section **(see illustration)**. **Note:** *It is good practice to replace the piston rings with new ones when an engine is being overhauled.*

Inspection

3 Lay out each piston with its ring set so the rings will be matched with the same piston and cylinder during the measurement procedure.

4 To measure the free end gap, lay the ring on a flat surface and measure the gap between the ends using a Vernier caliper **(see illustration)**. Compare the results to the specifications at the beginning of this Chapter and renew any ring that is outside its service limit.

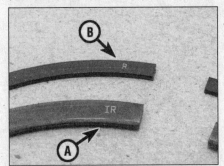

27.2a Top ring (A) and second ring (B) – note the mark on the end of each ring . . .

27.2b . . . and the difference in their profiles

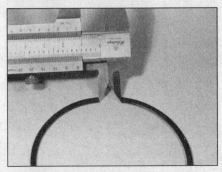

27.4 Measuring piston ring free end gap

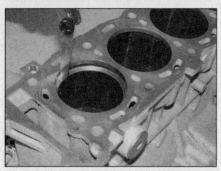

27.5 Measuring piston ring installed end gap

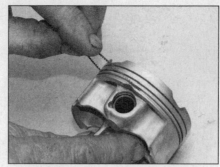

27.9a Fit the oil ring expander . . .

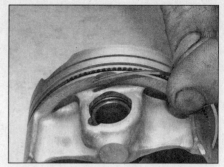

27.9b . . . then fit the lower side rail . . .

27.9c . . . and the upper side rail

27.11a Fit the second ring into its groove . . .

5 To measure the installed end gap, insert the ring into the top of the cylinder and square it up with the cylinder walls by pushing it in with the top of the piston. The ring should be about 20 mm below the top edge of the cylinder. Slip a feeler gauge between the ends of the ring to measure the gap and compare the result to the Specifications at the beginning of this Chapter **(see illustration)**.

6 If the gap is larger or smaller than specified, check that you have the correct rings before proceeding. Excess end gap is not critical unless it exceeds the service limit. Again, check that you have the correct rings for your engine.

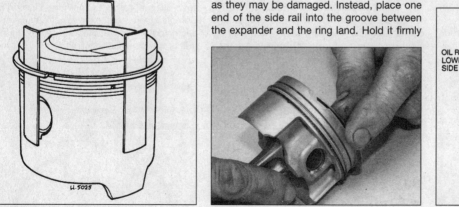

27.11b . . . old pieces of feeler gauge blade can be used to guide the rings over the piston . . .

7 Repeat the procedure for the other compression ring and then the compression rings in the other cylinders. Remember to keep the rings together with their matched pistons.

8 Refer to Section 26, Step 11 and measure the piston ring-to-groove clearance.

Installation

9 The oil control ring (lowest on the piston) is installed first. It is composed of three separate components; the expander and the upper and lower side rails. Slip the expander into the groove, positioning its ends so that they touch but do not overlap **(see illustration)**. Fit the lower side rail. Do not use a piston ring installation tool on the oil ring side rails as they may be damaged. Instead, place one end of the side rail into the groove between the expander and the ring land. Hold it firmly

27.12 . . . then fit the top ring

in place and slide a finger or thin blade around the piston while pushing the rail into the groove. Next, fit the upper side rail in the same manner.

10 After the oil control ring been installed, check that both its upper and lower side rails can be turned smoothly in the ring groove.

11 Fit the second compression ring into the middle groove in the piston with its letter facing up (see Step 2). Do not expand the ring any more than is necessary to slide it into place **(see illustration)**. To avoid breaking the ring, use old pieces of feeler gauge blade **(see illustration)**.

12 Fit the top compression ring in the same manner into the top groove in the piston with the letters facing up **(see illustration)**.

13 Once the rings are correctly installed, check they move freely without snagging and stagger their end gaps as shown **(see illustration)**.

28 Crankshaft and main bearings

Note: *To remove the crankshaft the engine must be removed from the frame.*

Removal

1 Separate the crankcases (see Section 19). Disconnect the piston/connecting

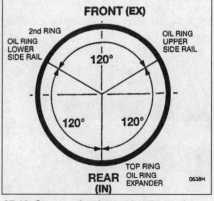

27.13 Stagger the ring end gaps as shown

28.3a Lift the crankshaft out of the crankcase

28.3b Remove the bearing shells if required

28.4 Note the position of the thrust bearings before removing them

rod assemblies from the crankshaft (see Section 25). Unless required, there is no need to remove them from the cylinders; push the rods up the bores so that they are clear of the crankshaft and wrap clean rag around the rods to prevent damage to the bores **(see illustration 25.4c)**.

2 On 750 models, remove the balancer shaft from the front of the crankcase (see Section 29).

3 Lift the crankshaft out of the upper crankcase **(see illustration)**. Remove the bearing shells if required but keep them in order **(see illustration)**.

4 The thrust bearings are located in the upper crankcase on each side of the centre main bearing housing. Note which side of the centre main bearing housing each thrust bearing fits – they are colour-coded for size and must be fitted in their original locations. Remove the thrust bearings for safe-keeping **(see illustration)**.

Inspection

5 Clean the crankshaft with a suitable solvent, paying particular attention to flush out the oil passages. If available, blow the crank dry with compressed air, and also blow through the oil passages.

6 Inspect the primary drive gear for wear or damage **(see illustration)**. If any of the gear teeth are excessively worn, chipped or broken,

the crankshaft must be replaced with a new one. On 750 models, inspect the balancer shaft drive gear.

7 Refer to Section 24 and examine the main bearing shells. If they are scored, badly scuffed or appear to have been seized, new shells must be installed. Always renew the main bearing shells as a set. If any are badly damaged, check the corresponding crankshaft journal. Evidence of extreme heat, such as discoloration, indicates that lubrication failure has occurred. Be sure to check the oil pump, pressure regulator and all oil holes and passages thoroughly before reassembling the engine.

8 Inspect the crankshaft journals, paying particular attention where damaged bearings have been discovered. If the journals are scored or pitted in any way a new crankshaft will be required. Note that undersize bearing shells are not available, precluding the option of re-grinding the crankshaft.

9 Place the crankshaft on V-blocks and check the runout at the main bearing journals using a dial gauge (see *Tools and Workshop Tips* in the *Reference* Section). Compare the reading to the maximum specified at the beginning of this Chapter. If the runout exceeds the limit, a new crankshaft must be installed.

Oil clearance check

10 Whether new bearing shells are being

fitted or the original ones are being re-used, the main bearing oil clearance should be checked before the engine is reassembled. Main bearing oil clearance is measured with a product known as Plastigauge. Note: *On 750 models, the balancer shaft bearing oil clearance can be checked at the same time if required (see Section 29).*

11 If not already done, remove the bearing shells from the crankcases.

12 Use a suitable solvent to clean the backs of the bearing shells and the bearing seats in both crankcases, and the main bearing journals on the crankshaft. Remove all traces of old sealant from the middle and upper crankcase mating surfaces with a suitable solvent

13 Press the bearing shells into their seats, ensuring that the tab on each shell engages in the notch in the crankcase **(see illustration 28.31)**. Make sure the bearings are fitted in the correct locations and take care not to touch bearing surfaces with your fingers.

14 Lay the crankshaft in position in the upper crankcase **(see illustration 28.3a)**. If removed, fit the dowels into the crankcase **(see illustration 19.12a)**.

15 Cut five appropriate size lengths of Plastigauge (they should be slightly shorter than the width of the crankshaft journals). Place a strip of Plastigauge along the centreline of each journal **(see illustration)**.

28.6 Check the primary drive gear (A) and on 750 models the balancer drive gear (B)

28.15 Lay a strip of Plastigauge along the centreline of each journal

28.19 Compare the width of the crushed
Plastigauge with the scale provided

28.21a Crankshaft journal size codes
(arrowed)

28.21b Measuring the crankshaft journals

Do not place Plastigauge over the oil holes in the crankshaft. **Note:** *It is essential that, throughout this procedure, the crankshaft does not rotate in the crankcase.*

16 Carefully fit the lower crankcase onto the upper crankcase, ensuring that the Plastigauge is not disturbed – if the transmission shafts and selector drum and forks have not been removed refer to Section 19, Steps 18 and 19 to ensure everything is correctly aligned for joining the crankcases **(see illustration 19.10)**. Make sure the dowels locate correctly and that the lower crankcase half is correctly seated. **Note:** *Do not tighten the crankcase bolts if the casing is not correctly seated.*

17 Clean the threads of the 9 mm crankshaft journal bolts and install them in their original locations **(see illustration 19.9)**. Tighten the bolts a little at a time in the numerical sequence shown, to the torque setting specified at the beginning of this Chapter (see Section 19, Steps 21 and 22).

18 Unscrew the crankshaft journal bolts a little at a time in the **reverse** order of the tightening sequence shown until they are all finger-tight, then remove the bolts. Carefully lift off the lower crankcase, making sure the Plastigauge is not disturbed.

19 Compare the width of the crushed Plastigauge on each crankshaft journal to the scale printed on the Plastigauge envelope to obtain the main bearing oil clearance **(see illustration)**. Compare the reading to the specifications at the beginning of this Chapter.

If the clearance is within the range specified and the bearings are in perfect condition, they can be reused.

20 Carefully scrape away all traces of the Plastigauge from the crankshaft journals and bearing shells using a fingernail or other object which will not score the bearing surfaces.

21 If the clearance is beyond the service limit, first check the crankshaft journal size code. The crankshaft journal size code is stamped on the outer left-hand crankshaft web and will be either an A, B or C **(see illustration)**. Measure the actual diameter of the crankshaft journal with a micrometer and compare the result with the Specifications at the beginning of this Chapter **(see illustration)**. For example, on 600 models, if the journal being measured is code A, the Specifications indicate that the service limit for that journal is 29.994 mm. If the journal diameter is larger than the service limit, new bearing shells can be fitted (see Steps 23 and 24). If the journal diameter is smaller than the service limit, the crankshaft must be replaced with a new one. Always renew all of the shells (on all five journals) at the same time.

22 Install the new shells and check the oil clearance once again.

Bearing shell selection

23 New shells for the main bearings are supplied on a selected fit basis. Size codes for the crankshaft journals are stamped on the outer left-hand crankshaft web and will be either an A, B or C **(see illus-**

tration 28.21a). The first (top) letter is for the outer left-hand journal, and so on. The corresponding bearing seat size codes are stamped into the rear of the upper crankcase and will be either an A, B or C **(see illustration)**. **Note:** *On 750 models, the bottom two code letters are for the balancer shaft bearings.*

24 A corresponding range of bearing shells is available. To select the correct shells, use the table to cross-refer the crankshaft journal size code with the crankcase seat size code to determine the colour-code for the shells required. For example, if the crankcase seat size code is B, and the crankshaft journal size code is C, then the bearing required is Yellow. The colour is marked on the side of the shell **(see illustration 25.27)**.

Crankcase seat code	Crankshaft journal code		
	A	B	C
A	Green	Black	Brown
B	Black	Brown	Yellow
C	Brown	Yellow	Blue

Thrust bearing check and selection

25 The thrust bearings are located in the upper crankcase between the crank webs and the centre main bearing housing. The thrust bearing clearance should be checked before the engine is reassembled.

26 Fit the thrust bearings **(see illustration 28.4)** then lay the crankshaft in the upper crankcase **(see illustration 28.3a)**. Push the crankshaft as far as it will go toward the left-hand (alternator) side of the crankcase so that there is no clearance between the crank and the right-hand thrust bearing. Insert a feeler gauge between the crank and the left-hand thrust bearing and measure the thrust bearing clearance **(see illustration)**. Compare the result with the Specifications at the beginning of this Chapter. If the clearance is excessive, adjust it as follows.

27 Remove the right-hand thrust bearing, then measure its thickness with a micrometer and compare the result with the Specifications at the beginning of this Chapter **(see**

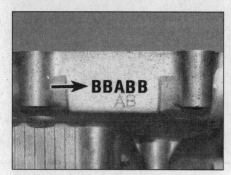

28.23 Crankshaft bearing seat size codes
(arrowed)

28.26 Measuring the clearance between
the crank and the left-hand thrust bearing

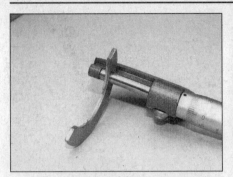

28.27 Measuring the thickness of the right-hand thrust bearing

28.28 Measure the gap between the crankcase and the web (arrowed)

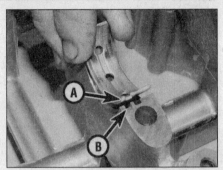

28.31 Ensure tab (A) locates in notch (B)

illustration). If the bearing is within the specifications, install it in its location, then follow Step 28. If the bearing is thinner than the specified size, fit a new bearing, then measure the thrust bearing clearance again (see Step 26). If the clearance is still excessive, follow Step 28. **Note:** *There is only one size for the right-hand thrust bearing, and its colour code is green.*

28 Remove the left-hand thrust bearing, then push the crankshaft as far as it will go toward the left-hand (alternator) side of the crankcase so that there is no clearance between the crank and the right-hand thrust bearing. Insert feeler gauges between the crank and the main bearing housing where the left-hand bearing fits, and measure the clearance **(see illustration).** Using the tables shown, select a new left-hand thrust bearing according to the clearance measured. For example, if the

clearance with the bearing removed is 2.495 mm, the bearing required is colour-coded blue. Re-check the clearance with the new bearings (see Step 26).

Thrust bearing selection table

Left-hand bearing clearance (bearing removed)	Bearing colour-code required
2.430 to 2.460 mm	Red
2.460 to 2.485 mm	Black
2.485 to 2.510 mm	Blue
2.510 to 2.535 mm	Green
2.535 to 2.560 mm	Yellow
2.560 to 2.585 mm	White

Installation

29 If removed, install the piston/connecting rod assemblies in the cylinders (see Section 25).

30 Ensure that the backs of the bearing shells, the bearing seats in the crankcases and the crankpin journals are clean. If new shells are being fitted, ensure that all traces of the protective grease are cleaned off using paraffin (kerosene). Dry the shells, seats and journals with a clean, lint-free cloth.

31 Install the shells, making sure the tab on each shell engages the notch in the bearing seat **(see illustration).** Make sure the bearings are fitted in their correct locations and take care not to touch any bearing surfaces with your fingers.

32 Lubricate the shells, preferably with molybdenum oil (a 50/50 mixture of molybdenum paste and clean engine oil) or clean engine oil.

33 Lubricate and fit the thrust bearings on each side of the centre main bearing housing, making sure the right-hand one is colour-coded green **(see illustration 28.4).** Make sure the oil grooves face out.

34 Lower the crankshaft into position in the upper crankcase, making sure the thrust bearings are not dislodged **(see illustration 28.3a).** Connect the piston/connecting rod assemblies to the crankshaft (see Section 25).

35 On 750 models, install the balancer shaft, making sure that it is correctly timed to the crankshaft (see Section 29).

36 Reassemble the crankcases (see Section 19).

29.2a Align the punch mark on the balancer with the square mark on the crankshaft . . .

29.2b . . . then lift the balancer shaft out

29.3 Remove the thrust washers

29.4a Note how the punch mark on the pinion aligns with the index mark on the balancer shaft . . .

29 Balancer shaft (750 models)

Removal

1 Separate the crankcases (see Section 19).

2 Turn the crankshaft until the punch mark on the balancer shaft pinion aligns with the index mark on the crankshaft gear, then lift the balancer shaft out of the upper crankcase **(see illustrations).**

3 Remove the thrust washer from each end of the shaft **(see illustration).**

4 Note how the punch mark on the balancer pinion aligns with the index mark on the balancer shaft **(see illustration).** Carefully pull

29.4b ... and how the ribs locate between the dampers

29.8 Check the shells (arrowed) in each crankcase half

29.13 Measuring the balancer shaft journal

the pinion off the shaft, noting how the shaft ribs locate between the dampers on the inside of the pinion (see illustrations).

Inspection

5 Clean the balancer shaft with a suitable solvent, paying particular attention to flush out the oil passage. If available, blow through the oil passage with compressed air.
6 Inspect the pinion for wear or damage. If any of the gear teeth are excessively worn, chipped or broken, the pinion must be renewed. Inspect the drive gear on the crankshaft (see illustration 28.6).
7 Check the dampers for signs of wear or deterioration and replace them with a new set if necessary.
8 Examine the balancer shaft bearing shells (see illustration). If they are scored, badly scuffed or appear to have been seized, new shells must be installed. Always replace the bearing shells as a set. If any are badly damaged, check the corresponding balancer shaft journal.
9 Examine the balancer shaft journals, paying particular attention where damaged bearings have been discovered. If the journals are scored or pitted in any way a new balancer shaft should be fitted.
10 Reassemble the shaft ensuring that the punch mark on the pinion aligns with the index mark on the shaft (see Step 4).

Oil clearance check

11 Whether new bearing shells are being fitted or the original ones are being re-used, the balancer shaft bearing oil clearance should

be checked before the engine is reassembled. Bearing oil clearance is measured with a product known as Plastigauge.
12 Follow Steps 12 to 20 in Section 28, and apply the same procedure for checking the crankshaft oil clearance to the balancer shaft. **Note:** *The balancer shaft oil clearance can be checked separately or at the same time as the crankshaft oil clearance if required.* Fit the thrust washers on the balancer shaft, then install the shaft in the crankcase (see illustrations 29.3 and 2b). Install the 9 mm crankshaft journal bolts and tighten them to the specified torque, then install the four 8 mm crankcase bolts on the balancer shaft housing and tighten them to the specified torque (see Section 19).
13 If the clearance is beyond the service limit, first check the balancer shaft journal size code. The journal size code is stamped on the body of the shaft and will be either an A or B. Measure the actual diameter of the shaft journal with a micrometer and compare the result with the Specifications at the beginning of this Chapter (see illustration). For example, if the journal being measured is code A, the Specifications indicate that the service limit for that journal is 22.984 mm. If the journal diameter is larger than the service limit, new bearing shells can be fitted (see Steps 15 and 16). If the journal diameter is smaller than the service limit, the shaft must be replaced with a new one. Always renew all of the shells (on both journals) at the same time.
14 Install the new shells and check the oil clearance once again.

Bearing shell selection

15 New shells for the balancer shaft bearings are supplied on a selected fit basis. Size codes for the shaft journals are stamped on the body of the shaft and will be either an A or B. The left-hand letter is for the left-hand journal, the right-hand letter is for the right-hand journal. The corresponding bearing seat size codes are stamped into the rear of the upper crankcase below the main bearing size codes and will be either an A or B (see illustration).
16 A corresponding range of bearing shells is available. To select the correct shells, use the table to cross-refer the balancer shaft journal size code with the crankcase seat size code to determine the colour code for the shells required. For example, if the crankcase seat size code is A, and the balancer shaft size code is B, then the bearing required is black. The colour is marked on the side of the shell (see illustration 25.27).

Crankcase seat code	Balancer shaft journal code	
	A	B
A	Green	Black
B	Black	Brown

Installation

17 Ensure that the backs of the bearing shells, the bearing seats in the crankcases and the balancer shaft journals are clean. If new shells are being fitted, ensure that all traces of the protective grease are cleaned off using paraffin (kerosene). Dry the shells, seats and journals with a clean, lint-free cloth.
18 Install the shells, making sure the tab on each shell engages the notch in the bearing seat (see illustration 29.8). Make sure the bearings are fitted in their correct locations and take care not to touch any bearing surfaces with your fingers.
19 Lubricate the shells with molybdenum oil (a 50/50 mixture of molybdenum paste and clean engine oil).
20 Fit the thrust washers on the balancer shaft (see illustration 29.3).
21 With the crankshaft installed, align the punch mark on the balancer shaft pinion with the index mark on the crankshaft gear (see illustration 29.2a), then install the balancer shaft (see illustration).
22 Reassemble the crankcases (see Section 19).

29.15 Balancer shaft bearing seat size codes (arrowed)

29.21 Align the marks and install the balancer shaft

30 Running-in procedure

1 Make sure the engine oil level and coolant level are correct (see *Pre-ride checks*). Make sure there is fuel in the tank.
2 Start the engine and let it run at fast idle until it reaches normal operating temperature. Check carefully that there are no oil and coolant leaks.

⚠ **Warning: If the oil pressure warning LED doesn't go off, or it comes on while the engine is running, stop the engine immediately.**

3 If a lubrication failure is suspected, stop the engine immediately and try to find the cause. If an engine is run without oil, even for a short period of time, severe damage will occur.
4 Make sure the transmission and controls, especially the throttle and brakes, function properly before road testing the machine.
5 Treat the machine gently for the first few miles to make sure oil has circulated throughout the engine and any new parts installed have started to seat.
6 Upon completion of the road test, and after the engine has cooled down completely, recheck the valve clearances (Chapter 1) and check the engine oil level and coolant level (see *Pre-ride checks*).
7 Even greater care is necessary if a major engine overhaul has been undertaken. In the case of a new crankshaft or piston and connecting rod assemblies, the bike will have to be run in as when new. This means greater use of the transmission and a restraining hand on the throttle until at least 1000 miles (1600 km) have been covered. There's no point in keeping to any set speed limit – the main idea is to keep from labouring the engine and to gradually increase performance up to the 1000 mile (1600 km) mark. These recommendations can be lessened to an extent when only a top-end overhaul has been undertaken. Experience is the best guide, since it's easy to tell when an engine is running freely. The following maximum engine speed limitations (above), which Suzuki provide for new motorcycles, can be used as a guide.

600 models		
Up to 500 miles (800 km)	8000 rpm max	Vary throttle position/speed
500 to 1000 miles (800 to 1600 km)	12,000 rpm max	Vary throttle position/speed. Use full throttle for short bursts
Over 1000 miles (1600 km)	16,000 rpm max	Do not exceed tachometer red line
750 models		
Up to 500 miles (800 km)	7500 rpm max	Vary throttle position/speed
500 to 1000 miles (800 to 1600 km)	11,000 rpm max	Vary throttle position/speed. Use full throttle for short bursts
Over 1000 miles (1600 km)	15,000 rpm max	Do not exceed tachometer red line

Chapter 3
Cooling system

Contents

Degrees of difficulty

Easy, suitable for novice with little experience	Fairly easy, suitable for beginner with some experience	Fairly difficult, suitable for competent DIY mechanic	Difficult, suitable for experienced DIY mechanic	Very difficult, suitable for expert DIY or professional

Specifications

Coolant
Mixture type and capacity ....   see Chapter 1

Pressure cap
Cap valve opening pressure...................................   15.4 to 19.5 psi (1.08 to 1.37 Bar)

Cooling fan
Cooling fan cut-in temperature ....   105°C approx.
Cooling fan cut-out temperature ....   100°C approx.

Engine coolant temperature (ECT) sensor
Resistance
  @ 20°C ....   2.450 K-ohms approx.
  @ 50°C ....   0.811 K-ohms approx.
  @ 80°C ....   0.318 K-ohms approx.
  @ 110°C ....   0.142 K-ohms approx.

Thermostat
Opening temperature...   82°C
Valve lift ....   8 mm (min) @ 95°C

Torque settings
Coolant inlet union bolts.....................................   10 Nm
Cooling fan mounting bolts ....   8 Nm
Engine coolant temperature (ECT) sensor ....   18 Nm
Thermostat cover bolts ....   10 Nm
Thermostat housing bolts....................................   10 Nm
Water pump cover screws....................................   5.5 Nm
Water pump impeller bolt....................................   8 Nm
Water pump mounting bolts..................................   10 Nm

2.2a Remove the cap

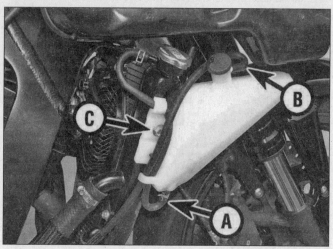

2.2b Radiator overflow hose (A), reservoir breather/overflow hose (B). Reservoir mounting bolt (C)

1 General information

The cooling system uses a water/antifreeze coolant to carry excess energy away from the engine in the form of heat. The cylinders are surrounded by a water jacket through which the coolant is circulated by thermo-syphonic action in conjunction with a water pump. The pump is mounted on the lower, left-hand side of the engine. Hot coolant flows from the pump, around the cylinders, to the thermostat and then to the radiator, where it is cooled by the passing air. It then flows through the water pump again and back to the engine where the cycle is repeated.

Coolant from the pump also flows through the oil cooler which is mounted on the front of the engine crankcases.

A thermostat is fitted in the system to prevent the coolant flowing through the radiator when the engine is cold, thus allowing the engine to reach normal operating temperature quickly. An electrically-controlled cooling fan is fitted behind the radiator to aid cooling in extreme conditions.

Coolant temperature information is supplied to the engine control module (ECM) and the instrument cluster display by the engine coolant temperature (ECT) sensor mounted in the rear of the cylinder head.

The complete cooling system is partially sealed and pressurised, the pressure being controlled by a spring-loaded valve in the radiator cap. By pressurising the coolant the boiling point is raised, preventing premature boiling in adverse conditions. The overflow pipe from the radiator is connected to a reservoir into which excess coolant is expelled under pressure. The discharged coolant automatically returns to the radiator when the engine cools.

⚠️ *Warning: Do not remove the pressure cap from the radiator when the engine is hot. Scalding hot coolant and steam may be blown out under pressure, which could cause serious injury. When the engine has cooled, place a thick rag, like a towel over the pressure cap; slowly rotate the cap anti-clockwise to allow any residual pressure to escape before removing the cap completely.*

⚠️ *Warning: Do not allow antifreeze to come in contact with your skin or painted surfaces of the motorcycle. Rinse off any spills immediately with plenty of water. Antifreeze is highly toxic if ingested. Never leave antifreeze lying around in an open container or in puddles on the floor; children and pets are attracted by its sweet smell and may drink it. Check with the local authorities about disposing of used antifreeze. Many communities will have collection centres for the safe disposal of antifreeze.*

Caution: At all times use the specified type of antifreeze, and always mix it with distilled water in the correct proportion. Antifreeze contains corrosion inhibitors which are essential to avoid damage to the cooling system. A lack of these inhibitors could lead to a build-up of corrosion which would block the coolant passages, resulting in overheating and severe engine damage. Distilled water must be used as opposed to tap water to avoid a build-up of scale which would also block the passages.

2 Coolant reservoir

1 The coolant reservoir is located on the inside of the right-hand fairing side panel.

Remove the panel for access (see Chapter 7).
2 Remove the reservoir cap **(see illustration)**. Place a suitable container underneath the reservoir, then release the clip securing the radiator overflow hose to the base of the reservoir **(see illustration)**. Detach the hose and allow the coolant to drain into the container.
3 Unscrew the reservoir mounting bolt and remove the reservoir, noting the routing of the hoses **(see illustration 2.2b)**. If required detach the reservoir breather/overflow hose from its union on the reservoir filler neck.
4 Installation is the reverse of removal. Make sure the hoses are correctly routed before tightening the mounting bolt **(see illustration 2.2b)**. On completion refill the reservoir as described in *Pre-ride checks*.

3 Cooling fan and fan relay

1 If the engine is overheating and the cooling fan isn't coming on, first check the coolant level (see *Pre-ride checks*). If the level is correct, check the cooling fan circuit fuse (see Chapter 8). If the fuse is blown, check the fan circuit for a short to earth (see *Wiring diagrams* at the end of Chapter 8). If the fuse is good, check the fan relay, then the fan motor, and then the ECT sensor, which acts as the fan switch via the ECM (see Section 4). If all components test good then check all the wiring and connectors in the relevant circuit, referring to electrical system fault finding at the beginning of Chapter 8 and to the wiring diagrams at the end of it.

Cooling fan relay

2 To access the relay on K6 and K7 models raise the fuel tank (see Chapter 4) – the relay is mounted on the front of the air filter housing

3.2a Cooling fan relay (arrowed) – K6 and K7 models

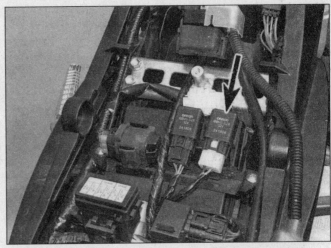

3.2b Cooling fan relay (arrowed) – K8 and K9 models

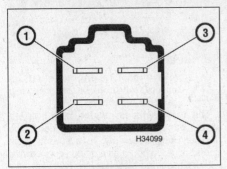

3.3 Cooling fan relay terminal identification

3.4 Disconnect the fan motor wiring connector (arrowed)

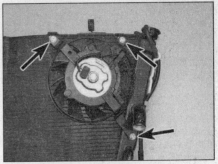

3.7 Cooling fan is secured by three bolts (arrowed)

on the left-hand side (see illustration). On K8 and K9 models remove the rider's seat (see Chapter 7) – the relay is mounted behind the battery on the left-hand side (see illustration).

3 Displace the relay and disconnect the wiring connector. Using a multimeter or test light, check for continuity between terminals 1 and 2 on the relay (see illustration). There should be no continuity. Now use jumper wires to connect the positive (+) terminal of a fully charged 12 volt battery to terminal 3 on the relay and the negative (-) battery terminal to terminal 4. There should now be continuity between terminals 1 and 2. If the relay fails either of the checks it must be replaced with a new one. If the relay is good check the fan motor and the ECT sensor

Cooling fan

Check

4 Remove the right-hand fairing side panel (see Chapter 7). Disconnect the fan motor wiring connector (see illustration). Check the connector for loose or broken wires and terminals.
5 Using a 12 volt battery and two jumper

wires, connect the battery positive (+) terminal to the blue wire terminal on the fan side of the wiring connector and the battery negative (-) terminal to the black wire terminal. Once connected the fan should operate. If it does not, then the fan motor is faulty.

Removal and installation

⚠ *Warning: The engine must be completely cool before carrying out this procedure.*

6 Remove the radiator (see Section 6).
7 Unscrew the three bolts securing the fan assembly to the radiator and remove the fan (see illustration).
8 Installation is the reverse of removal. Tighten the mounting bolts to the torque setting specified at the beginning of the chapter.

Check

1 The engine coolant temperature (ECT) sensor is located in the rear of the cylinder head on the left-hand side (see illustration). If

a sensor fault is indicated by the fuel injection system diagnostic process (see Chapter 4), carry out the preliminary checks as described in Chapter 4, Section 9.
2 To check the sensor resistance remove it from the cylinder head (see Steps 5 to 7).
3 Fill a small heatproof container with oil and place it on a stove. Using an ohmmeter set to the K-ohms scale, connect the meter probes to the sensor terminals, and using some wire or other support, suspend the sensor in the oil so that just the sensing portion and the

4.1 Engine coolant temperature (ECT) sensor wiring connector (arrowed)

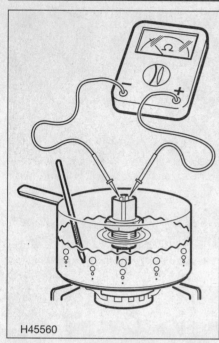

H45560

4.3 Coolant temperature sensor testing set-up

threads are submerged **(see illustration)**. Also place a thermometer capable of reading temperatures up to 140°C in the oil so that its bulb is close to the switch. **Note:** *None of the components should be allowed to touch the container directly.*

4 Check the meter reading and compare the

5.3 Undo the bolts and detach the cover . . .

5.5 Thermostat housing bolts (arrowed)

4.7 Unscrew the sensor using a spanner on the hex (arrowed)

result with the specifications at the beginning of this Chapter, then heat the oil slowly, stirring it gently.

⚠ **Warning: This must be done very carefully to avoid the risk of personal injury.**

As the temperature of the oil rises, the sensor resistance should fall. Check that the specified resistance is obtained at the correct temperature (see Specifications at the beginning of this Chapter). If the readings do not correspond, the sensor is faulty and must be replaced with a new one.

Renewal

⚠ **Warning: The engine must be completely cool before carrying out this procedure.**

5 The engine coolant temperature (ECT) sensor is located in the rear of the cylinder head on the left-hand side **(see illus-**

5.4 . . . and remove the thermostat

5.6 Thermostat should be closed at room temperature

tration 4.1)**. Raise the fuel tank, or remove it to improve access if required (see Chapter 4).

6 Disconnect the sensor wiring connector.

7 If required, drain the cooling system (see Chapter 1), otherwise place a rag on the crankcase underneath the sensor. Unscrew the sensor from the cylinder head **(see illustration)**. Discard the sealing washer as a new one must be fitted on reassembly.

8 Installation is the reverse of removal, noting the following:

● Fit a new sealing washer to the sensor.
● Tighten the sensor to the torque setting specified at the beginning of this Chapter.
● Top-up or refill the cooling system as necessary (see Chapter 1 and *Pre-ride checks*).

5 Thermostat

Removal

⚠ **Warning: The engine must be completely cool before carrying out this procedure.**

1 The thermostat is located in a housing on the back of the cylinder head below the throttle body assembly. It is automatic in operation and should give many years service without requiring attention. In the event of a failure, the valve will probably jam open, in which case the engine will take much longer than normal to warm up. Conversely, if the valve jams shut, the coolant will be unable to circulate and the engine will overheat. Neither condition is acceptable, and the fault must be investigated promptly.

2 Partially drain the cooling system (see Chapter 1). Raise the fuel tank, or remove it to improve access if required (see Chapter 4). On K8 and K9 California models remove the EVAP system purge control valve (see Chapter 4).

3 Undo the thermostat cover bolts and displace the cover **(see illustration)**. Slacken the clamp and detach the hose if required.

4 Withdraw the thermostat, noting how it fits **(see illustration)**.

5 If required, unscrew the bolts and displace the housing **(see illustration)**. Discard the O-ring – a new one must be used. Release the clip and detach the hose if required.

Check

6 Examine the thermostat visually before carrying out the test. If it remains in the open position at room temperature, it should be replaced with a new one **(see illustration)**.

7 Fill a small, heatproof container with cold water and place it on a stove. Using a piece of wire, suspend the thermostat in the water. Place a thermometer in the water so

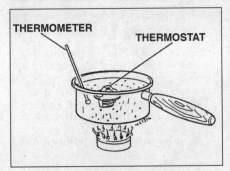

5.7 Thermostat testing set-up

6.2a Detach the hoses (arrowed) from the right-hand side . . .

6.2b . . . and the left-hand side (arrowed)

6.4 Unscrew the lower mounting bolt (arrowed)

6.5a Unscrew the upper bolt (arrowed) on each side . . .

that its bulb is close to the thermostat (see illustration). **Note:** *None of the components should be allowed to touch the container directly.*

8 Heat the water, noting the temperature when the thermostat opens, and compare the result with the specifications given at the beginning of this Chapter. Also check the amount the valve opens after it has been heated at 95°C for a few minutes and compare the measurement to the specifications. If the readings obtained differ from those given, the thermostat is faulty and must be replaced with a new one. .

9 In the event of thermostat failure, as an emergency measure only, it can be removed and the machine used without it. **Note:** *Take care when starting the engine from cold as it will take much longer than usual to warm up. Ensure that a new unit is installed as soon as possible.*

Installation

10 Installation is the reverse of removal, noting the following:

● If removed fit the housing using a new O-ring smeared with coolant, with the UP mark and hose union at the top, and tighten the bolts to the torque setting specified at the beginning of the Chapter (see illustration 5.5).

● Makes sure the rubber seal on the thermostat is correctly fitted and is in good condition (see illustration 5.7).

● Install the thermostat with the jiggle pin at the top (see illustration 5.4).

● Tighten the cover bolts to the specified torque setting (see illustration 5.3).
● Make sure the hoses are secure.
● Top up the cooling system (see *Pre-ride checks*).

6 Radiator

Removal

⚠️ *Warning: The engine must be completely cool before carrying out this procedure.*

1 Remove the fairing side panels (see Chapter 7). Drain the cooling system and reservoir (see Chapter 1). If required remove the reservoir (see Section 2).

2 Loosen the clips securing the coolant hoses

to the radiator and detach the hoses, noting where they fit (see illustrations).

3 Disconnect the fan motor wiring connector (see illustration 3.4).

4 Undo the radiator lower mounting bolt (see illustration).

5 Support the radiator, then undo the upper mounting bolts and remove the radiator (see illustrations). **Note:** *When removing components of the cooling system, be prepared to catch any residual fluids.*

6 If required remove the cooling fan (see Section 3). Note the spacers inside the bushes on the radiator mounting brackets and remove them for safekeeping (see illustration). If required, undo the bolt that secures the lower bracket to the crankcase and remove the bracket, noting how it locates (see illustration).

7 Check the radiator for damage and clear

6.5b . . . and remove the radiator

6.6a Note the spacers in the rubber bushes

6.6b Unscrew the bolt (arrowed) and remove the bracket if required

any dirt or debris that might obstruct airflow and inhibit cooling (see Chapter 1). Check the mounting bushes and fit new ones if they are damaged or deteriorated.

Installation

8 Installation is the reverse of removal, noting the following:

● Check the condition of the rubber bushes and replace them with new ones if necessary **(see illustration 6.6a)**.

● Make sure the spacers are fitted in the bushes **(see illustration 6.6a)**.

● Check the condition of the coolant hoses and the hose clips (see Chapter 1).

● On completion, refill the cooling system and check the level (see Chapter 1 and *Pre-ride checks*).

Pressure cap check

9 If problems such as overheating or loss of coolant occur, check the entire system as described in Chapter 1. The operation of the radiator cap pressure valve should be checked by a Suzuki dealer with the special tester required to do the job. If the cap is defective, replace it with a new one.

7 Water pump

Check

1 The water pump is located on the lower left-hand side of the engine. Check the area around the pump for signs of leakage.

7.7a Hold the impeller and unscrew the bolt (arrowed) . . .

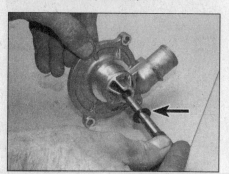

7.8 Withdraw the pump shaft – note the washer (arrowed)

7.2 Check the underside of the water pump for signs of leakage from the drain hole (arrowed)

2 To prevent leakage of water from the cooling system into the lubrication system a mechanical seal is fitted on the pump shaft behind the impeller. If the seal fails, a drain hole in the underside of the pump body allows the coolant to escape **(see illustrations)**. Look for telltale signs of leakage around the drain hole. To prevent oil entering the cooling system, an oil seal is installed on the shaft behind the mechanical seal. Do not remove the seals from the pump unnecessarily as once removed they cannot be reused.

Removal

3 Drain the coolant and the engine oil (see Chapter 1).
4 Loosen the clip securing the coolant hose to the pump housing and detach the hose.
5 Undo the bolts securing the pump to the

7.7b . . . and lift off the impeller

7.9a Remove the mechanical seal (arrowed)

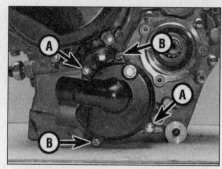

7.5 Unscrew the mounting bolts (A) and withdraw the pump. Pump cover screws (B)

crankcase and withdraw the pump **(see illustration)**. Discard the body O-ring.
6 If required, undo the cover screws and remove the cover.

Overhaul

7 Hold the impeller with some suitable grips, then unscrew the impeller bolt, noting the sealing washer and lock washer, and remove the impeller **(see illustrations)**. Inspect the sealing washer and replace it with a new one if damaged. If necessary for cleaning, remove the seal rings from the back of the impeller (a plastic one fits inside a rubber one), but take great care not to damage them as they are not listed as individual parts and come as an assembly with the impeller.
8 Withdraw the pump shaft from the rear of the pump body, noting the washer on the shaft **(see illustration)**. Check the shaft and its journal in the pump for wear and damage and replace the pump assembly with a new one if necessary.
9 To remove the seals, first pull the mechanical seal out of the pump body with a knife-edged bearing puller if available (see *Tools and Workshop Tips* in the reference Section), or using grips or pliers (the seal cannot be reused so do not worry about damaging it, but make sure you don't score the housing) **(see illustration)**. Next, lever out the oil seal using a small flat-bladed screwdriver, or push it out using a bar inserted from the back, noting how it fits **(see illustration)**. Take care not to damage or scratch the inside of the pump body.

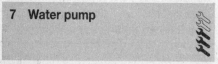

7.9b You can push the oil seal out from the back via the shaft hole (arrowed)

10 Lubricate the new oil seal lips with multi-purpose grease. Fit the oil seal with the marked side facing the mechanical seal. Carefully press the seal into its seat with a suitable sized socket. Now carefully press the new mechanical seal into place making sure the socket presses on the rim of the seal body, not the sprung seal itself **(see illustration 7.9a)**.

11 Slide the washer onto the pump shaft, then smear the shaft with molybdenum oil (50/50 molybdenum paste and engine oil) and insert it **(see illustration 7.8)**. Fit the new seal rings onto the back of the impeller **(see illustration)**. Fit the impeller onto the shaft **(see illustration 7.7b)**.

12 Install the convex side of the lock washer and the metal side of the sealing washer towards the head of the impeller bolt, then apply a suitable, non permanent thread locking compound to the bolt threads **(see illustration)**. Hold the impeller as before and tighten the bolt to the specified torque.

Installation

13 Installation is the reverse of removal, noting the following:
● Lubricate the pump cover O-ring with coolant before fitting it **(see illustration)**.
● Apply a smear of grease to the new pump body O-ring before fitting it **(see illustration)**.
● Align the slot in the water pump shaft with the drive tab on the oil pump shaft.
● Tighten the cover screws and pump mounting bolts to the specified torque settings.
● Fit the coolant hoses fully onto their unions and secure them with the clips.
● Replenish the coolant and the engine oil (see Chapter 1 and *Pre-ride checks*).

8 Coolant hoses and unions
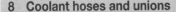

Removal

1 Before removing a hose, drain the coolant (see Chapter 1). **Note:** *When removing components of the cooling system, be prepared to catch any residual coolant.*

2 Use a screwdriver or small socket to loosen the larger-bore hose clips, then slide them back along the hose and clear of the union spigot. The smaller-bore hoses are secured by spring clips which can be expanded by squeezing their ends together with pliers.
Caution: The radiator unions are fragile. Do not use excessive force when attempting to remove the hoses.

7.11 Fit new seal rings (arrowed) to the impeller

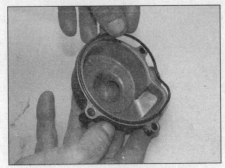

7.13a Fit a new O-ring into the groove in the cover

3 If a hose proves stubborn, release it by rotating it on its union before working it off. If all else fails, cut the hose with a sharp knife then slit it lengthways at the union so that it can be peeled off (see *Tools and Workshop Tips* in the reference Section). Whilst this means renewing the hose, it is preferable to buying a new radiator.

4 The coolant inlet union on the front of the cylinder block can be removed by unscrewing its bolts **(see illustration)**. If the union is removed, a new O-ring must be fitted.

Installation

5 Slide the clip onto the hose first. Where

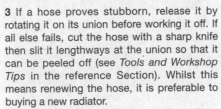

8.4 Coolant inlet union bolts (arrowed)

7.12 Make sure the washers are fitted as described

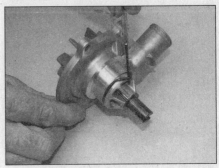

7.13b Fit a new O-ring into the groove in the body

> **HAYNES HiNT**
> *If the hose is difficult to push on its union, it can be softened by soaking it in very hot water, or alternatively a little soapy water can be used as a lubricant.*

present work the hose all the way onto its union as far as the raised stop **(see illustration)**.

6 Rotate the hose on its unions to settle it in position before sliding the clips into place and tightening them securely.

7 If removed, fit the coolant inlet union using a new O-ring smeared with coolant and tighten the bolts to the specified torque setting.

8.5 Work the hose on all the way to the stop (arrowed)

Chapter 4
Engine management system

Contents

Degrees of difficulty

Easy, suitable for novice with little experience	Fairly easy, suitable for beginner with some experience	Fairly difficult, suitable for competent DIY mechanic	Difficult, suitable for experienced DIY mechanic	Very difficult, suitable for expert DIY or professional

Specifications

General information
Cylinder identification (from left to right-hand side of the bike) 1–2–3–4
Firing order.. 1–2–4–3
Spark plugs .... see Chapter 1

Fuel
Grade
  600 European models............................ Unleaded, minimum 91 RON (Research Octane Number)
  600 US model.................................... Unleaded, minimum 87 ((R+M) /2 method)
  750 European models............................. Premium unleaded, minimum 95 RON (Research Octane Number)
  750 US models................................... Premium unleaded, minimum 90 ((R+M) /2 method)
Fuel tank capacity (including reserve)*
  K6 and K7 models .... 16.5 litres
  K8 and K9 models .... 17 litres
Reserve capacity (fuel warning light comes on)................. 3.5 litres (approx.)
*Fuel tanks on California models hold 0.5 litre less due to the EVAP components.

Fuel supply system
Operating pressure................................... 43 psi (2.97 Bars)

Fuel level sensor
Resistance
  K6 and K7 models
    In full position .... 179 to 185 ohms
    In empty position .... 3 to 5 ohms
  K8 and K9 models
    In full position .... 4.5 to 6.5 ohms
    In empty position .... 80 to 83 ohms

Throttle body

Identification marking
600K6 and K7 – California	01H1
600K6 and K7 – all other markets	01H0
600K8 and K9 – California	37H1
600K8 and K9 – all other markets	37H0
750K6 and K7 – California	02H1
750K6 and K7 – all other markets	02H0
750K8 and K9 – California	38H1
750K8 and K9 – all other markets	38H0

Bore diameter
600 models..	40 mm
750 models..	42 mm
Idle speed...	see Chapter 1
Fast idle speed – K6 and K7 models	1500 to 2000 rpm

Component test data

Atmospheric pressure (AP) sensor	
Input voltage...	4.5 to 5.5 V
Output voltage	3.6 V @ 760 mmHg
Crankshaft position (CKP) sensor	
Resistance	142 to 194 ohms
Peak voltage...	above 0.28 V
Engine coolant temperature (ECT) sensor	
Input voltage...	4.5 to 5.5 V
Output voltage	0.15 to 4.85 V
Resistance	approx. 2.45 K-ohms @ 20°C
Exhaust control valve (EXCV) servo position sensor	
Input voltage...	4.5 to 5.5 V
Output voltage	
K6 and K7 models	
Closed...	0.5 to 1.3 V
Open...	3.7 to 4.5 V
K8 and K9 models	
Closed...	0.45 to 1.4 V
Open...	3.6 to 4.55 V
Resistance	approx. 3.1 K-ohms
Gear position (GP) sensor voltage	above 0.6 V
Heated oxygen (HO2) sensor	
Resistance	
K6 and K7 models	4.0 to 5.0 ohms @ 23°C
K8 and K9 models	6.7 to 9.5 ohms @ 23°C
Output voltage	
At idle speed.......................................	less than 0.4 V
At 5000 rpm	more than 0.6 V
Idle speed control (ISC) valve resistance	approx. 80 ohms @ 20°C
Injector voltage..	Battery voltage (12 V approx)
Injector resistance	11 to 13 ohms @ 20°C
Intake air pressure (IAP) sensor	
Input voltage...	4.5 to 5.5 V
Output voltage	approx. 2.7 V at idle speed
Intake air temperature (IAT) sensor	
Input voltage...	4.5 to 5.5 V
Output voltage	0.15 to 4.85 V
Resistance	
K6 and K7 models	approx 2.45 K-ohms @ 20°C
K8 and K9 models	approx 2.58 K-ohms @ 20°C
PAIR system control valve solenoid resistance	
K6 and K7 models	18 to 22 ohms @ 20 to 30°C
K8 and K9 models	20 to 24 ohms @ 20 to 30°C
Secondary throttle position (STP) sensor	
Input voltage...	4.5 to 5.5 V
Output voltage	
Closed...	approx 0.6 V
Open...	approx 3.9 V
Resistance – K6 and K7 models	
Standard...	approx 4.69 K-ohms
Closed...	approx 0.5 K-ohms
Open...	approx 3.9 K-ohms

Component test data (continued)

Secondary throttle valve (STV) servo resistance .... approx 6.5 ohms
Throttle position (TP) sensor
   Input voltage... 4.5 to 5.5 V
   Output voltage
      Closed... 1.1 V approx
      Open.. 4.3 V approx
   Resistance – K6 and K7 models
      Standard.. approx 4.68 K-ohms
      Closed.. 1.1 K-ohms approx
      Open.. 4.3 K-ohms approx
Tip over (TO) sensor
   Resistance .... 16.5 to 22.3 K-ohms
   Voltage
      Upright .... 0.4 to 1.4 V approx
      At 65° angle .... 3.7 to 4.4 V approx

Ignition coils

Primary winding resistance .... 1.1 to 1.9 ohms
Secondary winding resistance
   K6 and K7 models .... 10.8 to 16.2 K-ohms
   K8 and K9 models .... 6.4 to 9.6 K-ohms
Primary peak voltage .... min 80 V when cranking

Torque settings

Camshaft position (CMP) sensor bolt .... 10 Nm
Exhaust system – K6 and K7 models
   Downpipe flange bolts .... 23 Nm
   Silencer clamp bolt.................................. 23 Nm
   Silencer mounting bolts .... 23 Nm
Exhaust system – K8 and K9 models
   Downpipe flange bolts .... 23 Nm
   Collector box bolts.................................. 23 Nm
   Silencer clamp bolt.................................. 23 Nm
   Silencer mounting bolts .... 25 Nm
   Heatshield screws .... 5.5 Nm
Fuel pump mounting bolts .... 10 Nm
Heated oxygen (HO2) sensor
   K6 and K7 model .... 48 Nm
   K8 and K9 models .... 25 Nm
TP and STP sensor screw .... 3.5 Nm

1 General information and precautions

General information

Fuel system

The fuel system consists of the fuel tank, incorporating the fuel pump, filter and pressure regulator, the fuel hose to the fuel rail on the throttle bodies, and the injectors that are located in each throttle body – two for each cylinder. The fuel pump is activated initially by the ignition switch and then by a relay. Fuel pressure is controlled within the pump by a pressure regulator. In the event of the machine falling over, a tip-over sensor cuts power to the fuel pump, injectors and ignition coils.

The entire fuel injection system is controlled by the engine control module (ECM) which monitors data sent from the various system sensors and adjusts fuel delivery to the engine accordingly. If a fault develops in the injection system, the FI warning LED illuminates on the instrument cluster, either on continuously or blinking depending on the severity of the fault, and FI is displayed on the LCD, either alternating with the temperature readout or continuously, depending on the severity of the fault. In the case of a minor fault (FI light on and LCD alternating between FI and engine temperature) the engine will continue to run enabling the machine to be ridden, although performance will be significantly reduced. For comprehensive fault diagnosis and certain service procedures, a Suzuki mode select switch (Pt. No. 09930-82720) is required.

The SDTV (Suzuki Dual Throttle Valve) fuel injection system uses two throttle valves and injectors in each throttle body. The main valve is actuated by the throttle cables from the handlebar twistgrip, the secondary valve is actuated by a servo controlled by the ECM for the purpose of smoothing airflow into the throttle body.

Ducts in the fairing feed air into the airbox which is housed under the fuel tank, and the air is then drawn through the filter and into the throttle bodies. An automatic fast idle system controls running from cold.

The exhaust system is a four-into-one design and incorporates an exhaust control valve (EXCV), operated by a servomotor, and a catalyst and heated oxygen sensor (HO2). All models feature a PAIR system which pulses filtered air into the exhaust ports to promote the burning of excess fuel in the exhaust gases, and on California models an EVAP emission control system prevents fuel vapour escaping into the atmosphere from the fuel tank.

Ignition system

The transistorised electronic ignition system is combined with the fuel injection system, both being controlled by the ECM (engine control module). The ignition system comprises a timing rotor, crankshaft position sensor (CKP sensor), engine control module (ECM) and ignition coils.

The triggers on the rotor, which is fitted to the right-hand end of the crankshaft, generate a signal in the CKP sensor as the crankshaft

rotates. The CKP sensor sends that signal to the ECM which, in conjunction with information received from the throttle position, gear position and engine coolant temperature sensors, calculates the ignition timing and supplies the ignition coils with the power necessary to produce a spark at the plugs. There is no provision for checking or adjusting the ignition timing. The ignition coil for each spark plug is incorporated in the spark plug cap.

The system incorporates a starter interlock circuit which will cut the ignition if the sidestand is put down whilst the engine is running and in gear, or if a gear is selected whilst the engine is running and the sidestand is down (see Chapter 8).

Maximum engine speed is restricted by the ECM to prevent engine damage.

Note: *Individual engine management system components can be checked but not repaired. If system troubles occur, and the faulty component can be isolated, the only cure for the problem in most cases is to replace the part with a new one. Keep in mind that most electronic parts, once purchased, cannot be returned. To avoid unnecessary expense, make very sure the faulty component has been positively identified before buying a new part.*

Precautions

⚠ *Warning: Petrol (gasoline) is extremely flammable, so take extra precautions when you work on any part of the fuel system. Don't smoke or allow open flames or bare light bulbs near the work area, and don't work in a garage where a natural gas-type appliance is present. If you spill any fuel on your skin, rinse it off immediately with soap and water. When you perform any kind of work on the fuel system, wear safety glasses and have a fire extinguisher suitable for a class B type fire (flammable liquids) on hand.*

Always perform service procedures in a well-ventilated area to prevent a build-up of fumes.

Never work in a building containing a gas appliance with a pilot light, or any other form of naked flame. Ensure that there are no naked light bulbs or any sources of flame or sparks nearby.

Do not smoke (or allow anyone else to smoke) while in the vicinity of petrol (gasoline) or of components containing it. Remember the possible presence of vapour from these sources and move well clear before smoking.

Check all electrical equipment belonging to the house, garage or workshop where work is being undertaken (see the Safety first! section of this manual). Remember that certain electrical appliances such as drills, cutters etc. create sparks in the normal course of operation and must not be used near petrol (gasoline) or any component containing it. Again, remember the possible presence of fumes before using electrical equipment.

Always mop up any spilt fuel and safely dispose of the rag used.

Any stored fuel that is drained off during servicing work must be kept in sealed containers that are suitable for holding petrol (gasoline), and clearly marked as such; the containers themselves should be kept in a safe place. Note that this last point applies equally to the fuel tank if it is removed from the machine; also remember to keep its filler cap closed at all times.

Read the Safety first! section of this manual carefully before starting work.

Owners of machines used in the US, particularly California, should note that their machines must comply at all times with Federal or State legislation governing the permissible levels of noise and of pollutants such as unburnt hydrocarbons, carbon monoxide etc. that can be emitted by those machines. All vehicles offered for sale must comply with legislation in force at the date of manufacture and must not subsequently be altered in any way which will affect their emission of noise or of pollutants.

In practice, this means that adjustments

may not be made to any part of the fuel, ignition or exhaust systems by anyone who is not authorised or mechanically qualified to do so, or who does not have the tools, equipment and data necessary to properly carry out the task. Also if any part of these systems is to be renewed it must be renewed with only genuine Suzuki components or by components which are approved under the relevant legislation. The machine must never be used with any part of these systems removed, modified or damaged.

2 Fuel tank

⚠ *Warning: Refer to the precautions given in Section 1 before starting work.*

Raise

1 Make sure the fuel cap is secure. Remove the rider's and passenger's seats (see Chapter 7). Remove the fuel tank prop from the storage space underneath the passenger's seat **(see illustration)**.
2 On K6 and K7 models carefully pull the back of each tank trim panel away to release the Velcro pads, then draw the panel to the rear to release the hook from the tab on the tank **(see illustrations)**.

2.1 Unclip and remove the fuel tank prop

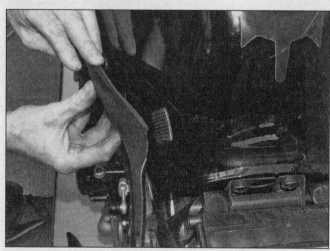

2.2a Pull the panel away to release the Velcro . . .

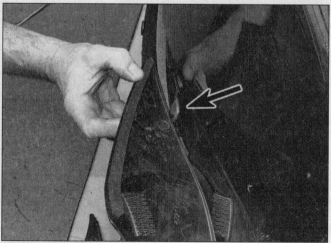

2.2b . . . then draw it back to free the hook from the tab (arrowed)

2.3a Undo the front mounting bolt

2.3b Pull the seat cowling out so the tank does not catch on it

2.3c Support the front of the tank with the prop

3 Undo the bolt securing the front of the fuel tank (see illustration). Raise the front of the tank, on K8 and K9 models pulling the front of the seat cowling out on each side so the tank trim panels fit inside them (see illustration), and support it with the prop, locating one end in the hole in the steering stem nut and the other in the collar in the mounting bolt hole (see illustration).

Removal

4 Make sure the ignition switch is OFF. Raise the tank (see above).

5 Pull the drain and breather hoses off their unions on the underside of the tank (see illustration).

6 Disconnect the fuel pump wiring connector (see illustration).

7 Place a rag underneath the fuel hose to catch any residual fuel. Release the clip on the fuel hose connector and disconnect the hose from the union on the fuel rail (see illustrations).

8 Remove the prop and lower the tank.

Undo the pivot bolt securing the tank bracket to the frame, then lift the tank away (see illustrations). Inspect the tank support rubbers for signs of damage or deterioration and replace them with new ones if necessary. Note the sleeve for the rear bolt and take care not to lose it (see illustration 2.9a).

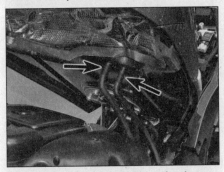

2.5 Detach the drain and breather hoses (arrowed)

Installation

9 Check that the tank mounting rubbers and the sleeve for the rear bolt are fitted (see illustration). Make sure the grommet and collar are in place in the tank's front mounting (see illustration).

2.6 Disconnect the fuel pump wiring connector

2.7a Release the clips . . .

2.7b . . . and detach the fuel hose connector

2.8a Unscrew the bolt (arrowed) . . .

2.8b . . . and remove the tank

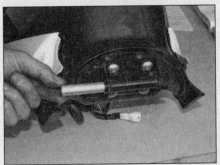

2.9a Make sure the rear bolt sleeve is in the bracket

2.9b Make sure the collar is in the front grommet

2.10 Align the holes and slide the bolt through

10 Carefully lower the fuel tank into position on the frame **(see illustration 2.8b)**. Align the sleeve in the bracket with the mounting lugs on the frame then slide the pivot bolt through and tighten it finger-tight **(see illustration)**.

11 Raise the front of the tank and support it with the prop **(see illustration 2.3c)**.

12 Align the fuel hose connector with the union on the bottom of the fuel pump and push it on fully so that the clip engages **(see illustration 2.7b)**.

13 Check the ignition switch is OFF, then connect the fuel pump wiring connector **(see illustration 2.6)**.

14 Push the breather and drain hoses fully onto their unions on the bottom of the tank **(see illustration 2.5)**.

15 Remove the prop and lower the tank. Fit the bolt with its washer and tighten the bolt **(see illustration 2.3a)**. Tighten the tank rear bolt.

16 Start the engine and check that there is no sign of fuel leakage, then turn it OFF.

17 Clip the fuel tank prop in the storage space underneath the passenger's seat, then install the seats **(see illustration 2.1)**.

Cleaning and repair

18 All repairs to the fuel tank should be carried out by a professional who has experience in this critical and potentially dangerous work. Even after cleaning and flushing the fuel system, explosive fumes can remain and ignite during repair of the tank.

19 If the fuel tank is removed from the bike, it should not be placed in an area where sparks or open flames could ignite the fumes coming

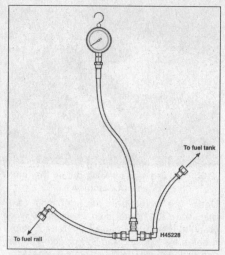

3.2 Fuel pressure gauge and hose set-up

out of the tank. Be especially careful inside garages where a natural gas-type appliance is located, because the pilot light could cause an explosion.

3 Fuel pressure check

> **Warning: Refer to the precautions given in Section 1 before starting work.**

Special Tool: *A fuel pressure gauge is required for this procedure.*

1 To check the fuel pressure, a suitable gauge, gauge hose and adapters are needed. Suzuki provides service tools (Pt. Nos. 09915-77331, 09915-74521, 09940-40211 and 09940-40220) for this purpose.

2 Raise the fuel tank, then disconnect the fuel hose from the fuel pump (see Section 2). Use the adapters to connect the gauge between the fuel tank and the fuel rail as shown **(see illustration)**.

3 Turn the ignition switch ON and check the pressure reading on the gauge. The pressure should be as specified at the beginning of this Chapter.

4 Turn the ignition OFF and disconnect the gauge and adapters. Use a rag to catch any

residual fuel as before. Reconnect the fuel hose to the pump (see Section 2).

5 If the pressure is too low, check for a leak in the fuel supply system, a blocked fuel filter (see Section 6), a faulty pressure regulator or a faulty fuel pump.

6 If the pressure is too high, either the pressure regulator or the fuel pump check valve is faulty.

7 Suzuki provides no test procedure for the pressure regulator. A new regulator is available as an integral part of the pump filter cartridge. Remove the pump and make sure the filter cartridge/regulator has not come loose from the pump assembly (this is unlikely), then if necessary disassemble the pump and replace the cartridge/regulator with a new one (see Section 6). The fuel check valve is an integral part of the pump and is not available separately.

4 Fuel pump relay

1 On K6 and K7 models, raise the fuel tank (see Section 2) – the relay is mounted on the front of the air filter housing on the right-hand side **(see illustration)**. On K8 and K9 models remove the rider's seat (see Chapter 7) – the relay is to the rear of the battery in the middle **(see illustration)**.

2 Displace the relay and disconnect the wiring connector. Using a multimeter or test light, check for continuity between terminals 1 and 2 on the relay **(see illustration)**. There should be no continuity. Now use jumper wires to connect the positive (+) terminal of a fully charged 12 volt battery to terminal 3 on the relay and the negative (-) battery terminal to relay terminal 4. There should be continuity shown across terminals 1 and 2. If the relay fails either of the checks, renew it.

5 Fuel pump

> **Warning: Refer to the precautions given in Section 1 before starting work.**

4.1a Fuel pump relay (arrowed) – K6 and K7 models

4.1b Fuel pump relay (arrowed) – K8 and K9 models

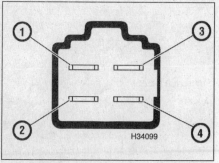

4.2 Fuel pump relay terminal identification

5.3a Fuel pump (arrowed) – K6 and K7 models

5.3b Fuel pump (arrowed) – K8 and K9 models

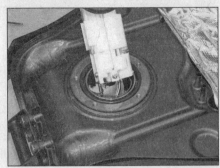

5.3c Carefully manoeuvre the pump out . . .

1 The fuel pump assembly, incorporating the pump, strainer, level sensor and filter cartridge/pressure regulator, is located inside the fuel tank. When the ignition is switched ON, it should be possible to hear the pump run for a few seconds until the system is up to pressure. If you can't hear anything, first check the fuse (see Chapter 8), then check the relay (see Section 4). If they are good, check the wiring and terminals for physical damage or loose or corroded connections and rectify as necessary (see the *Wiring Diagrams* at the end of Chapter 8). If the pump still will not run, check the tip-over (TO) sensor (see Section 10). If that is good, and assuming the ECM is OK, fit a new pump assembly – the pump itself is not available separately, though the strainer, level sensor and filter cartridge/pressure regulator all are. Note that if the pump has failed and you are buying a complete new pump assembly, before discarding the old assembly remove the strainer components, the level sensor, and the filter cartridge/pressure regulator and keep them as spares, just in case! (see Section 6).

Removal

2 The fuel pump is located inside the fuel tank. Remove the tank and drain it (see Section 2).
3 Turn the tank upside down and rest it on some clean rag to protect the paintwork. Undo the bolts securing the base to the underside of the tank and carefully lift out the pump, taking care not to snag the level sensor arm **(see illustrations)**. Discard the O-ring as a new one must be fitted on reassembly.
4 If required, disassemble the pump assembly to clean the strainer, replace the filter cartridge/pressure regulator, and check the operation of the level sensor (see Section 6).

Installation

5 Check that all the wiring terminals for the fuel pump and the level sensor are tight.
6 Smear the new O-ring lightly with grease and fit it into the recess around the aperture on the underside of the fuel tank **(see illustration)**.
7 Install the pump and align the holes in the base with the threaded holes in the tank – on

5.3d . . . taking care not to snag the sensor arm

K6 and K7 models the fuel hose union points to the right-hand side of the bike, and on K8 and K9 models it points to the left-hand side **(see illustration 5.3a or b)**. Apply a suitable thread locking compound to the bolts and tighten them finger-tight, then tighten them evenly and a little at a time in a criss-cross pattern to the torque setting specified at the beginning of this Chapter.
8 Install the fuel tank (see Section 2). Make sure there is no fuel leakage around the pump base.

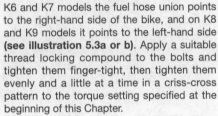

6 Fuel strainer, filter cartridge/pressure regulator, and fuel level sensor

⚠ **Warning: Refer to the precautions given in Section 1 before starting work.**

K6 and K7 models

Fuel strainer

1 Remove the fuel pump assembly (see Section 5).
2 Undo the nuts and remove the washers securing the pump and level sensor feed wires to the terminals on the base and detach the wires, noting their position **(see illustration overleaf)**. Undo the screws on the holding arms coming off the pump base and detach the pump and level sensor earth wires, then remove the clip nuts.
3 Remove the fuel level sensor (Step 15) –

5.6 Fit a new O-ring smeared with grease into the recess

although not actually necessary it is easy to damage the sensor arm and so removal is advised as a precaution.
4 Pull the pump assembly out of the base. Discard the O-ring on the base fuel union as a new one must be fitted on reassembly. Clean any sediment out of the pump base.
5 Clean any sediment off the strainer gauze with a soft brush or low pressure compressed air. If the strainer is damaged, or if there is sediment inside it, a new one should be fitted – release the clips and remove the fuel pump seat and rubber cushion, then remove the strainer from the bottom of the pump.
6 Install the components in the reverse order of disassembly, noting the following:
● Fit a new O-ring to the pump base fuel union and smear it with engine oil.
● Make sure the clip nuts are in place on both holding arms for the wire terminal retaining screws.
● Do not forget the washers with the wiring terminal nuts – the spring washer goes between the plain washer and the nut.

Fuel filter cartridge/pressure regulator

7 Remove the fuel pump assembly (see Section 5).
8 Remove the fuel level sensor (Step 15).
9 Release the earth wire clip **(see illustration 6.2)**.
10 Carefully separate the fuel filter cartridge/pressure regulator from the pump. Discard the rubber bush and the O-ring on the base fuel union as new ones must be used. There is no need to detach the fuel pressure regulator as

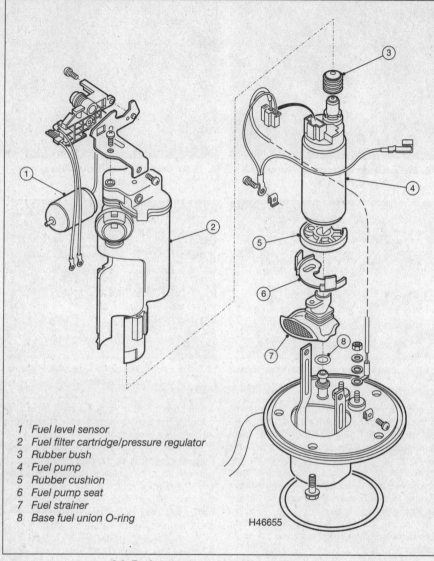

1 Fuel level sensor
2 Fuel filter cartridge/pressure regulator
3 Rubber bush
4 Fuel pump
5 Rubber cushion
6 Fuel pump seat
7 Fuel strainer
8 Base fuel union O-ring

H46655

6.2 Fuel pump assembly – K6 and K7 models

litres; when it drops to 1.0 litre the warning LED will remain on.

12 Remove the fuel pump assembly (see Section 5).

13 To check the sensor trace the wires from it and detach them from their terminals as in Step 2. Connect the probes of an ohmmeter to the wire terminals and measure the resistance of the sensor with the float in the raised (tank full) and lowered (tank empty) positions and compare the readings to the specifications at the beginning of the Chapter **(see illustrations 6.28a and b)**. Replace the sensor with a new one if necessary (Step 15).

14 If the tests show the level sensor to be good, check the wiring circuit to the instrument cluster (see Chapter 8).

15 To remove the sensor detach the wires as in Step 2, then undo the screws securing the sensor, separating it from its bracket if required. Note the routing of the wiring.

16 Installation is the reverse of removal.

K8 and K9 models

Fuel strainer

17 Remove the fuel pump assembly (see Section 5).

18 Detach the pump and level sensor feed wires from the terminals on the base, noting their position **(see illustration)**.

19 Remove the fuel level sensor (Step 30). Remove the fuel filter cartridge/pressure regulator (Step 25).

20 Pull the pump assembly off the base **(see illustration)**.

21 Remove the strainer from the bottom of the pump **(see illustration)**. Clean any sediment off the strainer gauze with a soft brush or low pressure compressed air. If the strainer is damaged, or if there is sediment inside it, a new one should be fitted.

22 Install the components in the reverse order of disassembly.

Fuel filter cartridge/pressure regulator

23 Remove the fuel pump assembly (see Section 5).

24 Remove the fuel level sensor (Step 30).

25 Carefully lever the fuel filter cartridge/ pressure regulator squarely up off the pump

it is an integral part of the filter cartridge and the new cartridge will come with one fitted.

11 Install the components in the reverse order of disassembly, noting the following:

● Fit a new rubber bush between the filter cartridge and the pump.

● Fit a new O-ring smeared with engine oil onto the pump base fuel union.

Fuel level sensor

Note: The fuel warning LED will flicker when the volume of fuel in the tank drops to 3.5

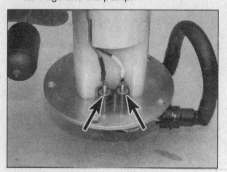

6.18 Detach the wires (arrowed)

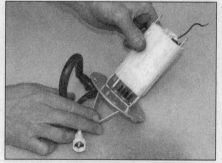

6.20 Pull the pump off the base

6.21 Remove and clean the strainer (arrowed)

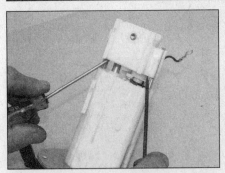

6.25a Lever the filter cartridge up off the pump and remove it

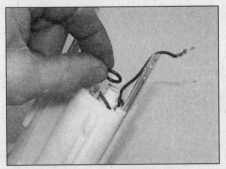

6.25b Remove the pump O-ring . . .

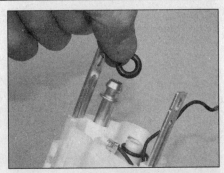

6.25c . . . and the base union O-ring and discard them

6.25d Remove the joint piece . . .

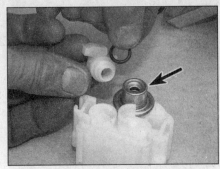

6.25e . . . and discard its O-ring. Fuel pressure regulator (arrowed)

using two screwdrivers **(see illustration)**. Remove the O-rings from the top of the pump and the base union and discard them as new ones must be used **(see illustrations)**. Remove the joint piece from the bottom of the filter cartridge and discard its O-ring. Do not detach the fuel pressure regulator as it is an integral part of the filter cartridge and the new cartridge will come with one fitted.

26 Install the components in the reverse order of disassembly, noting that new O-rings smeared with engine oil must be fitted onto the joint piece, the pump and the base fuel union **(see illustrations 6.25e, c and b)**.

Fuel level sensor

Note: *The fuel warning LED will flicker when the volume of fuel in the tank drops to 3.5 litres; when it drops to 1.5 litres the warning LED will remain on.*

27 Remove the fuel pump assembly (see Section 5).

28 To check the sensor connect the positive probe of an ohmmeter to the pink wire terminal on the base and the negative probe to the base itself and measure the resistance of the sensor with the float in the lowered (tank empty) and raised (tank full) positions **(see illustrations)**. Compare the readings to the specifications at the beginning of the Chapter. Replace the sensor with a new one if necessary (Step 30).

29 If the tests show the level sensor to be good, check the wiring circuit to the instrument cluster (see Chapter 8).

30 To remove the sensor detach the level sensor feed wire (pink) from its terminal on

the base and free it from its guide, noting its routing **(see illustration)**. Undo the screws securing the sensor and detach the pump and level sensor earth wires, noting which

connects where **(see illustrations)**. Separate the sensor from its bracket if required. Note the routing of the wiring.

31 Installation is the reverse of removal.

6.28a Connect the meter probes to the left-hand terminal and the base and measure the resistance in the empty position . . .

6.28b . . . and in the full position

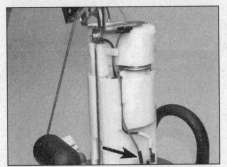

6.30a Detach the pink wire (arrowed) from the base and note its routing

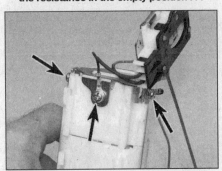

6.30b Undo the screws (arrowed) . . .

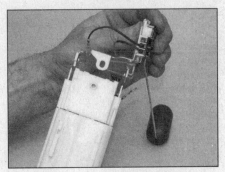

6.30c . . . and remove the sensor

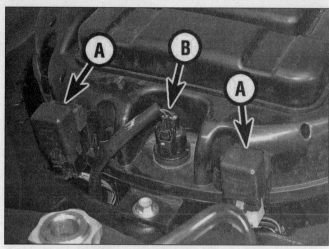

7.2a Displace the relays (A) and disconnect the wiring connector (B)

7.2b Remove the blanking cap (arrowed)

7 Air filter housing

Removal

1 Raise the fuel tank and support it with the prop, or for better access remove it altogether (see Section 2).

2 On K6 and K7 models displace the cooling fan and fuel pump relays from the front of the housing and disconnect the IAT sensor wiring connector (see illustration). Remove the blanking cap from the clamp screw access hole in each side of the frame (see illustration).

3 On K8 and K9 models insert a finger into the hole on the inside of the frame and press lightly against the inner end of the peg in the trim clip (see illustration) – this is to prevent the peg being pushed too far in and dropping inside the frame. Push the centre of the peg in from the outside, then draw the body of the clip out of the frame (see illustration).

4 Release the clip and disconnect the crankcase breather hose from the top of the housing (see illustration).

5 Loosen the clamp screws securing the housing to the throttle bodies – note that all 600 models and 750K6 models have four individual clamps (note their orientation), all other models have two paired clamps (see illustration). Undo the bolt securing the front of the housing to the frame, then lift the housing off the throttle bodies, making sure the clamps do not foul the fuel injector wiring connectors (see illustration). Note the seals between the housing inlets and the ducts in the frame.

6 On K6 and K7 models release the clip and disconnect the PAIR hose from the right-hand side of the housing (see illustration 7.7b).

7 On K8 and K9 models release the clips and disconnect the idle speed control valve hose from the back of the housing and the PAIR hose from the right-hand side, then disconnect the intake air temperature (IAT) sensor wiring connector from the left-hand side (see illustrations).

7.3a Place your finger behind the clip and push its centre in . . .

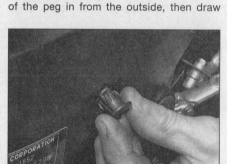

7.3b . . . then draw the body out of the frame

7.4 Detach the crankcase breather hose (arrowed)

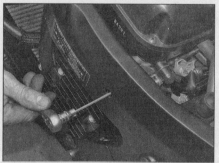

7.5a Slacken the clamp screws on each side via the access hole

7.5b Unscrew the bolt at the front

7.7a Detach the ISC valve hose . . .

7.7b . . . the PAIR hose . . .

7.7c . . . and the IAT sensor wiring connector

7.8a Fit the body into the hole . . .

7.8b . . . then fit the peg into the body

Installation

8 Installation is the reverse of removal. Make sure the inlet seals locate correctly against the ducts in the frame – there should be no gaps between them. Make sure all hoses and wiring are securely connected. On K8 and K9 models to refit the trim clip first draw the peg out of the body. Fit the body into the hole, then fit the peg into the body and push it in so it is flush **(see illustrations)**.

8 Fuel injection system description

1 The fuel injection system consists of two main component groups, the fuel supply circuit and the electronic control circuit.
2 The fuel supply circuit consists of the tank, pump and filter, pressure regulator and injectors. Fuel is pumped under pressure from the tank to the fuel rail, from which the individual injectors are fed. Operating pressure is maintained initially by the pump check valve and, once the engine is running, by the pressure regulator. The injectors spray pressurised fuel into the throttle bodies where it mixes with air and vaporises, before entering the cylinder where it is compressed and ignited.
3 The electronic control circuit consists of the engine control module (ECM), which operates and co-ordinates both the fuel injection and ignition systems, and the various sensors which provide the ECM with information on engine operating conditions.
4 The ECM monitors signals from the following sensors:
 Intake air temperature (IAT) sensor
 Intake air pressure (IAP) sensor
 Throttle position (TP) sensor
 Secondary throttle position (STP) sensor
 Camshaft position (CMP) sensor
 Crankshaft position (CKP) sensor
 Coolant temperature (ECT) sensor
 Atmospheric pressure (AP) sensor
 Gear position (GP) sensor
 Tip-over (TO) sensor
 Heated oxygen (HO2) sensor
5 Based on the information it receives, the ECM calculates the appropriate ignition and fuel requirements of the engine. By varying the length of the electronic pulse it sends to each injector, the ECM controls the length of time the injectors are held open and thereby the amount of fuel that is supplied to the engine. Fuel supply varies according to the engine's needs for starting, warming-up, idling, cruising and acceleration.
6 In the event of an abnormality in any of the sensor signals, the ECM will determine whether the engine can still be run safely. If it can, a back-up mode replaces the sensor signal with a fixed signal, restricting performance but allowing the bike to be ridden home or to a dealer. When this occurs, the LCD display in the instrument cluster will indicate the letters FI every two seconds (alternating with the coolant temperature reading), and the FI LED will come on. If the unit decides that the fault is too serious, the appropriate system will be shut down and the engine will not run. When this occurs, the LCD display in the instrument cluster will indicate the letters FI continuously, and the FI LED will flash. See Section 9 for fault diagnosis. Do not disconnect the wiring connectors from the ECM or disconnect the battery before accessing the fault codes as they will be erased.
7 The system incorporates two safety circuits. When the ignition is switched ON, the fuel pump runs for three seconds and pressurises the system. Thereafter the pump automatically switches off until the engine is started. The

9.2a On K6 and K7 models unscrew the bolts (arrowed) and displace the bridge . . .

9.2b . . . to access the connector

second circuit incorporates a tip-over sensor, which automatically switches off the fuel pump and cuts the ignition and injection circuits if the motorcycle falls over.

9.2c Remove the cover from the connector (K8/K9 model shown) . . .

9 Fuel injection system fault diagnosis

1 The system incorporates a self-diagnostic function whereby any faults are stored in the ECM memory. To access the appropriate fault code, a Suzuki mode select switch (Pt. No. 09930-82720) is required. The mode select switch is inexpensive and will be required for a number of testing procedures. **Note:** *Do not disconnect the battery, main fuse or ECM wiring connectors before recording the fault codes – the ECM memory is erased when they are disconnected.*

2 Remove the rider's seat (see Chapter 7). On K6 and K7 models undo the frame bridge bolts and move the bridge aside (see illustration). Locate the mode select switch wiring connector and remove the cover (see illustration). Make sure the ignition and the select switch are OFF. Connect the mode select switch (see illustration).

3 Start the engine, or if it will not start, crank the engine on the electric starter for at least 4 seconds. Turn the mode select switch ON (see illustration). The fault code(s) will be displayed on the LCD panel on the instrument cluster, in ascending order if there are more than on. Note the code(s) and identify the fault(s) from the table.

4 To check the fuel injection system components see Section 10.

5 Once the fault has been corrected, turn the ignition switch OFF (if not already done), then turn it back ON. If the fault has been cleared, the instrument display with indicate the code C00. Turn the mode select switch OFF and ignition switch OFF and disconnect the mode select switch. Refit the wiring connector cover and install the seat (see Chapter 7).

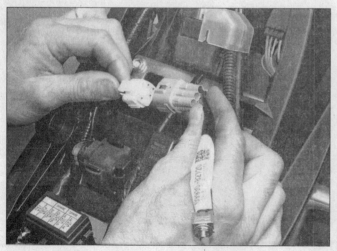

9.2d . . . and connect the mode select switch

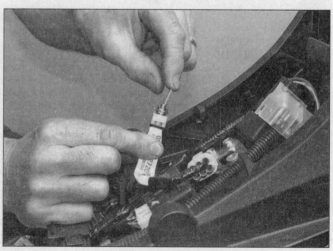

9.3 Turn the switch on

Fault code	Faulty component – symptoms	Possible causes
CHEC	No ECM signal – engine will not run	Kill switch OFF
		Faulty wiring or wiring connector
		Faulty ignition safety interlock system (clutch switch, sidestand switch, diode or gear position switch)
		Damaged ignition fuse
C00	No fault	System clear
C11	Camshaft position (CMP) sensor – engine will continue to run but will not restart once turned OFF	Faulty wiring or wiring connector
		Damaged sensor or intake cam pin
C12	Crankshaft position (CKP) sensor – engine will not run	Faulty wiring or wiring connector
		Damaged sensor or timing rotor
C13	Intake air pressure (IAP) sensor – engine will run, air pressure signal fixed at 760 mmHg	Faulty wiring or wiring connector
		Damaged sensor
C14	Throttle position (TP) sensor – engine will run, throttle position and ignition timing fixed	Faulty wiring or wiring connector
		Damaged sensor
C15	Engine coolant temperature (ECT) sensor – engine will run, coolant temperature signal fixed at 80°C	Faulty wiring or wiring connector
		Damaged sensor
C21	Intake air temperature (IAT) sensor – engine will run, air temperature signal fixed at 40°C	Faulty wiring or wiring connector
		Damaged sensor
C22	Atmospheric pressure (AP) sensor – engine will run, atmospheric pressure signal fixed at 760 mmHg	Faulty wiring or wiring connector
		Damaged sensor
C23	Tip-over (TO) sensor – engine will not run	Faulty wiring or wiring connector
		Damaged sensor
C24*	No. 1 cylinder ignition coil – engine will run on other 3 cylinders, fuel supply to No. 1 cylinder cut	Faulty wiring or wiring connector
		Damaged ignition coil
		Faulty power supply for the ignition system
C25*	No. 2 cylinder ignition coil – engine will run on other 3 cylinders, fuel supply to No. 2 cylinder cut	Faulty wiring or wiring connector
		Damaged ignition coil
		Faulty power supply for the ignition system
C26*	No. 3 cylinder ignition coil – engine will run on other 3 cylinders, fuel supply to No. 3 cylinder cut	Faulty wiring or wiring connector
		Damaged ignition coil
		Faulty power supply for the ignition system
C27*	No. 4 cylinder ignition coil – engine will run on other 3 cylinders, fuel supply to No. 4 cylinder cut	Faulty wiring or wiring connector
		Damaged ignition coil
		Faulty power supply for the ignition system
C28	Secondary throttle valve (STV) servo – engine will run, valve fixed in closed position	Faulty wiring or wiring connector
		Damaged servo motor
C29	Secondary throttle position (STP) sensor – engine will run, throttle valve fixed in closed position	Damaged sensor
C31	Gear position (GP) sensor – engine will run, signal fixed in 6th gear	Faulty wiring or wiring connector
		Damaged sensor
		Faulty gearchange mechanism
C32*	No. 1 fuel injector – engine will run on other 3 cylinders	Faulty wiring or wiring connector
		Damaged fuel injector
C33*	No. 2 fuel injector – engine will run on other 3 cylinders	Faulty wiring or wiring connector
		Damaged fuel injector
C34*	No. 3 fuel injector – engine will run on other 3 cylinders	Faulty wiring or wiring connector
		Damaged fuel injector
C35*	No. 4 fuel injector – engine will run on other 3 cylinders	Faulty wiring or wiring connector
		Damaged fuel injector
C36*	No. 1 secondary fuel injector – engine will run on other 3 cylinders	Faulty wiring or wiring connector
		Damaged fuel injector
C37*	No. 2 secondary fuel injector – engine will run on other 3 cylinders	Faulty wiring or wiring connector
		Damaged fuel injector
C38*	No. 3 secondary fuel injector – engine will run on other 3 cylinders	Faulty wiring or wiring connector
		Damaged fuel injector
C39*	No. 4 secondary fuel injector – engine will run on other 3 cylinders	Faulty wiring or wiring connector
		Damaged fuel injector

*The engine will not run when two or more ignition coils or fuel injectors fail

Fault code	Faulty component – symptoms	Possible causes
C40 K8 and K9 models	Idle speed control (ISC) valve – idle speed too low or high, engine will run	Faulty wiring or wiring connector
	Faulty valve	
C41	Fuel pump control system – engine will not run	Faulty wiring or wiring connector to pump and/or pump relay
		Faulty pump relay (see Section 4)
		Damaged fuel pump (see Section 5)
C42	Ignition switch or immobiliser (where fitted) – engine will not run	Faulty wiring or wiring connector
		Damaged switch or immobiliser (see Chapter 8 for switch and Section 23 for immobiliser)
C44	Heated oxygen sensor – signal fixed to normal, engine will run	Faulty wiring or wiring connector
		Faulty sensor
C46	Exhaust control valve (EXCV) servo – engine will run, valve fixed in fully open position	Faulty wiring or wiring connector
		Faulty control valve cable adjustment
		Damaged servo (see Section 16 for details)
C49	PAIR system control valve – valve inactive, engine will run	Faulty wiring or wiring connector
		Faulty control valve
		Damaged servo (see Section 18 for details)
C60	Cooling fan relay	Faulty wiring or wiring connector
		Faulty relay
C62 K8 and K9 California models	EVAP system purge control solenoid valve – engine will run	Faulty wiring or wiring connector
		Faulty valve
C91 K8 and K9 models	Speed sensor – engine will run	Faulty wiring or wiring connector
		Faulty sensor
C93 K8 and K9 models	Steering damper – no electronic control over damper, engine will run	Faulty wiring or wiring connector
		Faulty damper control valve – refer to Chapter 5

10 Fuel injection system sensors

1 If a fault is indicated on any of the system components, first check the wiring and connectors between the appropriate component and the engine control module (ECM) – refer to electrical system fault finding at the beginning of Chapter 8 and the *Wiring Diagrams* at the end. A continuity test of all wires will locate a break or short in any circuit. Inspect the terminals inside the wiring connectors and ensure they are not loose or corroded. Spray the inside of the connectors with a proprietary electrical terminal cleaner before reconnection. Also remove the sensor and check the sensor head, and clean it if it is dirty – an accumulation of dirt could affect the signal it transmits.

2 It is possible to undertake some checks on system components using a multimeter and comparing the results with the specifications at the beginning of this Chapter. **Note:** *Different meters may give slightly different results to those specified even though the component being tested is not faulty – do not consign a component to the bin before having it double-checked.* However, some faults will only become evident when a component is tested with a peak voltage tester, in which

case the checks should be undertaken by a Suzuki dealer.

3 If after a thorough check the source of a fault has not been identified, it is possible that the ECM itself is faulty. Suzuki provides no test specifications for the ECM. In order to determine conclusively that the unit is defective, it should be substituted with a known good one. If the problem is then rectified, the original unit is faulty. Note that Suzuki have their own (dealer only) SDS fault diagnosis software which provides a more in depth analysis and diagnosis of the system – if you cannot locate or rectify a fault take the bike to a dealer equipped with the system (not all of them will have it, so phone first).

Camshaft position (CMP) sensor

4 Make sure the ignition is OFF. Remove the air filter housing (see Section 7). The CMP sensor is in the middle of the valve cover at the front. Disconnect the wiring connector **(see illustration)**. Using an ohmmeter or multimeter check for a resistance between the sensor terminals, then check that there is no continuity between each terminal and earth (ground). Suzuki do specify a resistance for the sensor, but if it is zero or infinite then it is likely the sensor is faulty.

5 If the results are good, have the sensor peak voltage tested by a Suzuki dealer.

6 To remove the sensor unscrew its bolt **(see illustration)**. Discard the seal and use

10.4 Disconnect the camshaft position (CMP) sensor wiring connector (arrowed)

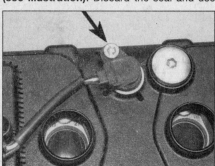

10.6 Unscrew the bolt (arrowed) and remove the sensor

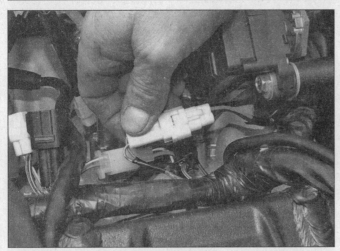

10.7 Trace the crankshaft position (CKP) sensor wiring to the connector

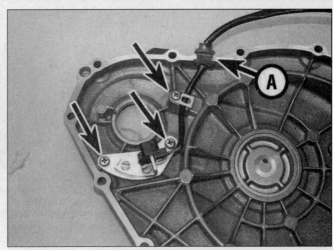

10.12 Undo the CKP sensor and wiring guide screws (arrowed), and free the wiring grommet (A)

a new one. On installation tighten the bolt to the torque setting specified at the beginning of the Chapter. To inspect the sensor tip and intake cam pin, remove the valve cover (see Chapter 2).

Crankshaft position (CKP) sensor

Check

7 Make sure the ignition is OFF. Raise the fuel tank (see Section 2). The CKP sensor is on the right-hand end of the crankshaft. Trace the wiring from the top of the clutch cover and disconnect it at the 2-pin connector with the black and green wires (**see illustration**). Using an ohmmeter or multimeter set to the ohms scale, measure the resistance between terminals on the sensor side of the connector. If the result is as specified, check that there is no continuity between each terminal and earth (ground).

8 If the results are good, have the sensor peak voltage tested by a Suzuki dealer.

Removal

9 Disconnect the battery negative (-) lead (see Chapter 8).

10 Trace the CKP sensor wiring back from the top of the clutch cover and disconnect it at the 2-pin connector with the black and green wires (**see illustration 10.7**). Free the wiring from any clips or ties and feed it through to the cover.

11 Remove the clutch cover (see Chapter 2).

12 Undo the screws securing the CKP sensor mounting plate and the screw securing the wiring clamp (**see illustration**). Remove the rubber wiring grommet from its recess, then remove the sensor assembly, noting how it fits.

13 Examine the timing rotor for signs of damage and install a new one if necessary (see Chapter 2, Section 11). **Note:** *The rotor is integral with the cam chain sprocket on the crankshaft.*

Installation

14 Fit the sensor assembly onto the cover

and tighten its screws (**see illustration 10.12**).

15 Apply a smear of sealant to the rubber wiring seal and fit the grommet in its recess in the crankcase. Locate the wiring under its clamp and tighten the clamp screw.

16 Install the clutch cover (see Chapter 2).

17 Route the wiring up to the connector and reconnect it (**see illustration 10.7**). Secure the wiring in any clips or ties.

18 Reconnect the battery negative (-) lead (see Chapter 8).

Intake air pressure (IAP) sensor

19 Make sure the ignition is OFF. Raise the fuel tank (see Section 2). The IAP sensor is mounted on a bracket on the right-hand end of the throttle bodies (**see illustration**). Check the condition of the vacuum hoses between the underside of the sensor and the throttle bodies (**see illustration**). If any hose is cracked or perished replace them all with a new set. Ensure each hose is a tight fit on its union.

10.19a Intake air pressure (IAP) sensor (arrowed)

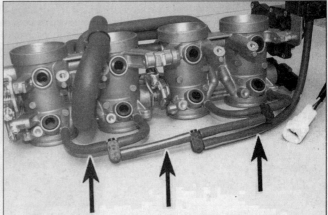

10.19b Check the complete hose arrangement and all the joints between the sensor and the throttle bodies (arrowed)

10.22a Displace the sensor . . .

10.22b . . . disconnect the wiring connector . . .

10.22c . . . and detach the hose from the underside

20 Disconnect the sensor wiring connector and turn the ignition ON (see illustration 10.22b). Connect the positive (+) probe of a voltmeter to the red wire terminal on the loom side of the wiring connector and the negative (-) probe first to earth (ground), then to the black/brown wire terminal to check the input voltage. Turn the ignition OFF. If the input voltage is not as specified, check the wiring to the ECM and the ECM connector terminals.

21 If the input voltage is good, reconnect the wiring to the sensor, then start the engine and allow it idle. Insert the positive (+) probe of a voltmeter into the green/black wire terminal in the connector and the negative (-) probe into the black/brown wire terminal to check the output voltage. If the result is as specified, take the sensor to a Suzuki dealer for vacuum testing.

22 To remove the IAP sensor, first displace the sensor, then disconnect the wiring connector and detach the vacuum hose (see illustrations). On installation, ensure the wiring connector terminals are clean and that the vacuum hose is a tight fit on the sensor union.

Throttle position (TP) sensor

Check

23 Make sure the ignition is OFF. Raise or remove the fuel tank (see Section 2), and if required for alternative access remove the right-hand fairing side panel (see Chapter 7). The TP sensor is located on the right-hand end of the throttle bodies and is the lower of

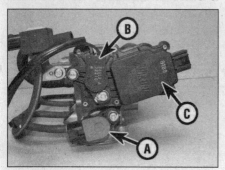

10.23 Throttle position (TP) sensor (A); secondary throttle position (STP) sensor (B); secondary throttle valve (STV) servo (C)

the two sensors (see illustration). Disconnect the wiring connector from the sensor (see illustration 11.5b). Turn the ignition ON and connect the positive (+) probe of a voltmeter to the red wire terminal in the connector and the negative (-) probe first to earth (ground), then to the black/brown wire terminal to check the input voltage. Turn the ignition OFF. If the input voltage is not as specified, check the wiring and connectors between the sensor and the ECM and the ECM connector terminals.

24 If the input voltage is good, check for continuity between the pink/black wire terminal in the sensor socket and earth (ground). There should be no continuity.

25 Turn the ignition ON and connect the probes of a voltmeter between the pink/black and black/brown wire terminals in the connector to check the output voltage, first with the throttle closed, then turn the twistgrip so that the throttle is fully open. Turn ignition OFF. If the results are not as specified, the sensor is faulty.

26 On K6 and K7 models, using an ohmmeter set to the K-ohms scale, measure the resistance between the pink/black and black/brown wire terminals in the sensor socket, first with the throttle closed, then turn the twistgrip so that the throttle is fully open. If the results are as specified, reconnect the wiring connector.

Removal

27 To remove the TP sensor, displace the throttle bodies from the intakes and disconnect the wiring connector (see Section 11) (see

10.31 Engine coolant temperature (ECT) sensor (arrowed)

illustration 11.5a). Mark the position of the sensor to aid installation, then undo the Torx screw and remove the sensor (see illustration 10.23). Note how the end of the throttle shaft engages the slot in the sensor. If the secondary throttle position (STP) sensor is also being removed make sure you mark them as to which is which.

Installation

28 Installation is the reverse of removal. Ensure that the throttle shaft engages correctly in the slot in the sensor and align any register marks before tightening the Torx screw to the torque setting specified at the beginning of this Chapter. Ensure the wiring connector terminals are clean.

29 To check and adjust the position of the TP sensor, first check the engine idle speed and adjust it if necessary (see Chapter 1). Turn the engine OFF and connect the mode select switch to the wiring connector (see Section 10). Remove the right-hand fairing side panel (see Chapter 7).

30 Start the engine. Turn the select switch ON. A code C00 will be displayed on the LCD panel on the instrument cluster with a line in front of it. If the line is in the mid-way position i.e. –C00, the TP sensor is adjusted correctly. If the line is above or below the mid-way position (‾C00 or _C00), loosen the sensor Torx screw and carefully rotate the sensor until the line is in the mid-way position. Tighten the Torx screw to the specified torque setting.

Engine coolant temperature (ECT) sensor

31 Make sure the ignition is OFF. Raise or remove the fuel tank (see Section 2). The ECT sensor is located in the rear of the cylinder head on the left-hand side (see illustration). Disconnect the sensor wiring connector and turn the ignition ON. Connect the positive (+) probe of a voltmeter to the black/blue wire terminal in the connector and the negative (-) probe first to earth (ground), then to the black/brown wire terminal to check the input voltage. Turn the ignition OFF. If the input voltage is not as specified, check the wiring to the ECM and the ECM connector terminals.

32 Using an ohmmeter or multimeter set to the K-ohms scale, measure the resistance between the terminals on the sensor itself

10.35a Intake air temperature (IAT) sensor (arrowed) – K6 and K7 models

10.35b Intake air temperature (IAT) sensor (arrowed) – K8 and K9 models

10.40 Undo the screws (arrowed) and remove the sensor

with the engine cold. If the result is not as specified, the sensor is faulty.

33 Reconnect the sensor wiring connector and turn the ignition ON. Measure the output voltage by inserting the voltmeter positive (+) probe into the black/blue wire terminal in the connector and the negative (-) probe to earth. If the result is not as specified, and the wiring and connector terminals are good, the sensor is faulty.

34 If the sensor is working correctly, the resistance should drop as the engine warms up. A check for sensor performance is described in Chapter 3, along with removal and installation details.

Intake air temperature (IAT) sensor

35 Make sure the ignition is OFF. Raise or remove the fuel tank (see Section 2). The IAT sensor is on the front of the air filter housing on K6 and K7 models **(see illustration)**, and on the left-hand side of it on K8 and K9 models **(see illustration)**.

36 Disconnect the sensor wiring connector and turn the ignition ON. Connect the positive (+) probe of a voltmeter to the dark green wire terminal in the connector and the negative (-) probe first to earth (ground), then to the black/brown wire terminal to check the input voltage. Turn the ignition OFF. If the input voltage is not as specified, check the wiring to the ECM and the ECM connector terminals.

37 Using an ohmmeter or multimeter set to the K-ohms scale, measure the resistance between the terminals on the sensor itself. If the result is not as specified, the sensor is faulty.

As with the ECT sensor (see Step 34), the IAT sensor resistance should drop as temperature increases. If required test the sensor in the same way as described in Chapter 3 – the resistance/temperature values are roughly the same (see Chapter 3 Specifications).

38 Reconnect the sensor wiring connector and turn the ignition ON. Measure the output voltage by inserting the voltmeter positive (+) probe into the dark green wire terminal in the connector and the negative (-) probe to earth. If the result is not as specified, and the wiring and connector terminals are good, the sensor is faulty.

39 To remove the sensor on K6 and K7 models raise the fuel tank (see Section 2). Pull the sensor out of its holding grommet in the air filter housing then disconnect the sensor wiring connector **(see illustration 10.35a)**. On installation, ensure the wiring connector terminals and sensor head are clean.

40 To remove the sensor on K8 and K9 models remove the air filter housing (see Section 7). Undo the screws and remove the sensor **(see illustration)**. On installation, ensure the wiring connector terminals and sensor head are clean.

Atmospheric pressure (AP) sensor

41 Make sure the ignition is OFF. Remove the rider's seat (see Chapter 7); the AP sensor is behind the battery positive (+) terminal **(see illustration)**.

42 Disconnect the sensor wiring connector and turn the ignition ON. Connect the positive (+) probe of a voltmeter to the red wire terminal

in the connector and the negative (-) probe first to earth (ground), then to the black/brown wire terminal to check the input voltage. Turn the ignition OFF. If the input voltage is not as specified, check the wiring to the ECM and the ECM connector terminals.

43 If the input voltage is good, reconnect the wiring to the sensor, then turn the ignition ON. Insert the positive (+) probe of a voltmeter into the green/yellow wire terminal in the connector and the negative (-) probe into the black/brown wire terminal to check the output voltage. Turn the ignition OFF.

44 If the output voltage is not as specified, the AP sensor air passage may be clogged with dirt. Disconnect the wiring connector and remove the sensor. Clean the outside of the sensor with a damp cloth and check the air passage for any obstruction, then retest the output voltage.

45 If the output voltage is as specified, take the sensor to a Suzuki dealer for vacuum testing.

Tip-over (TO) sensor

46 Make sure the ignition is OFF. On K6 and K7 models remove the seat cowling (see Chapter 7) – the TO sensor is on the back of the rear sub-frame **(see illustration)**. On K8 and K9 models remove the rider's seat (see Chapter 7) – the TO sensor is to the rear of the fusebox **(see illustration)**.

47 Disconnect the wiring connector from the sensor. Using an ohmmeter or multimeter set to the K-ohms scale, measure the resistance between the red and black/brown wire terminals on the sensor. Compare the result

10.41 Atmospheric pressure (AP) sensor (arrowed)

10.46a Tip-over (TO) sensor (arrowed) – K6 and K7 models

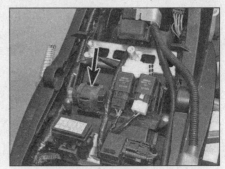

10.46b Tip-over (TO) sensor (arrowed) – K8 and K9 models

to that given in the Specifications at the beginning of this Chapter; if the result is good, reconnect the wiring connector.

48 Turn the ignition ON and insert the probes of a voltmeter into the black and black/brown wire terminals in the connector to check the voltage. If the result is as specified for the upright position, carefully unclip the sensor from its bracket and check the voltage reading when the sensor is leaned beyond 65° to one side and then to the other, this simulates the cut-off point reached if the motorcycle falls over – at each point the voltage should change to that specified for the leaned-over position. If not, the sensor is faulty.

49 To remove the sensor, first disconnect the wiring connector. Release the sensor from its bracket, noting which way round it fits. Installation is the reverse of removal – on K6 and K7 models make sure the arrow on the sensor points up **(see illustration 10.46a)**, and on K8 and K9 models make sure the UP mark is on the top **(see illustration)**.

Secondary throttle valve (STV) servo

50 Make sure the ignition is OFF. Remove the air filter housing (see Section 7) in order to view the throttle valves. The STV servo is on the right-hand end of throttle body assembly **(see illustration 10.23)**.

51 Turn the ignition ON and check that the secondary throttle valves move. Turn the ignition OFF. If the valves do not move, check the wiring from the servo to the ECM and check the ECM connector terminals.

52 Disconnect the STV servo wiring connector **(see illustration 11.5b)**. Check that there is no continuity between the terminals in the servo socket and earth (ground).

53 Using an ohmmeter or multimeter set to the ohms scale, measure the resistance first between the top two (white/black and green) wire terminals in the servo socket, then between the bottom two (pink/white and black/light green) wire terminals. If the result is not as specified, the STV servo is faulty. If the result is as specified, have the ECM checked by a Suzuki dealer.

54 The servo is an integral part of the throttle body assembly and must not be removed from it. The servo is not available separately, and so if it is faulty a new throttle body assembly must be obtained.

Secondary throttle position (STP) sensor

55 Make sure the ignition is OFF. Raise the fuel tank (see Section 2). The STP sensor is mounted on the right-hand end of the throttle body assembly and is the upper of the two sensors **(see illustration 10.23)**.

56 Disconnect the sensor wiring connector **(see illustration 11.2c)**. Turn the ignition ON. Connect the positive (+) probe of a voltmeter to the red wire terminal in the loom side of the wiring connector and the negative (-) probe first to earth (ground), then to the black/brown wire terminal to check the input voltage. Turn the ignition OFF. If the input voltage is not as specified, check the wiring to the ECM and the ECM connector terminals.

57 If the input voltage is good, check for continuity between the yellow wire terminal on the sensor side of the wiring connector and earth (ground). There should be no continuity.

58 On K6 and K7 models remove the air filter (see Chapter 1) and close the secondary throttle valves by finger pressure. Using an ohmmeter or multimeter set to the K-ohms scale, connect the positive (+) probe to the yellow wire terminal on the sensor side of the connector and the negative (-) probe to the black wire terminal and measure the sensor resistance. Now open the secondary throttle valves by finger pressure and measure the sensor resistance. Also check the standard resistance between the blue and black wire terminals on the sensor side of the connector.

59 Reconnect the sensor wiring connector and turn the ignition ON. Disconnect the STV servo wiring connector **(see illustration 11.5b)**. Insert the probes of a voltmeter into the yellow and black wire terminals in the sensor connector to check the output voltage while carefully closing and opening the throttle valves by finger pressure. If the output voltage is not as specified, and on K6 and K7 if the resistance readings weren't as specified, first check the sensor adjustment as follows.

60 Close the secondary throttle valves and loosen the sensor Torx mounting screw – displace the throttle bodies if required for access (see Section 11). Connect the voltmeter to the yellow and black wire terminals then adjust the position of the sensor until the closed output voltage reading is within specification;

tighten the Torx screw. If the specified resistance cannot be obtained, the STP sensor is faulty. If everything appears good take have a Suzuki dealer check the ECM.

61 To remove the sensor, first disconnect the wiring connector **(see illustration 11.2c)**. Mark the position of the sensor to aid installation, then undo the Torx screw and remove the sensor **(see illustration 10.23)**. Note how the end of the shaft engages the slot in the sensor. If the throttle position (TP) sensor is also being removed make sure you mark them as to which is which.

62 Installation is the reverse of removal. Apply a small quantity of grease to the slot in the throttle shaft and align the tab on the sensor with the slot before installing the motor cover. Check the position of the sensor (see Step 60), then tighten the Torx screw.

Gear position (GP) sensor

63 Support the bike on an auxiliary stand and raise the sidestand. Raise or remove the fuel tank (see Section 2). Ensure the engine kill switch is in the RUN position. The GP sensor is located on the left-hand side of the engine unit behind the front sprocket cover.

64 Trace the wiring from the sensor to the connector **(see illustration)**. Turn the ignition switch ON and insert the positive (+) probe of a voltmeter into the pink wire terminal in the connector and connect the negative (-) probe to the black/white wire terminal to check the output voltage. Select each gear in turn and check that the voltage is above the specified minimum in each gear. Turn the ignition OFF.

65 If the output voltage is not as specified, and the wiring and connectors are good, then the GP switch itself is faulty.

66 If the output voltage is as specified check the wiring from the sensor to the ECM and check the ECM connector terminals.

67 To remove the GP sensor, refer to Chapter 6 to remove the front sprocket cover, then refer to Chapter 2, Section 15, Steps 6 and 20 to remove and install the sensor.

Heated oxygen (HO2) sensor

68 Raise the fuel tank (see Section 2).

69 Disconnect the sensor wiring connector **(see illustration)**. Using a multimeter set to the ohms scale, measure the resistance

10.49 Make sure the UP mark is on top of the sensor

10.64 Gear position sensor wiring connector

10.69 Oxygen sensor wiring connector

10.72 Clamp the hoses (arrowed)

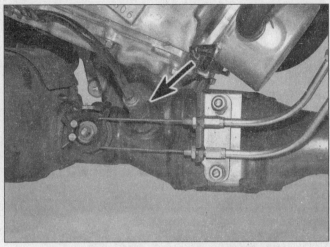

10.73 Unscrew and remove the sensor (arrowed)

between the two white wire terminals on the sensor side of the connector – note that the sensor must be at atmospheric temperature for a true reading. If not as specified replace the sensor with a new one.

70 Reconnect the wiring connector and turn the ignition switch on. Using a multimeter set to the voltage scale, connect the positive (+) probe between the orange/white wire terminal and the negative (-) probe to earth, and check for battery voltage (12V). If there is no voltage check the orange/white wire for a fault, referring to the wiring diagrams at the end of Chapter 8.

71 Start the engine and warm it up.

72 Using a multimeter set to the voltage scale, connect the positive (+) probe to the white/green wire terminal in the connector and the negative (-) probe to the black/brown wire terminal and measure the output voltage with the engine idling. If that is good remove the air filter housing (see Section 7) and clamp the PAIR system hoses **(see illustration)**. Recheck the output voltage with the engine running at 5000 rpm. If the voltage readings are not as specified replace the sensor with a new one. If they are, and all the wiring and connectors are good, have a Suzuki dealer check the ECM.

73 To remove the sensor remove the right-hand fairing side panel (see Chapter 7). Trace the wiring from the sensor and disconnect the wiring connector **(see illustration 10.69)**. Feed the wiring down to the sensor noting its routing and freeing it from any ties. Unscrew and remove the sensor **(see illustration)**. Take care not to drop the sensor, and keep the sensing portion on the bottom and the filter holes on the top free of dirt and dust. Installation is the reverse of removal. If the correct tools are available tighten the sensor to the torque setting specified at the beginning of the Chapter.

11 Throttle body removal and installation

⚠️ *Warning: Refer to the precautions given in Section 1 before starting work.*

Removal

1 Remove the fairing side panels (see Chapter 7), the fuel tank (see Section 2) and the air filter housing (see Section 7).

2 Release the cable-ties which secure the wiring to the fuel rail **(see illustration)**. Disconnect the wiring connectors from the secondary fuel injectors and the secondary throttle position (STP) sensor **(see illustrations)**. On K8 and K9 models disconnect the idle speed control (ISC) valve wiring connector **(see illustration)**.

3 On California models disconnect the EVAP system hose(s).

4 Loosen the clamp screws securing the throttle bodies to the intake adapters – note that 600K6 models have four individual clamps (note their orientation), all other models have

11.2a Release the cable-ties (arrowed)

11.2b Disconnect the secondary injector wiring connectors . . .

11.2c . . . and the STP sensor wiring connector

11.2d On K8 and K9 disconnect the wiring connector from the ISC valve on the front of the throttle bodies

11.4 Slacken the clamp screw(s) on each side

11.5a Disconnect the TP sensor wiring connector . . .

11.5b . . . the STV servo wiring connector . . .

two paired clamps **(see illustration)**. Ease the bodies up off the adapters so the remaining connectors are accessible.

5 Disconnect the primary fuel injector wiring connectors **(see illustration)**. Disconnect the throttle position (TP) sensor and secondary throttle valve (STV) servo wiring connectors **(see illustrations)**. Move the throttle body assembly wiring loom out of the way.

6 Detach the throttle cables (see Section 14), then remove the throttle bodies.

Installation

7 Installation is the reverse of removal, noting the following:
● Ensure the terminals in the connectors are clean and reconnect them firmly.
● Ensure the throttle bodies are fully engaged with the intake adapters on the cylinder head before tightening the clamps.
● Check the operation of the throttle cables and adjust them as necessary (see Chapter 1).
● Check the engine idle speed and on K6/K7 models adjust as necessary (see Chapter 1).

12 Throttle body overhaul

⚠️ *Warning: Refer to the precautions given in Section 1 before starting work.*

Disassembly

1 Note the arrangement and routing of all the hoses connected to the throttle bodies – if you have a digital camera take some pictures. Disconnect the vacuum hoses for the intake air pressure (IAP) sensor from the union on each throttle body and remove the IAP sensor and hose system **(see illustration 10.19b)**. On K8 and K9 models disconnect the ISC valve hoses **(see illustration 15.6)**. On California models also disconnect the EVAP system hose assembly.

2 Remove the fuel rail and injectors (see Section 13).

3 If required, remove the TP sensor and STP sensor (see Section 10). DO NOT remove the STV servo. On K8 and K9 models remove the ISC valve (see Section 15).

Caution: The throttle valves and secondary throttle valves must not be removed from the valve shafts.

Cleaning

Caution: Use only a petroleum based solvent or dedicated injector cleaner for throttle body cleaning. Don't use caustic cleaners.

4 Ensure that only metal components are submerged in cleaning solvent and always follow the manufacturer's recommendations as to cleaning time. If a spray cleaner is used, direct the spray into all passages.

5 After the cleaner has loosened and dissolved most of the varnish and other deposits, use a nylon-bristled brush to remove the stubborn deposits. Rinse the throttle bodies again, then dry them with compressed air.

6 Use compressed air to blow out all of the fuel and air passages.

Inspection

7 Check the throttle bodies for cracks or any other damage which may result in air getting in.

8 Check that the throttle valves move smoothly and freely in the bodies. Inspect the valve shafts and throttle bodies for wear. Check the condition of the valve shaft springs.

9 Check the throttle cable bracket, pulley and related components **(see illustration)**.

Reassembly

10 If removed, install the TP and STP sensors (see Section 10), and on K8 and K9 models

12.9 Check the throttle pulley components

11.5c . . . and the primary injector wiring connectors

the ISC valve (see Section 15).

11 Install the fuel injectors and fuel rail (see Section 13).

12 Connect the various hoses as noted on removal (Step 1).

13 Fuel rails and injectors

⚠️ *Warning: Refer to the precautions given in Section 1 before starting work.*

Check

1 Make sure the ignition is OFF. Raise or remove the fuel tank (see Section 2). Identify the faulty injector by the fault code (see Section 9). Disconnect the injector wiring connector **(see illustration 11.2b or 11.5c)**.
Note: *The injectors are numbered 1 to 4 from*

13.1 Checking injector resistance

13.6a Fuel rail screws (arrowed) – K6 and K7 models

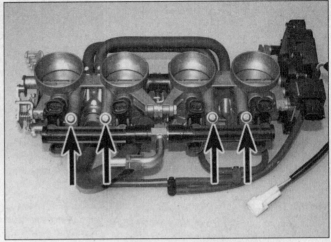

13.6b Fuel rail screws (arrowed) – K8 and K9 models

the left-hand to right-hand side of the engine. Using an ohmmeter or multimeter set to the ohms scale, measure the resistance between the terminals on the injector **(see illustration)**. If the result is as specified, check that there is no continuity between each terminal and earth (ground).

2 Turn the ignition ON. Connect the positive (+) probe of a voltmeter to the yellow/red wire terminal in the wiring connector and the negative (-) probe to earth (ground) to check the input voltage. **Note:** *Injector voltage can only be detected for 3 seconds after the ignition has been turned ON.* Turn the ignition OFF. If the input voltage is not as specified, refer to the *Wiring Diagrams* at the end of Chapter 8 and check for a fault in the yellow/red wire.

3 If the input voltage is as specified check, refer to the Wiring Diagrams at the end of Chapter 8 and check for a fault in the individual injector wiring.

Removal

Note: *The fuel injectors can be removed with the throttle bodies in place. If the bodies have been removed, ignore the Steps which do not apply.*

4 Remove the air filter housing (see Section 7). Disconnect the battery negative terminal (see Chapter 8).

13.6c Carefully remove the fuel rail assembly

5 Cut the cable-ties securing the wiring to the fuel rail and disconnect the individual fuel injector wiring connectors **(see illustrations 11.2a and b and 11.5c)**. Disconnect and move aside any hose that obstructs removal of the fuel rail.

6 Undo the screws securing the fuel rail assembly to the throttle bodies, noting the washers on K8 and K9 models **(see illustrations)**. Carefully lift the fuel rail off the throttle bodies – the injectors will come away with the rails **(see illustration)**. Remove and discard the injector seals.

7 As required pull the injectors out of the fuel rail, noting how they align and which fits

13.6d Remove the seals – new ones must be used

where – the primary and secondary injectors are different and must be returned to their original rail **(see illustration)**. Remove and discard each injector O-ring **(see illustration)**.

8 On K8 and K9 models, if required pull each rail section off the centre joint piece **(see illustration)**. Discard the O-rings.

9 Modern fuels contain detergents which should keep the injectors clean and free of gum or varnish from fuel residue. If an injector is suspected of being blocked, clean it through with injector cleaner. If the injector is clean but its performance is suspect, take it to a Suzuki dealer for assessment.

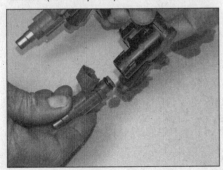

13.7a Pull each injector out of the fuel rail

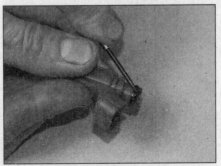

13.7b Remove the O-ring – a new one must be used

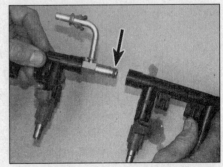

13.8 Separate each rail from the joint piece and discard the O-ring (arrowed)

13.12 The screws on K8 and K9 models have washers

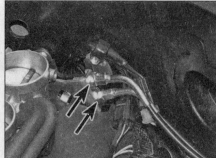

14.2a Slacken the locknuts (arrowed)

14.2b Free the throttle opening cable from the top of the bracket . . .

Installation

Note: *Apply a smear of clean engine oil to all new seals and O-rings before reassembly.*

10 On K8 and K9 models if separated assemble the fuel rails and their joint piece using new O-rings **(see illustration 13.8)**.

11 Fit a new O-ring onto each injector, then carefully press each injector into its fuel rail, aligning the wiring connector socket between the bosses on the injector socket in the rail **(see illustrations 13.7b and a)**. **Note:** *Avoid twisting the injectors when pushing them into the rail as this may damage the O-ring seals.*

12 Fit a new seal into each injector port in the throttle bodies **(see illustration 13.6d)**. Fit the fuel rails and injectors onto the throttle bodies, making sure each injector is correctly aligned before pressing the assembly into place **(see illustration 13.6c)**. Install and tighten the fuel

rail screws **(see illustration 13.6a or b)** – do not forget the washers on K8 and K9 models **(see illustration)**.

13 Connect the individual injector wiring connectors and secure the wiring loom to the fuel rail with cable-ties.

14 Install the remaining components in the reverse order of removal. On completion, start the engine and check carefully that there are no fuel leaks.

14 Throttle cables

Removal

1 Raise the fuel tank (see Section 2).

2 Loosen the locknuts securing the throttle cable adjusters in the bracket **(see illustration)**. Turn the adjusters out to thread the bottom nuts down and detach the cables, noting how they fit – the upper cable is the accelerator (throttle opening) cable, the lower cable is the decelerator (throttle closing) cable **(see illustrations)**. Disconnect the cables from the throttle pulley **(see illustrations)**.

3 Undo the cable retaining plate screw, noting how the plate locates around the front (throttle opening) cable elbow **(see illustration)**.

4 Undo the handlebar housing screws and separate the halves **(see illustration)**. Note how the pin locates in the hole in the handlebar. Detach the cable ends from the twistgrip pulley, noting how they fit, then pull the cables out of the lower half of the housing **(see illustration)**.

5 Draw the cables out and remove them

14.2c . . . then detach the cable end from the pulley

14.2d Free the throttle closing cable from the bottom of the bracket . . .

14.2e . . . then detach the cable end from the pulley

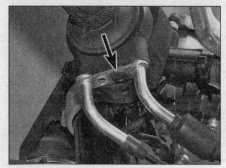

14.3 Remove the retainer plate screw (arrowed)

14.4a Undo the screws (arrowed) . . .

14.4b . . . then separate the switch housing and detach the cable ends (arrowed)

from the machine, noting their routing **(see illustration)**.

> **HAYNES HiNT**
> *Before removing the cables from the bike, tape the lower end of the new cable to the upper end of the old cable. Slowly pull the lower end of the old cable out, guiding the new cable down into position. Using this method will ensure the cables are routed correctly.*

Installation

6 Route the cables between the handlebar and the throttle bodies, making sure they are correctly routed – they must not interfere with any other component and should not be kinked or bent sharply **(see illustration 14.5)**.

7 Fit the throttle opening cable elbow into the front of the lower half of the handlebar housing and the closing cable elbow into the rear, then locate the open end of the retainer plate around the shoulder on the opening cable elbow and secure the plate with its screw **(see illustration 14.3)**.

8 Lubricate the end of each cable with multi-purpose grease. Fit the lower half of the handlebar housing onto the twistgrip pulley and attach the cable ends to the pulley **(see illustration 14.4b)**. Ensure the cables are correctly aligned on the pulley, then fit the upper half of the housing and join the halves – make sure the peg on the bottom half locates in the hole in the underside of the handlebar **(see illustration)**. Fit the screws and tighten them. Check that the twistgrip pulley turns freely.

9 Fit the lower end of each cable onto the throttle pulley; the throttle opening cable goes around the top of the pulley, the closing cable goes around the bottom **(see illustrations 14.2e, d, c and b)**.

10 Fit the cable adjusters into the bracket, ensuring the nuts are located on each side of the plate. Pull the adjusters up so the bottom nuts are captive in the bracket then thread the

14.5 Loosen the bolt (arrowed) and free the cables from the guide

adjusters all the way onto the bracket so there is no clearance between the adjusters and the locknuts. Adjust the cables as described in Chapter 1.

11 Lower the fuel tank (see Section 2).

12 Start the engine and check that the idle speed does not rise as the handlebars are turned. If it does, correct the problem before riding the motorcycle.

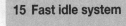

15 Fast idle system

K6 and K7 models

1 The fast idle mechanism is actuated by the STV servo when the engine is cold and should cancel automatically after a period determined by ambient and engine temperatures and lapsed time.

2 The engine should be cold. Start the engine and check the fast idle speed on the tachometer – it should be 1500 to 2000 rpm.

3 Leave the engine running and check that the fast idle speed reduces automatically as the engine warms, and falls to the normal idle speed for a warm engine. If necessary, adjust the idle speed (see Chapter 1).

4 The fast idle mechanism is pre-set at the factory and should not be adjusted. If the fast

14.8 Make sure the peg (arrowed) locates in its hole

idle speed is incorrect (see Specifications) adjustment must be made by a Suzuki dealer using a special test harness.

K8 and K9 models

Check

5 The fast idle speed is set by the idle speed control (ISC) valve in the throttle bodies. Idle speed should be faster when started from cold engine and should cancel automatically after a period determined by the ECM in accordance with information received from the various sensors in the fuel injection system.

6 The fast idle mechanism is pre-set at the factory using the SDS software and cannot be adjusted without it. If the fast idle speed is incorrect remove the air filter housing (see Section 7). Check that the ISC valve hoses are all securely connected and are in good condition **(see illustration)**. Make sure the valve wiring connector is secure and the wiring is good.

7 Disconnect the wiring connector **(see illustration)**. Using a multimeter set to test continuity check that there is no continuity between each terminal in the valve socket and earth.

8 Set the multimeter to ohms and measure the resistance of the valve, first between the blue and yellow wire terminals in the valve socket, and then between the green and brown

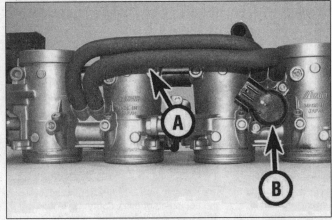

15.6 Check the ISC valve hoses (A) on the front of the throttle bodies. ISC valve (B)

15.7 Disconnect the wiring connector from the valve

wire terminals. In each case the resistance should be as specified at the beginning of the Chapter. If not the valve is faulty and should be replaced with a new one.

9 If necessary take the bike to a dealer equipped with the software for testing and adjustment.

ISC valve removal and installation

10 Remove the air filter housing (see Section 7) – the ISC valve is on the front of the throttle bodies on the left-hand end. If required to improve access displace or remove the throttle bodies (see Section 11).

11 If required pull the ISC hoses off their unions.

12 Undo the ISC valve screws and remove the valve. Remove and discard the O-ring.

13 Fit a new O-ring smeared with clean oil onto the valve. Install the valve and tighten the screws.

14 Fit the hoses, using new ones if necessary.

15 Install the throttle bodies if removed or displaced (see Section 11), and the air filter housing (see Section 7).

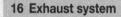

16 Exhaust system

 Warning: If the engine has been running the exhaust system will be very hot. Allow the system to cool before carrying out any work.

K6 and K7 models

Silencer removal

1 Make sure the ignition is OFF. Remove the fairing side panels (see Chapter 7).

2 Loosen the clamp securing the silencer to the downpipes **(see illustration)**.

3 Unscrew the bolts, one on the right-hand side and two on the left, securing the silencer to the frame **(see illustrations 16.47a and b)**.

4 Pull the silencer off the end of the downpipes and remove it.

5 Note the spacers fitted inside the bushes in each mount and remove them for safekeeping if required. Check the condition of the seal fitted between the downpipes and silencer and if necessary remove it so a new one can be fitted.

16.2 Slacken the clamp bolt (arrowed)

Silencer installation

6 Make sure the rubber bushes in the mounts are in good condition, and if not replace them with new ones. If removed, fit the spacers into the bushes from the inside. If necessary fit a new seal into the silencer. Make sure the clamp is in place on the end.

7 Fit the silencer onto the end of the downpipes. Fit the mounting bolts and tighten them to the specified torque, then tighten the clamp bolt to the specified torque **(see illustrations 16.47a and b and 16.2)**.

8 Run the engine and check that there are no exhaust gas leaks. Install the fairing side panels (see Chapter 7).

Downpipe assembly removal

9 Remove the fairing side panels (see Chapter 7). Displace the radiator forwards, using some rag to protect the mudguard (see Chapter 3) – there is no need to drain the cooling system or detach the hoses. If you prefer to have better clearance remove the radiator.

10 Raise the fuel tank (see Section 2). Trace the wiring from the heated oxygen sensor and disconnect the wiring connector **(see illustration 10.69)**. Feed the wiring down to the sensor noting its routing and freeing it from any ties. If required remove the sensor (see Section 10).

11 Unscrew the exhaust control valve servo pulley cable bracket nuts and detach the cables from the pulley **(see illustrations 16.46a and b)**.

12 Loosen the clamp securing the silencer to the downpipes **(see illustration 16.2)**.

13 Unscrew and remove the downpipe flange bolts from the cylinder head **(see illustration 16.48a)**. Draw the downpipes off the cylinder head and out of the silencer **(see illustration 16.48b)** – take care not to damage the radiator fins.

14 Remove the gaskets from the cylinder head exhaust ports and discard them as new ones must be fitted on reassembly **(see illustration 16.52)**. Check the condition of the seal fitted between the downpipes and silencer and if necessary remove it so a new one can be fitted.

Downpipe assembly installation

15 Apply a smear of grease to the new exhaust port gaskets to keep them in place, then place the gaskets in the ports **(see illustration 16.52)**. If necessary fit a new seal into the silencer. Make sure the clamp is in place on the end.

16 Manoeuvre the downpipe assembly into position so that it is located in the cylinder head and the silencer, then install the downpipe flange bolts and tighten them evenly to the torque setting specified at the beginning of this Chapter **(see illustrations 16.48b and a)**. Now tighten the clamp bolt to the specified torque **(see illustration 16.2)**.

17 Fit the cable ends into the control valve pulley, then fit the cable bracket and tighten its nuts **(see illustrations 16.46b and a)**.

18 If removed install the heated oxygen sensor (see Section 10). Otherwise feed the heated oxygen sensor wiring back up to its connector, making sure it is correctly routed, and reconnect it **(see illustration 10.69)**. Lower the fuel tank (see Section 2).

19 Install the radiator (see Chapter 3). Run the engine and check that there are no exhaust gas leaks.

20 Install the fairing side panels (see Chapter 7).

Complete system removal

21 Remove the fairing side panels (see Chapter 7). Displace the radiator forwards, using some rag to protect the mudguard (see Chapter 3) – there is no need to drain the cooling system or detach the hoses. If you prefer to have better clearance remove the radiator.

22 Raise the fuel tank (see Section 2). Trace the wiring from the heated oxygen sensor and disconnect the wiring connector **(see illustration 10.69)**. Feed the wiring down to the sensor noting its routing and freeing it from any ties. If required remove the sensor (see Section 10).

23 Unscrew the exhaust control valve servo pulley cable bracket nuts and detach the cables from the pulley **(see illustrations 16.46a and b)**.

24 Place a support under the silencer. Unscrew the bolts, one on the right-hand side and two on the left, securing the silencer to the frame **(see illustrations 16.47a and b)**.

25 Unscrew and remove the downpipe flange bolts from the cylinder head **(see illustration 16.48a)**. Draw the downpipes off the cylinder head and remove the system **(see illustration 16.48b)** – take care not to damage the radiator fins.

26 Remove the gaskets from the cylinder head exhaust ports and discard them as new ones must be fitted on reassembly **(see illustration 16.52)**.

27 Note the spacers fitted inside the bushes in each silencer mount and remove them for safekeeping if required.

Complete system installation

28 Make sure the rubber bushes in the mounts are in good condition, and if not replace them with new ones. If removed, fit the spacers into the bushes from the inside.

29 Apply a smear of grease to the new exhaust port gaskets to keep them in place, then place the gaskets in the ports **(see illustration 16.52)**.

30 Manoeuvre the exhaust system into position so that the downpipes are located in the cylinder head, then align the silencer mountings and slide the bolts through, tightening them finger-tight.

31 Fit the downpipe flange bolts and tighten them evenly to the torque setting specified at the beginning of this Chapter **(see illustration 16.48a)**. Now tighten the other bolts to the specified torque.

32 Fit the cable ends into the control valve

16.37 Undo the screws (arrowed) and remove the shield . . .

16.38 . . . then slacken the clamp bolt (arrowed)

16.39 Unscrew the nut, withdraw the bolt and remove the silencer

pulley, then fit the cable bracket and tighten its nuts **(see illustrations 16.46b and a)**.

33 If removed install the heated oxygen sensor (see Section 10). Otherwise feed the heated oxygen sensor wiring back up to its connector, making sure it is correctly routed, and reconnect it **(see illustration 10.69)**. Lower the fuel tank (see Section 2).

34 Install the radiator (see Chapter 3). Run the engine and check that there are no exhaust gas leaks.

35 Install the fairing side panels (see Chapter 7).

K8 and K9 models

Silencer removal

36 Make sure the ignition is OFF. Remove the fairing side panels (see Chapter 7).

37 Undo the heatshield screws and remove the shield **(see illustration)**.

38 Loosen the clamp securing the silencer to the collector box **(see illustration)**.

39 Unscrew the nut on the silencer bolt, then support the silencer, withdraw the bolt with its washer and pull the silencer off the end of the downpipes and remove it **(see illustration)**.

40 Note the spacer fitted inside the bush in the silencer mount and remove it for safekeeping if required. Check the condition of the seal fitted between the collector box and silencer and if necessary remove it so a new one can be fitted.

Silencer installation

41 Make sure the rubber bush in the silencer mount is in good condition, and if not replace

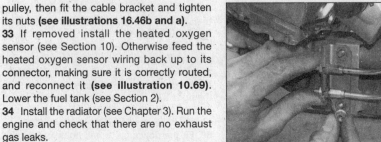

16.46a Unscrew the bracket nuts . . .

it with a new one. If removed, fit the spacer into the bush from the inside. If necessary fit a new seal onto the collector box stub pipe, with the chamfered end facing the rear. Make sure the clamp is in place on the silencer.

42 Fit the silencer onto the end of the collector box. Fit the mounting bolt with its washer and tighten the nut to the specified torque **(see illustration 16.39)**. Tighten the clamp bolt to the specified torque **(see illustration 16.38)**.

43 Run the engine and check that there are no exhaust gas leaks. Fit the heatshield **(see illustration 16.37)**. Install the fairing side panels (see Chapter 7).

Downpipe/collector box assembly removal

44 Remove the fairing side panels (see Chapter 7). Displace the radiator forwards, using some rag to protect the mudguard (see Chapter 3) – there is no need to drain the cooling system or detach the hoses. If you

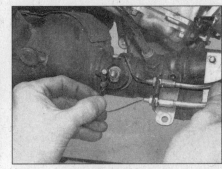

16.46b . . . and detach the cable ends from the pulley

prefer to have better clearance remove the radiator.

45 Raise the fuel tank (see Section 2). Trace the wiring from the heated oxygen sensor and disconnect the wiring connector **(see illustration 10.69)**. Feed the wiring down to the sensor noting its routing and freeing it from any ties. If required remove the sensor (see Section 10).

46 Unscrew the exhaust control valve servo pulley cable bracket nuts and detach the cables from the pulley **(see illustrations)**.

47 Undo the heatshield screws and remove the shield **(see illustration 16.37)**. Loosen the clamp securing the silencer to the collector box **(see illustration 16.38)**. Unscrew the bolts, one on the right-hand side and two on the left, securing the collector box to the frame **(see illustrations)**.

48 Unscrew and remove the downpipe flange bolts from the cylinder head **(see illustration)**.

16.47a Unscrew the bolt (arrowed) on the right-hand side . . .

16.47b . . . and the bolts (arrowed) on the left

16.48a Unscrew the bolts . . .

16.48b . . . and remove the downpipe assembly

16.52 Fit a new gasket into each exhaust port

16.63 Removing the complete system

Draw the downpipes off the cylinder head and the collector box off the silencer **(see illustration)** – take care not to damage the radiator fins.

49 Note the spacers fitted inside the bushes in each collector box mount and remove them for safekeeping if required. Check the condition of the seal fitted between the collector box and silencer and if necessary remove it so a new one can be fitted.

50 Remove the gaskets from the cylinder head exhaust ports and discard them as new ones must be fitted on reassembly **(see illustration 16.52)**.

Downpipe/collector box assembly installation

51 Make sure the rubber bushes in the collector box mounts are in good condition, and if not replace them with new ones. If removed, fit the spacers into the bushes from the inside. If necessary fit a new seal onto the collector box stub pipe, with the chamfered end facing the rear. Make sure the clamp is in place on the end.

52 Apply a smear of grease to the new exhaust port gaskets to keep them in place, then place the gaskets in the ports **(see illustration)**.

53 Manoeuvre the downpipe/collector box assembly into position so that it is located in the cylinder head and the silencer, then fit the collector box mounting bolts, tightening them finger-tight **(see illustration 16.47a and b)**. Fit the downpipe flange bolts and tighten them evenly to the torque setting specified at the beginning of this Chapter **(see illustration 16.48a)**. Now tighten the collector box bolts and the clamp bolt to the specified torque **(see illustration 16.38)**.

54 Fit the cable ends into the control valve pulley, then fit the cable bracket and tighten its nuts **(see illustrations 16.46b and a)**.

55 If removed install the heated oxygen sensor (see Section 10. Otherwise feed the heated oxygen sensor wiring back up to its connector, making sure it is correctly routed, and reconnect it **(see illustration 10.69)**. Lower the fuel tank (see Section 2).

56 Install the radiator (see Chapter 3). Run the engine and check that there are no

exhaust gas leaks. Fit the heat shield **(see illustration 16.37)**.

57 Install the fairing side panels (see Chapter 7).

Complete system removal

58 Remove the fairing side panels (see Chapter 7). Displace the radiator forwards, using some rag to protect the mudguard (see Chapter 3) – there is no need to drain the cooling system or detach the hoses. If you prefer to have better clearance remove the radiator.

59 Raise the fuel tank (see Section 2). Trace the wiring from the heated oxygen sensor and disconnect the wiring connector **(see illustration 10.69)**. Feed the wiring down to the sensor noting its routing and freeing it from any ties. If required remove the sensor (see Section 10).

60 Unscrew the exhaust control valve servo pulley cable bracket nuts and detach the cables from the pulley **(see illustrations 16.46a and b)**.

61 Place a support under the collector box. Unscrew the bolts, one on the right-hand side and two on the left, securing the collector box to the frame **(see illustrations 16.47a and b)**.

62 Unscrew the nut on the silencer bolt then withdraw the bolt with its washer **(see illustration 16.39)**.

63 Unscrew and remove the downpipe flange bolts from the cylinder head **(see illustration 16.48a)**. Draw the downpipes off the cylinder head and remove the system **(see illustration)** – take care not to damage the radiator fins.

64 Remove the gaskets from the cylinder head exhaust ports and discard them as new ones must be fitted on reassembly **(see illustration 16.52)**.

65 Note the spacers fitted inside the bushes in the silencer mount and each collector box mount and remove them for safekeeping if required.

Complete system installation

66 Make sure the rubber bushes in the mounts are in good condition, and if not replace them with new ones. If removed, fit the spacers into the bushes from the inside.

67 Apply a smear of grease to the new

exhaust port gaskets to keep them in place, then place the gaskets in the ports **(see illustration 16.52)**.

68 Manoeuvre the exhaust system into position so that the downpipes are located in the cylinder head **(see illustration 16.48b)**, then align the collector box mounts and slide the bolts through, tightening them finger-tight. Fit the silencer bolt with its washer and tighten the nut finger-tight **(see illustration 16.39)**.

69 Fit the downpipe flange bolts and tighten them evenly to the torque setting specified at the beginning of this Chapter **(see illustration 16.48a)**. Now tighten the other bolts to the specified torque.

70 Fit the cable ends into the control valve pulley, then fit the cable bracket and tighten its nuts **(see illustrations 16.46b and a)**.

71 If removed install the heated oxygen sensor (see Section 10). Otherwise feed the heated oxygen sensor wiring back up to its connector, making sure it is correctly routed, and reconnect it **(see illustration 10.69)**. Lower the fuel tank (see Section 2).

72 Install the radiator (see Chapter 3). Run the engine and check that there are no exhaust gas leaks.

73 Install the fairing side panels (see Chapter 7).

17 Exhaust control valve

> *Warning: If the engine has been running the exhaust system will be very hot. Allow the system to cool before carrying out any work.*

Special tool: *These procedures require the use of the Suzuki mode select switch (Pt. No. 09930-82720).*

Servo check

1 Make sure the ignition is OFF. On K6 and K7 models remove the seat cowling (see Chapter 7). On K8 and K9 models raise the fuel tank (see Section 2). Turn the ignition ON and observe the movement of the servo pulley and cables – the pulley should go from fully closed, to fully open, then to 30% open on K6 and K7 models and 60% open on K8 and K9

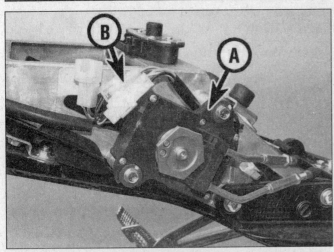

17.1a Exhaust control valve servo (A) and wiring connectors (B) – K6 and K7 models

17.1b Exhaust control valve servo (arrowed) and wiring connectors – K8 and K9 models

models **(see illustrations)**. Turn the ignition OFF. If the pulley does not move, disconnect the servo motor 2-pin wiring connector. Use jumper wires to connect the terminals of a 12V battery to the wire terminals on the servo side of the connector. The servo pulley should rotate in one direction. Now reverse the wire connections and ensure the pulley rotates in the other direction. If the pulley does not rotate, or only rotates in one direction, replace the servo with a new one. **Note:** *Disconnect the jumper wires as soon as the test is complete to avoid damaging the servo.*

2 If the pulley moves correctly when connected to the battery with jumper wires, check the wiring to the ECM for continuity and check the wiring connector terminals. If the pulley tries to move but cannot, either the cables or the valve in the exhaust could have jammed.

3 If a code displayed on the LCD panel on the instrument cluster indicates a fault with the servo, but the servo motor is good, first check and if necessary adjust the control valve cables (see below). If the fault code is still displayed after adjusting the cables, make sure the ignition is OFF and disconnect the servo 3-pin wiring connector.

4 Turn the ignition ON and connect the positive (+) probe of a voltmeter to the red wire terminal on the loom side of the wiring connector and the negative (-) probe first to earth (ground), then to the black/brown wire terminal to check the input voltage. Turn the ignition OFF. If the input voltage is not as specified, check the wiring to the ECM for continuity and check the wiring connector terminals.

5 If the input voltage is good, check for continuity between the yellow wire terminal on the servo side of the wiring connector and earth (ground). There should be no continuity.

6 Reconnect the servo 3-pin wiring connector. Connect the mode select switch (see Section 9). Turn the select switch ON and turn the ignition ON to position the servo in the adjustment position. Turn the ignition OFF. Disconnect the 3-pin wiring connector.

7 Using an ohmmeter or multimeter set to the K-ohms scale, connect the positive (+) probe to the yellow wire terminal on the servo side of the connector and the negative (-) probe to the white wire terminal and measure the resistance. If the result is not as specified with the servo in the adjustment position, the servo is faulty.

8 If the result is as specified, it is likely a fault exists in the servo output voltage. Adjust the cables as described in Steps 31 and 32 to set the correct output voltage.

Servo removal and installation

Removal

9 Make sure the ignition is OFF. On K6 and K7 models remove the seat cowling (see Chapter

17.11a EXCV cable adjusters (arrowed) – K6 and K7 models

7). On K8 and K9 models raise the fuel tank (see Section 2).

10 Connect the mode select switch (see Section 9). Turn the select switch ON and turn the ignition ON to position the control valve servo in the adjustment position (the cable end sockets in the pulley are central). Turn the ignition OFF. Disconnect the servo wiring connectors **(see illustration 17.1a or b)**.

11 Slacken the locknut on each cable adjuster and thread it all the way back, then measure the amount of exposed thread between them so they can be reset to the same position later **(see illustrations)**. Turn the adjusters in to provide maximum freeplay in the cables.

12 Undo the servo mounting bolts and remove the servo **(see illustration 17.1a or b)**.

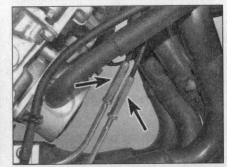

17.11b EXCV cable adjusters (arrowed) – K8 and K9 models

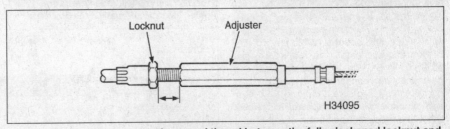

17.11c Measure the amount of exposed thread between the fully slackened locknut and the adjuster as shown

13 Hold the servo pulley using an adjustable spanner to prevent it turning and undo the pulley centre bolt. Remove the pulley from the servo motor with the cables attached. Note how the pulley aligns with the motor shaft. Detach the cables from the motor body and pulley noting how they locate and which fits where.

Installation

14 Make sure the servo shaft is positioned so the line is central at the top. Locate the cables on the servo and connect them to the pulley – refer to Step 21 or 22 for cable identification if you are not sure which fits where. Slide the pulley onto the shaft with the cable sockets at the top aligned with the line on the shaft. Counter-hold the pulley as on removal and tighten the bolt to the specified torque setting.

15 Fit the servo onto its mounts and tighten the bolts **(see illustration 17.1a or b)**. Connect the servo wiring connectors.

16 Turn the adjusters on the cables as required until the measured amount of exposed thread is set on each cable, then tighten the adjuster locknuts (see Step 11).

17 Remove the model select switch (see Section 9). On K6 and K7 models install the seat cowling (see Chapter 7). On K8 and K9 models lower the fuel tank (see Section 2).

Control valve inspection

18 Remove the right-hand fairing side panel (see Chapter 7).

19 Unscrew the exhaust control valve servo pulley cable bracket nuts and detach the cables from the pulley **(see illustrations 16.46a and b)**.

20 Check the operation of the control valve; it should turn smoothly and be held in the fully closed position by the return spring. Individual components are not available for the valve; if it is damaged or corroded the exhaust downpipe assembly must be replaced with a new one.

Cable removal, installation and adjustment

21 On K6 and K7 models the No. 1 cable is marked 01H0CL and fits into the upper socket in the servo pulley and the upper

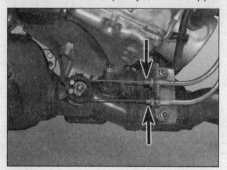

17.25 Measure the amount of exposed thread (arrowed) on the end of each cable elbow before detaching them

socket in the valve pulley **(see illustrations 17.1a and 17.25)**. The No. 2 cable is marked 01H0OP and fits into the lower socket in the servo pulley and the lower socket in the valve pulley.

22 On K8 and K9 models the No. 1 cable is marked 37H0CL and fits into the front socket in the servo pulley and the upper socket in the valve pulley **(see illustrations 17.1b and 17.25)**. The No. 2 cable is marked 37H0OP and fits into the rear socket in the servo pulley and the lower socket in the valve pulley.

Removal

23 Remove the right-hand fairing side panel (see Chapter 7).

24 Disconnect the cables from the servo pulley (see Steps 9 to 13).

25 Measure the amount of exposed thread on each cable in the bracket on the exhaust so they can be reset to the same position later **(see illustration)**. Slacken the locknuts and detach the cables from the bracket and pulley, noting which fits where.

Installation and adjustment

26 If the same cables are being re-fitted, connect the cable ends to the valve pulley on the exhaust then set the cables in the bracket on the exhaust so that the measured amount of exposed thread is set on each cable, then tighten the locknuts **(see illustration 17.25)** – see Step 21 or 22 for cable identification if you are not sure which fits where. Connect the cables to the servo pulley (see Steps 14 to 17).

27 If new cables are being fitted, connect the No. 1 cable end to the valve pulley on the exhaust then set the cable in the bracket on the exhaust on so that the measured amount of exposed thread is set, then tighten the locknut **(see illustration 17.25)** – see Step 21 or 22 for cable identification if you are not sure which fits where. Set the No. 1 cable straight, then loosen the adjuster locknut **(see illustration 17.11a or b)** and turn the adjuster to set the length of the exposed inner cable (servo motor end) to 41 to 42 mm on K6 and K7 models, and 44 to 45 mm on K8 and K9 models **(see illustration)**. Tighten the adjuster locknut.

28 Turn the adjuster on the No. 2 cable fully in. Connect the No. 2 cable end to the valve pulley on the exhaust then set the cable in the bracket on the exhaust so that the length of the exposed inner cable (servo motor end) is 60 to 61 mm on all models **(see illustration 17.27)**. Tighten the locknuts against the bracket.

29 Connect the cables to the servo pulley (see Steps 14 and 15). Now set the adjuster on the No. 2 cable so there is 11 to 12 mm of exposed thread, then tighten the locknut.

30 Make sure the mode select switch is OFF. Turn the ignition ON and check the movement of the servo pulley and cables. Turn the mode select switch ON and check the LCD display on the instrument cluster. If no fault code is displayed the cable adjustment is correct.

31 If fault code C46 is displayed, the cables need to be readjusted as follows to correct the output voltage. Turn the ignition off. Disconnect the servo 2-pin wiring connector **(see illustration 17.1a or b)**. Using a 12 volt battery and jumper wires, connect the +ve terminal of the battery to the pink wire terminal on the servo side of the connector and the –ve lead to the grey wire terminal. This sets the valve to its fully closed position – disconnect the battery as soon as the position is reached. Turn the ignition on. Using a multimeter connect the +ve probe to the yellow wire terminal in the servo 3-pin wiring connector, with it still connected, and the –ve probe to the black/brown wire terminal and measure the output voltage. It should be as specified for the closed position. If not, set the valve in adjustment position (Step 10). Slacken the locknut on the No. 1 cable adjuster **(see illustration 17.11a or b)** and turn the adjuster out a bit, then recheck the output voltage with the valve in the closed position as before. Repeat the procedure until the output voltage in the closed position is as specified. If C46 still comes up with the output voltage within the specified range but below 0.9 volts, readjust to between 0.9 and the upper value of the range.

32 Now connect the +ve terminal of the battery to the grey wire terminal on the servo side of the connector and the –ve lead to the pink wire terminal. This sets the valve to its fully open position – disconnect the battery as soon as the position is reached. Turn the ignition on. Using a multimeter connect the +ve probe to the yellow wire terminal in the servo 3-pin wiring connector, with it still connected, and the –ve probe to the black/brown wire terminal and measure the output voltage. It should be as specified for the open position. If not, set the valve in adjustment position (Step 10). Slacken the locknut on the No. 2 cable adjuster and turn the adjuster out a bit, then recheck the output voltage with the valve in the open position as before. Repeat

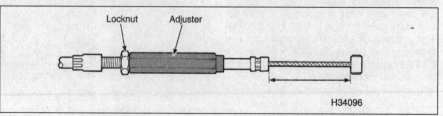

17.27 Set the exposed length of inner cable as specified

H34096

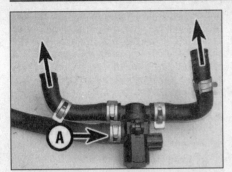

18.5 Air blown in via hose A should flow through the valve and out the hoses as shown

18.6 Apply 12V to the terminals (arrowed) and repeat the airflow check

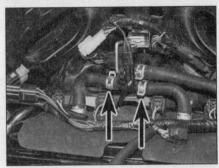

18.9 Detach the hoses (arrowed) from the control valve

the procedure until the output voltage in the open position is as specified.

33 If C46 still comes up with the output voltage within the specified range have the system checked by a Suzuki dealer.

Caution: Incorrect adjustment of the output voltage can damage the servo.

18 PAIR (pulse air supply) system

General information

1 To reduce the amount of unburned hydrocarbons released in the exhaust gases, a pulsed secondary air (PAIR) system is fitted. The system consists of the control valve (mounted above the valve cover), the reed valves (incorporated in the cylinder head) and the hoses between them and the air filter housing. The control valve is actuated electronically by the ECM.

2 Under certain operating conditions, the PAIR control valve allows filtered air to be drawn through it, the reed valves and cylinder head passages and into the exhaust ports. The air mixes with the exhaust gases, causing any unburned particles of the fuel in the

mixture to be burnt in the exhaust port/pipes. This process changes a considerable amount of hydrocarbons and carbon monoxide into relatively harmless carbon dioxide and water. The reed valves are fitted to prevent the flow of exhaust gases back into the control valve and air filter housing.

3 The system is not adjustable and requires no maintenance, except to ensure that the hoses are in good condition and are securely connected at each end, and that there is no build-up of carbon fouling the reed valves. Replace any hoses that are cracked, split or generally deteriorated, with new ones. The reed valves can be checked for any build-up of carbon by removing the valve cover (see Chapter 2) – if any is found, clean up the valves and their housings.

Testing

Control valve

4 Remove the valve from the motorcycle (see Steps 10 to 12).

5 Check the operation of the control valve by blowing through the air filter housing hose union; air should flow freely through the valve and out of the reed valve hoses **(see illustration)**.

6 Now connect battery voltage (12 volts) to the valve wiring connector terminals and

repeat the check **(see illustration)**; no air should now flow through the valve if it is functioning correctly.

7 Check the resistance of the control valve windings by connecting an ohmmeter between its wiring connector terminals and compare the reading obtained to that given in the Specifications. Replace the valve with a new one if faulty.

Reed valves

8 Remove the air filter housing (see Section 7).

9 Disconnect each reed valve hose from the control valve **(see illustration)**. Check the valve by blowing and sucking on the hose end. Air should flow through the hose only when blown down it and not when sucked back up. If this is not the case the reed valve is faulty. Check the other valve in the same way.

Component renewal

Control valve

10 Remove the air filter housing (see Section 7).

11 Detach the reed valve hoses from the unions on the valve cover then disconnect the wiring connector **(see illustration)**. Free the control valve from its mount and remove it **(see illustration)**.

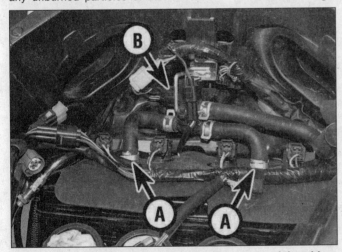

18.11a Detach the hoses (A) from the valve cover and the wiring connector (B) from the control valve . . .

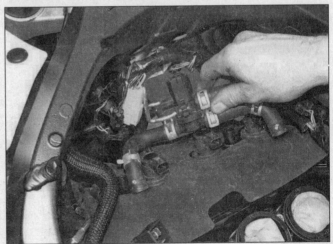

18.11b . . . then free the valve and remove it

12 Detach the hoses from the valve if required, noting which fits where.

13 Installation is the reverse of removal. Make sure the hoses are securely connected at each end.

Reed valves

14 Remove the valve cover (see Chapter 2) – this procedure incorporates removing the reed valves from the camshaft holders on the cylinder head.

15 Make sure the reed valves and their housings are clean. Check the reeds for cracks and make sure they seat correctly at rest.

16 Installation is the reverse of removal.

19 EVAP system (California models)

1 This system prevents the escape of fuel vapour into the atmosphere by storing it in a charcoal-filled canister.

2 When the engine is not running, excess fuel vapour from the tank passes, via the breather hose into the canister. When the engine is started, the vapour passes from the canister into the throttle bodies to be burned during the normal combustion process. On K6 and K7 models the vapour passes through a pressure control valve on its way from the tank to the canister. On K8 and K9 models the vapour passes through a purge control solenoid valve on its way from the canister to the throttle bodies.

3 The canister has a one way valve in its end which allows air to be drawn into the system as the volume of fuel decreases in the tank, but doesn't allow vapour to escape. The system also has a fuel shut-off valve which prevents any fuel escaping through it in the event of the bike falling over.

4 The system is not adjustable. Check that all the hoses are in good condition and are securely connected at each end. Replace any hoses that are cracked, split or generally deteriorated with new ones.

5 On K6 and K7 models the pressure control valve can be checked by disconnecting the hoses from it and blowing through it – remove the seat cowling for access (see Chapter 7). Note which way round the valve fits. Air should pass through the valve easily when blowing into it from the canister side, but it should be harder to blow through from the fuel tank side. If the performance of the control valve is suspect have it checked by a Suzuki dealer or replace it with a new one.

6 On K8 and K9 models the purge control solenoid valve can be checked by disconnecting the hoses and wiring connector from it and blowing through it, first through one hose union then the other – raise the fuel tank to access the valve (see Section 2). Air should pass through the valve easily in both directions. Now connect battery voltage (12 volts) across the valve wiring connector terminals and repeat the check; no air should flow through the valve in either direction if it is functioning correctly. If the performance of the control valve is suspect have it checked by a Suzuki dealer or replace it with a new one.

7 The fuel shut-off valve is located below the front of the battery. The valve should allow airflow in one direction (from the tank to the canister) only. To test it, disconnect the hoses and blow through the valve – it may be easier to disconnect the hoses from the tank and the pressure control valve on K6 and K7 models, and from the tank and the canister (remove the seat cowling for access) on K8 and K9 models.

Caution: Fuel vapour is toxic. A small amount of vapour will be present in the valve when it is removed from the bike. Take care not to inhale the vapour when checking the valve.

20 Ignition system check

⚠ *Warning: The energy levels in electronic systems can be very high. On no account should the ignition be switched on whilst the coils or plugs are being held. Shocks from the HT circuit can be most unpleasant. Secondly, it is vital that the engine is not turned over or run with any of the coils removed, and that the plugs are soundly earthed (grounded) when the system is checked for sparking. The system components can be seriously damaged if the HT circuit becomes isolated.*

1 As no means of adjustment is available, any failure of the system can be traced to failure of a system component or a simple wiring fault. Of the two possibilities, the latter is by far the most likely. In the event of failure, check the system in a logical fashion, as described below.

2 Remove the air filter housing (see Section 7). Referring to Section 10, trace the wiring from the cam position (CMP), crankshaft position (CKP), throttle position (TPS), engine coolant temperature (ECT) and gear position (GP) sensors to their respective wiring connectors and then to the ECM. Ensure that the connector terminals are clean and that the connectors are secure.

3 Check the battery condition and the ignition circuit fuse (see Chapter 8).

4 Refer to Section 22 and disconnect the ECM multi-pin wiring connectors, then turn the ignition ON. Connect the probes of a voltmeter between the orange/green (UK and European models) or orange/white (all other models) and the black/white wire terminals on the loom side of the wiring connector and check for battery input voltage (12V approx). Turn the ignition OFF. If the input voltage is not as specified, check the ignition switch, sidestand relay and engine stop switch (see Chapter 8).

5 Disconnect each ignition coil wiring connector **(see illustration)**. Clean the area around the coil seal to prevent any dirt falling into the spark plug channel, then pull the coils off the spark plugs and reconnect the wiring connectors **(see illustration)**. **Note:** *To avoid damaging the wiring, always disconnect the connectors before removing the coils. Do not attempt to lever the coils off the plugs or pull them off with pliers. Do not drop the coils.*

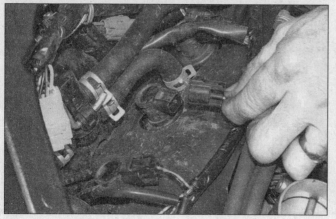

20.5a Disconnect the wiring connector . . .

20.5b . . . then pull the coil off the spark plug

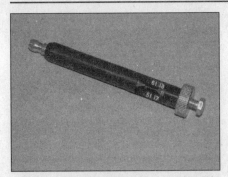

20.8 Adjustable ignition spark gap tester

6 Connect each coil to a known good spark plug and lay each plug back in its bore angled so the threads are earthed (grounded) against the cylinder head – NOT against the valve cover as it is magnesium.

Caution: Do not lay the plugs against the magnesium valve cover as its finish could be damaged.

⚠️ *Warning: Do not remove any of the spark plugs from the engine to perform this check – atomised fuel being pumped out of the open spark plug hole could ignite, causing severe injury!*

7 Having observed the above precautions, check that the kill switch is in the RUN position and the transmission is in neutral, then turn the ignition switch ON, pull the clutch lever in and turn the engine over on the starter motor. If the system is in good condition a regular, fat blue spark should be evident at each plug electrode. If the spark appears thin or yellowish, or is non-existent, further investigation will be necessary.

8 The ignition system must be able to produce a spark at each coil which is capable of jumping a particular size gap. A healthy system should produce a spark capable of jumping 8 mm. Use a commercially available adjustable ignition spark gap test tool to check the strength of the spark **(see illustration)**.

9 Connect one of the coils to the protruding

electrode on the test tool (all others must remain earthed as in Step 6), and clip the tool to a good earth (ground) on the engine (not the valve cover) or frame. Check that the kill switch is in the RUN position, turn the ignition switch ON and turn the engine over on the starter motor. If the system is in good condition a regular, fat blue spark should be seen to jump the gap between the test tool electrodes. Repeat the test on the other coils. If the test results are good the entire ignition system can be considered good. If one or more of the sparks appears thin or yellowish, or is non-existent, further investigation will be necessary. Turn the ignition OFF.

10 Ignition faults can be divided into two categories, namely those where the ignition system has failed completely, and those which are due to a partial failure. The likely faults are listed below, starting with the most probable source of failure. Work through the list systematically, referring to the relevant sections for details of the necessary checks and tests.

● Loose, corroded or damaged wiring connections, broken or shorted wiring between any of the component parts of the ignition system (see Chapter 8).
● Faulty spark plug, dirty or damaged plug electrodes, incorrect gap between electrodes, incorrect spark plug (see Chapter 1).
● Faulty ignition switch or engine stop switch (see Chapter 8).
● Faulty clutch switch, neutral switch, sidestand switch or relay and diodes (see Chapter 8).
● Faulty crankshaft position sensor (see Section 10).
● Faulty ignition coil.
● Faulty ECM.

11 If the above checks don't reveal the cause of the problem, have the ignition system tested by a Suzuki dealer.

21 Ignition coils

Removal

1 Remove the air filter housing (see Section 7). Disconnect the battery negative (-ve) lead.
2 Disconnect each ignition coil wiring connector **(see illustration 20.5a)**. Clean the area around the coil seal to prevent any dirt falling into the spark plug channel, then pull the coils off the spark plugs **(see illustration 20.5b)**. Note: *To avoid damaging the wiring, always disconnect the connectors before removing the coils. Do not attempt to lever the coils off the plugs or pull them off with pliers. Do not drop the coils.*

Check

3 Ensure the primary circuit terminals in the top of the coil and the spark plug terminal inside the coil are undamaged and free from corrosion.
4 Using an ohmmeter or multimeter set to the ohms scale, measure the coil primary resistance between the primary circuit terminals, connecting the positive (+ve) meter probe to the right-hand terminal **(see illustration)**. Compare the result with the specifications at the beginning of this Chapter.
5 Now set the meter to the K-ohms scale and measure the coil secondary resistance between the negative (-ve) primary circuit terminal (the left-hand terminal) and the spark plug terminal, connecting the positive (+ve) meter probe to the spark plug terminal **(see illustration)**. Compare the result with the specifications at the beginning of this Chapter.
6 If either of the results are not as specified the coil is probably faulty. Have the coil peak voltage tested by a Suzuki dealer to confirm this.

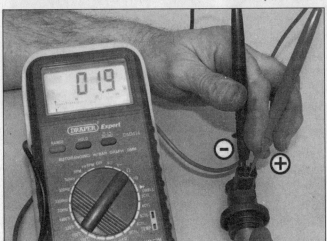

21.4 Measuring the coil primary resistance

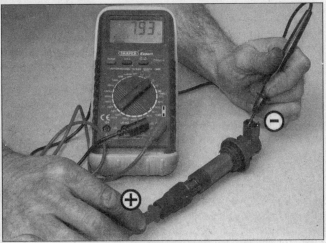

21.5 Measuring the coil secondary resistance

22.3a Displace the starter relay from its mount . . .

22.3b . . . then unscrew the bolt (arrowed) . . .

22.3c . . . and draw the sidestand/turn signal relay out . . .

22.3d . . . and position them both clear of the ECM

22.3e Release the strap (arrowed) . . .

22.3f . . . then lift the ECM out and disconnect the wiring connectors

Installation

7 Ensure the spark plug channels are free from any obstructions and press the coils fully home onto the spark plugs **(see illustration 20.5b)**.
8 Reconnect the wiring connectors **(see illustration 20.5a)**.
9 Connect the battery negative (-ve) lead and install the air filter housing.

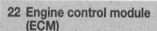

22 Engine control module (ECM)

1 If the testing procedures described in this Chapter indicate that all ignition and fuel injection system components are functioning correctly, yet a fault exists, take the machine to a Suzuki dealer for testing. No details are available for checking the ECM on home workshop equipment.
2 To remove the ECM, first remove the rider's seat (see Chapter 7) and disconnect the battery negative (-ve) lead. Remove the seat cowling (see Chapter 7).
3 On K6 and K7 models undo the frame cross-piece bolts and remove it **(see illustration 9.2a)**. Displace the starter relay and the sidestand/turn signal relay **(see illustrations)**. Free the rubber retainer **(see illustration)**. Draw the ECM out then disconnect the multi-pin wiring connectors **(see illustration)**.

4 On K8 and K9 models displace the starter relay, the tip-over (TO) sensor and the fuel pump and cooling fan relays. Undo the two screws and remove the holder. Draw the

ECM out then disconnect the multi-pin wiring connectors **(see illustrations)**.
5 Installation is the reverse of removal. Make sure the wiring connectors are clean and secure.

22.4a Displace the starter relay (arrowed) . . .

22.4b . . . and the relays and TO sensor (arrowed)

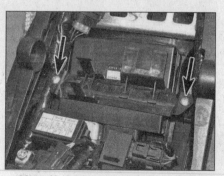

22.4c Undo the screws (arrowed) and remove the holder . . .

22.4d . . . then lift the ECM out and disconnect the wiring connectors

23 Immobiliser

Note: *The immobiliser is not fitted as standard on US and Canadian models*

1 The immobiliser verifies the authenticity of the key being used by matching its code with that of the ECM, and will not allow the engine to be started if the match is not exact.

2 When the ignition switch is turned on using the key and the kill switch is set to the RUN position a transponder in the key communicates with the immobiliser antennae around the ignition switch, and that in turn communicates with the ECM. The immobiliser light (key symbol) in the instrument cluster will flash a few times, the number of flashes corresponding to the number of keys registered to the system. If the match is made the immobiliser light (key symbol) in the instrument cluster comes on for two seconds. If there is a non-match or a problem the light flashes rapidly. If this happens, turn the ignition OFF then ON again as it is possible for radio interference to affect the communication process.

3 No further information is provided for the system. If there is a problem with a key, all keys are lost or the bike will not start and all other possible causes have been eliminated, take the bike to a Suzuki dealer.

24 Drive mode selector – K8 and K9 models

1 The drive model selector switch allows the rider to switch between three different engine mapping characteristics. Mode A, which is the standard and default mode, provides normal throttle response for maximum performance. Models B and C deliver progressively softer throttle response.

2 When the ignition switch is turned on and the kill switch is set to the RUN position mode A is automatically selected. To change mode start the engine and push the model selector for 2 seconds until the mode indicator shows A. Now switch from A to B to C to A and so on using the bottom switch, or from A to C to B to A and so on using the top switch. The engine must be running to change mode, but note that if you change mode while riding with the throttle open engine speed will change. Turning the kill switch or ignition switch off resets the system to mode A.

3 If there is a problem when changing modes the mode indicator blinks. If this happens, turn the engine off, then restart it and try again. If it happens again, first check the wiring and connectors to and in the handlebar switch housing (see Chapter 8). If all is good take the bike to a Suzuki dealer equipped with the SDS software – function of the system can only be checked with this.

Notes

Chapter 5
Frame and suspension

Contents

Degrees of difficulty

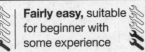

Easy, suitable for novice with little experience	Fairly easy, suitable for beginner with some experience	Fairly difficult, suitable for competent DIY mechanic	Difficult, suitable for experienced DIY mechanic	Very difficult, suitable for expert DIY or professional

Specifications

Front forks

Fork inner tube diameter	41 mm
Fork oil type	Showa SS05 fork oil
Fork oil capacity	
600K6 and K7 models	413 cc
600K8 and K9 models	410 cc
750K6 and K7 models	408 cc
750K8 and K9 models	418 cc
Fork oil level*	
600K6 and K7 models	107 mm
600K8 and K9 models	110 mm
750K6 and K7 models	112 mm
750K8 and K9 models	115 mm
Fork spring free length	
600K6 and K7 models	
Standard	268 mm
Minimum	262 mm
600K8 and K9 models	
Standard	266 mm
Minimum	260 mm
750K6 and K7 models	
Standard	264.8 mm
Minimum	259.5 mm
750K8 and K9 models	
Standard	264.6 mm
Minimum	259 mm
Fork tube protrusion above top yoke (not inc. top bolt).	5 mm

Oil level is measured from the top of the tube with the fork spring removed and the leg fully compressed.

Steering damper

Solenoid valve resistance	12.5 ohms @ 20°C
Solenoid valve voltage	approx. 10 volts

Rear suspension

Spring pre-load adjustment range	
Min pre-load	186.4 mm
Max pre-load	176.4 mm
Standard pre-load	
750 K8 and K9	182.3 mm
All other models	181.4 mm
Swingarm pivot bolt runout (max)	0.3 mm

Torque settings

Clutch lever clamp bolt	10 Nm
Fork clamp bolts (top and bottom yoke)	23 Nm
Fork compression damping adjuster	
K6 and K7 models	23 Nm
K8 and K9 models	18 Nm
Fork damper cartridge bolt	35 Nm
Fork top bolt	35 Nm
Front brake master cylinder clamp bolts	10 Nm
Handlebar clamp bolts	23 Nm
Rear brake peal holder bolt	35 Nm
Rear shock absorber nuts	50 Nm
Rear shock absorber upper mounting bracket nut	115 Nm
Rear suspension linkage arm-to-linkage rod nut	78 Nm
Rear suspension linkage arm-to-swingarm nut	98 Nm
Rear suspension linkage rod-to-frame nut	
K6 and K7 models	78 Nm
K8 and K9 models	98 Nm
Rider's footrest bracket bolts	23 Nm
Sidestand mounting bracket bolts	50 Nm
Sidestand pivot bolt	50 Nm
Sidestand pivot bolt nut	40 Nm
Steering damper mounting bolt and nut	23 Nm
Steering head bearing adjuster nut initial setting (see text)	45 Nm
Steering head bearing locknut	
K6 and K7 models	80 Nm
K8 and K9 models	90 Nm
Steering stem nut	90 Nm
Swingarm pivot bolt	15 Nm
Swingarm pivot nut	100 Nm
Swingarm pivot bolt locknut	90 Nm

1 General information

All models have a twin spar, box-section aluminium frame which uses the engine as a stressed member.

All models are fitted with upside-down coil-sprung and hydraulically-damped telescopic forks that are adjustable for spring pre-load, rebound and compression damping. All models are fitted with an hydraulic steering damper, that on K8 and K9 models is electronically controlled.

At the rear, an alloy swingarm acts on a single shock absorber via a three-way linkage. The shock absorber is adjustable for spring pre-load, rebound and compression damping on all models.

2 Frame inspection and repair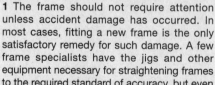

1 The frame should not require attention unless accident damage has occurred. In most cases, fitting a new frame is the only satisfactory remedy for such damage. A few frame specialists have the jigs and other equipment necessary for straightening frames to the required standard of accuracy, but even then there is no simple way of assessing to what extent the frame may have been over stressed.

2 After a high mileage, the frame should be examined closely for signs of cracking or splitting at the welded joints. Loose engine mounting bolts can cause ovaling or fracturing of the mounting points. Minor damage can often be repaired by specialised welding, depending on the extent and nature of the damage.

3 Remember that a frame that is out of alignment will cause handling problems. If, as the result of an accident, misalignment is suspected, it will be necessary to strip the machine completely so the frame can be thoroughly checked.

3 Footrests, brake pedal and gearchange lever

Rider's footrests

1 Remove the E-clip from the bottom of the footrest pivot pin, then withdraw the pivot pin and remove the footrest, noting the fitting of

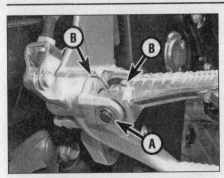

3.1 Remove the E-clip (A) and withdraw the pivot pin. Note the position of the return spring ends (B)

3.2a Unscrew the bracket bolts (arrowed) . . .

3.2b . . . the bracket can be mounted in three different positions using the different holes

the return spring (see illustration). Discard the E-clip if it is damaged and fit a new one on reassembly. On installation apply a small amount of grease to the pivot pin and make sure the E-clip is properly located in the groove in the pivot pin.

2 The rider's footrest brackets can be set in three different positions to suit rider preference. Unscrew the bolts securing the bracket to the bracket holder (see illustration). Clean the bolt threads and apply some fresh threadlock. Reposition the footrest assembly as required, then fit the bolts and tighten them to the torque setting specified at the beginning of the Chapter (see illustration). After moving the right-hand footrest assembly adjust the rear brake pedal height if required, and make sure the brake light switch comes on when it should, and adjust it if required – see Chapter 1, Section 10. After moving the left-hand assembly adjust the gearchange lever position and height as required (Steps 11 and 13).

Passenger footrests

3 Remove the E-clip from the bottom of the footrest pivot pin, then withdraw the pivot pin and remove the footrest, noting the

position of the detent plate, ball and spring (see illustration). Discard the E-clip if it is damaged and fit a new one on reassembly. Apply a small amount of grease to the pivot pin, detent plate and ball. Make sure the E-clip is properly located in the groove in the pivot pin.

Brake pedal

Removal

4 Unscrew the two bolts securing the footrest bracket to the frame, then turn the bracket round (see illustration 3.2a). Take care not to strain the brake hoses or the brake light switch wiring.
5 Unhook the brake pedal return spring and brake light switch spring from the bracket on the back of the brake pedal (see illustration).
6 Remove the split pin and washer from the clevis pin securing the brake pedal to the master cylinder pushrod (see illustration 3.5). Remove the clevis pin and separate the pedal from the pushrod.
7 Undo the brake pedal holder bolt, then remove the footrest/holder and pedal (see illustration 3.5). Slide the pedal off the holder.

Installation

8 Installation is the reverse of removal, noting the following:
● Apply grease to the brake pedal pivot.
● Align the lugs on the holder with the bracket.
● Clean the brake pedal holder bolt threads and apply some fresh threadlock. Tighten the bolt to the torque setting specified at the beginning of this Chapter.
● Use a new split pin on the clevis pin securing the brake pedal to the master cylinder pushrod and bend the split pin ends securely (see illustration 3.5).
● Clean the footrest bracket bolt threads and apply some fresh threadlock. Tighten the bolts to the torque setting specified at the beginning of this Chapter.
● Adjust the rear brake pedal height if required, and make sure the brake light switch comes on when it should, and adjust it if required – see Chapter 1, Section 10.

Gearchange lever

Removal

9 Loosen the gearchange linkage rod locknuts, then unscrew the rod and separate

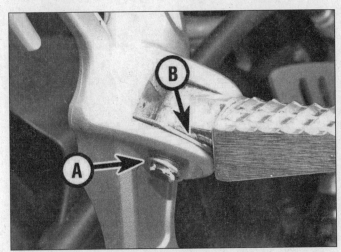

3.3 Remove the E-clip (A) and withdraw the pivot pin. Note the position of the detent plate, ball and spring (B)

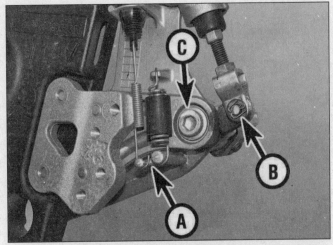

3.5 Unhook the springs from the bracket (A). Remove the split pin and washer (B) on the brake pedal clevis pin. Pedal holder bolt (C)

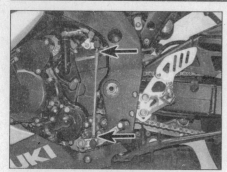

3.9 Loosen the locknuts (arrowed) and unscrew the rod

3.10 Remove the circlip and washer then slide the lever off

3.11 Unscrew the pivot (arrowed) – it can be placed in either of the other holes

● Apply grease to the gearchange lever pivot. Use a new circlip.
● Adjust the gearchange lever height as required by screwing the rod in or out of the lever and arm, then tighten the locknuts securely. Note that Suzuki specify a standard position for the lever tip of 65 to 75 mm below the top surface of the rider's footrest.

3.12 Unscrew the bolt and slide the arm off the shaft

4 Sidestand

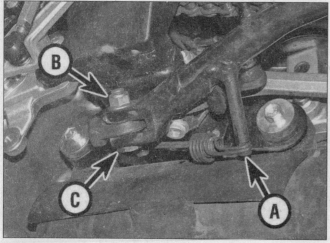

3.14 Set the gearchange lever tip position to the specified distance below the top surface of the footrest

it from the lever and the gearchange arm – the rod is reverse-threaded on one end and so will simultaneously unscrew from both lever and arm **(see illustration)**. Note the how far the rod is threaded into the lever and arm as this determines the height of the lever relative to the footrest.

10 Remove the circlip and washer from the end of the lever pivot and slide the lever off **(see illustration)**. Use a new circlip on installation.

11 To change the position of the gearchange lever unscrew the lever pivot **(see illustration)**. Clean the pivot threads and apply some fresh

threadlock. Reposition the pivot as required and tighten it.

12 If required undo the gearchange linkage arm pinch bolt and remove the arm from the shaft, noting any alignment marks **(see illustration)**. If no marks are visible, make your own before removing the arm so that it can be correctly aligned with the shaft on installation.

Installation

13 Installation is the reverse of removal, noting the following:

● If removed align the gearchange linkage arm with the shaft as noted on removal.

Removal

1 The sidestand pivots on a bracket which is bolted to the frame. Springs between the bracket and the stand ensure that it is held in the retracted or extended position.

2 Support the bike using an auxiliary stand. To remove the stand only, first unhook the springs **(see illustration)**. Undo the pivot bolt nut, then undo the pivot bolt and remove the stand.

3 To remove the bracket, unscrew the sidestand switch bolts and displace the switch **(see illustration)**. Undo the bolts securing the bracket to the frame.

4.2 Release the springs (A). Undo the nut (B) then unscrew the pivot bolt (C)

4.3 Sidestand switch bolts (arrowed)

5.2 Front brake light switch connector (arrowed) – K8/K9 type shown

5.3 Handlebar end-weight screw (arrowed)

5.4 Undo the reservoir bolt (A) and the clamp bolts (B)

Installation

4 If the sidestand bracket was removed, tighten its bolts to the specified torque setting.

5 Apply grease to the pivot bolt shank. Locate the stand on its bracket, then fit the bolt and tighten it to the specified torque. Now fit the nut and tighten it to the specified torque. Fit the springs onto their posts. Check that the springs are correctly located and hold the stand securely up when not in use – an accident is almost certain to occur if the stand extends while the machine is in motion.

6 Check the operation of the sidestand switch (see Chapter 8).

5 Handlebars and levers

Right handlebar removal

Note: *Unless the handlebar is being replaced with a new one the bar end-weight and twistgrip can be left in place.*

1 Raise or remove the fuel tank to prevent the possibility of damage (see Chapter 4).

2 Disconnect the brake light switch wiring connector(s) from the switch on the underside of the master cylinder (see illustration). Release the throttle cables from the twistgrip pulley (see Chapter 4). Position the switch/twistgrip housing away from the handlebar.

3 If required, undo the screw retaining the bar end-weight and remove the weight,

5.7a Disconnect the wiring connector (arrowed) . . .

5.7b . . . then undo the screws (arrowed) and detach the switch housing

then pull the twistgrip off the handlebar (see illustration).

4 Undo the bolt securing the brake fluid reservoir bracket to the handlebar (see illustration). Undo the front brake master cylinder clamp bolts and remove the clamp. Wrap the master cylinder and reservoir assembly in rag and position it clear of the handlebar. Make sure no strain is placed on the hose. Keep the fluid reservoir upright to prevent air entering the system.

5 Follow Steps 10 to 12 and remove the top yoke and handlebar.

Left handlebar removal

Note: *Unless the handlebar is being replaced with a new one the bar end-weight, grip and clutch lever/lever bracket can be left in place.*

6 Raise or remove the fuel tank to prevent the possibility of damage (see Chapter 4).

7 Disconnect the clutch switch wiring connector from the switch on the underside of the clutch lever bracket (see illustration). Undo the handlebar switch housing screws then separate the halves and position them away from the handlebar (see illustration).

8 Screw the clutch cable adjuster fully into the lever bracket (see illustration). Align the slots in the adjuster and the bracket, then pull the outer cable end out of the adjuster and release the inner cable from the lever (see illustration). If there is not enough slack in the cable to free it from the adjuster, remove the clutch lever (see Step 14).

9 If required, undo the screw retaining the bar end-weight and remove the weight, then peel the grip off the handlebar (see illustration). **Note:** *The grip will probably be stuck in place – it may be necessary to slit the grip with a sharp knife in order to remove it.* Loosen the

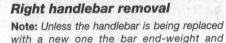

5.8a Create as much slack as possible . . .

5.8b . . . then detach the clutch cable as described

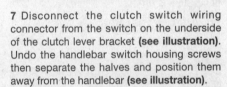

5.9a Handlebar end-weight screw (arrowed)

5.9b Clutch lever bracket clamp bolt (arrowed)

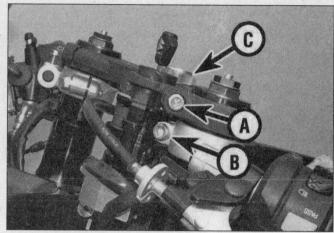

5.10 Fork clamp bolt (A), handlebar clamp bolt (B), steering stem nut (C)

clutch lever bracket bolt and slide the bracket off the handlebar (see illustration).

10 Loosen the fork clamp bolts in the top yoke (see illustration).

11 Undo the steering stem nut and remove the washer, noting which way up it fits. Ease the top yoke up off the fork tubes. Ensure no strain is placed on the wiring.

12 Loosen the handlebar clamp bolt, then ease the handlebar up and off the fork (see illustration 5.10).

Handlebar installation

13 Installation is the reverse of removal, noting the following:

- Fit the handlebars loosely on the forks, then fit the top yoke. Fit the steering stem nut washer with its tapered side facing onto the yoke, then fit the steering stem nut and tighten it to the torque setting specified at the beginning of the Chapter (see illustration). Now tighten the fork clamp bolts to the specified torque setting (see illustration 5.10).
- Slide the handlebar up against the underside of the top yoke, locating the lug on the top of the handlebar clamp in the hole, then tighten the handlebar clamp bolt to the specified torque (see illustration).
- Ensure the front brake master cylinder

clamp is installed with the UP mark facing up, and align the clamp joint with the punch mark on the top of the handlebar (see illustration). Tighten the top clamp bolt first. Tighten the clamp bolts to the specified torque.

- Align the clutch lever bracket clamp joint with the punch mark on the bottom of the handlebar (see illustration). Refer to Chapters 2 and 1 for installation and adjustment of the clutch cable.
- Refer to Chapter 4 for installation of the throttle cables.
- When fitting the switch housings locate the peg in the bottom half of each housing in the hole in the underside of the handlebar (see illustration).
- If removed, apply a suitable non-permanent locking compound to the handlebar end-weight retaining screws. If new grips are being fitted, secure them using a suitable adhesive.
- Check the operation of the front brake light switch and clutch switch before riding the motorcycle.

Handlebar levers

14 To remove the clutch lever, first screw the clutch cable adjuster fully into the lever bracket to provide maximum freeplay in the

5.13a Tighten the steering stem nut to the specified torque

5.13b Locate the lug in the hole (arrowed) in the underside of the yoke

5.13c Align the master cylinder clamp mating surfaces with the punch mark (arrowed)

5.13d Align the clutch bracket clamp mating surfaces with the punch mark (arrowed)

5.13e Locate the peg (arrowed) in the hole

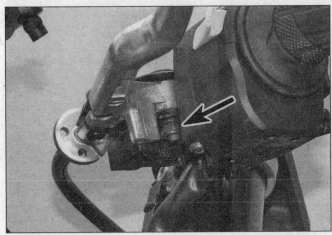

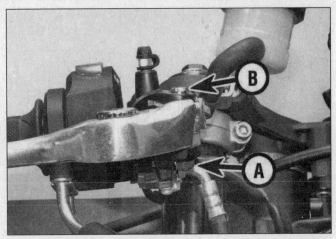

5.14 Unscrew the locknut (arrowed), then push the pivot bolt out

5.15 Unscrew the locknut (A) then undo the pivot screw bolt (B)

cable **(see illustration 5.8a)**. Align the slots in the adjuster and the bracket. Unscrew the lever pivot bolt locknut on the underside of the lever, then push the pivot bolt out and remove the lever, detaching the cable as you do **(see illustration)**.

15 To remove the front brake lever, undo the lever screw bolt locknut on the underside of the lever, then unscrew the pivot bolt and remove the lever **(see illustration)**.

16 Installation is the reverse of removal. Apply grease to the pivot shaft and the contact areas between the lever and its bracket, and on the brake lever apply silicone grease to the contact tip with the master cylinder pushrod. Grease the exposed end of the clutch cable and the cable socket in the lever. When fitting the brake lever tighten the screw, then counter-hold it and tighten the locknut. Adjust the clutch cable freeplay (see Chapter 1). Check the setting of the front brake lever span adjuster.

6 Fork removal and installation

Removal

1 Remove the fairing side panels, and if required for improved access the fairing (see Chapter 7).

2 Remove the front wheel (see Chapter 6). Remove the mudguard (see Chapter 7).

3 Work on each fork leg individually. Note the routing of the cables, wiring and hoses around the forks. If both fork legs are being removed, note which side fits where and mark them accordingly. When removing the right-hand fork unscrew the brake fluid reservoir bolt and displace the reservoir to access the clamp bolt in the top yoke **(see illustration 5.4)**.

4 Loosen but do not remove the fork clamp bolt in the top yoke and the handlebar clamp bolt **(see illustration 5.10)**.

5 If the forks are to be disassembled, or if the fork oil is being changed, note the current rebound damping adjuster setting then set it to its minimum (see Section 14), then loosen the fork top bolt **(see illustration)**.

6 Support the fork leg, then loosen but do not remove the clamp bolts in the bottom yoke **(see illustration)**. Remove the fork by twisting it and pulling it downwards, drawing the handlebar off the top as you do **(see illustration)**. Support the handlebars so they are out of the way.

Installation

7 Remove all traces of corrosion from the fork tubes and the yokes. Slide the fork leg up through the bottom yoke and handlebar clamp and into the top yoke **(see illustration 6.6b)**.

> **HAYNES HiNT** *If the fork legs are seized in the yokes, spray the area with penetrating oil and allow time for it to soak in before trying again.*

Set the top of the fork tube (where it meets the fork top bolt) 5 mm above the top yoke.

8 Tighten the clamp bolts in the bottom yoke to the torque setting specified at the beginning of the Chapter **(see illustration 6.6a)**. If the fork has been dismantled or if the fork oil has been changed, tighten the fork top bolt to the specified torque setting **(see illustration 6.5)**. Tighten the fork clamp bolt in the top yoke to the specified torque setting **(see illustration 5.10)**.

9 Slide the handlebar up against the underside of the top yoke, locating the lug on the top of the handlebar clamp in the hole, then tighten the handlebar clamp bolt to the specified torque **(see illustrations 5.13b and 5.10)**.

10 Install the remaining components in the reverse order of removal. If the fork has been dismantled or if the fork oil has been changed reset the rebound damping adjuster as required (see Section 14).

11 Check the operation of the front forks and brake before taking the machine on the road.

6.5 Slacken the fork top bolt while the fork is clamped in the bottom yoke

6.6a Loosen the fork clamp bolts (arrowed) in the bottom yoke . . .

6.6b . . . and remove the fork

7.3 Unscrew the fork top bolt

7.4a Home-made spacer holding tool and slotted washer

7.4b Fit the tool onto the spacer, then compress the spring and slide the washer under the nut

7 Fork oil change

Special Tool: *Special tools are needed to disassemble the forks. Suzuki produces service tools (spacer holder Pt. No. 09940-94930 and stopper plate Pt. No. 09940-94922) to do this. Alternatively, use the home-made set-up shown, making sure the tool is wide enough to fit over the tube (see illustration 7.4a).*

1 After a high mileage the fork oil will deteriorate and its damping and lubrication qualities will be impaired. Always change the oil in both fork legs.

2 Remove the fork leg; ensure that the top bolt is loosened while the leg is still clamped in the bottom yoke (see Section 6).

3 Support the fork leg upright and unscrew the top bolt from the top of the outer tube **(see illustration)**. Slide the outer tube down onto the inner tube.

4 Fit the spacer holder tool onto the spacer and thread the arms into the holes **(see illustrations)**. Press down on the spacer holder to compress the spring then fit the stopper plate or slotted washer between the top of the spacer seat and the exposed locknut on the bottom of the top bolt. Carefully release the pressure on the tool and allow the plate or slotted washer to rest against the underside of the locknut.

5 Counter-hold the locknut using one spanner and unscrew the top bolt assembly using another spanner on the flats on the bottom of the pre-load adjuster, then thread the top bolt off the damper rod and remove it,

drawing the damping adjuster rod out with it **(see illustration)**. Check the condition of the top bolt O-ring and replace it with a new one if necessary **(see illustration 7.15a)**.

6 Press down on the spacer holder and remove the plate or slotted washer, then carefully allow the spring to relax. Remove the spacer seat and the spacer **(see illustration)**. Withdraw the spring from the tube, noting which way up it fits **(see illustration)**.

7 Invert the fork leg over a suitable container and pump the fork tubes and damper rod to expel as much oil as possible **(see illustration)**.

8 Support the leg and allow it to drain for several minutes. Wipe any excess oil off the spring and spacer. If the fork oil contains metal particles inspect the fork components for signs of wear (see Section 8).

9 Stand the fork upright and slowly pour in the correct quantity and type of fork oil as specified at the beginning of this Chapter, keeping a hold on the damper rod to prevent it sinking **(see illustration)**. Secure the fork leg upright and if required fit a slotted washer under the locknut as shown to prevent the rod sinking into the tube, and allow it to stand for several minutes to allow all the air to escape. Now pump the rod again – once all the air is expelled you should feel stiff resistance when pumping the rod. Make sure all air is expelled from the damper cartridge at this stage.

10 Fully compress the fork outer tube and damper rod into the inner tube and measure the oil level from the top of the outer tube **(see**

7.5 Counter-hold the locknut and thread the top bolt off the rod

7.6a Remove the spacer seat and spacer . . .

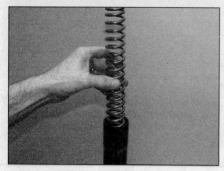

7.6b . . . and the spring

7.7 Drain all the old oil from the fork

7.9 Pour the fresh oil into the top of the tube

7.10 Measure the oil level with the fork held vertical

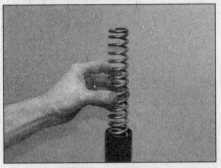

7.11a Fit the spring . . .

7.11b . . . then draw the rod out and tie some wire round to hold it up . . .

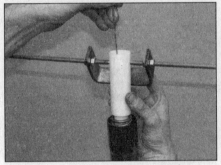

7.11c . . . while fitting the spacer . . .

7.11d . . . and the spacer seat

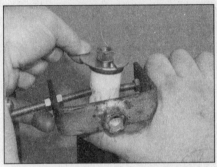

7.12 Fit the slotted washer between the spacer seat and the nut

illustration). Add or subtract oil until it is at the level specified at the beginning of this Chapter.

11 Install the spring with its tapered end upwards, sliding it over the damper rod **(see illustration)**. Draw the rod out and fit a piece of thin wire around the rod under the locknut to help keep it extended **(see illustration)**. Fit the spacer and the spacer seat, sliding them over the wire or holding tool if being used **(see illustrations)**.

12 Thread the locknut up to the top of the damper rod – this makes it easier to compress the spring and fit the washer or plate. Keeping the damper rod fully extended, press down on the spacer holder (see Step 4), then insert the stopper plate or slotted washer under the locknut **(see illustration)**. Remove the wire. Thread the locknut down to the bottom of the threads on the damper cartridge rod.

13 Insert the damping adjuster rod into the damper rod and thread the top bolt onto the damper rod all the way down until it seats lightly, using a spanner on the pre-load adjuster flats **(see illustration)**. Counter-hold the pre-load adjuster and tighten the locknut securely against it **(see illustration 7.5)**.

14 Press down on the spacer holder and remove the plate or slotted washer, then carefully release the spring pressure, and allow the spacer seat to rest on the underside of the top bolt. Remove the holding tool.

15 Make sure the top bolt O-ring is seated in its groove, and smear it with fork oil **(see illustration)**. Pull the outer tube all the way up off the inner tube and carefully screw the top bolt in, making sure it does not cross-thread **(see illustration)**. **Note:** *The top bolt can be tightened to the specified torque setting*

at this stage if the tube is held between the padded jaws of a vice. However, to avoid the risk of damaging the tube, a better method is to tighten the top bolt when the fork leg has been installed and is securely clamped in the bottom yoke (see Section 6).

16 Install the fork leg (see Section 6). Adjust the fork settings as required (see Section 14).

8 Fork overhaul

Disassembly

1 Always dismantle the fork legs separately to avoid interchanging parts. Store all

7.13 Fit the adjuster rod into the damper rod and thread the top bolt onto the damper rod

7.15a Check and lubricate the O-ring (arrowed)

7.15b Thread the top bolt into the tube

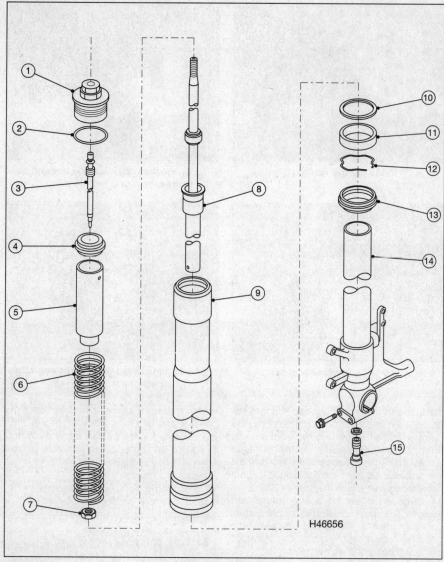

8.2 Slacken the damper cartridge bolt

8.1 Front fork components

1 Top bolt assembly
2 O-ring
3 Damping adjuster rod
4 Spacer seat
5 Spacer
6 Spring
7 Locknut
8 Damper cartridge
9 Outer tube
10 Washer
11 Oil seal
12 Retaining clip
13 Dust seal
14 Inner tube
15 Damper rod bolt and
   washer

components in separate, clearly marked containers **(see illustration)**.
2 Loosen, then lightly re-tighten, the damper cartridge bolt in the bottom of the fork slider bolt **(see illustration)**. If the bolt turns the damper cartridge with it rather than loosening from it, and an air wrench is not available, carry on and obtain a holding tool as described in Step 5.
3 Drain the fork oil (see Section 7, steps 3 to 8).
4 Draw the inner and outer tubes fully apart **(see illustration)**.
5 Remove the previously loosened damper cartridge bolt and its sealing washer from the bottom of the fork **(see illustration)**. Discard the washer as a new one must be fitted on reassembly. If the bolt did not loosen, note that a Suzuki service tool (Pt. No. 09940-30221) is available to hold the damper cartridge in place while the bolt is unscrewed; the tool passes down the fork tube, over the damper rod and engages the top of the cartridge body.
6 Withdraw the damper cartridge assembly from the inner tube **(see illustration)**.
7 Carefully prise the dust seal from the bottom of the outer tube **(see illustration)**. Remove the oil seal retaining clip **(see illustration)**.
8 Carefully prise out the oil seal using either a seal hook or an internal puller with slide-hammer attachment, or the Suzuki tool (Pt. No.09913-50121), taking great care not to damage the rim of the tube **(see illustrations)**. Remove the oil seal washer **(see illustration 8.17a)**. Discard the seals as new ones must be fitted on reassembly.

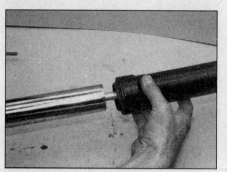

8.4 Separate the inner and outer tubes

8.5 Remove the damper cartridge bolt . . .

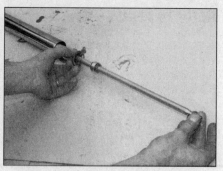

8.6 . . . then withdraw the damper

8.7a Remove the dust seal . . .

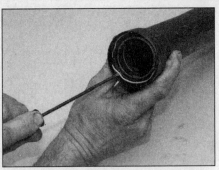

8.7b . . . followed by the retaining ring

8.8a Fit the puller under the seal . . .

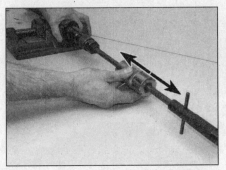

8.8b . . . then attach the slide-hammer . . .

8.8c . . . and use it to draw the seal out

8.12 Check the bushes (arrowed) for wear

9 If required unscrew the compression damping adjuster from the bottom of the fork. Discard its o-ring.

Inspection

10 Clean all parts in a suitable solvent and blow them dry with compressed air, if available.

11 Check the outer surface of the inner tube for score marks, scratches, flaking of the finish and excessive or abnormal wear. Look for creases and dents. Check the tube for runout using V-blocks and a dial gauge. Suzuki provides no specifications for runout. If the condition is suspect have it checked by a Suzuki dealer or suspension specialist. Replace the inner tubes in both forks with new ones if any are defects are found.

⚠ *Warning: If the inner tube is bent, replace it with a new one – it should not be straightened.*

12 Inspect the inside surface of the outer tube and the working surface of each bush for score marks, scratches and signs of excessive wear **(see illustration)**. If the bottom bush is worn it can be replaced with a new one, but note that if it is worn it is likely that the top bush is also worn, and this cannot be replaced with a new one as it is an integral part of the outer tube. If necessary obtain a new fork tube, and if it does not come already fitted with the bottom bush obtain that separately and carefully drive it into the tube until it is flush with the bottom of the oil seal washer seat.

13 Check the fork oil seal seat for nicks,

gouges and scratches. If damage is evident, leaks will occur. Also check the oil seal washer for damage or distortion and replace it with a new one if necessary.

14 Check the spring for cracks and other damage. Measure the spring free length and compare the measurement to the specifications at the beginning of this Chapter **(see illustration)**. If the spring is defective or has sagged below the service limit, fit new springs in both forks. Never fit only one new spring.

15 Check the damper cartridge assembly for damage and wear. Hold the cartridge and gently pump the rod in and out **(see illustration)**. If the rod does not move smoothly the assembly must be replaced with a new one.

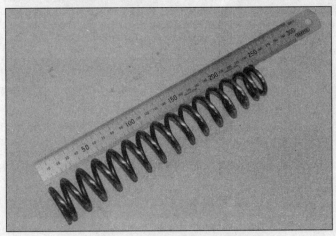

8.14 Measure the free length of the spring

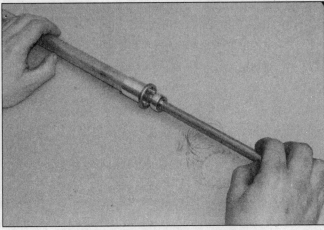

8.15 Check the action of the damper rod

8.17a Fit the oil seal washer . . .

8.17b . . . and the new seal . . .

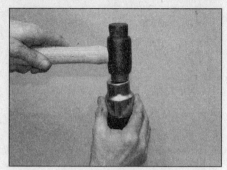

8.17c . . . using a suitable socket to drive it in

Reassembly

16 If removed fit a new O-ring smeared with clean fork oil onto the compression damping adjuster. Fit the adjuster and tighten it to the torque setting specified at the beginning of the Chapter.

17 Fit the oil seal washer into the bottom of the outer tube **(see illustration)**. Fit the new oil seal into the tube and tap it into place until it seats and the retaining clip groove is visible – tap it in using a suitable socket with walls thin enough so it sits only on the hard outer rim of the seal and not on the spring rim on the top **(see illustrations)**. If necessary you can use the old seal as an interface between the socket and the new seal, especially if your socket is not the ideal size.

18 Fit the retaining clip, making sure it locates correctly in its groove **(see illustration)**. Press the dust seal into the tube **(see illustration)**.

19 Insert the damper cartridge assembly into the fork until it contacts the bottom of the inner tube **(see illustration)**. Lubricate the inner surfaces of the new seals with the specified fork oil. Fit a new sealing washer onto the damper cartridge bolt and apply a few drops of a suitable non-permanent thread locking compound, then fit the bolt through the bottom of the outer tube and into the damper cartridge and tighten it to the torque setting specified at the beginning of this Chapter **(see illustrations)**.

20 Lubricate the inner tube and the bushes inside the outer tube with fork oil. Carefully insert the inner tube into the outer tube using a twisting motion – it is important to keep the tubes parallel or the seal lips could be damaged and leak **(see illustration)**.

21 Pour in the correct quantity and type of fork oil, and finish assembling the fork (see Section 7, Steps 9 to 15).

22 Install the fork leg (see Section 6). Adjust the fork settings as required (see Section 14).

9 Steering damper

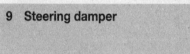

Removal

1 Remove the fairing (see Chapter 7). Remove the trim panel from the bottom yoke. On K8 and K9 models disconnect the wire connector from the solenoid valve on the damper body.

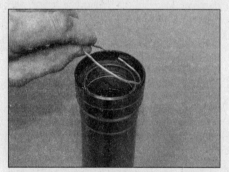

8.18a Fit the retaining clip . . .

8.18b . . . then the new dust seal

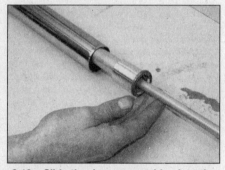

8.19a Slide the damper cartridge into the inner tube

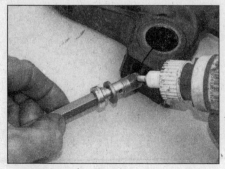

8.19b Fit the bolt using a new sealing washer . . .

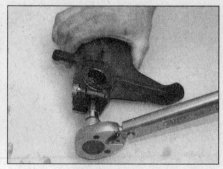

8.19c . . . and tighten it to the specified torque

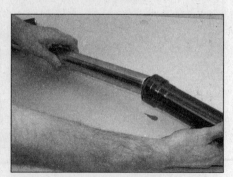

8.20 Fit the inner tube into the outer tube

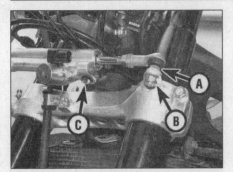

9.2 Counter-hold the hex (A) and unscrew the nut (B). Steering head bolt (C)

9.3 Take care not to lose the seals which could drop out

9.4 Clean and check the damper rod (arrowed)

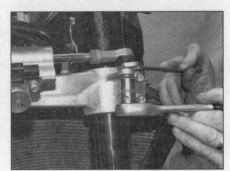

9.7 Counter-hold the hex with a spanner while loosening and tightening the nut

2 Counter-hold the hex on the damper stud on the upper side of its yoke mount then undo the nut **(see illustration and 9.7)**.

3 Undo the bolt securing the damper body to the steering head and remove the damper. Note the seals fitted each side of the bearing in the damper body **(see illustration)**.

Inspection

4 Clean the damper rod and inspect it for wear, score marks, oil leakage and corrosion **(see illustration)**. Damage to the surface of the rod will lead to oil loss and lack of damping. Pump the rod all the way in and out of the damper body. Movement should be slow and progressive and the rod should move smoothly. If the rod binds, or there is no resistance, or if there is oil leakage, fit a new damper.

5 Remove the seals if not already done and inspect the bearing in the damper body **(see**

illustration 9.4). If the centre is loose, press the bearing out and fit a new one, along with new seals.

6 On K8 and K9 models, if fault code C93 has been displayed (see Chapter 4), or if the operation of the damper is suspect, check the resistance of the solenoid valve by connecting the positive (+) probe of an ohmmeter or multimeter to the upper terminal in the damper wiring connector socket and the negative (-) probe to the lower terminal. If the resistance is not as specified at the beginning of the chapter replace the damper with a new one. If the resistance is good check the solenoid voltage by connecting the positive (+) probe of a voltmeter or multimeter to the white wire terminal in the wiring connector and the negative (-) probe to a good earth (ground) on the frame. Turn the ignition on – if the voltage is not as specified at the beginning of the chapter check the wiring connector for loose

or broken wires and terminals, then check the white wire between the connector and the ECM for continuity, referring to electrical system fault finding at the beginning of Chapter 8 and to the wiring diagrams at the end of it. If the voltage was good check the brown wire between the connector and the ECM.

Installation

7 Installation is the reverse of removal, noting the following:
● Lubricate the damper body bearing and seals with grease.
● Tighten the mounting nut and bolt to the specified torque setting – counter-hold the stud hex when tightening the nut **(see illustration)**.

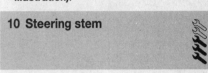

10 Steering stem

Removal

1 Remove the front forks (see Section 6) – it is best to remove the fairing as well as the side panels. Support the handlebars or tie them to the fairing bracket so they are out of the way – make sure no strain is placed on the brake hose, cables or wiring, and keep the fluid reservoir upright.

2 Remove the steering damper (see Section 9).

3 Raise or remove the fuel tank as preferred to avoid the possibility of damage (see Chapter 4).

4 Unscrew the bolt securing the front brake hose clamp to the bottom yoke **(see illustration)**.

5 If the top yoke needs to be removed from the bike completely rather than just being placed aside, remove the air filter housing (see Chapter 4) and disconnect the ignition switch and immobiliser (if fitted) wiring connector(s). Feed the wiring back to the switch noting its routing.

6 Unscrew and remove the steering stem nut and remove the washer, noting which way up it fits **(see illustration)**. Gently ease the top yoke upwards off the steering stem **(see illustration)**.

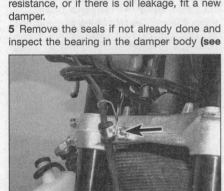

10.4 Unscrew the bolt (arrowed) and detach the brake hose

10.6a Unscrew the nut and remove the washer . . .

10.6b . . . then lift the top yoke off the steering stem

10.7a Remove the locknut . . .

10.7b . . . and washer

10.8a Unscrew the adjuster nut . . .

10.8b . . . remove the cover . . .

10.8c . . . and seal . . .

10.8d . . . then draw the stem out of the head

7 Unscrew the locknut using either a C-spanner, a peg spanner or a suitable drift located in one of the notches, then remove the washer **(see illustrations)**.

8 Support the bottom yoke then unscrew the adjuster nut, remove the bearing cover and seal, then lower the steering stem out of the steering head **(see illustrations)**.

9 Remove the upper bearing inner race and the upper bearing from the top of the steering head **(see illustration)**. Remove the lower bearing from the steering stem **(see illustration)**. **Note:** *Do not attempt to remove the outer races from the frame or the lower bearing from the steering stem unless new bearings are being installed.*

10 Remove all traces of old grease from the bearings and races and check them for wear or damage (see Section 11).

Installation

11 Apply general purpose grease to the inner races and to the outer races in the steering head, and work grease well into both the upper and lower bearings. Fit the lower bearing onto the steering stem **(see illustration 10.9b)**.

12 Carefully lift the steering stem up through the steering head and support it there **(see illustration 10.8d)**. Fit the upper bearing and inner race into the top of the steering head **(see illustration)**. Fit the seal and the bearing cover **(see illustrations 10.8c and b)**. Thread the adjuster nut onto the steering stem and tighten it finger-tight **(see illustration 10.8a)**.

13 If the Suzuki tool (Pt. Nos. 09940-14911 and 09940-14960) is available the adjuster nut can be tightened to the initial torque setting of 45 Nm to pre-load the bearings. Alternatively use a C-spanner to tighten the adjuster nut **(see illustration)**. Whichever method is use, now slacken off the adjuster nut by ¼ to ½ a turn, then turn the steering stem from lock to lock five or six times to settle the bearings and slacken the nut off by a further ¼ to ½ a turn.

Caution: Take great care not to apply excessive pressure to the bearings as this will cause their premature failure. If new

10.9a Remove the upper bearing and its inner race . . .

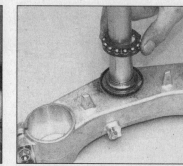

10.9b . . . and the lower bearing

10.12 Fit the upper bearing and the inner race into the top of the head

10.13 Tighten the adjuster nut as described

10.14 Fit the tab on the washer in the groove in the stem

11.3 Check the outer race (arrowed) in the top and bottom of the head

bearings have been fitted you may need to carry out the adjustment procedure several times to allow them to settle properly. The object is to set the adjuster nut so that the bearings are under a very light loading, just enough to remove any front to back freeplay.

14 Fit the washer onto the steering stem, aligning the tab on its inside with the groove in the stem **(see illustration)**. Fit the locknut and tighten it to the specified torque setting **(see illustration 10.7a)**.

15 Fit the top yoke onto the steering stem **(see illustration 10.6b)**. If disconnected feed the ignition switch and immobiliser (where fitted) wiring through to the connector(s), making sure it is correctly routed. Connect the wiring. Install the air filter housing (see Chapter 4).

16 Fit the steering stem nut washer with its tapered side facing onto the yoke, then fit the nut and tighten it finger-tight **(see illustration 10.6a)**. Temporarily install one of the fork legs to align the top and bottom yokes, and secure it by tightening the bottom yoke clamp bolts only. Tighten the steering stem nut to the specified torque setting. Remove the fork leg.

17 Attach the front brake hose clamp to the bottom yoke **(see illustration 10.4)**.

18 Install the steering damper (see Section 9).

19 Install the forks (see Section 6) and all remaining components in the reverse order of removal.

20 Carry out a check of the steering head bearing adjustment as described in Chapter 1, and if necessary re-adjust.

11 Steering head bearings

Inspection

1 Remove the steering stem (see Section 10).

2 Remove all traces of old grease from the bearings and races and check them for wear or damage.

3 The races should be polished and free from indentations **(see illustration)**. Inspect the bearing balls for signs of wear, pitting or discoloration, and examine the ball cages for signs of cracks or splits. If there are any signs of wear on any of the above components, both upper and lower bearing sets should be replaced with new ones. **Note:** *Do not attempt to remove the outer races from the frame or the lower bearing inner race from the steering stem unless new ones are being installed.*

Removal and installation

4 The outer races are an interference fit in the frame steering head and can be tapped out with a suitable drift – cut-outs are provided so good purchase can be made **(see illustrations)**. Tap firmly and evenly around each race to ensure that it is driven out squarely. It may prove advantageous to curve the end of the drift slightly to improve purchase on the exposed rim.

5 Alternatively, the outer races can be removed using a slide-hammer type bearing extractor – these can often be hired from tool shops.

6 Fit the new outer races preferably using a drawbolt arrangement, or a large diameter bearing driver **(see illustration)**. Ensure that the drawbolt washer or driver (as applicable) bears only on the outer edge of the race and does not contact the bearing seat.

> **HAYNES HiNT**
> *Installation of new bearing outer races is made much easier if the races are left overnight in the freezer. This causes them to contract slightly making them a looser fit.*

11.4a Drive the outer races out with a brass drift as shown . . .

11.4b . . . locating it in the cut-outs (arrowed)

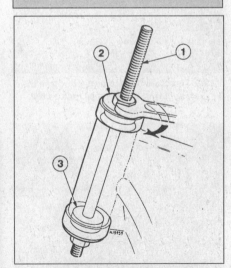

11.6 Drawbolt arrangement for fitting steering head bearing outer races

1 *Long bolt or threaded bar*
2 *Thick washer*
3 *Guide for lower outer race*

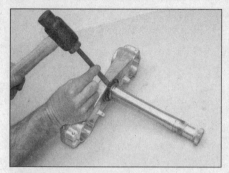

11.7a Tap under the race to create a gap . . .

11.7b . . . and carefully work it free . . .

7 To remove the inner race from the steering stem, thread an old nut onto the top of the steering stem to protect the threads, then lay the stem down onto the nut and carefully tap the race free with a chisel, then use two screwdrivers placed on opposite sides of the race to work it free **(see illustrations)**. If the bearing is firmly in place it will be necessary to use a bearing puller **(see illustration)**. Take the steering stem to a Suzuki dealer if required. Check the condition of the seal under the race and fit a new one if necessary.

8 Fit the seal, then fit the inner race onto the steering stem. A length of tubing with an internal diameter slightly larger than the steering stem will be needed to tap the bearing into position **(see illustration)**. Ensure that the drift bears only on the inner edge of the bearing and does not contact the balls or cage.

9 Install the steering stem (see Section 10).

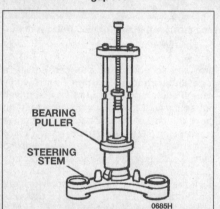

11.7c . . . you may have to use a puller

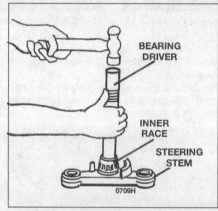

11.8 Install the race using a suitable driver or length of tubing

12 Rear shock absorber

Removal

1 Support the bike using an auxiliary stand. Position a support under the rear wheel so that it does not drop when the shock absorber is removed, but ensure that the weight of the machine is off the rear suspension so that the shock is not compressed.

2 Remove the exhaust silencer (see Chapter 4).

3 Unscrew the nut and withdraw the bolt securing the linkage rod ends to the suspension linkage arm **(see illustration)**.

4 Unscrew the nut and remove the bolt securing the bottom of the shock to the linkage arm, then pivot the linkage arm down **(see illustration)**.

5 Unscrew the nut and remove the bolt securing the linkage rod pivot to the frame and remove the linkage rod piece, on K8 and K9 models noting the washers fitted between the pivot and the frame **(see illustrations)**.

6 Unscrew the nut on the bolt securing the top of the shock to the upper mounting

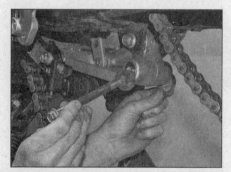

12.3 Unscrew the nut and withdraw the bolt securing the linkage rods to the linkage arm

12.4 Unscrew the nut, withdraw the bolt and swing the linkage arm down

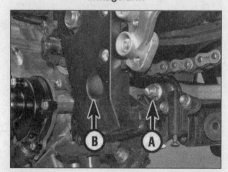

12.5a Unscrew the nut (A) – on K8/K9 insert a socket extension through the hole (B) for best access; K6/K7 models nut is on right-hand side

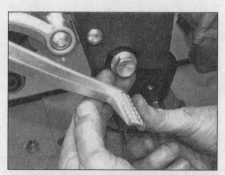

12.5b Withdraw the bolt, on K8/K9 pushing the pedal down for clearance – on K6/K7 withdraw the bolt via the hole in the frame 12.5a

12.5c Retrieve the washers as you remove the arm

12.6a Unscrew the nut (arrowed) . . .

12.6b . . . withdraw the bolt . . .

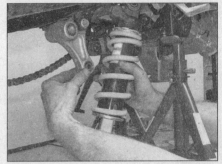

12.6c . . . and remove the shock absorber

bracket **(see illustration)**. Support the shock, withdraw the bolt and remove the shock **(see illustrations)**.

Inspection

7 Inspect the body of the shock absorber for signs of oil leakage and physical damage, and the coil spring for looseness, cracks or signs of fatigue.

8 Ensure the spring pre-load adjuster threads are clean.

9 Check the bush in the mounting at the upper end of the shock for wear and deterioration **(see illustration)**.

10 If the shock absorber is in any way damaged or worn a new one must be installed. Individual components are not available from Suzuki although it is worth checking whether the shock can be rebuilt by a suspension specialist.

11 Check the tightness of the shock absorber upper mounting bracket. If the bracket is loose, raise the fuel tank (see Chapter 4) and tighten the mounting bracket nut to the torque setting specified at the beginning of this Chapter **(see illustration)**.

12 If a new shock is required on K6 and K7 models, before disposing of the old one the nitrogen gas should be released as follows: lay the shock down with the release valve pointing away from you. Remove the cap from the valve. Select a suitable tool (such as a screwdriver with a small tip and a long shank) to depress the valve core, then cover the reservoir and your hands in rag and slowly release the gas by pushing on the valve core with the tip of the screwdriver.

Caution: If the shock is being scrapped, release the nitrogen gas first, in the way described. Wear suitable protective eye and hand gear such as goggles and gloves and direct the gas away from your body and face.

13 If a new shock is required on K8 and K9 models, there is no pressure release valve on the reservoir so you should take the shock to a Suzuki dealer or suspension specialist for disposal.

Installation

14 Installation is the reverse of removal, noting the following:

● Apply general purpose grease to the mounting bolts and to the bearings in the linkage arm.

● Install the upper mounting bolt first, but do not tighten the nut until the lower mounting bolt is installed.

● On K8 and K9 models insert the linkage rod pivot bolt from the right-hand side, and the shock absorber and linkage rod end-to-linkage arm bolts from the left **(see illustrations 12.5b, 12.4 and 12.3)**. Make sure the washers are fitted between the linkage rod pivot and the frame **(see illustration 12.5c)**.

● On K6 and K7 models insert all the bolts from the left-hand side.

● Tighten the mounting bolts to the torque settings specified at the beginning of this Chapter.

● Adjust the rear shock as required (see Section 14).

13 Rear suspension linkage

Removal

1 Support the bike using an auxiliary stand. Position a support under the rear wheel so that it does not drop when the suspension linkage is disconnected, but ensure that the weight of the machine is off the rear suspension so that the shock is not compressed.

2 Remove the exhaust silencer (see Chapter 4).

3 Unscrew the nut and remove the bolt securing the linkage rod ends to the linkage arm **(see illustration 12.3)**.

4 Unscrew the nut and remove the bolt securing the bottom of the shock absorber to the linkage arm **(see illustration 12.4)**.

5 Unscrew the nut and remove the bolt securing the linkage rod pivot to the frame and remove the linkage rod piece, on K8 and K9 models noting the washers fitted between the pivot and the frame **(see illustrations 12.5a, b and c)**.

6 Unscrew the nut and remove the bolt securing the linkage arm to the swingarm and remove the arm **(see illustration)**.

Inspection

7 Withdraw the spacers from the linkage arm and the linkage rod pivot, noting their different sizes – note that the needles for the bearing in the swingarm mount in the linkage arm are

12.9 Check the bush (arrowed) for wear

12.11 Shock absorber bracket nut (arrowed)

13.6 Unscrew the nut, withdraw the bolt and remove the arm

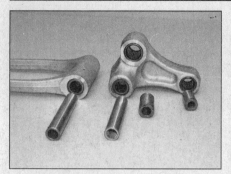

13.7 Withdraw the spacers from the linkage arm and rod pivot

14.1 Spring pre-load adjuster (arrowed)

14.2 Rebound damping adjuster (arrowed)

uncaged, and may therefore drop out as they are only held in by grease **(see illustration)**. Clean all the components thoroughly with a suitable solvent to remove all traces of dirt and old grease, but take great care with the uncaged needles. Remove any corrosion from the spacers with steel wool.

8 Inspect the components closely, looking for obvious signs of wear such as scoring and pitting, and for elongation of the bolt holes in the linkage rod ends. Apply clean oil to the spacers, then slip each one back into its bearing(s) and check that there is not an excessive amount of freeplay between them. Ensure the bearings turn smoothly without binding or grating. **Note:** *The long spacers in the linkage arm and that in the linkage rod pivot are supported by two needle roller bearings.*

9 Replace any components as required with new ones. Refer to *Tools and Workshop Tips (Section 5)* in the Reference section for more information on bearings and bearing removal and installation methods. **Note:** *The needle bearings should only be removed if new bearings are going to be fitted. Note the position of the bearings before removing them. The new bearings should be pressed or drawn into place and must not be driven into position. Position the single bearings centrally in their bores, noting that this should leave a gap of 0.5 mm at each side. Where two bearings are fitted, the gap between the outer edge of the bearing and the bore in the housing should be 1.0 mm.*

Installation

10 Installation is the reverse of removal, noting the following:

● Apply general purpose grease to the bearings, spacers and pivot bolts.

● On K8 and K9 models insert the linkage arm-to-swingarm bolt and the linkage rod pivot bolt from the right-hand side, and the shock absorber and linkage rod end-to-linkage arm bolts from the left **(see illustrations 13.6 12.5b, 12.4 and 12.3)**. Make sure the washers are fitted between the linkage rod pivot and the frame **(see illustration 12.5c)**.

● On K6 and K7 models insert all the bolts from the left-hand side.

● Tighten the nuts and bolts to the torque settings specified at the beginning of this Chapter.

● Check the operation of the rear suspension before taking the machine on the road.

14 Suspension adjustment

Caution: Always make sure the adjusters in both fork legs are set in corresponding positions.

Front fork spring pre-load

1 Spring pre-load is adjusted using a suitable spanner on the adjuster flats **(see illustration)**. The adjuster is located in the fork top bolt; turn the adjuster clockwise to increase pre-load and anti-clockwise to decrease it. The amount of pre-load is determined by the number of turns in from the minimum (fully turned out anti-clockwise) setting. The standard pre-load setting is seven turns in from the minimum setting. Turn the adjusters a small amount at a time until a suitable setting has been found.

Front fork rebound damping

2 Rebound damping is adjusted using a flat-bladed screwdriver in the slot in the adjuster in each fork top bolt **(see illustration)**. To set the standard setting turn the adjuster clockwise until it stops, then turn it anti-clockwise 1¾ turns on all 600 models and on 750K8 and K9 models, and 1½ turns

on 750K6 and K7 models, so that the punch marks align. To increase damping turn the adjuster clockwise, and to decrease it turn the adjuster anti-clockwise. Turn the adjusters a small amount at a time until a suitable setting has been found.

Front fork compression damping

3 On all 600 models and on 750K6 and K7 models compression damping is adjusted using a flat-bladed screwdriver in the slot in the adjuster located in the bottom of each fork **(see illustration)**. To set the standard setting turn the adjuster clockwise until it stops, then turn it anti-clockwise 1¾ turns so that the punch marks align. To increase damping turn the adjuster clockwise, and to decrease it turn the adjuster anti-clockwise. Turn the adjusters a small amount at a time until a suitable setting has been found.

4 On 750K8 and K9 models low speed compression damping is adjusted using a flat-bladed screwdriver in the slot in the adjuster located in the bottom of each fork **(see illustration)**. To set the standard setting turn the adjuster clockwise until it stops, then turn it anti-clockwise 2 turns so that the punch marks align. High speed compression damping is adjusted using a suitable spanner on the adjuster flats. To set the standard setting turn the adjuster clockwise until it stops, then turning it anti-clockwise 2 1/2 turns so that the punch marks align. To increase damping turn each adjuster clockwise, and to decrease it turn them anti-clockwise. Turn the adjusters a small amount at a time until a suitable setting has been found.

14.3 Compression damping adjuster (arrowed) – all 600 and 750K6 and K7 models

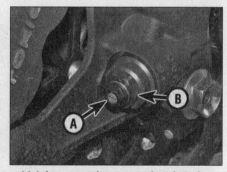

14.4 Low speed compression damping adjuster (A), high speed adjuster (B) – 750K8 and K9 models

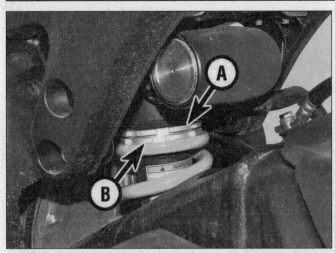

14.5 Slacken the locknut (A) then turn the adjuster nut (B) as required

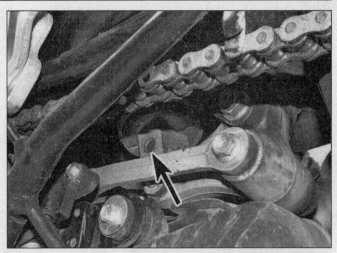

14.6 Rebound damping adjuster (arrowed)

Rear shock spring pre-load

5 Spring pre-load is adjusted by turning the adjuster ring nut on the shock absorber body. Position the motorcycle upright on an auxiliary stand and measure the spring length (from the top to bottom spring coils), then compare this to the standard pre-load figure given in the specifications. If adjustment is required, use a slim C-spanner to loosen the locknut, then turn the adjuster nut clockwise to increase pre-load or anti-clockwise to decrease it **(see illustration)**. Tighten the locknut securely after adjustment. **Note***: Do not set the spring length beyond the minimum and maximum pre-load settings* (see Specifications at the beginning of this Chapter).

Rear shock rebound damping

6 Rebound damping is adjusted using a flat-bladed screwdriver in the slot in the adjuster in the bottom of the shock absorber **(see illustration)**. To set the standard setting turn the adjuster clockwise until it stops, then turn it anti-clockwise 1 3/4 turns on 600K6 and K7 and 750K8 and K9 models, 1 1/2 turns on 750K6 and K7 models, and 2 turns on 600K8 and K9 models, so that the punch marks align. Turn the adjuster a small amount at a time until a suitable setting has been found.

Rear shock compression damping

7 Low speed compression damping is adjusted using a flat-bladed screwdriver in the slot in the adjuster in the top of the shock absorber **(see illustration)**. To set the standard setting turn the adjuster clockwise until it stops, then turning it anti-clockwise 2 turns on 750K8 and K9 models and 1 3/4 turns on all other models so that the punch marks align. High speed compression damping is adjusted using a suitable spanner on the adjuster flats.

To set the standard setting turn the adjuster clockwise until it stops, then turn it anti-clockwise 3 turns on all models so that the punch marks align. To increase damping turn the adjusters clockwise, and to decrease it turn them anti-clockwise. Turn the adjusters a small amount at a time until a suitable setting has been found.

15 Swingarm removal and installation

Removal

Special Tool: *A special tool is needed to unscrew the swingarm locknut – see Step 8.*
1 Remove the fairing side panels (see Chapter 7).
2 Remove the front sprocket (see Chapter 6). Rest the drive chain over the gearbox output shaft. **Note:** *The chain will come off with the swingarm. To remove the chain from the swingarm the chain must be split (see Chapter 6). Only split the chain if a new chain or new swingarm are to be fitted.*

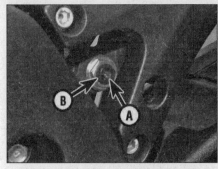

14.7 Low speed compression damping adjuster (A), high speed adjuster (B) – 750K8 and K9 models

3 Remove the rear wheel (see Chapter 6).
4 Unscrew the bolt securing the brake hose guide to the inside of the swingarm **(see illustration)**. Free the hose from the clip on the outside of the swingarm **(see illustration)**.
5 Displace the brake caliper bracket from the swingarm, noting how it locates.
6 Remove the rear shock absorber (see Section 12).
7 If required unscrew the nut and remove the bolt securing the linkage arm to the

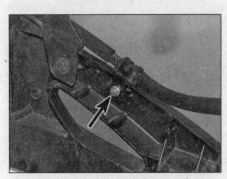

15.4a Unscrew the bolt (arrowed) . . .

15.4b . . . and release the clip to free the brake hose from the swingarm

15.8a This is the tool we made . . .

15.8b . . . to undo the swingarm pivot bolt locknut

A peg 'socket' can be made by cutting four sections out of the rim of the correct sized socket to form castellations that locate in the slots in the locknut – measure the width and depth of the slots to determine the size of the castellations needed. If an old socket is not available, a nut can be welded onto a piece of steel tube and pegs can then be cut into the other end of the tube rim in the same way (see illustration 15.8a).

15.9a You will need a large hex key or a tool made from nuts and bolts to counter-hold the pivot bolt . . .

15.9b . . . while unscrewing the nut

swingarm and remove the arm **(see illustration 13.6)**.

8 Undo the locknut on the right-hand end of

the swingarm pivot bolt **(see illustrations)**. Suzuki produce a service tool to fit the locknut (Pt. No. 09940-14940). Alternatively a similar tool can be made (see ***Tool Tip***).

9 Counter-hold the pivot bolt head using

a 19 mm hex key, then undo the nut on the left-hand end of the bolt **(see illustrations)**.

10 Support the swingarm, then unscrew the pivot bolt using the hex key until the threaded head is out of the frame. Withdraw the bolt and ease the swingarm out of the back of the frame, bringing the drive chain with it if not removed **(see illustration)**.

11 If required, remove the chainguard, the chain slider and the rear hugger from the swingarm **(see illustrations)**.

Installation

12 Clean the frame around the swingarm mountings and check that the pivot bolt is a good fit.

13 If removed, install the rear hugger, the chain slider and the chainguard **(see illustration 15.11d, c, b and a)**.

14 Ensure the bearings, collars and pivot bolt are lubricated with multi-purpose grease (see Section 16).

15 Offer up the swingarm, and if fitted pass

15.10 Unscrew and withdraw the pivot bolt and remove the swingarm

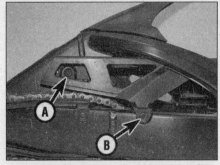

15.11a Release the trim clip (A) by pushing its centre in then drawing the body out, then unscrew the bolts (B) . . .

15.11b . . . to free the chainguard

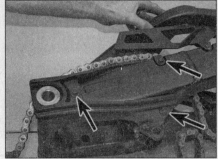

15.11c Chain slider is retained by three bolts (arrowed)

15.11d Rear hugger bolts (arrowed)

15.15 Feed the chain between the engine and frame and loop it over the output shaft

16.2a Check the chain adjusters . . .

16.2b . . . and the axle plate (arrowed)

the chain between the gearbox output shaft and the frame and rest it over the shaft **(see illustration)**.

16 Align the swingarm pivot with the frame mountings and insert the pivot bolt from the right-hand side **(see illustration 15.10)**. Tighten the pivot bolt to the torque setting specified at the beginning of this Chapter using the hex key **(see illustration 15.9a)**.

17 Fit the nut on the left-hand end of the pivot bolt, then counter-hold the bolt and tighten the nut to the specified torque setting **(see illustration 15.9b)**.

18 Fit the locknut on the right-hand end of the pivot bolt, then tighten the locknut to the specified torque setting **(see illustration 15.8b)**.

19 Install the remaining components in the reverse order of removal, noting the following:
● Refer to Sections 13 and 12 for the installation of the suspension linkage arm and the shock absorber, tightening the nuts to the specified torque settings.
● Check the drive chain slack (see Chapter 1).
● Check the operation of the rear suspension and brake before taking the machine on the road.

16 Swingarm inspection and bearing renewal

Inspection

1 Clean the swingarm with a suitable solvent, removing all traces of dirt, corrosion and grease.

2 Inspect the drive chain adjuster bolts and the bolt threads in the swingarm **(see illustration)**. Stripped threads in the swingarm can be repaired with a thread insert – see *'Tools and Workshop Tips'* in the Reference section. Inspect the axle plate on the inside of the swingarm end and fit a new one if it is gouged or distorted – clean the screw threads and apply some fresh threadlock on installation, and make sure the hole locates over the peg **(see illustration)**.

16.3a Remove the collars . . .

16.3b . . . and clean and check the bearings (arrowed)

3 Withdraw the collars from the needle roller bearings in both ends of the swingarm pivot **(see illustration)**. Remove any corrosion from the collars with steel wool. If necessary, wash old grease out of the bearings with a suitable solvent, then dry the bearings with compressed air, if available **(see illustration)**.

4 Inspect the components closely, looking for obvious signs of wear such as scoring and pitting. Apply clean oil to the collars, then slip each one back into its bearing and check that there is not an excessive amount of freeplay between the two. Ensure the bearings turn smoothly without binding or grating. If there is any doubt about the condition of the bearings have them checked by a Suzuki dealer or replace them with new ones (see below).

5 Clean the swingarm pivot bolt and check the bolt for wear at the points where it passes through the frame and the bearing spacers. Slide the bearing collars onto the pivot bolt and check that there is not an excessive amount of freeplay between the two.

6 Check the pivot bolt is straight by rolling it on a flat surface such as a piece of plate glass. If available, place the bolt in V-blocks and measure the runout using a dial gauge. If the runout exceeds the limit specified, fit a new one.

7 Lay the swingarm on the work surface and support it so that the pivot end is level (check this with a spirit level). Install the chain adjuster blocks and the wheel axle and check

the level of the axle. If the axle is not level, the swingarm is out of true and must be replaced with a new one.

Bearing renewal

Note: *The needle bearings should only be removed if new bearings are going to be fitted – removal of the bearings will destroy them.*

8 Remove the collars from the bearings **(see illustration 16.3a)**. Note the set position of the bearings before removing them.

9 Use a knife-edged puller to extract the bearings. Locate the bearing puller tool behind the inner edge of the first bearing to be removed – note that there is only a small clearance between the bearing and centre spacer in which to locate the puller edges. Operate the puller to draw the bearing out of the swingarm. The centre spacer can now be removed from inside the swingarm. Now use the same procedure to remove the bearing from the other side of the swingarm.

10 The new bearings should be pressed or drawn into place so that their stamped side faces outwards, and with the centre spacer fitted between them. In the absence of a press, a suitable drawbolt arrangement can be made up as described in *Tools and Workshop Tips (Section 5)* in the Reference section.

12 Lubricate each bearing and collars with grease before installing the swingarm.

Notes

Chapter 6
Brakes, wheels and final drive

Contents

Degrees of difficulty

Easy, suitable for novice with little experience	**Fairly easy,** suitable for beginner with some experience	**Fairly difficult,** suitable for competent DIY mechanic	**Difficult,** suitable for experienced DIY mechanic	**Very difficult,** suitable for expert DIY or professional

Specifications

Brakes

Brake fluid type	DOT 4
Disc minimum thickness	
Front	
K6 and K7 models	
Standard	5.3 to 5.7 mm
Service limit	5.0 mm
K8 and K9 models	
Standard	4.8 to 5.2 mm
Service limit	4.5 mm
Rear	
Standard	4.8 to 5.2 mm
Service limit	4.5 mm
Disc maximum runout (front and rear, all models)	0.3 mm
Caliper bore ID	
Front	
K6 and K7 models	
Lower	30.280 to 30.356 mm
Upper	34.010 to 34.086 mm
K8 and K9 models	
Lower	30.280 to 30.330 mm
Upper	32.080 to 32.130 mm
Rear (all models)	38.180 to 38.256 mm
Caliper piston OD	
Front	
K6 and K7 models	
Lower	30.150 to 30.200 mm
Upper	33.884 to 33.934 mm
K8 and K9 models	
Lower	30.167 to 30.200 mm
Upper	31.967 to 32.000 mm
Rear (all models)	38.098 to 38.148 mm

Brakes (continued)

Master cylinder bore ID
  Front
    K6 and K7 models .... 19.050 to 19.093 mm
    K8 and K9 models .... 17.460 to 17.503 mm
  Rear (all models).. 14.000 to 14.043 mm
Master cylinder piston OD
  Front
    K6 and K7 models .... 19.018 to 19.034 mm
    K8 and K9 models .... 17.417 to 17.444 mm
  Rear (all models).. 13.957 to 13.984 mm

Wheels

Maximum wheel runout (front and rear)
  Axial (side-to-side) .... 2.0 mm
  Radial (out-of-round) .... 2.0 mm
Maximum axle runout (front and rear) .... 0.25 mm

Tyres

Tyre pressures .... see *Pre-ride checks*
Tyre sizes
  Front .... 120/70 ZR 17 58W
  Rear .... 180/55 ZR 17 73W
Refer to the owners handbook or the tyre information label on the swingarm for approved tyre brands.

Final drive

Drive chain slack and lubricant .... see Chapter 1
Drive chain type
  600-K6 and K7 models................................. RK 525SMOZ7Y (114 links)
  600-K8 and K9 models................................. RK 525SMOZ8 (114 links)
  750 models... RK 525ROZ5Y (116 links)
Sprocket sizes
  600 models... 16 tooth front, 43 tooth rear
  750 models... 17 tooth front, 45 tooth rear

Torque settings

Brake caliper bleed valves .... 7.5 Nm
Brake master cylinder (front) bleed valve..................... 6 Nm
Brake hose banjo bolts...................................... 23 Nm
Front brake caliper body joining bolts .... 22 Nm
Front brake caliper mounting bolts
  K6 and K7 models .... 35 Nm
  K8 and K9 models .... 39 Nm
Front brake disc bolts
  K6 and K7 models .... 23 Nm
  K8 and K9 models .... 18 Nm
Front brake master cylinder clamp bolts .... 10 Nm
Front brake pad retaining pins
  K6 and K7 models .... 15 Nm
  K8 and K9 models .... 16 Nm
Front axle bolt .... 100 Nm
Front axle clamp bolts .... 23 Nm
Front sprocket nut .... 115 Nm
Rear axle nut .... 100 Nm
Rear brake caliper front slider pin
  K6 and K7 models .... 32 Nm
  K8 and K9 models .... 33 Nm
Rear brake caliper mounting bolt/slider pin
  K6 and K7 models .... 17 Nm
  K8 and K9 models .... 18 Nm
Rear brake pad retaining pin
  K6 and K7 models .... 15 Nm
  K8 and K9 models .... 16 Nm
Rear brake disc bolts .... 35 Nm
Rear brake master cylinder mounting bolts .... 10 Nm
Rear sprocket nuts .... 60 Nm
Speed sensor rotor... 25 Nm

2.1 Slacken the pad pins (arrowed) . . .

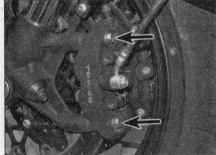

2.2a . . . then unscrew the bolts (arrowed) . . .

2.2b . . . and slide the caliper off the disc

1 General information

All models have hydraulically operated disc brakes, twin discs at the front and a single disc at the rear. The front calipers have four opposed pistons and the rear caliper has a single piston sliding caliper.

All models are fitted with cast alloy wheels designed for tubeless tyres only.

The drive to the rear wheel is by chain and sprockets.

Caution: Disc brake components rarely require disassembly. Do not disassemble components unless absolutely necessary. If an hydraulic brake hose is loosened or disconnected, the union sealing washers must be renewed and the system bled upon reassembly. Do not use solvents on internal brake components. Solvents will cause the seals to swell and distort. Use only clean DOT 4 brake fluid for cleaning. Use care when working with brake fluid as it can injure your eyes and it will damage painted surfaces and plastic parts.

2 Front brake pads

⚠ *Warning: The dust created by the brake system may contain asbestos, which is harmful to your health. Never blow it out with compressed air and don't inhale any of it. An approved filtering mask should be worn when working on the brakes.*

1 Slacken the pad retaining pins **(see illustration)**.
2 Unscrew the caliper mounting bolts and slide the caliper off the disc **(see illustrations)**. Free the brake hose from its guide and/or release the clip from the mudguard (according to side) to give more freedom of movement if required **(see illustration 3.2)**.
3 Unscrew and remove the pad pins, then remove the pads from the bottom of the caliper **(see illustrations)**. **Note:** *Do not operate the brake lever while the pads are out of the caliper.* If required and fitted, remove

2.3a Unscrew the pins . . .

2.3b . . . and remove the pads

the shim from the back of each pad, noting how it locates **(see illustration 2.11a)**.
4 The pad spring can stay in place unless you are overhauling the caliper – to remove the spring the pistons must be pushed all the way back into their bores to give clearance (see Step 9) **(see illustration 2.11b)**.
5 Inspect the surface of each pad for contamination and check that the friction material has not worn beyond its service limit (see Chapter 1, Section 10). If any pad is worn down to, or beyond, the service limit wear indicator (i.e. the wear indicator is no longer visible), is fouled with oil or grease, or heavily scored or damaged, fit a complete set of new pads. **Note:** *It is not possible to degrease the friction material; if the pads are contaminated in any way they must be replaced with new ones.*
6 If the pads are in good condition clean them carefully, using a fine wire brush which is completely free of oil and grease to remove all traces of road dirt, corrosion and glazing. Using

a pointed instrument, dig out any embedded particles of foreign matter. If required, spray with a dedicated brake cleaner to remove any dust.
7 Check the condition of the brake disc (see Section 4).
8 Remove all traces of corrosion from the pad pins and check them for wear and damage.
9 Clean around the exposed section of each piston to remove any dirt or debris that could cause the seals to be damaged. If new pads are being fitted, now push the pistons all the way back into the caliper to create room for them; if the old pads are still serviceable push the pistons in a little way. To push the pads back use finger pressure or a piece of wood as leverage, or place the old pads back in the caliper and use a metal bar or a screwdriver inserted between them, or use grips and a piece of wood, rag or card to protect the caliper body **(see illustration)**. Alternatively obtain a proper piston-pushing tool from a good tool supplier **(see illustration)**. It may

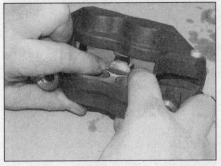

2.9a Push the pistons in using your fingers if possible

2.9b This is a commercially available piston pushing tool

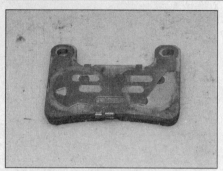

2.11a Make sure the shim is correctly fitted

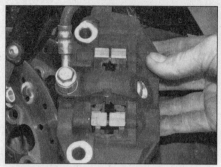

2.11b Fit the spring if removed making sure it locates correctly

2.13 Fit the bolts and tighten them to the specified torque

be necessary to remove the master cylinder reservoir cap, plate and diaphragm and siphon out some fluid (see *Pre-ride) checks*. If the pistons are difficult to push back, remove the bleed valve cap, then attach a length of clear hose to the bleed valve and place the open end in a suitable container, then open the valve and try again (see Section 11). Take great care not to draw any air into the system. If in doubt, bleed the brakes afterwards.

10 If any of the pistons appear seized, first block or hold the other pistons using wood or cable-ties, then apply the brake lever and check whether the piston in question moves at all. If it moves out but can't be pushed back in the chances are there is some hidden corrosion stopping it. If it doesn't move at all, or to fully clean and inspect the pistons, disassemble the caliper and overhaul it (see Section 3).

11 Where applicable fit the shim onto the back of each pad with the triangular mark pointing in the direction of disc rotation and making sure it locates correctly **(see illustration)**. If the pad spring was removed, make sure the pistons are fully recessed in their bores then fit the spring with its wider tang facing the top of the caliper **(see illustration)**.

12 Fit the pads into the caliper so the friction material on each pad faces the other. Press them up against the spring to align the holes, then insert the pad pins and secure them finger-tight at this stage **(see illustrations 2.3b and a)**.

13 Slide the caliper onto the disc making sure

the pads locate correctly on each side **(see illustration 2.2b)**. Install the caliper mounting bolts and tighten them to the torque setting specified at the beginning of the Chapter **(see illustration)**. Fit the brake hose into its guide and/or clip if removed **(see illustration 3.2)**.

14 Tighten the pad pins to the torque setting specified at the beginning of this Chapter **(see illustration 2.1)**.

15 Operate the brake lever until the pads contact with the disc. Check the level of fluid in the hydraulic reservoir and top-up if necessary (see *Pre-ride checks*).

16 Check the operation of the front brake before riding the motorcycle.

3 Front brake calipers

> ⚠️ **Warning: If a caliper is in need of an overhaul all old brake fluid should be flushed from the system. Also, the dust created by the brake system may contain asbestos that is harmful to your health. Never blow it out with compressed air and do not inhale any of it. An approved filtering mask should be worn when working on the brakes. Overhaul of the brake caliper must be done in a spotlessly clean work area to avoid contamination and possible failure of the brake hydraulic system components. Do not, under any circumstances, use petroleum-based solvents to clean brake parts. Use clean**

DOT 4 brake fluid, dedicated brake cleaner or denatured alcohol only, as described. To prevent damage from spilled brake fluid, always cover paintwork when working on the braking system, and mop up any spilled fluid straight away.**

Removal

Note: *If the calipers are being overhauled (usually due to sticking pistons or fluid leaks) read through the entire procedure first and make sure that you have obtained all the new parts required, including some new DOT 4 brake fluid.*

1 If the calipers are being overhauled, slacken the brake pad retaining pins **(see illustration 2.1)**. If the calipers are just being displaced from the forks as part of the wheel removal procedure, the brake pads can be left in place.

2 Free the brake hose from its guide and/or release the clip from the mudguard (according to side) to give more freedom of movement if required **(see illustration)**.

3 If the calipers are being completely removed or overhauled, unscrew the brake hose banjo bolt and detach the banjo union, noting its alignment with the caliper **(see illustration)**. When working on the right-hand caliper, note the double hose arrangement.

4 Wrap plastic foodwrap around the banjo union and secure the hose in an upright position to minimise fluid loss. Discard the sealing washers, as new ones must be fitted on reassembly.

5 Unscrew the caliper mounting bolts and slide the caliper off the disc **(see illustrations 2.2a and b)**. If the caliper is just being displaced, secure it to the motorcycle with a cable-tie to avoid straining the brake hose.

Note: *Do not operate the brake lever while either caliper is off the disc.*

6 If the caliper is being overhauled, remove the brake pads (see Section 2).

Overhaul

7 Clean the exterior of the caliper with denatured alcohol or brake system cleaner. Have some clean rag ready to catch any spilled brake fluid.

8 Unscrew the caliper body joining bolts and separate the halves, catching any residual fluid

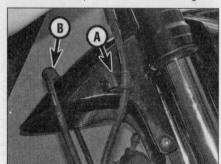

3.2 Free the hose from the guide (A) and/ or release the clip (B) to give freedom of movement

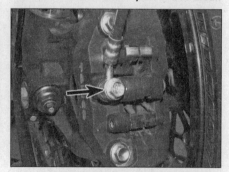

3.3 Brake hose banjo bolt (arrowed)

3.8 Caliper body joining bolts (arrowed)

3.9a Block the fluid inlet using a suitable bolt

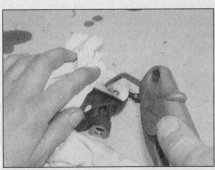

3.9b Apply compressed air to the fluid passage . . .

with the rag **(see illustration)**. Remove the fluid passage O-ring from whichever half it is in and discard it – fit a new one on reassembly **(see illustration 3.18a)**. If the bolts are too tight for the caliper to be held by hand fit it back onto the fork and tighten the mounting bolts, then undo the body joining bolts using a socket extension inserted from the opposite side of the wheel – take great care not to mark the wheel.

9 Place each caliper half piston side upwards on the bench. Find a suitable bolt and thread it into the banjo bolt bore in the outer half of the caliper **(see illustration)**. Get a wad of rag and hold it against the pistons as a cushion to protect your hand as the pistons are forced out. Apply compressed air gradually and progressively, starting with a fairly low pressure, to the fluid passage on the caliper joint and allow the pistons to ease out of their bores, controlling them with hand pressure and the rag **(see illustration)**. Make sure the pistons are displaced evenly, using pressure to block one while the other moves if necessary **(see illustration)**. Repeat the procedure for the other caliper half.

10 If a piston is stuck in its bore due to corrosion the caliper should be replaced with a new one. Do not resort to levering the piston out or gripping it with pliers.

11 Mark each piston and the caliper halves to ensure that the pistons can be matched to their original bores on reassembly. Note that two sizes of piston are used in each caliper half (see Specifications at the beginning of this Chapter).

3.9c . . . until the pistons are displaced

12 Remove the dust seals and the piston seals from the piston bores using a soft wooden or plastic tool to avoid scratching the bores **(see illustration)**. Discard the seals as new ones must be fitted on reassembly.

13 Clean the pistons and bores with clean DOT 4 brake fluid. If compressed air is available, blow it through the fluid galleries in the caliper to ensure they are clear (make sure it is filtered and unlubricated).

Caution: Do not, under any circumstances, use a petroleum-based solvent to clean brake parts.

14 Inspect the caliper bores and pistons for signs of corrosion, nicks and burrs and loss of plating. If surface defects are present, the pistons and/or the caliper assembly must be replaced with new ones. If a caliper is in poor condition, the other front caliper and the master cylinder should also be checked.

3.12 Remove the seals and discard them

15 Lubricate the new piston seals with clean brake fluid and fit them into their grooves **(see illustration)**. Note that there are two sizes of bore in each caliper and care must therefore be taken to ensure that the correct size seals are fitted to the correct bores (see Specifications). The same applies when fitting the new dust seals and pistons.

16 Lubricate the new dust seals with clean brake fluid and fit them into their grooves **(see illustration)**.

17 Lubricate the pistons with DOT 4 brake fluid and fit them, closed-end first, into the bores, taking care not to displace the seals **(see illustration)**. Using your thumbs, push the pistons all the way in, making sure they enter the bore squarely.

18 Lubricate the new fluid passage O-ring with brake fluid and fit it into its recess in

3.15 Fit the new piston seals . . .

3.16 . . . then the new dust seals . . .

3.17 . . . then fit the pistons

3.18a Fit the O-ring into its recess . . .

3.18b . . . then join the caliper halves

3.22 Always use new sealing washers

one half of the caliper **(see illustration)**. Join the two halves of the caliper body together, making sure the O-ring stays in place **(see illustration)**. Install the joining bolts and tighten them evenly to the torque setting specified at the beginning of this Chapter **(see illustration 3.8)**. If you can't tighten the bolts with the caliper held by hand fit it back onto the fork and tighten the mounting bolts, then tighten the body joining bolts using a socket extension inserted from the opposite side of the wheel – take great care not to mark the wheel.

Installation

19 If removed, install the brake pads (see Section 2).
20 Slide the caliper onto the brake disc, making sure the pads fit on each side of the disc **(see illustration 2.2b)**.
21 Install the caliper mounting bolts and tighten them to the torque setting specified at the beginning of this Chapter **(see illustration 2.13)**.
22 If removed, connect the brake hose(s) to the caliper, using new sealing washers on each side of each banjo fitting **(see illustration)**. Align the fitting as noted on removal **(see illustration 3.3)**. Tighten the banjo bolt to the specified torque setting.
23 Secure the brake hose assembly in the guide and fit the clip on the front mudguard **(see illustration 3.2)**.
24 Fill the fluid reservoir with new DOT 4 brake fluid (see *Pre-ride checks*). Refer to Section 11 and bleed the air and all old fluid from the system. Check that there are no

fluid leaks and test the operation of the brake before riding the motorcycle.

4   Front brake discs

Inspection

1 Inspect the surface of the disc for score marks and other damage. Light scratches are normal after use and won't affect brake operation, but deep grooves and heavy score marks will reduce braking efficiency and accelerate pad wear. If a disc is badly grooved it must be replaced with a new one.
2 The disc must not be allowed to wear down to a thickness less than the service limit as listed in this Chapter's Specifications. Check the thickness of the disc with a micrometer and replace it with a new one if necessary.
3 To check if the disc is warped, position the bike on an auxiliary stand with the front wheel raised off the ground. Mount a dial gauge to the fork leg, with the gauge plunger touching the surface of the disc about 10 mm from the outer edge **(see illustration)**. Rotate the wheel and watch the gauge needle, comparing the reading with the limit listed in the Specifications at the beginning of this Chapter. If the runout is greater than the service limit, check the wheel bearings for play (see Chapter 1). If the bearings are worn, install new ones (see Section 16) and repeat this check. If the disc runout is still excessive, a new pair of discs will have to be fitted.

Removal

4 Remove the wheel (see Section 14).
Caution: Don't lay the wheel down and allow it to rest on the disc – the disc could become warped. Set the wheel on wood blocks so the wheel rim supports the weight of the wheel.
5 If you are not replacing the disc with a new one, mark the relationship of the disc to the wheel, so it can be installed in the same position and on the same side as originally fitted. Unscrew the disc retaining bolts, loosening them evenly and a little at a time in a criss-cross pattern to avoid distorting the disc, then remove the disc **(see illustration)**.

Installation

6 Before installing the disc, make sure there is no dirt or corrosion where the disc seats on the hub. If the disc does not sit flat when it is bolted down, it will appear to be warped when checked or when the front brake is used.
7 Fit the disc onto the wheel with its marked side facing out, aligning the previously applied matchmarks (if you're reinstalling the original disc).
8 Clean the threads of the disc mounting bolts, then apply a suitable non-permanent thread locking compound. Install the bolts and tighten them evenly and a little at a time in a criss-cross pattern to the torque setting specified at the beginning of this Chapter. Clean the disc using acetone or brake system cleaner. If a new disc has been installed, remove any protective coating from its working surfaces and fit new brake pads.
9 Install the front wheel (see Section 14).
10 Operate the brake lever several times to bring the pads into contact with the disc. Check the operation of the brake before riding the motorcycle.

5   Front brake master cylinder

 Warning: If the brake master cylinder is in need of an overhaul all old brake fluid should be flushed from the system. Overhaul of the brake master cylinder must be done in a spotlessly

4.3 Checking disc runout with a dial gauge

4.5 The disc is secured by six bolts (arrowed)

5.1 Brake light switch wiring connector (arrowed) – K8/K9 type

5.2 Unscrew the reservoir bolt (A) then unscrew the clamp bolts (B)

clean work area to avoid contamination and possible failure of the brake hydraulic system components. Do not, under any circumstances, use petroleum-based solvents to clean brake parts. Use clean DOT 4 brake fluid, dedicated brake cleaner or denatured alcohol only, as described. To prevent damage from spilled brake fluid, always cover paintwork when working on the braking system, and mop up any spilled fluid straight away.

Removal

Note: *If the master cylinder is being overhauled (usually due to sticking or poor action, or fluid leaks) read through the entire procedure first and make sure that you have obtained all the new parts required, including some new DOT 4 brake fluid.*

1 Disconnect the wiring connector(s) from the brake light switch (see illustration).

2 If the master cylinder is just being displaced, ensure the fluid reservoir cap is secure. Undo the bolt securing the reservoir to the handlebar bracket (see illustration). Unscrew the master cylinder clamp bolts and remove the back of the clamp, noting how it fits, then position the master cylinder and reservoir assembly clear of the handlebar. Ensure no strain is placed on the hydraulic hose. Keep the reservoir upright to prevent air entering the system.

3 If the master cylinder is being overhauled, remove the brake lever (see Chapter 5).

4 Remove the reservoir cap clamp screw and clamp.

5 Unscrew the brake hose banjo bolt and detach the banjo union, noting its alignment with the master cylinder (see illustration). Wrap plastic foodwrap around the banjo union and secure the hose in an upright position to minimise fluid loss Discard the sealing washers as new ones must be fitted on reassembly. Wrap some rag around the master cylinder fluid outlet.

6 Undo the bolt securing the reservoir to the handlebar bracket (see illustration 5.2).

Unscrew the master cylinder clamp bolts and remove the back of the clamp, noting how it fits, then lift the master cylinder and reservoir away from the handlebar.

7 Unscrew the reservoir cap and remove the diaphragm plate and the diaphragm. Drain the brake fluid from the master cylinder and reservoir into a suitable container. Release the clip securing the reservoir hose to the union on the master cylinder and detach the hose (see illustration). Wipe any remaining fluid out of the reservoir with a clean rag.

8 If required, undo the screw securing the

brake light switch to the bottom of the master cylinder and remove the switch.

Overhaul

9 Inspect the reservoir hose for cracks or splits and replace it with a new one if necessary. If required remove the cap from the fluid reservoir hose union, then remove the circlip and detach the union from the master cylinder (see illustrations). Discard the O-ring as a new one must be fitted on reassembly – it is not part of the master cylinder rebuild kit and so must be obtained separately.

5.5 Unscrew the banjo bolt (arrowed)

5.7 Release the clip and detach the hose

5.9a Lift the cap off . . .

5.9b . . . to access the circlip

5.10 Remove the boot and pushrod where applicable from the end of the master cylinder piston . . .

5.11a . . . then depress the piston and remove the circlip . . .

5.11b . . . then draw out the piston . . .

10 Carefully remove the rubber boot from the master cylinder, bringing the pushrod with it **(see illustration)**.

11 Depress the piston and use circlip pliers to remove the circlip, then slide out the piston assembly, the spring and spring guide, noting how they fit **(see illustrations)**. If they are difficult to remove, apply low pressure compressed air to the brake fluid outlet. Lay the parts out in the proper order to prevent confusion during reassembly.

12 Clean the master cylinder with clean brake fluid. If compressed air is available, blow it through the fluid galleries to ensure they are clear (make sure the air is filtered and unlubricated).

Caution: Do not, under any circumstances, use a petroleum-based solvent to clean brake parts.

13 Check the master cylinder bore for corrosion, scratches, nicks and score marks.

If damage or wear is evident, the master cylinder must be replaced with a new one. If the master cylinder is in poor condition, then the calipers should be checked as well.

14 The dust boot, pushrod, circlip, piston components, spring and spring guide are all included in the master cylinder rebuild kit. Use all of the new parts, regardless of the apparent condition of the old ones. Lubricate the master cylinder bore with new brake fluid.

15 Smear the cup and seal with new brake fluid and if not already in place fit them into their grooves in the piston so their wider ends will fit into the master cylinder first **(see illustration)**.

16 Fit the spring guide into the end of the spring **(see illustration)**. Fit the spring guide and spring into the master cylinder **(see illustration 5.11c)**. Lubricate the piston with clean brake fluid and slide it into the master

cylinder and up against the spring **(see illustration 5.11b)**. Make sure the lips on the cup and seal do not turn inside out. Push the piston in to compress the spring and fit the new circlip into its groove **(see illustrations)**. Fit the rubber boot onto the pushrod so its narrow end lips locate in the groove **(see illustration 5.10)**. Smear the rounded end with silicone grease and locate it against the end of the piston, then press the boot into place **(see illustration)**.

17 If removed fit a new O-ring onto the fluid reservoir hose union, then press the union into the master cylinder and secure it with the circlip, using a new one if necessary **(see illustration 5.9b)**. Fit the cap over the circlip **(see illustration 5.9a)**.

18 Inspect the reservoir diaphragm and fit a new one if it is damaged or deteriorated or holed.

5.11c . . . and the spring

5.15 Make sure the cup and seal are correctly installed on the piston

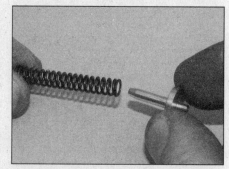

5.16a Fit the guide into the end of the spring

5.16b Push the piston into the bore . . .

5.16c . . . and hold it there while fitting the circlip

5.16d Feed the rim of the boot into the bore

5.20 Align the clamp mating surface with the punch mark

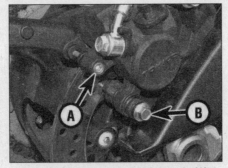

6.1a Slacken the pad retaining pin (A), then unscrew the bolt (B)

6.1b Pivot the caliper up and remove the pads

Installation

19 If removed, fit the brake light switch onto the bottom of the master cylinder, making sure the pin locates in the hole, and tighten the screw.

20 Attach the master cylinder to the handlebar, aligning the clamp joint with the punch mark on the top of the handlebar, then fit the back of the clamp with its UP mark facing up (**see illustration and 5.2**). Tighten the upper bolt to the torque setting specified at the beginning of this Chapter, followed by the lower bolt.

21 Locate the fluid reservoir on its bracket and tighten the bolt (**see illustration 5.2**). Connect the reservoir hose to the union on the master cylinder and secure it with the clip (**see illustration 5.7**).

22 Connect the brake hose to the master cylinder, using new sealing washers on each side of the banjo fitting. Align the hose as noted on removal (**see illustration 5.5**). Tighten the banjo bolt to the torque setting specified at the beginning of this Chapter.

23 Install the brake lever (see Chapter 5).

24 Connect the brake light switch wiring (**see illustration 5.1**).

25 Fill the fluid reservoir with new DOT 4 brake fluid (see *Pre-ride checks*). Refer to Section 11 and bleed the air and all old fluid from the system.

26 Check the operation of the front brake carefully and make sure there are no leaks before riding the motorcycle.

6 Rear brake pads

Warning: The dust created by the brake system may contain asbestos, which is harmful to your health. Never blow it out with compressed air and don't inhale any of it. An approved filtering mask should be worn when working on the brakes.

1 Slacken the pad retaining pin (**see illustration**). Unscrew the caliper rear mounting bolt/slider pin. Pivot the back of the caliper up off the disc and remove the pads, noting how they fit (**see illustration**).

2 Note the pad spring in the top of caliper and the pad guide on the caliper bracket and remove them if required for cleaning or replacement, noting how they fit (**see illustrations 7.17a and b**). Note: *Do not operate the brake pedal while the pads are out of the caliper.*

3 Inspect the surface of each pad for contamination and check that the friction material has not worn beyond its service limit (see Chapter 1, Section 10). If either pad is worn down to, or beyond, the service limit wear indicator (i.e. the wear indicator is no longer visible), is fouled with oil or grease, or heavily scored or damaged, fit a set of new pads. **Note:** *It is not possible to degrease the friction material; if the pads are contaminated in any way they must be replaced with new ones.*

4 If the pads are in good condition clean them carefully, using a fine wire brush which is completely free of oil and grease to remove all traces of road dirt and corrosion. Using a pointed instrument, dig out any embedded particles of foreign matter. If required, spray with a dedicated brake cleaner to remove any dust.

5 Check the condition of the brake disc (see Section 8).

6 Remove all traces of corrosion from the pad pin and check it for wear and damage.

7 Slide the caliper off the bracket (**see illustration**). Remove the collar from the rear slider pin boot (**see illustration**). Clean off all traces of corrosion and hardened grease from the collar, boots and pins. Check the slider pin boots for cracks and splits and replace them with new ones if necessary (see Section 7).

8 Clean around the exposed section of the piston to remove any dirt or debris that could cause the seals to be damaged. If new pads are being fitted, now push the piston all the

6.7a Slide the caliper off the bracket

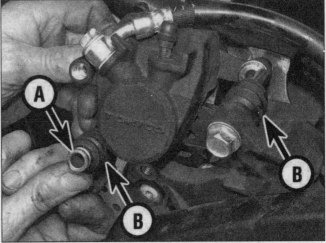

6.7b Remove the collar (A) and check the boots (B)

6.8 Push the piston in using your fingers if possible

6.12a Fit the pads onto the bracket . . . .

6.12b . . . making sure they locate correctly

way back into the caliper to create room for them; if the old pads are still serviceable push the piston in a little way. To push the piston back use finger pressure or a piece of wood as leverage, or place the old pads back in the caliper and use a metal bar or a screwdriver inserted between them, or use grips and a piece of wood, with rag or card to protect the caliper body **(see illustration)**. Alternatively obtain a proper piston-pushing tool from a good tool supplier **(see illustration 2.9b)**. It may be necessary to remove the master cylinder reservoir cap, plate and diaphragm and siphon out some fluid (see *Pre-ride) checks*. If the piston is difficult to push back, remove the bleed valve cap, then attach a length of clear hose to the bleed valve and place the open end in a suitable container, then open the valve and try again (see Section 11). Take great care not to draw any air into the system. If in doubt, bleed the brake afterwards.

9 If the piston appears seized, apply the brake pedal and check whether the piston moves at all. If it moves out but can't be pushed back in the chances are there is some hidden corrosion stopping it. If it doesn't move at all, or to fully clean and inspect the piston, disassemble the caliper and overhaul it (see Section 7).

10 Apply a smear of silicone based grease to the slider pins, rubber boots and collar. Fit the boots, making sure they locate correctly **(see illustration 6.7b)**. Fit the collar into the rear boot, making sure each end of the boot locates in the groove in the collar. Make sure

the pad spring and guide are correctly fitted **(see illustrations 7.17a and b)**. Slide the caliper onto the bracket **(see illustration 6.7a)**.

11 Lightly smear the back of the pad backing material and the edges of the backing material where it contacts the caliper body and the guide on the bracket with copper-based grease, making sure that none gets on the friction material. Also smear the pad pin.

12 Fit each pad onto the caliper bracket with the friction material facing the disc, making sure they locate correctly **(see illustrations)**. Pivot the caliper down over the pads. Fit the pad pin through the caliper and pads then fit the rear mounting bolt/slider pin **(see illustrations)**. Tighten the bolt and pin to the torque settings specified at the beginning of the Chapter.

13 Operate the brake pedal until the pads contact with the disc. Check the level of fluid in the hydraulic reservoir and top-up if necessary (see *Pre-ride checks*).

14 Check the operation of the rear brake before riding the motorcycle.

7 Rear brake caliper

⚠️ *Warning: If the caliper is in need of an overhaul all old brake fluid should be flushed from the system. Also, the dust created by the brake system may contain asbestos that is harmful to your health. Never*

blow it out with compressed air and do not inhale any of it. An approved filtering mask should be worn when working on the brakes. Overhaul of the brake caliper must be done in a spotlessly clean work area to avoid contamination and possible failure of the brake hydraulic system components. Do not, under any circumstances, use petroleum-based solvents to clean brake parts. Use clean DOT 4 brake fluid, dedicated brake cleaner or denatured alcohol only. To prevent damage from spilled brake fluid, always cover paintwork when working on the braking system, and mop up any spilled fluid straight away.

Removal

Note: *If the caliper is being overhauled (usually due to a sticking piston or fluid leaks) read through the entire procedure first and make sure that you have obtained all the new parts required, including some new DOT 4 brake fluid.*

1 If the caliper is being completely removed or overhauled, unscrew the brake hose banjo bolt and detach the banjo union, noting its alignment with the caliper **(see illustration)**. Wrap plastic foodwrap around the banjo union and secure the hose in an upright position to minimise fluid loss. Discard the sealing washers as new ones must be fitted on reassembly. Cover the top of the caliper with rag to catch the fluid inside the caliper.

2 Unscrew the brake pad retaining pin and the caliper rear mounting bolt/slider pin **(see illustration 6.1a)**.

6.12c Pivot the caliper down over the pads and fit the retaining pin . . .

6.12d . . . and the bolt

7.1 Unscrew the banjo bolt (arrowed)

7.7a Apply the compressed air as described . . .

7.7b . . . until the piston is displaced

7.9 Remove the seals and discard them

3 Pivot the caliper up then slide it off the bracket **(see illustration 6.7a).**

4 If required remove the brake pads, noting how they fit **(see illustration 6.1b).**

5 If required, remove the pad spring from the caliper, and if the pads have been removed the pad guide from the bracket, noting how they fit **(see illustrations 7.17a and b).**

Overhaul

6 Clean the exterior of the caliper with denatured alcohol or brake system cleaner. Have some clean rag ready to catch any spilled brake fluid.

7 Place a piece of wood between the piston and the caliper body – it should be just thick enough to stop the piston leaving the bore entirely **(see illustration).** Apply compressed air gradually and progressively, starting with a fairly low pressure, to the fluid inlet on the

caliper body and allow the piston to ease out of its bore, controlling it with the wood **(see illustration).**

8 If the piston is stuck in its bore due to corrosion the caliper should be replaced with a new one. Do not try to remove a piston by levering it out or by using pliers or other grips.

9 Remove the dust seal and the piston seal from the piston bore using a soft wooden or plastic tool to avoid scratching the bores **(see illustration).** Discard the seals as new ones must be fitted on reassembly.

10 Clean the piston and bore with clean DOT 4 brake fluid. If compressed air is available, blow it through the fluid passages in the caliper to ensure they are clear (make sure it is filtered and unlubricated).

Caution: Do not, under any circumstances, use a petroleum-based solvent to clean brake parts.

11 Inspect the caliper bore and piston for signs of corrosion, nicks and burrs and loss of plating. If surface defects are present, the piston and/or the caliper assembly must be replaced with new ones. If the caliper is in poor condition, the master cylinder should also be checked.

12 Remove the collar from the rear slider pin boot **(see illustration 6.7b).** Remove the slider pin boots. Clean off all traces of corrosion and hardened grease from the collar, boots and pins. Replace the rubber boots with new ones if they are damaged, deformed or deteriorated. Apply a smear of silicone based grease to all the components. Fit the boots, making sure they locate correctly. Fit the collar into the rear boot, making sure each end of the boot locates in the groove in the collar.

13 Lubricate the new piston seal with clean brake fluid and fit it into its groove in the caliper bore **(see illustrations).**

14 Lubricate the new dust seal with silicone grease and fit it into its groove in the caliper bore **(see illustration).**

15 Lubricate the piston with clean brake fluid and fit it, closed-end first, into the caliper bore, taking care not to displace the seals **(see illustration).** Using your thumbs, push the piston all the way in, making sure it enters the bore squarely **(see illustration).**

Installation

16 If the caliper has not been overhauled, refer to Step 12 and clean, check and re-grease the slider pins, boots and collar.

7.13a Lubricate the new piston seal . . .

7.13b . . . and fit it into the lower groove

7.14 Lubricate and fit the new dust seal into the upper groove . . .

7.15a . . . then lubricate and fit the piston . . .

7.15b . . . pushing it squarely all the way in

17 Make sure that the pad spring and pad guide are correctly fitted **(see illustrations)**.

18 If removed fit each brake pad onto the caliper bracket with the friction material facing the disc, making sure they locate correctly **(see illustrations 6.12a and b)**. Slide the caliper onto the bracket **(see illustration 6.7a)**.

19 Pivot the caliper down over the pads. Fit the pad pin through the caliper and pads then fit the rear mounting bolt/slider pin **(see illustrations 6.12c and d)**. Tighten the bolt and pin to the torque settings specified at the beginning of the Chapter.

20 If detached, connect the brake hose to the caliper, using new sealing washers on each side of the fitting. Align the hose as noted on removal **(see illustration 7.1)**. Tighten the banjo bolt to the torque setting specified at the beginning of the Chapter.

21 Fill the fluid reservoir with new DOT 4 brake fluid (see *Pre-ride checks*). Refer to Section 11 and bleed the air and all old fluid from the system. Check that there are no fluid leaks and test the operation of the brake before riding the motorcycle.

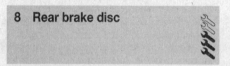

8 Rear brake disc

Inspection

1 Refer to Section 4 of this Chapter, noting that the dial gauge should be attached to the swingarm.

Removal

2 Remove the wheel (see Section 15).

Caution: Don't lay the wheel down and allow it to rest on the disc or sprocket – they could become warped. Set the wheel on wood blocks so the wheel rim supports the weight of the wheel.

3 If you are not replacing the disc, mark the

7.17a Make sure the pad spring (arrowed) is correctly fitted in the caliper . . .

relationship of the disc to the wheel so it can be installed in the same position. Unscrew the disc retaining bolts, loosening them evenly and a little at a time in a criss-cross pattern to avoid distorting the disc, then remove the disc **(see illustration)**.

Installation

4 Before installing the disc, make sure there is no dirt or corrosion where the disc seats on the hub. If the disc does not sit flat when it is bolted down, it will appear to be warped when checked or when the rear brake is used.

5 Install the disc on the wheel with its marked side facing out, aligning the previously applied matchmarks (if you're reinstalling the original disc).

6 Clean the threads of the disc mounting bolts, then apply a suitable non-permanent thread locking compound. Install the bolts and tighten them evenly and a little at a time in a criss-cross pattern to the torque setting specified at the beginning of this Chapter. Clean the disc using acetone or brake system cleaner. If a new disc has been installed, remove any protective coating from its working surfaces and fit new brake pads.

7 Install the rear wheel (see Section 15).

8 Operate the brake pedal several times to bring the pads into contact with the disc. Check the operation of the rear brake before riding the motorcycle.

7.17b . . . and the pad guide (arrowed) is correctly fitted on the bracket

9 Rear brake master cylinder

> *Warning: If the brake master cylinder is in need of an overhaul all old brake fluid should be flushed from the system. Overhaul of the brake master cylinder must be done in a spotlessly clean work area to avoid contamination and possible failure of the brake hydraulic system components. Do not, under any circumstances, use petroleum-based solvents to clean brake parts. Use clean DOT 4 brake fluid, dedicated brake cleaner or denatured alcohol only, as described. To prevent damage from spilled brake fluid, always cover paintwork when working on the braking system, and mop up any spilled fluid straight away.*

Removal

Note: *If the master cylinder is being overhauled (usually due to sticking or poor action, or fluid leaks) read through the entire procedure first and make sure that you have obtained all the new parts required, including some new DOT 4 brake fluid.*

1 Remove the split pin and washer from the clevis pin securing the master cylinder pushrod to the brake pedal **(see illustration)**.

8.3 Disc is secured by five bolts

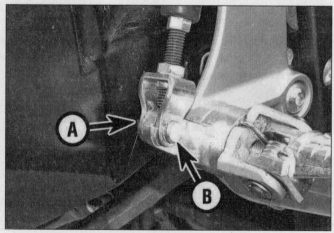

9.1 Remove the split pin and washer (A) and withdraw the clevis pin (B)

9.2a Unscrew the bolt and draw the reservoir out

Withdraw the clevis pin and separate the pushrod from the pedal. Discard the split pin as a new one must be fitted on reassembly.

2 Undo the bolt securing the fluid reservoir and draw it out from behind the frame **(see illustration)**. If the master cylinder is being overhauled undo the reservoir cover screws and remove the reservoir cover, plate and diaphragm **(see illustration)**. Pour the brake fluid into a suitable container. Release the clip securing the reservoir hose to the union on the master cylinder and detach the hose, being prepared to catch any residual fluid **(see illustration)**. Wipe any remaining fluid out of the reservoir with a clean rag.

3 Undo the brake hose banjo bolt and detach the banjo union, noting its alignment with the master cylinder **(see illustration)**. Once disconnected, wrap plastic foodwrap around the banjo union and secure the hose in an upright position to minimise fluid loss. Discard the sealing washers as new ones must be fitted on reassembly.

4 Undo the screws securing the heel plate and master cylinder to the footrest bracket and remove the master cylinder **(see illustration)**.

Overhaul

5 Inspect the reservoir hose for cracks or splits and replace it with a new one if necessary. If required release the circlip securing the fluid reservoir hose union and detach the union from the master cylinder. Discard the O-ring as a new one must be fitted on reassembly.

6 Carefully remove the dust boot from the master cylinder **(see illustration)**.

9.7b . . . the piston . . .

9.2b Remove the cover, plate and diaphragm and drain the reservoir . . .

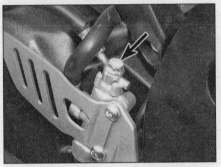

9.3 Brake hose banjo bolt (arrowed)

9.6 Draw the dust boot back . . .

7 Depress the pushrod and use circlip pliers to remove the circlip **(see illustration)**. Slide out the pushrod, piston assembly and spring, noting how they fit **(see illustrations)**. If they are difficult to remove, apply low pressure compressed air to the brake fluid outlet. Lay

9.7c . . . and the spring

9.2c . . . then release the clip (arrowed) and detach the hose

9.4 Master cylinder/heel plate screws (arrowed)

9.7a . . . then release the circlip and remove the pushrod . . .

the parts out in the proper order to prevent confusion during reassembly.

8 Mark the position of the clevis locknut on the pushrod, then loosen the locknut and thread the clevis nut, clevis and locknut off the pushrod **(see illustration)**. Remove the rubber boot.

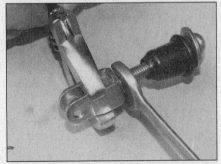

9.8 Hold the clevis to loosen the locknut

9.12a Make sure the seal is correctly fitted on the piston

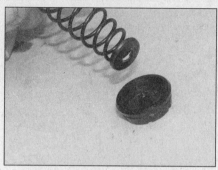

9.12b Fit the cup onto the end of the spring, locating the peg in the hole

9.13a Fit the spring . . .

9 Clean all parts with clean DOT 4 brake fluid. If compressed air is available, blow it through the fluid galleries to ensure they are clear (make sure the air is filtered and unlubricated). *Caution: Do not, under any circumstances, use a petroleum-based solvent to clean brake parts.*

10 Check the master cylinder bore for corrosion, scratches, nicks and score marks. If damage or wear is evident, the master cylinder must be replaced with a new one. If the master cylinder is in poor condition, then the caliper should be checked as well.

11 The dust boot, circlip, piston, seal, cup and spring are all included in the master cylinder rebuild kit. Use all of the new parts, regardless of the apparent condition of the old ones.

12 Smear the cup and seal with new brake fluid. If the seal is not already on the piston, fit it into its groove so the wider end will fit into

the master cylinder first (see illustration). Fit the cup onto the narrow end of the spring (see illustration). Lubricate the master cylinder bore with new brake fluid.

13 Fit the spring wide-end first into the master cylinder and push the cup in, making sure its lips do not turn inside out (see illustrations).

14 Lubricate the piston with clean brake fluid and slide it into the master cylinder and up against the cup and spring (see illustration). Make sure the lips on the seal do not turn inside out.

15 Slide the rubber boot onto the pushrod with its wider end facing the top of the rod. Fit the clevis locknut, the clevis and the clevis nut onto the master cylinder pushrod end (see illustration). Position the clevis as noted on removal, but leave the locknut finger-tight at this stage.

16 Smear some silicone grease onto the rounded end of the pushrod and locate it

against the end of the piston (see illustration). Push the piston in using the pushrod until the washer is beyond the circlip groove, then fit the new circlip, making sure it locates properly (see illustration 9.7a).

17 Fit the rubber boot into the master cylinder, making sure the lips are seated correctly in the bore and around the pushrod (see illustration).

18 If removed fit a new O-ring onto the fluid reservoir hose union, then press the union into the master cylinder and secure it with the circlip, using a new one if necessary.

Installation

19 Clean the master cylinder mounting bolt threads and apply some fresh threadlock. Locate the master cylinder on the inside of the footrest bracket, then fit the heel plate and tighten the bolts to the torque setting specified at the beginning of this Chapter (see illustration 9.4).

20 Align the brake pedal with the master cylinder pushrod clevis and install the clevis pin (see illustration 9.1). Fit the washer and a new split pin and bend the pin ends round the clevis pin. If the clevis position on the pushrod was disturbed during overhaul, check the brake pedal height (see Chapter 1, Section 10). Tighten the clevis locknut.

21 Align the brake hose as noted on removal and connect the hose to the master cylinder, using a new sealing washer on each side of the banjo fitting (see illustration 9.3). Tighten the banjo bolt to the torque setting specified at the beginning of this Chapter.

9.13b . . . making sure the cup locates correctly in the bore . . .

9.14 . . . then push the piston in

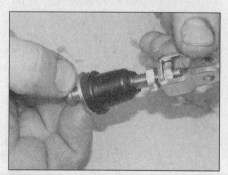

9.15 Thread the locknut and the clevis and its nut onto the pushrod

9.16 Fit the pushrod and secure it with the circlip

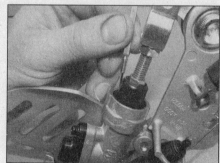

9.17 Make sure the boot rim locates correctly

11.2 Set-up for bleeding the brakes

11.4a Master cylinder bleed valve (arrowed)

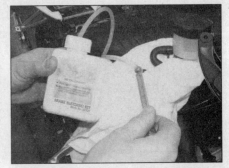

11.4b Bleeding the master cylinder

22 Connect the reservoir hose to the union on the master cylinder and secure it with the clip **(see illustration 9.2c)**. Check that the hose is secured with a clip at the reservoir end as well. If the clips have weakened, use new ones.

23 Fill the fluid reservoir with new DOT 4 brake fluid (see *Pre-ride checks*). Refer to Section 11 and bleed the air and all old fluid from the system. On completion fit the diaphragm, plate, cover and screws, then fit the reservoir back onto the bracket and tighten the bolt **(see illustrations 9.2b and a)**.

24 Check the operation of the rear brake carefully and make sure there are no leaks before riding the motorcycle.

10 Brake hoses and fittings

Inspection

1 Brake hose condition should be checked regularly and the hoses replaced with new ones at the specified interval (see Chapter 1).

2 Twist and flex the hoses while looking for cracks, bulges and seeping hydraulic fluid. Check extra carefully around the areas where the hoses connect with the banjo fittings, as these are common areas for hose failure.

3 Inspect the banjo fittings connected to the brake hoses. If the fittings are rusted, scratched or cracked, fit new hoses.

Removal and installation

4 The brake hoses have banjo fittings on each end. Cover the surrounding area with plenty of rags and place a suitable container at the bottom end of the hose. Unscrew the banjo bolt at each end of the hose, noting the alignment of the fitting with the master cylinder or brake caliper, and allow the fluid to drain into the container, also catching any residual fluid from the master cylinder or caliper with a rag **(see illustrations 3.3, 5.5, 7.1 and 9.3)**. Free the hose from any clips or guides and remove it, noting its routing. Discard the sealing washers. **Note:** *Do not operate the brake lever or pedal while a brake hose is disconnected.*

5 Position the new hose, making sure it isn't twisted or otherwise strained, and ensure

that it is correctly routed through any clips or guides and is clear of all moving components.

6 Check that the fittings align correctly, then install the banjo bolts, using new sealing washers on both sides of the fittings **(see illustration 3.22)**. Tighten the banjo bolts to the torque setting specified at the beginning of this Chapter.

7 Refill the reservoir with new DOT 4 brake fluid (see *Pre-ride checks*) and bleed the air from the system (see Section 11).

8 Check the operation of the brake carefully and make sure there are no leaks before riding the motorcycle.

11 Brake system bleeding and fluid change

Note: *If bleeding the system using the conventional method does not work sufficiently well, you can use a commercially available vacuum-type brake bleeding tool (see illustration 11.17) and repeat the procedure detailed below, following the manufacturers instructions for using the tool.*

Bleeding

1 Bleeding the brakes is simply the process of removing air from the brake fluid reservoir, the hose(s) and the brake caliper(s). Bleeding is necessary whenever a brake system hydraulic connection is loosened, after a component or hose is replaced with a new one, or when the master cylinder or caliper is overhauled. Leaks in the system may also allow air to enter, but

leaking brake fluid will reveal their presence and warn you of the need for repair.

2 To bleed the brakes, you will need some new DOT 4 brake fluid, a length of clear vinyl or plastic hose, a small container partially filled with clean brake fluid, some rags and a spanner to fit the brake caliper bleed valve **(see illustration)**.

3 Cover the fuel tank and other painted components to prevent damage in the event that brake fluid is spilled. Support the bike and position the handlebars as necessary so that each reservoir is level. When doing the rear brake displace the reservoir from its bracket and draw it out from behind the frame, then tie or support it so that there is no danger of it tipping over.

4 Refer to *Pre-ride checks* and remove the reservoir cap or cover, diaphragm plate and diaphragm. Slowly pump the brake lever (front brake) or pedal (rear brake) a few times, until no air bubbles can be seen floating up from the holes in the bottom of the reservoir. This bleeds the air from the master cylinder end of the line. Temporarily refit the reservoir cap or cover. The front master cylinder is fitted with a bleed valve as well as the calipers **(see illustration)** – if there is evidence of air in the system bleed the master cylinder as well as the calipers as described below **(see illustration)**.

5 Pull the dust cap off the bleed valve **(see illustrations)**. Attach one end of the clear vinyl or plastic hose to the bleed valve and submerge the other end in the clean brake fluid in the container **(see illustration 11.2)**. When

11.5a Front caliper bleed valve (arrowed)

11.5b Rear caliper bleed valve (arrowed)

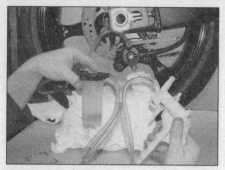

11.17 Using a vacuum pump to draw the fluid from or through the system

bleeding the front brakes, bleed the right-hand caliper first. **Note:** *To avoid damaging the bleed valve during the procedure, loosen it and then tighten it temporarily with a ring spanner before attaching the hose. With the hose attached, the valve can then be opened and closed either with an open-ended spanner, or by leaving the ring spanner located on the valve and fitting the hose above it.*

6 Check the fluid level in the reservoir. Do not allow the fluid level to drop below the lower mark during the procedure.

7 Carefully pump the brake lever or pedal three or four times and hold it in (front) or down (rear) while opening the bleed valve. When the valve is opened, brake fluid will flow out of the caliper into the clear tubing, and the lever will move toward the handlebar, or the pedal will move down. If there is air in the system there will be air bubbles in the brake fluid coming out of the caliper.

8 Tighten the bleed valve, then release the brake lever or pedal gradually. Repeat the process until no air bubbles are visible in the brake fluid leaving the caliper, and the lever or pedal is firm when applied. Keep an eye on the fluid level in the reservoir and top it up as required when it reaches the lower level line. On completion, disconnect the hose, then tighten the bleed valve to the torque setting specified at the beginning of this Chapter and install the dust cap. When bleeding the front brakes, start with the master cylinder (See Step 4), then do the right-hand caliper then the left-hand caliper.

 If it is not possible to produce a firm feel to the lever or pedal, the fluid may be aerated. Let the brake fluid in the system stabilise for a few hours and then repeat the procedure when the tiny bubbles in the system have settled out.

9 Top-up the reservoir, then install the diaphragm, diaphragm plate and cap or cover. Fit the rear reservoir onto its bracket and tighten the bolt. Wipe up any spilled brake fluid. Check the entire system for fluid leaks.

10 Check the operation of the brakes before riding the motorcycle.

Fluid change

11 Changing the brake fluid is a similar process to bleeding the brakes and requires the same materials plus a suitable tool for siphoning the fluid out of the reservoir. Also ensure that the container is large enough to take all the old fluid when it is flushed out of the system.

12 Follow Steps 3 and 5, then remove the reservoir cap or cover, diaphragm plate and diaphragm and siphon the old fluid out of the reservoir. Fill the reservoir with new DOT 4 brake fluid, then open the bleed valve and carefully pump the brake lever/pedal until new fluid (which will be lighter in colour) can be seen emerging from the caliper bleed valve – keep the reservoir topped-up with new fluid to above the LOWER level at all times or air may enter the system and greatly increase the length of the task.

13 If for some reason the new fluid does not pump through the system, close the bleed valve and pump the lever or pedal three or four times and hold it in (front) or down (rear) while opening the caliper bleed valve. When the valve is opened, brake fluid will flow out of the caliper into the clear tubing, and the lever will move toward the handlebar, or the pedal will move down. Tighten the bleed valve, then release the brake lever or pedal gradually. Repeat the process until new fluid can be seen emerging from the bleed valve.

 Old brake fluid is invariably much darker in colour than new fluid, making it easy to see when all old fluid has been expelled from the system.

14 Disconnect the hose, then tighten the bleed valve to the specified torque setting and fit the dust cap.

15 Top-up the reservoir, then install the diaphragm, diaphragm plate and cap or cover. Fit the rear reservoir onto its bracket and tighten the bolt. Wipe up any spilled brake fluid. Check the entire system for fluid leaks.

16 Check the operation of the brakes before riding the motorcycle.

Draining the system for overhaul

17 Draining the brake fluid is again a similar process to bleeding the brakes. The quickest and easiest way is to use a commercially available vacuum-type brake bleeding tool **(see illustration)** – follow the manufacturer's instructions. Otherwise follow the procedure described above for changing the fluid, but quite simply do not put any new fluid into the reservoir – the system fills itself with air instead. Alternatively you can just detach the brake hose at each end and allow the fluid to drain into a suitable container.

1 In order to carry out a proper inspection of the wheels, it is necessary to support the bike upright so that the wheel being inspected is raised off the ground. Position the motorcycle on an auxiliary stand. Clean the wheels thoroughly to remove mud and dirt that may interfere with the inspection procedure or mask defects. Make a general check of the wheels (see Chapter 1) and tyres (see *Pre-ride checks*).

2 Attach a dial gauge to the fork or the swingarm and position its tip against the side of the wheel rim. Spin the wheel slowly and check the axial (side-to-side) runout of the rim **(see illustration)**.

3 In order to accurately check radial (out of round) runout with the dial gauge, remove the wheel from the machine, and the tyre from the wheel. With the axle clamped in a vice and the dial gauge positioned on the top of the rim, the wheel can be rotated to check the runout **(see illustration 12.2)**.

4 An easier, though slightly less accurate, method is to attach a stiff wire pointer to the fork or the swingarm and position the end a fraction of an inch from the wheel rim where the wheel and tyre join. If the wheel is true, the distance from the pointer to the rim will be constant as the wheel is rotated. **Note:** *If wheel runout is excessive, check the wheel bearings very carefully before renewing the wheel.*

5 The wheels should also be inspected for cracks, flat spots on the rim and other damage.

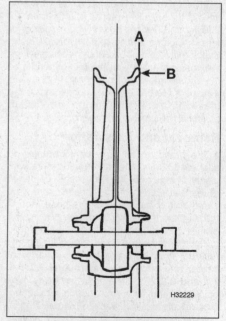

12.2 Check the wheel for radial (out-of-round) runout (A) and axial (side-to-side) runout (B)

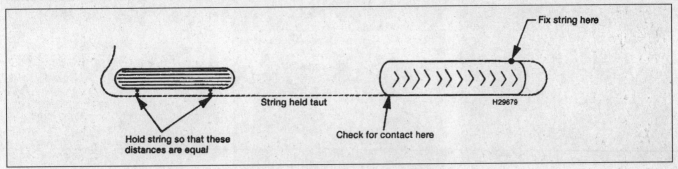

13.5 Wheel alignment check using string

Look very closely for dents in the area where the tyre bead contacts the rim. Dents in this area may prevent complete sealing of the tyre against the rim, which leads to deflation of the tyre over a period of time. If damage is evident, or if runout in either direction is excessive, the wheel will have to be renewed. Never attempt to repair a damaged cast alloy wheel.

13 Wheel alignment check

1 Misalignment of the wheels due to a bent frame or forks can cause strange and possibly serious handling problems. If the frame or forks are at fault, repair by a frame specialist or renewal are the only options.

2 To check wheel alignment you will need an assistant, a length of string or a perfectly straight piece of wood and a ruler. A plumb bob or spirit level for checking that the wheels are vertical will also be required.

3 In order to make a proper check of the wheels it is necessary to support the bike in an upright position, using an auxiliary stand. First ensure that the chain adjuster markings coincide on each side of the swingarm (see Chapter 1, Section 1). Next, measure the width of both tyres at their widest points. Subtract the smaller measurement from the larger measurement, then divide the difference by two. The result is the amount of offset that should exist between the front and rear tyres on both sides of the machine.

4 If a string is used, have your assistant hold one end of it about halfway between the floor and the rear axle, with the string touching the back edge of the rear tyre sidewall.

5 Run the other end of the string forward and pull it tight so that it is roughly parallel to the floor **(see illustration)**. Slowly bring the string into contact with the front edge of the rear tyre sidewall, then turn the front wheel until it is parallel with the string. Measure the distance from the front tyre sidewall to the string.

6 Repeat the procedure on the other side of the motorcycle. The distance from the front tyre sidewall to the string should be equal on both sides.

7 As previously mentioned, a perfectly straight length of wood or metal bar may be substituted for the string **(see illustration)**.

8 If the distance between the string and tyre is greater on one side, or if the rear wheel appears to be out of alignment, have your machine checked by a Suzuki dealer or frame specialist.

9 If the front-to-back alignment is correct, the wheels still may be out of alignment vertically.

10 Using a plumb bob or spirit level, check the rear wheel to make sure it is vertical. To do this, hold the string of the plumb bob against the tyre upper sidewall and allow the weight to settle just off the floor. If the string touches both the upper and lower tyre sidewalls and is perfectly straight, the wheel is vertical. If it is not, adjust the stand until it is.

11 Once the rear wheel is vertical, check the front wheel in the same manner. If both wheels are not perfectly vertical, the frame and/or major suspension components are bent.

14 Front wheel

Removal

Special tool: *A 24 mm Hex key is needed to counter-hold the axle while tightening the bolt. If one is not available you can make a tool using suitable nuts and bolts* **(see illustration 14.10)**.

1 Displace the front brake calipers (see Section 3). **Note:** *Do not operate the brake lever while the calipers are off the disc.*

2 Loosen the axle clamp bolts on the bottom of the right-hand fork **(see illustration)**.

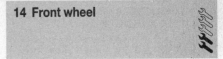

14.2 Loosen the clamp bolts (A) then unscrew the axle bolt (B)

Distance between gauge and tyre must be equal each side and front and back

Perfectly straight lengths of wood or metal bar

Rear tyre must be parallel to gauge at front and back

13.7 Wheel alignment check using a straight-edge

14.4a Loosen the clamp bolts (arrowed) . . .

14.4b . . . then withdraw the axle and remove the wheel

14.4c Remove the spacer for safekeeping

14.8 Fit the axle bolt and tighten it finger-tight

14.10 Counter-hold the axle using a suitable tool as shown

Unscrew the bolt from the right-hand end of the axle.

3 Using an auxiliary stand, support the motorcycle securely in an upright position with the front wheel off the ground – remove the fairing side panels if a support is being placed under the engine (see Chapter 7).

4 Loosen the axle clamp bolts on the bottom of the left-hand fork (see illustration). Support the wheel, then withdraw the axle from the left-hand side, tapping it out from the right using a suitable drift if required, making sure you don't damage the threads (see illustration). Remove the wheel from between the forks. Remove the spacer from the right-hand side of the wheel, noting how it fits (see illustration).

Caution: Don't lay the wheel down and allow it to rest on the disc – the disc could become warped. Set the wheel on wood blocks so the wheel rim supports the

weight of the wheel. Do not operate the brake lever with the wheel removed.

5 Clean the axle and remove any corrosion using steel wool. Check the axle is straight by rolling it on a flat surface such as a piece of plate glass. If available, place the axle in V-blocks and check for runout using a dial gauge. If the axle is bent or the runout exceeds the limit specified at the beginning of this Chapter, replace it with a new one.

6 Wipe any old grease off the bearing seals and check the condition of the seals and the wheel bearings (see Section 16).

Installation

7 Manoeuvre the wheel into position between the forks, making sure the directional arrows on both the wheel and tyre are pointing in the normal direction of rotation. Apply a thin coat of grease to the axle and to the lips of the bearing seals.

8 Fit the spacer into the seal on the right-hand side of the wheel (see illustration 14.4c). Lift the wheel and slide the axle through from the left-hand side (see illustration 14.4b). Fit the axle bolt and secure it finger-tight (see illustration).

9 Install the brake calipers (see Section 3).

10 Counter-hold the axle head using a suitable tool, and tighten the axle bolt to the torque setting specified at the beginning of the Chapter (see illustration). Now tighten the clamp bolts on the bottom of the right-hand fork to the specified torque (see illustration 14.2).

11 Move the motorcycle off the stand, apply the front brake and pump the front forks a few times to settle all components in position.

12 Tighten the clamp bolts on the left-hand fork to the specified torque setting (see illustration 14.4a).

13 Install the fairing side panels (see Chapter 7).

14 Check the operation of the front brake before riding the motorcycle.

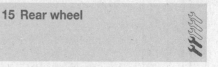

15 Rear wheel

Removal

1 Using an auxiliary stand, support the motorcycle securely in an upright position with the rear wheel off the ground – remove the fairing side panels if required (see Chapter 7).

2 If required remove the brake pads and displace the rear brake caliper (see Section 7) – they can be left mounted on the caliper bracket but it does make wheel installation a bit more fiddly. Note: Do not operate the brake pedal while the caliper is off the disc.

3 Slacken the drive chain (see Chapter 1). Unscrew the axle nut and remove the washer where fitted (see illustration).

4 Remove the chain adjuster block from the left-hand end of the axle, noting how it fits (see illustration 15.15b).

5 Support the wheel, then withdraw the axle and the right-hand adjuster block (see illustration). Lower the wheel to the ground.

6 Disengage the chain from the sprocket

15.3 Remove the axle nut and the washer where fitted

15.5 Support the wheel and withdraw the axle

15.6a Disengage the chain from the sprocket

15.6b Note how the caliper bracket locates

15.7a Remove the right-hand spacer . . .

then draw the wheel back and remove it **(see illustration)**. Note how the axle passes through the caliper mounting bracket, and detach it from the swingarm as you remove the wheel, noting how it locates **(see illustration)**.

7 Remove the axle spacers from each side of the hub, noting which fits where **(see illustrations)**. Remove the chain adjuster block from the axle, noting how the flats on the axle head fit into the recess in the block.

Caution: Don't lay the wheel down and allow it to rest on the disc or the sprocket – they could become warped. Set the wheel on wood blocks so the wheel rim supports the weight of the wheel. Do not operate the brake pedal with the wheel removed.

8 Clean the axle and remove any corrosion using steel wool. Check the axle is straight by rolling it on a flat surface such as a piece of plate glass. If available, place the axle in V-blocks and check for runout using a dial gauge. If the axle is bent or the runout exceeds the limit specified at the beginning of this Chapter, renew it.

9 Wipe all old grease off the bearing seals and check the condition of the seals and the wheel bearings (see Section 16).

Installation

10 Apply a thin coat of grease to the lips of each bearing seal, to the inside and the inner faces of the axle spacers, and to the axle.

11 Fit the plain spacer into the seal in the left-hand side of the hub and the shouldered spacer into the seal in the right **(see illustrations 15.7b and a)**. Slide the

15.7b . . . and the left-hand spacer, noting their difference

right-hand chain adjuster block onto the axle, making sure it is the correct way round.

12 Manoeuvre the wheel into position between the ends of the swingarm and locate the caliper bracket on its lug on the swingarm **(see illustration)**.

13 Engage the drive chain with the sprocket **(see illustration 15.6a)**.

14 Lift the wheel into position, making sure the caliper bracket and spacers stay in place and the bracket is correctly aligned with the wheel and the swingarm, and slide the axle through from the right-hand side **(see illustration 15.5)**.

15 Locate the right-hand chain adjuster block in the swingarm and the flats on the axle head between the raised sections on the block **(see illustration)**. Check that everything is correctly aligned, then fit the left-hand adjuster block **(see illustration)**. Fit the axle nut with its

15.12 If the caliper and pads are fitted make sure the disc fits between the pads

washer where fitted **(see illustration 15.3)**. Tighten the nut finger-tight.

16 Adjust the chain slack as described in Chapter 1.

17 Tighten the axle nut to the torque setting specified at the beginning of this Chapter. On US and Canadian models where fitted, insert a new split pin through the nut castellations and hole in the axle and bend its ends round the nut.

18 Install the brake caliper (see Section 7). Operate the brake pedal several times to bring the pads into contact with the disc. Check the operation of the brake before riding the motorcycle.

16 Wheel bearings

Caution: Don't lay the wheel down and allow it to rest on the disc or the sprocket – they could become warped. Set the wheel on wood blocks so the wheel rim supports the weight of the wheel, or keep the wheel upright. Don't operate the brake lever/pedal with the wheel removed.

Special tool: A knife-edged bearing puller with slide-hammer attachment will be required to extract the wheel bearings.

Note: Always renew the wheel bearings in sets, never individually. Avoid using a high pressure cleaner on the wheel bearing area.

Front wheel bearings

1 Remove the wheel (see Section 14).

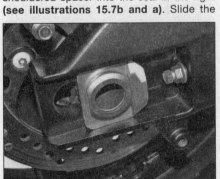

15.15a Make sure the adjuster block is the correct way round and the axle head locates correctly

15.15b Make sure the adjuster block is the correct way round

16.2 Lever out the bearing seals

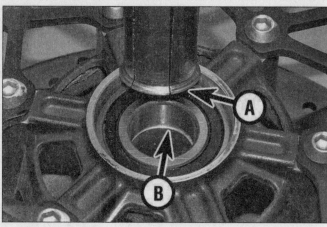

16.4a Locate the expanding edge (A) in the gap (B) and tighten the expander . . .

2 Lever out the bearing seal from each of the hub using a seal hook or a screwdriver and a piece of wood **(see illustration)**. Take care not to damage the hub. Discard the seals as new ones must be fitted on reassembly.

3 Inspect the bearings – check that the inner race turns smoothly and that the outer race is a tight fit in the hub (see *Tools and Workshop Tips (Section 5)* in the Reference Section). **Note:** *Do not remove the bearings unless they are going to be replaced with new ones – removal will destroy them.*

4 If the bearings are worn, remove them using an internal expanding puller with slide-hammer attachment, which can be obtained commercially or from Suzuki, part No. 09921-20240 (see *Tools and Workshop Tips*) **(see illustrations)**.

Assemble the puller, then hold the wheel down and remove the right-hand bearing.

5 Retrieve the spacer which fits between the bearings.

6 Either turn the wheel over and remove the left-hand bearing using the same procedure, or leave it the same way up and drive the left-hand bearing out using a suitable drift inserted from the right-hand side.

7 Thoroughly clean the hub area of the wheel with a suitable solvent and inspect the bearing seats for scoring and wear. If the seats are damaged, consult a Suzuki dealer before reassembling the wheel.

8 If the bearings are open-sided work some bearing grease into them. If they are sealed on one side only fit that side facing out. If they

are sealed on both sides fit the marked side facing out.

9 Use either a drawbolt arrangement (see *Tools and Workshop Tips*), a bearing driver or suitable socket to install the bearings **(see illustration)**. Ensure that the drawbolt washer or driver (as applicable) bears only on the outer edge of the race and does not mark the bearing housing.

10 Install the new right-hand bearing first. Ensure the bearing is fitted squarely and all the way in until it seats. When seated, turn the wheel over, fit the bearing spacer and then the new left-hand bearing.

11 Apply a smear of grease to the new seals, then press them into the hub **(see illustration)**. Level the seals with the rim with a small block of wood **(see illustration 16.23b)**.

12 Clean the brake discs using acetone or brake system cleaner, then install the wheel (see Section 14).

Rear wheel bearings

13 Remove the wheel (see Section 15). Lift the sprocket coupling out of the hub **(see illustration)**.

14 Lever out the bearing seal from the right-hand side of the hub using a seal hook or a flat-bladed screwdriver and a piece of wood **(see illustration)**. Take care not to damage the hub. Discard the seal as a new one should be fitted on reassembly.

16.4b . . . then use the slide-hammer attachment to draw the bearings out

16.9 Using a socket to drive the bearing in

16.11 Press the seal into place setting it flush with the rim

16.13 Lift the sprocket coupling off the wheel

16.14 Lever out the bearing seal

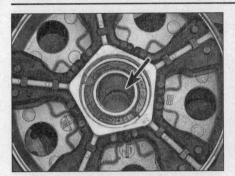

16.16a Locate the drift on the exposed inner race (arrowed) . . .

16.16b . . . and drive the bearing out

16.21 Using a socket to drive the bearing in

15 Inspect the bearings in both sides of the hub – check that the inner race turns smoothly and that the outer race is a tight fit in the hub (see *Tools and Workshop Tips (Section 5)* in the *Reference* section). **Note:** *Do not remove the bearings unless they are going to be replaced with new ones – removal will destroy them.*

16 If the bearings are worn, remove them as follows: lay the wheel on the blocks with its left-hand side facing down. Insert a metal rod (preferably a brass drift punch) through the centre of the upper bearing and locate it on the inner race of the lower bearing, pushing the spacer aside to expose it **(see illustration)**. Tap evenly around the rim to drive the bearing from the hub **(see illustration)**. The spacer should drop out once the bearing is free.

17 If it proves difficult or impossible to get your drift to purchase on the rim of the bearing, remove it using an internal expanding puller with slide-hammer attachment, which

can be obtained commercially or from Suzuki, Pt. No. 09921-20240 (see *Tools and Workshop Tips*) **(see illustrations 16.4a and b)**.

18 Turn the wheel over and drive out the remaining bearing using the same procedure.

19 Thoroughly clean the hub area of the wheel with a suitable solvent and inspect the bearing seats for scoring and wear. If the seats are damaged, consult a Suzuki dealer before reassembling the wheel.

20 If the bearings are open-sided work some bearing grease into them. If they are sealed on one side only fit that side facing out. If they are sealed on both sides fit the marked side facing out.

21 Use either a drawbolt arrangement (see *Tools and Workshop Tips*), a bearing driver or suitable socket to install the bearings **(see illustration)**. Ensure that the drawbolt washer or driver (as applicable) bears only on the outer edge of the race and does not mark the bearing housing.

22 Install the right-hand bearing first. Ensure the bearing is fitted squarely and all the way in until it seats. When seated, turn the wheel over, install the bearing spacer and then the left-hand new bearing.

23 Apply a smear of grease to the new seal, then press it into the right-hand side of the hub **(see illustration)**. Level the seal with the rim of the hub with a small block of wood **(see illustration)**.

24 Clean the brake disc using acetone or brake system cleaner, then install the wheel (see Section 15).

Sprocket coupling bearing

25 Remove the wheel (see Section 15). Lift the sprocket coupling out of the hub **(see illustration 16.13)**.

26 Remove the spacer from inside the sprocket coupling **(see illustration)**.

27 Lever out the bearing seal on the outside of the coupling using a seal hook or a flat-bladed screwdriver and a piece of wood **(see illustration)**. Take care not to damage the rim of the coupling. Discard the seal as a new one should be fitted on reassembly.

28 Inspect the bearing – check that the inner race turns smoothly and that the outer race is a tight fit in the coupling (see *Tools and Workshop Tips (Section 5)* in the Reference Section). **Note:** *Do not remove the bearing unless it is going to be replaced with a new one – removal will destroy it.*

29 Support the coupling on blocks of wood, sprocket side down, and drive the bearing out from the inside using a bearing driver or socket **(see illustration)**.

16.23a Press the seal into place . . .

16.23b . . . using a piece of wood as shown helps set the seal flush with the rim

16.26 Remove the spacer from inside the coupling

16.27 Lever out the bearing seal

16.29 Drive the bearing out from the inside

30 Thoroughly clean the bearing seat with a suitable solvent and inspect the seat for scoring and wear. If the seat is damaged, consult a Suzuki dealer before reassembling the wheel.

31 If the bearing is open-sided work some bearing grease into it. If it is sealed on one side only fit that side facing out. If it is sealed on both sides fit the marked side facing out.

32 Use either a drawbolt arrangement (see *Tools and Workshop Tips*), a bearing driver or suitable socket to install the bearing **(see illustration)**. Ensure that the drawbolt washer or driver (as applicable) bears only on the outer edge of the race and does not mark the bearing housing. Ensure the bearing is fitted squarely and all the way onto its seat.

33 Apply a smear of grease to the new seal, then press it into the coupling, using a bearing driver or suitable socket **(see illustration)**. Level the seal with the rim of the coupling with a small block of wood **(see illustration 16.23b)**.

34 Fit the bearing spacer into the bearing **(see illustration 16.26)**.

35 Check the sprocket coupling/rubber dampers (see Section 20), then fit the sprocket coupling into the wheel and install the wheel (see Section 15).

16.32 Using a socket to drive the bearing in

16.33 Press the seal into place setting it flush with the rim

17 Tyres

General information

1 The wheels fitted to all models are designed to take tubeless tyres only. Tyre sizes are given in the Specifications at the beginning of this chapter.

2 Refer to *Pre-ride checks* listed at the beginning of this manual for tyre maintenance.

Fitting new tyres

3 When selecting new tyres, refer to the tyre information in the Owner's Handbook. Ensure that front and rear tyre types are compatible, the correct size and correct speed rating; if necessary seek advice from a Suzuki dealer or tyre fitting specialist **(see illustration)**.

4 It is recommended that tyres are fitted by a motorcycle tyre specialist rather than attempted in the home workshop. This is particularly relevant in the case of tubeless tyres because the force required to break the seal between the wheel rim and tyre bead is substantial, and is usually beyond the capabilities of an individual working with normal tyre levers. Additionally, the specialist will be able to balance the wheels after tyre fitting.

5 Note that punctured tubeless tyres can

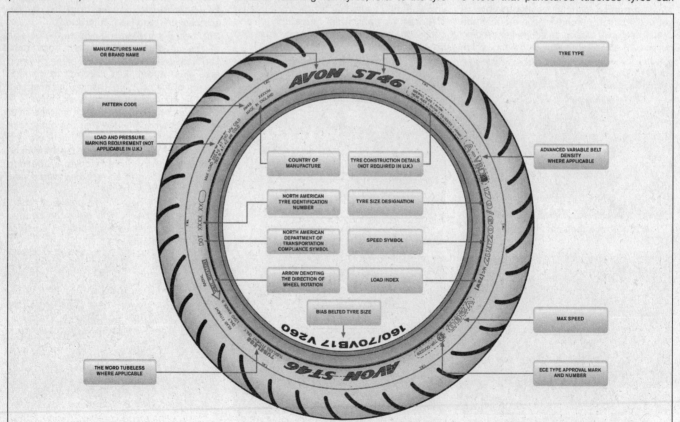

17.3 Common tyre sidewall markings

19.1 Undo the pinch bolt and slide the arm off the shaft

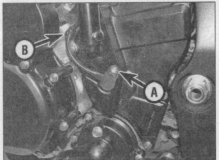

19.2 Unscrew the speed sensor bolt (A) and free the wiring from the clip (B)

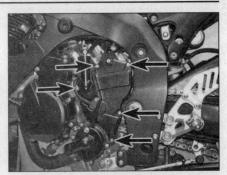

19.3a Undo the bolts (arrowed) and remove the sprocket cover

in some cases be repaired. Repairs must be carried out by a motorcycle tyre fitting specialist. Suzuki advise that a repaired tyre should not be used at speeds above 50 mph (80 kmh) for the first 24 hours, and not above 80 mph (130 kmh) thereafter.

18 Drive chain

Warning: NEVER install a drive chain which uses a clip-type (split) master link. ONLY use the correct tools to secure the riveted soft link – if you do not have access to such tools or do not have the skill to operate them correctly, have the chain installed by a Suzuki dealer.

Note: *Due to the swingarm design it is not possible to remove the chain complete. The drive chain has a riveted soft link which must be split using either the Suzuki service tool (Pt. No. 09922-22711) or a commercially-available drive chain cutting/staking tool.*

1 Remove the front sprocket cover (see Section 19).
2 Slacken the drive chain (see Chapter 1).
3 Refer to 'Tools and Workshop Tips (Section 8)' in the Reference section for details of how to identify the soft link, then split the chain at the soft link using the chain breaking tool. Note the chain's routing through the swingarm, then remove the chain from the bike.
4 When fitting the chain, route it through the swingarm and around the front sprocket,

leaving the two ends in a convenient position to work on. Assemble the new soft link and rivet it as described in Section 8 of *Tools and Workshop Tips*.
5 If fitting the original equipment RK chain, Suzuki specifies that the sideplate must be pressed into place so that the distance between the outer edges of the side plates is:
   600 models, 750K6 and K7 models
      18.6 to 18.9 mm
   750K8 and K9 models
      20.1 to 20.4 mm
6 After the soft link pins have been riveted in place, check the staked pin ends for any signs of cracking. If either of the pins have cracked the chain must be disassembled and another new soft link and O-rings fitted. If fitting the original equipment RK chain, Suzuki specifies that the diameter of the staked pins should be 5.45 to 5.85 mm.
7 Install the sprocket cover (see Section 19).
8 On completion, adjust and lubricate the chain (see Chapter 1).

19 Sprockets

Note: *Always renew the engine and rear wheel sprockets as a set, together with the drive chain.*

Removal

Front sprocket cover

1 Undo the gearchange linkage arm pinch

bolt and remove the arm from the shaft, noting any alignment marks **(see illustration)**. If no marks are visible, make your own before removing the arm so that it can be correctly aligned with the shaft on installation. Pivot the arm out of the way.
2 If required detach the clutch cable from the release lever and sprocket cover (see Chapter 2) – the cover can be supported or tied to one side with the cable still connected if preferred. If required unscrew the speed sensor bolt and draw the sensor out of the cover **(see illustration)**.
3 Undo the bolts securing the sprocket cover to the crankcase and displace or remove the cover **(see illustration)**. Note the position of the dowels and remove them for safekeeping if loose. Withdraw the clutch pushrod to prevent the possibility of accidentally bending it **(see illustration)**.

Front sprocket

4 Shift the transmission into gear, then have an assistant apply the rear brake whilst you undo the bolt securing the speed sensor rotor and remove the rotor **(see illustration)**.
5 Use the same method whilst you slacken the front sprocket nut, then remove the nut and washer **(see illustration)**. The sprocket nut is of the self-locking type. If the locking device is no longer effective, discard the nut and fit a new one on reassembly.
6 Slacken the drive chain (see Chapter 1). If the sprocket is to be reused mark its outer face so it can be installed the same way

19.3b Withdraw the clutch pushrod

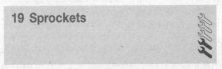

19.4 Undo the bolt (arrowed) and remove the speed sensor rotor

19.5 Unscrew the nut and remove the washer . . .

19.6 ... then disengage the chain and slide the sprocket off the shaft

19.8 The sprocket is secured by five nuts

19.12 Fit the rotor and bolt

round. Lift the chain off the sprocket and slide the sprocket off the shaft **(see illustration)**.

Rear sprocket

7 Remove the rear wheel (see Section 15). Lay it down on some wooden blocks – not on the disc. If the sprocket is to be reused mark its outer face so it can be installed the same way round.

8 Undo the sprocket nuts and remove the sprocket **(see illustration)**. If required, pull the sprocket coupling out of the hub and check the condition of the rubber dampers (see Section 20).

9 The sprocket nuts are the self-locking type. If the locking device is no longer effective, discard the nuts and fit new ones on reassembly.

Installation

Front sprocket and cover

10 Slide the sprocket onto the gearbox shaft and fit the chain around it **(see illustration 19.6)**; if the original sprocket is being refitted ensure it is installed the same way around as on removal. Take up some of the slack in the chain (see Chapter 1).

11 Clean the threads of the output shaft, then apply thread locking compound to the threads. Fit the washer and sprocket nut **(see illustration 19.5)**. Use the same method as on removal to prevent the sprocket turning, then tighten the nut to the torque setting specified at the beginning of the Chapter.

12 Fit the speed sensor rotor and its bolt **(see illustration)**; tighten the bolt to the specified torque setting.

13 Fit the remaining components in the reverse order of removal, noting the following:

● Lubricate each the end of the clutch pushrod with general purpose grease and make sure it locates correctly against the release mechanism in the cover **(see illustration 19.3b)**.

● Fit the cover locating dowels **(see illustration)**.

● Clean the speed sensor tip **(see illustration)**.

19.13a Make sure the dowels (arrowed) are in place . . .

● Align the gearchange linkage arm correctly with the shaft **(see illustration 19.1)**.

Rear sprocket

14 If removed, fit the sprocket coupling in the hub **(see illustration 16.13)**.

15 Fit the sprocket onto the coupling with its marked side facing out and install the sprocket nuts; if the original sprocket is being refitted ensure it is installed the same way around as on removal **(see illustration 19.8)**. Tighten the nuts evenly to the torque setting specified at the beginning of this Chapter.

16 Install the rear wheel (see Section 15).

20 Rear sprocket coupling/ rubber dampers

1 Remove the rear wheel (see Section 15).

2 The coupling walls should be a good fit between the dampers with no rotational freeplay – If there is freeplay the damper segments have compressed and should be replaced with a new set.

3 Pull the sprocket coupling out of the hub leaving the rubber dampers in place **(see illustration 16.13)**. Note the spacer inside the coupling bearing and remove it if it is loose **(see illustration 16.26)**.

4 Check the coupling for cracks and damage

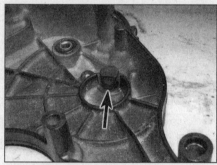

19.13b . . . and clean the sensor tip (arrowed) before fitting it

(see illustration). Also check the sprocket studs for damage and ensure they are secure in the coupling.

5 Lift the rubber dampers from the hub and check them for cracks, hardening and general deterioration. Replace the rubber dampers with a new set if necessary.

6 Checking and renewal procedures for the coupling bearing are described in Section 16.

7 Make sure the rubber dampers are correctly located in the hub.

8 Make sure the spacer is correctly installed in the coupling bearing, then press the coupling firmly into the hub.

9 Install the rear wheel (see Section 15).

20.4 Remove and check the damper segments

Chapter 7
Bodywork

Contents

Degrees of difficulty

| **Easy,** suitable for novice with little experience | | **Fairly easy,** suitable for beginner with some experience | | **Fairly difficult,** suitable for competent DIY mechanic | | **Difficult,** suitable for experienced DIY mechanic | | **Very difficult,** suitable for expert DIY or professional | |

---

1 General information

This Chapter covers the procedures necessary to remove and install the bodywork. Since many service and repair operations require the removal of the body panels, the procedures are grouped here and referred to from other Chapters.

In the case of damage to the bodywork, it is usually necessary to remove the broken component and replace it with a new (or used) one. The material that the body panels are composed of doesn't lend itself to conventional repair techniques. Note that there are however some companies that specialise in 'plastic welding' and there are a number of bodywork repair kits now available for motorcycles.

When attempting to remove any body panel, first study it closely, noting any fasteners and associated fittings, to be sure of returning everything to its correct place on installation. In some cases the aid of an assistant will be required when removing panels, to help avoid the risk of damage to paintwork. Once the evident fasteners have been removed, try to withdraw the panel as described but DO NOT FORCE IT – if it will not release, check that all fasteners have been removed and try again.

When installing a body panel, first study it closely, noting any fasteners and associated fittings removed with it, to be sure of returning everything to its correct place. Check that all fasteners are in good condition, including the trim clips and damping/rubber mounts; replace any faulty fasteners with new ones before the panel is reassembled. Check also that all mounting brackets are straight and repair them or replace them with new ones if necessary before attempting to install the panel.

Tighten the fasteners securely, but be careful not to overtighten any of them or the panel may break (not always immediately) due to the uneven stress.

Trim clips

1 Two types of plastic trim clip are used. The most common type has a centre pin which is pushed into the body of the clip to allow it to be drawn out of the panel **(see illustration)**. To install the clip, first depress the pawls of the clip body so that the centre pin extends from the body. Now fit the clip into its hole, then push the centre pin in so that it is flush with the clip head. The clip should now be locked in place.

2 The other type of trim clip (found on the underside of the fairing side panels) has a large circular head, with a removal slot in the body of the clip. Use a small, flat-bladed screwdriver to carefully ease the head out of the clip body, then draw the clip out of the panel. To install the clip, fit it into its hole with the head pulled out, then push the head in to lock the clip.

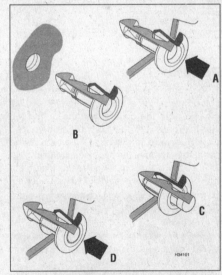

1.1 Centre pin type trim clip

To remove, push the centre pin in (A) to allow the clip body to be withdrawn from the panel (B).

To install, depress the clip pawls to extend the centre pin and insert it into the panel (C), then press the centre pin in flush with the body of the clip to lock it in place (D)

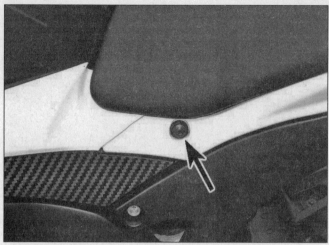

2.1a Unscrew the bolt (arrowed) on each side . . .

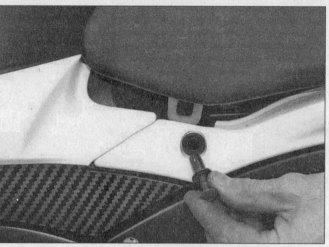

2.1b . . . noting the collars on K8 and K9 models . . .

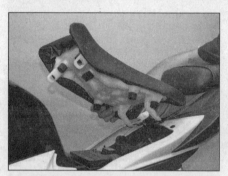

2.1c . . . and remove the seat

2.2a Turn the key to unlock the seat . . .

2.2b . . . note how the tabs at the back locate

2 Seats

Removal

1 To remove the rider's seat, first unscrew the bolt on each side at the front – on K8 and K9 models note the collars with the bolts **(see illustrations)**. Lift the front of the seat and draw it forward to disengage the tabs at the back, then remove the seat **(see illustration)**.
2 To remove the passenger seat, insert the ignition key into the seat lock located under the left-hand side of the seat cowling, and turn it to unlock the seat **(see illustration)**. Lift the front of the seat and draw it forward to disengage the tab(s) at the back, then remove the seat **(see illustration)**. **Note:** *A hard cover seat tail box may be fitted instead of the passenger seat.*

Installation

3 Installation is the reverse of removal, noting the following:
● Make sure the seat tab(s) are properly located.
● Press down on the front of the rider's seat to align the mounting bolt holes – do not forget the collars on K8 and K9 models.

● Push down on the passenger seat to engage the lock.

3 Seat cowling

Removal

1 Remove the seats (see Section 2).
2 Release the seat lock cable from the latch **(see illustration)**.
3 On K6 and K7 models, undo the screws and release the trim clips securing each side of the seat cowling **(see illustrations)**. Carefully pull

3.2 Release and detach the seat lock cable

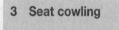

3.3a Undo the screws (arrowed) . . .

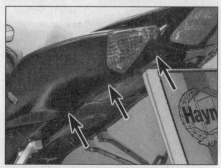

3.3b . . . and release the trim clips (arrowed) on each side

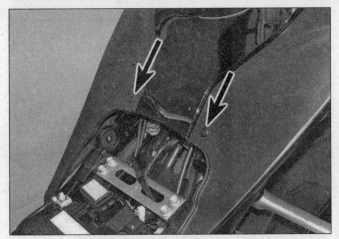

3.3c Release the trim clips (arrowed) . . .

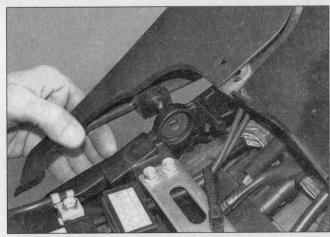

3.3d . . . then pull the pegs out of the grommets

the front away on each side to release the peg from the grommet (see illustration). Draw the cowling back and up on the right-hand side and disconnect the tail light wiring connector (see illustration). Draw the cowling off the bike. Take note how the seat rubbers and collars fit. If required detach each side piece from the centre piece, noting how it fits.

4 On K8 and K9 models, release the trim clips and remove the tail light trim panel, noting how it locates (see illustrations). Undo the screws and release the trim clips securing each side of the seat cowling (see illustrations). Draw the left-hand side of the cowling out and up to access and disconnect the wiring connector (see illustration). Draw the cowling back and lift it off the bike (see

3.3e Displace the cowling as described to disconnect the wiring connector . . .

3.3f . . . and remove the cowling

illustration). Take note how the seat rubbers and collars fit. If required detach the side

pieces from the centre piece, noting how it fits.

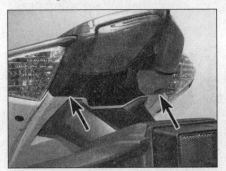

3.4a Release the trim clips (arrowed) . . .

3.4b . . . and remove the tail light trim

3.4c Undo the screws (arrowed) . . .

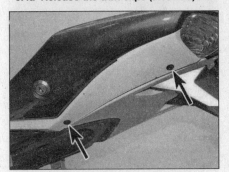

3.4d . . . and release the trim clips (arrowed) on each side

3.4e Displace the cowling as described to disconnect the wiring connector . . .

3.4f . . . and remove the cowling

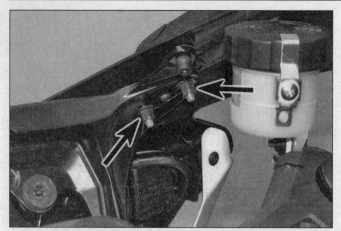

4.1 Slacken the nuts (arrowed)

4.2a Undo the screws (arrowed) . . .

4.2b . . . and remove the windshield

5.3 Disconnect the relevant wiring connector

5.4 Remove the mirror, noting the routing of the wiring

Installation

5 Installation is the reverse of removal. Check the operation of the tail/brake light before riding the motorcycle.

4 Windshield

1 Slacken the mirror mounting nuts **(see illustration)**.
2 Undo the screws and remove the windshield **(see illustrations)** – there are two different types of screw, the ones at the rear are different to those in the middle and at

the front. Note the threads for the screws are retained in rubber well-nuts.
3 Installation is the reverse of removal.

5 Mirrors

1 Remove the windshield (see Section 4).
2 Remove the instrument cluster (see Chapter 8).
3 Trace the turn signal wiring from the mirror base and disconnect it **(see illustration)**.
4 Undo the nuts and lift off the mirror, taking care not to snag the wiring as you draw it through and noting its routing **(see illustration)**.

5 Installation is the reverse of removal. Make sure the rubber pad is correctly in place on the fairing bracket.

6 Fairing panels

Fairing side panels

Removal

Note: *If both panels are being removed, remove the left-hand one first.*
1 Release the trim clip(s) securing the side panels together on the underside **(see illustrations)**.

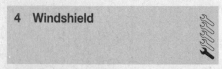
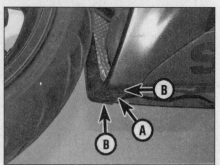

6.1a On K6 and K7 models release the centre trim clip (A) and one of the side clips (B) . . .

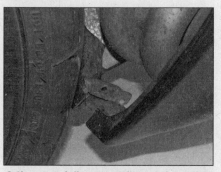

6.1b . . . and disengage the panels, noting how they fit together along with the brace plate

6.1c On K8 and K9 models release the trim clips (arrowed)

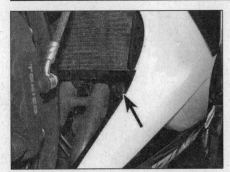

6.2a Release the trim clip (arrowed)

6.2b Undo the screw (arrowed) . . .

6.2c . . . on K6 and K7 the three screws (arrowed) . . .

2 To remove the left-hand side panel, release the trim clip securing the panel to the centre panel (**see illustration**). Undo the screws securing the panel to the fairing and the frame (**see illustrations**). Carefully pull the panel away to release the pegs from the grommets and remove the panel, noting how it engages with the fairing, the inner panel and the centre panel, and on K8 and K9 models draw the fuel tank drain and breather hoses out of their guides (**see illustrations**).

3 To remove the right-hand side panel, if the left-hand panel has not been removed, release the trim clip securing the left-hand panel to the centre panel (**see illustration 6.2a**). Undo the screws securing the panel to the fairing and the frame (**see illustrations 6.2b and c**). Carefully pull the panel away to release the pegs from the grommets and remove the

6.2d . . . or on K8 and K9 the two screws (arrowed)

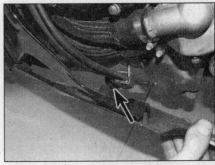

6.2e On K6 and K7 models release the bottom peg from its grommet (arrowed)

panel, bringing the centre panel with it, and noting how it engages with the fairing and the inner panel (**see illustrations 6.2e, f, g, h, i and j**).

4 If required release the trim clips securing the inner panel to the fairing under panel and remove the inner panel, noting how the peg on the upper inner end locates in the heat

6.2f Disengage the panel from the centre panel . . .

6.2g . . . the inner panel . . .

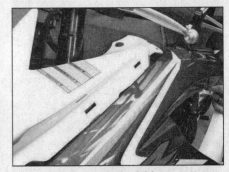

6.2h . . . and the fairing . . .

6.2i . . . and release the pegs from their grommets (arrowed) . . .

6.2j . . . and on K8 and K9 pull the grommet off the peg (arrowed) . . .

6.2k . . . and draw the hoses out of the guide

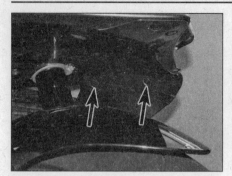

6.4a Release the trim clips and remove the panel . . .

6.4b . . . noting how it locates

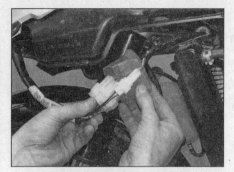

6.8a Disconnect the wiring connector(s) . . .

deflector panel on the front of the frame **(see illustrations)**.

Installation

5 Installation is the reverse of removal. Make sure each panel engages correctly with the fairing and the other panels Make sure the pegs on the upper inner ends of the inner panels locate correctly in the clips on each end of the deflector panel on the front of the frame and do not press into the fins on the radiator which are easily damaged **(see illustration 6.4b)**. On K8 and K9 models do not forget to feed the fuel tank drain and breather hoses through their guide **(see illustration 6.2k)**.

Fairing

Removal

6 Remove both mirrors (see Section 5).
7 Remove the fairing side panels and inner panels (see above).
8 Trace the wiring from the headlight assembly and disconnect it at the connector(s) **(see illustration)**. Release the wiring from its clip **(see illustration)**. On K8 and K9 models disconnect the steering damper wiring connector **(see illustration)**.
9 Remove the screw from each side **(see illustration)**.
10 Carefully draw the fairing forward **(see illustration)** – note how the pegs for the screws locate in the grommets on the fairing bracket. Note how the air ducts locate. Note

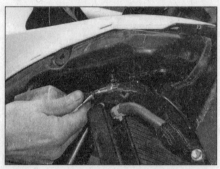

6.8b . . . and release the wiring from the air duct

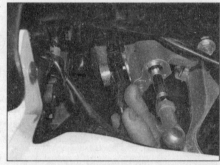

6.8c Disconnect the steering damper connector

6.9 Undo the screw (arrowed) on each side . . .

6.10 . . . and carefully remove the fairing

the rubber cushions located in the mirror mountings on the fairing bracket.
11 If required remove the air ducts and headlight assembly from the fairing (see Chapter 8). If

required unscrew the fairing bracket bolts and detach it from the frame **(see illustration)**. If required remove the trim panel from the underside of the bottom yoke **(see illustration)**.

6.11a Unscrew the nuts (arrowed), withdraw the bolts and remove the bracket

6.11b Unscrew the bolts (arrowed) and remove the trim panel

Installation

12 Installation is the reverse of removal, noting the following:

● If removed, tighten the fairing bracket mounting bolt nuts to 23 Nm **(see illustration 6.11a)**.

● If removed, fit the trim panel to the bottom yoke **(see illustration 6.11b)**.

● Make sure the rubber pad for each mirror is correctly in place on the fairing bracket.

● Ensure the pegs on the back of the headlight assembly locate correctly in the grommets on the fairing bracket **(see illustration)**.

● Make sure the air ducts locate correctly **(see illustration)**.

● Ensure the wiring connectors are firmly connected and the wiring is retained by its clip.

● Fit the rubber cushions for the mirror mountings before fitting the fairing.

7 Front mudguard

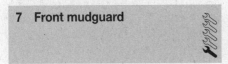

1 Remove the front wheel (see Chapter 6).
2 Release the right-hand brake hose from the clip on the mudguard **(see illustration)**. Ease the clip on the left-hand hose out of the mudguard **(see illustration)**.
3 Unscrew the two bolts securing the mudguard to the front of each fork and

6.12a Make sure the pegs locate in the grommets

remove the bolts **(see illustration)**. Unscrew the bolt securing the mudguard to the rear of each fork and remove the bolt, and on K6 and K7 models the rubber bush and spacer.

7.2a Release the brake hose assembly from the guide (arrowed)

7.2c ... and draw it out the top

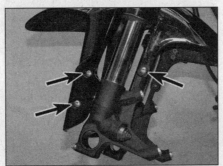

7.3 Unscrew the three bolts (arrowed) on each side ...

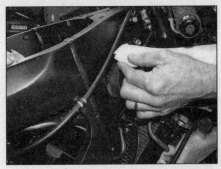

6.12b Make sure the air ducts locate correctly

4 Ease the mudguard forward and off the bike, squeezing the sides together to clear the forks **(see illustration)**.
5 Installation is the reverse of removal.

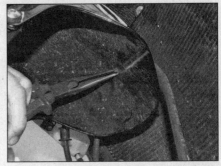

7.2b Use pliers to release the clip from the underside ...

7.4 ... and carefully draw the mudguard out from between the forks

Chapter 8
Electrical system

Contents

Degrees of difficulty

Easy, suitable for novice with little experience	**Fairly easy,** suitable for beginner with some experience	**Fairly difficult,** suitable for competent DIY mechanic	**Difficult,** suitable for experienced DIY mechanic	**Very difficult,** suitable for expert DIY or professional

Specifications

Battery

Type and capacity
  600 models. FTX9-BS, 12V 8Ah
  750 models. YT12A-BS, 12V 10Ah
Charging time
  Normal charge rate. . . . . 5 to 10 hours @ 1.2 A
  Quick charge rate . . . . 1 hour @ 5 A

Charging system

Battery current leakage . . . . 3 mA (max)
Alternator output
  Regulated voltage output. . . . . 14.0 to 15.5V @ 5000 rpm
  Unregulated voltage output (no-load). . . . . min. 65V AC @ 5000 rpm
Alternator stator coil resistance . . . . 0.2 to 1.0 ohms

Starter motor

Brush length
  Standard . . . . 10 mm
  Service limit (min) . . . . 6.5 mm

Starter relay

Resistance . . . . 3.0 to 6.0 ohms

Fuses

Main 30A
Headlight (high beam)
  K6 and K7 models 10A
  K8 and K9 models 15A
Headlight (low beam) 10A
Fuel pump 10A
Ignition
  K6 and K7 models 10A
  K8 and K9 models 15A
Signal
  K6 and K7 models 15A
  K8 and K9 models 10A
Fan 15A

Bulbs

Headlight
  K6 and K7 models
    HI beam 65W H9
    LO beam 55W H7
  K8 and K9 models
    HI beam . . . . 60W HB3 x 2
    LO beam 55W H11
Sidelight(s) 5W
Licence plate light 5W
Turn signal lights . . . . 21W x 4 (orange glass)
Brake/tail light . . . . LED
Instrument lights . . . . LED

Torque settings

Oil pressure switch . . . . 14 Nm
Starter motor mounting bolts . . . . 10 Nm

1 General information

All models have a 12-volt electrical system charged by a three-phase alternator with a separate regulator/rectifier.

The regulator maintains the charging system output within the specified range to prevent overcharging, and the rectifier converts the ac (alternating current) output of the alternator to dc (direct current) to power the lights and other components and to charge the battery. The alternator rotor is mounted on the left-hand end of the crankshaft.

The starter motor is mounted on top of the crankcase on the left-hand side. The starting system includes the motor, the battery, the relay, the clutch switch, gear position sensor and sidestand switch. If the engine kill switch is in the RUN position and the ignition switch is ON, the starter relay allows the starter motor to operate if the transmission is in neutral (neutral light on) and the clutch lever is

pulled in or, if the transmission is in gear, the side-stand is up and the clutch lever is pulled in.

Note: *Keep in mind that electrical parts, once purchased, cannot be returned. To avoid unnecessary expense, make very sure the faulty component has been positively identified before buying a replacement part.*

2 Electrical system fault finding

1 A typical electrical circuit consists of an electrical component, the switches, relays, etc, related to that component and the wiring and connectors that link the component to the battery and the frame.
2 Before tackling any troublesome electrical circuit, first study the wiring diagram thoroughly to get a complete picture of what makes up that individual circuit. Trouble spots, for instance, can often be narrowed down by noting if other components related to that circuit are operating properly or not. If

several components or circuits fail at one time, chances are the fault lies either in the fuse or in the common earth (ground) connection, as several circuits are often routed through the same fuse and earth (ground) connections.
3 Electrical problems often stem from simple causes, such as loose or corroded connections or a blown fuse. Prior to any electrical fault finding, always visually check the condition of the fuse, wires and connections in the problem circuit. Intermittent failures can be especially frustrating, since you can't always duplicate the failure when it's convenient to test. In such situations, a good practice is to clean all connections in the affected circuit, whether or not they appear to be good – where possible use a dedicated electrical cleaning spray along with sandpaper, wire wool or other abrasive material to remove corrosion, and a dedicated electrical protection spray to prevent further problems. All of the connections and wires should also be wiggled to check for looseness which can cause intermittent failure.
4 If you don't have a multimeter it is highly advisable to obtain one – they are not expensive and will enable a full range of

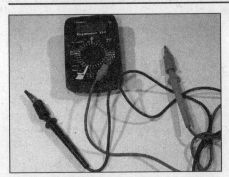

2.4a A digital multimeter can be used for all electrical tests

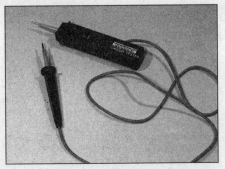

2.4b A battery-powered continuity tester

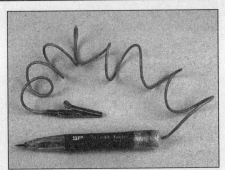

2.4c A simple test light is useful for voltage tests

electrical tests to be made. Go for a modern digital one with LCD display as they are easier to use. A continuity tester and/or test light are useful for certain electrical checks as an alternative, though are limited in their usefulness compared to a multimeter (see illustrations).

Continuity checks

5 The term continuity describes the uninterrupted flow of electricity through an electrical circuit. Continuity can be checked with a multimeter set either to its continuity function (a beep is emitted when continuity is found), or to the resistance (ohms / Ω) function, or with a dedicated continuity tester. Both instruments are powered by an internal battery, therefore the checks are made with the ignition OFF. As a safety precaution, always disconnect the battery negative (-) lead before making continuity checks, particularly if ignition switch checks are being made.

6 If using a multimeter, select the continuity function if it has one, or the resistance (ohms) function. Touch the meter probes together and check that a beep is emitted or the meter reads zero, which indicates continuity. If there is no continuity there will be no beep or the meter will show infinite resistance. After using the meter, always switch it OFF to conserve its battery.

7 A continuity tester can be used in the same

way – its light should come on or it should beep to indicate continuity in the switch ON position, but should be off or silent in the OFF position.

8 Note that the polarity of the test probes doesn't matter for continuity checks, although care should be taken to follow specific test procedures if a diode or solid-state component is being checked.

Switch continuity checks

9 If a switch is at fault, trace its wiring to the wiring connectors. Separate the connectors and inspect them for security and condition. A build-up of dirt or corrosion here will most likely be the cause of the problem – clean up and apply a water dispersant such as WD40, or alternatively use a dedicated contact cleaner and protection spray.

10 If using a multimeter, select the continuity function if it has one, or the resistance (ohms) function, and connect its probes to the terminals in the connector (see illustration). Simple ON/OFF type switches, such as brake light switches, only have two wires whereas combination switches, like the handlebar switches, have many wires. Study the wiring diagram to ensure that you are connecting to the correct pair of wires. Continuity should be indicated with the switch ON and no continuity with it OFF.

Wiring continuity checks

11 Many electrical faults are caused by damaged wiring, often due to incorrect routing or chaffing on frame components. Loose, wet

or corroded wire connectors can also be the cause of electrical problems.

12 A continuity check can be made on a single length of wire by disconnecting it at each end and connecting the meter or continuity tester probes to each end of the wire (see illustration). Continuity (low or no resistance – 0 ohms) should be indicated if the wire is good. If no continuity (high resistance) is shown, suspect a broken wire.

13 To check for continuity to earth in any earth wire connect one probe of your meter or tester to the earth wire terminal in the connector and the other to the frame, engine, or battery earth (-) terminal. Continuity (low or no resistance – 0 ohms) should be indicated if the wire is good. If no continuity (high resistance) is shown, suspect a broken wire or corroded or loose earth point (see below).

Voltage checks

14 A voltage check can determine whether power is reaching a component. Use a multimeter set to the dc voltage scale, or a test light. The test light is the cheaper component, but the meter has the advantage of being able to give a voltage reading.

15 Connect the meter or test light in parallel, i.e. across the load (see illustration).

16 First identify the relevant wiring circuit by referring to the wiring diagram at the end of this manual. If other electrical components share the same power supply (i.e. are fed from the same fuse), take note whether they are working correctly – this is useful information in deciding where to start checking the circuit.

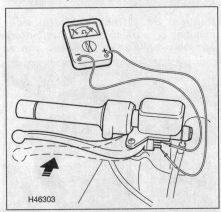

2.10 Continuity should be indicated across switch terminals when the lever is operated

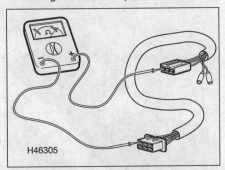

2.12 Wiring continuity check. Connect the meter probes across each end of the same wire

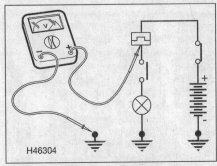

2.15 Voltage check. Connect the meter positive probe to the component and the negative probe to earth

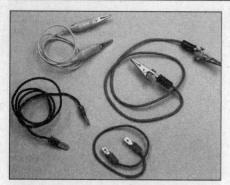

2.23 A selection of insulated jumper wires

17 If using a meter, check first that the meter leads are plugged into the correct terminals on the meter (red to positive (+ve), black to negative (-ve)). Set the meter to the dc volts function, where necessary at a range suitable for the battery voltage – 0 to 20 vdc. Connect the meter red probe (+ve) to the power supply wire and the black probe to a good metal earth (ground) on the motorcycle's frame or directly to the battery negative terminal. Battery voltage should be shown on the meter with the ignition switch, and if necessary any other relevant switch, ON.

18 If using a test light, connect its positive (+ve) probe to the power supply terminal and its negative (-ve) probe to a good earth (ground) on the motorcycle's frame. With the switch, and if necessary any other relevant switch, ON, the test light should illuminate.

19 If no voltage is indicated, work back towards the fuse continuing to check for voltage. When you reach a point where there is voltage, you know the problem lies between that point and your last check point.

Earth (ground) checks

20 Earth connections are made either directly to the engine or frame (such as the oil pressure switch which only has a positive feed) or by a separate wire into the earth circuit of the wiring harness. Alternatively a short earth wire is sometimes run from the component directly to the motorcycle's frame.

21 Corrosion is a common cause of a poor earth connection, as is a loose earth terminal fastener.

22 If total or multiple component failure is experienced, check the security of the main earth lead from the negative (-ve) terminal of the battery, the earth lead bolted to the engine, and the main earth point(s) on the frame. If corroded, dismantle the connection and clean all surfaces back to bare metal. Remake the connection and prevent further corrosion from forming by smearing battery terminal grease over the connection.

23 To check the earth of a component, use an insulated jumper wire to temporarily bypass its earth connection **(see illustration)** – connect one end of the jumper wire to the earth terminal or metal body of the component and the other end to the motorcycle's frame. If the circuit works with the jumper wire installed, the earth circuit is faulty.

24 To check an earth wire first check for corroded or loose connections, then check the wiring for continuity (Step 13) between each connector in the circuit in turn, and then to its earth point, to locate the break.

---

3 Battery removal, installation, inspection and maintenance

Caution: Be extremely careful when handling or working around the battery. The electrolyte is very caustic and an explosive gas (hydrogen) is given off when the battery is charging.

Removal and installation

1 Remove the rider's seat (see Chapter 7).

2 Unscrew the negative (-ve) terminal bolt first and disconnect the lead from the battery **(see illustration)**. Lift up the red insulating cover to access the positive (+ve) terminal, then unscrew the bolt and disconnect the lead. Lift the battery from the bike **(see illustration)**.

HAYNES HiNT *Battery corrosion can be kept to a minimum by applying a layer of battery terminal grease or petroleum jelly (Vaseline) to the terminals after the leads have been connected. DO NOT use a mineral based grease.*

3 On installation, clean the battery terminals and lead ends with a wire brush, knife or steel wool. Reconnect the leads, connecting the positive (+ve) terminal first.

4 Install the seat (see Chapter 7).

Inspection and maintenance

5 The battery is of the maintenance-free (sealed) type, therefore requiring no regular maintenance. However, the following checks should still be regularly performed.

6 Check the battery terminals for corrosion and make sure the leads are tight. If corrosion is evident, clean the terminals as described in Step 3.

7 Clean the battery case to prevent current leakage, which can discharge the battery over a period of time (especially when it sits unused). Wash the outside of the case with a solution of baking soda and water. Rinse the battery thoroughly, then dry it.

8 Look for cracks in the case and replace the battery with a new one if any are found. If acid has been spilled on the frame or battery box, neutralise it with a baking soda and water solution, dry it thoroughly, then touch up any damaged paint.

9 If the motorcycle sits unused for long periods of time, disconnect the leads from the battery terminals, negative (-ve) terminal first. Refer to Section 4 and charge the battery once every month to six weeks.

10 The condition of the battery can be assessed by measuring the voltage at the battery terminals **(see illustration)**. Connect the voltmeter positive (+ve) probe to the battery positive (+ve) terminal and the negative (-ve) probe to the battery negative (-ve) terminal. When fully charged there should be more than 12.5 volts present. If the voltage falls below 12.0 volts remove the battery and recharge it (see Section 4).

---

4 Battery charging

Caution: Be extremely careful when handling or working around the battery. The electrolyte is very caustic and an

3.2a Disconnect the negative lead (A) first, then the positive lead (B) . . .

3.2b . . . and lift the battery out

3.10 Connect a meter as described to check battery voltage

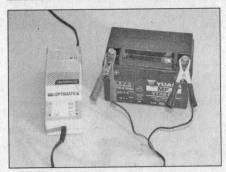

4.2 Battery connected to a charger

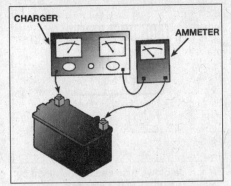

CHARGER

AMMETER

4.3 If the charger has no built-in ammeter, connect one in series as shown. DO NOT connect the ammeter between the battery terminals or it will be ruined

explosive gas (hydrogen) is given off when the battery is charging.

1 Ensure the battery charger is suitable for charging a 12 volt battery.

2 Remove the battery (see Section 3). Connect the charger to the battery, making sure that the positive (+ve) lead on the charger is connected to the positive (+ve) terminal on the battery, and the negative (-ve) lead is connected to the negative (-ve) terminal **(see illustration)**.

3 Suzuki recommend that the battery is charged at a rate of 1.2 amps for 5 to 10 hours. Exceeding this figure can cause the battery to overheat, buckling the plates and rendering it useless. If a basic charger without current control is used check that after a possible initial peak, the charge rate falls to a safe level **(see illustration)**. If the battery becomes hot during charging **stop**. Further charging will

cause damage. **Note:** *In emergencies the battery can be charged at a maximum rate of 5 amps for a period of 1 hour. However, this is not recommended and the low amp charge is by far the safer method of charging the battery.*

4 After charging, allow the battery to stand for 30 minutes, then measure its terminal voltage (see Section 3). If the voltage is below 12.5 volts, charge the battery again and repeat the voltage measuring process. If the voltage is still low, the battery is failing and should be replaced with a new one.

5 If the recharged battery discharges rapidly when left disconnected, it is likely that an

internal short caused by physical damage or sulphation has occurred. A new battery will be required. A good battery will tend to lose its charge at about 1% per day.

6 Install the battery (see Section 3).

7 If the motorcycle is unused for long periods of time, charge the battery once every month to six weeks and leave it disconnected.

5 Fuses

1 The electrical system circuits are protected by fuses of different ratings.

2 The main fuse is integral with the starter relay – on K6 and K7 models remove the rider's seat, and on K8 and K9 models remove the seat cowling to access it (see Chapter 7) **(see illustration)**. To access the main fuse, displace the starter relay from its mount and remove the relay cover **(see illustrations)**. A spare main fuse is housed in the starter relay cover **(see illustration)**.

3 The circuit fuses are housed in the fusebox, which is under the rider's seat – remove the seat for access (see Chapter 7) **(see illustration)**. The designation and rating of each fuse is marked on a label on the lid. To access the circuit fuses, unclip the lid **(see illustration)**. A spare circuit fuse of each rating is also housed in the fusebox.

4 The fuses can be removed and checked

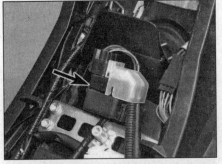

5.2a Starter relay (arrowed)

5.2b Remove the starter relay cover . . .

5.2c . . . to access the main fuse (arrowed)

5.2d A spare is housed in the cover (arrowed)

5.3a Fusebox (arrowed)

5.3b Unclip the fusebox lid to access the circuit fuses. Note the spares (arrowed)

5.4a Remove the fuse and check it . . .

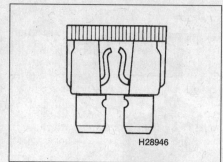

5.4b . . . a blown fuse can be identified by a break in the element

visually **(see illustration)**. If you can't pull the fuse out with your fingertips, use a pair of needle-nose pliers. A blown fuse is easily identified by a break in the element **(see illustration)**. Each fuse is clearly marked with its rating and must only be replaced with a fuse of the correct rating. If a spare fuse is used, always replace it with a new one so that a spare of each rating is carried on the bike at all times **(see illustrations 5.2d and 5.3b)**.

> ⚠ *Warning: Never put in a fuse of a higher rating or bridge the terminals with any other substitute, however temporary it may be. Serious damage may be done to the circuit, or a fire may start.*

5 If a new fuse blows immediately, be sure to check the wiring circuit very carefully for evidence of a short-circuit. Look for bare wires and chafed, melted or burned insulation.

6 Occasionally a fuse will blow or cause an open-circuit for no obvious reason. Corrosion of the fuse ends and fusebox terminals may occur and cause poor fuse contact. If this happens, remove the corrosion with a wire brush or wire wool, then spray the fuse ends and terminals with electrical contact cleaner.

6 Lighting system check

1 The battery provides power for operation of the headlight, tail light, brake light and instrument cluster lights. If none of the lights

6.5a Headlight relay (arrowed)

operate, always check battery voltage before proceeding. Low battery voltage indicates either a faulty battery or a defective charging system. Refer to Section 3 for battery checks and Section 27 for charging system tests. Also, check the fuses (see Section 5). When checking for a blown filament in a bulb, it is advisable to back up a visual check with a continuity test of the filament as it is not always apparent that a bulb has blown. When testing for continuity, remember that on some bulbs it is the metal body of the bulb that is the earth (ground).

Headlight

2 If the headlight fails to work, first check the bulb and the bulb terminals (see Section 7), and then the headlight high beam or low beam fuse (see Section 5). On K8 and K9 models next check the headlight relay (see Step 5). Next check for battery voltage at the headlight wiring connector with a test light or multimeter – connect the negative (-ve) probe of the multimeter to earth (ground) and the positive (+ve) probe either to the high beam connector terminal (black/yellow wire) or the low beam connector terminal (black/brown wire) with the ignition switch ON. Don't forget to select either high or low beam at the handlebar switch while conducting this test.

3 If no voltage is indicated at either terminal, check the wiring between the headlight connector, HI/LO switch and the ignition switch, then check the switches themselves. Refer to the *Wiring Diagrams* at the end of this Chapter.

4 If voltage is indicated, check for continuity

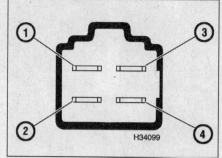

6.5b Headlight relay terminal identification

in the black/white wire to earth (ground). If there is no continuity, check the earth (ground) circuit for a broken or poor connection.

5 To check the relay on K8 and K9 models remove the seat cowling (see Chapter 7) – the relay is mounted on the left-hand side of the rear sub-frame **(see illustration)**. Displace the relay and disconnect the wiring. Using an ohmmeter or continuity tester, check for continuity between the 1 and 2 terminals on the relay **(see illustration)**. There should be no continuity (infinite resistance). Now use jumper wires to connect the positive (+ve) terminal of a 12V battery to the 3 terminal on the relay and the negative (-ve) terminal to the 4 relay terminal, and again check for continuity between the A and B terminals. There should be continuity (zero resistance). If there is no continuity, fit a new relay.

Sidelight

6 If the sidelight bulb fails to work, first check the bulb, the bulb terminals and wiring connector (see Section 7), then the signal fuse (see Section 5). Next check for voltage at the sidelight wiring connector with a test light or multimeter – connect the negative (-ve) probe of the multimeter to earth (ground) and the positive (+ve) probe to the brown wire terminal with the ignition switch ON.

7 If no voltage is indicated, check the wiring between the connector and the ignition switch, then check the switch. Refer to the *Wiring Diagrams* at the end of this Chapter.

8 If voltage is indicated, check for continuity in the black/white wire to earth (ground). If there is no continuity, check the earth (ground) circuit for a broken or poor connection.

Tail light

9 If the tail light fails to work, first check the wiring connector (see Section 9), then the signal fuse (see Section 5). Next check for voltage on the supply side of the wiring connector with a test light or multimeter – connect the negative (-ve) probe of the multimeter to earth (ground) and the positive (+ve) probe to the brown wire terminal with the ignition switch ON.

10 If no voltage is indicated, check the wiring between the connector and the ignition switch, then check the switches themselves. Refer to the *Wiring Diagrams* at the end of this Chapter.

11 If voltage is indicated, check for continuity between the black/white wire terminal and earth (ground). If there is no continuity, check the earth (ground) circuit for a broken or poor connection. If all is good the LED has probably failed, which means a new tail light unit must be fitted (see Section 10).

Brake light

12 If the brake light fails to work, first check the wiring connector (see Section 9), then the signal fuse (see Section 5). Next check for voltage on the supply side of the wiring connector with a test light or multimeter

– connect the negative (-) probe of the multimeter to earth (ground) and the positive (+) probe to the white/black wire terminal with the ignition switch ON and the brake lever pulled in or the pedal depressed.

13 If no voltage is indicated, check the wiring between the connector, the brake light switches and the ignition switch, then check the brake light switches (see Section 14). Refer to the *Wiring Diagrams* at the end of this Chapter.

14 If voltage is indicated, check for continuity in the black/white wire to earth (ground). If there is no continuity, check the earth (ground) circuit for a broken or poor connection. If all is good the LED has probably failed, which means a new tail light unit must be fitted (see Section 10).

Licence plate light

15 If the light fails to work, first check the bulb and the bulb terminals and the wiring connector (see Section 9), then the signal fuse (see Section 5). Next check for voltage on the supply side of the wiring connector with a test light or multimeter – connect the negative

(-) probe of the multimeter to earth (ground) and the positive (+) probe to the brown wire terminal with the ignition switch ON.

16 If no voltage is indicated, check the wiring between the connector and the ignition switch, then check the switches themselves. Refer to the *Wiring Diagrams* at the end of this Chapter.

17 If voltage is indicated, check for continuity in the blue wire to earth (ground). If there is no continuity, check the earth (ground) circuit for a broken or poor connection.

Turn signal lights

18 If one light fails to work, check the bulb and the bulb terminal first, then the wiring connector (see Section 11). If none of the turn signals work, first check the signal fuse.

19 If the fuse is good, see Section 13 for the turn signal circuit check.

Instrument cluster and warning lights

20 The instrument cluster and warning lights are LEDs. If an LED fails, and a fault cannot be traced anywhere else in the system, a new

instrument cluster board will have to be fitted (see Section 15).

7 Headlight bulbs and sidelight bulb(s)

Note: *The headlight bulbs are of the quartz-halogen type. Do not touch the bulb glass as skin acids will shorten the bulb's service life. If the bulb is accidentally touched, it should be wiped carefully with a rag soaked in methylated spirit and dried before fitting. Always use a paper towel or dry cloth when handling new bulbs to prevent injury if the bulb should break and to increase bulb life.*

Headlight bulbs – K6 and K7 models

Low beam

1 Remove the instrument cluster (see Section 15).

2 Disconnect the wiring connector then remove the rubber cover, noting how it fits **(see illustrations)**.

7.2a **Disconnect the wiring connector . . .**

7.2b **. . . and remove the rubber cover**

7.3a **Release the retaining clip . . .**

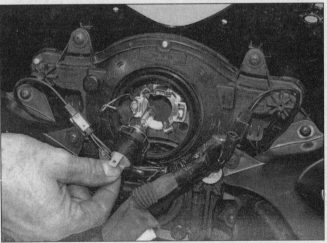
7.3b **. . . and withdraw the bulbholder**

7.8 Disconnect the wiring connector

7.9a Turn the bulb unit anti-clockwise ...

7.9b ... and withdraw it from the headlight

7.12a There are two sidelights (arrowed)

7.12b Pull the bulbholder out ...

3 Release the bulb retaining clip, noting how it fits, then remove the bulb **(see illustrations)**.
4 Fit the new bulb into the headlight, making sure it locates correctly, and secure it in position with the retaining clip.
5 Fit the rubber cover, making sure it is correctly seated. Connect the wiring connector.
6 Check the operation of the bulb.
7 Install the instrument cluster (see Section 15).

Main beam

8 Disconnect the wiring connector from the bulb **(see illustration)**.

9 Turn the bulb unit anti-clockwise to release it then withdraw it **(see illustrations)**.
10 Fit the bulb into the headlight and turn it clockwise to lock it. Connect the wiring connector.
11 Check the operation of the bulb.

Sidelight

12 Carefully pull the relevant bulbholder out of the headlight using long-nosed pliers **(see illustrations)**.
13 Carefully pull the bulb out of the holder **(see illustration)**.

14 Fit the new bulb into the holder, then fit the holder into its socket in the headlight.
15 Check the operation of the sidelight.

Headlight bulbs – K8 and K9 models

Low beam

16 The low beam bulb is the centre of the three headlight bulbs **(see illustration)**. Remove the instrument cluster for access (see Section 15).
17 Disconnect the wiring connector from the bulb unit.
18 Turn the bulb unit anti-clockwise to release it then withdraw it.
19 Fit the bulb into the headlight and turn it clockwise to lock it. Connect the wiring connector.
20 Check the operation of the bulb.
21 Install the instrument cluster (see Section 15).

Main beam

22 There are two main beam bulbs **(see illustration 7.16)**. Disconnect the wiring

7.13 ... then remove the bulb

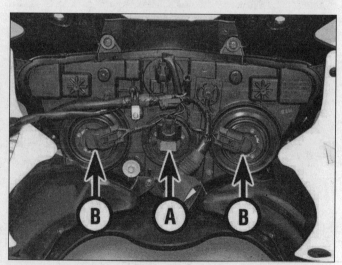

7.16 Low beam bulb (A), main beam bulbs (B)

7.22 Disconnect the wiring connector

7.23a Turn the bulb unit anti-clockwise . . .

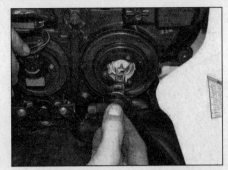

7.23b . . . and withdraw it from the headlight

7.27 Release the cover . . .

7.28 . . . then withdraw the bulbholder . . .

7.29 . . . and remove the bulb

connector from the relevant bulb unit **(see illustration)**.
23 Turn the bulb unit anti-clockwise to release it then withdraw it **(see illustrations)**.
24 Fit the bulb into the headlight and turn it clockwise to lock it. Connect the wiring connector.
25 Check the operation of the bulb.

Sidelight

26 Remove the instrument cluster (see Section 15).
27 Turn the cover anti-clockwise to release it **(see illustration)**.

28 Carefully pull the bulbholder out of the headlight using long-nosed pliers **(see illustration)**.
29 Carefully pull the bulb out of the holder **(see illustration)**.
30 Fit the new bulb into the holder, then fit the holder into its socket in the headlight.
31 Fit the cover onto the headlight and turn it clockwise to lock it. Connect the wiring connector.
32 Check the operation of the sidelight.
33 Install the instrument cluster (see Section 15).

8 Headlight

Removal

K6 and K7 models

1 Remove the fairing (see Chapter 7).
2 Undo the screws and remove the bottom section of the fairing **(see illustrations)**.
3 Release the trim clip securing each air duct

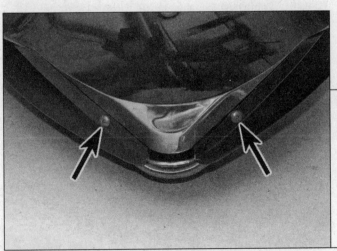

8.2a Undo the screws (arrowed) . . .

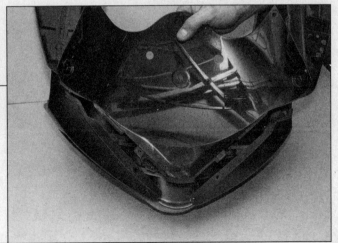

8.2b . . . and remove the bottom panel

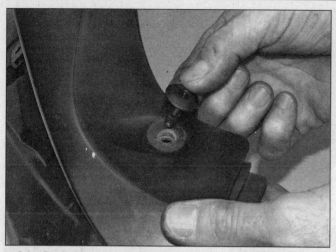

8.3a Push the centre of the clip in then draw the body out . . .

8.3b . . . and remove the air duct

to the side section of the fairing and remove the air ducts **(see illustrations)**.

4 Undo the screws securing each side section and remove them, noting how they locate **(see illustrations)**.

5 Undo the screws securing the headlight assembly inside the fairing **(see illustrations)**. Carefully pull the headlight out, noting how the rubber grommets locate over the screw posts.

K8 and K9 models

6 Remove the fairing (see Chapter 7).

7 Release the trim clips and remove the bottom section of the fairing **(see illustrations)**.

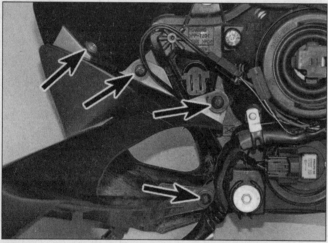

8.4a Undo the screws (arrowed) . . .

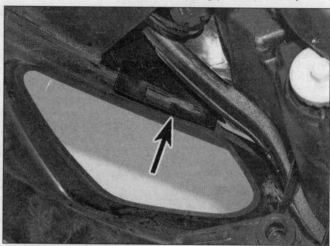

8.4b . . . note how the tab at the front locates (arrowed) . . .

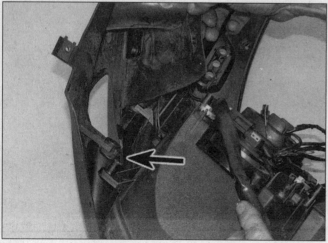

8.4c . . . and how the grommet locates over the peg (arrowed)

8.5 Undo the screws (arrowed) and remove the headlight

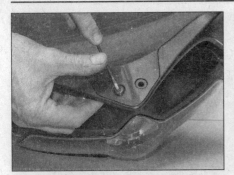

8.7a Release the trim clips by pushing the centre in and drawing the body out . . .

8.7b . . . and remove the bottom panel

8.8a Undo the screw (arrowed)

Carefully lift the fairing from the top of the headlight, freeing the pegs from the grommets and releasing the Velcro patches **(see illustration)**.

Installation

11 Installation is the reverse of removal, noting the following:

- Make sure the rubber grommets are in good condition, and fit new ones if necessary.
- Spray some suitable lubricant onto the rubber grommets to help them onto the posts.
- Make sure the headlight wiring is correctly routed **(see illustration)**.
- Check the operation of the headlight and sidelight.
- Check the headlight aim.

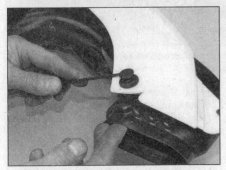

8.8b Lever the centre of the clip up . . .

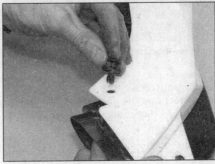

8.8c . . . then draw the body out . . .

8 Release the screw and trim clip securing each air duct to the side section of the fairing and remove the air ducts **(see illustrations)**.
9 Undo the screws securing each side section

and remove them, noting how they locate **(see illustration)**.
10 Undo the screws securing the bottom trim section and remove it **(see illustrations)**.

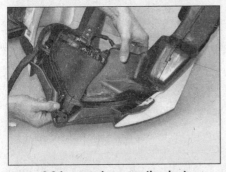

8.8d . . . and remove the duct

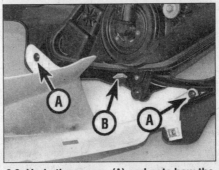

8.9 Undo the screws (A) and note how the tabs locates (B)

8.10a Undo the screws (arrowed) . . .

8.10b . . . and remove the bottom section

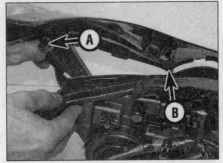

8.10c On each side pull the peg (A) from the grommet and release the Velcro patch (B)

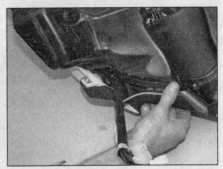

8.11 On K8 and K9 models make sure the wiring goes between the left-hand air duct and the fairing as shown

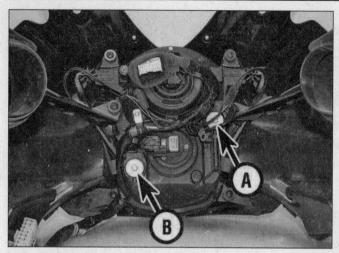

8.13a Headlight beam adjusters on K6 and K7 models – horizontal (A), vertical (B)

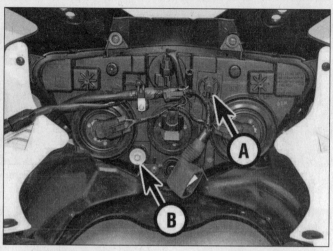

8.13b Headlight beam adjusters on K8 and K9 models – horizontal (A), vertical (B)

Headlight aim

Note: *An improperly adjusted headlight may cause problems for oncoming traffic or provide poor, unsafe illumination of the road ahead. Before adjusting the headlight aim, be sure to consult with local traffic laws and regulations – for UK models refer to MOT Test Checks in the Reference section.*

12 The headlight beams can adjusted both horizontally and vertically. Before making any adjustment, check that the tyre pressures are correct and the suspension is adjusted as required. Make any adjustments to the headlight aim with the machine on level ground, with the fuel tank half full and with an assistant sitting on the seat. If the bike is usually ridden with a passenger, have a second assistant to do this.

13 Adjust the beams horizontally first, then vertically. Locate each adjuster and turn them as required using a suitable screwdriver – the horizontal adjuster is on the upper right-hand side of the headlight unit, and the vertical adjuster is on the lower left-hand side (**see illustrations**).

9   Tail/brake/licence plate bulbs

Tail and brake lights

1 The tail and brake lights are LEDs. If an LED fails, and a fault cannot be traced anywhere else in the circuit (see Section 6), a new tail light assembly will have to be fitted (see Section 10).

Licence plate light

2 Unscrew the two nuts on the inside of the mudguard and draw the light unit off (**see illustration**). Undo the two screws on the back and remove the cover (**see illustrations**).

3 Push the bulb in and twist it anti-clockwise to release it (**see illustration**).

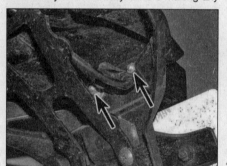

9.2a Unscrew the nuts (arrowed) . . .

9.2b . . . then displace the unit and undo the screws (arrowed) . . .

9.2c . . . and remove the cover

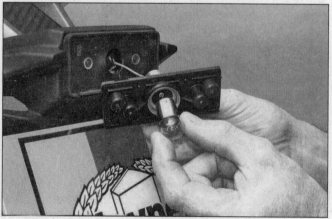

9.3 Push in and twist the bulb to remove it

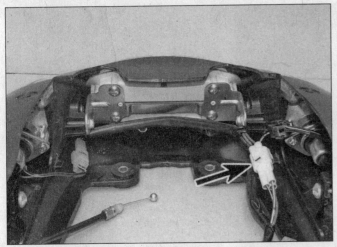

10.2 Disconnect the wiring connector – K6/K7 shown

10.3 Tail light screws (arrowed) – K8/K9 shown

4 Check the terminals for corrosion and clean them if necessary.
5 Line up the pins of the new bulb with the slots in the holder, then push the bulb in and turn it clockwise until it locks into place. Fit the cover, making sure the seal is correctly seated, then fit the light unit and tighten the nuts.

10 Tail light assembly

1 Remove the seat cowling (see Chapter 7).
2 Disconnect the tail light wiring connector **(see illustration)**.
3 Undo the screws and carefully withdraw the tail light assembly from the seat cowling **(see illustration)**.
4 Installation is the reverse of removal.

11 Turn signal bulbs

> **HAYNES HiNT**
> *If the socket contacts are dirty or corroded, scrape them clean and spray with electrical contact cleaner before a new bulb is installed.*

Front

1 Remove the screw securing the turn signal to the mirror and draw it out, noting how it fits **(see illustrations)**.
2 Twist the bulbholder anti-clockwise to release it from the lens **(see illustration)**. Push the bulb into the holder and twist it anti-clockwise to release it **(see illustration)**.

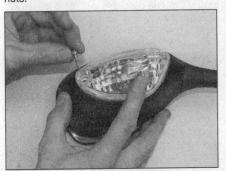

11.1a Undo the screw . . .

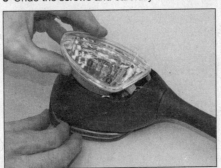

11.1b . . . and remove the turn signal

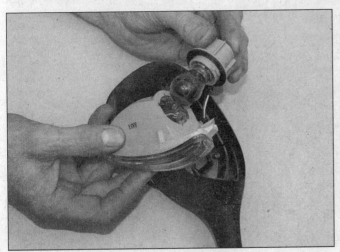

11.2a Release the bulbholder . . .

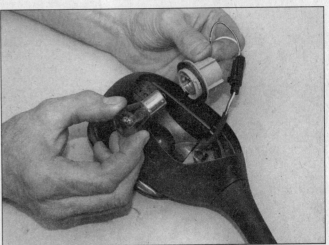

11.2b . . . and remove the bulb

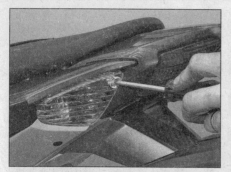

11.6a Undo the screw . . .

11.6b . . . and detach the lens

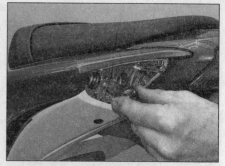

11.7 Push the bulb in and twist it anti-clockwise to remove it

3 Check the terminal inside the socket for corrosion and clean it if necessary.

4 Line up the pins of the new bulb with the slots in the holder, then push the bulb in and turn it clockwise until it locks into place. Fit the holder into the lens and turn it clockwise to secure it.

5 Fit the turn signal into the mirror and secure it with the screw.

Rear

6 Undo the screw securing the lens and detach the lens from the housing **(see illustrations)**.

7 Push the bulb into the holder and twist it anti-clockwise to release it **(see illustration)**.

8 Check the terminal inside the socket for corrosion and clean it if necessary.

9 Line up the pins of the new bulb with the slots in the holder, then push the bulb in and turn it clockwise until it locks into place.

10 Fit the lens and secure it with the screw.

12.2 Disconnect the wiring connector

12 Turn signal assemblies

Front

1 Remove the screw securing the turn signal to the mirror and draw it out, noting how it fits **(see illustrations 11.1a and b)**.

2 Disconnect the turn signal wiring connector **(see illustration)**.

3 Installation is the reverse of removal. Check the operation of the turn signals.

Rear

4 Remove the seat cowling (see Chapter 7). Remove the tail light (see Section 10).

5 Disconnect the wiring connector **(see illustration)**.

6 Undo the screws securing the turn signal

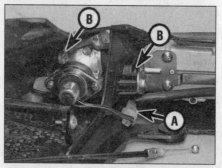

12.5 Disconnect the wiring connector (A) then undo the screws (B)

and remove it – if required detach the side piece of the seat cowling from the centre piece.

7 Installation is the reverse of removal. Check the operation of the turn signals.

13 Turn signal circuit check

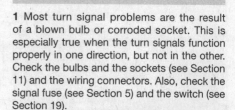

1 Most turn signal problems are the result of a blown bulb or corroded socket. This is especially true when the turn signals function properly in one direction, but not in the other. Check the bulbs and the sockets (see Section 11) and the wiring connectors. Also, check the signal fuse (see Section 5) and the switch (see Section 19).

2 The battery provides power for operation of the turn signal lights, so if they do not operate, also check the battery voltage. Low battery voltage indicates either a faulty battery or a defective charging system. Refer to Section 3 for battery checks and Section 27 for charging system tests.

3 If all the above are good, check the integral turn signal/sidestand relay – on K6 and K7 models remove the rider's seat to access it (see Chapter 7), then unscrew the relay holder bolt and draw the relay out from under the centre section of the rear sub-frame **(see illustrations)**; on K8 and K9 models remove the seat cowling (see Chapter 7) – the relay is on the left-hand side of the rear sub-frame **(see illustration)**.

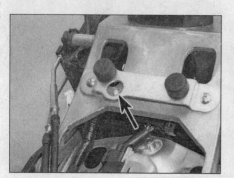

13.3a Unscrew the bolt (arrowed) . . .

13.3b . . . and draw the relay out

13.3c Turn signal/sidestand relay (arrowed) – K8 and K9 models

14.2 Disconnect the wiring connector(s) (arrowed)

14.6 Undo the screw (arrowed) and remove the switch

4 Make sure the ignition is OFF. Pull the relay out of its connector. Turn the ignition ON, then connect the positive (+ve) probe of a voltmeter to the brown wire terminal in the relay connector and the negative (-ve) probe to a good earth (ground) and check for battery voltage. Turn the ignition OFF.

5 If there is no voltage, check the wiring from the connector to the ignition switch for continuity.

6 If there is voltage, install the relay and use a test light to check the output from the light blue wire terminal on the relay. Ensure the test light is earthed and turn the ignition ON; the light should flash. If the light does not flash, replace the relay with a new one.

7 If the light flashes, check the wiring and connectors between the relay, the turn signal switch and the turn signal lights.

14 Brake light switches

Check

1 Before checking the switches, check the brake light circuit (see Section 6).

2 The front brake light switch is mounted on the underside of the brake master cylinder. Disconnect the wiring connector(s) from the switch **(see illustration)**. Using a continuity tester, connect the probes to the terminals of the switch. With the brake lever at rest, there should be no continuity. With the brake lever applied, there should be continuity. If the switch does not behave as described, replace it with a new one.

3 The rear brake light switch is mounted on the inside of the rider's right-hand footrest bracket above the brake pedal **(see illustration 14.8)**. Raise the fuel tank (see Chapter 4), then trace the wiring from the switch and disconnect it at the connector. Using a continuity tester, connect the probes to the terminals on the switch side of the connector. With the brake pedal at rest, there should be no continuity. With the brake pedal applied, there should be continuity. If the switch does not behave as described, replace it with a new one.

4 If the switches are good, check for voltage at the black/red wire terminal (front brake switch) or the orange/green wire terminal (rear brake switch) on the connector with the ignition switch ON – there should be battery voltage. If there's no voltage present, check the wiring between the switch and the ignition switch (see the *Wiring Diagrams* at the end of this Chapter). If there is voltage, check the wiring and connectors between the switch and the tail/brake light unit.

Removal and installation

Front brake switch

5 The switch is mounted on the underside of the brake master cylinder. Disconnect

the wiring connector(s) from the switch **(see illustration 14.2)**.

6 Undo the screw securing the switch and remove it **(see illustration)**.

7 Installation is the reverse of removal. The switch isn't adjustable.

Rear brake switch

8 The switch is mounted on the inside of the rider's right-hand footrest bracket above the brake pedal **(see illustration)**. Raise the fuel tank (see Chapter 4), then trace the wiring from the switch and disconnect it at the connector.

9 Detach the lower end of the switch spring from the brake pedal, then hold the adjusting nut and unscrew and remove the switch – for best access unscrew the footrest bracket bolts and displace the bracket.

10 Installation is the reverse of removal. Make sure the brake light is activated just before the rear brake pedal takes effect. If adjustment is necessary, hold the switch and turn the adjusting nut until the brake light is activated as required.

15 Instrument cluster removal and installation

1 Unscrew the bolt securing the instrument cluster, then pull the cluster up to free the two pegs on the back from the grommets **(see illustrations)**.

14.8 Rear brake light switch (arrowed)

15.1a Unscrew the bolt (arrowed) . . .

15.1b . . . then pull the cluster off its mounts . . .

15.2 . . . and disconnect the wiring connector

2 Pull back the boot on the instrument cluster wiring connector and disconnect the connector **(see illustration)**.

3 Installation is the reverse of removal. Check the condition of the grommets and fit new ones if they are damaged or deteriorated.

16 Instrument check

Note: *The tachometer, LCD display and LEDs are integral with the instrument panel printed* circuit board (PCB) – separate components for the PCB are not available, but the PCB is available separately from the cover and housing.

Speedometer and speed sensor

Check

1 If the speedometer, odometer or trip meter fail to work, take the motorcycle to a Suzuki dealer for assessment. Special equipment is needed to check the operation of the speedometer and the speed sensor.

Renewal

2 Remove the instrument cluster (see Section 15). If required, undo the screws on the back of the instrument cluster to separate the front cover, instrument panel and rear cover **(see illustrations)**. Further dismantling is not possible.

3 To remove the speed sensor, first raise the fuel tank (see Chapter 4). Trace the wiring from the sensor and disconnect it at the connector **(see illustration)**. Free the wiring from any clips and feed it down to the sensor, noting its routing.

4 Undo the screw securing the sensor to the sprocket cover and withdraw the sensor **(see illustration)**. If required, remove the sprocket cover and check the condition of the speed sensor rotor (see Chapter 6, Section 19).

Tachometer

Check

5 Suzuki provides no data for testing the tachometer. If the tachometer fails to work, take the motorcycle to a Suzuki dealer for assessment.

6 In normal operation, when the ignition is first turned ON, the tachometer pointer will swing to full scale and then return to zero. This is part of the instrument's self checking procedure. If the tachometer pointer fails to return to zero (which may occur in very low temperatures), and switching the ignition off then on again does not return it, it can be reset as follows.

7 Make sure the ignition is OFF. Hold the ADJ button ON and turn the ignition ON. Release the ADJ button three to five seconds after turning the ignition ON, then press the ADJ button twice within four seconds. If the tachometer is working correctly, the tachometer needle should now be at zero. The whole reset procedure should be completed within ten seconds. Turn the ignition OFF.

Renewal

8 Remove the instrument cluster (see Section 15). If required, remove the instrument panel from the case (see Step 2).

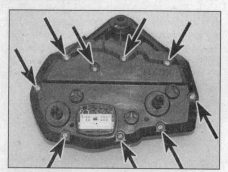

16.2a Undo the screws (arrowed) . . .

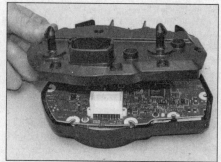

16.2b . . . then remove the housing . . .

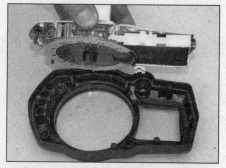

16.2c . . . and lift the panel out of the front cover

16.3 Disconnect the wiring connector – K8 shown

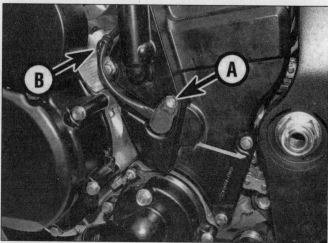

16.4 Speed sensor mounting bolt (A) and wiring clip (B)

Coolant temperature LED and display

Check

9 Ensure that the engine coolant temperature (ECT) sensor is working correctly (see Chapter 3, Section 4). Special equipment is needed to check the operation of the LED and LCD display circuits. If any of the circuits fail to work, take the motorcycle to a Suzuki dealer for assessment.

Renewal

10 See Step 2.

Oil pressure LED and symbol

Check

11 When the ignition is first turned ON and before the engine is started, the oil warning symbol and the warning LED should come on. When the engine is started they should extinguish. This is part of the instrument's self checking procedure.

12 If the display and light do not come on, turn the ignition OFF and disconnect the wiring connector from the oil pressure switch (see Section 17). Turn the ignition ON and earth (ground) the wiring connector on the crankcase – the warning LED should come on and the oil warning symbol should flicker. If the LED and warning symbol do not come on, the instrument panel should be renewed, although first check the wire between the oil pressure switch and instruments for continuity.

13 If the warning symbol and warning LED come on when the engine is running, and this is not due to low oil level or low oil pressure, disconnect the oil pressure switch wiring connector (see Section 17), then turn the ignition ON; the display and light should be out. If they are on, the wire between the switch and instrument cluster must be earthed (grounded) at some point.

Renewal

14 See Step 2.

Fuel level warning LED

Check

15 When the ignition is first turned ON and before the engine is started, the fuel warning LED should come on for three seconds. This is part of the instrument's self checking procedure. The fuel warning light will flicker when the volume of fuel in the tank drops to approximately 3.5 litres; when it drops to 1.0 litre on K6 and K7 models or 1.5 litres on K8 and K9 models the warning light will remain on.

16 If the LED does not come on, check the wiring from the base of the fuel tank to the instrument cluster for continuity (see *Wiring Diagrams* at the end of this Chapter). Also check the operation of the fuel level sensor (see Chapter 4, Section 6).

17 If the wiring and level sensor are in good order, the fuel level warning LED is faulty.

Renewal

18 See Step 2.

17 Oil pressure switch

Check

1 Before checking the switch, make sure the display functions as described in Section 16. The oil pressure switch is screwed into the front of the crankcase on the left-hand side of the. Remove the left-hand fairing side panel to access it (see Chapter 7).

2 Pull the rubber boot off the switch **(see illustration)**. Undo the screw (according to model) and detach the wiring connector. Turn the ignition ON and check for voltage at the wiring connector. If there is voltage, earth (ground) the connector on the crankcase and check that the oil warning symbol and warning LED come on.

3 Now touch the connector to the terminal

on the switch and check that the oil warning symbol and warning LED come on. If the display and warning light do not come on, the switch must be assumed faulty and a new one must be fitted.

Removal and installation

4 Remove the left-hand fairing side panel (see Chapter 7). Drain the engine oil (see Chapter 1).

5 Pull the rubber boot off the switch. Undo the screw and detach the wiring connector **(see illustration 17.2)**. Unscrew the switch and withdraw it from the crankcase.

6 Apply a suitable sealant (Suzuki-Bond 1207B or equivalent) to the threads near the switch body, then thread it into the crankcase and tighten it to the torque setting specified at the beginning of this Chapter.

7 Attach the wiring connector and tighten the screw. Fit the boot.

8 Fill the engine with the correct type and quantity of oil (see Chapter 1). Start the engine and check that there are no leaks around the switch.

9 Install the fairing side panel (see Chapter 7).

18 Ignition switch

⚠️ *Warning: To prevent the risk of short circuits, disconnect the battery negative (-ve) lead before making any ignition switch checks.*

Check

1 Remove the air filter housing (see Chapter 4). Trace the wiring from the ignition switch and disconnect it at the connector **(see illustration)**.

2 Using an ohmmeter or a continuity tester, check the continuity of the connector terminal pairs (see the *Wiring Diagrams* at the end of

17.2 Pull the boot off, undo the screw and detach the wiring connector

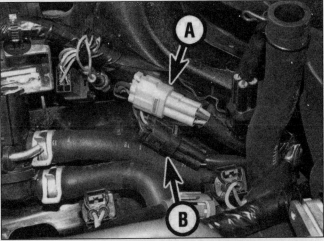

18.1 Ignition switch wiring connector (A), immobiliser wiring connector (B)

18.5 Unscrew the bolt (arrowed) and free the wiring

19.3a Right-hand switch housing wiring connectors (arrowed) – K8 shown

19.3b Left-hand switch housing wiring connector (arrowed) – K8 shown

this Chapter). Continuity should exist between the terminals connected by a solid line in the switch box diagram when the switch is in the indicated position.

3 If the switch fails any of the tests, replace it with a new one.

Removal and installation

Note: *The bolts used to secure the ignition switch to the top yoke are of a special Torx type which have a raised pip in their centre. Ensure that you have the necessary Torx bit to undo them (Pt. No. 09930-11920 from Suzuki, or commercially available equivalent).*

4 Remove the fairing (see Chapter 7).

5 Remove the air filter housing (see Chapter 4). Disconnect the ignition switch wiring connector, and where fitted the immobiliser wiring connector **(see illustration 18.1)**. Free the wiring from its guide(s) and feed it through to the switch **(see illustration)**. Undo the special Torx bolts used to mount the ignition switch to the underside of the top yoke and remove the switch.

6 Where fitted and if required remove the immobiliser from the top of the switch by undoing its two screws.

7 Installation is the reverse of removal, noting the following:

● Clean the switch mounting bolts and apply a suitable non-permanent thread locking compound.

● Make sure the wiring is correctly routed and securely connected.

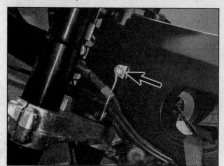

19.9 Unscrew the bolt (arrowed) and free the wiring

19 Handlebar switches

Check

1 Generally speaking, the switches are reliable and trouble-free. Most troubles, when they do occur, are caused by dirty or corroded contacts, but wear and breakage of internal parts is a possibility that should not be overlooked. If breakage does occur, the entire switch and related wiring harness will have to be renewed, since individual parts are not available.

2 The switches can be checked for continuity using an ohmmeter or a continuity test light. Always disconnect the battery negative (-ve) lead, which will prevent the possibility of a short circuit, before making the checks.

3 Remove the air filter housing (see Chapter 4). Trace the wiring harness of the switch in question back to its connector and disconnect it **(see illustrations)**.

4 Check for continuity between the terminals of the connector on the switch side, with the switch in the various positions (i.e. switch OFF – no continuity, switch ON – continuity) – see the switch boxes in the *Wiring Diagrams* at the end of this Chapter.

5 If the continuity check indicates a problem exists, remove the switch and spray the switch contacts with electrical contact cleaner (see Section 20). If they are accessible, the contacts can be scraped clean with a

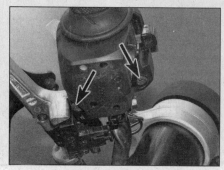

19.11 Switch housing screws (arrowed)

knife or polished with crocus cloth. If switch components are damaged or broken, it will be obvious when the switch is disassembled.

Removal

Right-hand switch

6 If the switch is to be removed from the bike, rather than just displaced from the handlebar, remove the air filter housing (see Chapter 4). Trace the wiring harness of the switch in question back to its connector and disconnect it **(see illustration 19.3a)**. Work back along the harness, freeing it from its guide, noting its correct routing **(see illustration 18.5)**.

7 Disconnect the front brake light switch wiring connector(s) **(see illustration 14.2)**.

8 Disconnect the throttle cables from the twistgrip (see Chapter 4, Section 14) – this procedure includes switch removal.

Left-hand switch

9 If the switch is to be removed from the bike, rather than just displaced from the handlebar, remove the air filter housing (see Chapter 4). Trace the wiring harness of the switch in question back to its connector and disconnect it **(see illustration 19.3b)**. Work back along the harness, freeing it from its guide, noting its correct routing **(see illustration)**.

10 Disconnect the clutch switch wiring connector **(see illustration 22.2)**.

11 Undo the screws on the underside of the housing and detach the halves from the handlebar **(see illustration)**.

Installation

12 Installation is the reverse of removal. Refer to Chapter 4 for installation of the throttle cables. Make sure the locating pin fits into the hole in the handlebar.

20 Gear position sensor (neutral switch)

Note: *The neutral LED in the instrument cluster is activated by the gear position (GP) sensor which is part of the fuel injection system. For full details of the GP sensor see Chapter 4, Section 10.*

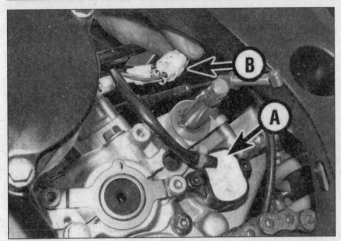

20.1 Gear position sensor (A) and its wiring connector (B)

21.2 Disconnect the wiring connector (arrowed) – K6 shown

Check

1 Raise the fuel tank (see Chapter 4). Trace the wiring from the GP sensor on the lower left-hand side of the engine and disconnect it at the connector **(see illustration)**. Make sure the transmission is in neutral, then turn the ignition ON. With the connector disconnected, the neutral LED should be out. If not, the wire between the connector and instrument cluster must be earthed (grounded) at some point.

2 If the neutral LED doesn't come on with the transmission in neutral, refer to the *Wiring Diagrams* at the end of this Chapter and check the blue/black wire from the instrument cluster to the diode in the turn signal/sidestand relay assembly for continuity, then check the blue wire from the diode to the gear position sensor for continuity. Check the diode as described in the next section. Check the black/white wire for continuity to earth.

3 Also check that when in neutral there is continuity between the blue and black/ white wire terminals on the switch side of the connector, and no continuity when a gear is selected. If not, and the wiring is good, the switch is faulty.

4 If the fuel injection system self-diagnostic function indicates a fault in the GP sensor, refer to Chapter 4 and check the sensor output voltage.

Removal and installation

5 Refer to Chapter 2, Section 15.

---

21 Sidestand switch, relay and diodes

Sidestand switch

1 The sidestand switch is mounted on the sidestand bracket. The switch is part of the safety circuit which prevents or stops the engine running if the transmission is in gear whilst the sidestand is down, and prevents the engine from starting if the transmission is in gear unless the sidestand is up and the clutch lever is pulled in.

2 Raise the fuel tank (see Chapter 4). Trace the wiring from the switch and disconnect it at the connector **(see illustration)**.

3 Check the operation of the switch using an ohmmeter or continuity test light. Connect the meter between the terminals on the switch side of the connector – meter positive (+ve) probe to the green wire terminal and negative (-ve) probe to the black/white wire terminal. With the sidestand up there should be continuity (zero resistance) between the terminals, with the stand down there should be no continuity (infinite resistance).

4 If the switch does not perform as expected, check that the fault is not caused by a sticking switch plunger due to the ingress of road dirt; spray the switch with a water dispersant aerosol **(see illustration)**. If the switch still does not work it is defective and must be replaced with a new one.

5 If the switch is good, check the sidestand relay (Steps 11 to 13) and diodes (Step 14). Also check the wiring between the various components (see *Wiring Diagrams* at the end of this Chapter).

6 To remove the switch, first disconnect the switch wiring (see Step 2). Feed the wiring back to the switch noting its routing and freeing it from any clips or ties.

7 Unscrew the bolts securing the switch and remove it **(see illustration)**.

21.4 Check the operation of the switch plunger

21.7 Switch is secured by two bolts (arrowed)

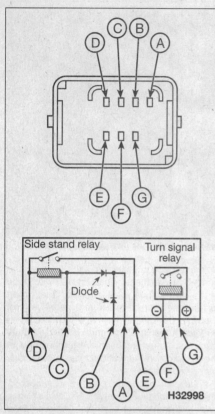

21.12 Turn signal/sidestand relay and diode terminal identification

8 Fit the new switch onto the bracket, then apply a suitable non-permanent thread locking compound to the bolt threads and tighten them.

9 Make sure the wiring is correctly routed up to the connector and retained by clips and ties. Reconnect the wiring connector.

10 Install the fuel tank (see Chapter 4).

Sidestand relay

11 On K6 and K7 models remove the rider's seat to access the relay (see Chapter 7), then unscrew the relay holder bolt and draw the relay out from under the centre section of the rear sub-frame (see illustrations 13.3a and b). On K8 and K9 models remove the seat cowling (see Chapter 7) – the relay is on the left-hand side of the rear sub-frame (see illustration 13.3c).

12 Pull the relay out of its connector. Using an ohmmeter or continuity tester, check for continuity between the D and E terminals on the relay (see illustration). There should be no continuity (infinite resistance).

13 Now use jumper wires to connect the positive (+ve) terminal of a 12V battery to the D terminal on the relay and the negative (-ve) battery terminal to the C relay terminal, and again check for continuity between the D and E terminals. There should now be continuity (zero resistance). If there is no continuity, fit a new relay.

Diodes

14 The diodes are integral with the sidestand/turn signal relay. Access the relay (see Step 11) and pull it off its connector.

15 Using a diode tester, connect the positive (+ve) probe to C terminal of the diode and the negative (-) probe to A terminal (see illustration 21.12). The tester should show 0.4 to 0.6 volts. Now reverse the probes. The tester should show its own battery voltage. Repeat the tests between B terminal and A terminal. The same results should be achieved. If it doesn't behave as stated, install a new relay.

16 If the diodes are good, check the other components in the starter interlock (safety) circuit (clutch switch, gear position switch, sidestand switch and relay) as described in the relevant sections of this Chapter. If all components are good, check the wiring between the various components (see the *wiring diagrams* at the end of this book).

22 Clutch switch

Check

1 The clutch switch is on the underside of the clutch lever bracket. The switch is part of the safety circuit and the lever must be pulled in (switch on) to allow the engine to be started.

2 To check the switch, disconnect the wiring connector (see illustration). Connect the probes of an ohmmeter or a continuity test light to the two switch terminals. With the clutch lever pulled in, there should be continuity (zero resistance). With the clutch lever out, there should be no continuity (infinite resistance).

3 If the switch is good, check the other components in the starter circuit as described in the relevant sections of this Chapter. If all components are good, check the wiring between the various components (see the *Wiring Diagrams* at the end of this Chapter).

Removal and installation

4 Disconnect the wiring connector from the clutch switch (see illustration 22.2). Undo the screw securing the switch to the clutch lever bracket and remove the switch (see illustration).

5 Installation is the reverse of removal. The switch isn't adjustable.

23 Horn

Check

1 The horn is mounted on the front of the frame on the left-hand side. Remove the left-hand fairing side panel (see Chapter 7).

22.2 Clutch switch wiring connector (arrowed)

22.4 Undo the screw (arrowed) and remove the switch

23.2a Unscrew the bolts (arrowed) . . .

23.2b . . . then draw the assembly out and disconnect the horn wiring connectors

2 On K6 and K7 models unscrew the horn/regulator/rectifier bracket bolts and draw the assembly out **(see illustration)**. Disconnect the wiring connectors from the horn **(see illustration)**.

3 On K8 and K9 models disconnect the wiring connectors from the horn **(see illustration 23.8)**.

4 Using jumper wires, apply battery voltage directly to the terminals on the horn. If the horn sounds, check the switch (see Section 19) and the wiring between the switch and the horn (see the *Wiring Diagrams* at the end of this Chapter).

5 If the horn doesn't sound, install a new one.

Removal and installation

6 Remove the left-hand fairing side panel (see Chapter 7).

7 On K6 and K7 models unscrew the horn/regulator/rectifier bracket bolts and draw the assembly out **(see illustration 23.2a)**.

Disconnect the wiring connectors from the horn **(see illustration 23.2b)**. Undo the bolt and remove the horn **(see illustration)**.

8 On K8 and K9 models disconnect the wiring connectors from the horn **(see illustration)**. Undo the bolts and remove the horn.

9 Install the horn in reverse sequence. Test the operation of the horn.

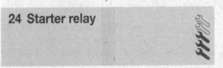

24 Starter relay

23.7 Unscrew the bolt (arrowed) and remove the horn

Check

1 If the starter circuit is faulty, first check the main and ignition fuses (see Section 5).

2 To access the starter relay, on K6 and K7 models remove the rider's seat, and on K8 and K9 models remove the seat cowling (see Chapter 7). Disconnect the battery negative (-ve) lead (see Section 3). Unclip the starter

relay and remove the plastic cover **(see illustrations 5.2a and b)**.

3 Undo the bolt securing the starter motor lead to its terminal on the relay and disconnect the lead, then position the lead away from the terminal **(see illustration)**. Reconnect the battery negative (-ve) lead. With the ignition

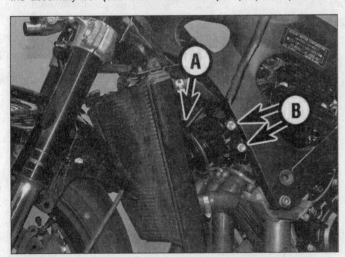

23.8 Horn wiring connectors (A) and mounting bolts (B)

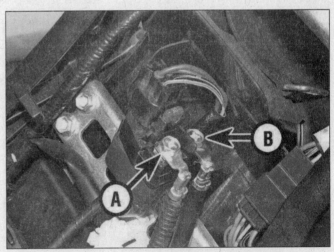

24.3 Battery lead (A) and starter motor lead (B)

24.4 Disconnect the starter relay wiring connector and check for battery voltage as described

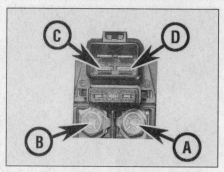

24.6a Starter relay terminal identification

24.6b Set-up for checking the starter relay for continuity

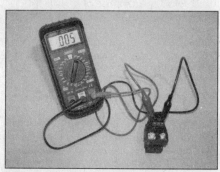

24.7 Measuring the starter relay resistance

ON, the engine kill switch in the RUN position, the transmission in neutral and the clutch pulled in, press the starter switch. The relay should be heard to click. Turn the ignition OFF.

4 If the relay doesn't click, disconnect the relay wiring connector and insert the positive (+ve) probe of a voltmeter into the yellow/green wire terminal in the connector and the negative (-ve) probe into the black/yellow wire terminal **(see illustration)**. Check for battery voltage with the ignition ON, kill switch in the RUN position, clutch lever pulled in and starter switch pressed. If no voltage is present, check the terminals in the wiring connector, the wiring (see *Wiring Diagrams* at the end of this Chapter) and the other components in the starter circuit as described in the relevant sections of this Chapter.

5 If there is voltage present, test the relay. Ensure the ignition is OFF and disconnect the battery negative (-ve) lead. Undo the bolts securing the starter motor and battery leads to the relay, noting where they fit, and remove the relay **(see illustration 24.3)**.

6 Set a multimeter to the ohms scale and connect it across the relay's starter motor and battery lead terminals (A and B) **(see illustration)**. Use jumper wires to connect the positive (+ve) terminal of a 12V battery to

the C terminal on the relay and the negative (-ve) battery terminal to the D relay terminal **(see illustration)**. The relay should be heard to click and there should be continuity (zero resistance) shown on the meter. Disconnect the battery. **Note:** *Do not apply battery voltage to the relay for more than 5 seconds to avoid damaging the relay coil.*

7 Now use the multimeter set to the ohms scale to measure the resistance between the relay's C and D terminals and compare the result with the Specifications at the beginning of this Chapter **(see illustration)**. If the result of either test is not as specified, the relay is faulty and must be replaced with a new one.

Removal and installation

8 To access the starter relay, on K6 and K7 models remove the rider's seat, and on K8 and K9 models remove the seat cowling (see Chapter 7). Disconnect the battery negative (-ve) lead.

9 Unclip the starter relay is from its location and remove the plastic cover **(see illustration 5.2a and b)**. Disconnect the relay wiring connector **(see illustration 24.4)**. Undo the bolts securing the starter motor and battery leads to the relay, noting where they fit and remove the relay **(see illustration 24.3)**.

10 Installation is the reverse of removal. Make sure the terminal bolts are tight.

25 Starter motor removal and installation

Removal

1 Disconnect the battery negative (-ve) lead (see Section 3). Remove the fuel tank (see Chapter 4).

2 Pull back the rubber boot on the starter motor terminal. Undo the nut securing the lead to the motor and disconnect the lead **(see illustration)**.

3 Undo the two bolts securing the starter motor to the crankcase **(see illustration)**.

25.2 Displace the boot then unscrew the nut and disconnect the terminal lead

25.3 Unscrew the two bolts (arrowed) . . .

4 Slide the starter motor out of the crankcase, using a screwdriver as leverage if necessary, and remove it from the machine **(see illustration)**. Remove the O-ring on the end of the starter motor and discard it as a new one must be fitted on reassembly.

Installation

5 Fit a new O-ring into the groove in the end of the starter motor **(see illustration)**. Apply a smear of engine oil or grease to the O-ring.
6 Manoeuvre the motor into position and slide it into the crankcase **(see illustration 25.4)**. Ensure that the starter motor teeth mesh correctly with those of the starter idle/reduction gear.
7 Install and tighten the bolts **(see illustration 25.3)**.
8 Connect the starter lead to the terminal and secure it with the nut **(see illustration 25.2)**. Fit the rubber boot.
9 Install the fuel tank (see Chapter 4).

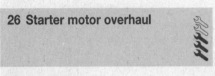

26 Starter motor overhaul

Disassembly

1 Remove the starter motor (see Section 25).
2 Note the alignment marks between the main housing and the front and rear covers, or make your own if they aren't clear **(see illustration)**.
3 Unscrew the two long bolts and withdraw them from the starter motor **(see illustration)**. Check the condition of the O-rings and replace them with new ones if necessary.
4 Wrap some insulating tape around the teeth on the end of the starter motor shaft – this will protect the oil seal from damage as the front cover is removed. Remove the front cover, then slide the shims off the shaft and

remove the cover O-ring **(see illustration)**. Remove the tabbed washer from inside the front cover, noting how it fits **(see illustration 26.19c)**.
5 Remove the rear cover and brushplate assembly, then slide the shims off the shaft and remove the cover O-ring **(see illustration)**. The brushes are under spring pressure and will probably pop out when the cover is removed.
6 Draw the main housing off the armature, noting that it is held by the attraction of the magnets **(see illustration)**.
7 Noting the correct fitted location of each component, unscrew the terminal nut and remove it along with its washer and insulating

25.4 . . . and remove the starter motor

25.5 Fit a new O-ring

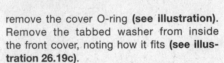
26.2 Note the alignment marks . . .

26.3 . . . then unscrew and remove the long bolts (arrowed)

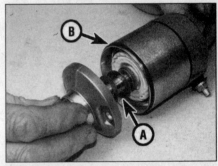
26.4 Remove the front cover, the shims (A) and the O-ring (B)

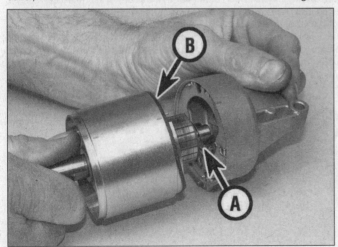
26.5 Remove the rear cover, the shims (A) and the O-ring (B)

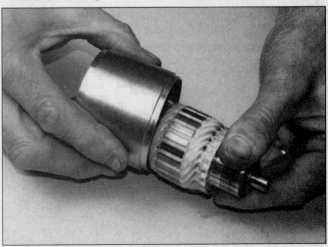
26.6 Draw the main housing and armature apart

26.7a Unscrew the terminal nut and remove the plain washer and insulating washers

26.7b Withdraw the terminal and brushplate from the cover

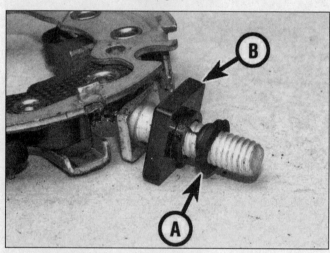

26.7c O-ring (A) and insulator piece (B)

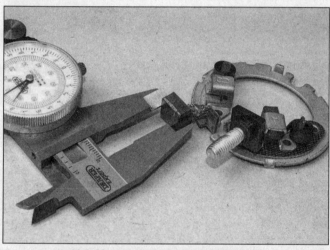

26.8 Measure the length of each brush

washers **(see illustration)**. Withdraw the terminal and brushplate assembly from the rear cover, noting how it fits **(see illustration)**. Note the O-ring and insulator piece on the bolt and remove them if required. Replace the O-ring with a new one if necessary

Inspection

8 The parts of the starter motor that are most likely to require attention are the brushes. Lift the springs, withdraw the brushes and measure

their length **(see illustration)**. Replace the brush plate with a new one if the brushes have worn down to the minimum length specified at the beginning of the Chapter, or if they are cracked, chipped, or otherwise damaged. Ensure the brushes are firmly attached to their terminals.
9 Inspect the commutator bars on the armature for scoring, scratches and discoloration. The commutator can be cleaned and polished with crocus cloth – do not use sandpaper or emery paper **(see illustration)**.

After cleaning, wipe away any residue with a cloth soaked in electrical system cleaner or denatured alcohol. Check that the insulation between each bar is below the level of the bars **(see illustration)**. If not, carefully scrape some away.
10 Using an ohmmeter or a continuity test light, check for continuity between the commutator bars **(see illustration)**. Continuity (zero resistance) should exist between each bar and all of the others. Also, check for

26.9a Check the commutator bars . . .

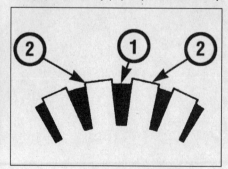

26.9b . . . and make sure the insulation (1) is below the level of the bars (2)

26.10a Checking for continuity between the commutator bars

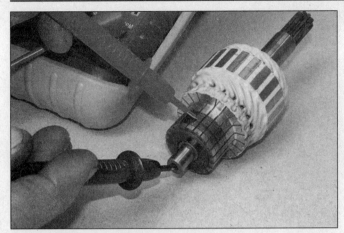

26.10b There should be no continuity between the commutator bars and the armature shaft

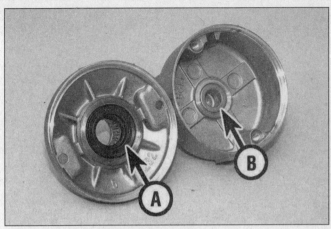

26.13 Check the seal and bearing (A) in the front cover and the bush (B) in the rear cover

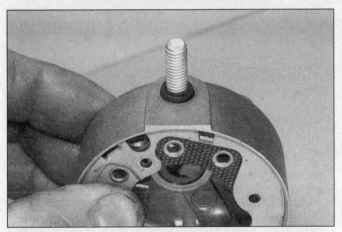

26.16 Fit the terminal O-ring between the bolt and the cover

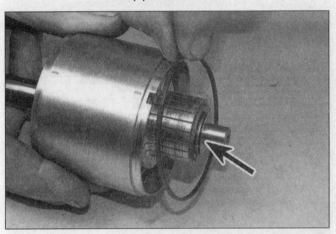

26.18a Fit the shims (arrowed) onto the shaft and the O-ring onto the housing . . .

continuity between the commutator bars and the armature shaft **(see illustration)**. There should be no continuity (infinite resistance) between the commutator and the shaft. If the checks indicate otherwise, the armature is defective.

11 When the starter motor is assembled check for continuity between the terminal bolt and the rear cover. There should be no continuity (infinite resistance).

12 Check the front end of the armature shaft for worn, cracked, chipped and broken teeth. If the shaft is damaged or worn, install a new armature.

13 Check the bearing and oil seal in the front cover and the bush in the rear cover for wear and damage **(see illustration)**. Individual components are not available; fit new covers if necessary.

14 Check the terminal insulating washers, insulator piece and O-ring for signs of deterioration and renew them if necessary.

Reassembly

15 Fit the brushes into their holders and place the spring ends onto the brushes. Check that the brushes slide freely in the holders.

16 Fit the insulator piece onto the

terminal bolt, then fit the O-ring **(see illustration 26.7c)**. Insert the terminal through the rear cover and fit the brushplate assembly into the cover, making sure it is correctly located **(see illustration 26.7b)**. Make sure the O-ring fits between the terminal bolt and the cover **(see illustration)**. Fit the insulating washers over the terminal, then fit the plain washer and the nut and tighten the nut **(see illustration 26.7a)**.

17 Fit the armature into the housing – it will

be forcefully drawn in by the magnets **(see illustration 26.6)**.

18 Slide the shims onto the rear of the armature shaft, then fit the rear cover O-ring **(see illustration)**. Apply a smear of molybdenum disulphide grease to the shaft end and insert it carefully into the rear cover, locating the brushes on the commutator as you do, and making sure the tab aligns with the cut-out **(see illustrations)**. Check that each brush is securely pressed against the commutator by its spring.

26.18b . . . then fit the rear cover, making sure the brushes locate correctly against the commutator bars . . .

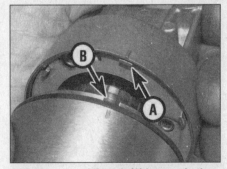

26.18c . . . and the tab (A) locates in the cut-out (B)

26.19a Fit the O-ring onto the main housing ...

26.19b ... the shims onto the shaft ...

26.19c ... and the tabbed washer onto the cover

26.20 Fit the long bolts with their O-rings

19 Fit the O-ring onto the front of the main housing, using a new one if necessary **(see illustration)**. Fit the shims onto the armature shaft **(see illustration)**. Apply a smear of grease to the lips of the front cover oil seal and fit the special washer into the cover, making sure its tabs locate correctly **(see illustration)**.

20 Fit the cover, aligning the marks made on removal **(see illustration 26.4)**. Install the long bolts with their O-rings and tighten them **(see illustration)**. Remove the insulating tape from around the teeth on the shaft.

21 Install the starter motor (see Section 25).

27 Charging system testing

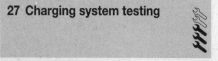

1 If the performance of the charging system is suspect, the system as a whole should be checked first, followed by testing of the individual components. **Note:** *Before beginning the checks, make sure the battery is* *fully charged and that all system connections are clean and tight.*

2 Checking the output of the charging system and the performance of the various components within the charging system requires the use of a multimeter (with voltage, current, resistance checking facilities). If a multimeter is not available, the job of checking the charging system should be left to a Suzuki dealer.

3 When making the checks, follow the procedures carefully to prevent incorrect connections or short circuits resulting in irreparable damage to electrical system components.

Leakage test

Caution: Always connect an ammeter in series, never in parallel with the battery, otherwise it will be damaged. Do not turn the ignition ON or operate the starter motor when the ammeter is connected – a sudden surge in current will blow the meter's fuse.

4 Ensure the ignition is OFF, then remove the rider's seat and disconnect the battery negative (-ve) lead.

5 Set the multimeter to the Amps function and connect its negative (-ve) probe to the battery negative (-ve) terminal, and positive (+ve) probe to the disconnected negative (-ve) lead **(see illustration)**. Always set the meter

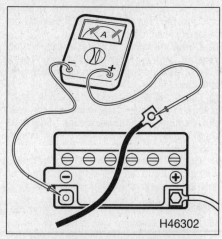

H46302

27.5 Checking the charging system leakage rate. Connect the meter as shown

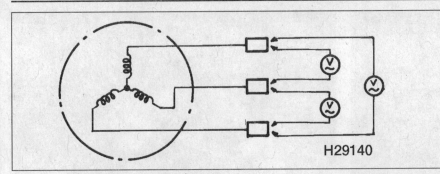

27.11 Alternator unregulated output voltmeter test connections

to a high amps range initially and then bring it down to the mA (milli Amps) range; if there is a high current flow in the circuit it may blow the meter's fuse.

6 Battery current leakage should not exceed the maximum limit (see Specifications). If a higher leakage rate is shown there is a short circuit in the wiring, although if an alarm is fitted its current draw should be taken into account. Disconnect the meter and reconnect the battery negative (-ve) lead.

7 If leakage is indicated, refer to *Wiring Diagrams* at the end of this Chapter to systematically disconnect individual electrical components and repeat the test until the source is identified.

Output test

8 Remove the rider's seat (see Chapter 7), then start the engine and warm it up.

9 To check the regulated (DC) voltage output, allow the engine to idle with the headlight main beam (HI) turned ON. Connect a multimeter set to the 0 – 20 volts DC scale across the terminals of the battery. Connect the positive (+ve) meter probe to battery positive (+ve) terminal and the negative (-ve) meter probe to the battery negative (-ve) terminal **(see illustration 3.10)**.

10 Slowly increase the engine speed to 5000 rpm and note the reading obtained. Compare the result with the Specification at the beginning of this Chapter. If the regulated voltage output is outside the specification, check the alternator and the regulator (see Sections 28 and 29).

11 To check the unregulated voltage output, displace the air filter housing to access the wiring connector, but leave the IAT sensor wiring connector connected (see Chapter 4). Trace the wiring back from the top of the alternator cover on the left-hand side of the engine to the wiring connector with the three yellow wires and disconnect it **(see illustration 28.2a or b)**. Start the engine and increase the engine speed to 5000 rpm, then using a multimeter set to 0 – 250 volts AC range, connect the meter probes to one pair of terminals at a time on the alternator side of the wiring connector **(see illustration)**. Make a note of the three readings obtained.

12 Compare the result with the Specification at the beginning of this Chapter. If the

> **HAYNES HINT** *Clues to a faulty regulator are constantly blowing bulbs, with brightness varying considerably with engine speed, and battery overheating.*

unregulated voltage output is outside the specification, check the alternator and the regulator (see Sections 28 and 29).

28 Alternator check

1 Remove the air filter housing (see Chapter 4).

2 Trace the wiring back from the top of the alternator cover on the left-hand side of the engine and disconnect it at the connector with the three yellow wires **(see illustrations)**.

3 Using a multimeter set to the ohms scale, connect the meter probes to one pair of terminals at a time on the alternator side of the wiring connector and measure the resistance between the terminals. Make a note of the three readings obtained. Now check for continuity between each terminal and ground (earth).

4 If the stator coil windings are in good condition the three readings should be within the range shown in the Specifications at the beginning of this Chapter and there should be no continuity (infinite resistance) between any of the terminals and ground (earth). If not, the alternator stator coil assembly is faulty and should be renewed. **Note:** *Before condemning the stator coils, check the fault is not due to damaged wiring between the connector and coils.*

29 Regulator/rectifier

1 On K6 and K7 models the regulator/rectifier is mounted on the front of the left-hand frame section on a bracket that also carries the horn. On K8 and K9 models the regulator/rectifier is mounted on a bracket that is bolted to the inside of the left-hand frame section.

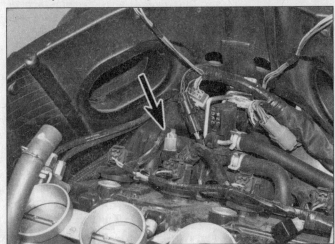

28.2a Alternator wiring connector (arrowed) – K6 and K7 models

28.2b Alternator wiring connector (arrowed) – K8 and K9 models

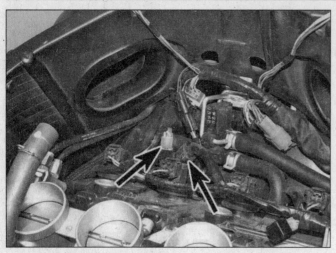

29.3a Regulator/rectifier wiring connectors (arrowed) – K6 and K7 models

29.3b Regulator/rectifier wiring connectors (arrowed) – K8 and K9 models

Unit: V

Connect negative probe of tester to:	Connect **positive** probe of tester to:						
	B/R 1	B/R 2	B 1	B 2	B 3	B/W 1	B/W 2
B/R 1		0	0.4-0.7	0.4-0.7	0.4-0.7	0.5-1.2	0.5-1.2
B/R 2	0		0.4-0.7	0.4-0.7	0.4-0.7	0.5-1.2	0.5-1.2
B 1	>1.4	>1.4		>1.4	>1.4	0.4-0.7	0.4-0.7
B 2	>1.4	>1.4	>1.4		>1.4	0.4-0.7	0.4-0.7
B 3	>1.4	>1.4	>1.4	>1.4		0.4-0.7	0.4-0.7
B/W 1	>1.4	>1.4	>1.4	>1.4	>1.4		0
B/W 2	>1.4	>1.4	>1.4	>1.4	>1.4	0	

H46658

> (greater than)

29.4a Regulator/rectifier test data and terminal identification – K6 and K7 models

B Black   B/R Black/red   B/W Black/white

Unit: V

Connect negative probe of tester to:	Connect **positive** probe of tester to:						
	B/R 1	B/R 2	B 1	B 2	B 3	B/W 1	B/W 2
B/R 1		0	0.2-0.9	0.2-0.9	0.2-0.9	0.3-1.0	0.3-1.0
B/R 2	0		0.2-0.9	0.2-0.9	0.2-0.9	0.3-1.0	0.3-1.0
B 1	>1.4	>1.4		0.5-1.2	0.5-1.2	0.1-0.8	0.1-0.8
B 2	>1.4	>1.4	0.5-1.2		0.5-1.2	0.1-0.8	0.1-0.8
B 3	>1.4	>1.4	0.5-1.2	0.5-1.2		0.1-0.8	0.1-0.8
B/W 1	>1.4	>1.4	0.3-1.0	0.3-1.0	0.3-1.0		0
B/W 2	>1.4	>1.4	0.3-1.0	0.3-1.0	0.3-1.0	0	

H46657

> (greater than)

29.4b Regulator/rectifier test data and terminal identification – K8 and K9 models

B Black   B/R Black/red   B/W Black/white

Check

2 Remove the rider's seat and disconnect the battery negative (-ve) lead (see Section 3).

3 Remove the air filter housing (see Chapter 4). Trace the wiring from the regulator/rectifier and disconnect it at the connectors (**see illustrations**).

4 Using a multimeter set to diode test, measure the voltage between the various terminals on the regulator/rectifier side of the wiring connector as shown in the table for your model (**see illustrations**). Note: *Depending on the multimeter used for the test, the results may vary from the specified figures. However, as long as the variance is constant, the test will give an indication of the condition of the regulator/rectifier. If the readings do not compare closely with those shown in the table, have the regulator/rectifier tested by a Suzuki dealer.*

5 If the regulator/rectifier appears to be good, check the wiring between the battery, regulator/rectifier and alternator, and the wiring connectors (see *Wiring Diagrams* at the end of this Chapter).

Removal and installation

6 Remove the rider's seat and disconnect the battery negative (-ve) lead (see Section 3). Remove the left-hand fairing side panel (see Chapter 7).

7 Remove the air filter housing (see Chapter 4). Trace the wiring from the regulator/rectifier and disconnect it at the connectors (**see illustration 29.3a or b**).

8 On K6 and K7 models undo the two bolts securing the regulator/rectifier/horn bracket, then draw the assembly out and disconnect the horn wiring connectors (**see illustrations 23.2a and b**). Unscrew the nuts, withdraw the bolts and detach the regulator/rectifier from the bracket (**see illustration**). Note the collars in the rubber grommets and remove them

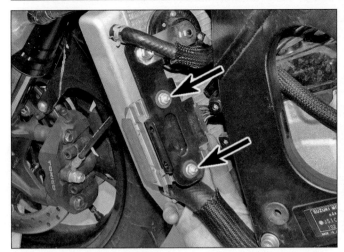

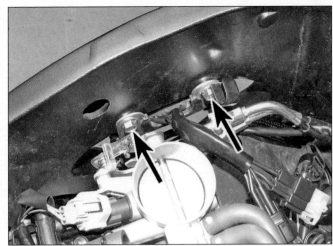

29.8 Unscrew the nuts (arrowed) to free the regulator/rectifier

29.9 Unscrew the bolts (arrowed) to free the regulator/rectifier

for safekeeping with the bolts. Check the condition of the grommets and replace them with new ones if necessary.

9 On K8 and K9 models undo the two bolts securing the regulator/rectifier bracket and remove the assembly **(see illustration)**. Unscrew the nuts, withdraw the bolts and detach the regulator/rectifier from the bracket. Note the collars in the rubber grommets and remove them for safekeeping with the bolts. Check the condition of the grommets and replace them with new ones if necessary.

10 Install the new unit in a reverse of the removal procedure.

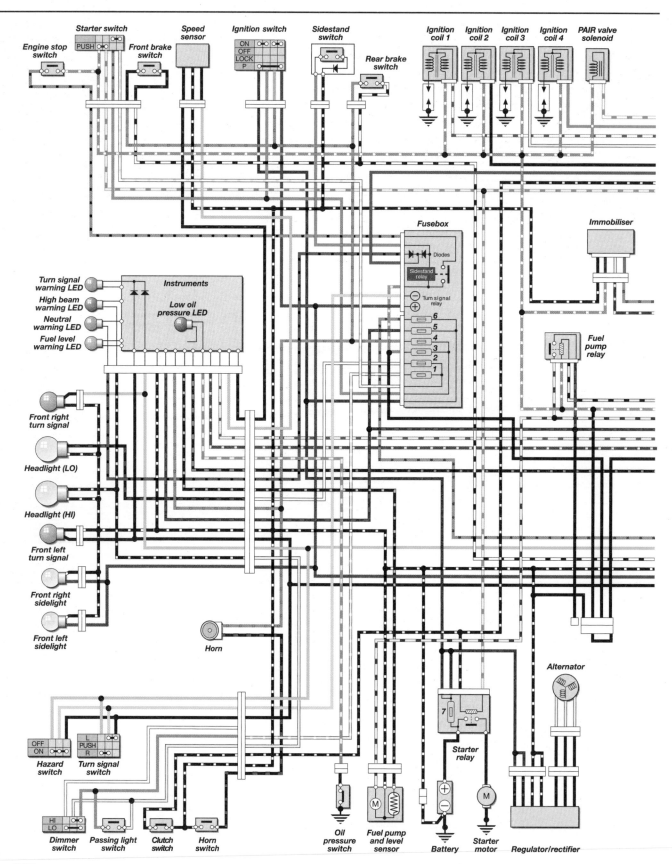

GSX-R600/750 K6 and K7 Europe

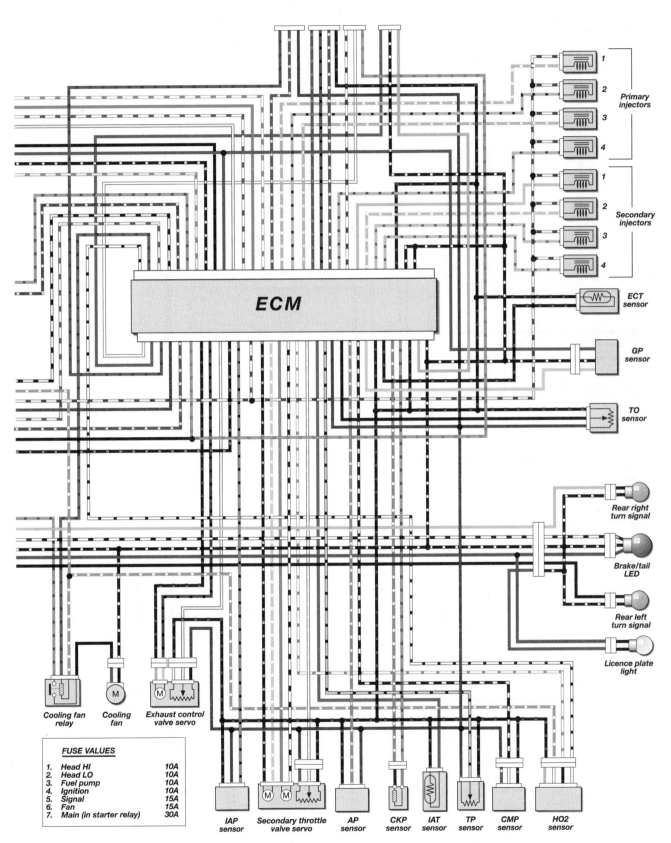

GSX-R600/750 K6 and K7 Europe

H33888

FUSE VALUES

1. Head HI — 10A
2. Head LO — 10A
3. Fuel pump — 10A
4. Ignition — 10A
5. Signal — 15A
6. Fan — 15A
7. Main (in starter relay) — 30A

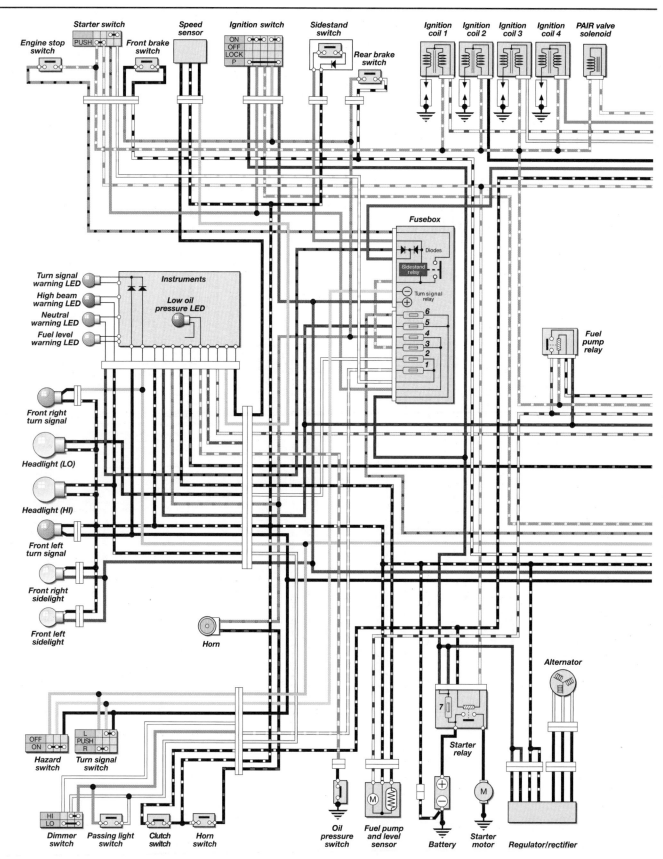

H33889

GSX-R600/750 K6 and K7 US

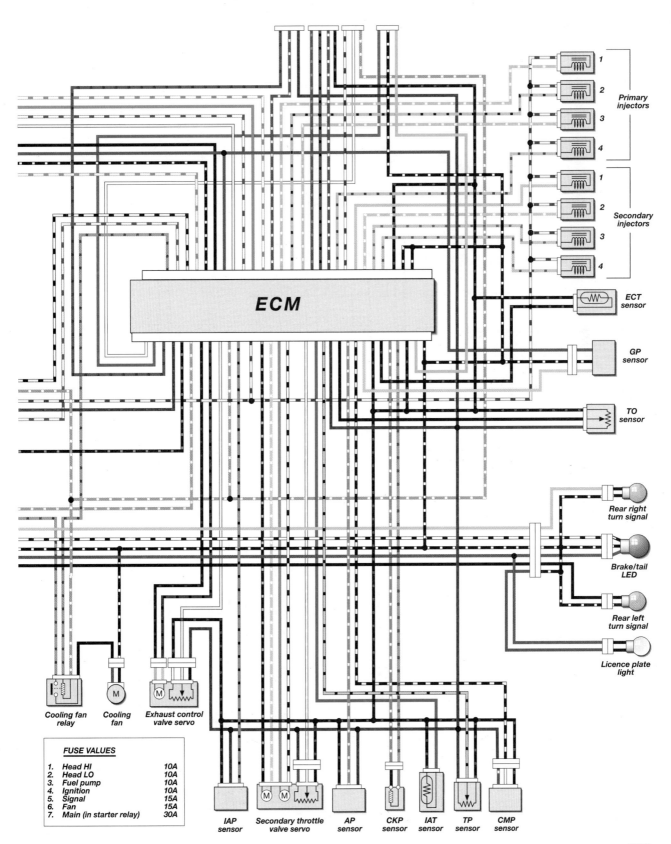

GSX-R600/750 K6 and K7 US

H33890

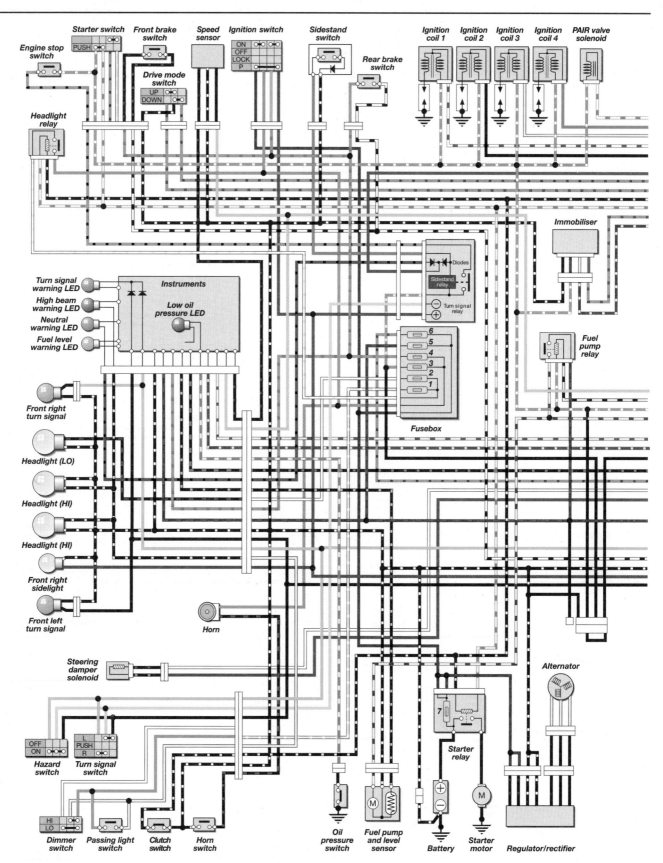

H33891

GSX-R600/750 K8 and K9 Europe

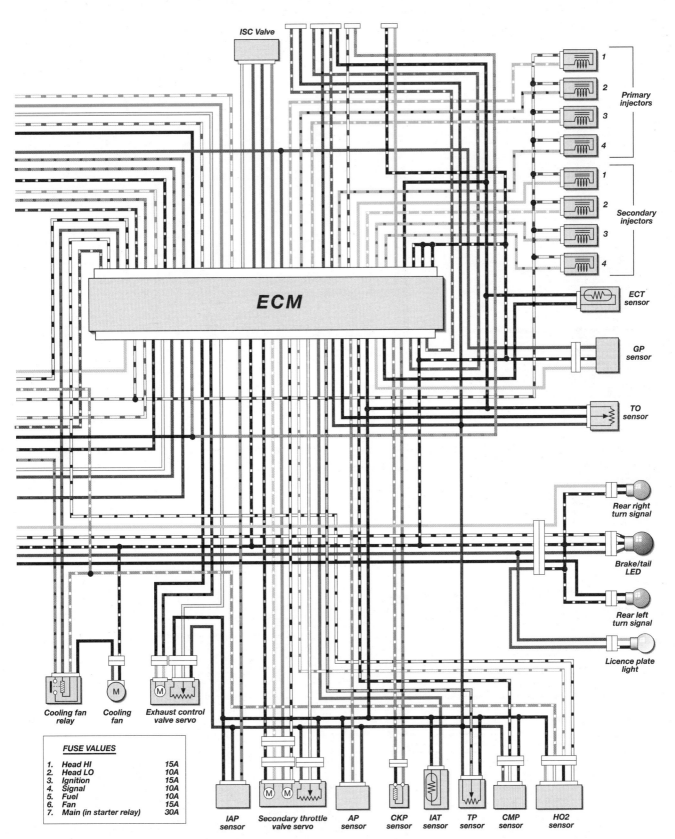

ISC Valve

ECM

Primary injectors

1
2
3
4

Secondary injectors

1
2
3
4

ECT sensor

GP sensor

TO sensor

Rear right turn signal

Brake/tail LED

Rear left turn signal

Licence plate light

Cooling fan relay

Cooling fan

Exhaust control valve servo

IAP sensor

Secondary throttle valve servo

AP sensor

CKP sensor

IAT sensor

TP sensor

CMP sensor

HO2 sensor

FUSE VALUES

1.	Head HI	15A
2.	Head LO	10A
3.	Ignition	15A
4.	Signal	10A
5.	Fuel	10A
6.	Fan	15A
7.	Main (in starter relay)	30A

GSX-R600/750 K8 and K9 Europe

H33892

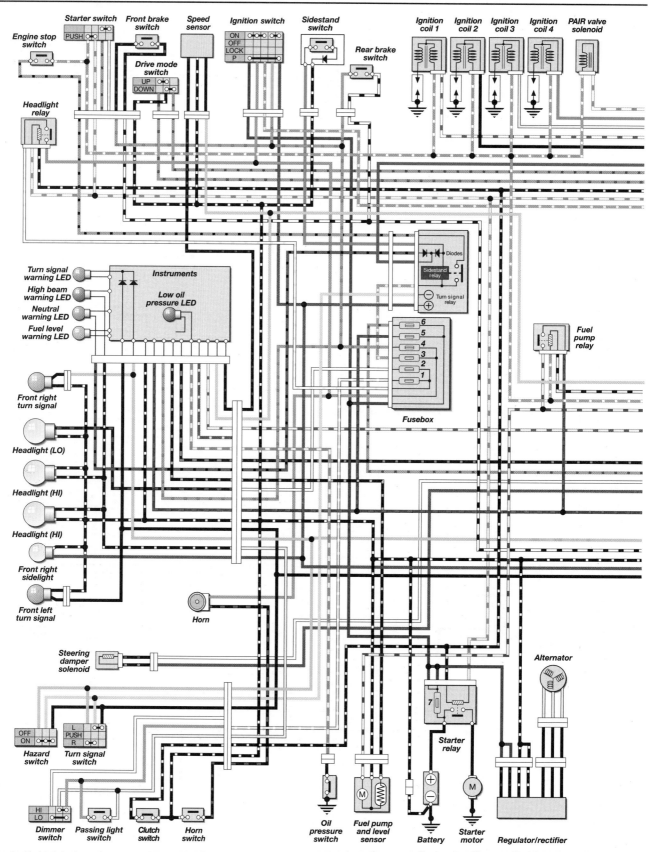

H33893

GSX-R600/750 K8 and K9 US

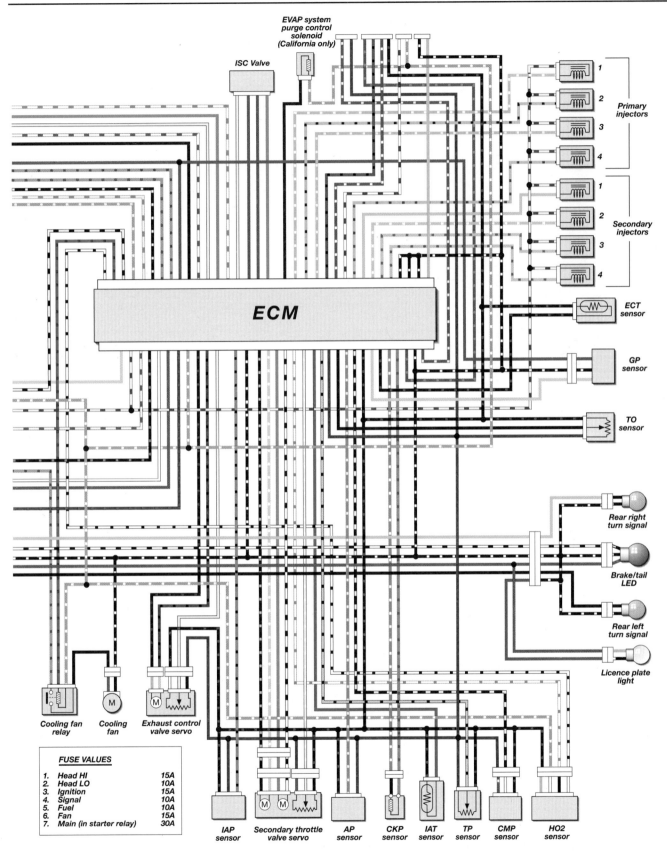

EVAP system
purge control
solenoid
(California only)

ISC Valve

Primary
injectors

1
2
3
4

Secondary
injectors

1
2
3
4

ECM

ECT
sensor

GP
sensor

TO
sensor

Rear right
turn signal

Brake/tail
LED

Rear left
turn signal

Licence plate
light

Cooling fan
relay

Cooling
fan

Exhaust control
valve servo

FUSE VALUES

1. Head HI   15A
2. Head LO   10A
3. Ignition   15A
4. Signal   10A
5. Fuel   10A
6. Fan   15A
7. Main (in starter relay) 30A

IAP
sensor

Secondary throttle
valve servo

AP
sensor

CKP
sensor

IAT
sensor

TP
sensor

CMP
sensor

HO2
sensor

GSX-R600/750 K8 and K9 US

H33894

Notes

Reference

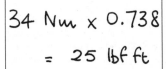

Buying tools

A toolkit is a fundamental requirement for servicing and repairing a motorcycle. Although there will be an initial expense in building up enough tools for servicing, this will soon be offset by the savings made by doing the job yourself. As experience and confidence grow, additional tools can be added to enable the repair and overhaul of the motorcycle. Many of the specialist tools are expensive and not often used so it may be preferable to hire them, or for a group of friends or motorcycle club to join in the purchase.

As a rule, it is better to buy more expensive, good quality tools. Cheaper tools are likely to wear out faster and need to be renewed more often, nullifying the original saving.

> **Warning: To avoid the risk of a poor quality tool breaking in use, causing injury or damage to the component being worked on, always aim to purchase tools which meet the relevant national safety standards.**

The following lists of tools do not represent the manufacturer's service tools, but serve as a guide to help the owner decide which tools are needed for this level of work. In addition, items such as an electric drill, hacksaw, files, soldering iron and a workbench equipped with a vice, may be needed. Although not classed as tools, a selection of bolts, screws, nuts, washers and pieces of tubing always come in useful.

For more information about tools, refer to the Haynes *Motorcycle Workshop Practice Techbook* (Bk. No. 3470).

Manufacturer's service tools

Inevitably certain tasks require the use of a service tool. Where possible an alternative tool or method of approach is recommended, but sometimes there is no option if personal injury or damage to the component is to be avoided. Where required, service tools are referred to in the relevant procedure.

Service tools can usually only be purchased from a motorcycle dealer and are identified by a part number. Some of the commonly-used tools, such as rotor pullers, are available in aftermarket form from mail-order motorcycle tool and accessory suppliers.

Maintenance and minor repair tools

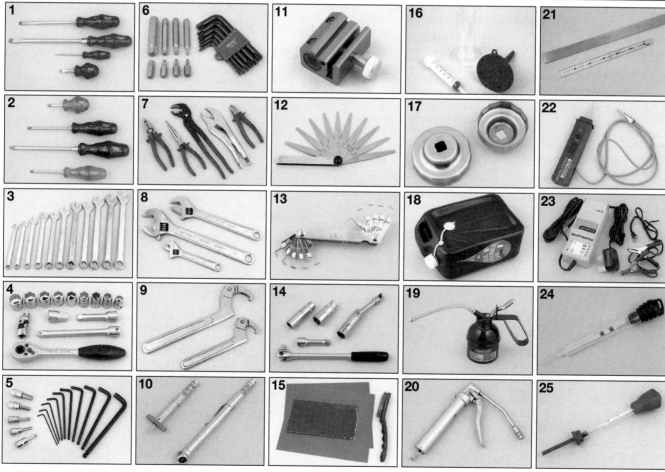

1   Set of flat-bladed screwdrivers
2   Set of Phillips head screwdrivers
3   Combination open-end and ring spanners
4   Socket set (3/8 inch or 1/2 inch drive)
5   Set of Allen keys or bits
6   Set of Torx keys or bits
7   Pliers, cutters and self-locking grips (Mole grips)
8   Adjustable spanners
9   C-spanners
10 Tread depth gauge and tyre pressure gauge
11 Cable oiler clamp
12 Feeler gauges
13 Spark plug gap measuring tool
14 Spark plug spanner or deep plug sockets
15 Wire brush and emery paper
16 Calibrated syringe, measuring vessel and funnel
17 Oil filter adapters
18 Oil drainer can or tray
19 Pump type oil can
20 Grease gun
21 Straight-edge and steel rule
22 Continuity tester
23 Battery charger
24 Hydrometer (for battery specific gravity check)
25 Anti-freeze tester (for liquid-cooled engines)

Repair and overhaul tools

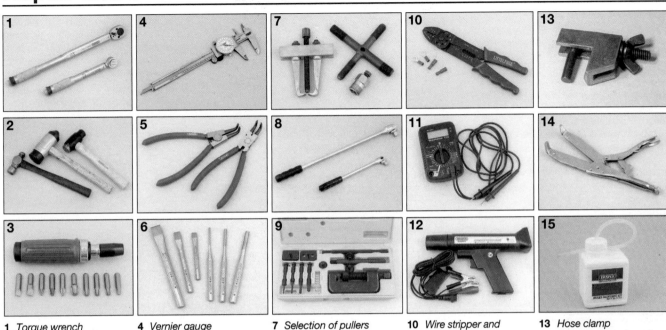

1 Torque wrench
  (small and mid-ranges)
2 Conventional, plastic or
  soft-faced hammers
3 Impact driver set

4 Vernier gauge
5 Circlip pliers (internal and
  external, or combination)
6 Set of cold chisels
  and punches

7 Selection of pullers
8 Breaker bars
9 Chain breaking/
  riveting tool set

10 Wire stripper and
   crimper tool
11 Multimeter (measures
   amps, volts and ohms)
12 Stroboscope (for
   dynamic timing checks)

13 Hose clamp
   (wingnut type shown)
14 Clutch holding tool
15 One-man brake/clutch
   bleeder kit

Specialist tools

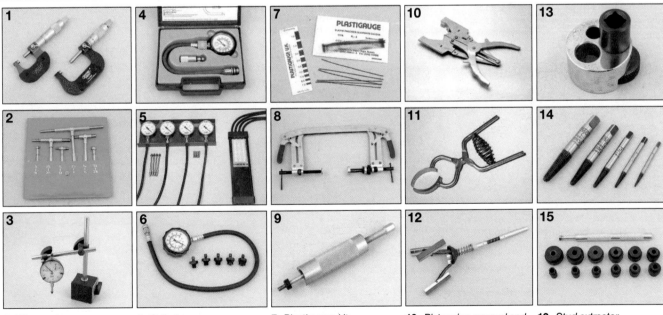

1 Micrometers
  (external type)
2 Telescoping gauges
3 Dial gauge

4 Cylinder
  compression gauge
5 Vacuum gauges (left) or
  manometer (right)
6 Oil pressure gauge

7 Plastigauge kit
8 Valve spring compressor
  (4-stroke engines)
9 Piston pin drawbolt tool

10 Piston ring removal and
   installation tool
11 Piston ring clamp
12 Cylinder bore hone
   (stone type shown)

13 Stud extractor
14 Screw extractor set
15 Bearing driver set

1 Workshop equipment and facilities

The workbench

● Work is made much easier by raising the bike up on a ramp - components are much more accessible if raised to waist level. The hydraulic or pneumatic types seen in the dealer's workshop are a sound investment if you undertake a lot of repairs or overhauls **(see illustration 1.1)**.

1.1 Hydraulic motorcycle ramp

● If raised off ground level, the bike must be supported on the ramp to avoid it falling. Most ramps incorporate a front wheel locating clamp which can be adjusted to suit different diameter wheels. When tightening the clamp, take care not to mark the wheel rim or damage the tyre - use wood blocks on each side to prevent this.
● Secure the bike to the ramp using tie-downs **(see illustration 1.2)**. If the bike has only a sidestand, and hence leans at a dangerous angle when raised, support the bike on an auxiliary stand.

1.2 Tie-downs are used around the passenger footrests to secure the bike

● Auxiliary (paddock) stands are widely available from mail order companies or motorcycle dealers and attach either to the wheel axle or swingarm pivot **(see illustration 1.3)**. If the motorcycle has a centrestand, you can support it under the crankcase to prevent it toppling whilst either wheel is removed **(see illustration 1.4)**.

1.3 This auxiliary stand attaches to the swingarm pivot

1.4 Always use a block of wood between the engine and jack head when supporting the engine in this way

Fumes and fire

● Refer to the Safety first! page at the beginning of the manual for full details. Make sure your workshop is equipped with a fire extinguisher suitable for fuel-related fires (Class B fire - flammable liquids) - it is not sufficient to have a water-filled extinguisher.
● Always ensure adequate ventilation is available. Unless an exhaust gas extraction system is available for use, ensure that the engine is run outside of the workshop.
● If working on the fuel system, make sure the workshop is ventilated to avoid a build-up of fumes. This applies equally to fume build-up when charging a battery. Do not smoke or allow anyone else to smoke in the workshop.

Fluids

● If you need to drain fuel from the tank, store it in an approved container marked as suitable for the storage of petrol (gasoline) **(see illustration 1.5)**. Do not store fuel in glass jars or bottles.

1.5 Use an approved can only for storing petrol (gasoline)

● Use proprietary engine degreasers or solvents which have a high flash-point, such as paraffin (kerosene), for cleaning off oil, grease and dirt - never use petrol (gasoline) for cleaning. Wear rubber gloves when handling solvent and engine degreaser. The fumes from certain solvents can be dangerous - always work in a well-ventilated area.

Dust, eye and hand protection

● Protect your lungs from inhalation of dust particles by wearing a filtering mask over the nose and mouth. Many frictional materials still contain asbestos which is dangerous to your health. Protect your eyes from spouts of liquid and sprung components by wearing a pair of protective goggles **(see illustration 1.6)**.

1.6 A fire extinguisher, goggles, mask and protective gloves should be at hand in the workshop

● Protect your hands from contact with solvents, fuel and oils by wearing rubber gloves. Alternatively apply a barrier cream to your hands before starting work. If handling hot components or fluids, wear suitable gloves to protect your hands from scalding and burns.

What to do with old fluids

● Old cleaning solvent, fuel, coolant and oils should not be poured down domestic drains or onto the ground. Package the fluid up in old oil containers, label it accordingly, and take it to a garage or disposal facility. Contact your local authority for location of such sites or ring the oil care hotline.

OIL CARE
FOLLOW THE CODE
OIL BANK LINE
0800 66 33 66
www.oilbankline.org.uk

Note: It is antisocial and illegal to dump oil down the drain. To find the location of your local oil recycling bank, call this number free.

In the USA, note that any oil supplier must accept used oil for recycling.

2 Fasteners -
screws, bolts and nuts

Fastener types and applications

Bolts and screws

● Fastener head types are either of hexagonal, Torx or splined design, with internal and external versions of each type **(see illustrations 2.1 and 2.2)**; splined head fasteners are not in common use on motorcycles. The conventional slotted or Phillips head design is used for certain screws. Bolt or screw length is always measured from the underside of the head to the end of the item **(see illustration 2.11)**.

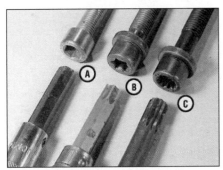

2.1 Internal hexagon/Allen (A), Torx (B) and splined (C) fasteners, with corresponding bits

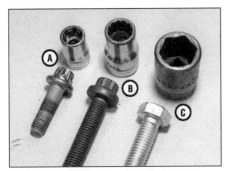

2.2 External Torx (A), splined (B) and hexagon (C) fasteners, with corresponding sockets

● Certain fasteners on the motorcycle have a tensile marking on their heads, the higher the marking the stronger the fastener. High tensile fasteners generally carry a 10 or higher marking. Never replace a high tensile fastener with one of a lower tensile strength.

Washers (see illustration 2.3)

● Plain washers are used between a fastener head and a component to prevent damage to the component or to spread the load when torque is applied. Plain washers can also be used as spacers or shims in certain assemblies. Copper or aluminium plain washers are often used as sealing washers on drain plugs.

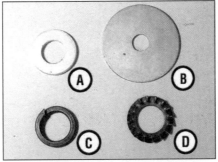

2.3 Plain washer (A), penny washer (B), spring washer (C) and serrated washer (D)

● The split-ring spring washer works by applying axial tension between the fastener head and component. If flattened, it is fatigued and must be renewed. If a plain (flat) washer is used on the fastener, position the spring washer between the fastener and the plain washer.

● Serrated star type washers dig into the fastener and component faces, preventing loosening. They are often used on electrical earth (ground) connections to the frame.

● Cone type washers (sometimes called Belleville) are conical and when tightened apply axial tension between the fastener head and component. They must be installed with the dished side against the component and often carry an OUTSIDE marking on their outer face. If flattened, they are fatigued and must be renewed.

● Tab washers are used to lock plain nuts or bolts on a shaft. A portion of the tab washer is bent up hard against one flat of the nut or bolt to prevent it loosening. Due to the tab washer being deformed in use, a new tab washer should be used every time it is disturbed.

● Wave washers are used to take up endfloat on a shaft. They provide light springing and prevent excessive side-to-side play of a component. Can be found on rocker arm shafts.

Nuts and split pins

● Conventional plain nuts are usually six-sided **(see illustration 2.4)**. They are sized by thread diameter and pitch. High tensile nuts carry a number on one end to denote their tensile strength.

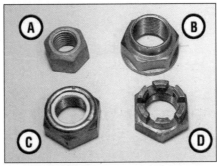

2.4 Plain nut (A), shouldered locknut (B), nylon insert nut (C) and castellated nut (D)

● Self-locking nuts either have a nylon insert, or two spring metal tabs, or a shoulder which is staked into a groove in the shaft - their advantage over conventional plain nuts is a resistance to loosening due to vibration. The nylon insert type can be used a number of times, but must be renewed when the friction of the nylon insert is reduced, ie when the nut spins freely on the shaft. The spring tab type can be reused unless the tabs are damaged. The shouldered type must be renewed every time it is disturbed.

● Split pins (cotter pins) are used to lock a castellated nut to a shaft or to prevent slackening of a plain nut. Common applications are wheel axles and brake torque arms. Because the split pin arms are deformed to lock around the nut a new split pin must always be used on installation - always fit the correct size split pin which will fit snugly in the shaft hole. Make sure the split pin arms are correctly located around the nut **(see illustrations 2.5 and 2.6)**.

2.5 Bend split pin (cotter pin) arms as shown (arrows) to secure a castellated nut

2.6 Bend split pin (cotter pin) arms as shown to secure a plain nut

Caution: If the castellated nut slots do not align with the shaft hole after tightening to the torque setting, tighten the nut until the next slot aligns with the hole - never slacken the nut to align its slot.

● R-pins (shaped like the letter R), or slip pins as they are sometimes called, are sprung and can be reused if they are otherwise in good condition. Always install R-pins with their closed end facing forwards **(see illustration 2.7)**.

**2.7 Correct fitting of R-pin.
Arrow indicates forward direction**

Circlips (see illustration 2.8)

● Circlips (sometimes called snap-rings) are used to retain components on a shaft or in a housing and have corresponding external or internal ears to permit removal. Parallel-sided (machined) circlips can be installed either way round in their groove, whereas stamped circlips (which have a chamfered edge on one face) must be installed with the chamfer facing away from the direction of thrust load **(see illustration 2.9)**.

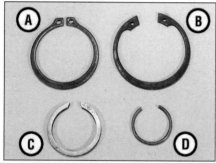

2.8 External stamped circlip (A), internal stamped circlip (B), machined circlip (C) and wire circlip (D)

● Always use circlip pliers to remove and install circlips; expand or compress them just enough to remove them. After installation, rotate the circlip in its groove to ensure it is securely seated. If installing a circlip on a splined shaft, always align its opening with a shaft channel to ensure the circlip ends are well supported and unlikely to catch **(see illustration 2.10)**.

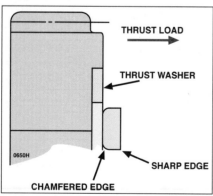

2.9 Correct fitting of a stamped circlip

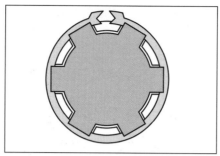

**2.10 Align circlip opening
with shaft channel**

● Circlips can wear due to the thrust of components and become loose in their grooves, with the subsequent danger of becoming dislodged in operation. For this reason, renewal is advised every time a circlip is disturbed.

● Wire circlips are commonly used as piston pin retaining clips. If a removal tang is provided, long-nosed pliers can be used to dislodge them, otherwise careful use of a small flat-bladed screwdriver is necessary. Wire circlips should be renewed every time they are disturbed.

Thread diameter and pitch

● Diameter of a male thread (screw, bolt or stud) is the outside diameter of the threaded portion **(see illustration 2.11)**. Most motorcycle manufacturers use the ISO (International Standards Organisation) metric system expressed in millimetres, eg M6 refers to a 6 mm diameter thread. Sizing is the same for nuts, except that the thread diameter is measured across the valleys of the nut.

● Pitch is the distance between the peaks of the thread **(see illustration 2.11)**. It is expressed in millimetres, thus a common bolt size may be expressed as 6.0 x 1.0 mm (6 mm thread diameter and 1 mm pitch). Generally pitch increases in proportion to thread diameter, although there are always exceptions.

● Thread diameter and pitch are related for conventional fastener applications and the accompanying table can be used as a guide. Additionally, the AF (Across Flats), spanner or socket size dimension of the bolt or nut **(see illustration 2.11)** is linked to thread and pitch specification. Thread pitch can be measured with a thread gauge **(see illustration 2.12)**.

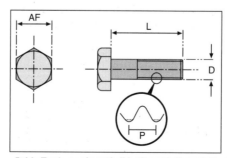

2.11 Fastener length (L), thread diameter (D), thread pitch (P) and head size (AF)

**2.12 Using a thread gauge
to measure pitch**

AF size	Thread diameter x pitch (mm)
8 mm	M5 x 0.8
8 mm	M6 x 1.0
10 mm	M6 x 1.0
12 mm	M8 x 1.25
14 mm	M10 x 1.25
17 mm	M12 x 1.25

● The threads of most fasteners are of the right-hand type, ie they are turned clockwise to tighten and anti-clockwise to loosen. The reverse situation applies to left-hand thread fasteners, which are turned anti-clockwise to tighten and clockwise to loosen. Left-hand threads are used where rotation of a component might loosen a conventional right-hand thread fastener.

Seized fasteners

● Corrosion of external fasteners due to water or reaction between two dissimilar metals can occur over a period of time. It will build up sooner in wet conditions or in countries where salt is used on the roads during the winter. If a fastener is severely corroded it is likely that normal methods of removal will fail and result in its head being ruined. When you attempt removal, the fastener thread should be heard to crack free and unscrew easily - if it doesn't, stop there before damaging something.

● A smart tap on the head of the fastener will often succeed in breaking free corrosion which has occurred in the threads **(see illustration 2.13)**.

● An aerosol penetrating fluid (such as WD-40) applied the night beforehand may work its way down into the thread and ease removal. Depending on the location, you may be able to make up a Plasticine well around the fastener head and fill it with penetrating fluid.

**2.13 A sharp tap on the head of a fastener
will often break free a corroded thread**

● If you are working on an engine internal component, corrosion will most likely not be a problem due to the well lubricated environment. However, components can be very tight and an impact driver is a useful tool in freeing them (see illustration 2.14).

2.14 Using an impact driver to free a fastener

● Where corrosion has occurred between dissimilar metals (eg steel and aluminium alloy), the application of heat to the fastener head will create a disproportionate expansion rate between the two metals and break the seizure caused by the corrosion. Whether heat can be applied depends on the location of the fastener - any surrounding components likely to be damaged must first be removed (see illustration 2.15). Heat can be applied using a paint stripper heat gun or clothes iron, or by immersing the component in boiling water - wear protective gloves to prevent scalding or burns to the hands.

2.15 Using heat to free a seized fastener

● As a last resort, it is possible to use a hammer and cold chisel to work the fastener head unscrewed (see illustration 2.16). This will damage the fastener, but more importantly extreme care must be taken not to damage the surrounding component.

Caution: Remember that the component being secured is generally of more value than the bolt, nut or screw - when the fastener is freed, do not unscrew it with force, instead work the fastener back and forth when resistance is felt to prevent thread damage.

2.16 Using a hammer and chisel to free a seized fastener

Broken fasteners and damaged heads

● If the shank of a broken bolt or screw is accessible you can grip it with self-locking grips. The knurled wheel type stud extractor tool or self-gripping stud puller tool is particularly useful for removing the long studs which screw into the cylinder mouth surface of the crankcase or bolts and screws from which the head has broken off (see illustration 2.17). Studs can also be removed by locking two nuts together on the threaded end of the stud and using a spanner on the lower nut (see illustration 2.18).

2.17 Using a stud extractor tool to remove a broken crankcase stud

2.18 Two nuts can be locked together to unscrew a stud from a component

● A bolt or screw which has broken off below or level with the casing must be extracted using a screw extractor set. Centre punch the fastener to centralise the drill bit, then drill a hole in the fastener (see illustration 2.19). Select a drill bit which is approximately half to three-quarters the

2.19 When using a screw extractor, first drill a hole in the fastener . . .

diameter of the fastener and drill to a depth which will accommodate the extractor. Use the largest size extractor possible, but avoid leaving too small a wall thickness otherwise the extractor will merely force the fastener walls outwards wedging it in the casing thread.

● If a spiral type extractor is used, thread it anti-clockwise into the fastener. As it is screwed in, it will grip the fastener and unscrew it from the casing (see illustration 2.20).

2.20 . . . then thread the extractor anti-clockwise into the fastener

● If a taper type extractor is used, tap it into the fastener so that it is firmly wedged in place. Unscrew the extractor (anti-clockwise) to draw the fastener out.

 Warning: Stud extractors are very hard and may break off in the fastener if care is not taken - ask an engineer about spark erosion if this happens.

● Alternatively, the broken bolt/screw can be drilled out and the hole retapped for an oversize bolt/screw or a diamond-section thread insert. It is essential that the drilling is carried out squarely and to the correct depth, otherwise the casing may be ruined - if in doubt, entrust the work to an engineer.

● Bolts and nuts with rounded corners cause the correct size spanner or socket to slip when force is applied. Of the types of spanner/socket available always use a six-point type rather than an eight or twelve-point type - better grip

2.21 Comparison of surface drive ring spanner (left) with 12-point type (right)

is obtained. Surface drive spanners grip the middle of the hex flats, rather than the corners, and are thus good in cases of damaged heads **(see illustration 2.21)**.

● Slotted-head or Phillips-head screws are often damaged by the use of the wrong size screwdriver. Allen-head and Torx-head screws are much less likely to sustain damage. If enough of the screw head is exposed you can use a hacksaw to cut a slot in its head and then use a conventional flat-bladed screwdriver to remove it. Alternatively use a hammer and cold chisel to tap the head of the fastener around to slacken it. Always replace damaged fasteners with new ones, preferably Torx or Allen-head type.

A dab of valve grinding compound between the screw head and screw-driver tip will often give a good grip.

Thread repair

● Threads (particularly those in aluminium alloy components) can be damaged by overtightening, being assembled with dirt in the threads, or from a component working loose and vibrating. Eventually the thread will fail completely, and it will be impossible to tighten the fastener.

● If a thread is damaged or clogged with old locking compound it can be renovated with a thread repair tool (thread chaser) **(see illustrations 2.22 and 2.23)**; special thread

2.22 A thread repair tool being used to correct an internal thread

2.23 A thread repair tool being used to correct an external thread

chasers are available for spark plug hole threads. The tool will not cut a new thread, but clean and true the original thread. Make sure that you use the correct diameter and pitch tool. Similarly, external threads can be cleaned up with a die or a thread restorer file **(see illustration 2.24)**.

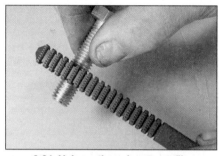

2.24 Using a thread restorer file

● It is possible to drill out the old thread and retap the component to the next thread size. This will work where there is enough surrounding material and a new bolt or screw can be obtained. Sometimes, however, this is not possible - such as where the bolt/screw passes through another component which must also be suitably modified, also in cases where a spark plug or oil drain plug cannot be obtained in a larger diameter thread size.

● The diamond-section thread insert (often known by its popular trade name of Heli-Coil) is a simple and effective method of renewing the thread and retaining the original size. A kit can be purchased which contains the tap, insert and installing tool **(see illustration 2.25)**. Drill out the damaged thread with the size drill specified **(see illustration 2.26)**. Carefully retap the thread **(see illustration 2.27)**. Install the

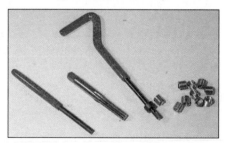

2.25 Obtain a thread insert kit to suit the thread diameter and pitch required

2.26 To install a thread insert, first drill out the original thread . . .

2.27 . . . tap a new thread . . .

2.28 . . . fit insert on the installing tool . . .

2.29 . . . and thread into the component . . .

2.30 . . . break off the tang when complete

insert on the installing tool and thread it slowly into place using a light downward pressure **(see illustrations 2.28 and 2.29)**. When positioned between a 1/4 and 1/2 turn below the surface withdraw the installing tool and use the break-off tool to press down on the tang, breaking it off **(see illustration 2.30)**.

● There are epoxy thread repair kits on the market which can rebuild stripped internal threads, although this repair should not be used on high load-bearing components.

Thread locking and sealing compounds

● Locking compounds are used in locations where the fastener is prone to loosening due to vibration or on important safety-related items which might cause loss of control of the motorcycle if they fail. It is also used where important fasteners cannot be secured by other means such as lockwashers or split pins.

● Before applying locking compound, make sure that the threads (internal and external) are clean and dry with all old compound removed. Select a compound to suit the component being secured - a non-permanent general locking and sealing type is suitable for most applications, but a high strength type is needed for permanent fixing of studs in castings. Apply a drop or two of the compound to the first few threads of the fastener, then thread it into place and tighten to the specified torque. Do not apply excessive thread locking compound otherwise the thread may be damaged on subsequent removal.

● Certain fasteners are impregnated with a dry film type coating of locking compound on their threads. Always renew this type of fastener if disturbed.

● Anti-seize compounds, such as copper-based greases, can be applied to protect threads from seizure due to extreme heat and corrosion. A common instance is spark plug threads and exhaust system fasteners.

---

3 Measuring tools and gauges

Feeler gauges

● Feeler gauges (or blades) are used for measuring small gaps and clearances **(see illustration 3.1)**. They can also be used to measure endfloat (sideplay) of a component on a shaft where access is not possible with a dial gauge.

● Feeler gauge sets should be treated with care and not bent or damaged. They are etched with their size on one face. Keep them clean and very lightly oiled to prevent corrosion build-up.

3.1 Feeler gauges are used for measuring small gaps and clearances - thickness is marked on one face of gauge

● When measuring a clearance, select a gauge which is a light sliding fit between the two components. You may need to use two gauges together to measure the clearance accurately.

Micrometers

● A micrometer is a precision tool capable of measuring to 0.01 or 0.001 of a millimetre. It should always be stored in its case and not in the general toolbox. It must be kept clean and never dropped, otherwise its frame or measuring anvils could be distorted resulting in inaccurate readings.

● External micrometers are used for measuring outside diameters of components and have many more applications than internal micrometers. Micrometers are available in different size ranges, eg 0 to 25 mm, 25 to 50 mm, and upwards in 25 mm steps; some large micrometers have interchangeable anvils to allow a range of measurements to be taken. Generally the largest precision measurement you are likely to take on a motorcycle is the piston diameter.

● Internal micrometers (or bore micrometers) are used for measuring inside diameters, such as valve guides and cylinder bores. Telescoping gauges and small hole gauges are used in conjunction with an external micrometer, whereas the more expensive internal micrometers have their own measuring device.

External micrometer

Note: *The conventional analogue type instrument is described. Although much easier to read, digital micrometers are considerably more expensive.*

● Always check the calibration of the micrometer before use. With the anvils closed (0 to 25 mm type) or set over a test gauge (for

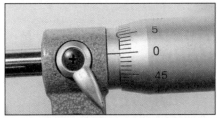

3.2 Check micrometer calibration before use

the larger types) the scale should read zero **(see illustration 3.2)**; make sure that the anvils (and test piece) are clean first. Any discrepancy can be adjusted by referring to the instructions supplied with the tool. Remember that the micrometer is a precision measuring tool - don't force the anvils closed, use the ratchet (4) on the end of the micrometer to close it. In this way, a measured force is always applied.

● To use, first make sure that the item being measured is clean. Place the anvil of the micrometer (1) against the item and use the thimble (2) to bring the spindle (3) lightly into contact with the other side of the item **(see illustration 3.3)**. Don't tighten the thimble down because this will damage the micrometer - instead use the ratchet (4) on the end of the micrometer. The ratchet mechanism applies a measured force preventing damage to the instrument.

● The micrometer is read by referring to the linear scale on the sleeve and the annular scale on the thimble. Read off the sleeve first to obtain the base measurement, then add the fine measurement from the thimble to obtain the overall reading. The linear scale on the sleeve represents the measuring range of the micrometer (eg 0 to 25 mm). The annular scale

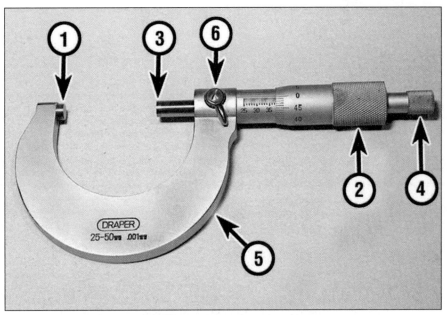

3.3 Micrometer component parts

1 Anvil	3 Spindle	5 Frame
2 Thimble	4 Ratchet	6 Locking lever

on the thimble will be in graduations of 0.01 mm (or as marked on the frame) - one full revolution of the thimble will move 0.5 mm on the linear scale. Take the reading where the datum line on the sleeve intersects the thimble's scale. Always position the eye directly above the scale otherwise an inaccurate reading will result.

In the example shown the item measures 2.95 mm (see illustration 3.4):

Linear scale	2.00 mm
Linear scale	0.50 mm
Annular scale	0.45 mm
Total figure	**2.95 mm**

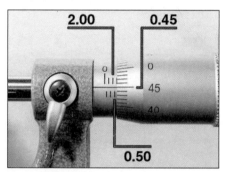

3.4 Micrometer reading of 2.95 mm

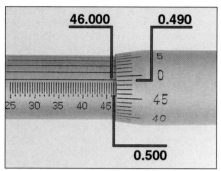

3.5 Micrometer reading of 46.99 mm on linear and annular scales . . .

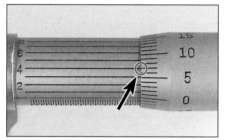

3.6 . . . and 0.004 mm on vernier scale

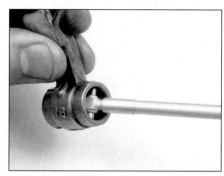

3.7 Expand the telescoping gauge in the bore, lock its position . . .

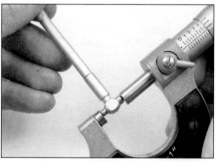

3.8 . . . then measure the gauge with a micrometer

Most micrometers have a locking lever (6) on the frame to hold the setting in place, allowing the item to be removed from the micrometer.
● Some micrometers have a vernier scale on their sleeve, providing an even finer measurement to be taken, in 0.001 increments of a millimetre. Take the sleeve and thimble measurement as described above, then check which graduation on the vernier scale aligns with that of the annular scale on the thimble **Note:** *The eye must be perpendicular to the scale when taking the vernier reading - if necessary rotate the body of the micrometer to ensure this.* Multiply the vernier scale figure by 0.001 and add it to the base and fine measurement figures.

In the example shown the item measures 46.994 mm (see illustrations 3.5 and 3.6):

Linear scale (base)	46.000 mm
Linear scale (base)	00.500 mm
Annular scale (fine)	00.490 mm
Vernier scale	00.004 mm
Total figure	**46.994 mm**

Internal micrometer

● Internal micrometers are available for measuring bore diameters, but are expensive and unlikely to be available for home use. It is suggested that a set of telescoping gauges and small hole gauges, both of which must be used with an external micrometer, will suffice for taking internal measurements on a motorcycle.
● Telescoping gauges can be used to measure internal diameters of components. Select a gauge with the correct size range, make sure its ends are clean and insert it into the bore. Expand the gauge, then lock its position and withdraw it from the bore (see illustration 3.7). Measure across the gauge ends with a micrometer (see illustration 3.8).
● Very small diameter bores (such as valve guides) are measured with a small hole gauge. Once adjusted to a slip-fit inside the component, its position is locked and the gauge withdrawn for measurement with a micrometer (see illustrations 3.9 and 3.10).

Vernier caliper

Note: *The conventional linear and dial gauge type instruments are described. Digital types are easier to read, but are far more expensive.*
● The vernier caliper does not provide the precision of a micrometer, but is versatile in being able to measure internal and external diameters. Some types also incorporate a depth gauge. It is ideal for measuring clutch plate friction material and spring free lengths.
● To use the conventional linear scale vernier, slacken off the vernier clamp screws (1) and set its jaws over (2), or inside (3), the item to be measured (see illustration 3.11). Slide the jaw into contact, using the thumb-wheel (4) for fine movement of the sliding scale (5) then tighten the clamp screws (1). Read off the main scale (6) where the zero on the sliding scale (5) intersects it, taking the whole number to the left of the zero; this provides the base measurement. View along the sliding scale and select the division which

3.9 Expand the small hole gauge in the bore, lock its position . . .

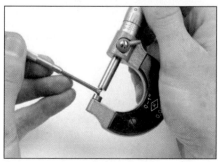

3.10 . . . then measure the gauge with a micrometer

lines up exactly with any of the divisions on the main scale, noting that the divisions usually represents 0.02 of a millimetre. Add this fine measurement to the base measurement to obtain the total reading.

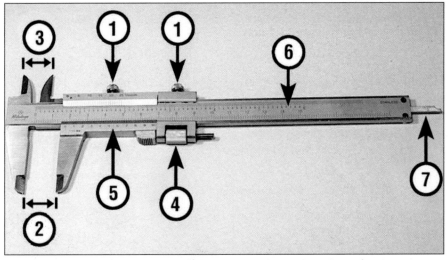

3.11 Vernier component parts (linear gauge)

1	Clamp screws	3	Internal jaws	5	Sliding scale	7	Depth gauge
2	External jaws	4	Thumbwheel	6	Main scale		

In the example shown the item measures 55.92 mm **(see illustration 3.12)**:

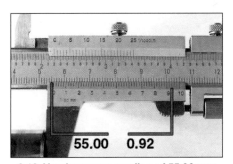

3.12 Vernier gauge reading of 55.92 mm

Base measurement	55.00 mm
Fine measurement	00.92 mm
Total figure	**55.92 mm**

● Some vernier calipers are equipped with a dial gauge for fine measurement. Before use, check that the jaws are clean, then close them fully and check that the dial gauge reads zero. If necessary adjust the gauge ring accordingly. Slacken the vernier clamp screw (1) and set its jaws over (2), or inside (3), the item to be measured **(see illustration 3.13)**. Slide the jaws into contact, using the thumbwheel (4) for fine movement. Read off the main scale (5) where the edge of the sliding scale (6) intersects it, taking the whole number to the left of the zero; this provides the base measurement. Read off the needle position on the dial gauge (7) scale to provide the fine measurement; each division represents 0.05 of a millimetre. Add this fine measurement to the base measurement to obtain the total reading.

In the example shown the item measures 55.95 mm **(see illustration 3.14)**:

Base measurement	55.00 mm
Fine measurement	00.95 mm
Total figure	**55.95 mm**

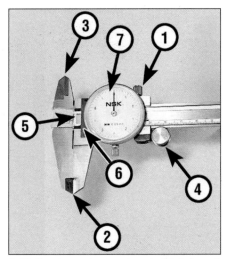

3.13 Vernier component parts (dial gauge)

1	Clamp screw	5	Main scale
2	External jaws	6	Sliding scale
3	Internal jaws	7	Dial gauge
4	Thumbwheel		

3.14 Vernier gauge reading of 55.95 mm

Plastigauge

● Plastigauge is a plastic material which can be compressed between two surfaces to measure the oil clearance between them. The width of the compressed Plastigauge is measured against a calibrated scale to determine the clearance.

● Common uses of Plastigauge are for measuring the clearance between crankshaft journal and main bearing inserts, between crankshaft journal and big-end bearing inserts, and between camshaft and bearing surfaces. The following example describes big-end oil clearance measurement.

● Handle the Plastigauge material carefully to prevent distortion. Using a sharp knife, cut a length which corresponds with the width of the bearing being measured and place it carefully across the journal so that it is parallel with the shaft **(see illustration 3.15)**. Carefully install both bearing shells and the connecting rod. Without rotating the rod on the journal tighten its bolts or nuts (as applicable) to the specified torque. The connecting rod and bearings are then disassembled and the crushed Plastigauge examined.

3.15 Plastigauge placed across shaft journal

● Using the scale provided in the Plastigauge kit, measure the width of the material to determine the oil clearance **(see illustration 3.16)**. Always remove all traces of Plastigauge after use using your fingernails.

Caution: Arriving at the correct clearance demands that the assembly is torqued correctly, according to the settings and sequence (where applicable) provided by the motorcycle manufacturer.

3.16 Measuring the width of the crushed Plastigauge

Dial gauge or DTI (Dial Test Indicator)

● A dial gauge can be used to accurately measure small amounts of movement. Typical uses are measuring shaft runout or shaft endfloat (sideplay) and setting piston position for ignition timing on two-strokes. A dial gauge set usually comes with a range of different probes and adapters and mounting equipment.

● The gauge needle must point to zero when at rest. Rotate the ring around its periphery to zero the gauge.

● Check that the gauge is capable of reading the extent of movement in the work. Most gauges have a small dial set in the face which records whole millimetres of movement as well as the fine scale around the face periphery which is calibrated in 0.01 mm divisions. Read off the small dial first to obtain the base measurement, then add the measurement from the fine scale to obtain the total reading.

In the example shown the gauge reads 1.48 mm (see illustration 3.17):

Base measurement	1.00 mm
Fine measurement	0.48 mm
Total figure	**1.48 mm**

3.17 Dial gauge reading of 1.48 mm

● If measuring shaft runout, the shaft must be supported in vee-blocks and the gauge mounted on a stand perpendicular to the shaft. Rest the tip of the gauge against the centre of the shaft and rotate the shaft slowly whilst watching the gauge reading (see illustration 3.18). Take several measurements along the length of the shaft and record the

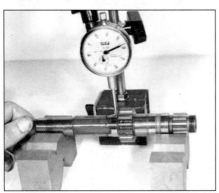

3.18 Using a dial gauge to measure shaft runout

maximum gauge reading as the amount of runout in the shaft. **Note:** *The reading obtained will be total runout at that point - some manufacturers specify that the runout figure is halved to compare with their specified runout limit.*

● Endfloat (sideplay) measurement requires that the gauge is mounted securely to the surrounding component with its probe touching the end of the shaft. Using hand pressure, push and pull on the shaft noting the maximum endfloat recorded on the gauge (see illustration 3.19).

3.19 Using a dial gauge to measure shaft endfloat

● A dial gauge with suitable adapters can be used to determine piston position BTDC on two-stroke engines for the purposes of ignition timing. The gauge, adapter and suitable length probe are installed in the place of the spark plug and the gauge zeroed at TDC. If the piston position is specified as 1.14 mm BTDC, rotate the engine back to 2.00 mm BTDC, then slowly forwards to 1.14 mm BTDC.

Cylinder compression gauges

● A compression gauge is used for measuring cylinder compression. Either the rubber-cone type or the threaded adapter type can be used. The latter is preferred to ensure a perfect seal against the cylinder head. A 0 to 300 psi (0 to 20 Bar) type gauge (for petrol/gasoline engines) will be suitable for motorcycles.

● The spark plug is removed and the gauge either held hard against the cylinder head (cone type) or the gauge adapter screwed into the cylinder head (threaded type) (see illustration 3.20). Cylinder compression is measured with the engine turning over, but not running - carry out the compression test as described in

3.20 Using a rubber-cone type cylinder compression gauge

Fault Finding Equipment. The gauge will hold the reading until manually released.

Oil pressure gauge

● An oil pressure gauge is used for measuring engine oil pressure. Most gauges come with a set of adapters to fit the thread of the take-off point (see illustration 3.21). If the take-off point specified by the motorcycle manufacturer is an external oil pipe union, make sure that the specified replacement union is used to prevent oil starvation.

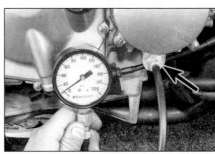

3.21 Oil pressure gauge and take-off point adapter (arrow)

● Oil pressure is measured with the engine running (at a specific rpm) and often the manufacturer will specify pressure limits for a cold and hot engine.

Straight-edge and surface plate

● If checking the gasket face of a component for warpage, place a steel rule or precision straight-edge across the gasket face and measure any gap between the straight-edge and component with feeler gauges (see illustration 3.22). Check diagonally across the component and between mounting holes (see illustration 3.23).

3.22 Use a straight-edge and feeler gauges to check for warpage

3.23 Check for warpage in these directions

● Checking individual components for warpage, such as clutch plain (metal) plates, requires a perfectly flat plate or piece or plate glass and feeler gauges.

4 Torque and leverage

What is torque?

● Torque describes the twisting force about a shaft. The amount of torque applied is determined by the distance from the centre of the shaft to the end of the lever and the amount of force being applied to the end of the lever; distance multiplied by force equals torque.

● The manufacturer applies a measured torque to a bolt or nut to ensure that it will not slacken in use and to hold two components securely together without movement in the joint. The actual torque setting depends on the thread size, bolt or nut material and the composition of the components being held.

● Too little torque may cause the fastener to loosen due to vibration, whereas too much torque will distort the joint faces of the component or cause the fastener to shear off. Always stick to the specified torque setting.

Using a torque wrench

● Check the calibration of the torque wrench and make sure it has a suitable range for the job. Torque wrenches are available in Nm (Newton-metres), kgf m (kilograms-force metre), lbf ft (pounds-feet), lbf in (inch-pounds). Do not confuse lbf ft with lbf in.

● Adjust the tool to the desired torque on the scale (see illustration 4.1). If your torque wrench is not calibrated in the units specified, carefully convert the figure (see *Conversion Factors*). A manufacturer sometimes gives a torque setting as a range (8 to 10 Nm) rather than a single figure - in this case set the tool midway between the two settings. The same torque may be expressed as 9 Nm ± 1 Nm. Some torque wrenches have a method of locking the setting so that it isn't inadvertently altered during use.

4.1 Set the torque wrench index mark to the setting required, in this case 12 Nm

● Install the bolts/nuts in their correct location and secure them lightly. Their threads must be clean and free of any old locking compound. Unless specified the threads and flange should be dry - oiled threads are necessary in certain circumstances and the manufacturer will take this into account in the specified torque figure. Similarly, the manufacturer may also specify the application of thread-locking compound.

● Tighten the fasteners in the specified sequence until the torque wrench clicks, indicating that the torque setting has been reached. Apply the torque again to double-check the setting. Where different thread diameter fasteners secure the component, as a rule tighten the larger diameter ones first.

● When the torque wrench has been finished with, release the lock (where applicable) and fully back off its setting to zero - do not leave the torque wrench tensioned. Also, do not use a torque wrench for slackening a fastener.

Angle-tightening

● Manufacturers often specify a figure in degrees for final tightening of a fastener. This usually follows tightening to a specific torque setting.

● A degree disc can be set and attached to the socket (see illustration 4.2) or a protractor can be used to mark the angle of movement on the bolt/nut head and the surrounding casting (see illustration 4.3).

4.2 Angle tightening can be accomplished with a torque-angle gauge . . .

4.3 . . . or by marking the angle on the surrounding component

Loosening sequences

● Where more than one bolt/nut secures a component, loosen each fastener evenly a little at a time. In this way, not all the stress of the joint is held by one fastener and the components are not likely to distort.

● If a tightening sequence is provided, work in the REVERSE of this, but if not, work from the outside in, in a criss-cross sequence (see illustration 4.4).

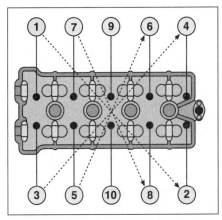

4.4 When slackening, work from the outside inwards

Tightening sequences

● If a component is held by more than one fastener it is important that the retaining bolts/nuts are tightened evenly to prevent uneven stress build-up and distortion of sealing faces. This is especially important on high-compression joints such as the cylinder head.

● A sequence is usually provided by the manufacturer, either in a diagram or actually marked in the casting. If not, always start in the centre and work outwards in a criss-cross pattern (see illustration 4.5). Start off by securing all bolts/nuts finger-tight, then set the torque wrench and tighten each fastener by a small amount in sequence until the final torque is reached. By following this practice,

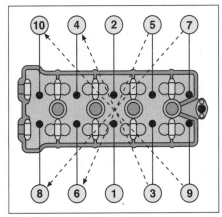

4.5 When tightening, work from the inside outwards

the joint will be held evenly and will not be distorted. Important joints, such as the cylinder head and big-end fasteners often have two- or three-stage torque settings.

Applying leverage

● Use tools at the correct angle. Position a socket wrench or spanner on the bolt/nut so that you pull it towards you when loosening. If this can't be done, push the spanner without curling your fingers around it **(see illustration 4.6)** - the spanner may slip or the fastener loosen suddenly, resulting in your fingers being crushed against a component.

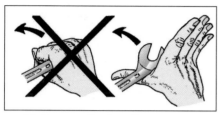

4.6 If you can't pull on the spanner to loosen a fastener, push with your hand open

● Additional leverage is gained by extending the length of the lever. The best way to do this is to use a breaker bar instead of the regular length tool, or to slip a length of tubing over the end of the spanner or socket wrench.
● If additional leverage will not work, the fastener head is either damaged or firmly corroded in place (see *Fasteners*).

5 Bearings

Bearing removal and installation

Drivers and sockets

● Before removing a bearing, always inspect the casing to see which way it must be driven out - some casings will have retaining plates or a cast step. Also check for any identifying markings on the bearing and if installed to a certain depth, measure this at this stage. Some roller bearings are sealed on one side - take note of the original fitted position.
● Bearings can be driven out of a casing using a bearing driver tool (with the correct size head) or a socket of the correct diameter. Select the driver head or socket so that it contacts the outer race of the bearing, not the balls/rollers or inner race. Always support the casing around the bearing housing with wood blocks, otherwise there is a risk of fracture. The bearing is driven out with a few blows on the driver or socket from a heavy mallet. Unless access is severely restricted (as with wheel bearings), a pin-punch is not recommended unless it is moved around the bearing to keep it square in its housing.

● The same equipment can be used to install bearings. Make sure the bearing housing is supported on wood blocks and line up the bearing in its housing. Fit the bearing as noted on removal - generally they are installed with their marked side facing outwards. Tap the bearing squarely into its housing using a driver or socket which bears only on the bearing's outer race - contact with the bearing balls/rollers or inner race will destroy it **(see illustrations 5.1 and 5.2)**.
● Check that the bearing inner race and balls/rollers rotate freely.

5.1 Using a bearing driver against the bearing's outer race

5.2 Using a large socket against the bearing's outer race

Pullers and slide-hammers

● Where a bearing is pressed on a shaft a puller will be required to extract it **(see illustration 5.3)**. Make sure that the puller clamp or legs fit securely behind the bearing and are unlikely to slip out. If pulling a bearing

5.3 This bearing puller clamps behind the bearing and pressure is applied to the shaft end to draw the bearing off

off a gear shaft for example, you may have to locate the puller behind a gear pinion if there is no access to the race and draw the gear pinion off the shaft as well **(see illustration 5.4)**.

> *Caution: Ensure that the puller's centre bolt locates securely against the end of the shaft and will not slip when pressure is applied. Also ensure that puller does not damage the shaft end.*

5.4 Where no access is available to the rear of the bearing, it is sometimes possible to draw off the adjacent component

● Operate the puller so that its centre bolt exerts pressure on the shaft end and draws the bearing off the shaft.
● When installing the bearing on the shaft, tap only on the bearing's inner race - contact with the balls/rollers or outer race with destroy the bearing. Use a socket or length of tubing as a drift which fits over the shaft end **(see illustration 5.5)**.

5.5 When installing a bearing on a shaft use a piece of tubing which bears only on the bearing's inner race

● Where a bearing locates in a blind hole in a casing, it cannot be driven or pulled out as described above. A slide-hammer with knife-edged bearing puller attachment will be required. The puller attachment passes through the bearing and when tightened expands to fit firmly behind the bearing **(see illustration 5.6)**. By operating the slide-hammer part of the tool the bearing is jarred out of its housing **(see illustration 5.7)**.
● It is possible, if the bearing is of reasonable weight, for it to drop out of its housing if the casing is heated as described opposite. If this

5.6 Expand the bearing puller so that it locks behind the bearing . . .

5.7 . . . attach the slide hammer to the bearing puller

method is attempted, first prepare a work surface which will enable the casing to be tapped face down to help dislodge the bearing - a wood surface is ideal since it will not damage the casing's gasket surface. Wearing protective gloves, tap the heated casing several times against the work surface to dislodge the bearing under its own weight **(see illustration 5.8)**.

5.8 Tapping a casing face down on wood blocks can often dislodge a bearing

● Bearings can be installed in blind holes using the driver or socket method described above.

Drawbolts

● Where a bearing or bush is set in the eye of a component, such as a suspension linkage arm or connecting rod small-end, removal by drift may damage the component. Furthermore, a rubber bushing in a shock absorber eye cannot successfully be driven out of position. If access is available to a engineering press, the task is straightforward. If not, a drawbolt can be fabricated to extract the bearing or bush.

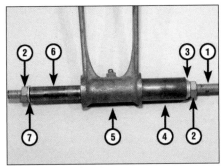

5.9 Drawbolt component parts assembled on a suspension arm

1 Bolt or length of threaded bar
2 Nuts
3 Washer (external diameter greater than tubing internal diameter)
4 Tubing (internal diameter sufficient to accommodate bearing)
5 Suspension arm with bearing
6 Tubing (external diameter slightly smaller than bearing)
7 Washer (external diameter slightly smaller than bearing)

5.10 Drawing the bearing out of the suspension arm

● To extract the bearing/bush you will need a long bolt with nut (or piece of threaded bar with two nuts), a piece of tubing which has an internal diameter larger than the bearing/bush, another piece of tubing which has an external diameter slightly smaller than the bearing/bush, and a selection of washers **(see illustrations 5.9 and 5.10)**. Note that the pieces of tubing must be of the same length, or longer, than the bearing/bush.

● The same kit (without the pieces of tubing) can be used to draw the new bearing/bush back into place **(see illustration 5.11)**.

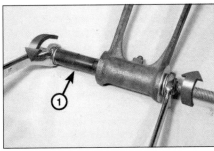

5.11 Installing a new bearing (1) in the suspension arm

Temperature change

● If the bearing's outer race is a tight fit in the casing, the aluminium casing can be heated to release its grip on the bearing. Aluminium will expand at a greater rate than the steel bearing outer race. There are several ways to do this, but avoid any localised extreme heat (such as a blow torch) - aluminium alloy has a low melting point.

● Approved methods of heating a casing are using a domestic oven (heated to 100°C) or immersing the casing in boiling water **(see illustration 5.12)**. Low temperature range localised heat sources such as a paint stripper heat gun or clothes iron can also be used **(see illustration 5.13)**. Alternatively, soak a rag in boiling water, wring it out and wrap it around the bearing housing.

> ⚠ **Warning: All of these methods require care in use to prevent scalding and burns to the hands. Wear protective gloves when handling hot components.**

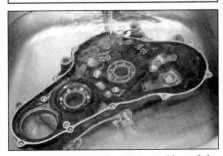

5.12 A casing can be immersed in a sink of boiling water to aid bearing removal

5.13 Using a localised heat source to aid bearing removal

● If heating the whole casing note that plastic components, such as the neutral switch, may suffer - remove them beforehand.

● After heating, remove the bearing as described above. You may find that the expansion is sufficient for the bearing to fall out of the casing under its own weight or with a light tap on the driver or socket.

● If necessary, the casing can be heated to aid bearing installation, and this is sometimes the recommended procedure if the motorcycle manufacturer has designed the housing and bearing fit with this intention.

● Installation of bearings can be eased by placing them in a freezer the night before installation. The steel bearing will contract slightly, allowing easy insertion in its housing. This is often useful when installing steering head outer races in the frame.

Bearing types and markings

● Plain shell bearings, ball bearings, needle roller bearings and tapered roller bearings will all be found on motorcycles (see illustrations 5.14 and 5.15). The ball and roller types are usually caged between an inner and outer race, but uncaged variations may be found.

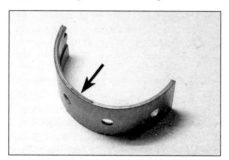

5.14 Shell bearings are either plain or grooved. They are usually identified by colour code (arrow)

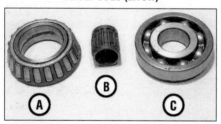

5.15 Tapered roller bearing (A), needle roller bearing (B) and ball journal bearing (C)

● Shell bearings (often called inserts) are usually found at the crankshaft main and connecting rod big-end where they are good at coping with high loads. They are made of a phosphor-bronze material and are impregnated with self-lubricating properties.

● Ball bearings and needle roller bearings consist of a steel inner and outer race with the balls or rollers between the races. They require constant lubrication by oil or grease and are good at coping with axial loads. Taper roller bearings consist of rollers set in a tapered cage set on the inner race; the outer race is separate. They are good at coping with axial loads and prevent movement along the shaft - a typical application is in the steering head.

● Bearing manufacturers produce bearings to ISO size standards and stamp one face of the bearing to indicate its internal and external diameter, load capacity and type (see illustration 5.16).

● Metal bushes are usually of phosphor-bronze material. Rubber bushes are used in suspension mounting eyes. Fibre bushes have also been used in suspension pivots.

5.16 Typical bearing marking

Bearing fault finding

● If a bearing outer race has spun in its housing, the housing material will be damaged. You can use a bearing locking compound to bond the outer race in place if damage is not too severe.

● Shell bearings will fail due to damage of their working surface, as a result of lack of lubrication, corrosion or abrasive particles in the oil (see illustration 5.17). Small particles of dirt in the oil may embed in the bearing material whereas larger particles will score the bearing and shaft journal. If a number of short journeys are made, insufficient heat will be generated to drive off condensation which has built up on the bearings.

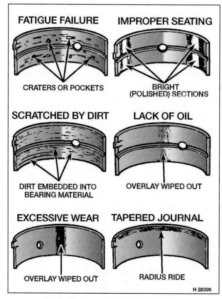

5.17 Typical bearing failures

● Ball and roller bearings will fail due to lack of lubrication or damage to the balls or rollers. Tapered-roller bearings can be damaged by overloading them. Unless the bearing is sealed on both sides, wash it in paraffin (kerosene) to remove all old grease then allow it to dry. Make a visual inspection looking to dented balls or rollers, damaged cages and worn or pitted races (see illustration 5.18).

● A ball bearing can be checked for wear by listening to it when spun. Apply a film of light oil to the bearing and hold it close to the ear - hold the outer race with one hand and spin the inner

5.18 Example of ball journal bearing with damaged balls and cages

5.19 Hold outer race and listen to inner race when spun

race with the other hand (see illustration 5.19). The bearing should be almost silent when spun; if it grates or rattles it is worn.

6 Oil seals

Oil seal removal and installation

● Oil seals should be renewed every time a component is dismantled. This is because the seal lips will become set to the sealing surface and will not necessarily reseal.

● Oil seals can be prised out of position using a large flat-bladed screwdriver (see illustration 6.1). In the case of crankcase seals, check first that the seal is not lipped on the inside, preventing its removal with the crankcases joined.

6.1 Prise out oil seals with a large flat-bladed screwdriver

● New seals are usually installed with their marked face (containing the seal reference code) outwards and the spring side towards the fluid being retained. In certain cases, such as a two-stroke engine crankshaft seal, a double lipped seal may be used due to there being fluid or gas on each side of the joint.

● Use a bearing driver or socket which bears only on the outer hard edge of the seal to install it in the casing - tapping on the inner edge will damage the sealing lip.

Oil seal types and markings

● Oil seals are usually of the single-lipped type. Double-lipped seals are found where a liquid or gas is on both sides of the joint.
● Oil seals can harden and lose their sealing ability if the motorcycle has been in storage for a long period - renewal is the only solution.
● Oil seal manufacturers also conform to the ISO markings for seal size - these are moulded into the outer face of the seal **(see illustration 6.2)**.

6.2 These oil seal markings indicate inside diameter, outside diameter and seal thickness

7 Gaskets and sealants

Types of gasket and sealant

● Gaskets are used to seal the mating surfaces between components and keep lubricants, fluids, vacuum or pressure contained within the assembly. Aluminium gaskets are sometimes found at the cylinder joints, but most gaskets are paper-based. If the mating surfaces of the components being joined are undamaged the gasket can be installed dry, although a dab of sealant or grease will be useful to hold it in place during assembly.
● RTV (Room Temperature Vulcanising) silicone rubber sealants cure when exposed to moisture in the atmosphere. These sealants are good at filling pits or irregular gasket faces, but will tend to be forced out of the joint under very high torque. They can be used to replace a paper gasket, but first make sure that the width of the paper gasket is not essential to the shimming of internal components. RTV sealants should not be used on components containing petrol (gasoline).
● Non-hardening, semi-hardening and hard setting liquid gasket compounds can be used with a gasket or between a metal-to-metal joint. Select the sealant to suit the application: universal non-hardening sealant can be used on virtually all joints; semi-hardening on joint faces which are rough or damaged; hard setting sealant on joints which require a permanent bond and are subjected to high temperature and pressure. **Note:** *Check first if the paper gasket has a bead of sealant*

impregnated in its surface before applying additional sealant.
● When choosing a sealant, make sure it is suitable for the application, particularly if being applied in a high-temperature area or in the vicinity of fuel. Certain manufacturers produce sealants in either clear, silver or black colours to match the finish of the engine. This has a particular application on motorcycles where much of the engine is exposed.
● Do not over-apply sealant. That which is squeezed out on the outside of the joint can be wiped off, whereas an excess of sealant on the inside can break off and clog oilways.

Breaking a sealed joint

● Age, heat, pressure and the use of hard setting sealant can cause two components to stick together so tightly that they are difficult to separate using finger pressure alone. Do not resort to using levers unless there is a pry point provided for this purpose **(see illustration 7.1)** or else the gasket surfaces will be damaged.
● Use a soft-faced hammer **(see illustration 7.2)** or a wood block and conventional hammer to strike the component near the mating surface. Avoid hammering against cast extremities since they may break off. If this method fails, try using a wood wedge between the two components.

Caution: If the joint will not separate, double-check that you have removed all the fasteners.

7.1 If a pry point is provided, apply gently pressure with a flat-bladed screwdriver

7.2 Tap around the joint with a soft-faced mallet if necessary - don't strike cooling fins

Removal of old gasket and sealant

● Paper gaskets will most likely come away complete, leaving only a few traces stuck on

Most components have one or two hollow locating dowels between the two gasket faces. If a dowel cannot be removed, do not resort to gripping it with pliers - it will almost certainly be distorted. Install a close-fitting socket or Phillips screwdriver into the dowel and then grip the outer edge of the dowel to free it.

the sealing faces of the components. It is imperative that all traces are removed to ensure correct sealing of the new gasket.
● Very carefully scrape all traces of gasket away making sure that the sealing surfaces are not gouged or scored by the scraper **(see illustrations 7.3, 7.4 and 7.5)**. Stubborn deposits can be removed by spraying with an aerosol gasket remover. Final preparation of

7.3 Paper gaskets can be scraped off with a gasket scraper tool . . .

7.4 . . . a knife blade . . .

7.5 . . . or a household scraper

7.6 Fine abrasive paper is wrapped around a flat file to clean up the gasket face

7.7 A kitchen scourer can be used on stubborn deposits

the gasket surface can be made with very fine abrasive paper or a plastic kitchen scourer **(see illustrations 7.6 and 7.7)**.

● Old sealant can be scraped or peeled off components, depending on the type originally used. Note that gasket removal compounds are available to avoid scraping the components clean; make sure the gasket remover suits the type of sealant used.

8 Chains

Breaking and joining final drive chains

● Drive chains for all but small bikes are continuous and do not have a clip-type connecting link. The chain must be broken using a chain breaker tool and the new chain securely riveted together using a new soft rivet-type link. Never use a clip-type connecting link instead of a rivet-type link, except in an emergency. Various chain breaking and riveting tools are available, either as separate tools or combined as illustrated in the accompanying photographs - read the instructions supplied with the tool carefully.

> ⚠ **Warning: The need to rivet the new link pins correctly cannot be overstressed - loss of control of the motorcycle is very likely to result if the chain breaks in use.**

● Rotate the chain and look for the soft link. The soft link pins look like they have been

8.1 Tighten the chain breaker to push the pin out of the link . . .

8.2 . . . withdraw the pin, remove the tool . . .

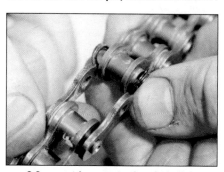

8.3 . . . and separate the chain link

deeply centre-punched instead of peened over like all the other pins **(see illustration 8.9)** and its sideplate may be a different colour. Position the soft link midway between the sprockets and assemble the chain breaker tool over one of the soft link pins **(see illustration 8.1)**. Operate the tool to push the pin out through the chain **(see illustration 8.2)**. On an O-ring chain, remove the O-rings **(see illustration 8.3)**. Carry out the same procedure on the other soft link pin.

> **Caution: Certain soft link pins (particularly on the larger chains) may require their ends to be filed or ground off before they can be pressed out using the tool.**

● Check that you have the correct size and strength (standard or heavy duty) new soft link - do not reuse the old link. Look for the size marking on the chain sideplates **(see illustration 8.10)**.

● Position the chain ends so that they are engaged over the rear sprocket. On an O-ring

8.4 Insert the new soft link, with O-rings, through the chain ends . . .

8.5 . . . install the O-rings over the pin ends . . .

8.6 . . . followed by the sideplate

chain, install a new O-ring over each pin of the link and insert the link through the two chain ends **(see illustration 8.4)**. Install a new O-ring over the end of each pin, followed by the sideplate (with the chain manufacturer's marking facing outwards) **(see illustrations 8.5 and 8.6)**. On an unsealed chain, insert the link through the two chain ends, then install the sideplate with the chain manufacturer's marking facing outwards.

● Note that it may not be possible to install the sideplate using finger pressure alone. If using a joining tool, assemble it so that the plates of the tool clamp the link and press the sideplate over the pins **(see illustration 8.7)**. Otherwise, use two small sockets placed over

8.7 Push the sideplate into position using a clamp

8.8 Assemble the chain riveting tool over one pin at a time and tighten it fully

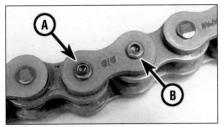

8.9 Pin end correctly riveted (A), pin end unriveted (B)

the rivet ends and two pieces of the wood between a G-clamp. Operate the clamp to press the sideplate over the pins.

● Assemble the joining tool over one pin (following the maker's instructions) and tighten the tool down to spread the pin end securely **(see illustrations 8.8 and 8.9)**. Do the same on the other pin.

> ⚠️ **Warning: Check that the pin ends are secure and that there is no danger of the sideplate coming loose. If the pin ends are cracked the soft link must be renewed.**

Final drive chain sizing

● Chains are sized using a three digit number, followed by a suffix to denote the chain type **(see illustration 8.10)**. Chain type is either standard or heavy duty (thicker sideplates), and also unsealed or O-ring/X-ring type.

● The first digit of the number relates to the pitch of the chain, ie the distance from the centre of one pin to the centre of the next pin **(see illustration 8.11)**. Pitch is expressed in eighths of an inch, as follows:

8.10 Typical chain size and type marking

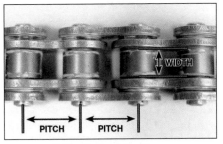

8.11 Chain dimensions

Sizes commencing with a 4 (eg 428) have a pitch of 1/2 inch (12.7 mm)
Sizes commencing with a 5 (eg 520) have a pitch of 5/8 inch (15.9 mm)
Sizes commencing with a 6 (eg 630) have a pitch of 3/4 inch (19.1 mm)

● The second and third digits of the chain size relate to the width of the rollers, again in imperial units, eg the 525 shown has 5/16 inch (7.94 mm) rollers **(see illustration 8.11)**.

9 Hoses

Clamping to prevent flow

● Small-bore flexible hoses can be clamped to prevent fluid flow whilst a component is worked on. Whichever method is used, ensure that the hose material is not permanently distorted or damaged by the clamp.

a) A brake hose clamp available from auto accessory shops **(see illustration 9.1)**.
b) A wingnut type hose clamp **(see illustration 9.2)**.

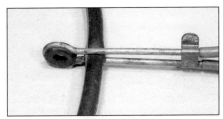

9.1 Hoses can be clamped with an automotive brake hose clamp . . .

9.2 . . . a wingnut type hose clamp . . .

c) Two sockets placed each side of the hose and held with straight-jawed self-locking grips **(see illustration 9.3)**.
d) Thick card each side of the hose held between straight-jawed self-locking grips **(see illustration 9.4)**.

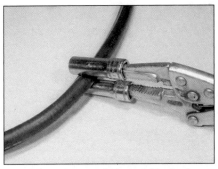

9.3 . . . two sockets and a pair of self-locking grips . . .

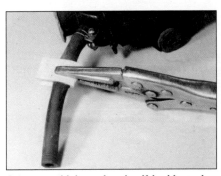

9.4 . . . or thick card and self-locking grips

Freeing and fitting hoses

● Always make sure the hose clamp is moved well clear of the hose end. Grip the hose with your hand and rotate it whilst pulling it off the union. If the hose has hardened due to age and will not move, slit it with a sharp knife and peel its ends off the union **(see illustration 9.5)**.

● Resist the temptation to use grease or soap on the unions to aid installation; although it helps the hose slip over the union it will equally aid the escape of fluid from the joint. It is preferable to soften the hose ends in hot water and wet the inside surface of the hose with water or a fluid which will evaporate.

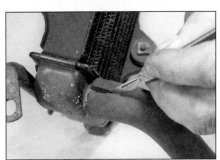

9.5 Cutting a coolant hose free with a sharp knife

Introduction

In less time than it takes to read this introduction, a thief could steal your motorcycle. Returning only to find your bike has gone is one of the worst feelings in the world. Even if the motorcycle is insured against theft, once you've got over the initial shock, you will have the inconvenience of dealing with the police and your insurance company.

The motorcycle is an easy target for the professional thief and the joyrider alike and the official figures on motorcycle theft make for depressing reading; on average a motorcycle is stolen every 16 minutes in the UK!

Motorcycle thefts fall into two categories, those stolen 'to order' and those taken by opportunists. The thief stealing to order will be on the look out for a specific make and model and will go to extraordinary lengths to obtain that motorcycle. The opportunist thief on the other hand will look for easy targets which can be stolen with the minimum of effort and risk.

Whilst it is never going to be possible to make your machine 100% secure, it is estimated that around half of all stolen motorcycles are taken by opportunist thieves. Remember that the opportunist thief is always on the look out for the easy option: if there are two similar motorcycles parked side-by-side, they will target the one with the lowest level of security. By taking a few precautions, you can reduce the chances of your motorcycle being stolen.

Security equipment

There are many specialised motorcycle security devices available and the following text summarises their applications and their good and bad points.

Once you have decided on the type of security equipment which best suits your needs, we recommended that you read one of the many equipment tests regularly carried out by the motorcycle press. These tests compare the products from all the major manufacturers and give impartial ratings on their effectiveness, value-for-money and ease of use.

No one item of security equipment can provide complete protection. It is highly recommended that two or more of the items described below are combined to increase the security of your motorcycle (a lock and chain plus an alarm system is just about ideal). The more security measures fitted to the bike, the less likely it is to be stolen.

Lock and chain

Pros: *Very flexible to use; can be used to secure the motorcycle to almost any immovable object. On some locks and chains, the lock can be used on its own as a disc lock (see below).*

Cons: *Can be very heavy and awkward to carry on the motorcycle, although some types will be supplied with a carry bag which can be strapped to the pillion seat.*

● Heavy-duty chains and locks are an excellent security measure **(see illustration 1)**. Whenever the motorcycle is parked, use the lock and chain to secure the machine to a solid, immovable object such as a post or railings. This will prevent the machine from being ridden away or being lifted into the back of a van.

● When fitting the chain, always ensure the chain is routed around the motorcycle frame or swingarm **(see illustrations 2 and 3)**. Never merely pass the chain around one of the wheel rims; a thief may unbolt the wheel and lift the rest of the machine into a van, leaving you with just the wheel! Try to avoid having excess chain free, thus making it difficult to use cutting tools, and keep the chain and lock off the ground to prevent thieves attacking it with a cold chisel. Position the lock so that its lock barrel is facing downwards; this will make it harder for the thief to attack the lock mechanism.

Ensure the lock and chain you buy is of good quality and long enough to shackle your bike to a solid object

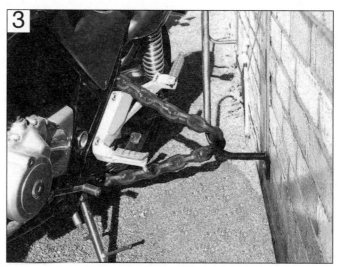

Pass the chain through the bike's frame, rather than just through a wheel . . .

. . . and loop it around a solid object

U-locks

Pros: *Highly effective deterrent which can be used to secure the bike to a post or railings. Most U-locks come with a carrier which allows the lock to be easily carried on the bike.*

Cons: *Not as flexible to use as a lock and chain.*

● These are solid locks which are similar in use to a lock and chain. U-locks are lighter than a lock and chain but not so flexible to use. The length and shape of the lock shackle limit the objects to which the bike can be secured **(see illustration 4)**.

Disc locks

Pros: *Small, light and very easy to carry; most can be stored underneath the seat.*

Cons: *Does not prevent the motorcycle being lifted into a van. Can be very embarrassing if you*

U-locks can be used to secure the bike to a solid object – ensure you purchase one which is long enough

forget to remove the lock before attempting to ride off!

● Disc locks are designed to be attached to the front brake disc. The lock passes through one of the holes in the disc and prevents the wheel rotating by jamming against the fork/brake caliper **(see illustration 5)**. Some are equipped with an alarm siren which sounds if the disc lock is moved; this not only acts as a theft deterrent but also as a handy reminder if you try to move the bike with the lock still fitted.

● Combining the disc lock with a length of cable which can be looped around a post or railings provides an additional measure of security **(see illustration 6)**.

Alarms and immobilisers

Pros: *Once installed it is completely hassle-free to use. If the system is 'Thatcham' or 'Sold Secure-approved', insurance companies may give you a discount.*

Cons: *Can be expensive to buy and complex to install. No system will prevent the motorcycle from being lifted into a van and taken away.*

● Electronic alarms and immobilisers are available to suit a variety of budgets. There are three different types of system available: pure alarms, pure immobilisers, and the more expensive systems which are combined alarm/immobilisers **(see illustration 7)**.
● An alarm system is designed to emit an audible warning if the motorcycle is being tampered with.
● An immobiliser prevents the motorcycle being started and ridden away by disabling its electrical systems.
● When purchasing an alarm/immobiliser system, check the cost of installing the system unless you are able to do it yourself. If the motorcycle is not used regularly, another consideration is the current drain of the system. All alarm/immobiliser systems are powered by the motorcycle's battery; purchasing a system with a very low current drain could prevent the battery losing its charge whilst the motorcycle is not being used.

A typical disc lock attached through one of the holes in the disc

A disc lock combined with a security cable provides additional protection

A typical alarm/immobiliser system

Indelible markings can be applied to most areas of the bike – always apply the manufacturer's sticker to warn off thieves

Chemically-etched code numbers can be applied to main body panels . . .

. . . again, always ensure that the kit manufacturer's sticker is applied in a prominent position

Security marking kits

Pros: *Very cheap and effective deterrent. Many insurance companies will give you a discount on your insurance premium if a recognised security marking kit is used on your motorcycle.*

Cons: *Does not prevent the motorcycle being stolen by joyriders.*

● There are many different types of security marking kits available. The idea is to mark as many parts of the motorcycle as possible with a unique security number **(see illustrations 8, 9 and 10)**. A form will be included with the kit to register your personal details and those of the motorcycle with the kit manufacturer. This register is made available to the police to help them trace the rightful owner of any motorcycle or components which they recover should all other forms of identification have been removed. Always apply the warning stickers provided with the kit to deter thieves.

Ground anchors, wheel clamps and security posts

Pros: *An excellent form of security which will deter all but the most determined of thieves.*

Cons: *Awkward to install and can be expensive.*

● Whilst the motorcycle is at home, it is a good idea to attach it securely to the floor or a solid wall, even if it is kept in a securely locked garage. Various types of ground anchors, security posts and wheel clamps are available for this purpose **(see illustration 11)**. These security devices are either bolted to a solid concrete or brick structure or can be cemented into the ground.

Permanent ground anchors provide an excellent level of security when the bike is at home

Security at home

A high percentage of motorcycle thefts are from the owner's home. Here are some things to consider whenever your motorcycle is at home:

✔ Where possible, always keep the motorcycle in a securely locked garage. Never rely solely on the standard lock on the garage door, these are usual hopelessly inadequate. Fit an additional locking mechanism to the door and consider having the garage alarmed. A security light, activated by a movement sensor, is also a good investment.

✔ Always secure the motorcycle to the ground or a wall, even if it is inside a securely locked garage.
✔ Do not regularly leave the motorcycle outside your home, try to keep it out of sight wherever possible. If a garage is not available, fit a motorcycle cover over the bike to disguise its true identity.
✔ It is not uncommon for thieves to follow a motorcyclist home to find out where the bike is kept. They will then return at a later date. Be aware of this whenever you are returning

home on your motorcycle. If you suspect you are being followed, do not return home, instead ride to a garage or shop and stop as a precaution.
✔ When selling a motorcycle, do not provide your home address or the location where the bike is normally kept. Arrange to meet the buyer at a location away from your home. Thieves have been known to pose as potential buyers to find out where motorcycles are kept and then return later to steal them.

Security away from the home

As well as fitting security equipment to your motorcycle here are a few general rules to follow whenever you park your motorcycle.
✔ Park in a busy, public place.
✔ Use car parks which incorporate security features, such as CCTV.

✔ At night, park in a well-lit area, preferably directly underneath a street light.
✔ Engage the steering lock.
✔ Secure the motorcycle to a solid, immovable object such as a post or railings with an additional lock. If this is not possible,

secure the bike to a friend's motorcycle. Some public parking places provide security loops for motorcycles.
✔ Never leave your helmet or luggage attached to the motorcycle. Take them with you at all times.

Lubricants and fluids

A wide range of lubricants, fluids and cleaning agents is available for motor-cycles. This is a guide as to what is available, its applications and properties.

Four-stroke engine oil

● Engine oil is without doubt the most important component of any four-stroke engine. Modern motorcycle engines place a lot of demands on their oil and choosing the right type is essential. Using an unsuitable oil will lead to an increased rate of engine wear and could result in serious engine damage. Before purchasing oil, always check the recommended oil specification given by the manufacturer. The manufacturer will state a recommended 'type or classification' and also a specific 'viscosity' range for engine oil.

● The oil 'type or classification' is identified by its API (American Petroleum Institute) rating. The API rating will be in the form of two letters, e.g. SG. The S identifies the oil as being suitable for use in a petrol (gasoline) engine (S stands for spark ignition) and the second letter, ranging from A to J, identifies the oil's performance rating. The later this letter, the higher the specification of the oil; for example API SG oil exceeds the requirements of API SF oil. **Note:** *On some oils there may also be a second rating consisting of another two letters, the first letter being C, e.g. API SF/CD. This rating indicates the oil is also suitable for use in a diesel engines (the C stands for compression ignition) and is thus of no relevance for motorcycle use.*

● The 'viscosity' of the oil is identified by its SAE (Society of Automotive Engineers) rating. All modern engines require multigrade oils and the SAE rating will consist of two numbers, the first followed by a W, e.g.

10W/40. The first number indicates the viscosity rating of the oil at low temperatures (W stands for winter – tested at –20°C) and the second number represents the viscosity of the oil at high temperatures (tested at 100°C). The lower the number, the thinner the oil. For example an oil with an SAE 10W/40 rating will give better cold starting and running than an SAE 15W/40 oil.

● As well as ensuring the 'type' and 'viscosity' of the oil match the recommendations, another consideration to make when buying engine oil is whether to purchase a standard mineral-based oil, a semi-synthetic oil (also known as a synthetic blend or synthetic-based oil) or a fully-synthetic oil. Although all oils will have a similar rating and viscosity, their cost will vary considerably; mineral-based oils are the cheapest, the fully-synthetic oils the most expensive with the semi-synthetic oils falling somewhere in-between. This decision is very much up to the owner, but it should be noted that modern synthetic oils have far better lubricating and cleaning qualities than traditional mineral-based oils and tend to retain these properties for far longer. Bearing in mind the operating conditions inside a modern, high-revving motorcycle engine it is highly recommended that a fully synthetic oil is used. The extra expense at each service could save you money in the long term by preventing premature engine wear.

● As a final note always ensure that the oil is specifically designed for use in motorcycle engines. Engine oils designed primarily for use in car engines sometimes contain additives or friction modifiers which could cause clutch slip on a motorcycle fitted with a wet-clutch.

Two-stroke engine oil

● Modern two-stroke engines, with their high power outputs, place high demands on their oil. If engine seizure is to be avoided it is essential that a high-quality oil is used. Two-stroke oils differ hugely from four-stroke oils. The oil lubricates only the crankshaft and piston(s) (the transmission has its own lubricating oil) and is used on a total-loss basis where it is burnt completely during the combustion process.

● The Japanese have recently introduced a classification system for two-stroke oils, the JASO rating. This rating is in the form of two letters, either FA, FB or FC – FA is the lowest classification and FC the highest. Ensure the oil being used meets or exceeds the recommended rating specified by the manufacturer.

● As well as ensuring the oil rating matches the recommendation, another consideration to make when buying engine oil is whether to purchase a standard mineral-based oil, a semi-synthetic oil (also known as a synthetic blend or synthetic-based oil) or a fully-synthetic oil. The cost of each type of oil varies considerably; mineral-based oils are the cheapest, the fully-synthetic oils the most expensive with the semi-synthetic oils falling somewhere in-between. This decision is very much up to the owner, but it should be noted that modern synthetic oils have far better lubricating properties and burn cleaner than traditional mineral-based oils. It is therefore recommended that a fully synthetic oil is used. The extra expense could save you money in the long term by preventing premature engine wear, engine performance will be improved, carbon deposits and exhaust smoke will be reduced.

● Always ensure that the oil is specifically designed for use in an injector system. Many high quality two-stroke oils are designed for competition use and need to be pre-mixed with fuel. These oils are of a much higher viscosity and are not designed to flow through the injector pumps used on road-going two-stroke motorcycles.

Transmission (gear) oil

● On a two-stroke engine, the transmission and clutch are lubricated by their own separate oil bath which must be changed in accordance with the Maintenance Schedule.
● Although the engine and transmission units of most four-strokes use a common lubrication supply, there are some exceptions where the engine and gearbox have separate oil reservoirs and a dry clutch is used.
● Motorcycle manufacturers will either recommend a monograde transmission oil or a four-stroke multigrade engine oil to lubricate the transmission.
● Transmission oils, or gear oils as they are often called, are designed specifically for use in transmission systems. The viscosity of these oils is represented by an SAE number, but the scale of measurement applied is different to that used to grade engine oils. As a rough guide a SAE90 gear oil will be of the same viscosity as an SAE50 engine oil.

Shaft drive oil

● On models equipped with shaft final drive, the shaft drive gears are will have their own oil supply. The manufacturer will state a recommended 'type or classification' and also a specific 'viscosity' range in the same manner as for four-stroke engine oil.
● Gear oil classification is given by the number which follows the API GL (GL standing for gear lubricant) rating, the higher the number, the higher the specification of the oil, e.g. API GL5 oil is a higher specification than API GL4 oil. Ensure the oil meets or

exceeds the classification specified and is of the correct viscosity. The viscosity of gear oils is also represented by an SAE number but the scale of measurement used is different to that used to grade engine oils. As a rough guide an SAE90 gear oil will be of the same viscosity as an SAE50 engine oil.
● If the use of an EP (Extreme Pressure) gear oil is specified, ensure the oil purchased is suitable.

Fork oil and suspension fluid

● Conventional telescopic front forks are hydraulic and require fork oil to work. To ensure the forks function correctly, the fork oil must be changed in accordance with the Maintenance Schedule.
● Fork oil is available in a variety of viscosities, identified by their SAE rating; fork oil ratings vary from light (SAE 5) to heavy (SAE 30). When purchasing fork oil, ensure the viscosity rating matches that specified by the manufacturer.
● Some lubricant manufacturers also produce a range of high-quality suspension fluids which are very similar to fork oil but are designed mainly for competition use. These fluids may have a different viscosity rating system which is not to be confused with the SAE rating of normal fork oil. Refer to the manufacturer's instructions if in any doubt.

Brake and clutch fluid

● All disc brake systems and some clutch systems are hydraulically operated. To ensure correct operation, the hydraulic fluid must be changed in accordance with the Maintenance Schedule.
● Brake and clutch fluid is classified by its DOT rating with most motorcycle manufacturers specifying DOT 3 or 4 fluid. Both fluid types are glycol-based and can be mixed together without adverse effect; DOT 4 fluid exceeds the requirements of DOT 3

fluid. Although it is safe to use DOT 4 fluid in a system designed for use with DOT 3 fluid, never use DOT 3 fluid in a system which specifies the use of DOT 4 as this will adversely affect the system's performance. The type required for the system will be marked on the fluid reservoir cap.
● Some manufacturers also produce a DOT 5 hydraulic fluid. DOT 5 hydraulic fluid is silicone-based and is not compatible with the glycol-based DOT 3 and 4 fluids. Never mix DOT 5 fluid with DOT 3 or 4 fluid as this will seriously affect the performance of the hydraulic system.

Coolant/antifreeze

● When purchasing coolant/antifreeze, always ensure it is suitable for use in an aluminium engine and contains corrosion inhibitors to prevent possible blockages of the internal coolant passages of the system. As a general rule, most coolants are designed to be used neat and should not be diluted whereas antifreeze can be mixed with distilled water to provide a coolant solution of the required strength. Refer to the manufacturer's instructions on the bottle.
● Ensure the coolant is changed in accordance with the Maintenance Schedule.

Chain lube

● Chain lube is an aerosol-type spray lubricant specifically designed for use on motorcycle final drive chains. Chain lube has two functions, to minimise friction between the final drive chain and sprockets and to prevent corrosion of the chain. Regular use of a good-quality chain lube will extend the life of the drive chain and sprockets and thus maximise the power being transmitted from the transmission to the rear wheel.
● When using chain lube, always allow some time for the solvents in the lube to evaporate before riding the motorcycle. This will minimise the amount of lube which will

'fling' off from the chain when the motorcycle is used. If the motorcycle is equipped with an 'O-ring' chain, ensure the chain lube is labelled as being suitable for use on 'O-ring' chains.

Degreasers and solvents

● There are many different types of solvents and degreasers available to remove the grime and grease which accumulate around the motorcycle during normal use. Degreasers and solvents are usually available as an aerosol-type spray or as a liquid which you apply with a brush. Always closely follow the manufacturer's instructions and wear eye protection during use. Be aware that many solvents are flammable and may give off noxious fumes; take adequate precautions when using them (*see Safety First!*).

● For general cleaning, use one of the many solvents or degreasers available from most motorcycle accessory shops. These solvents are usually applied then left for a certain time before being washed off with water.

Brake cleaner is a solvent specifically designed to remove all traces of oil, grease and dust from braking system components. Brake cleaner is designed to evaporate quickly and leaves behind no residue.

Carburettor cleaner is an aerosol-type solvent specifically designed to clear carburettor blockages and break down the hard deposits and gum often found inside carburettors during overhaul.

Contact cleaner is an aerosol-type solvent designed for cleaning electrical components. The cleaner will remove all traces of oil and dirt from components such as switch contacts or fouled spark plugs and then dry, leaving behind no residue.

Gasket remover is an aerosol-type solvent designed for removing stubborn gaskets from engine components during overhaul. Gasket remover will minimise the amount of scraping required to remove the gasket and therefore reduce the risk of damage to the mating surface.

Spray lubricants

● Aerosol-based spray lubricants are widely available and are excellent for lubricating lever pivots and exposed cables and switches. Try to use a lubricant which is of the dry-film type as the fluid evaporates, leaving behind a dry-film of lubricant. Lubricants which leave behind an oily residue will attract dust and dirt which will increase the rate of wear of the cable/lever.

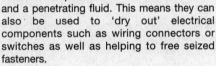

● Most lubricants also act as a moisture dispersant and a penetrating fluid. This means they can also be used to 'dry out' electrical components such as wiring connectors or switches as well as helping to free seized fasteners.

Greases

● Grease is used to lubricate many of the pivot-points. A good-quality multi-purpose grease is suitable for most applications but some manufacturers will specify the use of specialist greases for use on components such as swingarm and suspension linkage bushes. These specialist greases can be purchased from most motorcycle (or car) accessory shops; commonly specified types include molybdenum disulphide grease, lithium-based grease, graphite-based grease, silicone-based grease and high-temperature copper-based grease.

Gasket sealing compounds

● Gasket sealing compounds can be used in conjunction with gaskets, to improve their sealing capabilities, or on their own to seal metal-to-metal joints. Depending on their type, sealing compounds either set hard or stay relatively soft and pliable.

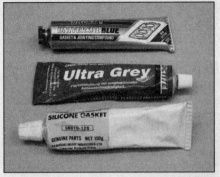

● When purchasing a gasket sealing compound, ensure that it is designed specifically for use on an internal combustion engine. General multi-purpose sealants available from DIY stores may appear visibly similar but they are not designed to withstand the extreme heat or contact with fuel and oil encountered when used on an engine (*see 'Tools and Workshop Tips' for further information*).

Thread locking compound

● Thread locking compounds are used to secure certain threaded fasteners in position to prevent them from loosening due to vibration. Thread locking compounds can be purchased from most motorcycle (and car) accessory shops. Ensure the threads of the both components are completely clean and dry before sparingly applying the locking compound (*see 'Tools and Workshop Tips' for further information*).

Fuel additives

● Fuel additives which protect and clean the fuel system components are widely available. These additives are designed to remove all traces of deposits that build up on the carburettors/injectors and prevent wear, helping the fuel system to operate more efficiently. If a fuel additive is being used, check that it is suitable for use with your motorcycle, especially if your motorcycle is equipped with a catalytic converter.

● Octane boosters are also available. These additives are designed to improve the performance of highly-tuned engines being run on normal pump-fuel and are of no real use on standard motorcycles.

Conversion factors

Length (distance)

Inches (in)	x 25.4	= Millimetres (mm)	x 0.0394	=	Inches (in)
Feet (ft)	x 0.305	= Metres (m)	x 3.281	=	Feet (ft)
Miles	x 1.609	= Kilometres (km)	x 0.621	=	Miles

Volume (capacity)

Cubic inches (cu in; in^3)	x 16.387	= Cubic centimetres (cc; cm^3)	x 0.061	=	Cubic inches (cu in; in^3)
Imperial pints (Imp pt)	x 0.568	= Litres (l)	x 1.76	=	Imperial pints (Imp pt)
Imperial quarts (Imp qt)	x 1.137	= Litres (l)	x 0.88	=	Imperial quarts (Imp qt)
Imperial quarts (Imp qt)	x 1.201	= US quarts (US qt)	x 0.833	=	Imperial quarts (Imp qt)
US quarts (US qt)	x 0.946	= Litres (l)	x 1.057	=	US quarts (US qt)
Imperial gallons (Imp gal)	x 4.546	= Litres (l)	x 0.22	=	Imperial gallons (Imp gal)
Imperial gallons (Imp gal)	x 1.201	= US gallons (US gal)	x 0.833	=	Imperial gallons (Imp gal)
US gallons (US gal)	x 3.785	= Litres (l)	x 0.264	=	US gallons (US gal)

Mass (weight)

Ounces (oz)	x 28.35	= Grams (g)	x 0.035	=	Ounces (oz)
Pounds (lb)	x 0.454	= Kilograms (kg)	x 2.205	=	Pounds (lb)

Force

Ounces-force (ozf; oz)	x 0.278	= Newtons (N)	x 3.6	=	Ounces-force (ozf; oz)
Pounds-force (lbf; lb)	x 4.448	= Newtons (N)	x 0.225	=	Pounds-force (lbf; lb)
Newtons (N)	x 0.1	= Kilograms-force (kgf; kg)	x 9.81	=	Newtons (N)

Pressure

Pounds-force per square inch (psi; lbf/in^2; lb/in^2)	x 0.070	= Kilograms-force per square centimetre (kgf/cm^2; kg/cm^2)	x 14.223	=	Pounds-force per square inch (psi; lbf/in^2; lb/in^2)
Pounds-force per square inch (psi; lbf/in^2; lb/in^2)	x 0.068	= Atmospheres (atm)	x 14.696	=	Pounds-force per square inch (psi; lbf/in^2; lb/in^2)
Pounds-force per square inch (psi; lbf/in^2; lb/in^2)	x 0.069	= Bars	x 14.5	=	Pounds-force per square inch (psi; lbf/in^2; lb/in^2)
Pounds-force per square inch (psi; lbf/in^2; lb/in^2)	x 6.895	= Kilopascals (kPa)	x 0.145	=	Pounds-force per square inch (psi; lbf/in^2; lb/in^2)
Kilopascals (kPa)	x 0.01	= Kilograms-force per square centimetre (kgf/cm^2; kg/cm^2)	x 98.1	=	Kilopascals (kPa)
Millibar (mbar)	x 100	= Pascals (Pa)	x 0.01	=	Millibar (mbar)
Millibar (mbar)	x 0.0145	= Pounds-force per square inch (psi; lbf/in^2; lb/in^2)	x 68.947	=	Millibar (mbar)
Millibar (mbar)	x 0.75	= Millimetres of mercury (mmHg)	x 1.333	=	Millibar (mbar)
Millibar (mbar)	x 0.401	= Inches of water (inH$_2$O)	x 2.491	=	Millibar (mbar)
Millimetres of mercury (mmHg)	x 0.535	= Inches of water (inH$_2$O)	x 1.868	=	Millimetres of mercury (mmHg)
Inches of water (inH$_2$O)	x 0.036	= Pounds-force per square inch (psi; lbf/in^2; lb/in^2)	x 27.68	=	Inches of water (inH$_2$O)

Torque (moment of force)

Pounds-force inches (lbf in; lb in)	x 1.152	= Kilograms-force centimetre (kgf cm; kg cm)	x 0.868	=	Pounds-force inches (lbf in; lb in)
Pounds-force inches (lbf in; lb in)	x 0.113	= Newton metres (Nm)	x 8.85	=	Pounds-force inches (lbf in; lb in)
Pounds-force inches (lbf in; lb in)	x 0.083	= Pounds-force feet (lbf ft; lb ft)	x 12	=	Pounds-force inches (lbf in; lb in)
Pounds-force feet (lbf ft; lb ft)	x 0.138	= Kilograms-force metres (kgf m; kg m)	x 7.233	=	Pounds-force feet (lbf ft; lb ft)
Pounds-force feet (lbf ft; lb ft)	x 1.356	= Newton metres (Nm)	x 0.738	=	Pounds-force feet (lbf ft; lb ft)
Newton metres (Nm)	x 0.102	= Kilograms-force metres (kgf m; kg m)	x 9.804	=	Newton metres (Nm)

Power

Horsepower (hp)	x 745.7	= Watts (W)	x 0.0013	=	Horsepower (hp)

Velocity (speed)

Miles per hour (miles/hr; mph)	x 1.609	= Kilometres per hour (km/hr; kph)	x 0.621	=	Miles per hour (miles/hr; mph)

Fuel consumption*

Miles per gallon (mpg)	x 0.354	= Kilometres per litre (km/l)	x 2.825	=	Miles per gallon (mpg)

Temperature

Degrees Fahrenheit = (°C x 1.8) + 32   Degrees Celsius (Degrees Centigrade; °C) = (°F - 32) x 0.56

It is common practice to convert from miles per gallon (mpg) to litres/100 kilometres (l/100km), where mpg x l/100 km = 282

About the MOT Test

In the UK, all vehicles more than three years old are subject to an annual test to ensure that they meet minimum safety requirements. A current test certificate must be issued before a machine can be used on public roads, and is required before a road fund licence can be issued. Riding without a current test certificate will also invalidate your insurance.

For most owners, the MOT test is an annual cause for anxiety, and this is largely due to owners not being sure what needs to be checked prior to submitting the motorcycle for testing. The simple answer is that a fully roadworthy motorcycle will have no difficulty in passing the test.

This is a guide to getting your motorcycle through the MOT test. Obviously it will not be possible to examine the motorcycle to the same standard as the professional MOT tester, particularly in view of the equipment required for some of the checks. However, working through the following procedures will enable you to identify any problem areas before submitting the motorcycle for the test.

It has only been possible to summarise the test requirements here, based on the regulations in force at the time of printing. Test standards are becoming increasingly stringent, although there are some exemptions for older vehicles. More information about the MOT test can be obtained from the TSO publications, *How Safe is your Motorcycle* and *The MOT Inspection Manual for Motorcycle Testing*.

Many of the checks require that one of the wheels is raised off the ground. If the motorcycle doesn't have a centre stand, note that an auxiliary stand will be required. Additionally, the help of an assistant may prove useful.

Certain exceptions apply to machines under 50 cc, machines without a lighting system, and Classic bikes - if in doubt about any of the requirements listed below seek confirmation from an MOT tester prior to submitting the motorcycle for the test.

Check that the frame number is clearly visible.

Electrical System

Lights, turn signals, horn and reflector

✔ With the ignition on, check the operation of the following electrical components. **Note:** *The electrical components on certain small-capacity machines are powered by the generator, requiring that the engine is run for this check.*

a) *Headlight and tail light. Check that both illuminate in the low and high beam switch positions.*

b) *Position lights. Check that the front position (or sidelight) and tail light illuminate in this switch position.*

c) *Turn signals. Check that all flash at the correct rate, and that the warning light(s) function correctly. Check that the turn signal switch works correctly.*

d) *Hazard warning system (where fitted). Check that all four turn signals flash in this switch position.*

e) *Brake stop light. Check that the light comes on when the front and rear brakes are independently applied. Models first used on or after 1st April 1986 must have a brake light switch on each brake.*

f) *Horn. Check that the sound is continuous and of reasonable volume.*

✔ Check that there is a red reflector on the rear of the machine, either mounted separately or as part of the tail light lens.

✔ Check the condition of the headlight, tail light and turn signal lenses.

Headlight beam height

✔ The MOT tester will perform a headlight beam height check using specialised beam setting equipment **(see illustration 1)**. This equipment will not be available to the home mechanic, but if you suspect that the headlight is incorrectly set or may have been maladjusted in the past, you can perform a rough test as follows.

✔ Position the bike in a straight line facing a brick wall. The bike must be off its stand, upright and with a rider seated. Measure the height from the ground to the centre of the headlight and mark a horizontal line on the wall at this height. Position the motorcycle 3.8 metres from the wall and draw a vertical

Headlight beam height checking equipment

line up the wall central to the centreline of the motorcycle. Switch to dipped beam and check that the beam pattern falls slightly lower than the horizontal line and to the left of the vertical line **(see illustration 2)**.

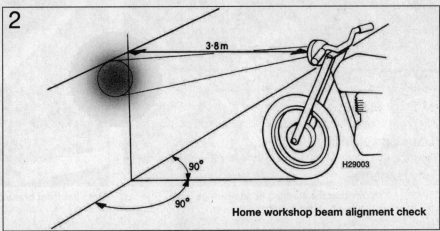

3·8 m

90°

90°

H29003

Home workshop beam alignment check

Exhaust System and Final Drive

Exhaust

✔ Check that the exhaust mountings are secure and that the system does not foul any of the rear suspension components.

✔ Start the motorcycle. When the revs are increased, check that the exhaust is neither holed nor leaking from any of its joints. On a linked system, check that the collector box is not leaking due to corrosion.

✔ Note that the exhaust decibel level ("loudness" of the exhaust) is assessed at the discretion of the tester. If the motorcycle was first used on or after 1st January 1985 the silencer must carry the BSAU 193 stamp, or a marking relating to its make and model, or be of OE (original equipment) manufacture. If the silencer is marked NOT FOR ROAD USE, RACING USE ONLY or similar, it will fail the MOT.

Final drive

✔ On chain or belt drive machines, check that the chain/belt is in good condition and does not have excessive slack. Also check that the sprocket is securely mounted on the rear wheel hub. Check that the chain/belt guard is in place.

✔ On shaft drive bikes, check for oil leaking from the drive unit and fouling the rear tyre.

Steering and Suspension

Steering

✔ With the front wheel raised off the ground, rotate the steering from lock to lock. The handlebar or switches must not contact the fuel tank or be close enough to trap the rider's hand. Problems can be caused by damaged lock stops on the lower yoke and frame, or by the fitting of non-standard handlebars.

✔ When performing the lock to lock check, also ensure that the steering moves freely without drag or notchiness. Steering movement can be impaired by poorly routed cables, or by overtight head bearings or worn bearings. The tester will perform a check of the steering head bearing lower race by mounting the front wheel on a surface plate, then performing a lock to lock check with the weight of the machine on the lower bearing (see illustration 3).

✔ Grasp the fork sliders (lower legs) and attempt to push and pull on the forks (see

Front wheel mounted on a surface plate for steering head bearing lower race check

illustration 4). Any play in the steering head bearings will be felt. Note that in extreme cases, wear of the front fork bushes can be misinterpreted for head bearing play.

✔ Check that the handlebars are securely mounted.

✔ Check that the handlebar grip rubbers are secure. They should by bonded to the bar left end and to the throttle cable pulley on the right end.

Front suspension

✔ With the motorcycle off the stand, hold the front brake on and pump the front forks up and down (see illustration 5). Check that they are adequately damped.

Checking the steering head bearings for freeplay

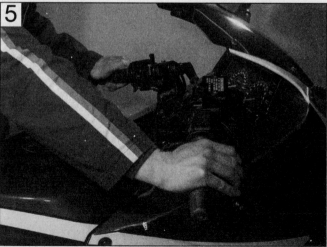

Hold the front brake on and pump the front forks up and down to check operation

6

Inspect the area around the fork dust seal for oil leakage (arrow)

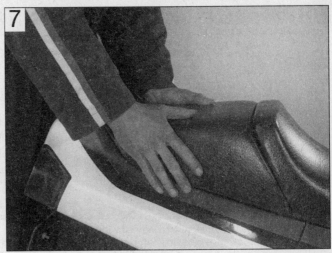

7

Bounce the rear of the motorcycle to check rear suspension operation

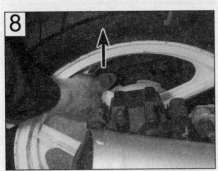

8

Checking for rear suspension linkage play

✔ Inspect the area above and around the front fork oil seals **(see illustration 6)**. There should be no sign of oil on the fork tube (stanchion) nor leaking down the slider (lower leg). On models so equipped, check that there is no oil leaking from the anti-dive units.

✔ On models with swingarm front suspension, check that there is no freeplay in the linkage when moved from side to side.

Rear suspension

✔ With the motorcycle off the stand and an assistant supporting the motorcycle by its handlebars, bounce the rear suspension **(see illustration 7)**. Check that the suspension components do not foul on any of the cycle parts and check that the shock absorber(s) provide adequate damping.

✔ Visually inspect the shock absorber(s) and check that there is no sign of oil leakage from its damper. This is somewhat restricted on certain single shock models due to the location of the shock absorber.

✔ With the rear wheel raised off the ground, grasp the wheel at the highest point and attempt to pull it up **(see illustration 8)**. Any play in the swingarm pivot or suspension linkage bearings will be felt as movement. **Note:** *Do not confuse play with actual suspension movement.* Failure to lubricate suspension linkage bearings can lead to bearing failure **(see illustration 9)**.

✔ With the rear wheel raised off the ground, grasp the swingarm ends and attempt to move the swingarm from side to side and forwards and backwards - any play indicates wear of the swingarm pivot bearings **(see illustration 10)**.

9

Worn suspension linkage pivots (arrows) are usually the cause of play in the rear suspension

10

Grasp the swingarm at the ends to check for play in its pivot bearings

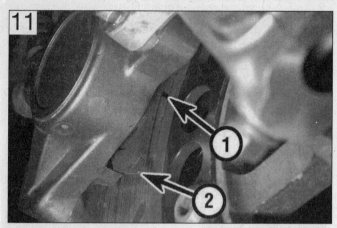

Brake pad wear can usually be viewed without removing the caliper. Most pads have wear indicator grooves (1) and some also have indicator tangs (2)

On drum brakes, check the angle of the operating lever with the brake fully applied. Most drum brakes have a wear indicator pointer and scale.

Brakes, Wheels and Tyres

Brakes

✔ With the wheel raised off the ground, apply the brake then free it off, and check that the wheel is about to revolve freely without brake drag.

✔ On disc brakes, examine the disc itself. Check that it is securely mounted and not cracked.

✔ On disc brakes, view the pad material through the caliper mouth and check that the pads are not worn down beyond the limit **(see illustration 11)**.

✔ On drum brakes, check that when the brake is applied the angle between the operating lever and cable or rod is not too great **(see illustration 12)**. Check also that the operating lever doesn't foul any other components.

✔ On disc brakes, examine the flexible hoses from top to bottom. Have an assistant hold the brake on so that the fluid in the hose is under pressure, and check that there is no sign of fluid leakage, bulges or cracking. If there are any metal brake pipes or unions, check that these are free from corrosion and damage. Where a brake-linked anti-dive system is fitted, check the hoses to the anti-dive in a similar manner.

✔ Check that the rear brake torque arm is secure and that its fasteners are secured by self-locking nuts or castellated nuts with split-pins or R-pins **(see illustration 13)**.

✔ On models with ABS, check that the self-check warning light in the instrument panel works.

✔ The MOT tester will perform a test of the motorcycle's braking efficiency based on a calculation of rider and motorcycle weight. Although this cannot be carried out at home, you can at least ensure that the braking systems are properly maintained. For hydraulic disc brakes, check the fluid level, lever/pedal feel (bleed of air if its spongy) and pad material. For drum brakes, check adjustment, cable or rod operation and shoe lining thickness.

Wheels and tyres

✔ Check the wheel condition. Cast wheels should be free from cracks and if of the built-up design, all fasteners should be secure. Spoked wheels should be checked for broken, corroded, loose or bent spokes.

✔ With the wheel raised off the ground, spin the wheel and visually check that the tyre and wheel run true. Check that the tyre does not foul the suspension or mudguards.

✔ With the wheel raised off the ground, grasp the wheel and attempt to move it about the axle (spindle) **(see illustration 14)**. Any play felt here indicates wheel bearing failure.

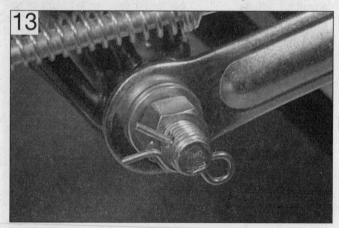

Brake torque arm must be properly secured at both ends

Check for wheel bearing play by trying to move the wheel about the axle (spindle)

Checking the tyre tread depth

Tyre direction of rotation arrow can be found on tyre sidewall

Castellated type wheel axle (spindle) nut must be secured by a split pin or R-pin

Two straightedges are used to check wheel alignment

✔ If the tyre sidewall carries a direction of rotation arrow, this must be pointing in the direction of normal wheel rotation (see illustration 16).

✔ Check that the wheel axle (spindle) nuts (where applicable) are properly secured. A self-locking nut or castellated nut with a split-pin or R-pin can be used (see illustration 17).

✔ Wheel alignment is checked with the motorcycle off the stand and a rider seated. With the front wheel pointing straight ahead, two perfectly straight lengths of metal or wood and placed against the sidewalls of both tyres (see illustration 18). The gap each side of the front tyre must be equidistant on both sides. Incorrect wheel alignment may be due to a cocked rear wheel (often as the result of poor chain adjustment) or in extreme cases, a bent frame.

✔ Check the tyre tread depth, tread condition and sidewall condition (see illustration 15).

✔ Check the tyre type. Front and rear tyre types must be compatible and be suitable for road use. Tyres marked NOT FOR ROAD USE, COMPETITION USE ONLY or similar, will fail the MOT.

General checks and condition

✔ Check the security of all major fasteners, bodypanels, seat, fairings (where fitted) and mudguards.

✔ Check that the rider and pillion footrests, handlebar levers and brake pedal are securely mounted.

✔ Check for corrosion on the frame or any load-bearing components. If severe, this may affect the structure, particularly under stress.

Sidecars

A motorcycle fitted with a sidecar requires additional checks relating to the stability of the machine and security of attachment and swivel joints, plus specific wheel alignment (toe-in) requirements. Additionally, tyre and lighting requirements differ from conventional motorcycle use. Owners are advised to check MOT test requirements with an official test centre.

Preparing for storage

Before you start

If repairs or an overhaul is needed, see that this is carried out now rather than left until you want to ride the bike again.

Give the bike a good wash and scrub all dirt from its underside. Make sure the bike dries completely before preparing for storage.

Engine

● Remove the spark plug(s) and lubricate the cylinder bores with approximately a teaspoon of motor oil using a spout-type oil can (see illustration 1). Reinstall the spark plug(s). Crank the engine over a couple of times to coat the piston rings and bores with oil. If the bike has a kickstart, use this to turn the engine over. If not, flick the kill switch to the OFF position and crank the engine over on the starter (see illustration 2). If the nature on the ignition system prevents the starter operating with the kill switch in the OFF position,

remove the spark plugs and fit them back in their caps; ensure that the plugs are earthed (grounded) against the cylinder head when the starter is operated (see illustration 3).

⚠️ **Warning: It is important that the plugs are earthed (grounded) away from the spark plug holes otherwise there is a risk of atomised fuel from the cylinders igniting.**

> **HAYNES HINT** *On a single cylinder four-stroke engine, you can seal the combustion chamber completely by positioning the piston at TDC on the compression stroke.*

● Drain the carburettor(s) otherwise there is a risk of jets becoming blocked by gum deposits from the fuel (see illustration 4).

● If the bike is going into long-term storage, consider adding a fuel stabiliser to the fuel in the tank. If the tank is drained completely, corrosion of its internal surfaces may occur if left unprotected for a long period. The tank can be treated with a rust preventative especially for this purpose. Alternatively, remove the tank and pour half a litre of motor oil into it, install the filler cap and shake the tank to coat its internals with oil before draining off the excess. The same effect can also be achieved by spraying WD40 or a similar water-dispersant around the inside of the tank via its flexible nozzle.

● Make sure the cooling system contains the correct mix of antifreeze. Antifreeze also contains important corrosion inhibitors.

● The air intakes and exhaust can be sealed off by covering or plugging the openings. Ensure that you do not seal in any condensation; run the engine until it is hot,

Squirt a drop of motor oil into each cylinder

Flick the kill switch to OFF . . .

. . . and ensure that the metal bodies of the plugs (arrows) are earthed against the cylinder head

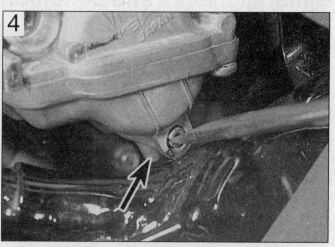

Connect a hose to the carburettor float chamber drain stub (arrow) and unscrew the drain screw

Exhausts can be sealed off with a plastic bag

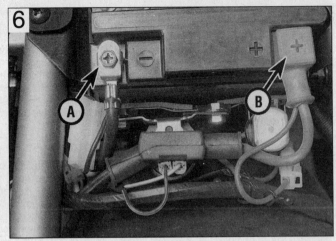

Disconnect the negative lead (A) first, followed by the positive lead (B)

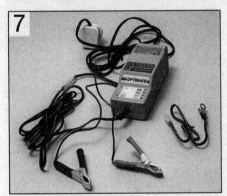

Use a suitable battery charger - this kit also assess battery condition

then switch off and allow to cool. Tape a piece of thick plastic over the silencer end(s) **(see illustration 5)**. Note that some advocate pouring a tablespoon of motor oil into the silencer(s) before sealing them off.

Battery

● Remove it from the bike - in extreme cases of cold the battery may freeze and crack its case **(see illustration 6)**.

● Check the electrolyte level and top up if necessary (conventional refillable batteries). Clean the terminals.
● Store the battery off the motorcycle and away from any sources of fire. Position a wooden block under the battery if it is to sit on the ground.
● Give the battery a trickle charge for a few hours every month **(see illustration 7)**.

Tyres

● Place the bike on its centrestand or an auxiliary stand which will support the motorcycle in an upright position. Position wood blocks under the tyres to keep them off the ground and to provide insulation from damp. If the bike is being put into long-term storage, ideally both tyres should be off the ground; not only will this protect the tyres, but will also ensure that no load is placed on the steering head or wheel bearings.
● Deflate each tyre by 5 to 10 psi, no more or the beads may unseat from the rim, making subsequent inflation difficult on tubeless tyres.

Pivots and controls

● Lubricate all lever, pedal, stand and

footrest pivot points. If grease nipples are fitted to the rear suspension components, apply lubricant to the pivots.
● Lubricate all control cables.

Cycle components

● Apply a wax protectant to all painted and plastic components. Wipe off any excess, but don't polish to a shine. Where fitted, clean the screen with soap and water.
● Coat metal parts with Vaseline (petroleum jelly). When applying this to the fork tubes, do not compress the forks otherwise the seals will rot from contact with the Vaseline.
● Apply a vinyl cleaner to the seat.

Storage conditions

● Aim to store the bike in a shed or garage which does not leak and is free from damp.
● Drape an old blanket or bedspread over the bike to protect it from dust and direct contact with sunlight (which will fade paint). This also hides the bike from prying eyes. Beware of tight-fitting plastic covers which may allow condensation to form and settle on the bike.

Getting back on the road

Engine and transmission

● Change the oil and replace the oil filter. If this was done prior to storage, check that the oil hasn't emulsified - a thick whitish substance which occurs through condensation.
● Remove the spark plugs. Using a spout-type oil can, squirt a few drops of oil into the cylinder(s). This will provide initial lubrication as the piston rings and bores comes back into contact. Service the spark plugs, or fit new ones, and install them in the engine.

● Check that the clutch isn't stuck on. The plates can stick together if left standing for some time, preventing clutch operation. Engage a gear and try rocking the bike back and forth with the clutch lever held against the handlebar. If this doesn't work on cable-operated clutches, hold the clutch lever back against the handlebar with a strong elastic band or cable tie for a couple of hours **(see illustration 8)**.
● If the air intakes or silencer end(s) were blocked off, remove the bung or cover used.
● If the fuel tank was coated with a rust

Hold clutch lever back against the handlebar with elastic bands or a cable tie

preventative, oil or a stabiliser added to the fuel, drain and flush the tank and dispose of the fuel sensibly. If no action was taken with the fuel tank prior to storage, it is advised that the old fuel is disposed of since it will go off over a period of time. Refill the fuel tank with fresh fuel.

Frame and running gear

● Oil all pivot points and cables.
● Check the tyre pressures. They will definitely need inflating if pressures were reduced for storage.
● Lubricate the final drive chain (where applicable).
● Remove any protective coating applied to the fork tubes (stanchions) since this may well destroy the fork seals. If the fork tubes weren't protected and have picked up rust spots, remove them with very fine abrasive paper and refinish with metal polish.
● Check that both brakes operate correctly. Apply each brake hard and check that it's not possible to move the motorcycle forwards, then check that the brake frees off again once released. Brake caliper pistons can stick due to corrosion around the piston head, or on the sliding caliper types, due to corrosion of the slider pins. If the brake doesn't free after repeated operation, take the caliper off for examination. Similarly drum brakes can stick

due to a seized operating cam, cable or rod linkage.
● If the motorcycle has been in long-term storage, renew the brake fluid and clutch fluid (where applicable).
● Depending on where the bike has been stored, the wiring, cables and hoses may have been nibbled by rodents. Make a visual check and investigate disturbed wiring loom tape.

Battery

● If the battery has been previously removal and given top up charges it can simply be reconnected. Remember to connect the positive cable first and the negative cable last.
● On conventional refillable batteries, if the battery has not received any attention, remove it from the motorcycle and check its electrolyte level. Top up if necessary then charge the battery. If the battery fails to hold a charge and a visual checks show heavy white sulphation of the plates, the battery is probably defective and must be renewed. This is particularly likely if the battery is old. Confirm battery condition with a specific gravity check.
● On sealed (MF) batteries, if the battery has not received any attention, remove it from the motorcycle and charge it according to the information on the battery case - if the battery fails to hold a charge it must be renewed.

Starting procedure

● If a kickstart is fitted, turn the engine over a couple of times with the ignition OFF to distribute oil around the engine. If no kickstart is fitted, flick the engine kill switch OFF and the ignition ON and crank the engine over a couple of times to work oil around the upper cylinder components. If the nature of the ignition system is such that the starter won't work with the kill switch OFF, remove the spark plugs, fit them back into their caps and earth (ground) their bodies on the cylinder head. Reinstall the spark plugs afterwards.
● Switch the kill switch to RUN, operate the choke and start the engine. If the engine won't start don't continue cranking the engine - not only will this flatten the battery, but the starter motor will overheat. Switch the ignition off and try again later. If the engine refuses to start, go through the fault finding procedures in this manual. **Note:** *If the bike has been in storage for a long time, old fuel or a carburettor blockage may be the problem. Gum deposits in carburettors can block jets - if a carburettor cleaner doesn't prove successful the carburettors must be dismantled for cleaning.*

● Once the engine has started, check that the lights, turn signals and horn work properly.

● Treat the bike gently for the first ride and check all fluid levels on completion. Settle the bike back into the maintenance schedule.

This Section provides an easy reference-guide to the more common faults that are likely to afflict your machine. Obviously, the opportunities are almost limitless for faults to occur as a result of obscure failures, and to try and cover all eventualities would require a book. Indeed, a number have been written on the subject.

Successful troubleshooting is not a mysterious 'black art' but the application of a bit of knowledge combined with a systematic and logical approach to the problem. Approach any troubleshooting by first accurately identifying the symptom and then checking through the list of possible causes, starting with the simplest or most obvious and progressing in stages to the most complex.

Take nothing for granted, but above all apply liberal quantities of common sense.

The main symptom of a fault is given in the text as a major heading below which are listed the various systems or areas which may contain the fault. Details of each possible cause for a fault and the remedial action to be taken are given, in brief, in the paragraphs below each heading. Further information should be sought in the relevant Chapter.

1 Engine doesn't start or is difficult to start

- [ ] Starter motor doesn't rotate
- [ ] Starter motor rotates but engine does not turn over
- [ ] Starter works but engine won't turn over (seized)
- [ ] No fuel flow
- [ ] Engine flooded
- [ ] No spark or weak spark
- [ ] Compression low
- [ ] Stalls after starting
- [ ] Rough idle

2 Poor running at low speed

- [ ] Spark weak
- [ ] Fuel/air mixture incorrect
- [ ] Compression low
- [ ] Poor acceleration

3 Poor running or no power at high speed

- [ ] Firing incorrect
- [ ] Fuel/air mixture incorrect
- [ ] Compression low
- [ ] Knocking or pinking
- [ ] Miscellaneous causes

4 Overheating

- [ ] Engine overheats
- [ ] Firing incorrect
- [ ] Fuel/air mixture incorrect
- [ ] Compression too high
- [ ] Engine load excessive
- [ ] Lubrication inadequate
- [ ] Miscellaneous causes

5 Clutch problems

- [ ] Clutch slipping
- [ ] Clutch not disengaging completely

6 Gearchanging problems

- [ ] Doesn't go into gear, or lever doesn't return
- [ ] Jumps out of gear
- [ ] Overselects

7 Abnormal engine noise

- [ ] Knocking or pinking
- [ ] Piston slap or rattling
- [ ] Valve noise
- [ ] Other noise

8 Abnormal driveline noise

- [ ] Clutch noise
- [ ] Transmission noise
- [ ] Final drive noise

9 Abnormal frame and suspension noise

- [ ] Front end noise
- [ ] Shock absorber noise
- [ ] Brake noise

10 Oil pressure warning LED comes on

- [ ] Engine lubrication system
- [ ] Electrical system

11 Excessive exhaust smoke

- [ ] White smoke
- [ ] Black smoke
- [ ] Brown smoke

12 Poor handling or stability

- [ ] Handlebar hard to turn
- [ ] Handlebar shakes or vibrates excessively
- [ ] Handlebar pulls to one side
- [ ] Poor shock absorbing qualities

13 Braking problems

- [ ] Brakes are spongy, don't hold
- [ ] Brake lever or pedal pulsates
- [ ] Brakes drag

14 Electrical problems

- [ ] Battery dead or weak
- [ ] Battery overcharged

1 Engine doesn't start or is difficult to start

Starter motor doesn't rotate

☐ Engine kill switch OFF.
☐ Fuse blown. Check main fuse and ignition circuit fuse (Chapter 8).
☐ Battery voltage low. Check and recharge battery (Chapter 8).
☐ Starter motor defective. Make sure the wiring to the starter is secure. Make sure the starter relay clicks when the start button is pushed. If the relay clicks, then the fault is in the wiring or motor (see Chapter 8).
☐ Starter switch not contacting. The contacts could be wet, corroded or dirty. Disassemble and clean the switch (Chapter 8).
☐ Wiring open or shorted. Check all wiring connections and harnesses to make sure that they are dry, tight and not corroded. Also check for broken or frayed wires that can cause a short to ground (earth) (see *Wiring diagrams*, Chapter 8).
☐ Ignition switch defective. Check the switch and renew it if it is defective (see Chapter 8).
☐ Engine kill switch defective. Check for wet, dirty or corroded contacts. Clean or renew the switch as necessary (see Chapter 8).
☐ Faulty gear position sensor, sidestand switch or clutch switch. Check the wiring to each switch and the switch itself (see Chapter 8).
☐ Faulty sidestand relay or diode (Chapter 8).
☐ Fuel injection system shutdown due to system fault (Chapter 4).

Starter motor rotates but engine does not turn over

☐ Starter motor clutch defective. Inspect and repair or renew (see Chapter 2).
☐ Damaged idler or starter gears. Inspect and renew the damaged parts (see Chapter 2).

Starter works but engine won't turn over (seized)

☐ Seized engine caused by one or more internally damaged components. Failure due to wear, abuse or lack of lubrication. Damage can include seized valves, followers, camshafts, pistons, crankshaft, connecting rod bearings, or transmission gears or bearings. Refer to Chapter 2 for engine disassembly.

No fuel flow

☐ No fuel in tank.
☐ Fuel tank breather hose obstructed.
☐ Fuel pump faulty, or the fuel filter is blocked (see Chapter 4).
☐ Fuel hose clogged. Remove the fuel hose and carefully blow through it. Check the fuel filter for damage.
☐ Fuel rail or injector clogged. For all of the injectors to be clogged, either a very bad batch of fuel with an unusual additive has been used, or some other foreign material has entered the tank. Check the fuel filter. In some cases, if a machine has been unused for several months, the fuel turns to a varnish-like liquid which can cause an injector needle to stick to its seat. Drain the tank and fuel system (Chapter 4).

Engine flooded

☐ Injector needle valve worn or stuck open. A piece of dirt, rust or other debris can cause the needle to seat improperly, causing excess fuel to be admitted to the throttle body. In this case, the injector should be cleaned and the needle and seat inspected (see Chapter 4). If the needle and seat are worn, then the leaking will persist and the parts should be renewed.
☐ Starting technique incorrect. Under normal circumstances (i.e. if all the components of the fuel injection system are good) the machine should start with the throttle closed.

No spark or weak spark

☐ Ignition switch OFF.
☐ Engine kill switch turned to the OFF position.
☐ Ignition or kill switch shorted. This is usually caused by water, corrosion, damage or excessive wear. The switches can be disassembled and cleaned with electrical contact cleaner. If cleaning does not help, renew the switches (see Chapter 8).
☐ Battery voltage low. Check and recharge the battery as necessary (Chapter 8).
☐ Ignition coil not making good contact. Make sure that the coils fit snugly over the plug ends.
☐ Spark plugs dirty, defective or worn out. Locate reason for fouled plugs using spark plug condition chart on the inside back cover and follow the plug maintenance procedures (see Chapter 1).
☐ Incorrect spark plugs. Wrong type or heat range. Check and install correct plugs (see Chapter 1).
☐ Ignition coil defective. Test and renew if necessary (Chapter 4).
☐ Fuel injection system shutdown due to system fault (Chapter 4).
☐ Camshaft position (CMP) sensor defective (see Chapter 4).
☐ Crankshaft position (CKP) sensor defective (see Chapter 4).
☐ Engine control module (ECM) defective (see Chapter 4).
☐ Wiring shorted or broken between:
   a) *Ignition switch and engine kill switch (or blown fuse)*
   b) *ECM and engine kill switch*
   c) *ECM and ignition coils*
   d) *ECM and CKP sensor*
☐ Make sure that all wiring connections are clean, dry and tight. Look for chafed and broken wires (see Chapters 4 and 8).

Compression low

☐ Spark plugs loose. Remove the plugs and inspect their threads. Reinstall and tighten securely (see Chapter 1).
☐ Cylinder head not sufficiently tightened down. If a cylinder head is suspected of being loose, then there's a chance that the gasket or head is damaged if the problem has persisted for any length of time. The head bolts should be tightened to the proper torque and in the correct sequence (Chapter 2).
☐ Improper valve clearance. This means that the valve is not closing completely and compression pressure is leaking past the valve. Check and adjust the valve clearances (Chapter 1).
☐ Cylinder and/or piston worn. Excessive wear will cause compression pressure to leak past the rings. This is usually accompanied by worn rings as well. A top-end overhaul is necessary (Chapter 2).
☐ Piston rings worn, weak, broken, or sticking. Broken or sticking piston rings usually indicate a lubrication or fuelling problem that causes excess carbon deposits to form on the pistons and rings. Top-end overhaul is necessary (Chapter 2).
☐ Piston ring-to-groove clearance excessive. This is caused by excessive wear of the piston ring lands. Piston renewal is necessary (Chapter 2).
☐ Cylinder head gasket damaged. If a head is allowed to become loose, or if excessive carbon build-up on the piston crown and combustion chamber causes extremely high compression, the head gasket may leak. Retorquing the head is not always sufficient to restore the seal, so gasket renewal is necessary (Chapter 2).
☐ Cylinder head warped. This is caused by overheating or improperly tightened head bolts. Machine shop resurfacing or head renewal is necessary (Chapter 2).
☐ Valve spring broken or weak. Caused by component failure or wear; the springs must be renewed (Chapter 2).
☐ Valve not seating properly. This is caused by a bent valve (from over-revving or improper valve adjustment), burned valve or seat (improper fuelling) or an accumulation of carbon deposits on the seat (from fuelling or lubrication problems). The valves must be cleaned and/or renewed (Chapter 2).

1 Engine doesn't start or is difficult to start (continued)

Stalls after starting

☐ Faulty ISC mechanism. Check the operation of the fast idle mechanism on K6/K7 models (see Chapter 4).

☐ Engine idle speed incorrect. Turn idle adjusting screw until the engine idles at the specified rpm – K6/K7 models (Chapter 1).

☐ Ignition malfunction (see Chapter 4).

☐ Fuel injection system malfunction (see Chapter 4).

☐ Fuel contaminated. The fuel can be contaminated with either dirt or water, or can change chemically if the machine has been unused for several months. Drain the tank and fuel system (Chapter 4).

☐ Intake air leak. Check for loose throttle body-to-inlet manifold connections, loose or damaged PAIR vacuum hose, or on K6/K7 models missing vacuum gauge blanking caps (Chapter 4).

Rough idle

☐ Idle speed incorrect (see Chapter 1).

☐ Ignition fault (see Chapter 4).

☐ Throttle valves not synchronised – K6/K7 models (see Chapter 1).

☐ Fuel injection system malfunction (see Chapter 4).

☐ Fuel contaminated. The fuel can be contaminated with either dirt or water, or can change chemically if the machine has been unused for several months. Drain the tank and the fuel system (Chapter 4).

☐ Intake air leak. Check for loose throttle body-to-inlet manifold connections, loose or damaged PAIR vacuum hose, or on K6/K7 models missing vacuum gauge blanking caps (Chapter 4).

☐ Air filter clogged. Clean or renew the air filter element (Chapter 1).

2 Poor running at low speeds

Spark weak

☐ Battery voltage low. Check and recharge battery (see Chapter 8).

☐ Ignition coils not making good contact. Make sure that the coils fit snugly over the plug ends.

☐ Spark plugs dirty, defective or worn out. Locate reason for fouled plugs using spark plug condition chart on the inside back cover and follow the plug maintenance procedures (see Chapter 1).

☐ Incorrect spark plugs. Wrong type or heat range. Check and install correct plugs (see Chapter 1).

☐ Ignition coil defective. Test and renew if necessary (see Chapter 4).

Fuel/air mixture incorrect

☐ Fuel tank breather hose obstructed.

☐ Fuel pump faulty, or the fuel filter is blocked (see Chapter 4).

☐ Fuel hose clogged. Remove the fuel hose and carefully blow through it. Check the fuel filter for damage.

☐ Fuel rail or injector clogged. For all of the injectors to be clogged, either a very bad batch of fuel with an unusual additive has been used, or some other foreign material has entered the tank. Check the fuel filter. In some cases, if a machine has been unused for several months, the fuel turns to a varnish-like liquid which can cause an injector needle to stick to its seat. Drain the tank and fuel system (Chapter 4).

☐ Intake air leak. Check for loose throttle body-to-inlet manifold connections and loose or damaged vacuum hoses (Chapter 4).

☐ Air filter clogged. Renew the air filter element (Chapter 1).

Compression low

☐ Spark plugs loose. Remove the plugs and inspect their threads. Reinstall and tighten securely (see Chapter 1).

☐ Cylinder head not sufficiently tightened down. If a cylinder head is suspected of being loose, then there's a chance that the gasket or head is damaged if the problem has persisted for any length of time. The head bolts should be tightened to the proper torque and in the correct sequence (Chapter 2).

☐ Improper valve clearance. This means that the valve is not closing completely and compression pressure is leaking past the valve. Check and adjust the valve clearances (Chapter 1).

☐ Cylinder and/or piston worn. Excessive wear will cause compression pressure to leak past the rings. This is usually accompanied by worn rings as well. A top-end overhaul is necessary (Chapter 2).

☐ Piston rings worn, weak, broken, or sticking. Broken or sticking piston rings usually indicate a lubrication or fuelling problem that causes excess carbon deposits to form on the pistons and rings. Top-end overhaul is necessary (Chapter 2).

☐ Piston ring-to-groove clearance excessive. This is caused by excessive wear of the piston ring lands. Piston renewal is necessary (Chapter 2).

☐ Cylinder head gasket damaged. If the head is allowed to become loose, or if excessive carbon build-up on the piston crown and combustion chamber causes extremely high compression, the head gasket may leak. Retorquing the head is not always sufficient to restore the seal, so gasket renewal is necessary (Chapter 2).

☐ Cylinder head warped. This is caused by overheating or improperly tightened head bolts. Machine shop resurfacing or head renewal is necessary (Chapter 2).

☐ Valve spring broken or weak. Caused by component failure or wear; the springs must be renewed (Chapter 2).

☐ Valve not seating properly. This is caused by a bent valve (from over-revving or improper valve adjustment), burned valve or seat (improper fuelling) or an accumulation of carbon deposits on the seat (from fuelling or lubrication problems). The valves must be cleaned and/or renewed (Chapter 2).

Poor acceleration

☐ Timing not advancing. The crankshaft position sensor (CKP) or the engine control module (ECM) may be defective (see Chapter 4). If so, they must be renewed.

☐ Throttle valves not synchronised on K6/K7 models (see Chapter 1).

☐ Engine oil viscosity too high. Using a heavier oil than that recommended in Chapter 1 can damage the oil pump or lubrication system and cause drag on the engine.

☐ Brakes dragging. Usually caused by debris which has entered the brake caliper piston seals, or from a warped disc or bent axle (see Chapter 6).

3 Poor running or no power at high speed

Firing incorrect

- [ ] Ignition coils not making good contact. Make sure that the coils fit snugly over the plug ends and that the wiring is secure.
- [ ] Spark plugs dirty, defective or worn out. Locate reason for fouled plugs using spark plug condition chart on the inside back cover and follow the plug maintenance procedures (see Chapter 1).
- [ ] Incorrect spark plugs. Wrong type or heat range. Check and install correct plugs (see Chapter 1).
- [ ] Ignition coil defective. Test and renew if necessary (see Chapter 4).
- [ ] Faulty ECM (engine control module) (see Chapter 4.

Fuel/air mixture incorrect

- [ ] Fuel tank breather hose obstructed.
- [ ] Fuel pump faulty, or the fuel filter is blocked (see Chapter 4).
- [ ] Fuel hose clogged. Remove the fuel hose and carefully blow through it. Check the fuel filter for damage.
- [ ] Fuel rail or injector clogged. For all of the injectors to be clogged, either a very bad batch of fuel with an unusual additive has been used, or some other foreign material has entered the tank. Check the fuel filter. In some cases, if a machine has been unused for several months, the fuel turns to a varnish-like liquid which can cause an injector needle to stick to its seat. Drain the tank and fuel system (Chapter 4).
- [ ] Intake air leak. Check for loose throttle body-to-inlet manifold connections and loose or damaged vacuum hoses (Chapter 4).
- [ ] Air filter clogged. Renew the air filter element (Chapter 1).

Compression low

- [ ] Spark plugs loose. Remove the plugs and inspect their threads. Reinstall and tighten securely (see Chapter 1).
- [ ] Cylinder head not sufficiently tightened down. If a cylinder head is suspected of being loose, then there's a chance that the gasket or head is damaged if the problem has persisted for any length of time. The head bolts should be tightened to the proper torque and in the correct sequence (Chapter 2).
- [ ] Improper valve clearance. This means that the valve is not closing completely and compression pressure is leaking past the valve. Check and adjust the valve clearances (Chapter 1).
- [ ] Cylinder and/or piston worn. Excessive wear will cause compression pressure to leak past the rings. This is usually accompanied by worn rings as well. A top-end overhaul is necessary (Chapter 2).
- [ ] Piston rings worn, weak, broken, or sticking. Broken or sticking piston rings usually indicate a lubrication or fuelling problem that causes excess carbon deposits to form on the pistons and rings. Top-end overhaul is necessary (Chapter 2).
- [ ] Piston ring-to-groove clearance excessive. This is caused by excessive wear of the piston ring lands. Piston renewal is necessary (Chapter 2).

- [ ] Cylinder head gasket damaged. If a head is allowed to become loose, or if excessive carbon build-up on the piston crown and combustion chamber causes extremely high compression, the head gasket may leak. Retorquing the head is not always sufficient to restore the seal, so gasket renewal is necessary (Chapter 2).
- [ ] Cylinder head warped. This is caused by overheating or improperly tightened head bolts. Machine shop resurfacing or head renewal is necessary (Chapter 2).
- [ ] Valve spring broken or weak. Caused by component failure or wear; the springs must be renewed (Chapter 2).
- [ ] Valve not seating properly. This is caused by a bent valve (from over-revving or improper valve adjustment), burned valve or seat (improper fuelling) or an accumulation of carbon deposits on the seat (from fuelling or lubrication problems). The valves must be cleaned and/or renewed (Chapter 2).

Knocking or pinking

- [ ] Carbon build-up in combustion chamber. Use of a fuel additive that will dissolve the adhesive bonding the carbon particles to the piston crown and chamber is the easiest way to remove the build-up. Otherwise, the cylinder head will have to be removed and decarbonised (Chapter 2).
- [ ] Incorrect or poor quality fuel. Old or improper grades of fuel can cause detonation. This causes the pistons to rattle, thus the knocking or pinking sound. Drain old fuel and always use the recommended fuel grade.
- [ ] Spark plug heat range incorrect. Uncontrolled detonation indicates the plug heat range is too hot. The plug in effect becomes a glow plug, raising cylinder temperatures. Install the proper heat range plug (Chapter 1).
- [ ] Improper air/fuel mixture. This will cause the cylinders to run hot, which leads to detonation. A blockage in the fuel system or an air leak can cause this imbalance (see Chapter 4).

Miscellaneous causes

- [ ] Throttle valve doesn't open fully. Adjust the throttle twistgrip freeplay (see Chapter 1).
- [ ] Clutch slipping due loose or worn clutch components (see Chapter 2).
- [ ] Timing not advancing. The crankshaft position sensor (CKP) or the engine control module (ECM) may be defective (see Chapter 4). If so, they must be renewed.
- [ ] Engine oil viscosity too high. Using a heavier oil than the one recommended in Chapter 1 can damage the oil pump or lubrication system and cause drag on the engine.
- [ ] Brakes dragging. Usually caused by debris which has entered the brake caliper piston seals, or from a warped disc or bent axle (see Chapter 6).

4 Overheating

Engine overheats

☐ Coolant level low. Check and add coolant (see *Pre-ride checks*).
☐ Leak in cooling system. Check cooling system hoses and radiator for leaks and other damage. Repair or renew parts as necessary (see Chapter 3).
☐ Faulty thermostat. Check and renew as described in Chapter 3.
☐ Faulty radiator cap. Remove the cap and have it pressure tested.
☐ Coolant passages clogged. Have the entire system drained and flushed, then refill with fresh coolant.
☐ Water pump defective. Remove the pump and check the components (see Chapter 3).
☐ Clogged or damaged radiator fins (see Chapter 3).
☐ Faulty cooling fan, fan switch, or relay (see Chapter 3).

Firing incorrect

☐ Wrongly connected ignition coil wiring.
☐ Spark plugs dirty, defective or worn out. Locate reason for fouled plugs using spark plug condition chart on the inside back cover and follow the plug maintenance procedures (see Chapter 1).
☐ Incorrect spark plugs. Wrong type or heat range. Check and install correct plugs (see Chapter 1).
☐ Ignition coil defective. Test and renew if necessary (see Chapter 5).
☐ Faulty ECM (engine control module) (see Chapter 4).

Fuel/air mixture incorrect

☐ Fuel tank breather hose obstructed.
☐ Fuel pump faulty, or the fuel filter is blocked (see Chapter 4).
☐ Fuel hose clogged. Remove the fuel hose and carefully blow through it. Check the fuel filter for damage.
☐ Fuel rail or injector clogged. For all of the injectors to be clogged, either a very bad batch of fuel with an unusual additive has been used, or some other foreign material has entered the tank. Check the fuel filter. In some cases, if a machine has been unused for several months, the fuel turns to a varnish-like liquid which can cause an injector needle to stick to its seat. Drain the tank and fuel system (Chapter 4).
☐ Intake air leak. Check for loose throttle body-to-intake manifold connections and loose or damaged vacuum hoses (Chapter 4).
☐ Air filter clogged. Renew the air filter element (Chapter 1).

Compression too high

☐ Carbon build-up in combustion chamber. Use of a fuel additive that will dissolve the adhesive bonding the carbon particles to the piston crown and chamber is the easiest way to remove the build-up. Otherwise, the cylinder head will have to be removed and decarbonised (Chapter 2).
☐ Improperly machined head surface or installation of incorrect gasket during engine assembly.

Engine load excessive

☐ Clutch slipping due loose or worn clutch components (see Chapter 2).
☐ Engine oil level too high. Too much oil will cause pressurisation of the crankcase and inefficient engine operation. Check Specifications and drain to proper level (see Chapter 1 and *Pre-ride checks*).
☐ Engine oil viscosity too high. Using a heavier oil than the one recommended in Chapter 1 can damage the oil pump or lubrication system as well as cause drag on the engine.
☐ Brakes dragging. Usually caused by debris which has entered the brake caliper piston seals, or from a warped disc or bent axle (see Chapter 6).

Lubrication inadequate

☐ Engine oil level too low. Friction caused by intermittent lack of lubrication or from oil that is overworked can cause overheating. The oil provides a definite cooling function in the engine. Check the oil level (see *Pre-ride checks*).
☐ Low engine oil pressure. Check the oil pressure (see Chapter 2).
☐ Blocked oil filter or oil cooler (see Chapter 2).
☐ Poor quality engine oil or incorrect viscosity or type. Oil is rated not only according to viscosity but also according to type. Some oils are not rated high enough for use in this engine. Check the Specifications section and change to the correct oil (Chapter 1).

Miscellaneous causes

☐ Modification to exhaust system. Most aftermarket exhaust systems cause the engine to run leaner, which make them run hotter. When installing an accessory exhaust system, always check with the manufacturer/supplier as to whether the ECM requires re-mapping.

5 Clutch problems

Clutch slipping

☐ Insufficient clutch cable freeplay. Check and adjust (see Chapter 1).

☐ Clutch plates worn or warped. Overhaul the clutch assembly (see Chapter 2).

☐ Clutch springs broken or weak. Old or heat-damaged (from slipping clutch) springs should be renewed (Chapter 2).

☐ Faulty clutch release mechanism. Renew any defective parts (see Chapter 2).

☐ Clutch centre or housing unevenly worn. This causes improper engagement of the plates. Renew the damaged or worn parts (see Chapter 2).

Clutch not disengaging completely

☐ Excessive clutch cable freeplay. Check and adjust (see Chapter 1).

☐ Clutch plates warped or damaged. This will cause clutch drag, which in turn will cause the machine to creep. Overhaul the clutch assembly (see Chapter 2).

☐ Clutch springs fatigued or broken. Check and renew the springs (see Chapter 2).

☐ Engine oil deteriorated. Old, thin oil will not provide proper lubrication for the plates, causing the clutch to drag. Renew the oil and filter (see Chapter 1).

☐ Engine oil viscosity too high. Using a heavier oil than recommended in Chapter 1 can cause the plates to stick together. Change to the correct weight oil.

☐ Clutch housing bearing seized on the transmission input shaft. Lack of lubrication, severe wear or damage can cause the bearing to seize. Overhaul of the clutch, and perhaps transmission, may be necessary to repair the damage (see Chapter 2).

☐ Faulty clutch release mechanism. Renew any defective parts (see Chapter 2).

☐ Loose clutch centre nut. Causes housing and centre misalignment putting a drag on the engine. Engagement adjustment continually varies. Overhaul the clutch assembly (see Chapter 2).

6 Gearchanging problems

Doesn't go into gear or lever doesn't return

☐ Clutch not disengaging (see above).

☐ Gearchange mechanism stopper arm spring weak or broken, or arm roller broken or worn. Renew the spring or arm (see Chapter 2).

☐ Selector fork(s) bent, worn or seized. Overhaul the transmission (see Chapter 2).

☐ Gear(s) stuck on shaft. Most often caused by a lack of lubrication or excessive wear in transmission bearings and bushes. Overhaul the transmission (see Chapter 2).

☐ Selector drum binding. Caused by lubrication failure or excessive wear. Renew the drum and bearing (see Chapter 2).

☐ Gearchange mechanism return spring weak or broken (see Chapter 2).

☐ Gearchange linkage arm broken. Splines stripped out of arm or shaft, caused by a loose linkage arm pinch bolt or from dropping the machine (see Chapter 2).

Jumps out of gear

☐ Selector fork(s) worn (see Chapter 2).

☐ Selector fork groove(s) in selector drum worn (see Chapter 2).

☐ Gear pinion dogs or dog slots worn or damaged. The gear pinions should be inspected and renewed. No attempt should be made to repair the worn parts.

Overselects

☐ Gearchange mechanism stopper arm spring weak or broken, or arm roller broken or worn. Renew the spring or arm (see Chapter 2).

☐ Gearchange mechanism return spring weak or broken (see Chapter 2).

7 Abnormal engine noise

Knocking or pinking

☐ Carbon build-up in combustion chamber. Use of a fuel additive that will dissolve the adhesive bonding the carbon particles to the piston crown and chamber is the easiest way to remove the build-up. Otherwise, the cylinder head will have to be removed and decarbonised (Chapter 2).

☐ Incorrect or poor quality fuel. Old or improper grades of fuel can cause detonation. This causes the piston to rattle, thus the knocking or pinking sound. Drain old fuel and always use the recommended fuel grade.

☐ Spark plug heat range incorrect. Uncontrolled detonation indicates the plug heat range is too hot. The plug in effect becomes a glow plug, raising cylinder temperatures. Install the proper heat range plug (Chapter 1).

☐ Improper air/fuel mixture. This will cause the cylinders to run hot, which leads to detonation. A blockage in the fuel system or an air leak can cause this imbalance (see Chapter 4).

Piston slap or rattling

☐ Cylinder-to-piston clearance excessive. Cylinder and/or piston worn, usually accompanied by worn rings as well. A top-end overhaul is necessary (see Chapter 2).

☐ Piston ring(s) worn, broken or sticking. Overhaul the top-end (see Chapter 2).

☐ Piston pin, piston pin bore or connecting rod small-end worn from high mileage or seized due to lack of lubrication (see Chapter 2).

☐ Piston seizure damage. Usually from lack of lubrication or overheating. Renew the pistons and upper crankcase, as necessary (see Chapter 2).

☐ Connecting rod big-end clearance excessive. Caused by excessive wear or lack of lubrication. Renew worn parts.

☐ Connecting rod bent. Caused by over-revving, trying to start a badly flooded engine or from ingesting a foreign object into the combustion chamber. Renew the damaged parts (Chapter 2).

Valve noise

☐ Incorrect valve clearances – check and adjust (see Chapter 1).

☐ Valve spring broken or weak. Check and renew weak valve springs (see Chapter 2).

☐ Camshaft or camshaft journals in the cylinder head worn or damaged. Lubrication failure at high rpm is usually the cause of damage due to insufficient oil or failure to change the oil at the recommended intervals. Since there are no replaceable bearings in the head, the head itself will have to be renewed (see Chapter 2).

Other noise

☐ Cylinder head gasket leaking. Check around the joint for blowing with the engine running.

☐ Exhaust pipe leaking at cylinder head connection. Caused by incorrect fit of pipe(s), loose exhaust flange or a damaged gasket. All exhaust system fasteners should be tightened evenly and carefully to avoid leaks (see Chapter 4).

☐ Crankshaft runout excessive. Caused by a bent crankshaft (from over-revving) or damage from an upper cylinder component failure. Can also be attributed to dropping the machine on either of the crankshaft ends.

☐ Engine mounting bolts loose – ensure all the bolts are tightened to the specified torque settings (see Chapter 2).

☐ Crankshaft bearings worn (see Chapter 2).

☐ Cam chain rattle, due to worn chain or defective tensioner. Also worn chain tensioner/guide blades (see Chapter 2).

8 Abnormal driveline noise

Clutch noise

☐ Clutch housing/friction plate clearance excessive (Chapter 2).
☐ Wear between the clutch housing splines and input shaft splines (Chapter 2).
☐ Worn release bearing (Chapter 2).

Transmission noise

☐ Bearings worn. Also includes the possibility that the shafts are worn. Overhaul the transmission (Chapter 2).
☐ Gears worn or chipped (Chapter 2).
☐ Metal chips jammed in gear teeth. Probably pieces from a broken clutch, gear or selector mechanism that were picked up by the gears. This will cause early bearing failure (Chapter 2).
☐ Engine oil level too low. Causes a howl from transmission. Also affects engine power and clutch operation (see *Pre-ride checks*).

Final drive noise

☐ Chain not adjusted properly (Chapter 1).
☐ Front or rear sprocket loose. Tighten fasteners (Chapter 6).
☐ Sprockets and/or chain worn. Renew sprockets and chain (Chapter 6).
☐ Rear sprocket warped. Renew sprocket (Chapter 6).
☐ Rubber dampers in rear wheel worn (Chapter 6).

9 Abnormal frame and suspension noise

Front end noise

☐ Low fluid level or improper viscosity oil in forks. This can sound like spurting and is usually accompanied by irregular fork action (Chapter 5).
☐ Spring weak or broken. Makes a clicking or scraping sound. Fork oil, when drained, will have a lot of metal particles in it (Chapter 5).
☐ Steering head bearings loose or damaged. Clicks when braking. Check and adjust or renew as necessary (Chapters 1 and 5).
☐ Fork yoke clamp bolts loose – ensure all the bolts are tightened to the specified torque (Chapter 5).
☐ Forks bent. Good possibility if machine has been dropped. Renew forks (Chapter 5).
☐ Front axle or axle pinch bolts loose. Tighten them to the specified torque (Chapter 6).
☐ Loose or worn wheel bearings. Check and renew as needed (Chapters 1 and 6).

Shock absorber noise

☐ Fluid level incorrect. Indicates a leak caused by defective seal. Shock will be covered with oil. Renew shock or seek advice on repair from a suspension specialist (Chapter 5).
☐ Defective shock absorber with internal damage. This is in the body of the shock and can't be remedied. The shock must be renewed or rebuilt (Chapter 5).

☐ Bent or damaged shock body. Renew the shock (Chapter 5).
☐ Loose or worn suspension linkage components. Check and renew as necessary (Chapter 5).

Brake noise

☐ Squeal caused by pad shim not installed or positioned correctly (where fitted) (Chapter 6).
☐ Squeal caused by dust on brake pads. Usually found in combination with glazed pads. Clean using brake cleaning solvent (Chapter 6).
☐ Pads glazed. Caused by excessive heat from prolonged hard use or from contamination. DO NOT use sandpaper, emery cloth, carborundum cloth or any other abrasive to roughen the pad surfaces as abrasives will stay in the pad material and damage the disc. A very fine flat file can be used, but pad renewal is suggested as a cure (Chapter 6).
☐ Contamination of brake pads. Oil or brake fluid can cause the brake pads to chatter or squeal. Fit new pads. Identify the cause of the contamination, especially check the caliper piston seals for leaking fluid. Clean disc thoroughly with brake system cleaner (Chapter 6).
☐ Disc warped. Can cause a chattering, clicking or intermittent squeal. Usually accompanied by a pulsating lever and uneven braking. Renew the disc (Chapter 6).
☐ Loose or worn wheel bearings. Check and renew as needed (Chapters 1 and 6).

10 Oil pressure warning LED comes on

Engine lubrication system

☐ Engine oil level low. Inspect for leak or other problem causing low oil level and add recommended oil (see *Pre-ride checks*).

☐ Engine oil pump defective, blocked oil strainer gauze or failed pressure regulator. Carry out an oil pressure check (Chapter 2).

☐ Engine oil viscosity too low. Very old, thin oil or an improper weight of oil used in the engine. Change to correct oil (Chapter 1).

☐ Camshaft or crankshaft journals worn. Excessive wear causing drop in oil pressure. Abnormal wear could be caused by oil starvation at high rpm from low oil level or improper weight or type of oil (Chapter 1).

Electrical system

☐ Oil pressure switch defective. Check the switch according to the procedure in Chapter 8. Renew it if it is defective.

☐ Oil pressure warning LED or symbol defective. Check for pinched, shorted, disconnected or damaged wiring (Chapter 8).

11 Excessive exhaust smoke

White smoke

☐ Piston rings worn or broken, causing oil from the crankcase to be pulled past the piston into the combustion chamber. Renew the rings (Chapter 2).

☐ Cylinders worn or scored. Caused by overheating or oil starvation. Install a new upper crankcase (Chapter 2).

☐ Valve oil seal damaged or worn. Renew oil seals (Chapter 2).

☐ Valve guide worn. Perform a complete valve job (Chapter 2).

☐ Engine oil level too high, which causes the oil to be forced past the rings. Drain oil to the proper level (see Chapter 1 and *Pre-ride checks*).

☐ Head gasket broken between oil return and cylinder. Causes oil to be pulled into the combustion chamber. Renew the head gasket and check the head for warpage (Chapter 2).

☐ Abnormal crankcase pressurisation which forces oil past the rings, usually caused by a clogged breather.

Black smoke

☐ Air filter clogged. Clean or renew the element (Chapter 1).

☐ Fuel injection system malfunction (Chapter 4).

Brown smoke

☐ Air filter poorly sealed or not installed (Chapter 1).

☐ Fuel injection system malfunction (Chapter 4).

12 Poor handling or stability

Handlebar hard to turn

☐ Steering head bearing adjuster nut too tight. Check adjustment as described in Chapter 1.

☐ Bearings damaged. Roughness can be felt as the bars are turned from side-to-side. Renew bearings (Chapter 5).

☐ Races dented or worn. Denting results from wear in only one position (e.g., straight ahead), from a collision or hitting a pothole or from dropping the machine. Renew bearings (Chapter 5).

☐ Steering stem lubrication inadequate. Causes are grease getting hard from age or being washed out by high pressure car washes. Disassemble steering head and repack bearings (Chapter 5).

☐ Steering stem bent. Caused by a collision, hitting a pothole or by dropping the machine. Renew damaged part. Don't try to straighten the steering stem (Chapter 5).

☐ Front tyre air pressure too low (see *Pre-ride checks*).

☐ Faulty steering damper. Remove the damper and see if the problem is solved, and if so check the damper (Chapter 5).

Handlebar shakes or vibrates excessively

☐ Tyres worn or out of balance (Chapter 6).

☐ Swingarm bearings worn. Renew worn bearings (Chapter 5).

☐ Failed steering damper (Chapter 5).

☐ Wheel rim(s) warped or damaged. Inspect wheels for runout (Chapter 6).

☐ Wheel bearings worn. Worn front or rear wheel bearings can cause poor tracking. Worn front bearings will cause wobble (Chapters 1 and 6).

☐ Fork yoke clamp bolts or handlebar clamp bolts loose. Tighten them to the specified torque (Chapter 5).

☐ Engine mounting bolts loose. Will cause excessive vibration with increased engine rpm – ensure all the bolts are tightened to the specified torque settings (see Chapter 2).

Machine pulls to one side

☐ Frame bent. Definitely suspect this if the machine has been dropped. May or may not be accompanied by cracking near the steering head, swingarm mountings or engine mountings. Renew the frame (Chapter 5).

☐ Wheels out of alignment. Caused by improper location of axle spacers or from bent steering stem or frame (Chapter 5).

☐ Forks bent. Disassemble the forks and renew the damaged parts (Chapter 5).

☐ Swingarm bent or twisted. Renew the arm (Chapter 5).

☐ Fork oil level uneven. Check and add or drain as necessary (Chapter 5).

Poor shock absorbing qualities

☐ Too hard:
   a) Suspension settings incorrect.
   b) Fork oil level excessive (Chapter 5).
   c) Fork oil viscosity too high. Use a lighter oil (see the Specifications in Chapter 5).
   d) Fork tube bent. Causes a harsh, sticking feeling (Chapter 5).
   e) Fork internal damage (Chapter 5).
   f) Shock shaft or body bent or damaged (Chapter 5).
   g) Shock internal damage.
   h) Tyre pressure too high (Pre-ride checks).

☐ Too soft:
   a) Suspension settings incorrect (Chapter 5).
   b) Fork oil level too low (Chapter 5).
   c) Fork oil viscosity too light (Chapter 5).
   d) Fork springs weak or broken (Chapter 5).
   e) Fork or shock oil leaking (Chapter 5).
   f) Shock internal damage (Chapter 5).

13 Braking problems

Brakes are spongy, don't hold

- ☐ Low brake fluid level (see *Pre-ride checks*).
- ☐ Air in hydraulic system. Caused by inattention to master cylinder fluid level or by leakage. Locate problem and bleed brakes (Chapter 6).
- ☐ Pad or disc worn (Chapters 1 and 6).
- ☐ Contaminated pads. Caused by contamination with oil, grease, brake fluid, etc. Fit new pads. Identify the cause of the contamination, especially check the caliper piston seals for leaking fluid. Clean disc thoroughly with brake system cleaner (Chapter 6).
- ☐ Brake fluid deteriorated. Fluid is old or contaminated. Drain system, replenish with new fluid and bleed the system (Chapter 6).
- ☐ Master cylinder internal seals worn or damaged causing fluid to bypass (Chapter 6).
- ☐ Master cylinder bore scratched by foreign material or broken spring. Repair or renew master cylinder (Chapter 6).
- ☐ Disc warped. Renew disc (Chapter 6).

Brake lever or pedal pulsates

- ☐ Disc warped. Renew disc (Chapter 6).
- ☐ Axle bent. Renew axle (Chapter 6).
- ☐ Brake caliper bolts loose – tighten the bolts to the specified torque (Chapter 6).
- ☐ Wheel warped or otherwise damaged (Chapter 6).
- ☐ Wheel bearings damaged or worn (Chapters 1 and 6).

Brakes drag

- ☐ Master cylinder piston seized. Caused by wear or damage to piston or cylinder bore (Chapter 6).
- ☐ Lever balky or stuck. Check pivot and lubricate (Chapter 6).
- ☐ Brake caliper piston seized in bore. Caused by corrosion or ingestion of dirt past deteriorated seal (Chapter 6).
- ☐ Rear brake caliper slider pins seized (Chapter 6).
- ☐ Brake pad damaged. Pad material separated from backing plate. Usually caused by faulty manufacturing process or from contact with chemicals. Renew pads (Chapter 6).
- ☐ Pads improperly installed (Chapter 6).
- ☐ Brake caliper incorrectly installed (Chapter 6).

14 Electrical problems

Battery dead or weak

- ☐ Battery faulty. Caused by sulphated plates which are shorted through sedimentation. Confirm with battery condition check (Chapter 8).
- ☐ Broken battery terminal making only occasional contact.
- ☐ Battery leads making poor contact (Chapter 8).
- ☐ Load excessive. Caused by addition of high wattage lights or other electrical accessories.
- ☐ Ignition switch defective. Switch either grounds (earths) internally or fails to shut off system. Renew the switch (Chapter 8).
- ☐ Regulator/rectifier defective (Chapter 8).
- ☐ Alternator stator coil open or shorted (Chapter 8).
- ☐ Charging system fault. Check for excessive current leakage (Chapter 8).
- ☐ Wiring faulty. Wiring grounded (earthed) or connections loose in ignition, charging or lighting circuits (Chapter 8).

Battery overcharged

- ☐ Regulator/rectifier defective. Overcharging is noticed when battery gets excessively warm (Chapter 8).
- ☐ Battery faulty. Confirm with battery condition check (Chapter 8).
- ☐ Battery amperage too low, wrong type or size of battery. Install manufacturer's specified amp-hour battery to handle charging load (Chapter 8).

A

ABS (Anti-lock braking system) A system, usually electronically controlled, that senses incipient wheel lockup during braking and relieves hydraulic pressure at wheel which is about to skid.

Aftermarket Components suitable for the motorcycle, but not produced by the motorcycle manufacturer.

Allen key A hexagonal wrench which fits into a recessed hexagonal hole.

Alternating current (ac) Current produced by an alternator. Requires converting to direct current by a rectifier for charging purposes.

Alternator Converts mechanical energy from the engine into electrical energy to charge the battery and power the electrical system.

Ampere (amp) A unit of measurement for the flow of electrical current. Current = Volts ÷ Ohms.

Ampere-hour (Ah) Measure of battery capacity.

Angle-tightening A torque expressed in degrees. Often follows a conventional tightening torque for cylinder head or main bearing fasteners **(see illustration)**.

Angle-tightening cylinder head bolts

Antifreeze A substance (usually ethylene glycol) mixed with water, and added to the cooling system, to prevent freezing of the coolant in winter. Antifreeze also contains chemicals to inhibit corrosion and the formation of rust and other deposits that would tend to clog the radiator and coolant passages and reduce cooling efficiency.

Anti-dive System attached to the fork lower leg (slider) to prevent fork dive when braking hard.

Anti-seize compound A coating that reduces the risk of seizing on fasteners that are subjected to high temperatures, such as exhaust clamp bolts and nuts.

API American Petroleum Institute. A quality standard for 4-stroke motor oils.

Asbestos A natural fibrous mineral with great heat resistance, commonly used in the composition of brake friction materials. Asbestos is a health hazard and the dust created by brake systems should never be inhaled or ingested.

ATF Automatic Transmission Fluid. Often used in front forks.

ATU Automatic Timing Unit. Mechanical device for advancing the ignition timing on early engines.

ATV All Terrain Vehicle. Often called a Quad.

Axial play Side-to-side movement.

Axle A shaft on which a wheel revolves. Also known as a spindle.

B

Backlash The amount of movement between meshed components when one component is held still. Usually applies to gear teeth.

Ball bearing A bearing consisting of a hardened inner and outer race with hardened steel balls between the two races.

Bearings Used between two working surfaces to prevent wear of the components and a build-up of heat. Four types of bearing are commonly used on motorcycles: plain shell bearings, ball bearings, tapered roller bearings and needle roller bearings.

Bevel gears Used to turn the drive through 90°. Typical applications are shaft final drive and camshaft drive **(see illustration)**.

Bevel gears are used to turn the drive through 90°

BHP Brake Horsepower. The British measurement for engine power output. Power output is now usually expressed in kilowatts (kW).

Bias-belted tyre Similar construction to radial tyre, but with outer belt running at an angle to the wheel rim.

Big-end bearing The bearing in the end of the connecting rod that's attached to the crankshaft.

Bleeding The process of removing air from an hydraulic system via a bleed nipple or bleed screw.

Bottom-end A description of an engine's crankcase components and all components contained there-in.

BTDC Before Top Dead Centre in terms of piston position. Ignition timing is often expressed in terms of degrees or millimetres BTDC.

Bush A cylindrical metal or rubber component used between two moving parts.

Burr Rough edge left on a component after machining or as a result of excessive wear.

C

Cam chain The chain which takes drive from the crankshaft to the camshaft(s).

Canister The main component in an evaporative emission control system (California market only); contains activated charcoal granules to trap vapours from the fuel system rather than allowing them to vent to the atmosphere.

Castellated Resembling the parapets along the top of a castle wall. For example, a castellated wheel axle or spindle nut.

Catalytic converter A device in the exhaust system of some machines which converts certain pollutants in the exhaust gases into less harmful substances.

Charging system Description of the components which charge the battery, ie the alternator, rectifer and regulator.

Circlip A ring-shaped clip used to prevent endwise movement of cylindrical parts and shafts. An internal circlip is installed in a groove in a housing; an external circlip fits into a groove on the outside of a cylindrical piece such as a shaft. Also known as a snap-ring.

Clearance The amount of space between two parts. For example, between a piston and a cylinder, between a bearing and a journal, etc.

Coil spring A spiral of elastic steel found in various sizes throughout a vehicle, for example as a springing medium in the suspension and in the valve train.

Compression Reduction in volume, and increase in pressure and temperature, of a gas, caused by squeezing it into a smaller space.

Compression damping Controls the speed the suspension compresses when hitting a bump.

Compression ratio The relationship between cylinder volume when the piston is at top dead centre and cylinder volume when the piston is at bottom dead centre.

Continuity The uninterrupted path in the flow of electricity. Little or no measurable resistance.

Continuity tester Self-powered bleeper or test light which indicates continuity.

Cp Candlepower. Bulb rating commonly found on US motorcycles.

Crossply tyre Tyre plies arranged in a criss-cross pattern. Usually four or six plies used, hence 4PR or 6PR in tyre size codes.

Cush drive Rubber damper segments fitted between the rear wheel and final drive sprocket to absorb transmission shocks **(see illustration)**.

Cush drive rubbers dampen out transmission shocks

D

Degree disc Calibrated disc for measuring piston position. Expressed in degrees.

Dial gauge Clock-type gauge with adapters for measuring runout and piston position. Expressed in mm or inches.

Diaphragm The rubber membrane in a master cylinder or carburettor which seals the upper chamber.

Diaphragm spring A single sprung plate often used in clutches.

Direct current (dc) Current produced by a dc generator.

Decarbonisation The process of removing carbon deposits - typically from the combustion chamber, valves and exhaust port/system.

Detonation Destructive and damaging explosion of fuel/air mixture in combustion chamber instead of controlled burning.

Diode An electrical valve which only allows current to flow in one direction. Commonly used in rectifiers and starter interlock systems.

Disc valve (or rotary valve) A induction system used on some two-stroke engines.

Double-overhead camshaft (DOHC) An engine that uses two overhead camshafts, one for the intake valves and one for the exhaust valves.

Drivebelt A toothed belt used to transmit drive to the rear wheel on some motorcycles. A drivebelt has also been used to drive the camshafts. Drivebelts are usually made of Kevlar.

Driveshaft Any shaft used to transmit motion. Commonly used when referring to the final driveshaft on shaft drive motorcycles.

E

Earth return The return path of an electrical circuit, utilising the motorcycle's frame.

ECU (Electronic Control Unit) A computer which controls (for instance) an ignition system, or an anti-lock braking system.

EGO Exhaust Gas Oxygen sensor. Sometimes called a Lambda sensor.

Electrolyte The fluid in a lead-acid battery.

EMS (Engine Management System) A computer controlled system which manages the fuel injection and the ignition systems in an integrated fashion.

Endfloat The amount of lengthways movement between two parts. As applied to a crankshaft, the distance that the crankshaft can move side-to-side in the crankcase.

Endless chain A chain having no joining link. Common use for cam chains and final drive chains.

EP (Extreme Pressure) Oil type used in locations where high loads are applied, such as between gear teeth.

Evaporative emission control system Describes a charcoal filled canister which stores fuel vapours from the tank rather than allowing them to vent to the atmosphere. Usually only fitted to California models and referred to as an EVAP system.

Expansion chamber Section of two-stroke engine exhaust system so designed to improve engine efficiency and boost power.

F

Feeler blade or gauge A thin strip or blade of hardened steel, ground to an exact thickness, used to check or measure clearances between parts.

Final drive Description of the drive from the transmission to the rear wheel. Usually by chain or shaft, but sometimes by belt.

Firing order The order in which the engine cylinders fire, or deliver their power strokes, beginning with the number one cylinder.

Flooding Term used to describe a high fuel level in the carburettor float chambers, leading to fuel overflow. Also refers to excess fuel in the combustion chamber due to incorrect starting technique.

Free length The no-load state of a component when measured. Clutch, valve and fork spring lengths are measured at rest, without any preload.

Freeplay The amount of travel before any action takes place. The looseness in a linkage, or an assembly of parts, between the initial application of force and actual movement. For example, the distance the rear brake pedal moves before the rear brake is actuated.

Fuel injection The fuel/air mixture is metered electronically and directed into the engine intake ports (indirect injection) or into the cylinders (direct injection). Sensors supply information on engine speed and conditions.

Fuel/air mixture The charge of fuel and air going into the engine. See **Stoichiometric ratio**.

Fuse An electrical device which protects a circuit against accidental overload. The typical fuse contains a soft piece of metal which is calibrated to melt at a predetermined current flow (expressed as amps) and break the circuit.

G

Gap The distance the spark must travel in jumping from the centre electrode to the side electrode in a spark plug. Also refers to the distance between the ignition rotor and the pickup coil in an electronic ignition system.

Gasket Any thin, soft material - usually cork, cardboard, asbestos or soft metal - installed between two metal surfaces to ensure a good seal. For instance, the cylinder head gasket seals the joint between the block and the cylinder head.

Gauge An instrument panel display used to monitor engine conditions. A gauge with a movable pointer on a dial or a fixed scale is an analogue gauge. A gauge with a numerical readout is called a digital gauge.

Gear ratios The drive ratio of a pair of gears in a gearbox, calculated on their number of teeth.

Glaze-busting see **Honing**

Grinding Process for renovating the valve face and valve seat contact area in the cylinder head.

Gudgeon pin The shaft which connects the connecting rod small-end with the piston. Often called a piston pin or wrist pin.

H

Helical gears Gear teeth are slightly curved and produce less gear noise that straight-cut gears. Often used for primary drives.

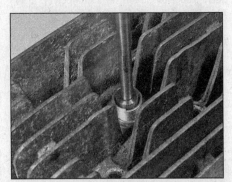

Installing a Helicoil thread insert in a cylinder head

Helicoil A thread insert repair system. Commonly used as a repair for stripped spark plug threads **(see illustration)**.

Honing A process used to break down the glaze on a cylinder bore (also called glaze-busting). Can also be carried out to roughen a rebored cylinder to aid ring bedding-in.

HT (High Tension) Description of the electrical circuit from the secondary winding of the ignition coil to the spark plug.

Hydraulic A liquid filled system used to transmit pressure from one component to another. Common uses on motorcycles are brakes and clutches.

Hydrometer An instrument for measuring the specific gravity of a lead-acid battery.

Hygroscopic Water absorbing. In motorcycle applications, braking efficiency will be reduced if DOT 3 or 4 hydraulic fluid absorbs water from the air - care must be taken to keep new brake fluid in tightly sealed containers.

I

lbf ft Pounds-force feet. An imperial unit of torque. Sometimes written as ft-lbs.

lbf in Pound-force inch. An imperial unit of torque, applied to components where a very low torque is required. Sometimes written as in-lbs.

IC Abbreviation for Integrated Circuit.

Ignition advance Means of increasing the timing of the spark at higher engine speeds. Done by mechanical means (ATU) on early engines or electronically by the ignition control unit on later engines.

Ignition timing The moment at which the spark plug fires, expressed in the number of crankshaft degrees before the piston reaches the top of its stroke, or in the number of millimetres before the piston reaches the top of its stroke.

Infinity (∞) Description of an open-circuit electrical state, where no continuity exists.

Inverted forks (upside down forks) The sliders or lower legs are held in the yokes and the fork tubes or stanchions are connected to the wheel axle (spindle). Less unsprung weight and stiffer construction than conventional forks.

J

JASO Quality standard for 2-stroke oils.

Joule The unit of electrical energy.

Journal The bearing surface of a shaft.

K

Kickstart Mechanical means of turning the engine over for starting purposes. Only usually fitted to mopeds, small capacity motorcycles and off-road motorcycles.

Kill switch Handebar-mounted switch for emergency ignition cut-out. Cuts the ignition circuit on all models, and additionally prevent starter motor operation on others.

km Symbol for kilometre.

kmh Abbreviation for kilometres per hour.

L

Lambda (λ) sensor A sensor fitted in the exhaust system to measure the exhaust gas oxygen content (excess air factor).

Lapping see **Grinding**.
LCD Abbreviation for Liquid Crystal Display.
LED Abbreviation for Light Emitting Diode.
Liner A steel cylinder liner inserted in a aluminium alloy cylinder block.
Locknut A nut used to lock an adjustment nut, or other threaded component, in place.
Lockstops The lugs on the lower triple clamp (yoke) which abut those on the frame, preventing handlebar-to-fuel tank contact.
Lockwasher A form of washer designed to prevent an attaching nut from working loose.
LT Low Tension Description of the electrical circuit from the power supply to the primary winding of the ignition coil.

M

Main bearings The bearings between the crankshaft and crankcase.
Maintenance-free (MF) battery A sealed battery which cannot be topped up.
Manometer Mercury-filled calibrated tubes used to measure intake tract vacuum. Used to synchronise carburettors on multi-cylinder engines.
Micrometer A precision measuring instrument that measures component outside diameters **(see illustration)**.

Tappet shims are measured with a micrometer

MON (Motor Octane Number) A measure of a fuel's resistance to knock.
Monograde oil An oil with a single viscosity, eg SAE80W.
Monoshock A single suspension unit linking the swingarm or suspension linkage to the frame.
mph Abbreviation for miles per hour.
Multigrade oil Having a wide viscosity range (eg 10W40). The W stands for Winter, thus the viscosity ranges from SAE10 when cold to SAE40 when hot.
Multimeter An electrical test instrument with the capability to measure voltage, current and resistance. Some meters also incorporate a continuity tester and buzzer.

N

Needle roller bearing Inner race of caged needle rollers and hardened outer race. Examples of uncaged needle rollers can be found on some engines. Commonly used in rear suspension applications and in two-stroke engines.
Nm Newton metres.
NOx Oxides of Nitrogen. A common toxic pollutant emitted by petrol engines at higher temperatures.

O

Octane The measure of a fuel's resistance to knock.
OE (Original Equipment) Relates to components fitted to a motorcycle as standard or replacement parts supplied by the motorcycle manufacturer.
Ohm The unit of electrical resistance. Ohms = Volts ÷ Current.
Ohmmeter An instrument for measuring electrical resistance.
Oil cooler System for diverting engine oil outside of the engine to a radiator for cooling purposes.
Oil injection A system of two-stroke engine lubrication where oil is pump-fed to the engine in accordance with throttle position.
Open-circuit An electrical condition where there is a break in the flow of electricity - no continuity (high resistance).
O-ring A type of sealing ring made of a special rubber-like material; in use, the O-ring is compressed into a groove to provide the sealing action.
Oversize (OS) Term used for piston and ring size options fitted to a rebored cylinder.
Overhead cam (sohc) engine An engine with single camshaft located on top of the cylinder head.
Overhead valve (ohv) engine An engine with the valves located in the cylinder head, but with the camshaft located in the engine block or crankcase.
Oxygen sensor A device installed in the exhaust system which senses the oxygen content in the exhaust and converts this information into an electric current. Also called a Lambda sensor.

P

Plastigauge A thin strip of plastic thread, available in different sizes, used for measuring clearances. For example, a strip of Plastigauge is laid across a bearing journal. The parts are assembled and dismantled; the width of the crushed strip indicates the clearance between journal and bearing.
Polarity Either negative or positive earth (ground), determined by which battery lead is connected to the frame (earth return). Modern motorcycles are usually negative earth.
Pre-ignition A situation where the fuel/air mixture ignites before the spark plug fires. Often due to a hot spot in the combustion chamber caused by carbon build-up. Engine has a tendency to 'run-on'.
Pre-load (suspension) The amount a spring is compressed when in the unloaded state. Preload can be applied by gas, spacer or mechanical adjuster.
Premix The method of engine lubrication on older two-stroke engines. Engine oil is mixed with the petrol in the fuel tank in a specific ratio. The fuel/oil mix is sometimes referred to as "petroil".
Primary drive Description of the drive from the crankshaft to the clutch. Usually by gear or chain.
PS Pfedestärke - a German interpretation of BHP.
PSI Pounds-force per square inch. Imperial measurement of tyre pressure and cylinder pressure measurement.
PTFE Polytetrafluroethylene. A low friction substance.

Pulse secondary air injection system A process of promoting the burning of excess fuel present in the exhaust gases by routing fresh air into the exhaust ports.

Q

Quartz halogen bulb Tungsten filament surrounded by a halogen gas. Typically used for the headlight **(see illustration)**.

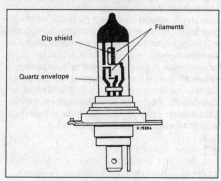

Quartz halogen headlight bulb construction

R

Rack-and-pinion A pinion gear on the end of a shaft that mates with a rack (think of a geared wheel opened up and laid flat). Sometimes used in clutch operating systems.
Radial play Up and down movement about a shaft.
Radial ply tyres Tyre plies run across the tyre (from bead to bead) and around the circumference of the tyre. Less resistant to tread distortion than other tyre types.
Radiator A liquid-to-air heat transfer device designed to reduce the temperature of the coolant in a liquid cooled engine.
Rake A feature of steering geometry - the angle of the steering head in relation to the vertical **(see illustration)**.

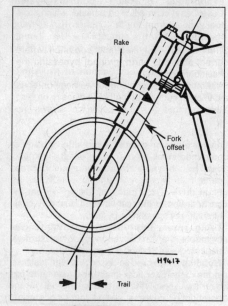

Steering geometry

Rebore Providing a new working surface to the cylinder bore by boring out the old surface. Necessitates the use of oversize piston and rings.

Rebound damping A means of controlling the oscillation of a suspension unit spring after it has been compressed. Resists the spring's natural tendency to bounce back after being compressed.

Rectifier Device for converting the ac output of an alternator into dc for battery charging.

Reed valve An induction system commonly used on two-stroke engines.

Regulator Device for maintaining the charging voltage from the generator or alternator within a specified range.

Relay A electrical device used to switch heavy current on and off by using a low current auxiliary circuit.

Resistance Measured in ohms. An electrical component's ability to pass electrical current.

RON (Research Octane Number) A measure of a fuel's resistance to knock.

rpm revolutions per minute.

Runout The amount of wobble (in-and-out movement) of a wheel or shaft as it's rotated. The amount a shaft rotates 'out-of-true'. The out-of-round condition of a rotating part.

S

SAE (Society of Automotive Engineers) A standard for the viscosity of a fluid.

Sealant A liquid or paste used to prevent leakage at a joint. Sometimes used in conjunction with a gasket.

Service limit Term for the point where a component is no longer useable and must be renewed.

Shaft drive A method of transmitting drive from the transmission to the rear wheel.

Shell bearings Plain bearings consisting of two shell halves. Most often used as big-end and main bearings in a four-stroke engine. Often called bearing inserts.

Shim Thin spacer, commonly used to adjust the clearance or relative positions between two parts. For example, shims inserted into or under tappets or followers to control valve clearances. Clearance is adjusted by changing the thickness of the shim.

Short-circuit An electrical condition where current shorts to earth (ground) bypassing the circuit components.

Skimming Process to correct warpage or repair a damaged surface, eg on brake discs or drums.

Slide-hammer A special puller that screws into or hooks onto a component such as a shaft or bearing; a heavy sliding handle on the shaft bottoms against the end of the shaft to knock the component free.

Small-end bearing The bearing in the upper end of the connecting rod at its joint with the gudgeon pin.

Spalling Damage to camshaft lobes or bearing journals shown as pitting of the working surface.

Specific gravity (SG) The state of charge of the electrolyte in a lead-acid battery. A measure of the electrolyte's density compared with water.

Straight-cut gears Common type gear used on gearbox shafts and for oil pump and water pump drives.

Stanchion The inner sliding part of the front forks, held by the yokes. Often called a fork tube.

Stoichiometric ratio The optimum chemical air/fuel ratio for a petrol engine, said to be 14.7 parts of air to 1 part of fuel.

Sulphuric acid The liquid (electrolyte) used in a lead-acid battery. Poisonous and extremely corrosive.

Surface grinding (lapping) Process to correct a warped gasket face, commonly used on cylinder heads.

T

Tapered-roller bearing Tapered inner race of caged needle rollers and separate tapered outer race. Examples of taper roller bearings can be found on steering heads.

Tappet A cylindrical component which transmits motion from the cam to the valve stem, either directly or via a pushrod and rocker arm. Also called a cam follower.

TCS Traction Control System. An electronically-controlled system which senses wheel spin and reduces engine speed accordingly.

TDC Top Dead Centre denotes that the piston is at its highest point in the cylinder.

Thread-locking compound Solution applied to fastener threads to prevent slackening. Select type to suit application.

Thrust washer A washer positioned between two moving components on a shaft. For example, between gear pinions on gearshaft.

Timing chain See **Cam Chain.**

Timing light Stroboscopic lamp for carrying out ignition timing checks with the engine running.

Top-end A description of an engine's cylinder block, head and valve gear components.

Torque Turning or twisting force about a shaft.

Torque setting A prescribed tightness specified by the motorcycle manufacturer to ensure that the bolt or nut is secured correctly. Undertightening can result in the bolt or nut coming loose or a surface not being sealed. Overtightening can result in stripped threads, distortion or damage to the component being retained.

Torx key A six-point wrench.

Tracer A stripe of a second colour applied to a wire insulator to distinguish that wire from another one with the same colour insulator. For example, Br/W is often used to denote a brown insulator with a white tracer.

Trail A feature of steering geometry. Distance from the steering head axis to the tyre's central contact point.

Triple clamps The cast components which extend from the steering head and support the fork stanchions or tubes. Often called fork yokes.

Turbocharger A centrifugal device, driven by exhaust gases, that pressurises the intake air. Normally used to increase the power output from a given engine displacement.

TWI Abbreviation for Tyre Wear Indicator. Indicates the location of the tread depth indicator bars on tyres.

U

Universal joint or U-joint (UJ) A double-pivoted connection for transmitting power from a driving to a driven shaft through an angle. Typically found in shaft drive assemblies.

Unsprung weight Anything not supported by the bike's suspension (ie the wheel, tyres, brakes, final drive and bottom (moving) part of the suspension).

V

Vacuum gauges Clock-type gauges for measuring intake tract vacuum. Used for carburettor synchronisation on multi-cylinder engines.

Valve A device through which the flow of liquid, gas or vacuum may be stopped, started or regulated by a moveable part that opens, shuts or partially obstructs one or more ports or passageways. The intake and exhaust valves in the cylinder head are of the poppet type.

Valve clearance The clearance between the valve tip (the end of the valve stem) and the rocker arm or tappet/follower. The valve clearance is measured when the valve is closed. The correct clearance is important - if too small the valve won't close fully and will burn out, whereas if too large noisy operation will result.

Valve lift The amount a valve is lifted off its seat by the camshaft lobe.

Valve timing The exact setting for the opening and closing of the valves in relation to piston position.

Vernier caliper A precision measuring instrument that measures inside and outside dimensions. Not quite as accurate as a micrometer, but more convenient.

VIN Vehicle Identification Number. Term for the bike's engine and frame numbers.

Viscosity The thickness of a liquid or its resistance to flow.

Volt A unit for expressing electrical "pressure" in a circuit. Volts = current x ohms.

W

Water pump A mechanically-driven device for moving coolant around the engine.

Watt A unit for expressing electrical power. Watts = volts x current.

Wear limit see **Service limit**

Wet liner A liquid-cooled engine design where the pistons run in liners which are directly surrounded by coolant **(see illustration).**

Wet liner arrangement

Wheelbase Distance from the centre of the front wheel to the centre of the rear wheel.

Wiring harness or loom Describes the electrical wires running the length of the motorcycle and enclosed in tape or plastic sheathing. Wiring coming off the main harness is usually referred to as a sub harness.

Woodruff key A key of semi-circular or square section used to locate a gear to a shaft. Often used to locate the alternator rotor on the crankshaft.

Wrist pin Another name for gudgeon or piston pin.

Note: *References throughout this index are in the form - "Chapter number" • "Page number"*

Haynes Motorcycle Manuals – The Complete List

Title		Book No
APRILIA RS50 (99 – 06) & RS125 (93 – 06)		4298
Aprilia RSV1000 Mille (98 – 03)	◆	4255
Aprilia SR50		4755
BMW 2-valve Twins (70 -96)	◆	0249
BMW F650	◆	4761
BMW K100 & 75 2-valve models (83 - 96)	◆	1373
BMW F800 (F650) Twins (06 – 10)	◆	4872
BMW R850, 1100 & 1150 4-valve Twins (93 – 06)	◆	3466
BMW R1200 (04 – 09)	◆	4598
BMW R1200 dohc Twins (10 – 12)	◆	4925
BSA Bantam (48 – 71)		0117
BSA Unit Singles (58 – 72)		0127
BSA Pre-unit Singles (54 – 61)		0326
BSA A7 & A10 Twins (47 – 62)		0121
BSA A50 & A65 Twins (62 – 73)		0155
CHINESE, Taiwanese & Korean Scooters		4768
Chinese, Taiwanese & Korean 125cc motorcyles		4781
Pulse/Pioneer Adrenaline, Sinnis Apache, Superbyke RMR (07 – 14)	◇◆	5750
DUCATI 600, 620, 750 & 900 2-valve V-twins (91 – 05)	◆	3290
Ducati Mk III & Desmo singles (69 – 76)	◇	0445
Ducati 748, 916 & 996 4-valve V-twins (94 – 01)	◆	3756
GILERA Runner, DNA, Ice & SKP/Stalker (97 – 11)		4163
HARLEY-DAVIDSON Sportsters (70 – 10)	◆	2534
Harley-Davidson Shovelhead & Evolution Big Twins (70 -99)	◆	2536
Harley-Davidson Twin Cam 88, 96 & 103 models (99 – 10)	◆	2478
HONDA NB, ND, NP & NS50 Melody (81 -85)	◇	0622
Honda NE/NB50 Vision & SA50 Vision Met-in (85-95)	◇	1278
Honda MB, MBX, MT & MTX50 (80 – 93)		0731
Honda C50, C70 & C90 (67 – 03)		0324
Honda XR50/70/80/100R & CRF50/70/80/100F (85 – 07)		2218
Honda XL/XR 80, 100, 125, 185 & 200 2-valve models (78 – 87)		0566
Honda H100 & H100S Singles (80 – 92)	◇	0734
Honda 125 Scooters (00 – 09)		4873
Honda ANF125 Innova Scooters (03 -12)	◆	4926
Honda CB/CD125T & CM125C Twins (77 – 88)	◇	0571
Honda CBF125 (09 – 14)	◆	5540
Honda CG125 (76 – 07)	◇	0433
Honda NS125 (86 – 93)	◇	3056
Honda CBR125R (04 – 10)		4620
Honda CBR125R, CBR250R & CRF250L/M (11 – 14)	◆	5919
Honda MBX/MTX125 & MTX200 (83 – 93)	◇	1132
Honda XL125V & VT125C (99 – 11)		4899
Honda CD/CM185 200T & CM250C 2-valve Twins (77 – 85)		0572
Honda CMX250 Rebel & CB250 Nighthawk Twins (85 – 09)	◇	2756
Honda XL/XR 250 & 500 (78 – 84)		0567
Honda XR250L, XR250R & XR400R (86 – 04)		2219
Honda CB250 & CB400N Super Dreams (78 – 84)	◇	0540
Honda CR Motocross Bikes (86 – 07)		2222
Honda CRF250 & CRF450 (02 – 06)		2630
Honda CBR400RR Fours (88 – 99)	◇◆	3552
Honda VFR400 (NC30) & RVF400 (NC35) V-Fours (89 – 98)	◇◆	3496
Honda CB500 (93 – 02) & CBF500 (03 – 08)	◇	3753
Honda CB400 & CB550 Fours (73 – 77)		0262
Honda CX/GL500 & 650 V-Twins (78 – 86)		0442
Honda CBX550 Four (82 – 86)	◇	0940
Honda XL600R & XR600R (83 – 08)	◆	2183
Honda XL600/650V Transalp & XRV750 Africa Twin (87 – 07)	◆	3919
Honda CB600 Hornet, CBF600 & CBR600F (07 – 12)	◆	5572
Honda CBR600F1 & 1000F Fours (87 – 96)	◆	1730
Honda CBR600F2 & F3 Fours (91 – 98)	◆	2070
Honda CBR600F4 (99 – 06)	◆	3911
Honda CB600F Hornet & CBF600 (98 – 06)	◇◆	3915
Honda CBR600RR (03 – 06)	◆	4590
Honda CBR600RR (07 -12)	◆	4795
Honda CB650 sohc Fours (78 – 84)		0665
Honda NTV600 Revere, NTV650 & NT650V Deauville (88 – 05)	◇◆	3243
Honda Shadow VT600 & 750 (USA) (88 – 09)		2312
Honda NT700V Deauville & XL700V Transalp (06 -13)	◆	5541
Honda CB750 sohc Four (69 – 79)		0131
Honda V45/65 Sabre & Magna (82 – 88)		0820
Honda VFR750 & 700 V-Fours (86 – 97)	◆	2101
Honda VFR800 V-Fours (97 – 01)	◆	3703
Honda VFR800 V-Tec V-Fours (02 – 09)	◆	4196
Honda CB750 & CB900 dohc Fours (78 – 84)		0535
Honda CBF1000 (06 -10) & CB1000R (08 – 11)	◆	4927
Honda VTR1000 Firestorm, Super Hawk & XL1000V Varadero (97 – 08)	◆	3744
Honda CBR900RR Fireblade (92 – 99)	◆	2161
Honda CBR900RR Fireblade (00 – 03)	◆	4060
Honda CBR1000RR Fireblade (04 – 07)	◆	4604
Honda CBR1000RR Fireblade (08 – 13)	◆	5688
Honda CBR1100XX Super Blackbird (97 – 07)	◆	3901
Honda ST1100 Pan European V-Fours (90 – 02)	◆	3384
Honda ST1300 Pan European (02 -11)	◆	4908
Honda Shadow VT1100 (USA) (85 – 07)		2313
Honda GL1000 Gold Wing (75 – 79)		0309
Honda GL1100 Gold Wing (79 – 81)		0669
Honda Gold Wing 1200 (USA) (84 - 87)		2199
Honda Gold Wing 1500 (USA) (88 – 00)		2225
Honda Goldwing GL1800	◆	2787
KAWASAKI AE/AR 50 & 80 (81 – 95)		1007
Kawasaki KC, KE & KH100 (75 – 99)		1371
Kawasaki KMX125 & 200 (86 – 02)	◇	3046
Kawasaki 250, 350 & 400 Triples (72 – 79)		0134
Kawasaki 400 & 440 Twins (74 – 81)		0281
Kawasaki 400, 500 & 550 Fours (79 – 91)		0910
Kawasaki EN450 & 500 Twins (Ltd/Vulcan) (85 – 07)		2053
Kawasaki ER-6F & ER-6N (06 -10)	◆	4874
Kawasaki EX500 (GPZ500S) & ER500 (ER-5) (87 – 08)	◆	2052
Kawasaki ZX600 (ZZ-R600 & Ninja ZX-6) (90 – 06)	◆	2146
Kawasaki ZX-6R Ninja Fours (95 – 02)	◆	3451
Kawasaki ZX-6R (03 – 06)	◆	4742
Kawasaki ZX600 (GPZ600R, GPX600R, Ninja 600R & RX) & ZX750 (GPX750R, Ninja 750R) (85 – 97)	◆	1780
Kawasaki 650 Four (76 – 78)		0373
Kawasaki Vulcan 700/750 & 800 (85 – 04)	◆	2457
Kawasaki Vulcan 1500 & 1600 (87 – 08)	◆	4913
Kawasaki 750 Air-cooled Fours		0574
Kawasaki ZR550 & 750 Zephyr Fours (90 – 97)	◆	3382
Kawasaki Z750 & Z1000 (03 – 08)	◆	4762
Kawasaki ZX750 (Ninja ZX-7 & ZXR750) Fours (89 – 96)	◆	2054
Kawasaki Ninja ZX-7R & ZX-9R (94 – 04)	◆	3721
Kawasaki 900 & 1000 Fours (73 – 77)		0222
Kawasaki ZX900, 1000 & 1100 Liquid-cooled Fours (83 – 97)	◆	1681
Kawasaki ZX-10R (04 – 10)	◆	5542
KTM EXC Enduro & SX Motocross (00 – 07)	◆	4629
LAMBRETTA Scooters (58 – 00)	◆	5573
MOTO GUZZI 750, 850 & 1000 V-Twins (74 – 78)		0339
MZ ETZ models (81 – 95)	◇	1680
NORTON 500, 600, 650 & 750 Twins (57 – 70)		0187
Norton Commando (68 – 77)		0125
PEUGEOT Speedfight, Trekker & Vivacity Scooters (96 – 08)	◇	3920
Peugeot V-Clic, Speedfight 3, Vivacity 3, Kisbee & Tweet (08 – 14)	◇◆	5751
PIAGGIO (Vespa) Scooters (91 – 09)	◇	3492
SUZUKI GT, ZR & TS50 (77 – 90)	◇	0799
Suzuki TS50X (84 – 00)	◇	1599
Suzuki 100, 125, 185 & 250 Air-cooled Trail bikes (79 – 89)		0797
Suzuki GP100 & 125 Singles (78 – 93)	◇	0576
Suzuki GS, GN, GZ & DR125 Singles (82 – 05)	◇	0888
Suzuki Burgman 250 & 400 (98 – 11)	◆	4909
Suzuki GSX-R600/750 (06 – 09)	◆	4790
Suzuki 250 & 350 Twins (68 – 78)		0120
Suzuki GT250X7, GT200X5 & SB200 Twins (78 – 83)	◇	0469
Suzuki DR-Z400 (00 – 10)	◆	2933
Suzuki GS/GSX250, 400 & 450 Twins (79 – 85)		0736
Suzuki GS500 Twin (89 – 08)	◆	3238
Suzuki GS550 (77 – 82) & GS750 Fours (76 – 79)		0363
Suzuki GS/GSX550 4-valve Fours (83 – 88)		1133
Suzuki SV650 & SV650S (99 – 08)	◆	3912
Suzuki DL650 V-Strom & SFV650 Gladius (04 – 13)	◆	5643
Suzuki GSX-R600 & 750 (96 – 00)	◆	3553
Suzuki GSX-R600 (01 – 03), GSX-R750 (00 – 03) & GSX-R1000 (01 – 02)	◆	3986
Suzuki GSX-R600/750 (04 – 05) & GSX-R1000 (03 – 06)	◆	4382
Suzuki GSF600, 650 & 1200 Bandit Fours (95 – 06)	◆	3367
Suzuki Intruder, Marauder, Volusia & Boulevard (85 – 09)	◆	2618
Suzuki GS850 Fours (78 – 88)		0536
Suzuki GS1000 Four (77 – 79)		0484
Suzuki GSX-R750, GSX-R1100 (85 – 92) GSX600F, GSX750F, GSX1100F (Katana) Fours (88 – 96)	◆	2055
Suzuki GSX600/750F & GSX750 (98 – 02)	◆	3987
Suzuki GS/GSX1000, 1100 & 1150 4-valve Fours (79 – 88)		0737
Suzuki TL1000S/R & DL V-Strom (97 – 04)	◆	4083
Suzuki GSF650/1250 Bandit & GSX650/1250F (07 – 14)	◆	4798
Suzuki GSX1300R Hayabusa (99 – 14)	◆	4184
Suzuki GSX1400 (02 – 08)	◆	4758
TRIUMPH Tiger Cub & Terrier (52 – 68)		0414
Triumph 350 & 500 Unit Twins (58 – 73)		0137
Triumph Pre-Unit Twins (47 – 62)		0251
Triumph 650 & 750 2-valve Unit Twins (63 – 83)		0122
Triumph 675 (06 – 10)	◆	4876
Triumph Tiger 800 (10 – 14)	◆	5752
Triumph 1050 Sprint, Speed Triple & Tiger (05 -13)	◆	4796
Triumph Trident & BSA Rocket 3 (69 – 75)		0136
Triumph Bonneville (01 – 12)	◆	4364
Triumph Daytona, Speed Triple, Sprint & Tiger (97 – 05)	◆	3755
Triumph Triples & Fours (carburetor engines) (91 – 04)	◆	2162
VESPA P/PX125, 150 & 200 Scooters (78 – 12)		0707
Vespa GTS125, 250 & 300 (05 – 10)		4898
Vespa Scooters (59 – 78)		0126
YAMAHA DT50 & 80 Trail Bikes (78 – 95)	◇	0800
Yamaha T50 & 80 Townmate (83 – 95)	◇	1247
Yamaha YB100 Singles (73 – 91)	◇	0474
Yamaha RS/RXS 100 & 125 Singles (74 – 95)		0331
Yamaha RD & DT125LC (82 – 87)	◇	0887
Yamaha TZR125 (87 – 93) & DT125R (88 – 07)	◇	1655
Yamaha TY50, 80, 125 & 175 (74 – 84)	◇	0464
Yamaha XT & SR125 (82 – 03)	◇	1021
Yamaha YBR125 & XT125R/X (05 – 13)		4797
Yamaha YZF-R125 (08 – 11)	◆	5543
Yamaha Trail Bikes (81 – 03)		2350
Yamaha 2-stroke Motocross Bikes (86 – 06)		2662
Yamaha YZ & WR 4-stroke Motocross Bikes (98 – 08)		2689
Yamaha 250 & 350 Twins (70 – 79)		0040
Yamaha XS250, 360 & 400 sohc Twins (75 – 84)		0378
Yamaha RD250 & 350LC Twins (80 – 82)		0803
Yamaha RD350 YPVS Twins (83 – 95)		1158
Yamaha RD400 Twin (75 – 79)		0333
Yamaha XT, TT & SR500 Singles (75 – 83)		0342
Yamaha XZ550 Vision V-Twins (82 – 85)		0821
Yamaha FJ, FX, XY & YX600 Radian (84 – 92)		2100
Yamaha XT660 & MT-03 (04 – 11)	◆	4910
Yamaha XJ600S (Diversion, Seca II) & XJ600N Fours (92 – 03)	◆	2145
Yamaha XJ6 & FZ6R (09 – 15)	◆	5889
Yamaha YZF600R Thundercat & FZS600 Fazer (96 – 03)	◆	3702
Yamaha FZ-6 Fazer (04 – 08)	◆	4751
Yamaha YZF-R6 (99 – 02)	◆	3900
Yamaha YZF-R6 (03 – 05)	◆	4601
Yamaha YZF-R6 (06 – 13)	◆	5544
Yamaha 650 Twins (70 – 83)		0341
Yamaha XJ650 & 750 Fours (80 – 84)		0738
Yamaha XS750 & 850 Triples (76 – 85)		0340
Yamaha TDM850, TRX850 & XTZ750 (89 – 99)	◇◆	3450
Yamaha YZF750R & YZF1000R Thunderace (93 – 00)	◆	3720
Yamaha FZR600, 750 & 1000 Fours (87 – 96)	◆	2056
Yamaha XV (Virago) V-Twins (81 – 03)	◆	0802
Yamaha XVS650 & 1100 Drag Star/V-Star (97 – 05)	◆	4195
Yamaha XJ900F Fours (83 – 94)	◆	3239
Yamaha XJ900S Diversion (94 – 01)	◆	3739
Yamaha YZF-R1 (98 – 03)	◆	3754
Yamaha YZF-R1 (04 – 06)	◆	4605
Yamaha FZS1000 Fazer (01 – 05)	◆	4287
Yamaha FJ1100 & 1200 Fours (84 – 96)	◆	2057
Yamaha FJR1300 (01 – 13)	◆	5607
Yamaha XJR1200 & 1300 (95 – 06)	◆	3981
Yamaha V-Max (85 – 03)	◆	4072
ATVs		
Honda ATC 70, 90, 110, 185 & 200 (71 – on)		0565
Honda Rancher, Recon & TRX250EX ATVs		2553
Honda TRX300 Shaft Drive ATVs (88 – 00)		2125
Honda Foreman (95 – 11)		2465
Honda TRX300EX, TRX400EX & TRX450R/ER ATVs (93 – 06)		2318
Kawasaki Bayou 220/250/300 & Prairie 300 ATVs (86 – 03)		2351
Polaris ATVs (85 – 97)		2302
Polaris ATVs (98 – 07)		2508
Suzuki/Kawasaki/Artic Cat ATVs (03 – 09)		2910
Yamaha YFS200 Blaster ATV (88 – 06)		2317
Yamaha YFM350 & YFM400 (ER & Big Bear) ATVs (87 – 09)		2126
Yamaha YFZ450 & YFZ450R (04 – 10)		2899
Yamaha Banshee and Warrior ATVs (87 – 10)		2314
Yamaha Kodiak and Grizzly ATVs (93 – 05)		2567
ATV Basics		10450
SCOOTERS		
Twist and Go (automatic transmission) Scooters Service and Repair Manual	◇	4082
TECHBOOK SERIES		
Motorcycle Basics Techbook (2nd edition)		3515
Motorcycle Electrical Techbook (3rd edition)		3471
Motorcycle Fuel Systems Techbook		3514
Motorcycle Maintenance Techbook		4071
Motorcycle Modifying		4272
Motorcycle Workshop Practice Techbook (2nd edition)		3470

◇ = not available in the USA ◆ = Superbike

The manuals on this page are available through good motorcycle dealers and accessory shops.
In case of difficulty, contact: **Haynes Publishing**
(UK) **+44 1963 442030** (USA) **+1 805 498 6703**
(SV) **+46 18 124016**
(Australia/New Zealand) **+61 2 8713 1400**

MCL 07.05.15

Preserving Our Motoring Heritage

< The Model J Duesenberg Derham Tourster. Only eight of these magnificent cars were ever built – this is the only example to be found outside the United States of America

Almost every car you've ever loved, loathed or desired is gathered under one roof at the Haynes Motor Museum. Over 300 immaculately presented cars and motorbikes represent every aspect of our motoring heritage, from elegant reminders of bygone days, such as the superb Model J Duesenberg to curiosities like the bug-eyed BMW Isetta. There are also many old friends and flames. Perhaps you remember the 1959 Ford Popular that you did your courting in? The magnificent 'Red Collection' is a spectacle of classic sports cars including AC, Alfa Romeo, Austin Healey, Ferrari, Lamborghini, Maserati, MG, Riley, Porsche and Triumph.

A Perfect Day Out

Each and every vehicle at the Haynes Motor Museum has played its part in the history and culture of Motoring. Today, they make a wonderful spectacle and a great day out for all the family. Bring the kids, bring Mum and Dad, but above all bring your camera to capture those golden memories for ever. You will also find an impressive array of motoring memorabilia, a comfortable 70 seat video cinema and one of the most extensive transport book shops in Britain. The Pit Stop Cafe serves everything from a cup of tea to wholesome, home-made meals or, if you prefer, you can enjoy the large picnic area nestled in the beautiful rural surroundings of Somerset.

> John Haynes O.B.E., Founder and Chairman of the museum at the wheel of a Haynes Light 12.

< The 1936 490cc sohc-engined International Norton – well known for its racing success

The Museum is situated on the A359 Yeovil to Frome road at Sparkford, just off the A303 in Somerset. It is about 40 miles south of Bristol, and 25 minutes drive from the M5 intersection at Taunton.
Open 9.30am - 5.30pm (10.00am - 4.00pm Winter) 7 days a week, *except Christmas Day, Boxing Day and New Years Day*
Special rates available for schools, coach parties and outings Charitable Trust No. 292048